ANGELS ALWAYS COME ON TIME

Chaim Linder
with Mark Linder

ISBN: 978-1-4834-7662-9 (sc)
ISBN: 978-1-4834-7661-2 (hc)
ISBN: 978-1-4834-7663-6 (e)

Lulu Publishing Services rev. date: 03/02/2018

PREFACE
New York 1996

My father was only a child when, in the winter of 1879, he said goodbye forever to his home in Poland and, with his mother, father, and two sisters, began an overland journey that brought them, three months later, to the gates of Jerusalem.

My father's age at the time and the exact date of the journey are uncertain, as was the journey itself. With a half dozen other families, a bedraggled caravan of souls lifted not on the wings of eagles but slowly and desperately on foot and horse cart, they made their way through cold and hostile lands. They traveled on a timeworn route established long ago by crusaders, traders, and generations of exiles. Though others were to follow, thousands upon thousands in tidal waves of humanity, my father and his parents were among the first of the Russian Pale to leave behind a land that, however inhospitable and cruel, had been their home for hundreds of years. Their faith in a divine benevolence—a benevolence that had yet to rescue them from ages of hateful, murderous persecution—seems remarkable to me as I sit safe and warm in my writing room in New York, now an old man tapping out my long-hoarded memories of people long dead, whose hopes and loves are yet very much alive.

Their stories, full of despair and loss and rich in courage, strength, and triumph, are mine to tell.

*

My grandparents and their children—my father and his sisters—began their journey in the latter half of the nineteenth century, but they had been on the road for almost two thousand years.

They lived in Plotsk, a village not far from Warsaw, in the part of Poland close to the German border. Searching my family's past, I have discovered that their book is full of empty pages; whatever records they kept were informal ones, such as dates written on the flyleaf of my grandfather's prayer book, meager jottings in the ledger of his village synagogue. Fearing all authority, they kept themselves hidden, leaving so few traces that they almost disappeared as the flowing years, like a ceaseless tide, wore away the fragile veneer of memory. Their lives were hard and short, each new generation struggling for light, the future a precious gem locked within time's tight purse. In each generation, as evil swept across Europe and consumed them with bitter fire, they would rise, sift through their ashes, and begin anew.

They left few footprints of their passage, and I shall attempt to redeem them from oblivion with these tales of their lives, and of other lives that theirs touched.

As I said, they lived in Plotsk, Poland, but that wasn't really where they kept their hopes and yearnings. Always there was a promise—a simple hope, a name, and a holy place—to which they would someday return: Jerusalem.

To return to a place implies time already spent there, yet for my grandparents and for the little boy my father was then, Jerusalem existed only as a collective memory carried by generations of men and women—a dream, but more real. It was strange, this attachment to a place they had never seen, but it sustained them as they trudged through the cold, wet winter of 1879.

But I write ahead of myself.

I am eighty-nine years old, and my hands tremble, but my fingers are still firm on the keys. Some of what I recount is of the time before my time. What I know of this past comes from the distant world of childhood, gleanings of faraway fields that, summoned by memory's call, raise themselves from dormancy. I am merely the reaper, walking through meadows of the past. I sit for long hours, compelled, obsessed. I want, as all writers do, my words to bring a world into being and bring the dead to life. I fear that I presume powers I do not possess, that my skills are inadequate. I fear too that I will not have the time to complete the task.

My stories require me to leave the present and step into the past.

This is a convention of storytelling--to begin at a point of embarkation, and travel through realms and times returning, at the very end, to that place where I began. So I sit at the electric typewriter one of my sons gave me as a present, and I am gratified that my trembling fingers, trained on a linotype, retain much of their cleverness.

*

This writing has taken more effort than I expected.

For nearly forty-five years, I spent my days at linotype composition, editing and pasting up English, Hebrew, and Yiddish books, magazines, dictionaries, newspapers, short stories, and all manner of printed material. When I retired in February 1978 at the age of seventy-one, I began to write, first in long hand and then on this electric typewriter. The change from linotype to typewriter was painfully slow. Not only is the typewriter's keyboard much different from a linotype's, but also, I was writing my own words, not merely rearranging and correcting those of others. I was determined to write directly in English, a new experience for a printer such as myself, who first set manuscripts in Hebrew and Yiddish before translating them into English.

I wasn't prepared for the task.

At the Mea Shearim Talmud Torah and in the Lubavitcher yeshiva in Jerusalem, where I received my education, I wasn't taught to write in any language. Occasionally—I can recall three or four instances—I was instructed to copy the Hebrew aleph-bet on tracing paper, but for the most part, my rebbes (teachers) advised me to practice writing on my own. What child takes on extra schoolwork voluntarily? Left to my own devices, I practiced little, turning my attention instead to arithmetic, whose sequences of numbers and operations of division and addition were more congenial than arranging letters into words and words into sentences. Only after my father left Jerusalem for America in 1925 and my mother insisted I become her correspondence secretary did I, with much effort, acquire any literary skills.

I was, I see now, fortunate to have my mother as my teacher. She knew nothing about writing—or reading, for that matter—but she spurred my efforts on with her unique kind of encouragement.

"When a baby starts to talk," she assured me, "only his parents understand what he's saying. Don't worry that others won't understand; Abba will be able to read what you scribble."

My mother called her weekly letters "a paper bridge," and she cautioned me not to "overload the bridge with unnecessary words."

Thus, I learned the essentials of clarity and purpose.

In these pages, I will try to follow her advice.

But again, my pen races ahead.

BOOK 1

Poland

Adapt the mores and constitution of the country
in which you find yourself, but be steadfast in
upholding the religion of your fathers, too.

—Moses Mendelssohn

CHAPTER 1

My grandfather Fishel Linder was born in 1850 in Poland. The exact date is unknown but thought to be in the early spring, sometime around Passover. His parents, like all Hasidic Jews, yearned for a big family, but had no choice but to accept God's will that their blessings be limited to a single son. As a child in Jerusalem, I knew my grandfather only in his mature years, yet now, white-haired myself, I see him vividly as a little boy living with his mother and father in a busy, well-ordered household in his home in Plotsk.

My grandfather's first memories—which have become mine, too, for I heard them often in the flickering light of a kerosene lantern—were like dreams, images and events distant and inexact, fading yet enduring.

He told me that before he could talk and before he understood what was said, he knew the voices of his mother and father and of many other men and women. At times, the voices were soft and comforting; sometimes they were full of passion; and other times, they held something close to tears. There was much singing too, songs full of their own special passion.

Soon, when he was able to distinguish one sound from another, he learned that much of the passion was associated with particular sounds, mere puffs of air called words: *Poland*, *Palestine*, and *Jerusalem*. He learned that words were strange and powerful things that possessed a special life of their own and were capable of filling people's hearts and inspiring men and women to song, tears, and argument. He came to attach those specific words with the men and women who spoke them, and soon there was no difference between them. The men and women were the words, and the words were their passions, and so his days were filled at all times with this great, tumbling vocal life.

Because he was a child, he knew nothing of the world, barely knew that a world outside his house existed, but he sensed that these words referred to real things beyond themselves, and that this unknown world would have a profound effect on his life and the lives of those around him.

This is what my grandfather Fishel Linder experienced as a child in Plotsk, and later, my father—and I too, even later in Jerusalem—experienced. Immersed in the sounds and passions, I heard the same talking and singing.

Even as a child, my grandfather Fishel yearned to live in the land of Israel. It was not called Israel then; maps show it as either Palestine or a territory belonging to a succession of empires—Babylonian, Persian, Assyrian, Greek, Roman, Macedonian, Christian, Turkish. After the Romans destroyed the second temple more than two thousand years ago and sent the Jews into sorrowful exile, Israel did not exist as a country. The world calls it exile, but we give it another name: the diaspora, or the dispersion—a casting to the winds. Yet down through the millennia, the stones of the Old City sent forth a soft, murmurous song. In thought and prayer, in mind, heart, and soul, there was the call to return to Jerusalem.

My grandfather Fishel grew up in relatively prosperous surroundings. His father was the manager of a large estate owned by a rich Polish aristocrat, a poritz. Like many other Jews who were legally prohibited from owning land, my great-grandfather Moshe used his talents and skills in the service of others. The poritz, a country squire preoccupied with such aristocratic activities as hunting, womanizing, and, above all, drinking, was confident that his manager, the Jew Moshe, wouldn't cheat him. A Jew simply wouldn't dare risk the certain punishment, which would include a little extra touch of harshness reserved especially for Jews.

In those days, hotels and inns were rare, and the Linder home was always open to Jewish travelers. Many of those visitors during the 1860s and '70s were emissaries from Jerusalem, collectors traveling the international routes on behalf of the many charitable institutions in the Holy Land. These collectors arrived on their annual schedules at my grandfather's house and stayed for weeks at a time, calling on households and synagogues in Plotsk and other nearby villages in an endless quest for funds.

Young Fishel loved these emissaries from Jerusalem. During the long winter nights, he sat with them at the long supper table and listened to their tales about the faraway Holy Land, the Turks and the Arabs there, the holy wonders of the ancient city, and the magic of its golden light.

One story made him cry.

One of the collectors, an older man with a long white beard and deep dark eyes who came every year just after the High Holy Days, told Fishel about the Shechinah.

"It is written, my little boy, that at the Kotel Ha'Maravi, the Western Wall of the Second Temple, the Shechinah appears every night precisely at midnight—except on the Sabbath and holy days—and there weeps because it was forced to leave Jerusalem when the temple was destroyed."

Fishel listened with trembling heart.

"The Shechinah is lonely and full of pain. Bereft of its home and forced to wander about this cold world, the divine spirit promises that one day it shall return to Jerusalem." The man's deep dark eyes looked into Fishel's. "I have heard twice the Shechinah crying."

"What does it sound like?"

"It is a low sound like the wind. Or like a lost child looking for its home. I myself heard it at the Wall."

"I will go to Yerushalayim," said Fishel, "and tell the Shechinah not to be sad."

"Yes, you must. The more there are at the Kotel, the quicker the Shechinah will return."

The next day, the collector left for Krakow, carrying a letter of introduction from Fishel's father.

Curious, Fishel went into the tiny room where the man was staying and looked about. The room had a narrow bed, a low table near the bed, and a small chest. There was a candle on the table, with white drippings on the flat piece of stone that was its holder. On the chest were a few items of clothing: a shirt and long underpants, two *seforim* (prayer books), and a little tin box. Fishel stepped closer. The box was small and plain, about the size of a grown man's closed fist. Fishel looked at it for a while before picking it up. It was old and slightly rusted. He held it to his ear and shook it. There was something in it. He shook it again. It belonged to the collector, but it couldn't be a secret, or he wouldn't have left it in plain sight. With awkward child's fingers, Fishel pried off the tight cover.

Inside was a brown powder.

He bent and put his nose to it. It had a faint aroma, almost a perfume. He poked the granules with his finger. The earth was dry and light, almost as fine as the flour his mother used to make challah, with not a single pebble in it.

"Fishel."

Startled, he almost dropped the box. He turned. His mother was watching him.

He put the box down immediately. He looked at her, expecting to see anger or irritation in her face, but there was none.

She stood silently in the doorway while he put the cover back on the box and put it back exactly where he had found it.

Then, standing near the small, low bed, he asked, "Why does he carry earth with him?"

"It's from Yerushalayim." She called the Holy City by its Hebrew name.

"But why?"

"If he were to die while he was away from Yerushalayim, he would have to be buried someplace else. But this earth is from the Mount of Olives. They would sprinkle the earth in his eyes, and it would be the same as being buried there."

"Why didn't he take it with him to Krakow?"

"Because he didn't expect to die." His mother smiled and shook her head. "And if he died in Krakow, there'd still be time to bring the earth to him."

Fishel nodded and walked out of the room. For the three days the collector was gone, Fishel was nervous. His mother was not concerned enough. The collector was old, as his long white beard indicated. If death caught him in Krakow, he would have to be buried within twenty-four hours, as was the custom, and someone would have to jump on a horse and bring the earth to him, or he would be lost to all time. Every morning and evening, Fishel went to the doorway and stared at the tin box that held the precious earth from the Mount of Olives, the Jewish burial ground on the sloping hill just east of the Old City.

At last, the collector returned, full of life and hungry. Fishel was glad. He watched the man gobble down his mother's food. He wished the man would take the box whenever he left, for it seemed to him that leaving it behind was a great risk.

As a child in Poland, Fishel was isolated and protected. He knew little of the outside world, which, full of a simmering hate that had from time to time erupted with a hot, violent fury, had not yet ravaged his little village. During the long, cold winters, he and a few other boys from the small Jewish community in Plotsk stayed indoors and were tutored by a private rebbe who taught them to read the prayer books and the Torah, also known as the Five Books of Moses. (Jews refer to the Bible not as the Old Testament but as the Tanakh, an acronym made from the Hebrew letters of each of the five books.)

During the summer, the time of heavy lumbering, Fishel went to live with his father in a small cabin. He loved the summers with his father in the endless forests of Poland. He loved to watch the lumberjacks—two strong men swinging heavy, sharp axes. With sharp blows, they'd sing and grunt in a loud, rhythmic song while attacking a giant tree until, with a loud shout and a roaring thunder of the heavy trunk, the tree came crashing down in full leaf, shattering other smaller trees, shaking the earth, and sending up clouds of dust and leaf. From other trees, flocks of birds scattered wildly from their nests and flew around in terrified circles, screaming and twitting. Slowly, the heavy dust settled, and the birds, bereft of their homes, flew away to look for other places to nest. It was terrifying and wonderful and sad—the frightened birds and the mighty tree, a live and towering creature, now lying upon the forest floor, broken and destroyed.

His father tried to console him. "We must cut the trees. It's necessary for people to live."

Fishel was full of tears.

"We will make lumber from the trees and houses from the wood," his father explained.

Fishel watched the men cut off the branches with axes and saws as they prepared the logs for hauling. The horses waited, snorting and tramping the earth. The heavy logs, with fresh open wounds that oozed sap, were chained, and straining horses gleaming with summer sweat pulled them along rough-cut forest paths down to the river, where the men loaded them onto flat barges and tied them down to be shipped across stormy waters. At the sawmill, his father explained, the logs would be cut into thick planks, and then carpenters would shape and trim them into boards, and houses would be built, in which people would live.

"And so you see how the tree has new life and gives life to us. Our house keeps us warm in the winter, and we share it with our guests from Jerusalem."

Yet still, Fishel was sad, for a fallen tree never rose, nor did its branches ever hold the nests of birds or have leaves for shade.

*

After his bar mitzvah at the age of thirteen, my grandfather attended a yeshiva in Plotsk, where he began what was to be a lifelong study of the Torah and the Talmud, which are the commentaries upon the Torah. These studies were conducted in Yiddish, the primary language of Polish Jews.

Yiddish, which uses the Hebrew alphabet, is a relatively new language—a mere 1,100 years old—and traces its origins to German, Hebrew, Aramaic, and Italian. In the Middle Ages, when Jews migrated to Eastern Europe, Yiddish incorporated many elements of the Slavic languages, and still later, in America, it borrowed English vocabulary and usage.

The devout viewed languages other than Yiddish and Hebrew as unnecessary and somewhat dangerous, leading one down the path of secularism. Fishel's parents faced a dilemma. As part of a community small in number, confined within tight geographical boundaries, constrained by many legal restrictions, and assaulted by a hostile, fearful population, they could choose, as many did, to build an even higher protective fence against the world, retreating into their small, cramped village.

But the world was ignored at one's peril, and holiness, however desirable, was not by itself sufficient, so his parents hired a private teacher who taught him how to write Hebrew and read and write Polish and German. Furthermore, Fishel's parents hired a second tutor to teach him arithmetic, an indispensable skill for those wishing to make their way in the world.

While a student in the yeshiva, Fishel boarded in the household of a family friend. This friend, Baruch, owned a successful hardware and stationery emporium in Plotsk. Fishel was filled with wonder when he visited the store for the first time. He walked up and down the aisles, looking at the hammers, screwdrivers, wrenches, screws, nails, papers, pens, and envelopes, marveling at all these man-made things, worldly implements. He studied the customers—men with purpose, their purses holding wealth—and paid close attention as they did business with Baruch. Most of all, he studied the way his father's friend handled the customers. To one, he smiled; to another, he did not; and to a third, he offered a smile of a different degree. Always polite, he adjusted his tone and aspect to each customer's personality and needs.

This, thought Fishel, *is what the world is about.*

When, a month later, Baruch had to go to Warsaw to buy merchandise, he asked his young boarder if he wanted to see what a city was. Fishel jumped at the chance.

Early in the morning, before the sun rose, they set out on a horse-drawn cart. They rode first on a small dirt road, then on a wider road, and then still on another, this one paved and full of travelers. Fishel was filled with wonder and curiosity. This was different from being in the forest with his father.

"You will soon see," Baruch told him, "what a city is."

Indeed, by evening, they were in Warsaw, the capital of Poland. They stayed overnight in an inn attached to a synagogue, and the next morning Fishel went with Baruch to the warehouses to observe how he ordered supplies, negotiated prices, and made payments, and Fishel saw again a different aspect of life. Fishel loved and admired his father and was fascinated by the life of the forest, but now he knew there were different paths he might choose from.

In the spring, Fishel returned to his parents' house for the Passover holiday. His mother and father greeted him as if he were a long-lost traveler, which, in a way, he was. For the first day, he felt separate and apart, but after a night in his own bed he woke his own self, truly home. His mother and aunts bustled about, cleaning every nook and cranny, every corner and cupboard, ridding the house of every last crumb of bread before setting out the Passover dishes and utensils. The sights, smells, and sounds of home filled Fishel's heart with an unexpected joy. At last, the night of the first Seder arrived, his large family, along with emissaries from Jerusalem, sat down at the long table. At the Seder, children show off their education by offering commentary and expla-nations of the different aspects of the Pesach rituals, and though Fishel was not a child in terms of years, he was his parents' only child, so he spoke on various points. One of the guests was a distinguished rabbi from Jerusalem seeking funds in Europe for an impoverished orphanage in Palestine. The rabbi listened, nodding in approval, and complimented young Fishel on his intelligence and knowledge.

They finished the Seder, drinking the required four goblets of wine, and then sang the final prayers, giving thanks for the meal and all that was good in their lives and in the world.

"Next year," they sang, "in Jerusalem."

That was their fervent hope, uttered over many centuries, and ev-eryone at the table sang the phrase again and again, their voices rising until the rafters shook.

"Next year in Jerusalem!"

As they sang, the distinguished rabbi from Jerusalem looked hard and long at Fishel and, catching the teenager's eye, smiled at him. At last, after all the guests had gone to bed, the rabbi spoke to Fishel.

"Your father says you are a good student at the yeshiva. You learn easily."

"It seems that I do."

"Do you like your studies?"

Fishel hesitated. He liked memorizing the Torah and the commentary around it and enjoyed the analysis of the fine points of behavior. Yet he liked studying arithmetic and language just as much, perhaps even more so.

The rabbi waited as Fishel gathered his thoughts. He knew that his father and the rabbi had been talking about him. Fishel remained silent, not because he had nothing to say but because he did not wish to offend the distinguished rabbi from Jerusalem by speaking the truth. The study of Torah was the highest of all possible endeavors, and if he wished, he could become a professional scholar, sitting for long days with other scholars and then teaching young boys as he had been taught. It was a secure, safe life, a life of study and piety.

Finally, Fishel spoke.

"I don't think I could devote myself to a life of study and nothing else."

"Do you want to stay here and learn your father's trade?"

Again, Fishel remained silent. It would be safe to be tucked away in Plotsk, where things stayed the same forever and where war, political unrest, and social upheaval were only clouds gathering in the east, in distant Russia, with an occasional ominous rumble from Germany in the west. Poland was their special place, secure and timeless.

The rabbi was watching him with kind eyes that did not blink, and Fishel knew that decisions about his life had been made, though he didn't know what they were. He felt a surge of despair. He wasn't even fourteen, and his life was no longer his own. His career would be chosen for him, and soon a young woman, a girl no older than he, would be selected from one of the families in Plotsk to be his wife. He would become like his father, and the girl, whoever she was, would be just like his mother. They would live there in Plotsk, grow old, and die, and his children would repeat the process forever. He was a small part in a great scheme, and the rabbi and his father were going to assign him his place in the world.

The rabbi waited. Fishel took a deep breath and spoke his truth.

"My father has given me a good life, and if I stayed here and learned how to manage the forest, I know I would succeed, and I would try to give my children the same good life. But I'm not certain that it is the life for me."

"Yes, your father thought so too."

A great burden was suddenly lifted from Fishel's heart. He spoke a second truth. "Yet I'm not sure what I would do to earn a living."

"Now is not the time for you to decide." The rabbi looked into Fishel's gray eyes. "The world has a place for you."

A week later, when the Passover holiday was over and the rabbi was preparing to go, he took Fishel aside.

"I have spoken to the head of a yeshiva in Warsaw," the rabbi said, "and if you wish, you will be able to study there."

Ah, Warsaw!

Young as he was, Fishel understood what was happening. The rabbi and his father had talked, and now he was being prepared. He was more than a mere boy; he was part of something greater than all of them.

"I would like to go to Warsaw."

"There are many good things there," the rabbi said, his eyes filled with a kindly light. "And other things not so good. You will have to choose among them."

Now the rabbi had to leave. He was going west into Germany on a long journey, and he was anxious to begin, the sooner to return to Jerusalem.

*

By modern modes of travel, Warsaw is not far from Plotsk, a mere hour's journey, but distance then was measured not in miles but in invisible boundaries. Leaving his little village on a journey of possibility, Fishel crossed vast divides of culture.

Like many cities, Warsaw was a place of both opportunity and danger. The young scholar, boarding in the Warsaw home of one of the merchant's business associates, removed from his family's influence and no longer confined to his little village, felt truly free for the first time in his young life.

I, now an elderly gentleman in New York, know what Fishel, my grandfather, felt, for I felt it too when, as a young man of twenty-two, having crossed an ocean, I found myself standing on a street corner in New York on a cold winter night in 1929, a stranger in a wonderful land.

But my father is impatient to tell his tale.

The year was 1873, and Poland was a vibrant and tumultuous land of contrasts and contradictions. Are not many times and places so? The latter half of the nineteenth century was in deep ferment; contrary forces existed side by side, tugging and pushing, and all of Europe, especially Poland, was in turmoil. During the previous hundred years, a rolling wave of warfare had carved Poland into various political and geographic entities. First, Austria and Prussia divided the Polish Commonwealth, as it was called, parceling out the land. In 1807, the Grand Duchy of Warsaw was created, but after the Congress of Vienna in 1815, the duchy was annexed by Russia and renamed the Kingdom of Poland. The czar, contrary to his usual autocratic impulses, gave this Kingdom a great deal of autonomy. Comprised mostly of ethnic Poles, Warsaw soon became the center of Polish politics and culture, steadily growing in economic power.

Throughout history, the Jewish population—more so than the general citizenry—was buffeted by potent political, economic, and social forces, forcing them into endless accommodations and adjustments. The young yeshiva scholar Fishel found himself in a maelstrom of contradictory impulses; his need for security and his desire to retain his primal identity were soon at odds with the lure of cosmopolitan variety and the excitement of the unknown. This was life!

The growth of the Jewish population in Poland during the nineteenth century was striking. The population doubled to approximately

14 percent by 1897 and, in keeping with general demographic trends, became increasingly urbanized. Throughout history, men and women have been drawn to cities, for a critical mass of citizenry is often indispensable for the creative process. This movement into the cities, especially pronounced for Jews, was also the result of forces unique to their minority status—official government decrees directing Jews to live in specific places. The disappearance of traditional nonurban Jewish vocations, such as farming and guild work, again due to prejudicial treatment, drove many Jews from the countryside. By midcentury, almost half of the kingdom's urban population was Jewish. Slowly but surely, a small but potent Jewish professional class began to emerge, coexisting alongside a substantial proletarian class of merchants and workers. It was an exciting time to be alive, and Polish Jews partook of, gave energy to, and were shaped by the many political and social movements of the latter half of nineteenth-century Europe. Indeed, all of Europe was a boiling, bubbling cauldron. Darwin and Marx had published their grand theories, and men and women debated with great heat and passion, and some nonsense, the virtues of socialism versus capitalism versus communism. Growing industrialization and technological progress were measured against a vanishing agricultural society, kingship fought democracy, believers fought atheists, women fought men, and everyone looked at the Jew with suspicion.

The center of this rich brew was Warsaw, in whose streets, synagogues, coffeehouses, and study halls one found the academics, political theorists, lawyers and bankers, and Zionists and socialists, communists, and assimilationists. The Jewish population was subject to powerful forces particular to their distinct minority position. Attempting to maintain a distinct identity while living within a greater host society, particularly a society hostile and xenophobic, creates a certain tension. Though this tension gives rise to great intellectual and artistic achievement, maintaining one's balance on these shifting, heaving sands is often exhausting. Fishel, in the midst of this ferment, grew strong, yet often wished for less stress so that so much strength wouldn't be necessary.

Poland also was the birthplace of the Hasidic movement, which sought to tap into the charismatic and mystical aspects of Judaism, and was soon felt throughout Eastern Europe as a distinct and compelling force.

As the center of this emerging Hasidic movement, Warsaw had many Hasidic rabbis, or rebbes, each of them the leader of a group of disciples, called a *kryzleck*. Each kryzleck, made up of as few as a dozen families or as many as five hundred, had its own synagogue. Some of these synagogues were rich, ornate structures, but most were small inner-city buildings converted into houses of prayer. Each synagogue needed only the Torah scroll, the ark to house it, and a small raised platform, a bema, on which the ark stood. Chairs or benches for the faithful completed the furnishings. Since Warsaw, like most cities, had no public transportation of any sort and the only mode of travel was by foot, the disciples and their families lived as close as possible to the synagogue, which facilitated twice daily attendance at prayer services. The immediate area around each synagogue became, in a sense, its own village, with strong ties to a particular rebbe.

Few, if any, government services were available, so each kryzleck tried to help its members. They established scholarships for young men in the form of boarding allowances; provided small amounts of monies for widows and orphans; formed groups of volunteers to visit the sick and dying, considered a moral responsibility in Jewish ethics; provided burial services for those who died too poor to afford them. Thus, the kryzleck became its own little city-state.

The great city of Warsaw held many cosmopolitan temptations, but Fishel resisted them. Most important were his studies, for the acquisition of knowledge, both spiritual and practical, was his primary goal. Despite the new freedoms of urban life, he knew his future was ordained: he would marry, continue his studies, and find some kind of work, while his wife, whoever she was to be, would raise their children and manage their household. There were no other options. In the strictly segregated world of Orthodox Judaism in which Fishel moved, men and women were kept apart until they married, and flesh being what it was, it was imperative to couple them off without undue delay. The thoughts of the pious might reach to heaven, but it was an indisputable fact that the sexual impulse was powerful, and it was best to confine it within the formal arrangement of marriage.

A shadchan, or matchmaker, would make marital arrangements in consultation with the two sets of parents. Seemingly despotic, the usual rules of human conduct prevailed, and softened this autocratic edge. Most parents would not force a marriage on a reluctant child, particularly a daughter, for it was recognized that an unhappy young bride could wreak havoc on a household's harmony. Thus, the woman often held an implicit veto power. Inexperience played its part. Despite the exception here and there, sexual experience was limited, and most men and women could not measure one partner against another. So one did not know what one was missing, if anything.

It never occurred to Fishel to find a woman on his own. The social mechanisms that allow for the intermingling of the sexes did not then exist in the Hasidic culture. Moreover, the idea of happiness and self-fulfillment that characterizes today's intimate social relations was not a priority in Fishel's time. Life was hard; the emphasis was on survival, and it was best to begin quickly the business of breeding and continuity. Thus, Fishel's future was ordained in its general outline; the specifics of times and places and the particulars of his as yet unknown wife and life would unfold in due course.

His immediate future was to be found in the study rooms of the Warsaw yeshiva, under the auspices of the Lubavitcher Hasidim. The yeshiva in Warsaw was large, its students worldlier, and Fishel kept to himself at first. But books were expensive treasures, so students were paired off in order to share their texts. The study partners sat close together, both for ease of reading and, because coal was expensive, for warmth during the cold Polish winters.

He learned easily. Yeshiva study is similar to legal training. The codes of Jewish ethics are derived from the Torah, and refined in the voluminous writings of the Talmud. Situations are posed—ethical conundrums such as, for instance, what kind of response is required by someone who comes across a valuable lost item—and an analysis of the situation is undertaken. The student is expected to follow the give-and-take of the argument. Precedent is cited, famous rabbis are invoked.

There are minority and majority interpretations, and though much weight is given to the majority, the minority interpretation is always noted, if not entirely respected. Through years of study, at times repetitious and tedious study, the student develops a method of inquiry by which the larger world may be examined and interpreted.

In the Warsaw yeshiva, Fishel's study partner was another teenage boy, Yitzhak Haggis. Yitzhak, who was sixteen, barely two years older than Fishel, was already formally engaged—that is, a marriage contract had been signed—to a young woman from Warsaw. His bride was Rivka Lederberg, and Fishel recognized the name at once. Her father was Tzvi Yehuda Lederberg. The name Lederberg is derived from the German *Leder*, meaning, "leather. The Lederbergs, one of the wealthiest families in Warsaw, were manufacturers of leather products; their company employed several hundred workers. The match had come about, Yitzhak explained to Fishel, when the bride's father had visited the yeshiva and the *rosh* (the head, or principal) decided to do a little matchmaking of his own. He recommended Yitzhak Haggis as a suitable partner for the leather mogul's older daughter. Inquiries were made as to the pedigree of the young man, and negotiations were entered into.

"My father signed the contract three months ago."

Fishel wished him mazel tov, or good luck.

"Rivka has a younger sister," Yitzhak Haggis said.

Fishel said nothing.

"Her name is Esther."

Fishel could only smile and look away. The thought of being the father of little children and coming home to a woman and sharing her bed had never entered his adolescent head. Neither he nor his study partner even had beards.

"You'll meet her when you come for the Shabbos meal," his friend said. "You'll see. Esther's very pretty."

Yitzhak Haggis also came from a small village outside Warsaw, and soon the two young innocents became fast friends. Sometimes alone but often together, Fishel explored the teeming European metropolis that was Warsaw. The city was crowded with people and carts, commerce and art existed side by side, men and women walked about in modern dress. The Jewish quarter was no less alive; the Jews there were aggressive and dynamic, walking through the streets as free men and women, citizens of a brave new world.

But soon Fishel saw that this bright, wonderful world was not what it seemed.

Beneath the gloss of urban worldliness, the Jewish population was beset with poverty and persecution. The poverty was not only material but also of the soul. Poland was infected with a severe anti-Semitism, and the daily insults and persecutions to which Jews were subjected pained his spirit. He learned at too young an age that the joy of life was lost when men and women lived in fear and anxiety. He saw how men and women, because the hatred was relentless and pervasive, turned it back upon themselves, blighting their own lives with self-contempt. The blight was all around him, and it made him sad and angry.

In his explorations of Warsaw, Fishel discovered that there were secular Jews as well as religious ones. He came to know too the entire range of spiritual response that led, in one direction to a blind religiosity, and in the other to an equally blind secularism, which brought one, at last, to abject self-denial. He met with the pious Hasidim, who danced with a heavenly joy, and joined in their dance, and he then talked with the passionate socialists who preached an atheistic one-world philosophy and was able to grasp the logic of the argument without agreeing with either the premise or the conclusion.

Though Fishel was tempted by the vision of a life without boundaries, his own faith never faltered. There was something far greater than oneself, greater even than collective humanity.

It was the Shechinah, the Divine Presence, sometimes called Ha Shem (the Name).

He also saw many Jews leaving Poland. He understood their urgency; fear and persecution abounded. Most of them left for the New Land, America, and only a few, usually the devout and the dreamers, dared the hazards of a journey to Ha Eretz, the Land.

Which, in geo-political terms, did not exist then and had not existed since the Roman legions destroyed the Second Temple and exiled the Jewish people almost two thousand years earlier.

It was then called Palestine, the Roman name derived from the Philistines, the warriors of Gaza who had made iron weapons and whom King David had defeated.

*

"You will come Friday night, of course?"

"Of course."

"You know that Esther looks forward to your visits."

Fishel said nothing and looked down at the open book between them. Soon after his marriage, Yitzhak's beard had come in dark and thick, and now he spoke often of his wife and her younger sister, the pretty Esther. The Lederberg house was always full of Sabbath guests, many of them young men from the Lubavitcher community whose expressions of admiration for the pretty young Esther, though limited by strict rules of decorum, could not be disguised. Esther Lederberg was a highly desirable match, not merely for her looks but also for the generous dowry she would bring.

"Come early this time," said Yitzhak.

"Let us begin," Fishel said, and he moved the book closer to his friend, whose eyesight was not as good as his. He looked down at the portion of the Mishnah they were studying, and he smiled. The order was Nashim (Women), and the text dealt with laws related to marriage and divorce. Fishel began reading out loud, and soon, alternating phrases and sentences, with voices pitched to the other, their gentle, rhythmic recital of the text became a murmurous duet between them. Around them, the other young men murmured and sang too, and the room became full of rising and falling male voices, a soft, eternal song much like the gentle roll of a ceaseless tide.

*

Tzvi Lederberg—the name Tzvi is Hebrew for a male deer, a stag— had three children: a son and two daughters, Rivka, the older, and her younger sister, Esther. Esther had been born with a twin sister, but the infant girl had died on the day of their birth. Tzvi Lederberg, a devout Hasid, had given his son a traditional education: much study of the Torah and Talmud, with only limited exposure to areas of secular knowledge deemed essential--a touch of arithmetic, some Polish. The great universities of Europe were not for ordinary people, especially not for Jews, and few men and women had more than the most cursory knowledge of the sciences, history, and literature. Besides, what would one do with such knowledge other than go hungry?

Although many Hasidim possessed a deep distrust of worldliness, the Lederberg household held a few surprises for Fishel. Their brother's wardrobe was restricted to the plain, serviceable black suit, white shirt, and black hat that remain the sartorial standard of the Polish Hasid to this day, but Fishel took immediate note of the Lederberg sisters' more stylish clothing. It was modest to be sure, but held a touch of modernity and flair. Fishel sensed another difference: the two sisters were educated. In addition to Yiddish and Hebrew, they spoke Polish and German. German in particular was a sign of high education and fine manners, a must for any young woman of wealth and position who wished to consider herself modern and intelligent. It was not unusual for young Orthodox women to be more exposed to academic study than their brothers, for many Hasidim who were conservative in the schooling of their male children were more liberal with their daughters. One would have expected the opposite, but men, carriers of the religious flame, were kept close to the spiritual, while women, with fewer formal religious obligations, were allowed more leeway. There was no formal, organized schooling for women, so a system of private tutoring evolved for the express purpose of educating young women in a safe, supervised setting.

Also, it was recognized that young women were, too often, bored. An intelligent, inquiring mind needed stimulation, and the closed, cramped existence that was the lot of most women in the latter half of the nineteenth century often produced deep resentment and depression. The world could not be shut out, and it was best to allow it in, albeit in controlled doses.

Both Lederberg sisters were intelligent and pretty, and Rivka, as a married woman, could tease Fishel with impunity. She called him a bookworm, which was a curious accusation to make against a young

Hasidic scholar. When her older sister made fun of him, Esther would look away and sometimes leave the room.

Actually, Rivka's accusation against Fishel could also be applied to her sister, who was an obsessive reader herself. When Esther wasn't holding a German or Hebrew text, she carried a siddur, a prayer book. Religious, she prayed three times a day. Once, Fishel had come upon her standing at the window with a prayer book in both hands, her lips moving silently. Older now, his beard beginning to darken, Fishel felt his heart filling whenever he and Esther were in the same room. Last week, he had watched silently from the doorway while she, a pretty young woman in her European dress, studied a book of the Talmud. Yitzhak had told him that she also read poetry and had even tried to write her own verses.

But it was not for him to talk to her of a future together, and she was so quiet and reserved whenever he was near that he did not know what to think.

I know all this because it has been passed to me across two generations, told to me by my own father, who heard it from his. We all agreed that it was extraordinary, really, that my pious, devout Hasidic grandfather married a woman who wrote her own poetry, and in German! I pass this on so that my adult children will know that once upon a time, their great-grandparents were young, with lives full of all the improbable and wonderful things that young lives contain.

And yes, my dear sons, your mother, my dancing girl, and I, were young once.

But I shall continue with the past.

*

Around the dinner table in the Lederberg household, the conversation turned always to the one burning question of the Jewish community of Warsaw, and perhaps of all Poland: "What does our future hold?"

There were many answers, none of them satisfactory. Among the Hasidic groups in Warsaw were those who argued that there was no future at all for the Jews in the Diaspora, even in Poland, and that the only safe place was in Jerusalem, where they could lead lives according to the dictates of Torah. But the land of milk and honey was far from paradise, and no one except the most blind, unrealistic dreamers had any doubts about the difficulties of life in Jerusalem. The collectors told tales of dire poverty and harsh conditions. They perhaps exaggerated some of the stories in order to open the purse strings of their audience, but the stories were true in the essentials. The Ottoman Turks ruled over the land with a harsh, violent hand. There was little justice and less mercy, and Jews as well as Arabs suffered relentless oppression.

Some Hasidim insisted the Jews should remain in Poland and wait for the Messiah. They cited the Holy Scriptures to prove that only when the world was redeemed would the dispersed children of Israel be brought to Jerusalem upon the wings of eagles. Until then, it was prudent to remain in place and do the best one could, living, suffering, and dying; surely this was God's will.

There were still others who argued that Jews should indeed get out of Poland, but why go to a hostile, impoverished Palestine, when America, a safer, more welcoming land, was just across the ocean? Many of these New Landers were flirting with an intellectually motivated assimilation, which they called international socialism. Jews were not, they pointed out, the only poor and downtrodden people who were persecuted and denied their rights. All humanity needed help. "Let us join forces with the world's oppressed," they exhorted. "Let us give up all claims to a special status, and not only will the world benefit by our contributions, but the so-called Jewish problem, with all its attendant woes, will, without Jews, instantly disappear."

The elder Lederberg, listening to this endless flow of argument and discussion and, one evening in the year 1874, finishing their third and final meal of the Sabbath, announced his decision to his family.

"We will leave Poland and go to live in Jerusalem."

The silence in the room was profound. Out of the corner of his eye, Fishel could see Esther looking at him.

"I am a realist," Lederberg continued. "There's no bright future for us in Poland, perhaps no future at all. Yet I am not naive about our prospects in Jerusalem. But a hard life there with hope is better than a sweet life here without any."

Yitzhak and his wife agreed. "We will go too."

Fishel spoke. "And I as well, when I am ready."

When Fishel looked up, Esther's glowing eyes were upon him.

Immediately, preparations for departure began. There was much to do. First, the Lederbergs had to sell or liquidate the huge leather company. As to be expected, the full value of the enterprise was not realized, for the various Polish laws pertaining to land sales and fund transfers discriminated against Jewish interests. Yet even with those restrictions, the monies raised were substantial, ensuring the financial security of the family in their new home.

But of far greater importance to Tzvi Lederberg were his children's futures. He would not leave until his son and younger daughter, Esther, were married. He was gripped by a new sense of urgency. Anti-Semitism was growing, and the Polish government was showing more hostility. Though the age of organized state-sponsored pogroms was not yet upon them, roving bands of angry Poles, drunk and full of mocking hate, were beating up Jews in Plotsk, while from the east, from Russia, there came ominous intimations.

"If we stay longer, we will be trapped," Lederberg said. He decided he and his wife must leave immediately and establish a presence in Jerusalem; his children would follow with their spouses and families. His son, Elezar, was already formally engaged. His older daughter and her new husband, Yitzhak Haggis, were prepared to immigrate as soon as Yitzhak finished his studies. The most pressing concern was his younger daughter, Esther. His house was full of yeshiva students, all eager to wed an attractive, young, virtuous woman from a wealthy, respected family; surely from among them a groom might be found.

*

Tzvi Yehuda Lederberg went to Jerusalem in 1875. Later that same year, his older daughter, Rivka, and her husband, Yitzhak, left Poland too, followed within a month by his son, Elezar, and his new wife, Alta.

Fishel Linder and Esther were married shortly thereafter; they lived in Warsaw for another four years and left Poland in the winter of 1879 with their three young children: their daughters, Miriam and Rachel, and a son, Yehaskel Elimelech.

Yehaskel was the youngest of their children, just three years old, and his first name meant, in Hebrew, "God has given strength."

Though his mother preferred to call him by his full name, his father and others called him simply, Haskel.

He was my father.

CHAPTER 2

My mother, Reizel Reisman, was also a child when she left Poland. The dates are, again, uncertain, but it is accurate to say that the Reisman family made the journey in 1879 or 1880, carried to the shores of Palestine on the first great wave of European migration.

The Reismans were from Warsaw too; pious Hasidim, they were devoted followers of the rebbe of Gur. A Hasidic rebbe serves a special function to his followers and their families. Often a figure of great physical presence and psychological intuitiveness, the rebbe and his charismatic spirituality are the binding force that knits his congregants into a large family of devoted souls. In a world of uncertainty, danger, disease, and mishap, the rebbe encourages, guides, reassures, and consoles. Since Judaism is a religion very much of this world, the rebbe is also something of a corporate executive, overseeing a staff of subordinates who accumulate and distribute resources within their congregation. The rebbe was traditionally also something of a shadchan, a matchmaker. One Hasid with a sixteen-year-old son and another with a fifteen-year-old daughter—or the ages of the boy and girl might be reversed—might find their families, within a year, intertwined through marriage.

My maternal grandparents, however, were not matched by a shadchan. Once he turned thirteen, Netanel Reisman accompanied his father on an annual sojourn to Gur, where they spent the month of Tishri with their spiritual leader, the rebbe of Gur.

The journey from Warsaw to Gur took two days, and father and son stayed overnight in a small inn whose owner was also a Gur Hasid. The inn was not big. In fact, it was merely a large house. The lower level had a small reception room, a large eating area and small kitchen, and two bedrooms. The upper floor had three small bedrooms, one of which was used for travelers. The accuracy of these details is incontrovertible, for my maternal grandfather, Netanel Reisman, regarded these events as the most important of his life, and his memory of them remained precise to the last day of his life. Because he wanted to preserve them in the minds of others—how else does one achieve immortality? —he told me the story of his marriage over and over, impressing upon me every detail, etching it indelibly.

The owners of the inn had two children, a son named David and, as fate would have it, a daughter. She was named Nechama. Nechama was her mother's helper at the inn. She had long golden hair; bright eyes; and a big, happy smile that shone upon all travelers and was, according to my grandfather Netanel, of incomparable beauty.

Now, even as a teenager, Netanel had a beautiful singing voice, a prized possession among Hasidim, for the Divine Presence welcomed all forms of joyous expression. Singing was prized most highly. However, this was a special kind of singing in which the soul rushed from the mouth in fountains of melody, an offering to the Divine. Once the singing began, there had to be dancing. And not just any dancing, such as ballroom waltzes or minuets, but a tumultuous, joyous, energized dancing in which all the body was filled with melody and limb, heart, and soul moved in bodily prayer.

So, always there was singing and dancing, especially if the Hasidim were on the way to Gur and their souls were aflame with expectation. At the inn after supper, Netanel Reisman sang, while the other Hasidim clapped and then began dancing, first in place and then around the table in a long line. Soon they needed more room. They pushed the table to the wall, and the dancing began in earnest while Netanel sang and sang, his powerful voice filling the inn with a sound that was not of this world. All the while, Nechama moved carefully among the men, never touching them, listening to Netanel's wonderful voice.

Well, a pious young man with a good voice was halfway there, and one thing led to another. Two years after Netanel's bar mitzvah, he and Nechama were married. They were both almost sixteen years old, a perfect age to have children.

They had many. Ten months after they were married, Nechama gave birth to twins, but both girls died in their second month. Twelve more children followed, six of whom died within their first year. Of the six who survived, only four of them, two boys and two girls, lived long enough that their names are remembered, and they are Chaim, Yisrael Yitzhak, Golda, and Reizel.

Reizel was to be my mother.

A number of years after their marriage, Nechama's parents died, and the inn passed to her and Netanel, bringing them a considerable income. Like her mother before her, Nechama took charge of everything. Though his heart wasn't in it, Netanel made himself useful, becoming a mingler and schmoozer. He greeted the guests, smiling at them and conversing, and he occasionally sang a melody.

He had a strong spiritual inclination—after all, his name meant, "God has given"—and traveled often to Gur to be with the other Hasidim and his beloved rebbe. There he sang and danced, and he'd return home with new melodies to sing in his synagogue, where he was the cantor—that is, the official singer for the congregation during prayer service. This is usually a paid position, but Netanel would not accept money for any service done in God's name. He did, however, earn a few pennies as a scribe. He had clear handwriting and could write Hebrew and Yiddish. The men and women of his village came to his little office in his wife's inn, and Netanel would write the words they spoke, sometimes in Polish but almost always in Yiddish. He knew enough Latin letters, as English was called, to address envelopes to America.

Like many pious men, Netanel Reisman had a lifelong dream to live in Jerusalem. A number of Hasidic families in the Gur religious community had already migrated to Eretz Yisrael—with the consent and blessing of the rebbe, of course. Unlike the strict constructionists who took the Torah literally, the rebbe of Gur was both devout and pragmatic. He didn't see any contradiction between the belief that the Messiah would eventually deliver the far-flung Jewish people to the land of Israel and the migration in the meanwhile of individual Jews to Jerusalem.

"You shall be our scouts," the rebbe told them, "as were the men who Moses sent to spy out the land of Canaan."

However, the dream is often more compelling than the reality, and neither Nechama nor Netanel was ready to leave their comfortable home and prosperous business. The years of childbirth, the pains and sorrows of so many infant deaths, and the effort needed to manage their large household had tired them. The tales of hardship brought by an endless stream of collectors had tempered their enthusiasm for the Holy Land.

But the times were troubling. Poland was changing. Life wasn't easy for anyone, but for the Jews, an extra portion of persecution and humiliation was thrown in for good measure. By the end of the nineteenth century, Netanel, Nechama, and their children, as well as five million other Jews, were living in Eastern Europe, most of them in the Pale of Settlement. They were confined, really, for they had no freedom to leave. News reached the ears of Netanel and Nechama about Cossack attacks, of drunken, angry men raging through the Pale, looting and killing. The Reismans were unaware that the age of pogroms was about to burst upon them, but Netanel did know that it was only a matter of time before the violence spread into the western areas of the Pale.

With ever increasing urgency, other families were fleeing, but Netanel and Nechama stayed. The Messiah might not come for a long time, but they were prepared to await his arrival in the comfort of their inn.

CHAPTER 3

Recorded Polish history begins in the tenth century, when tribes known as the Polanie—that is, tillers of the soil—began their conquest and settlement of lands along the Baltic coast and Carpathian Mountains. During the early Middle Ages, Poland was ruled by a small group of families, an oligarchy transferring power through hereditary rights.

The earliest record of a substantial Jewish presence in Poland goes back to the late eleventh century, when itinerant Jewish merchants plied their trade on well-established routes running east and west. The arrival of these first Jews was due in part to the growth of commerce and urban settlement in Europe but was mostly the result of harsh persecution in the west.

Christianity was, and remains, the dominant religion of Europe. Its influence is pervasive in all political, economic, legal, and social institutions. The Christian population could count on some degree of constancy—an enduring, eternal state of affairs built upon church doctrine. Nothing, however, stayed the same for the Jews for long. At times, they were treated well, but most often, they were not. Displaced, vilified, and forcibly converted, their goods confiscated and their lives proscribed with edicts, the Jewish communities fled to the east until, with conditions worsening, they tramped west again.

Over the centuries, the Tartars invaded, the Russians and the Swedes fought, and the Prussians and Austrians overran the land. The Kazakhs raged in all directions. Poland was positioned most precariously, the corridor between the Europeans on the west and the Russians and Tartars to the east. The land was divided up and parceled out, and then reconstituted as the various European nations battered and bludgeoned each other in a perennial cycle of war and conquest.

Early feudal Europe was a relatively benign era for the Jews of France, Germany, England, and Italy, but only relatively. Life was hard for everyone, but because the church was the most powerful, cohesive institution of the age, life was more difficult for those whose religious persuasion did not permit them to function within its confines. However, rays of enlightenment did penetrate the darkness. Thus, Pope Gregory the Great prohibited the forced conversion of Jews, while Theodoric of Italy and Charlemagne, emperor of France, actually invited Jews to settle within their lands.

But why this newfound, if temporary, acceptance of the Jews by Theodoric and Charlemagne? Historians hypothesize that perhaps there were simply not enough people. Birth and mortality rates were about equal, and disease, injury, warfare, poverty, and a host of other ills had reduced the population to the bare minimum necessary for societal survival. In 1066, William the Conqueror put forth the word that Jews were welcome in England. Other kingdoms and territories followed suit—not that the Jews were suddenly viewed in favorable light, for they were still nonbelievers or, more accurately from the Christian theological viewpoint, disbelievers. However, Jews, though of a lesser spiritual status, were people of high economic value.

This more welcoming attitude was the product, somewhat paradoxically, of an earlier ostracism. Discrimination was part of the legal and social fabric of the Dark Ages, and Jews were prohibited from holding high government positions, intermarrying, joining craft guilds, or testifying against Christians in court. In all times, contradictions abounded, and these legal limitations proved a curious advantage. Barred from many trades, Jews entered the fields of banking and commerce. Slowly and grudgingly, as feudal Europe evolved into a more complex and commerce-oriented society, Jewish bankers and merchants, who over many decades had created a far-flung multinational system of trade, became indispensable to the economy.

The good times, such as they were, did not last. Soon there came another terror in the form of the armed knight wielding the sword of righteousness, his heart full of sanctimonious rage. The age of the Crusades, from 1095 to 1272, saw the wheel of fortune carry European Jewry on another bloody downward turn. Seeking to free the Holy Land of Muslim rule and claiming Jerusalem as the spiritual capital of world Christianity, the eight Crusades visited yet another reign of violence and persecution upon the world, and during a series of particularly bloody massacres, warrior zealots laid waste to the Jewish communities of the Rhineland. The survivors, among them my nameless ancestors, fled east.

With the end of the Crusades and the gradual decline of feudalism, many Jews returned to Germany and France to build their lives anew.

History, however, was not yet finished with my people.

Many political, social, economic, and psychological elements combined to put Jews in a tighter bind. The general population was barely literate, fearful of the dark and anything different, and ignorant of natural phenomena. Food was scarce, and disease and violence were everywhere. In this miasma of fear and anger, theologians elevated xenophobia to a form of religious expression. The Jew, decreed by religious fiat to be the eternal outsider, might have been tolerated but was never loved. Holy writ ordained that he be treated badly—just punishment for his infidel ways—but not dealt with so viciously that he would pick up and leave.

There's an art to this nuanced animosity, and European society developed it to a sublime level. A touch of spite was introduced when the Fourth Lateran Council of Pope Innocent III decreed that Jews must wear special markings so that the population might have identifiable targets upon which to vent their frustrations. The fourteenth century was an especially ugly time. Bad weather and meager harvests brought Europe to the point of starvation. Recurrent visitations of the black plague decimated the population and foretold the end of days. Someone had to be blamed, and the Jews were accused of poisoning the wells and casting spells. During this time, the first charges of ritual blood murders and accusations of desecration of the Host reared their ugly heads. As Christians slowly took over more of the commercial and banking functions that were previously the monopoly of Jews, the Jewish presence was no longer required. Soon the age of expulsions began, and country after country cast out their offending disbelievers. An element of avarice added impetus to the expulsions, for inevitably, before the Jews were expelled or killed, their wealth, meager as it was, was taken from them.

In response, the Linders and tens of thousands of others picked themselves up and left Germany, tramping eastward once again into what is now Poland and Lithuania. I see them in their bitter flight, men, women, and children with hollow eyes, a stream of pitiful humanity fleeing through the corridors of history, searching for haven.

At last, my ancestors settled in Plotsk, where, by all accounts, they lived for many generations in what passed, for them, as peace and stability. By today's standards of civilized living, their lives were not quite peaceful and not at all stable. There was, however, a measure of predictability. Accustomed to oppression, they learned to cope. They learned too that though there were ups and downs in all things, events, for them, tended to go from bad to worse.

Thus, Russian expansion westward during the seventeenth and eighteenth centuries incorporated more and more of Poland's Jewish population into Russia's empire. Never tolerant of its minorities, the czars now had a great many more of them, and in the late 1700s, Catherine the Great decreed that all Jews must live within a defined territory, known as the Pale of Settlement, which included much of Poland. Resettlement was necessary, and by the 1770s, as the Jewish population conformed to the czarina's decree, more Jews lived in the Pale than in all of Europe.

Life was not especially pleasant. Of the more than five million Jews in the Russian Empire, more than 90 percent were confined in the Pale of Settlement. The Pale itself was constantly shrinking as a result of czarist edicts, which led to an ever diminishing pool of resources and ever increasing impoverishment. It was more than mere economics. Prevented from interacting with the outside world and forced to depend on their own meager resources, the prisoners of the Pale were caught in a downward spiral of isolation and depression.

Then, as the nineteenth century drew to a close, the Cossacks rampaged through the forests, looting and killing.

From the countries of Western Europe and especially from the Pale of Settlement, Jews fled by the tens of thousands. They ran from poverty, discrimination, and violence. They fled too from the czarist draft. Forced military conscription was a Russian tradition, and those unfortunate enough to be dragooned into the Imperial Army were lost forever. Conscripts, especially Jews, were immediately forced to become Russians: they underwent conversion to Christianity, voluntarily or not, and were sent to remote regions of the vast Russian empire to serve for periods of twenty-five years or until death, whichever came first.

From 1880 to 1917, it is estimated that more than two million Jews fled from the Pale of Settlement and the surrounding territories. Most of them, along with more than the twenty million other souls who emigrated from Europe during that time, found their way to the United States. About two hundred thousand went to Great Britain, half that many went to Canada. It is estimated that about forty thousand went to South Africa. About three hundred thousand of those leaving the Pale retraced earlier migratory patterns and returned to the countries of Western Europe.

Of all these teeming multitudes, only a few thousand went to Palestine. One of them was my father, Haskel Linder, and, leaving Poland somewhat later, my mother, Reizel Reisman. They were both young children when they set out on their impossible journey. The two families did not know each other in Poland, and neither Haskel nor Reizel had any idea that the other existed, nor did they have the slightest idea what life had in store for them in the narrow, ancient stone alleys of Jerusalem.

Chapter 4

According to received wisdom, Israel is the center of the world, and Jerusalem is the center of Israel. My grandparents, therefore, were aiming for the precise center of the universe when they left Poland.

They were also committing a criminal act, for by decree of the czarina, no one was allowed to enter or leave a village of the Pale without formal permission. Though no papers were provided, money, however, did change hands, and Fishel and Esther Linder and their three children—Miriam, Rachel, and Haskel—disappeared into the winter's night, carrying only what they could strap to their backs.

For the young Haskel, the three-month journey was a long, nightmarish dream. Beneath a bleak winter sky, they trudged on muddy roads, passing through villages and forests. He was cold and hungry, day and night. At first, they traveled alone, making their way south through the populated areas of the Pale, Radom and Lublin, and receiving shelter from the Jewish families in the shtetls. The roads were safe during the day. They traveled south through the Pale, paying off local officials at various checkpoints and hoarding their money.

Presently, they reached the town of Brody, a major gathering point for Jews fleeing the Pale. From there, paid guides took the migrants over the Austria-Hungarian border under cover of night. Once on the other side, most of them headed west, the poorest on foot and those who could afford it by horse caravan or train. In Berlin, Vienna, and Frankfurt, their ranks were swollen by other streams of Jews fleeing from Russia and Romania, a ceaseless tide of humanity flowing to the ports of Western Europe.

If they were fortunate, the overland journey would take weeks; more often, the journey lasted months. The weather was changeable, and disease and injury delayed entire families. They had to bribe every minor government official and border guard. When their money ran out, they found other means of continuing. At times, their spirits faltered, but always, their will drove them forward. In Hamburg, Bremen, Antwerp, and Amsterdam, they boarded whatever oceangoing transport they could buy and bribe their way onto. Most went to the United States of America. Once on board the great vessels, they knew they had reached sanctuary. America would take them in and give them a new life.

There was no such happy anticipation for those going to Jerusalem; the Linders and, a number of years later, the Reismans, belonged to that small group of migrants who, leaving Brody, continued overland south through the Pale to the Black Sea. There they hoped to find a steamer that would take them to Palestine, a land where, in addition to the ancient stores of milk and honey, they would partake of large portions of uncertainty and poverty.

Leaving Brody, the Linders began the part of the journey that was most dangerous. Its villages were few and far between, and the population was more hostile. The Linders, together with another family from Warsaw, made up a small caravan of a dozen determined souls, and wended their way south to the Black Sea, to the port of Odessa, where they hoped to buy passage to Palestine.

Haskel's father tried to keep everyone's spirits high, but the fear was always there, along with the cold that pressed from outside and the hunger that rose from within

"I was very frightened," Haskel said. "On the road, we were silent whenever we met someone, and only our father spoke. We had to give money to everyone. My father put the money in different parts of his clothing—a little in his shoe, some in the lining of his jacket. He had secret pockets everywhere. That way, the robbers wouldn't get everything. We were never robbed, though if we had been attacked, all those secret hiding places would have meant nothing. My mother—your grandmother Esther—had two pairs of gold earrings and a bracelet that she kept hidden in the hem of her dress. We didn't have many clothes, just what we wore—a few layers. We became very dirty, but we had no choice. When it rained or snowed, we found a place to protect ourselves and waited until the rain or snow stopped, and then we continued walking. We ate what we could. We wanted the food to be kosher, but we took what we found. When life is at stake, you are permitted everything. The men didn't stop to pray. It was too dangerous, and besides, we never had a minyan, so my father and the other man spoke the prayers as we walked along. We were always tired, but everyone was too exhausted to complain. I know now that it was more terrible for the adults because they knew how bad things were. A few times, we had to hide in the forest and be very quiet until the drunken peasants passed.

"At the end, it started getting warmer, and we had some sunny days, but we were still cold and hungry all the time. And when we finally got to Odessa, we had to wait a week until there was a boat. It was going to Syria, and the other family decided to wait for another boat, but our money was running out. My father said that it was better to take what you had than wait for the perfect thing that might not happen. You shouldn't ask for miracles when you can do things yourself. He said that like the Israelites in the desert, we should just keep moving, and the closer we got to Jerusalem, the sooner we could rest. And besides, he said, no one was going to part the sea for us."

Odessa was a major port of departure, and desperate Jewish immigrants crowded its docks, hoping to buy passage to Palestine. Trieste, on the northern end of the Adriatic, was another such port, as was Sevastopol, where hordes of Russian Jews gathered in the middle of the Black Sea.

"Your grandfather Fishel was one of those desperate men. We spent a week in Odessa in a tiny room in a house next to a synagogue," my father, Haskel, told me many years later. "Only our father went out into the streets. He went out every day and came back at night with food and whatever news there was. There would be a boat soon, he had heard, but no one could say exactly when. We stayed inside day and night and would go out only with our mother to go to the public toilet. The streets were crowded and dirty. My sisters and I held on to our mother's dress or her hands, and we walked very fast and then returned to our room just as quickly. Every day our father came back with reports promising a boat soon, and then one evening, he came back to the room and told us to get ready immediately. We didn't have much to pack, and we were ready in fifteen minutes. Outside, it was very dark, and we walked very fast through the streets to the harbor. My older sister pulled me along. I don't remember the name of the boat. I don't think the name was ever mentioned. It wasn't important. I remember how big the boat looked in the dark, but of course, I was a child and had never seen such a boat before.

"We followed my father to where a yellow lantern was glowing. There was a man waiting for us at the ladder, and before we climbed up, my father took money out of his shoe and handed it over. The boat was a big black wall. 'Haskel, go up,' my father said, and I put a foot on the ladder and then a hand and pulled myself up and went through a door cut in the side of the wall. The boat smelled of oil and smoke. A man led us through a dark, narrow hall to a tiny dark room. It was very hot, and the smell of smoke and oil was very strong. Our father came in and closed the door.

"'We are on our way,' he said, and even in the dark, I saw that his eyes were shiny with tears."

The voyage from Odessa to Syria took three weeks. After a day, Haskel and his sisters were allowed to leave the room and stand on deck. They looked silently at the sailors, who looked silently back at them. The boat stopped at half a dozen ports to pick up and discharge cargo and passengers. At every port, Fishel withdrew money from one of his hiding places and handed it over to one of the boat's officers, who presumably used it to bribe port officials and kept a percentage for himself, perhaps all of it. On the third day, the boat entered the narrow straits of the Bosporus. Haskel was amazed. The city of Istanbul shone in the morning sun, and he saw mighty palaces of stone and light. On the other side of the boat, his father was praying, facing toward Jerusalem, his eyes closed.

They ate all their meals in their little, airless dark room. Their mother separated the kosher food from the unkosher. When in doubt, they simply ate. At least they weren't cold anymore. With each passing day, the air grew warmer, and the sun grew brighter. They went south along the coast of Greece, weaving their way through sunny islands sitting in the dark blue water. In another week, they landed in Syria. There they waited for another boat due to arrive in a day or perhaps a month. If they had the money and were willing to take the risk, they could hire a guide and armed guards to take them overland into Palestine. For two days, Fishel and Esther debated the merits of the alternatives and couldn't arrive at any decision. Then fortune smiled upon them. The day before they were due to land, the ship's officer told Fishel that the boat would continue on to Jaffa and that for a small additional fee, regrettably unavoidable, the captain would take them that extra distance and, for yet another fee, would allow them to disembark there. Again, Fishel reached into his clothing and handed over more money.

The next hurdle was the entry into the Ottoman Empire. Accommodating the local Arab population, the Turks had a restrictive immigration policy: no new immigrant was allowed into Palestine as a permanent resident. Considering how desolate and poor the country was and how great the need for development was, one would have thought the Turks would encourage immigration, but, apparently not.

However, for a small fee, a visit of three months was permitted. The traveler handed over the money and received in return a red slip of paper with an official scribble showing the date and port of entry. The red slip was perpetually renewable upon payment of an additional sum, so one was constantly shelling out baksheesh to the local officials. However, if the traveler could prove he was returning to the country of his birth, there were no time restrictions upon his visit. This was an age when the use of passports and formal entry permits and visas was not yet in effect in that part of the world, perhaps because the low level of literacy rendered written material useless, so proof of citizenship was a function of one's appearance. The immigration official standing at the docks could recognize a native by his clothing and language, and with a little baksheesh changing hands, all manner of fashions and accents passed the test.

The standard approach was to buy, either from the ship's captain or from one of the vendors in a small boat that would sail out to meet the freighter, a two-piece wardrobe consisting of a Turkish caftan, a long robe tied with a sash, and a red hat, a tarboosh, with a black tassel. In addition, the immigrant was taught a specific phrase in Arabic: *"Ana Ibn belad,"* which, roughly translated, means, "I am a son of the country." Women and children, a man's property, passed through the gates in silence. All this, in addition to a gift of one Turkish rial, about a dollar, granted the traveler de facto citizenship.

For the Linders, however, entry was even simpler. Their boat arrived in Jaffa at midnight, and having paid the last bribe to the ship's officer, they simply climbed down another rope ladder, got into a small boat, and were rowed to shore after paying the two Arab oarsmen a few pennies. Stepping onto the sands of Jaffa, Fishel and his family were met by a friend of Yitzhak Haggis. The Jewish community had worked out their own accommodation with the Turks. Discreet payments of baksheesh had been made, and the few local Arab guards and Turkish government officials drinking their thick, sweet morning coffee were not in the least interested in the tired, bedraggled Linder family wading through the surf in the predawn light. Led through the streets by the friend, the Linders, tired and disoriented, with little Haskel staring about in wonder, disappeared into Jaffa without a trace.

They rested in Jaffa for three days, staying with relatives who had left Plotsk some time earlier and, being less Orthodox, settled in Jaffa rather than Jerusalem. On the morning after the third day, Fishel and his family rose before sunrise to begin their ascent to Jerusalem.

The roads in Palestine were then unsafe, and they rode in a long caravan of wagons. It was a mild spring day, and the donkeys pulled with a slow and steady pace. Riding in the swaying, dipping wagon, they sat very still and and expectant. At last, their long, cold journey was coming to an end. What a change it was from the harsh Polish winter! On the sloping hills and alongside the road were trees with thick clusters of white blossoms. They breathed in the cool morning air, and sweetness filled their lungs. "Apricot trees," the driver of the wagon told them. "Soon they will have delicious fruits on every bough." They sat in the swaying wagon, looking about. The morning air was cool and damp, but they could feel the hesitant warmth on their faces.

For a long time, the caravan traveled on flat, winding roads. On either side of them were little villages of stone and sun-dried brick. Camels rested on the sandy earth, and herds of goats tended by Arabs in long robes were grazing on every patch of green. From the opposite direction came many travelers, some on foot and others on donkeys and camels. Once they were passed by a group of marching soldiers in tan uniforms, men with mustaches and guns.

Haskel turned to watch them go by.

"They are Turkish soldiers," his father told him. "But look—we are climbing to the sky."

The ascent had been barely noticeable for a while, but now the donkeys were laboring, and when he turned to look back, Haskel saw that they were moving steadily uphill. In his father's eyes was a different look. It was the look he had when, back in Poland, they sang songs about going to Yerushalayim.

Slowly, as the line of donkey carts climbed higher on the dirt road that led up into the foothills of Judea, the sun too climbed, until it was a bright yellow ball in the clear sky.

"Abba," said Haskel, pointing. "Father, I see gold. Is that Yerushalayim?"

"It's only the sun on the mountains," his father replied, smiling. Jerusalem, the City of Gold, was not yet in sight. "But soon we will be there."

However, it would be a while yet as, with deliberate pace, they traveled the beaten dirt road that left the coastal plain of the Mediterranean Sea and wound inland on a gradual incline toward the Judean hills. Jerusalem, built on one of the highest peaks in Judea, rose 2,500 feet, half a mile, above the surrounding countryside. The drivers coaxed their beasts upward, and soon, as the soft morning light hardened into clear, bright sunshine, the sun burned off the cool mists.

Without warning, the ascent became much steeper. Haskel turned to look back again and saw how high they had gone. Now the donkeys were laboring, pulling their carts with slow determination. The distance from Jaffa to Jerusalem was a short thirty miles or so, but the steepest ascent was yet to come.

The sun was bright and hot, a desert sun, yet the air at that higher elevation remained cool and clear. Below in the sandy desert, the goats looked like black stones. Their caravan rode higher and higher along a winding road that dipped through a small valley, leveled off for a while, and climbed again into the clear blue sky.

"I'm hungry, Abba," said Haskel, and his sisters took up his cry.

"Soon we will be able to stop," their mother told them. "Soon."

But the mule drivers did not stop. They had to reach the city by nightfall, before the gates of Jerusalem were closed and locked, and already the sun was on their backs, casting their shadows in front.

Fishel was hungry too, and Esther reached into one of her bags and pulled out flat, soft bread and then raisins and dates. It was strange food for the young children from Poland, and they ate it slowly, not quite knowing what to make of it.

Suddenly, the shadows were even longer, and the drivers urged their animals on with quick flicks of their whips. Knowing the dangers of being caught on the road when night fell, the donkeys picked up their pace. Only a few travelers passed them in the opposite direction, and they too were hurrying through the growing dusk. Above them in the east, the jagged stones and the cedars were lit with a glowing evening light, but below, in the ravines and wadis, the shadows were darkening. It would soon be darker than it ever had been in Haskel's village in Poland. On a moonless night such as this, the black of the desert would be absolute; neither starlight nor a lantern would help. The sun was sinking quickly. Higher and higher they went, the hard dirt road turning one way and then turning sharply in the other. Their drivers urged the tired beasts on, but gently, for a donkey had a mind of its own.

"Look!" Haskel's father was excited. "There!" Haskel turned and lifted his eyes, and a sudden thrill seized him. The falling sun threw its dying light against the ancient wall, and the massive stones were aflame with a golden light.

His mother cried out, "*Baruch HaShem!*" (Bless the Name!).

The caravan slowed to a crawl and then came to a complete stop. Haskel peered into the growing darkness. In front of them was a long line of donkey carts, horses, and camels. The walls of the Old City gleamed in the evening light.

The animals were growing anxious, for they too were afraid of the night. Haskel and his sisters had fallen asleep. Esther and Fishel raised their heads and stared at the massive walls. After hundreds of years of exile, with generation upon generation wandering over the face of

Europe, they were at last returning home—and just in time too, for all the gates of Old Jerusalem were about to be sealed tightly against the night, to be reopened only at dawn.

At last, they passed through the gate, and in a small open square just inside, they stepped out of their cart. They took their few possessions off the cart and put them on the stones. Torches and lanterns lit the square. Roused from their sleep, Haskel and his sisters looked around. Fishel turned at the sound of his name. There was Yitzhak Haggis, smiling. Fishel embraced him, his tears flowing.

CHAPTER 5

Meanwhile, back in Warsaw, Netanel and Nechama couldn't make up their minds. They wanted to go to Jerusalem but did not want to leave Poland.

Especially hard for Netanel was the thought of giving up his annual pilgrimage to Gur, where, leaving the cares of the inn behind, he would spend a glorious, happy month celebrating the High Holy Days.

Among all the pleasures of Gur, what Netanel loved most was the singing. Every year there were new songs to learn, as well as new melodies for the old favorites. All of Gur anticipated Netanel's arrival every Rosh Hashanah. He had a beautiful high tenor, and when he burst into song he was lifted out of this world, and the other Hasidim, joining in, rose on the wings of his wonderful voice.

If he were to leave his little village in Poland, he would be just another Hasid with a good voice; nothing special, for Jerusalem was full of powerful singers. For there, the holiness of the air tempered the vocal cords to a fine edge.

His wife, Nechama, had hesitations too. She loved Jerusalem with all her heart and soul, and her love was bred of true and pure feeling. Like many women, she didn't read or write any language, including Hebrew, but growing up in a pious household, she had learned the prayers and blessings by heart. What came out of her mouth was a confused babble of Hebrew, Yiddish, and Polish, but she knew that God understood. In her daily prayers and blessings, the names of Zion, Jerusalem, and Israel were always on her lips. Though she had no idea where they were or how they were configured as to shape and size, for she had never seen a map, they took up large areas of her heart.

Thus, Netanel and Nechama continued to dwell in Poland, yearning for Jerusalem.

This might have gone on forever had a miracle not occurred.

Nechama became gravely ill.

Usually, a disease is not considered a miracle, but it's only in the totality of an event that the miraculous becomes evident.

The illness came suddenly and struck with devastating force. For two weeks, Nechama hovered between life and death. Word went out to Gur, and all the Hasidim there prayed for her recovery. Her condition did not improve. The rebbe of Gur himself used his considerable powers of supplication in an attempt to soften fate's impending harsh decree, but even that did not suffice. In addition to the heavenly requests, the world of science was not neglected, and a large sum was spent to bring a renowned doctor from Warsaw.

But to no avail.

When the situation appeared hopeless, the true miracle began unfolding.

A poor but exceedingly pious Hasid passing through Warsaw was persuaded to make a special trip to see Nechama before she died. It was understood that such a man, whose piety and poverty were of great and equal weight, might possess a more effective cure than a rich doctor from the big city. The Hasid, a tall man with an unruly dark beard, was brought into the sick room. In the dim candlelight, he studied Nechama as she lay near death. His eye held a bright, dancing fire that was stronger and brighter than the glowing coals in the little stove that barely warmed the room. He looked around and up and down, and his eye fixed upon the corner near the door. He drew back, frowning, his eye full of even brighter fire. The dark angel was waiting impatiently in the shadows.

He ordered everyone from the room, including Netanel, and for an hour all that was heard was the Hasid's murmurous prayers. Then all was silent. The door opened, and the pious Hasid beckoned. Netanel stepped in. His wife lay motionless on her bed, her eyes closed.

"I shall now prescribe a two-part cure," said the pious Hasid.

"Yes, yes, anything."

The first holy drug consisted of a generous donation to one of Jerusalem's Hasidic institutions of higher learning.

With only the slightest hesitation, Netanel agreed. "And the other?"

The second part of the cure was a promise from the sick woman that she would convince her husband, Netanel, to leave Poland and settle in Jerusalem.

"This both of you must to do joyfully, for there is little blessing in a deed done without enthusiasm."

What was there to discuss? Right then and there, Netanel and the pious Hasid settled the matter of the donation, after which Nechama, with great effort, sat up in bed and looked around.

Within an hour, with new color in her cheeks, she was already packing.

On their last day in Poland, Nechama, Netanel, and their children went to the family cemetery. Several rows of graves belonged to them, for their grandparents and parents were buried there, as well as sisters, brothers, aunts, uncles, and, most recently and most painfully, their own children.

Nechama's heart was full of a bottomless sorrow as she stood before the stones.

"You never answered me, but I could always talk to you." Her tears fell on the gravestones. "Now I won't be able to even talk to you."

"Yes you will, Imma," said her young daughter Reizel. "They aren't here. You can always talk to them wherever you are."

But Nechama could not be consoled.

Family circles in Jerusalem were never certain just how many children Nechama gave birth to, nor was it known how many were still alive when they left Warsaw. Some say they left with six children; others say only five. However, one fact is known: Nechama and Netanel came to Jerusalem with four healthy children. What happened on the journey to Palestine regarding the others was never revealed.

Some say they died on the overland trip and were buried in unknown graves; others say the two children, or the one, died on the boat from Trieste and were buried at sea. No one ever asked Nechama to give numbers or dates. Pious men and women did not regard these specifics as important, for numbers were always changing, and dates were insignificant points of time in eternity's vast expanse.

Furthermore, questions about past sorrows were unnecessary, especially when new ones came so thick and fast.

Leaving Poland, the Reismans journeyed overland with a large group of Jewish migrants heading south to the Black Sea. Loaded with heavy packs on their shoulders, they walked day and night through bright sun and dark, moonless nights. They slept in open fields. Passing through Jewish shtetls, they were given food and shelter.

In Trieste, they waited a week for a boat to take them to Palestine. At last, boarding with their children, Netanel raised his beautiful voice in a melody of thanksgiving. They were truly on their way at last. On the second day at sea, their youngest son complained of a headache. Nechama pressed her lips to his forehead and felt only slight warmth. She was not concerned. The little boy was overexcited, nothing more. But every time she kissed him, the fever increased, until his skin burned her lips. Her alarm grew. She had lost too many children in Poland to the Dark Angel. *Not here*, she prayed. *Not at sea!*

As the boy's condition worsened, Nechama became confused and angry. They had been told that migration to Jerusalem was a good and holy deed, and that anyone performing such a deed was protected against evil. Their undertaking had been further blessed by the rebbe of Gur, and his pious disciples had sent them off with prayers and song. Why then was her young son caught in a raging fever?

She prayed night and day, asking not for the boy's recovery but for an even smaller miracle. *Spare my son until the ship reaches Jaffa*, she prayed. *Send an angel to stay the hand of Death so that he may die on land and be buried in the bosom of the earth.*

All the Jewish passengers were present when Netanel wrapped his son with a tallit, a prayer shawl, and, with one long, wrenching cry, cast him overboard. In their little hovel of a cabin, Nechama wept.

Ah, but tears always come in bitter waves.

Three days later, another son succumbed even more rapidly to the fever, and his father cast the child into the sea, to be swallowed forever by the deep waters.

The ship took them directly to Jaffa, and from there, Netanel and Nechama, with their four surviving children, joined the stream of new arrivals ascending to Jerusalem.

*

That is how Reizel, together with her family, came to leave her home in Poland, much as Haskel left his, both of them to travel their separate, perilous ways to Jerusalem.

BOOK 2

Jerusalem

As the navel is set in the center of the human body,
so is the land of Israel the navel of the world ...
and Jerusalem is the center of the land of Israel,
and the sanctuary in the center of Jerusalem,
and the holy place in the center of the sanctuary,
and the ark in the center of the holy place,
and the foundation stone before the holy place,
because from it the world was founded.

—Midrash Tanchuma, Qedoshim

CHAPTER 6

Fishel and his family spent their first night in Jerusalem in the home of his father-in-law, Tzvi Lederberg, the leather merchant from Warsaw. The house was full of men and women eager for news about Poland, and they talked far into the night until, exhausted and happy, the new arrivals went to bed and rested securely and warmly for the first time in more than three months.

Early the next morning, Fishel walked through the streets with a welcoming entourage and went to a nearby synagogue for morning prayers. The walls of the Old City were touched with morning light, and the gold dome of the Great Mosque shone like a second sun. There was light everywhere, for Jerusalem is built on the crest of the Judean hills, and its ancient stones catch the sun throughout the day. The light is most lovely at dawn and dusk, when the sun strikes with full and level force, bringing out the burnished flame hidden in the desert stone. As Fishel was led to prayers on that bright and chilly morning, he marveled at such heavenly radiance. The dew sparkled like diamonds on the earth, and the walls glowed like precious metal.

At last, he understood why they called Jerusalem the City of Gold.

At the doors of the synagogue, the men stepped aside so that he might enter first. There he was called up to the Torah for an aliyah, which means an ascent, for the ark in which the Torah is kept is on a raised platform called a bema, so that reading the Holy Scriptures is akin to going up to Jerusalem.

With his prayer shawl on and his tefillin, or phylacteries, wound round his arm and forehead, Fishel acknowledged his family's safe passage over land and sea.

"Blessed are you, God our God, Sovereign of the universe, who has given favors to the undeserving and has shown us every kindness."

The congregation responded, "May God, who has shown you every blessing, deal with you always with kindness."

After the service, Fishel returned to his temporary home in Jerusalem and, led by an even larger group of friends and family, went with his wife and children to the Kotel Ha'Maravi, the Western Wall, to offer more prayers of thanksgiving.

Later that first day, while his family rested, Fishel set out to explore his new home. The night before, at the Jaffa Gate, he had been overwhelmed by the towering city in the setting sun, but that morning, while he walked to the synagogue, his jubilation gave way to dismay. The morning light carried a special blessing, and from the very stones holiness had risen, but now, navigating these dark, narrow, and twisting alleyways, he was depressed.

One must not, he knew, compare the dirty and malodorous streets of the Old City to the open, clean spaces in Plotsk or to the wide, long boulevards in Warsaw. Such comparisons were not appropriate. From listening to the emissaries from Jerusalem, he knew of the city's problems, but after anticipating so much holiness and beauty, he was saddened to see how bad things really were. Certainly, Warsaw had its share of the poor and unemployed; the armed and dangerous; and crowded, run-down neighborhoods, but the pervasive dirt and poverty in the walled city of Old Jerusalem was much worse. The streets weren't really streets but dark, twisting mazes of stone and mud. Without any municipal building codes, people had built without regard for aesthetics or safety, cutting off the light and air and cramping the streets even more. Without public toilets of any kind, every dark corner and narrow alley had become a bathroom, and the holy stones reeked of human waste. Beggars were everywhere, as were thieves and pickpockets. Arabs with daggers in their belts and armed Turkish soldiers, scowling and menacing, walked about with a challenging swagger, and he dared not meet their threatening eyes.

Expecting a city of vibrant, ancient holiness, he was stunned by the paucity of the Jewish presence. More than fifteen hundred years of Muslim and Christian conquest had taken their toll. Everywhere were churches and mosques crowding upon one another, towering structures that blotted out the sun and dwarfed the few synagogues, which were poor and shabby in comparison. Meandering slowly through the dark, twisting alleys, Fishel found himself close to tears, though that morning they were not tears of joy.

He and his wife had been living in a false dream. As a child, he had sat in his parents' house in Poland, listening to the emissaries from the east tell wonderful stories of the Holy Land. Their words had grown wings on him, and he had longed to soar upon the golden light of Jerusalem. He had come to live in this holy place to be yet another link in a golden chain that his people had been forging for thousands of years. But the evidence of his senses could not be denied. Was this what they wanted for themselves and their children—this small, dark, malodorous, dirty place? This walled city so alien and dangerous? With eyes blinded by despair, he found his way home.

Esther needed but one glance to see that he was upset.

"Tell me what is wrong."

She listened as Fishel told her what he had seen, and she listened to his fears and uncertainties.

"Oh, my husband, my dear husband," she told him. "There is no turning back now. We have burned all our bridges to Poland, and they cannot be rebuilt."

"I know. I do not want to return."

"We will make the best of it," she said. "With God's help, we will build here."

CHAPTER 7

Jews know the wall that Fishel had visited that morning as the Kotel Ha'Maravi, the Western Wall. Its stones are the last vestiges of the Second Temple built twenty-five hundred years earlier by Jews returning from their Babylonian exile, an exile that had lasted for almost a hundred years. King Solomon had built the First Temple five hundred before that, not only as a symbol of faith and religiosity but also a demonstration of Israelite power and wealth. Such glory did not endure, however, and the Babylonians swallowed the Kingdom of Israel, its people exiled, the temple looted.

In due course, the wheel of fortune turned again, and Babylon fell to the sword of Cyrus the Great of Persia. Cyrus, a tolerant despot, believing he was following a great prophecy, allowed the Israelites to return to their homeland, as it is written in the concluding words of the Torah:

> Now in the first year of Cyrus king of Persia, that the word of the Lord by the mouth of Jeremiah might be accomplished, the Lord stirred up the spirit of Cyrus king of Persia, that he made a proclamation throughout all his kingdom, and put it also in writing, saying: "Thus says the Cyrus king of Persia: All the kingdoms of the earth hath the Lord, the God of Heaven, given me, and God hath charged me to build Him a house in Jerusalem, which is in Judah. Whosoever there is among you of all His people—the Lord his God be with him—let him go up."

So the exiles returned, reconstructed the walls of Jerusalem, and built a Second Temple.

No sooner had the Israelites reestablished their nation than the Macedonians, eager for conquest, showed up, and in short order, the Persian Empire fell to Alexander the Great. Too busy with the exciting business of killing and conquering to give much thought to governing, Alexander left the kingdom of Judah to itself. After his early death, however, his generals fought for the spoils. Ptolemy seized the rich prize of Palestine, whose strategic position astride the important trade routes provided a wealth of taxes and fees.

Soon a new military force, the Seleucids, deposed the Macedonians, and were in turn vanquished by the Greeks, who rapidly became the dominant seafaring power.

The Greeks were somewhat possessive about their many gods and didn't care for or understand the concept of monotheism. Indeed, recognition of a single higher nonhuman power is often a threat to tyrants, petty or otherwise, who recognize no greater authority than themselves. The Greeks took action. Using the Syrians as proxies, the Greek governor of the region, Antiochus, attacked Jerusalem and, in the year 167 BC, 2,200 years ago, sacked but did not destroy the Second Temple.

The wheel of fortune, turning incessantly, loosed a new force upon the world, which rapidly gathering strength, burst upon the world with an explosion of military might and seductive culture. Nothing could stop the invincible legions of Rome.

The Romans installed Herod as king of Judah, and the land was incorporated into the province of Syria, called Palestina. The Romans, their presence stretched thin over a vast empire, granted local populations a good amount of autonomy as long as they paid their taxes and did not challenge Roman rule, and they allowed the Jews a good amount of religious freedom, permitting them to continue their own judicial and legislative practices.

These concessions to local rule whetted rather than quenched Jewish aspiration for true freedom, and led by a fanatical sect of zealots, a revolutionary movement rose, challenging the supremacy of Roman rule.

About that time, a new religion was making itself felt. Beginning as a Jewish sect at whose center was a martyred charismatic preacher, this religion made steady inroads in Palestine, further challenging Roman authority.

In the year 70, after three years of fierce Jewish rebellion, the brilliant

Roman general, Titus, led his legions against Jerusalem and destroyed the city and Second Temple.

Jewish aspirations for freedom were not dampened, and partisans continued to harass the Romans until, fifty years later, a ragtag army of zealots attacked the Roman garrison, only to be crushed by Hadrian. Desiring to end these pesky, bloody challenges, the Romans prohibited all forms of Jewish study and practice. The province of Judah was absorbed into Syria-Palestine, Jerusalem was renamed Aelia Capitolina, and all Jews, upon penalty of death, were forbidden to venture within sight of Jerusalem.

Once a year, however, on the date of the destruction of the temple, the Romans permitted the outcasts to gather at the last remnant of their once mighty temple, the Western Wall, to pray. Because so much lamentation and tears are offered to its ancient stones, the world often refers to the Kotel as the Wailing Wall.

Without a state of their own, thus lacking a geographical center, Jewish existence was dependent upon intangibles, and nationalistic impulses were replaced by a cultural identity. The early exiles of Babylon, whose creative, scholarly endeavors had never ceased, stepped forth to create an inner self. With a powerful awareness of their mission, they identified and codified the cultural, intellectual, and spiritual aspects of Judaism, creating a system of ethics based upon biblical concepts of good and evil. In this way, they were able to link the spiritual impulse with the social good, infusing secular behavior with religious precepts. The rabbi and the synagogue replaced the priest and the temple, and animal sacrifice, a ritual of Second Temple Judaism, ceased to exist.

Events continued to unfold.

As Christianity spread, the Roman Empire underwent dramatic changes. With Constantine's conversion to the new religion in the year 330, interest in Jerusalem surged. Pilgrims flooded into Palestine, bringing a new prosperity to the devastated region. Most remaining Jewish sites were overrun in a wave of intense Christian proselytizing. When Rome fell to the Mongol hordes and its far-flung empire disintegrated, Palestine and the surrounding areas came under the control of a succession of eastern powers, finally becoming part of the Arab-Muslim empire after the Arab conquest of Jerusalem in 638.

The Muslim conquerors then proclaimed Jerusalem to be the third-most-important site in Islam, after Mecca and Medina. Islamic rulers destroyed or built over Christian sites and the few remaining Jewish sites, and the last vestiges of the Jewish presence disappeared in a sea of Islamic fervor.

Yet hope endured.

Throughout centuries of conflict and destruction, the Jewish population found cautious haven in all the corners of the world. In Palestine too there were hidden pockets of Judaism, secret libraries and discreet study halls with a holy Torah held in a makeshift ark. The traditions and customs dwelt in the shadows, waiting for another day. Meanwhile, Jews went to Rome, England, France, and the Rhineland. They went east too, to the lands of Byzantium, where they found refuge in Jewish communities dating back fifteen hundred years. To Russia too they went, and even farther east to China.

In the decades following the Muslim conquest, Palestine became a raging battlefield as Muslim leaders fought each other for control of Jerusalem and its lucrative trade routes. More bloodshed followed during the age of the Crusades, when Europe's kings sent their armies of knights and mercenaries to capture the prize of Jerusalem. The knights met with varying success, winning here and losing there, until the Muslim warrior Saladin defeated them in 1187 at the decisive Battle of Hattin. Arab-Muslims retained control of Palestine until early in the sixteenth century, when the Ottoman Turks destroyed the Mameluke forces and began four hundred years of Turkish dominance. Dividing Palestine into administrative entities, they parceled out the land and its resources to local leaders, asking in return obedience and tax revenues. With Christian pilgrims prohibited and the Jewish community in tatters, Palestine became, in effect, a lost world for the next three hundred years. An inhospitable and impoverished place, Jerusalem remained an under populated and isolated land with little wealth and almost no hope.

In that sad, depressed corner of the Ottoman Empire, upon the stones of Jerusalem's ancient streets, Fishel stood in the year 1879, his heart full of despair.

Yet there was hope still. A spark of the Divine Presence remained, and as he walked through the Jewish quarter, his step became livelier the closer he came to the Western Wall.

CHAPTER 8

"Come into partnership with me."

Fishel Linder sat in the home of his brother-in-law, Yitzhak Haggis. It was midafternoon, and the two men were drinking coffee in the Turkish style, dark and strong, the grinds and sugar settling into a soft, sweet mass at the bottom of the little ceramic cups.

"The store is doing well and will do better," continued Yitzhak. "There's enough for two families to make a living."

"I don't have any money to invest."

His brother-in-law waved his hand in dismissal. "I'm not asking for money. When you have it—and that time will come—you'll give it to me."

Fishel was silent. If he were to accept the offer, it would make life much simpler.

"Let me think about it," he said, and the two men sipped their coffee and left it at that.

Fishel knew that his father-in-law would gladly give him the money to buy into the business and become a full partner.

Tzvi Lederberg had come to Jerusalem three years earlier, and what he saw had also appalled him. The greater part of the Jewish community lived in dire poverty, dependent entirely on the charity that the collectors brought back from Europe. A practical as well as a pious man, Tzvi Lederberg knew that true help, lasting help, came from oneself. As an entrepreneur, he knew that the best antidote to poverty was not to redistribute wealth but to create it.

The area was as economic wasteland. Manufacturing and commerce, essential for a healthy economic base, were practically nonexistent. The per capita income was below subsistence levels. There was no market for imported goods, and there was a severe dearth of general merchandise, without which a merchant class could not exist. Compounding the problem was the lack of any export trade.

The Jewish community of Jerusalem was even more unproductive than the general population. Holiness—of which there were three different, distinct brands: Jewish, Muslim, and Christian—was Jerusalem's major commodity, but it commanded a very low price.

Tzvi Lederberg made a business decision.

In Poland, he had done a great deal of exporting and importing, and he knew that the value of goods increased in proportion to the distance they traveled and the need they satisfied.

He knew too that the citizens of Jerusalem were unaware of the vast array of practical devices available and were therefore willing to live without many items that the rest of the world considered essential. Once these goods were imported into the city, however, there would be a tremendous demand for them.

Without hesitation, he decided to open a store.

"But what will we sell?" his son, Yitzhak, asked.

"Stationery," replied the elder Lederberg. "Look around, and see what is needed. Paper goods, writing materials, pens and pencils, envelopes, and business stationery—receipt booklets, ledgers and notebooks, and accounting books." He knew what a business required. "Carbon sheets for copies, erasers, ink bottles, glue, and wax. Invoices and address forms," he continued. "And file folders so that people can keep track of their papers."

Yitzhak asked, "And just where are we going to get all these precious items?"

"From Germany and Czechoslovakia," replied Lederberg. "And from England. I have contacts everywhere."

Indeed, the store was an instant success, and by the time his son-in-law, Fishel Linder, arrived, Yitzhak was the owner of a flourishing business.

But when Fishel thought about the proposed partnership, he knew that however well they got along as friends, they would clash as partners—Yitzhak wanted to retain the right of decision making.

Instead, Fishel wanted a business for himself.

Lederberg approved. He liked this young man who was married to his younger daughter. He liked his intelligence, the way he thought large, and especially the way he talked to people— calm and respectful, honest and direct.

"Would you like to open another stationery store?" Lederberg sat with Fishel one evening, exploring the possibilities.

"I thought of that, but why compete with family? When I walk around Jerusalem, I see a need for something else."

"Yes?"

"I want to open a hardware store. It would be more expensive to import the goods, but the markup would be greater. Some things are impossible to find." Fishel's voice held a new excitement. "Like matches. No one has matches. And pots and pans. A good set of plates would be like gold! I've already found a good location."

Lederberg looked at the young man with admiration. This yeshiva student had a head for practical matters. His daughter had chosen wisely.

"Of course, I would have to borrow the money from you."

"*Ganz gut*," said Lederberg. "All's well. A hardware store is an excellent choice."

There was no written contract and barely an oral agreement. Lederberg would make the loan gladly, and, of course, after a few years the loans would be forgiven. A man did what he could for his children and did it without desire for profit. He would sometimes, if necessary, even take a loss. Besides, at some point in the future, the grandchildren would get everything anyway.

Fishel had a good head for marketing too. He located his new enterprise in the major shopping area of Old Jerusalem and negotiated a lease for a big, square store on a corner, the better to attract trade. When his stock came in from Europe, Turkey, and Greece, he displayed the merchandise so that customers could see all his wares with one long glance. The store had a huge window in the roof, and sunlight poured in all day, giving his goods shine and sparkle. Next to his store was a row of little shops that sold many varieties of spices. Cinnamon, cloves, allspice, nutmeg, and dozens of other exotic spices were displayed on the narrow street in open barrels and burlap sacks, spreading pleasant aromas all around. This street was the center of the spice trade, so when people wanted to know where Fishel's hardware store was, they would be told to go to Bsomim Gass, the Spice Street. Most Jerusalem streets were not identified by written signs but were known for their offerings. For instance, the street leading through the Damascus Gate, so called because the road from it went north to Damascus, was also the street on which olives from Shomrom were brought into Jerusalem, so it was called the Street of Olives, Khan el Zeit.

Fishel was a keen observer of the local scene, and he sold goods that were scarce in Jerusalem: starch; blue dyes; potash; glue; tin, copper, and iron pots, pans, and kettles; utensils of all kinds, including knives, forks, spoons, and serving items, such as ladles and spatulas, which were in short supply and expensive. He imported kerosene stoves, with the wide wicks that gave a hot, broad flame; tools, such as hammers, pliers, and screwdrivers; and a hundred other items that were manna from heaven to the deprived inhabitants.

Needless to say, his store was an immediate success; his many customers, Jew and non-Jew, flocked to Bsomim Gass to see what marvels they might acquire.

With success came a problem: language.

The Jewish population comprised about two-thirds of the inhabitants of Old Jerusalem. Most of the others were Arabs, with only a small number of Christians living within the walls. These different groups used a dozen different languages and just as many dialects.

The Jews themselves were divided into two main groups. There were the Sephardim, who were of African Arab descent. They spoke Hebrew with a distinct, hard accent, and weren't comfortable with the softer, more European Hebrew, which the Ashkenazi preferred. The Sephardim knew little Yiddish, which was Fishel's native tongue and the language of preference for the Ashkenazi, whose numbers were far less than the Sephardic Jews. The Ashkenazi reserved Hebrew for prayer and study, using it for secular discourse only under duress.

Compounding the confusion of tongues, many Jerusalemites spoke only the language of their native country, which, for the Sephardim, was usually an Arabic dialect. Walking the streets of the Old City, Fishel thought he had wandered into the land of Babel.

In order to survive, Fishel became adept at shifting from Ashkenazi Hebrew to the Sephardic dialect. He picked up Arabic quickly, as well as some Turkish. German and Polish were his native tongues, as was Yiddish, of course. French too was useful, and he found himself speaking a few words of that most curious language.

The Arabs were his best customers—not the local Jerusalem Arabs, who were poor and scarcely had enough bread to eat. The Arabs who shopped in his store were the rich farmers, the effendis, and landowners. They came to Jerusalem on their beautiful horses, with their wives behind on camels or donkeys or, more often, following on foot, covered from head to toe with beautiful beaded dresses, their faces hidden by veils. These rich Arabs bought lavishly, and they didn't bargain.

They were also difficult. They had money, and they demanded obeisance and were often insulting and brusque, for to them he was nothing more than an ignoble merchant. The men brought their wives into the store and let them pick and choose from Fishel's merchandise while they stood and watched with heavy, possessive eyes. Fishel was careful not to look at the women or speak to them. Sometimes a rich Arab would throw the money to the floor, not in anger but as a way of showing how meaningless such sums were, and Fishel would wait for the man to leave before picking up the gold and silver coins. The men always returned, because his store held wonders that were unavailable anywhere else in Jerusalem.

Among those wonders were plain, simple wooden matches. Candles and lanterns provided all light in Jerusalem, in all of Palestine, and all cooking was done over little kerosene stoves and in charcoal-fired ovens. Jerusalemites were in constant need of an ember, and used little tin boxes to carry live coals from one house to another. During the day, especially in the morning and evening, children would go from house to house, as I did as a child, begging for fire.

Matches were in great demand.

The wooden sort were hard to find and expensive. People hoarded them like gold. Fishel imported them from Turkey, but the supply was spotty, and the quality was often poor.

One shipment was particularly bad.

"These are no good." Benjamin Cohen stood at the counter, holding a small cardboard box. Cohen was a holy scribe, a maker of Torah scrolls, and worked by candlelight.

"Not good?"

"See for yourself."

Fishel took the box. The match tips, of blue sulfur and phosphorous, were cracked and grainy.

"Go ahead. Try," said Cohen.

Fishel struck a match on the abrasive strip on the box. The blue tip sizzled without igniting and put forth a faint acrid smell.

"Aha!" Cohen's eyes shone with vindication. "Try another."

Fishel did, with the same result.

"They aren't worth bubkes." (Goat droppings)

Fishel tried a third match. Cohen was right.

"I'll give you a new box," said Fishel.

"Ach, they're all wet. Look at the box. Here, look. You see the watermark?"

Cohen was right again. The carton was water stained. When Fishel and Cohen examined his inventory, they saw that the matches had indeed been exposed to water. They discussed the possibilities: maybe the container had fallen into the water when being loaded; maybe it had sat out on the dock during a rainstorm; or maybe, suggested Cohen, the workers in the factory in Turkey had urinated on them. Whatever the reason, all the matches were useless.

Other customers came back too. Without matches, how could one light candles, especially for the Sabbath? How could one read at night or cook, and how would one light a cigarette or hookah?

Fishel pondered the problem.

"I need matches," he said to his brother-in-law later that afternoon.

"I can give you a case."

"I need more."

"You can get them from Damascus. I know a supplier there."

"How long will it take?"

Yitzhak Haggis shrugged. "A month maybe. More certain, two."

"I need them now. My customers are dependent on me."

Yitzhak Haggis shrugged again. Man proposed; God disposed.

Fishel was thinking. "I have an idea," he said.

The next morning at eleven o'clock, when the sun was shining brightly in a clear blue sky, conditions common in Jerusalem, Fishel stood outside his hardware store on Spice Street and held up an object to the sun. He made a big show of examining the object, turning it over above his head, holding it against the light, moving it this way and that, breathing on it, and cleaning it with a soft white cloth.

Passersby stopped to watch his curious behavior.

He continued examining the object as more and more people gathered around. He put down the object and turned to the small crowd. "Does anyone have a cigarette to light?"

After a moment of silence, a man's voice spoke in Arabic. "Light mine."

Fishel put out his hand. The man stepped forward. He wore the usual Arab robe of white cotton and a white kaffiyeh, or headdress, secured with a double coil of black braid. He held out a stubby Turkish cigarette. Such cigarettes were strong and biting.

Fishel took it in his left hand and, holding the magnifying glass in his right, adjusted it so that a bright circle of light touched the end of the cigarette.

The crowd held its breath as Fishel moved the magnifying glass so that the circle got smaller.

The crowd closed around him.

The light was now a bright pinpoint on the end of the cigarette. A thin curl of smoke rose from the cigarette. The crowd moved in tighter, peering in wonder. Fishel puffed his cheeks and blew, and the paper flared into fire.

"Ah!"

"Your cigarette, sir," said Fishel, handing it back to the owner.

From the wooden box at his feet, Fishel took out a half dozen magnifying glasses and held them up. They had lenses about two inches in diameter, mounted in holders of brass. He had imported them from Czechoslovakia months ago for reading purposes, but they had not sold, for not many people could read. Now they flew out of his hands.

Word about the latest miracle on Spice Street spread rapidly throughout Jerusalem, and by the evening he had sold his entire stock of two hundred magnifying glasses. When his next shipment came two months later, they sold out within a week. Shortly thereafter, a new shipment of perfectly good matches arrived from his supplier in Turkey, and demand for the miracle device fell off.

Fortune was kind to Fishel and Esther Linder. After hardly a year in Jerusalem, they had a good home and a profitable business.

Esther loved their spacious home. It had a big front yard for the children to play in, large rooms with high-arched ceilings, many windows, and a narrow but long balcony across the width of the house.

Esther's favorite place was the balcony. From it, she could see most of the Holy City, and when she stood at the railing, she could also see the slope of the Mount of Olives and the Jewish cemetery outside the walls. There were no graves in the Old City, for it was a holy place where death was not allowed in. Besides, there were so many of the dead, where would you put them all? Whenever she could spare time from her busy day, Esther sat on the balcony, whispered prayers, and then sang psalms to herself, giving thanks for her good life and asking that it continue.

Esther never complained. Everything was directed by God's finger, and whatever happened was meant to be. Her one discontent, however, was her failure to keep up with her secret studies. In Warsaw, whenever she'd had a few minutes to herself, she had dared to open one of her husband's books and try to make sense of the complicated tract. Here in Jerusalem, she was too busy with housekeeping and helping Fishel in the store, but soon she would dare again.

Her first winter in Jerusalem was a pleasant surprise. Compared to the long, cold, snow-filled winters in Poland, this weather, though windy and full of rain, was mild. Others complained constantly of the chill, and it was true that there was no way to heat the houses in Jerusalem; there were no fireplaces or room stoves to burn wood or coal. There was, in fact, no wood or coal to burn, for the land was semi desert. Indeed, Esther missed the endless forests of Poland; she missed their fresh, leafy green fragrance; the rustling songs of boughs in the wind;

and the chirping melodies of birds. None of the houses in Jerusalem had kitchen stoves; most cooking was done on little kerosene pots or outdoor grills. Bread and challah, the twisted egg bread of the Sabbath, were baked in a few large central bakeries to which the women brought the unbaked dough they had prepared at home. They returned later to retrieve the fragrant golden loaves, which were still warm from the bakers' ovens.

Jerusalem's climate was special. The city was perched atop the high Judean Mountains, and its days were full of sunshine while the nights were cool and crisp. The houses, constructed of stone and mortar, had thick, heavy walls thought to be good insulation. The opposite was really true, for stonewalls without wood or other coverings transmitted the cold easily and became damp with condensation. During cold spells, the only way to stay warm was to put on as many layers of clothing as you could and, when that didn't work, try to ignore the chill.

Her husband's business was doing well. Fishel could have expanded his hardware store on Spice Street or opened another, but his real interests lay elsewhere. He devoted a good deal of time and energy to community work and an equal amount to study. Mornings and evenings found him at the synagogue for prayer service, followed by an hour of Talmudic study in the morning and two additional hours in the evening.

And her children were thriving. The food and climate of Jerusalem seemed to make them healthier. Miriam, who had not grown for years, suddenly shot up a few inches, and all the clothing she had brought from Warsaw no longer fit. That was just as well, for the styles were different there. Esther was reluctant to part with the old clothing, if only for the memories. She decided to keep one or two items and give the rest to charity.

Esther had a mother's adoring eye, but an honest one. Both daughters were nice looking; Rachel was prettier, and Miriam was more practical but good looking enough. As a mother, Esther thought constantly of the future. It was never too early to plan. Would her daughters have husbands? What men were available? The matchmakers would consider the girls a find, but she would insist upon waiting for men who were special. But, once married, would they be fertile?

Esther loved her daughters, but for her son, she had a special love. Hopes for Haskel and his future filled her heart and mind.

Esther sometimes compared herself to Hannah of the Bible, who, barren for many years, prayed for a child. Hannah's prayers were answered, for she conceived in her old age and gave birth to a boy, Samuel, whom she brought to the Holy Temple in Jerusalem to offer him in holy service. The boy grew up to become the prophet Samuel and, fulfilling a divine purpose, anointed Saul as the first king of Israel.

Esther had wanted many children, but after she gave birth to two daughters, the doctors had told her that another pregnancy would be dangerous. However, she'd conceived and given birth to Haskel. Had he been a girl, she would have risked her life again, for she wanted to have a son. When he was born, they named him after the Hasidic rebbe of Kuzmeir, a little village near Plotsk. His full name was Yehaskel Elimelech, which, translated from the Hebrew, meant, "God shall hold you" and "God the king."

Her husband and all their family and friends called him by the last two syllables of his first name: Haskel.

*

My father was somewhat shorter than most children his age, but he was strong and healthy and was spared many of the dreaded childhood diseases that killed or scarred others. Full of energy, he started walking at an early age, and he had my grandfather's gift of language and began talking before it was expected. As was the custom, he was introduced to religious study when he was barely four years old. Coming from a family that was well off, he had a personal tutor, a melamed. The melamed had three other students. Private lessons were not in favor, because it was thought that one learned more, and faster, in a small group in which the children interacted with each other. Besides, even for his parents, private lessons would have been too expensive.

Esther was proud of her son. It was a pride she kept to herself. One must not tempt fate by carrying on too much about one's happiness and success. Esther was aware of the existence of unseen, unkind forces, and it was prudent to hide one's good fortune from the evil eye. In due time, as a tree grew and bore fruit, the world would see how good and noble her son was. Soon the matchmakers would come round, and her son would continue the march of the generations.

CHAPTER 9

The history of Jerusalem is the story of humanity, a tale as timeless, varied, complex, and contradictory as human nature itself.

In the City of Peace, there was perpetual strife.

In the hearts of those who preached joy and redemption was a deep despair.

In a city whose inhabitants sang of eternal life flowed a river of death and disease.

Amid the great wealth of the world's mighty religions, there was inescapable poverty.

It seemed to be ever so.

The most obvious aspects of Jerusalem were its poverty and filth.

In good measure, this poverty was a product of its religiosity. A philosophy that sets the spiritual above all else tends to negate the material, for the soul is not well served by worldly pleasures. Many of the pious viewed the present as a temporary passage to a happy eternity, rendering long-term economic progress meaningless. Indeed, why plan for a future that one hopes will not come to pass? The demands of commerce were incompatible with religious scruples; the profit motive was seen as greed, and the satisfaction of physical needs a rejection of holiness.

If poverty and need were the signs of holiness, Palestine certainly qualified as one of the holiest places on earth.

Mark Twain, who toured Palestine in 1867, a short time before Fishel Linder stepped through the Jaffa Gate, described the region as a "desolate country ... given over wholly to weeds—a silent mournful expanse ... A desolation is here that not even imagination can grace ... There was hardly a tree or shrub anywhere. Even the olive and the cactus, those fast friends of a worthless soil, had almost deserted the country."

According to an earlier traveler, Alphonse de Lamartine, Jerusalem was part of this desolation. He wrote in 1835,

> Outside the gates of Jerusalem we saw indeed no living
> object, heard no living sound, we found the same void,
> the same silence … as we should have expected before
> the entombed gates of Pompeii … a complete eternal
> silence reigns in this town, on the highways, in the
> country … the tomb of a whole people.

Fishel had read neither Twain nor de Lamartine, but the sad truth of their observations echoed in his own thoughts. It seemed to him that many religious Jews came to Jerusalem not to live but to die. Their most ardent wish was to be laid to rest on the Mount of Olives, and they lived their lives as close as possible to their chosen gravesite. He walked through the old, twisted streets of Jerusalem, looking into the yeshivas and synagogues where the Orthodox, young and old, studied and prayed, waiting for the Messiah.

That was all well and good, but surely one was allowed to make life more pleasant while waiting.

In fact, one had a duty to do so.

Fishel regarded himself as an observant Jew, but while yearning for the joys of the world to come, he acknowledged the undeniable reality of the here and now. Many of the pious viewed the spiritual and the physical worlds as separate and distinct and believed that one could not live in both places simultaneously.

But he believed that the two worlds, the spiritual and the physical, were really one and the same. The separation was a mere construct, for the Supreme Being who'd brought forth heaven and earth from the formless dark made all things equal, and men and women of flesh and blood were sanctified by that same Being.

Besides, did not Jewish ethics teach that a good deed created heaven on earth, bringing the two worlds together by joining God's with that of men? Furthermore, acts of loving kindness enhanced the worth of both worlds, for then men and women were elevated not only in God's eyes but also in their own, if indeed one could even think of the Supreme Being as possessing eyes. It was apparent that only through the acts of men and women was the world made a better place, and no one could argue that the world did not need improvement.

Most certainly, Jerusalem needed much repair. There were no public utilities—no electric or gas service and no private plumbing of any sort. The population preferred alleys and corners to the few filthy public toilets. People lit their homes with lanterns or candles and cooked with kerosene. Without water or facilities for bathing, people bathed infrequently, if they bathed at all, and only in public baths. As a child during and after World War I, I went once a week to the public baths with my father, Haskel. Water was scarce, and its distribution system was primitive and unreliable. Later, during the British mandate, the utility systems were slowly modernized, but for many years, centuries even, full-body bathing was a luxury enjoyed only by the very privileged or those fortunate enough to dwell where water was plentiful. People went for weeks or even months without bathing.

There were no municipal services, such as garbage collection or street cleaning. Potable water for drinking and cooking was obtained in a few central public squares. Like Rachel at the well, women and children gathered at the spigots with their water jugs, and it was common in the Old City to see them balancing urns and buckets of precious water on their hips and shoulders.

Without electricity, refrigeration was impossible. In the desert heat, food was highly perishable and was bought and prepared for immediate consumption. The food supply chain was primitive, and fresh produce and meat were hard to come by and expensive, especially kosher meat. In the battle against spoilage and waste, a great deal of expertise was required of the housewife, and good kitchen management became the cornerstone of a successful household economy. An efficient woman knew how to make ends more than meet, procuring and combining ingredients so that the whole was greater than the sum of its parts. Needless to say, kitchen work took up a good part of one's day—rather, a good part of the woman's day, for most of life's tasks, great and small, public and private, were assigned by gender.

However, many cultures, especially in urban settings, allow for some gender stretching. The Jewish community in Jerusalem was no exception. Though few men cooked, they often shopped, and though women were not required to study Talmud or learn to read, many did, even if they did it in secret. Because Orthodox men were expected to dedicate their lives to sitting and studying, women were active in the commercial aspects of life, and often became shopkeeper and owner.

In the subsistence economy of Jerusalem, nothing was ever thrown away. Recycling was the norm. Clothes, shoes especially, were treated with reverence and passed down or sometimes up and often across family lines. Furniture was rotated among households. Pots and pans, plates and bowls, and knives and forks were precious items carried from place to place, even across oceans. A broken plate was cause for lamentation. A porcelain serving plate with a crack was brought to the shop of a fixer, who, using a fine porcelain drill and steel clips held in place with a mix of glue and ground ceramic, stapled it together. Copper and iron pots were tinned and retinned. Scraps of cloth and lengths of thread were kept for another day. Paper, a treasured commodity, was never destroyed but was transmuted, with the alchemy of necessity, from one form to another; a paper bag would be cut up for letter writing or crumpled and stuffed into the toe of a shoe to provide a snug fit for the smaller foot of a younger brother.

Daily life was full of potential disasters. Minor cuts and respiratory infections blossomed overnight into fatal infections. A contaminated water supply spread typhus and diphtheria. The discovery of penicillin during the First World War was a miracle of major proportions. Travel of any sort was problematic. The internal combustion engine did not make significant inroads into Palestine until after the First World War, and the only means of transportation was some sort of foot power, either two-legged or four, the latter consisting of an assortment of camels, horses, and donkeys. On the road, dangers lurked around every hill, and the lone traveler was an easy target. Surrounded by ancient walls, Jerusalem was an oasis of safety in a desert of dangers. During the day, travelers hired their own guards or relied upon Turkish army patrols to keep the robbers away, but at night the roads and the hills around the city belonged to roving bands of thieves. Venturing out of the walled city at night was considered especially foolhardy.

Bandits were after loot, and women—hopefully young women, but any age would do. According to Muslim law, a man was allowed four wives, and many rich Arabs had two or three, while the poor men, of whom there were many, often had none. Kidnapping was common, so women remained indoors, going out only in groups or under the protection of men.

The tourist trade, vital to the economy of Jerusalem today, did not exist either. So harsh were conditions and so scarce were civilized amenities that few tourists ventured into the region.

In the streets of Jerusalem, beggars were everywhere.

And the sacred structures were in varying states of dilapidation and decay.

Jerusalem had nothing the world wanted, unless one counted its vast supply of holiness, which, arguably a truly priceless commodity, was not readily converted into cash.

Everywhere Fishel looked, he saw deprivation and hopelessness. His heart was heavy and his thoughts were in turmoil. Especially vexing was the sad condition of the Ashkenazi, the European Jews. Their Sephardic counterparts, the Jews from Arab countries, were more adept and practical. They were workers who didn't shy from hard manual labor, and many were traders who imported textiles from Syria and Egypt, which were known for the long, silky fibers of their cotton, and then sold their goods both wholesale and retail.

In contrast, the European Jewish community was top heavy with rabbis and students trying to become rabbis. Many men, disdaining all worldly aspirations, devoted themselves to fasting and prayer. They looked down upon their Sephardic brethren as too materialistic and uneducated.

Thus, two walls surrounded Jerusalem's Old City. One, a stone wall, was the physical structure that gave shape to the city and, once its gates were closed at nightfall, kept its inhabitants safe and secure within.

The other wall, the spiritual wall, was not made of stone or wood but was even more difficult to breach.

The first and only place to live for the devout European Hasid was within both walls. The closer one lived to the Kotel Ha'Maravi, the Western Wall, the closer was one to God. So attached was the ultra-Orthodox Jew to these sacred stones that he would not leave the Old City except when compelled by exceptional and urgent need; it was not uncommon to hear an elderly resident boast that he had never slept a single night outside the city walls.

There he would live, and there he would die.

In death too, the devout stayed as close to the ancient stones as possible. On the Mount of Olives was a cemetery that had been the burial ground of Jews for thousands of years. Facing east, its slope was touched every morning with the light of the newly risen sun. According to legend, the Messiah was to come from the east, his trumpet and heavenly fire heralding the approach of the Divine Presence. Then the bones of the dead would knit together and dance, and the dead would rise to life eternal, ushering in the world to come.

There was no clear picture of what exactly this new era would bring, but those souls fortunate enough to be buried on the Mount of Olives, facing east, would be the first to experience the Messiah and, thus, the first to rise from the grave; the pious wanted to get a jump on immortality. Should one be caught more than a day's journey from Jerusalem when death came, burial on the Mount of Olives would be impossible, for Jewish custom was to inter the body within twenty-four hours to prevent the dead body from being an object of veneration and a cult of death from developing. There were times, however, when travel was necessary, as when the collectors roamed Europe in pursuit of donations. In those cases, as Fishel had discovered when he was a child, a tin box of holy earth from Jerusalem would suffice.

Thus, for the truly devout, Jerusalem was the center of the physical world and the navel of their existence. The stone perimeter ringing the Old City separated the sacred from the profane. Inside was a special spiritual world, a living holiness found nowhere else on earth. Distances in the Old City were measured not in miles, yards, feet, or inches, but in gradients of prayer, sacrifice, and devotion. The devout Hasid lived not in a place of length, width, and height but in an intangible but real spiritual dimension.

However, as Fishel was learning, though the Divine Spirit might reside in the hearts and minds of its pious inhabitants, filling them with joy and light, the heavenly sun penetrated the narrow, dark, malodorous allies of the Old City but rarely.

*

One of Jerusalem's most pressing problems was the extreme shortage of housing.

In 1850, it was estimated the Jewish population of Jerusalem numbered 1,500. By 1868, with the total population of Jerusalem about twenty-five thousand souls, half were Jewish, with seven thousand mainstream Christians, five thousand Muslims, and a scattering of other religious sects making up the rest. They were stuffed into a tiny walled space where a good portion of the real estate consisted of massive churches, glorious mosques, and, to a much lesser degree, Jewish synagogues and institutions of learning. As the nineteenth century drew to a close, one religion or another claimed every square inch of the Old City. Among the Christians, the various sects—Greek Orthodox, Russian Orthodox, Protestants, Catholics, and Latvians—were in perpetual and bitter competition with each other for space and prestige, and from time to time, riots would break out over some perceived encroachment or insult regarding a sect's territory or prerogative.

All these houses of worship, when added to the assorted collections of holy stones and sites of biblical significance, limited residential living to a fraction of the real estate. With space so tight, houses were built over the narrow streets and alleys, blocking the healing sun and cleansing rains.

All attempts by the Jewish community to increase their real estate holdings were frustrated by the Ottoman Turks, who would not allow a greater Jewish presence in their Muslim empire. In the 1850s and '60s, the Jewish community, wanting to reclaim some of the Old City and counter the ever-intensifying activities of well-financed Christian missionaries, built a number of small hospitals outside the Jewish quarter. Funded by Dutch and German philanthropists, other projects followed, and soon more construction—of an extremely limited nature—expanded the traditional living quarters of the Jewish community to include areas outside the Old City.

The new projects were unable to keep up with the influx of immigrants. Living conditions were already intolerable, and with every boat arriving in Jaffa and every immigrant caravan making its slow way down from Syria, the crowding became worse. The Jewish population of the Old City increased dramatically during the last twenty-five years of the nineteenth century as Hasidic families fleeing the pogroms in Russian and Poland chose Palestine as their new home. New arrivals flooded the dark, dirty alleys and hovels, wanting only to dwell within the sacred walls. Compounding the problem, the Jewish birth rate was high. Six children per family were reasonable; a dozen was a blessing. A slightly higher level of hygiene, diet, and medical care in the Jewish community increased infant survival, adding to the congestion.

Somewhat paradoxically, the ultra religious community viewed the abominable situation in a positive light, as poverty was, to them, an index of piety. The Jerusalem emissaries traveling the routes of Europe exploited these terrible conditions in their appeals for charity, but seeing it firsthand, Fishel and others who did not believe in the redemptive powers of squalor were determined to alleviate this terrible situation.

Some progress had already been made. Earlier immigrants had banded together in small self-help groups and pooled their resources. Their experiences in the small, isolated shtetls of Europe, where they had learned to govern themselves, served them well in Palestine. Bound by common language and custom, the immigrants established their own societies, called kolels. Fishel was elected the president of Kolel Warsaw, an organization formed by Polish immigrants that helped new arrivals from Poland with temporary housing and subsistence grants. Jerusalem had many such kolels, federations organized by country of origin in which immigrants found a sympathetic ear and a familiar tongue. Jews from Hungary belonged to Kolel Hungary; the Romanians belonged to Kolel Romania, and so forth. The Jewish immigrants from Poland, soon to number in the thousands, formed kolels from their various cities, Warsaw being the largest of them. Kolel Warsaw in Jerusalem was one of the largest and most successful associations

Underemployed and with little or no disposable income, people were eager to give charity in the form of work, and almost all services of the kolel were provided by volunteers. The largest kolels were organized along corporate lines, with a president, or memunah, and an executive board elected by the members, and was governed by a printed constitution and a set of bylaws. Changes in the constitution were proposed, debated, and then voted on by the entire membership. Every male member of the kolel was entitled to vote, and elections for the various offices were held every two years by secret ballot.

The major obstacles to Jewish expansion were Turkish laws prohibiting Jews from purchasing land both inside the Old City and outside its walls. The Ottomans tolerated Jews inside the Jewish quarter in old Jerusalem but, responding to demands by the Arab mufti of Jerusalem, did not allow any formal expansion beyond the gates. Without new housing, Jewish immigration would come to a standstill; Jewish residents had to find a way to break out of the stony confines.

According to an old Jewish adage, God sends the cure before the plague strikes, and against the disease of discrimination, God had sent the potent medicine of baksheesh. With money passing from Jewish hands to Turkish palms, miracles were accomplished, and here and there, with the use of middlemen and secret contracts, land was bought outside the walls.

Earlier, before the arrival of Fishel Linder and his family, a group of Ashkenazi Jews had bought land and built an apartment complex outside the Old City, northeast of the Damascus Gate. Bounded on the south by the Ethiopian church and on the west by the Romanian church, the complex, called the Mea Shearim, consisted of one hundred small apartments. The name Mea Shearim means "One Hundred Gates," though there were, in fact, only four major entry points. Most likely, the gates referred to the apartment doors, which were heavy and gate-like. The houses were one story, and were attached to each other side by side, forming a walled fortress with the exterior gates the only entrances to the interior courtyard. As were the gates of the Old City, the four gates of the Mea Shearim were closed during the night, keeping their residents safe and secure.

The distance from the Jaffa Gate to the new apartments was just a little more than a mile, not far in actual distance but light-years away in spirituality. To the ultra-Orthodox, moving outside the ancient walls was a rejection of the past, a purposeful distancing from God that left the offender open to dangers of all sorts, not the least of which were crime and ambush.

The dangers were real. The Turkish authorities did not provide any police protection or army patrols outside the Old City, and one passed through the ancient gates at one's peril. Visiting the Mea Shearim was considered an adventure into the wilderness. There were no paved roads, and the narrow earthen path winding out of the Old City wasn't even wide enough for a horse-drawn wagon. Donkeys and horses walked single file, moving aside to let a heavily laden beast pass. People walked in groups with heavy, wooden canes and iron bars wrapped in leather, and used them to beat off attacks by small bands of Bedouin thieves who, hiding in ravines or behind the many small hills, regarded those foolish enough to be caught in the open as fair prey. Whips were used to frighten off the roaming packs of wild dogs and the occasional coyote.

When the Mea Shearim was first built, it was a daring, cosmopolitan place to live: fancy European gas lanterns lit the streets, a movie theater with magic lantern shows entertained all of Jerusalem, and a number of fashion shows displayed the latest European styles to the locals. Inhabited by Jews of a lesser piety, the Mea Shearim was dubbed the Paris of the Orient and became the prototype for more housing erected outside the walled city. Though these complexes didn't have protective walls, the houses were built around an inner square and, attached one to the other, formed a continuous outer wall of solid stone and cement, in effect creating a self-contained fortress. A big open market and a smattering of small stores were usually inside the square.

Yet, by the first decade of the twentieth century, the Mea Shearim had become a bastion of Hasidism and ultra-Orthodoxy. A number of Talmud Torahs, religious elementary schools, and yeshivas for educating young men replaced the movie theater and the various houses of entertainment. A public bath and an attached mikvah, used by women for ritual bathing, were constructed. Inside the gates were also a few large synagogues and a number of smaller ones, called shtiblech, where the services were performed at a faster pace than in the bigger synagogues so that worshippers who had other things to do were assured of a quick departure. Among the faithful, these shtiblech were referred to as prayer factories.

The success of the Mea Shearim showed that it was possible to survive and even thrive outside the protective walls of Jerusalem, and other apartment complexes were erected on the hills west and north of the city. Most of them were built in the basic courtyard design of the Mea Shearim, the most simple and effective way of creating a safe, self-contained community. Slowly but surely, a ring of housing complexes grew on the hilly perimeter outside the Old City, enclosing Jerusalem within a second wall of more modern structures. Either by design or subconscious motive, the houses were built mostly of stones taken from the surrounding hillsides so that new construction, at least outwardly, was consistent with the old. Thus, Jerusalem retained its special look, from the color and texture of its facades to the various and wonderful roof lines of its churches and mosques, all exposed to the golden sun of morning and the bronze light of dusk.

Even as people moved out of the walled city, Old Jerusalem remained the center of Jewish life. Regional and local government agencies were located there, as were most of the Jewish institutions of culture and learning. However, the outlying communities thrived. Schools were built, and hospitals and libraries opened their doors. The busy markets of the different apartment complexes added to the general economic well being. By the end of the nineteenth century, from dawn till dusk, there was a steady stream of people leaving and entering the gates of the Old City, moving up and down the hills on horses and donkeys laden with all manner of goods and produce.

It was in this community that I was born, and where I was to play on its streets; pray and study in its synagogues, Talmud Torahs and yeshivas; and, later, to leave in my search to find my place in the world.

CHAPTER 10

After living all her life in her inn in Poland, Nechama was miserable in her small, cramped apartment in Jerusalem. She feared the narrow dark alleys and the Arabs with their faces half hidden in their kaffiyehs, and she refused to let her two daughters, Golda Leah and Reizel, walk in the Old City without a male escort.

The other Hasidim welcomed her husband, Netanel, and her two sons, who had their father's voice, with open arms. The older son, Chaim, had an exceptionally powerful voice and soon was known as the *shaggas ha'ari chazen*, the cantor with the roar of a lion.

Within a few weeks of his arrival in Palestine, Netanel had found work. He could read Hebrew, Polish, and German and could write all three in a clean, legible hand. In a society where most men and women were barely literate, such skills commanded a price, and he was soon earning a living as a clerk and translator. After finishing his workday at five, he then spent two hours every evening, Sunday through Thursday, studying Torah. He'd return home at about eight o'clock for a late supper.

Slowly, Nechama adjusted to her life in the Old City. In spite of her fears, she had to admit that things were good. "Baruch HaShem," she often said. "Bless the Name. We entered Jerusalem with the right foot and did not have to apply for charity."

Every day, Nechama prayed using the prayer book she had brought from Warsaw, in which the Hebrew had been transliterated into Yiddish script, so she could pronounce the Hebrew by reading the Yiddish. Actually, she didn't know how to read, but the constant repetition over many years had rendered the text irrelevant, and though her eye followed the print and her fingers turned the pages, the words really passed from her heart to her tongue. Her house was crowded with guests, as it had been in the old days in Poland. Nechama was known for her lavish table and her home-baked challah, the sweet braided Sabbath bread without which no holiday was complete. It was so good that Netanel often had to admonish his hungry Hasidim—it seems they were always hungry, perhaps because they sang and danced with such fervor—not to jump on the challah, reminding them to save room for the other delicious foods to come.

Those years in my grandparents' home were wonderful and full of life. I remember that, suddenly, one of the men would begin singing, and my grandfather Netanel would then take up the melody, soon joined by his son with the roar of the lion. Then the other son would sing, and soon the dancing would start, with the men snaking around the table with their hands on the shoulders of the Hasidim in front of them, as Netanel and both his sons, my uncles, lifted their voices. The women stood back and clapped the rhythm. The men danced and danced, their black caftans flapping and their long, curled earlocks bouncing up and down like happy springs of coiled metal, as their voices poured forth in praise of HaShem, the Name.

But Nechama could not put aside her past. The memory of her children resting in a cemetery in Warsaw and the two sons buried at sea was always with her. She lived in constant fear that ill fortune would befall her four surviving children.

Wishing to protect them and give herself ease, she went to the Kotel twice a week, Monday and Thursday, and prayed for the health and safety of her family. As she stood at the wall with her siddur, the ancient prayers tumbling from her lips, her fears vanished. She wept, but the tears were tears of comfort. After closing her siddur, she would return to her home in the Old City with a happy heart, certain that her four surviving children were going to remain in this world for a long time.

Having emigrated from Warsaw, Nechama and Netanel automatically became registered members of Kolel Warsaw and were put on the long wait list for an apartment in a new development called Batei Warsaw, the Houses of Warsaw, which was under construction just west of the Mea Shearim. There would be thirty-six units, one of which would be given to Netanel, Nechama, and their four children, rent-free. Until then, they had to make do with their dark, cramped apartment in the Old City, making the best of it.

An additional difficulty, at least at first, was their neighbor. Netanel and Nechama lived in a building occupied by both Ashkenazi and Sephardic Jews, two groups that usually kept to themselves. Both groups spoke Hebrew but with distinct differences in pronunciation and rhythm. Their foods were different too; the Ashkenazi favored European cuisine, and the Sephardim favored Arabic. Their dress was dissimilar: the Hasidim affected the eighteenth-century look of the Polish aristocrat—long black caftans and tight pants with stockings showing—while the Sephardim favored long, flowing, colorful robes. Further, regarding religious observance, the Orthodox Hasidim viewed their Sephardic brothers with skepticism. In matters great and small, the Sephardim—sometimes referred to as Oriental Jews—were more relaxed. For instance, though all pious men had beards, the Sephardim trimmed theirs, but the Ashkenazi did not.

Their neighbors were the Simontovs, who had migrated from Iraq. The father, Shlomo, had owned a business in Baghdad that imported wool and silk; he could have stayed in Iraq and enjoyed a comfortable life, but heeding a timeless call of Jerusalem, he had brought his family to that dangerous, impoverished land. With his wealth and business skills, Shlomo Simontov soon established a major enterprise in Jerusalem, importing fabrics and ready-made apparel.

The Simontov store stocked a large line of ready-made clothes, which were expensive but necessary commodities, for not all citizens had the skills or time to sew their own. Most of his trade, however, was in unfinished fabric, and the Simontov store was a treasure trove of exotic cloth, bolts of silks from China and India, cottons from Egypt and Morocco, wool from England and Scotland, and fancy prints of deep, rich colors from France and Germany. Nechama often took her daughters, Golda Leah and Reizel, with her to the store, where they bought cloth to be sewn into dresses, blouses, sheets and pillowcases and napkins.

The younger sister, Reizel, was more interested in looking than buying. The colors and textures fascinated her, and while her mother and older sister made their selections and bargained, Reizel walked around the store, her eyes caressing the many colors and patterns while her hands reached out and touched the silks, cottons, and wools, her fingers tingling with pleasure. Observing the customers and the clerks discussing the different fabrics and negotiating prices, she began to learn about the different types of material, their uses, and their worth.

Soon, as Golda and Reizel got older, Nechama let her two daughters go out together in the Old City and do the household shopping. It was important that they learn the fine points of selection and purchase, especially bargaining, for their ordained roles as wives and mothers required these skills. The Simontov store was one of their favorite places, and they'd often go there just to wander through the wonderful fabrics.

By the way, my mother's name is pronounced as if it's spelled Rayz'l. In linguistics, the *ei* is known as a diphthong—that is, a double vowel that takes on special characteristics. Thus, Reizel sounds like Rayz'l.

Reizel was an adventurer, and had no fear of Jerusalem's streets. Often, she walked the full length of the long, crowded market, the souk, in the Old City, discovering stores with things she had never seen: Arabian lanterns and carved furniture, intricately patterned rugs, bright paintings, and carved stones and jewels set in golden frames. She was fascinated with the open-air cafes and would walk slowly, breathing in the aromas of strong coffee, rising tobacco smoke from the hookahs, and sizzling meats roasting on open charcoal fires, food forbidden to her by Jewish dietary rules. Music poured from the inner darkness—strange, hypnotic melodies. It was a great sin to listen to the music and an even greater one to enjoy it, but she walked slowly. She had a routine, keeping her favorite place for last. With her anticipation building as she approached Spice Street, she would slow down to delay the pleasure. Suddenly, displayed in open sacks and barrels, their colors as rich as Simontov's fabrics, were the barrels of spices. Their fragrances were strong even in winter, and on summer days they were intensified by the hot sunlight so that their vapors enveloped her in a cloud of strange perfume, making her dizzy.

Her mother knew that Reizel was different.

Nechama listened to her younger daughter nag her father to teach her how to write Hebrew.

"Abba," she insisted, "show me how to write the aleph-bet."

Netanel was dismissive. "Why do you need it? You're not going to use it."

"I want to know."

"You don't need it."

"Show me, Abba."

"Later," he told her, but they both knew that later would never come.

She envied her two brothers and was angry that they had private tutors who taught them how to write Hebrew and how to write the Latin alphabet so that they could address letters to Europe and America. Seeking to quench her thirst for knowledge, every Sabbath afternoon, when her father sat with her brothers over a passage of the Talmud, she stood by the door and listened. Sometimes, excited by what she heard, she would step into the room and ask a question.

"Eh? What's this?" Her father was always surprised. "Have you been listening?"

Always, she remained fascinated by the Old City and would walk up and down the narrow, crowded souk, steeping herself in the sights, sounds, and smells of the bustling market. She thought often of her future, of the unknown young man she would marry, and how she would have her own wonderful store on a street in Jerusalem.

Chapter 11

Arriving in Jerusalem, Fishel and Esther Linder had started a new calendar, for they thought of their lives as beginning anew the evening they stepped through the Jaffa Gate.

Now the calendar was five years old.

Five difficult yet rewarding years had passed, with much to be grateful for.

Esther loved the Old City. This was the city of David, whose beautiful psalms she knew by heart and sang to herself as she walked to the Kotel Ha'Maravi, the Western Wall. Her feet touched the same stones the prophets and temple priests had walked on, and she prayed at the same holy places where they had prayed. In Poland, her father had been rich, and all her material needs had been satisfied, but in Jerusalem she was satisfied with little. She wore the same clothing she had carried all the way from Plotsk, with the exception of shoes, which wore out quickly on the rough stone streets of the Old City.

Her husband spent most of his day at his hardware store, and when he wasn't there he was either studying Torah or occupied with charitable and community activities. Whenever she needed money, she went to the drawer in the dining room table and took what she needed. Her two daughters, Miriam and Rachel, would soon be young women. Miriam, who was fourteen years old, was short and stout and had a light complexion; her most striking features were her large green eyes and big, open smile. Miriam liked to stay home, helping her mother cook and clean, shopping with her to the open-air markets. The younger sister, Rachel, twelve, was tall and slender. She liked to go to her father's hardware store, spend the afternoon there, and return home when the store closed for the day.

Her son, Haskel, was Esther's pride and joy. Nine years old now, he was never home. He left early in the morning with his father for morning prayers at the synagogue, ate breakfast there, and then went off to cheder, elementary school, for morning and afternoon lessons.

Later, he'd join his father at the synagogue for early evening prayers. The two of them, father and young son, would walk home together and eat supper with the rest of the family.

Fishel too was content.

He believed that the hand of the Almighty had brought him out of exile in Poland and led him to the holy city of Jerusalem. His material success was also part of this divine goodness, for it allowed him to give charity to the needy and serve his community. His generosity was not limited to monetary donations; his skills in business and his reputation for integrity brought him respect and position, and the opportunity for other good works. The year before, he had been elected, for the second time, the president of Kolel Warsaw, which was now the largest kolel in Jerusalem, and he had just been appointed the mukhtar, the official representative of the kolel at meetings of the Greater City Council. In addition, the congregation at his synagogue had voted him gabbai, or president.

On a more personal but equally satisfying level, his wealth would allow him to marry off his two daughters in a manner befitting the Linder family's status in the community.

There were times when he feared his contentment was too great and his success too easy. The Torah was full of cautionary tales, and one didn't need to go beyond the first book of the Bible, B'reshit (Genesis), to learn the appropriate lesson. Jacob, the first patriarch, was content with his life in Canaan. He married the woman he loved, and made peace with his hostile neighbors. His twelve sons were strong and prosperous, their flocks increasing. Then, suddenly, disaster struck. His sons brought him a bloody robe, and he recognized it immediately as the coat of many colors he had given his favorite child, Joseph.

"It is my son's coat," Jacob cried. "Joseph is without doubt rent in pieces."

Fishel did not dwell on this sad tale, for he did not want to tempt fate.

He thought, *I shall be content with my lot, for the hand of the Almighty is in all things. For I am part of something greater than myself.*

Indeed, he was; he was part of that first great wave of European

Jewish immigration to wash over the ancient land. Between 1882 and 1903, more than twenty-five thousand new immigrants, led by impassioned Zionists hoping to reclaim their homeland, arrived in Jerusalem. But, despite housing projects, such as the Mea Shearim and the Warsaw Houses, the Old City was bursting at the seams. The situation could not be ignored. The lack of adequate housing forced people to live in such overcrowded conditions that both their physical health and psychological well being were at risk. Pedestrian and animal travel in the narrow, teeming streets was impossible, and even the donkeys were feeling the effects of overcrowding, kicking and bucking against the press of people.

Kolel Warsaw had finally finished their housing project outside the Old City, and already every unit was occupied. Under pressure from the Arab mufti of Jerusalem, and reacting to the extreme overcrowding in Jerusalem, the Turkish authorities were threatening to end all Jewish immigration. Quick, decisive action was needed, but local resources were inadequate for further expansion. Help had to come from the Diaspora, from the Jews in Europe and America. Collectors had to be sent forth.

Fishel turned down the request of the kolel that he return to Poland to raise funds. He had left Plotsk never expecting, nor wanting, to return. Jerusalem was the cornerstone of his new life. His family, business, and very soul were centered in this place of prophets and kings, a patch of land so small and crowded yet so infinitely large as to encompass eternity.

If he were to go back to Poland, he'd be gone for years, and his hardware store, upon which his family depended for survival, and allowed much of his charitable generosity, wouldn't survive without him. He would have to liquidate his business and become a paid servant of the kolel.

He was asked again, and again declined. He had reached his limit of sacrifice; not even for the welfare of his community would he abandon Jerusalem.

There was also a moral principle involved. He had learned it from his father, Moshe, who was buried now in Poland: "Do not allow," his father had told him, "any charity work to become a source of material benefit or income to yourself, for that corrupts the mitzvah, the good deed." Following this precept, Fishel had worked for the community without recompense of any kind, and had on many occasions covered kolel expenses out of his own pocket. A good deed, he believed, must be pure, completely free of self-interest, and untainted by worldly gain.

Yet a third time a delegation of rabbis and community leaders tried to persuade him, and a third time, Fishel refused.

Then his brother-in-law came to him. After expanding and moving his stationery store closer to the Jaffa Gate, which was now the center of commerce in the Old City, Yitzhak had become one of the wealthiest men in Jerusalem. He was also a real estate developer, and had bought property in the Old City. It was a tricky business, requiring bribes and secret contracts in order to get around Arab objections and Ottoman restrictions. He had bought land outside of Jaffa as well, in Petah Tikva, a town east of Tel Aviv, where Jewish settlers had established a farming collective and planted the first orange groves.

"Fishel, you must go back to Poland."

"Must? There is no must."

"Conditions here are dire; the need is great."

"There are others who could do the job as well. My family needs me."

"Believe me, they'll survive without you. The kolel will take care of them."

"I will not go to Poland to raise money while my family in Jerusalem has to receive charity. And I know what will happen—no matter how much money is collected, there will be a need for more, always more, and I will be asked to stay."

"I know, I know. But listen, I've thought about it, and I have a plan."

Fishel sighed. His brother-in-law had a plan for everything. "Okay, tell me your plan."

Yitzhak Haggis smiled, sensing he had won. "It's very simple," he said.

As Fishel expected, his brother-in-law's plan was anything but.

He would liquidate his hardware business and return to Poland, where he would limit his fund-raising to the specific goal of financing a housing project in New Jerusalem, as the area outside the walled city was called. Upon his return to Jerusalem, he would assume the management of Yitzhak's stationery story, drawing a salary commensurate with his managerial responsibilities. Equally important, Yitzhak would assume the costs of Fishel's trip to Poland, including the salary he would have earned had he stayed behind as the manager of the stationery store, so Fishel's family would not need any charity.

"Well," said Fishel, "I see you covered all my objections."

"*Nu?* So?"

"I am reluctant, but it seems to be my destiny. I will go to Poland."

Yitzhak Haggis was jubilant.

*

Fishel was gone more than two years. It was a strange and moving experience for him, and there were many times when he wished he had never returned to his birthplace. In the small village of Plotsk, nothing had changed, yet everything was different. Many had left, and many had stayed. In the cemetery, new markers stood garish and bright in the winter sun alongside the old, faded gravestones. He stood upon the cold, frozen earth and recited the Kaddish over his parents' graves, and wept.

It was not Poland that had changed; he was not the same man who had left. Returning from his new home in Jerusalem to stand upon the earth of his childhood, this rich, fertile soil that had brought forth the lush forests through which he had run as a little boy, he knew more than ever that he belonged in Jerusalem. The streets and houses were the same, the little synagogues were still standing, and the people went about their business. However, a sense of foreboding filled the air. His lungs choked on its heaviness, and there were times when, while walking the streets of Warsaw, he could not draw breath. Everywhere people were leaving, some to Palestine, many to America. The violence was growing; the anti-Semitism was more blatant and unapologetic. In the coffeehouses in Warsaw and the institutions of Jewish learning, the debates raged as when he had been a yeshiva student: "Should we stay in Poland and assimilate, or stay and remain distinct? Should we leave in the face of violence, or should we stay and fight for our rights? Should we fight as people, as Jews, or as both?"

Fishel listened and shook his head as he listened to the same endless arguments and the same unsatisfactory theories.

There was no hope here

But there was money, and his trip was a great financial success, and he returned to Jerusalem with sufficient funds to buy the land Kolel Warsaw needed for their new apartments outside the walled city. The building project went ahead, and a great number of dignitaries and rabbis were present at the groundbreaking ceremony outside the gates of the Old City. A prayer of gratitude was offered, followed by another prayer for the continuity and health of the community. Then my grandfather Fishel was given the honor of placing two gold French Napoleons under the carved granite cornerstone.

Even as the flow of Jews out of the Old City was accelerating, their political and economic power as a community grew as new immigrants arrived from Europe. Still, there were those who questioned the entire concept of a Jewish state. The last decade of the nineteenth century, as Zionism propelled Jewish immigration, saw a great debate taking shape. In Jerusalem, as in Warsaw, thinkers and theorists tried to answer an existential question: What was the place of the Jew in the world? A second and even more fundamental question had raised its head: What was the role of the Jew in Jerusalem?

There was a third more practical, pressing question: Which of the three great religions had the most valid claim to Jerusalem?

Some saw the Christians and Muslims as latecomers who, through force of arms, had ousted the Jews from their ancient homeland, destroying their temples and killing the inhabitants in the name of their own God. They pointed out the Christians and Muslims had other holy places, while the Jews possessed only one: Jerusalem. History could not be denied: the Jewish presence in Jerusalem, from the time of Joshua, David, and the prophets, had been continuous, interrupted only by war and forced exile. Over hundreds of years of Ottoman rule, Palestine had become a wasteland. Jerusalem had become a dying and neglected city, a place pilgrims visited if they dared, where armies clashed in the sands.

And in the last decades of Turkish rule, Palestine had been incorporated into Greater Syria, further eroding its national identity. All decisions affecting Jerusalem were made in Damascus, a distant and alien city. Suddenly, when the Jewish people began their long-delayed return to their homeland, others raised a hue and cry.

*

Some of the changes Fishel noted upon his return to Jerusalem after two years were for the better. Commerce in the Old City had grown tremendously, and the stationery store he now was managing had been enlarged and was flourishing. In the streets and in the shops and synagogues, Fishel heard other languages: Hungarian, Russian, and more English.

His successful fund-raising had enhanced his prestige and authority, and a number of institutions wanted his managerial services. At first tempted by the offers, he eventually declined. His two years away from home and family had taught him how important his wife and children were to him, and he wanted to balance the needs of the community with those of his own family.

Another change, a most rewarding one, was the new maturity of his children. It had been only two years since he'd left—how the days in Poland had dragged, even as the years of self-imposed exile had flown— and now Miriam, Rachel, and Haskel were practically young adults.

"The matchmakers are knocking at our door," Esther told him.

"Ah, and who have they suggested?"

She gave him a few names, one or two of which Fishel recognized.

"Nu?" he said.

"We shall wait for the perfect match," Esther said.

"Ah, but perfection is hard to find, so let's not wait too long."

Fishel had become impatient since his return, for the world seemed a more precarious place, and he wanted to take the good now rather than wait for an ideal heaven. His faith was deeper, but his sense of uncertainty was too, and he wanted his children to find spouses and start their families as soon as possible.

Esther, whose life in Jerusalem had gone on without change or disruption, felt no such urgency.

"Soon we will have a shidduch," she assured her husband, referring to a marriage contract. "Our daughters are good catches."

Indeed, they were both attractive and intelligent, and their family was pious and respected. Furthermore, the Linder girls would bring good dowries. The dowry, or bridal price, consisted of a number of items. First, the bride's family was required to provide enough money to set the new couple up in a house or get them started in a business. Second, there was also the monthly stipend, or kest, usually granted for a period of two years, during which time the young husband would refrain from work in order to study the Torah and Talmud, building his reputation in the religious community. It was expected, of course, that the couple would have children immediately and frequently, and the kest would be expected to cover the household expenses.

"Soon we will have a shidduch," Esther had said, and indeed, the two sisters were quickly matched and married. The young grooms, however, were somewhat unusual choices for a Hasidic family such as the Linders. Both Miriam and Rachel married secularized young men. Though both lived well within the accepted norms of Orthodoxy and observancy, they were more engaged in the secular world than was customary. Certain members of Fishel's congregation disapproved, but he spoke in praise of both grooms, and the objectors were silenced. Fishel was open-minded, not only acknowledging that differences were good, but also arguing that the Orthodox community must always expand its horizons.

With both precious daughters successfully matched, Esther turned all her attention to finding the perfect young woman for Haskel. Almost sixteen but with only a trace of beard, he looked much younger than his years. But his mind was mature, his reasoning sharp, and he was one of the best students in the Hasidic Yeshiva Hayei Olam. He was now a tutor himself, instructing some of the younger students.

Haskel was hardly at home, and for that reason perhaps, his mother, Esther, fussed over her darling son even more. Sparing no expense, she dressed Haskel in the finest clothing available. At one point, even

Fishel, who never paid attention to household doings, objected to her lavishness. But Esther had plans for her only son. She insisted he not spend any time in his father's store, for a stationery store, or any retail establishment, was not the proper place for a young, studious, pious Hasid with a glorious future.

However, as Haskel matured, he drew closer to his father. Despite Esther's disapproval of his interest in the business world, Haskel liked the energy of the marketplace and enjoyed working in the big stationery store near the Jaffa Gate, which his father now managed. There, as his father had when he himself was a young man in Poland, Haskel discovered that the world of commerce had something of genuine value; the store took him beyond the self-contained world of religious study, and was in fact, the place to practice what the books taught—how to live in the real world and deal with people.

Approaching his seventeenth birthday, Haskel was adept enough to please both his parents.

At home, he was the son of his mother, quiet and polite; in the bustling stationery store, which he visited often, he was his father's son, engaged and talkative.

In addition, the young Haskel had a third, more private persona: at the Hayei Olam Yeshiva, he was their star pupil.

CHAPTER 12

Netanel and Nechama were concerned; their daughter, Reizel, nearly twenty years old, was not married.

This was truly a cause for alarm.

Their three other children were married. They were especially pleased with Golda Leah's husband, Shlomo Wertheimer. An immigrant from Hungary, he was a rabbi and a scholar researching old Hebrew manuscripts. His work took him to libraries and museums around the world, where he exhumed ancient, forgotten manuscripts and brought them back to life. He was not, however, regarded in high esteem by the ultra-Orthodox community in Jerusalem, who felt a secular library was no place for a pious Hasidic rabbi, not to mention a museum full of statuary and graven images, idols not much different from the golden calf.

"I would be pleased to have another groom such as Shlomo Wertheimer for our Reizel," said Nechama, "but it seems she's going to make herself into an old maid."

"Sha, sha," replied Netanel. "She'll be under the chuppah soon."

It wasn't that no one wanted to marry her. On the contrary, the matchmakers had knocked at their door any number of times, but Reizel had let all prospects slip away. It was too bad for the matchmakers, her father said. But the proposed grooms had been in the middle range of desirability. And now some of the better matchmakers had stricken her from their lists.

Apparently, Reizel didn't care; she had her own mind and wasn't going to marry anyone she didn't want, and neither her mother nor her father had the heart to force her into a match against her will.

"She's getting worse," Nechama said to her husband. "Golda Leah told me what she said."

Her older sister was Reizel's confidante.

"Well, what did she say?"

"She said she doesn't care if she doesn't get married." Nechama shook her head and rolled her eyes. "She told Golda Leah that she wasn't for sale."

Netanel sighed. "It will happen, God willing."

Nechama would not be calmed. "She's going to be twenty. And we're not rich."

Reizel was the youngest of their children, and her time to wed had come and was almost gone. Most marriage contracts were signed when the couple was in their late teens; sixteen was regarded as just the right age for a girl to marry. By the time a woman was Reizel's age, she should have had at least two children running around the house and a third on the way.

"I asked her," Nechama said, "how much longer she needs to make up her mind, and she said that she isn't ready."

"Reizel has a head on her shoulders. Believe me, she knows what she wants."

"Let her want it soon."

"God willing, she will be married soon."

"God is willing," his wife retorted. "It's our daughter who's not."

Netanel shook his head. All things were divinely inspired, and he told his wife a story.

"An all-powerful king in a distant land summoned a rabbi. 'Rabbi,' the king said, 'God created heaven and earth in six days, but what has he done lately?'

"'God spends most of his time making matches between men and women,' the rabbi replied.

"'What's so special about that? I can be a matchmaker too.'

"'Many have tried and failed.'

"'I am the all-powerful king,' said the king, and he dismissed the rabbi.

"Shortly thereafter, one of his trusted ministers became a widower, and the all-powerful king decided to find him a new wife and prove the rabbi wrong. So he disguised himself in non-powerful clothing and secretly left his palace in search of a wife for the minister. He walked through the marketplace, passing many eligible women, but he didn't stop until he saw a beautiful girl arranging pastries in a bakery. 'Aha,' said the all-powerful king, 'she will be the wife of my trusted minister.'

"The king entered the bakery and bought a large assortment of pastries, and he told the beautiful woman, who was single, that he wished her to personally deliver the pastries to his minister. The king took from his purse a dozen gold coins and a sealed letter, telling the woman that she must give the letter to the minister when she delivered the pastries. The woman agreed, and the king left, feeling even more powerful. The letter informed the minister that it was the king's wish that he marry the woman carrying the pastries.

"In due course, hearing news of the marriage, the king summoned the rabbi and called for his minister, telling him to bring his new wife.

"The king sat upon his throne with the rabbi at his side as the minister and his wife entered. The all-powerful king's mouth dropped open. The woman was not the beautiful young woman from the pastry shop but a considerably older woman who was not at all beautiful.

"'Who is this woman you have married?' the king demanded.

"'Sire,' replied the minister, 'she is the woman who brought the pastries and your letter commanding me to marry her.'

"The king turned to the woman and demanded an explanation.

"'The young woman in the pastry shop, my lord,' she said, 'cut her finger while slicing some bread and was bleeding too heavily to deliver the pastries, so I went in her place.'

"The king turned to the rabbi. 'You are right,' he said. 'Only God can be a matchmaker.'

"So you see," said Netanel, "she will be married to the right man, God willing."

"Baruch HaShem," replied Nechama. "Just let God will it soon."

"Amen," murmured Netanel.

"And another thing," said his wife, "where does she go all day by herself?"

*

Three times a week, Reizel would leave without telling anyone and walk through the souk. She took her time, stopping here and there to look at the merchandise on one side of the street, and turning back to gaze at the stores on the other side. She loved the sights, sounds, and smells of the busy, crowded marketplace. The stores were open to the street, their goods spread on tables and hanging from above. Often, she stopped and listened to the bargaining between seller and buyer—loud, heated exchanges often accompanied by oaths, challenges, curses, and blessings. Sometimes a fight broke out, with the men slapping at each other and an occasional fist rose, but usually it was a contest of wit and will; cleverness was important, endurance the key. The merchant had to resist until the customer was about to leave for good—often, the first walk-away was a ruse—while the buyer had to be careful not to antagonize the merchant and risk not getting the goods at any price. It was part of the grown-up world, a world she had yet to enter.

One of Reizel's favorite places was the fabric store of their neighbor, Shlomo Simontov, the Iraqi merchant, who always had a smile for her. She would walk slowly among his shelves, touching the cotton, wool, and velvet and the shimmering satins and bright silks, and she would dream—not of making dresses for herself but of owning such a store, buying and selling as a grown woman with a home and life of her own.

Usually, the Simontov apparel store was her last stop before hurrying home, but once in a while she walked to the end of the souk and into the open square near the Jaffa Gate. On the left of the square was the ancient Citadel, and near it was David's Tower; on the right were a number of large stores. She'd walk past them, looking in through their windows, lingering.

This day, however, she had business to conduct for her father, and she walked quickly through the crowded market to the stationery store of Yitzhak Haggis, now managed by Fishel Linder, or, as he was sometimes called, Reb Plotsker.

Every month for the last half year, Reizel had bought writing supplies for her father and brother. Today, she had to buy ink—not just any ink, but three specific colors. Her father, Netanel, worked for a Jerusalem charity, and when he got a donation, he wrote out a receipt.

For a small donation, he wrote a simple receipt in black ink; for a larger sum, blue; and for a donation over a certain amount, he wrote a receipt using a fancy, decorative script in bright scarlet ink, indicating the largesse of the donor. Entering, Reizel looked around and, before making her purchases, took time to stroll up and down the aisles.

From his desk, where he had been studying a tractate of the Talmud, Fishel Linder looked up. He recognized the girl. She came in regularly and bought pens, paper, inks, and blotters. She had made a favorable impression on him. The store had a one-price policy, but that didn't stop the customers from bargaining. But this young woman never haggled. As always, watching her today, he was surprised to see her, for it was unusual for a young woman to come alone to a store so close to the Jaffa Gate, far from the Jewish quarter, where, he assumed, she must live. If she lived outside the walls in one of the newer housing projects, she was even more adventurous.

As she picked out her merchandise, Fishel saw his son entering, and a smile lit his face. He closed his book and stood as Haskel walked down the long aisle to where Fishel had his small open office—a desk, two chairs, a low filing cabinet, a second cabinet with three drawers.

"Abba, *guten tag*" (Father, good day). They spoke in Yiddish, the preferred and often only language of the Orthodox community.

Fishel asked his son how his day had gone, and as usual, Haskel had attended morning prayers, had breakfast, and studied, taken a break for lunch, studied some more. Now he'd come to the stationery story to help his father. In an hour, they would close the store and walk together to their little synagogue for evening prayers.

The young woman had made her selections and was waiting at the counter. Fishel would normally have taken her money, but because Haskel was there, he stayed at his desk. Like all strictly Orthodox men, Fishel avoided physical contact with any woman other than his wife, even in the fleeting exchange of money over a counter.

At the counter, Haskel tallied the young woman's merchandise on a small pad. From his desk, Fishel watched, noting how tall and poised the young woman stood. She was dressed well but modestly, with a touch of color in the scarf covering her hair, which, uncut, signaled her unmarried state. He watched her reach into her purse and put the money on the counter quietly and simply. His son picked up the money, counted it, and then picked change out of the cash box and placed the coins on the counter. The woman picked them up, put them in her purse, and then placed the inks and two pens in the cloth shopping bag hanging from the sash around her waist. She looked into his son's eyes for a moment, nodded, and left.

Fishel had a fleeting thought, a mere wisp of a question: *Who is this young woman?* But it was gone in an instant, because his attention returned to the open book on his desk, and he lowered his eyes and continued reading.

On the way home from evening prayers, Fishel again thought of the young woman.

She! The strange girl! She could be my son's wife.

Haskel was walking alongside, humming the last melody of the service, and Fishel glanced at him out of the corner of his eye. His son was younger than the girl, but they had looked at each other and had not panicked. She had been in the store two other times when his son was there, and they had exchanged similar looks. *Yes, a definite look!*

It was unthinkable for the two young people to talk to each other, but that look was enough.

Was it part of a grand plan?

The thought was so powerful that Fishel felt he had been struck by lightning.

"What did you say, Abba?"

Fishel shook his head. Without knowing, he had murmured a prayer of thanksgiving, albeit with a cautious tone.

When next the strange girl entered his store, Fishel paid her more attention. He asked her what she needed and made the change himself, taking the money off the counter and putting the change on it. He wanted to know more, but strict rules of comportment did not permit questions. He thought of following her home, but that too was unacceptable.

Then, a month later, the young woman came again, this time just after lunch. As luck would have it, Haskel, who usually came later, appeared shortly; he was going to the yeshiva and, on impulse, had stopped in to wish his father a good day.

On the lookout now, Fishel watched the two young people. They were careful not to pay each other too much attention, but he thought he sensed something there.

But maybe not. Maybe.

Just then, on his way to a potential client, Mordecai the shadchan, matchmaker, hurried by in the street. A coincidence perhaps? Perhaps a miracle? As the all-powerful king had learned, matches were made in heaven. Construe it as a divine nudge. Worldly miracles, especially relatively minor ones such as this, often had a human agent. Was Mordecai an angel in disguise just waiting for this opportunity? At any rate, the timing was perfect, and something, another inexplicable impulse, prompted the shadchan to peer into the stationery store.

Mordecai had a keen eye for certain things, for that was how he earned his living and, seeing the two young people standing on either side of the counter, he stopped dead in his tracks. This was most unusual—a young man and a young woman facing each other in a store. He moved closer to the window. They were not just any young man and young woman but, of all possible young men and young women, Haskel Linder and Reizel Reisman!

Quickly and nervously, not wishing to reveal his interest to any competitors who might be passing by, Mordecai walked away. He ducked into a corner, pulled out his notebook, and jotted a few notes in his own code, which not even his wife knew. This tattered little black notebook was his parnassah, his livelihood. Its pages were worn, smudged, and covered with tiny, cryptic marks. God forbid it should ever fall into his competitor's hand.

Mordecai hurried on, not wishing to be late for the interview with the family of a prospective bride. The matchmaker knew every family in Old Jerusalem who had a son or daughter of marriageable age, and knew many of the families living outside the gates. He knew the Linders, or, as they were sometimes called, the Plotskers, and had already approached Esther Linder with names of young women for her son. She had turned him down without so much of a thought. He had also gone to Nechama

Reisman with more than a few names of fine young men for her daughter and had no better luck there. However, it had never occurred to him, until through the store window, he had seen Haskel and Reizel looking at each other over the counter, that the two of them could be a match.

He stopped dead in his tracks.

I have to think this over, he told himself.

If he didn't approach this situation absolutely correctly, he would fail. Usually, he went to the girl's parents first, but this time he'd visit the prospective groom's parents, the Linders. It was always the boy's mother who was the toughest nut. And he'd change strategy and go to the father this time, because he knew from three previous attempts that Esther was the sort of mother who believed that no girl was good enough to marry her darling son, the prince Haskel.

But when should I do it?

He stood on the street, shaking with excitement, and fear.

If he had seen the possibilities, it was only a matter of time before some other busybody shadchan would put two and two together and beat him to the punch. Delay was fatal.

Mordecai spun around, walked quickly back to the store, peered through the window. The girl wasn't there, neither was the boy. Pulled by the hand of fate, Mordecai stepped into the store and asked for Reb Fishel Plotsker Linder. An employee pointed down the long, narrow aisle. Mordecai saw Fishel sitting at his desk, deeply absorbed in an open book. Interrupting a pious Hasid during holy study was unthinkable, but this was more important than philosophy, ethics, or religious theory—this was life!

Barely able to contain himself, Mordecai walked quietly but boldly down the aisle. Fishel didn't even raise his head. The shadchan stood at the desk.

Be polite, be dignified. Fishel Linder is a respected scholar and a successful businessman.

Mordecai took a deep breath. "The girl!" he shrieked. "The girl!"

Fishel jerked up and almost fell off his chair.

"Reb Fishel, your son!"

Confused, Fishel stared at the shadchan. Who did not know

Mordecai? But the man's wild look and hysterical manner alarmed him. Had something happened? "My son? What girl?"

"Netanel Reisman's daughter. The girl who buys the pens and ink. She was just here!"

Fishel's mouth dropped.

"A good girl," Mordecai said, calming down. "Intelligent, respectful, modest."

Ah, thought Fishel, a flush of pleasure spreading over his face.

"And a good family," continued the shadchan, lowering his voice to a conspiratorial whisper. "Religious, hardworking. Not a breath of scandal."

Fishel, president of Kolel Warsaw, knew the Reismans, for the father did clerical work for the kolel. They were indeed a good, religious family without false pride or pretense—and without a penny to their name.

"A match," the shadchan said, "that will bring mutual happiness to all parties."

Remaining silent, Fishel nodded slowly.

Mordecai smelled great interest, if not victory. "Nu?"

Containing his own excitement, Fishel stood and extended his hand. "I shall talk to my wife tonight."

In the street, Mordecai's fingers trembled as he wrote in his pad.

Wasting no time, but waiting until evening prayers were concluded, the shadchan raced to the Reismans that very night and quickly got approval from Netanel and Nechama, who were overjoyed that a groom such as Haskel Linder, a young scholar from a distinguished and established family, had been proposed for their daughter.

"And the Linders?" asked Netanel. His brow wrinkled with concern; he could not afford even a fraction of the dowry such a groom would command.

"We'll see," replied Mordecai with a little smile, implying that all would be well.

Leaving the Reismans with the couple already wed, even if it was only in his hopeful imagination, Mordecai made his way home, practically dancing with joy on the ancient stones. This match was going to be smooth sailing all the way to the chuppah. But then his heart stopped and his feet became leaden. The girl was very picky. She had said no many times before.

But had he not seen with his own two eyes the way they had looked at each other over the counter?

Once more, the shadchan's step became light; his heart beat high and strong. He must go home and celebrate with his wife—but again Mordecai stopped in midstep. *The boy's mother!* He struck his forehead with the palm of his right hand—a hard, stinging blow to remind him of the pitfalls of false optimism. Esther Linder was impossible to please when it came to her son.

But the shadchan had seen the approval in Reb Fishel's eyes and felt it in his firm handshake. But the issue of the dowry could derail the entire project!

Anyone observing Mordecai would have thought that the poor shadchan was afflicted with a rare sort of neurological impairment: he walked a little distance, stopped abruptly to strike his forehead and mutter to himself, then turned around and retraced his steps. He stopped again, stood immobile, then abruptly took off with a joyous stride, head high and humming to himself, only to stop yet again to look up to the dark heavens and roll his eyes, shaking his head and sighing. In such a syncopated and strange manner did the shadchan make his way home, where, to his wife's amazement, he collapsed into his chair, demanded supper, and then alternated between eating voraciously and pushing away his plate, muttering to himself before taking up his knife and fork again. He refused to divulge even to his wife the cause of his strange behavior.

A few days later, Mordecai was invited to the house of the Linders. This was a good sign, but it quickly became apparent that the sailing was not going to be as smooth as he'd hoped.

Mordecai sat down, nervous under Esther Linder's disapproving eye, and waited.

Esther did all the talking.

"The family is not well off."

"Piety is not measured by the bank account."

"The father is a clerk, I hear."

"And he writes, believe me, like a ancient scribe."

"My son is only seventeen," Esther continued.

"A good age to start a family," replied Mordecai.

"He's still a boy."

"But mature beyond his years."

"The girl is almost twenty, isn't she?"

The matchmaker shrugged, held out his hand, and rocked it. A year here, a year there—did it matter in the long run?

Esther was silent, a bad sign. The shadchan glanced at Fishel, who gave him a quick wink.

Fishel had noted the way his son looked at the girl, and he was determined that no one, not even his wife, would spoil this new proposal. Life was short, happiness elusive. He wanted his son to have what he wanted, and he had told his wife not to dismiss this proposal too quickly.

"Well," said Esther at last, "whatever her age, the younger the better." She stood and left the table.

It wasn't a firm no, and two days later, when Mordecai returned, there was a definite maybe.

Esther said, "so, it's time for them to meet. Maybe they won't like each other."

Fishel and the shadchan exchanged glances, and Mordecai kept his mouth shut. If Esther Linder knew that the young woman had been wandering about the streets of Old Jerusalem without an escort, and had been in their store, she would call off the match then and there.

"Yes," agreed the shadchan, "they have to meet."

With all parties consenting, Mordecai took out his tattered little notepad, entered a little code, and arranged the time and place for the couple's supposedly first meeting.

The next week, Fishel and Reizel met at the Kotel Ha'Maravi, the Western Wall. The shadchan had selected Tuesday, the third day of the week, a lucky day. It was early in the morning, and only a few people were present. Haskel came alone, and Reizel was accompanied by her sister, Golda.

Facing the ancient stones, the teenage boy and young woman stood ten feet apart, separated by a low wooden fence. They both held open siddurs, pretending to pray, but, for them, the pages were completely blank. Instead, they exchanged careful but promising glances. After half an hour of this pious and heartfelt devotion, they smiled at each other and closed their books.

Reizel and her sister left the Kotel first; Haskel waited a few minutes before leaving, not wanting to follow them through the streets. Home, Golda Leah gave her mother her impressions of the young Haskel. In response to her mother's questions, however, Reizel didn't offer a word. Nechama took her silence as a yes, for her daughter would not have hesitated to reject this newest potential bridegroom, as she had rejected a half dozen already.

However, the matchmaker wasn't home free yet. A few days later, Haskel's mother and her older sister visited the Reisman household to interview the proposed bride. It did not go well.

Reizel knew they had come to expose her as unlearned and ignorant. Esther Linder and her sister spoke Yiddish with a thick German accent, which poor Reizel found hard to understand. In addition, the two older women mixed their conversation with Hebrew quotations from the Bible, which further put the young woman at a disadvantage.

Rivka wore expensive clothing and jewelry, and around her head there hovered a cloud of strong, sweet perfume. Nor did they call her by her pretty name; instead, they addressed her in overly refined and delicate tones as "my dear child."

But she wasn't their child.

Obviously, the boy's mother was against the shidduch.

"My dear child," said Rivka, "tell us—how far is Jerusalem from Jaffa?"

"Why, as far as Jaffa is from Jerusalem."

"Yes, of course. And, my dear child, with what do we eat gefilte fish?"

"With a fork, of course."

"My dear child," said Esther, correcting her, "we eat gefilte fish with challah."

Reizel controlled her temper.

"Tell us, child—who was Jacob's grandfather."

"Abraham."

"Moses's sister?"

"Miriam."

"Isaac's grandfather?

"Terah."

"Queen Esther's uncle?"

"Mordecai."

"How many daughters did Jacob have?"

"He had no daughters."

"My dear child, he had one—Dinah."

"I am mistaken then."

"Who was the second king of Israel?"

"Solomon."

"No, it was David. Solomon was his son."

"I am mistaken again."

As the questions continued, Reizel kept her temper down, but the last straw came when they asked her if she knew how to write Yiddish or Hebrew.

Reizel flushed deeply. It was her shame that she could not. "I was not taught, even though I wanted to learn. I know the aleph-bet."

"My dear child, can you at least write your name?"

Without another word, Reizel got up and left the room. Outside, she turned her face to the stonewall, and wept tears of anger and sorrow.

*

It was the custom in those days for the groom's parents to thoroughly investigate the prospective bride. Not only was the bride herself investigated, but her immediate family was put under the microscope; the groom's parents would send forth their relatives to quietly, but thoroughly, question friends and neighbors.

The investigation was expected and, at times, welcome. Marriage was an important event that impacted the larger community; families were joined, wealth was transferred. The children from their union would become members of the religious community, enlarging it and ensuring its continuity. Unlike today, there were few formal depositories of information, and all parties were concerned that there be no legal, social, or medical obstacles preventing the couple from fulfilling their personal and public duties.

However, it was the bride and her family that bore the brunt of this detective work. Most girls were brought up in the seclusion of their homes under the strict supervision of their mothers, protected by their entire family. Girls were escorted everywhere, and their movements outside the home were limited. For a young woman to wander about the streets of Jerusalem, as Reizel did, was unusual. There were dangers real and physical, and reputation was at risk.

Young boys and men led lives much less sheltered. Little boys had more freedom to wander off and play, and as new apartment complexes were built outside the Old City's walls, they were allowed to explore without fear. Their freedom was curtailed, however, by their religious and academic obligations. At about four years of age, Hasidic boys attended school for most of the day, and by five, in addition to their studies, they were expected in synagogue for morning and evening prayers. Every Friday afternoon, a boy joined his father in the public baths; bathing was a requirement under rabbinical law. As the boy matured, he spent less time at home and more time interacting with adults. At the age of thirteen, he became a bar mitzvah, a son of good deeds, and was expected to participate fully in the religious and social life of the community. Consequently, when a matchmaker proposed a match, the boy was well known to the father and the other male relatives of the bride, but the girl was something of a mystery.

When Fishel heard his wife's report of her interview with Reizel, including the questions the girl had missed and her lack of reading and writing skills, he became angry.

"My dear wife," he said, controlling himself, "I must remind you what is written in the Ethics of the Fathers: 'One must not look at the flask but at what is in it.'"

"But she is—"

"There are no buts." His usual even-tempered tone now held genuine anger. "She is a good young woman from a good and pious family, and she will make our Haskel a good wife."

He was determined to bring this shidduch to completion; he had seen his son and the girl look at each other in the store, and after their meeting at the Kotel, Fishel knew that his son would be happy with her, even if she barely knew the aleph-bet. But many women could not read or write. She could learn. Certainly she was different, walking about on her own, a young woman unafraid. The girl's family was without scandal or blemish. Never had he heard a word of gossip or malice attributed to them, nor were their names ever linked to impiety. True, their fortunes had declined since their arrival in Jerusalem, but they carried themselves with dignity, and they were beautiful singers, especially the younger son with a voice like the roar of a lion.

Whatever his wife thought of Reizel, he would make sure the match would happen.

On the evening after the interview, after services in the synagogue, Fishel and Netanel Reisman sat down for a long conversation.

After which, walking home, Netanel could have wept for joy. He knew young Haskel well—who didn't know the son of Fishel Linder? He was a short, good-looking young man who was quiet and thoughtful, and when he spoke his voice was sure and pleasant. The status of the Linders within the Hasidic community was high. The family was well off, modest too, even though the older sister flaunted her wealth and could be somewhat imposing. But most importantly, his dear daughter Reizel wanted the boy. At last, thought Netanel as he walked home that night, at *last*. He had put on a cheerful, optimistic face for his wife, but he had feared that his daughter was destined to be unwed and grow old, living a life of loneliness, despair, and danger. *Not anymore*, he told himself as he spoke a prayer of thanksgiving to the dark night full of stars. *At last, my dear Reizel will be safe.*

*

A date was set for signing the kinyon, the marriage contract, when the parents and a select group of relatives of both families were to meet to discuss the details of the dowry. Once settled, the kinyon would be drawn up and signed, and a date would be set for the wedding.

Until the dowry was resolved, Mordecai was on pins and needles. The Linder-Reisman match was to be the greatest accomplishment of his career—who would have thought it possible? And his reputation was already enhanced. His little black notepad had served him well. However, for such a catch as Haskel Linder, a rich dowry would be expected, and the Reismans were of modest means. The negotiations could still fall apart.

By custom, the parties convened in the home of the future bride. Present were the immediate family members and their spouses, and three men from the Hasidic community unrelated to either the bride or groom. One of them would write the contract, the kinyon, and the other two would sign as witnesses.

The Reismans made lavish preparations; the home was decorated, the table held a feast not to be touched until the kinyon was signed. As was Orthodox custom, the men and women were in separate rooms. If it had been up to Esther, the dowry price for her son, Haskel, would have been impossibly high. She had said more than once, "my son should be weighed in gold." Netanel Reisman was too poor to meet even a modest bridal price, and the assembled families held their breath as the two fathers sat down at the table, face to face.

The shadchan also did not breath. Writing a kinyon was a long and tense procedure. Often, seemingly minor details became major obstacles; disagreements were exaggerated, tempers and egos flared, and the match would fall apart. But Fishel was determined not to let anything thwart this marriage, and he was a skilled and experienced businessman.

He looked up and cleared his throat.

"Reb Fishel, please," said one of the Hasidim.

"I wish to make a clear and brief statement."

The men fell silent. The women in the side room gathered in the door.

"I speak on behalf of my son, Yehaskel Elimelech. The groom doesn't ask for any dowry or any kest. Further, he has asked that his parents, Esther and myself, assume the costs of the wedding."

There was a surprised murmur from the assembled guests. With open mouth, Netanel Reisman stared at Fishel.

"However," said Fishel, "it is impossible not to give anything."

Netanel nodded vigorously. Family honor insisted that the bride's family give something, or they would be looked upon as beggars.

"So. The parents of the bride will give a set of seforim, books, required by the groom in furtherance of his studies. And they shall be twenty volumes of Talmud Bavli, a complete set of the Mishnah Torah by Maimonides, and the Arbah'ah Turim by Rabbi Ya'akov ben Asher."

As Fishel spoke, the only sound was the scratch of the quill on parchment as his words were recorded. His was not an inexpensive request. Holy books such as these were produced in limited editions and were handed down through the generations; their typeface was special, the paper was costly, and their bindings were of the finest leather.

At last, with the details settled and the kinyon signed by the bride and groom, both sets of parents, and the two witnesses, Haskel spoke. As was customary, he had prepared a presentation on a topic of rabbinical law, known as the halachah. This might seem like a rather esoteric anti-climax to a nuptial drama, but the focus of these proceedings, at least the public focus, was not on the two young people but on something greater than themselves. There would be time for them later, time for living together and for conception, childbirth, work, children, family and friends. For now, the small group gave their attention to the spiritual aspects of life and listened as young Haskel, his beard barely showing, analyzed and interpreted a fine point of Jewish law. His voice was soft and musical; his soft gray eyes were alive. Reizel watched and listened, a smile on her face.

The complete list of titles and authors that Fishel requested might be found on the kinyon that remains in the possession of my family in Jerusalem. The parchment is a hundred years old, faded and cracked, but the black ink is legible, as are all the signatures, especially that of Reizel, who had practiced for many hours, so that she might sign her name.

*

The wedding was held in the winter of 1898 at the home of Yitzhak Haggis, in the Old City of Jerusalem. My grandfather Fishel's prominence in the religious and philanthropic life of the city made the marriage a public event, and the celebration lasted an entire week. At the conclusion of the festivities, friends and relatives escorted the young couple to their marital home in the newly built Warsaw Houses. Snaking through the streets and out the Jaffa Gate, a long line of black-garbed, fur-hatted Hasidim sang and danced behind Haskel and Reizel, finally putting them on chairs and carrying them, a king and queen on their simple thrones, through the gates of their apartment. Once inside, they set the chairs on the stone floors and, with shouts of "Mazel tov!" and much laughter, left them to their new lives.

Chapter 13

Just west of the Mea Shearim, the Warsaw Houses—in Hebrew, Batei Warsaw—were similar to a modern condominium; each apartment a separate unit. They were modern and appealing, especially in contrast to the old, cramped, lightless apartments in the Old City. The walls were of thick concrete, with stonework around the doors and windows and iron gates on the yards and windows.

My parents' home, which was mine too for twenty-two years, had three interior rooms and a small exterior kitchen in a small front yard. Immediately inside our front door was a long, narrow room. On the left was another room, the *kleine shtibl*, the small room, while at the end of the long, narrow room was a door opening into the *grosse shtub*, or the large room. The kitchen—or, more accurately, the exterior cooking room—was a structure of wood and tin attached to the front wall of the house. Inside the kitchen, which one entered from the yard, was a freestanding brick oven with four open burners. We used coal, when it was available, or, most often, charcoal, in the firebox under the burners.

Inside the house, the grosse shtub, the big room in the rear, had three windows overlooking Mea Shearim Road, a wide dirt path that snaked into other roads leading to the Jaffa Gate of the Old City. To the west, Mea Shearim Road led to a wilderness of unpopulated hills and fields. The windows of the grosse shtub faced north and, combined with the poor insulating qualities of stone and the lack of any central heat, made the room extremely cold and damp in the winter. This room was big enough to have three closets built side by side on the long wall. The other two rooms—the long, narrow one and the small front room off to the side—both faced south, and each had a single narrow window. The floor was made of big slabs of polished granite, which was easy to clean but very cold. It was covered with assorted area rugs, which we swept with a stiff broom, or hung from a clothesline in the yard and beat as clean as we could.

The grosse shtub, with the windows and closets, served many

purposes, not all of them compatible. It was the main bedroom, a dining room when the house was filled with guests, and a general all-purpose overflow room. Our furnishings were meager--two separate beds, a round wooden table with eight chairs, and a small chest of drawers with an attached mirror. One closet held the wardrobe of my parents, and the other two closets stored assorted linens and dishes to be used for Pesach (Passover), when we shifted from leavened bread to matzo. In this big room was a large bookcase that held the seforim my father had received for his dowry.

Because the houses of Batei Warsaw were built on a relatively steep hill, we had a small cellar beneath the large room. Its entrance was above ground, facing north on Mea Shearim Road. We used the cellar, which extended into the hill about ten feet, to store odds and ends, extra furnishings, and an emergency supply of food. Our general poverty insured that the cellar was often empty.

Neither Old nor New Jerusalem had a central sewer system, and none of the homes Batei Warsaw had running water or any sort of toilet facilities. On top of the low hill facing the houses was a communal outhouse, a hut of wood and tin that was divided into four small rooms the size of large closets, the meaning of *large* being relative to the tight confines of the cramped Old City. Each compartment had a hole in the ground. It was not the most pleasant of places, and men and even women often used the most convenient wall or alley as an alternative. People were afraid to use the public toilets during the night, as there were no lights of any kind, and found it too cold and unpleasant during the winter, when temperatures sometimes hovered near freezing.

Reizel needed time to adjust to life outside Jerusalem's walls. The Mea Shearim's large central market was just a short walk away, but she missed the teeming souk of the Old City, with the Arab, Jewish, and Armenian merchants shouting out their wares and daring their customers to enter into a bargaining bout. She also missed the big stationery store and Simontov's fabric store. She missed especially the Street of Spices with the aromas so strong they were sweet colors in the air.

Though just a short walk from the crowded Mea Shearim, the land around the Warsaw Houses was wild and undeveloped. The unpaved streets were no more than beaten paths, and from their new home in Batei Warsaw, Haskel had to walk the long, dusty two miles to the yeshiva in the Old City. For safety and company, he walked with a group of young men; the two strongest carried cudgels against an assortment of dangers, animal and human.

From her front door, Reizel could see the high, rolling hill on whose crest was the big flourmill that was Jerusalem's main source of grain and bread. On windy days, the air carried the smells of fresh-ground wheat and corn, and from the mill's high stacks thick, fragrant clouds blew over her. From the back of her house, looking out the windows that opened onto Mea Shearim Road, Reizel gazed upon long stretches of fields of wheat and corn. During the spring and summer, the corn and wheat gave a lush green color to the otherwise dry land, and in the winter, after the harvest, the Arabs brought their sheep and goats to graze on the cuttings, and the flutes of the shepherds echoed throughout the valley.

But here, in the middle of Batei Warsaw, it was quiet and lonely.

At night, most often during the winter, she heard the barking and cries of jackals and wild dogs.

In the spring, strong, gusty winds brought heavy rains to the hills of Jerusalem, and in the summer, hot, dry air sweeping in from the desert mixed with the warm, sultry air of the Mediterranean and filled the sky with storm clouds. Then thunder and lightning rolled across the hills as heaven waged war with earth, and at the first thunderous explosions, Reizel would utter a prayer praising God for creating the heavens and all contained therein. Often, she thought of David's psalm, of the valley of the shadow of death, as the water rushed down the hills toward her gate, tumbling dark torrents racing toward her, and she would sigh with relief as the water swept past her gate, sparing her home.

Her new life in Batei Warsaw had a routine. During the week, Haskel was hardly home. He rose early and went to the main synagogue in the Mea Shearim for morning prayers, ate a light breakfast there, and then marched with his small gang of Hasidim to the Old City to the Yeshiva Hayei Olam, where he taught teenage boys barely younger than himself the rudiments of the Talmud. He came home just before sunset to freshen up, then left immediately for evening prayers, staying for another hour for more study. Finally, about eight o'clock, he returned for the night, and he and Reizel had supper together.

The Sabbath and the days leading up to it were a wonderful interlude.

Thursday morning, Reizel began preparations. In the morning, she baked the challah and sweet cakes they would eat on Friday night and Shabbos. In the afternoon, she went to the open food market in Mea Shearim, where the women and their young daughters crowded round the stalls to bargain with the vendors over potatoes, carrots, onions, and slivers of meat. They'd carry everything home wrapped and sealed. On Friday morning, she prepared the three Sabbath meals. Since cooking, or work of any sort, was forbidden on the day of rest, it was necessary to finish preparations by sunset. Hurrying about, she then cleaned the house, washing the floors and windows, and laid out her special dress.

On Friday, the yeshiva closed its doors at noon, and Haskel returned early; on the way home, he bought wine for the Sabbath Kiddush, the ritual of sanctification. Once home, he prepared the oil lamps that Reizel would light before dark, for it was forbidden to make any sort of fire on the Sabbath. While she set the supper table, Haskel polished his black shoes and then went outside to the kitchen and put enough coal in the oven to last through the night and into the next day. On the stove, in heavy covered pots, was the special Sabbath cholent, a stew of beans, potatoes, and bits of beef, which would simmer through the night. After finishing his chores, he trimmed his fingernails and, moving fast, lest the clock catch him, dressed quickly and went to the mikvah for his weekly bath.

From there, he hurried home, where he put on his Sabbath finery. Every Friday, twenty minutes before sunset, the sound of the shofar was heard throughout Batei Warsaw and the Mea Shearim, the haunting melody of the ram's horn ushering in the Sabbath and bringing the day of rest into the yards and gates of the inhabitants and into their hearts. Inside her clean, sparkling home, Reizel had already put on her special Sabbath dress, while Haskel, wearing his silk caftan and fur-trimmed streimel, hurried to the synagogue.

At home, Reizel waited for his return. The oil lamps cast warm shadows everywhere and the savory foods and sweet challah filled the house with delicate smells. Home at last, Haskel and Reizel ate supper, and then they got into bed. It was thought a blessing to make love at such a time, a time of peace and rest, for this world had already been created for them, and now, with the oil lamps glowing and the black night full of deep quiet, it was for them to create their own special world of man and woman.

Everything was new to them—their home in Batei Warsaw, the furniture, their clothing. They were new to themselves and new to each other. The wind, the rain, the thunder and lightning, and the mountains of dark rushing water—all were new and wonderful to Reizel.

*

Another event of 1898 had more far-reaching consequences than the marriage of Haskel and Reizel, not just on the lives of those who lived in Batei Warsaw or Old Jerusalem but on the rest of the world as well.

Fishel Linder was sitting at his desk in the rear of the stationery store, when his brother-in-law, Yitzhak Haggis, entered, excited.

"The Kaiser is coming!"

"The Kaiser?" Fishel looked up from his ledger. "Which Kaiser?"

Fishel, like many devout Hasidim, did not pay much attention to the political world of faraway Europe, whose rulers came and went with great frequency and clamor, all of them temporary and insignificant when compared to the eternal God and the ageless wisdom of the holy books.

"Kaiser Wilhelm of Prussia," Yitzhak Haggis told him.

"Ah, Prussia." *Men of war.*

"He's making a special trip to Jerusalem. He wants to meet the sultan."

"Why doesn't the sultan go to the Kaiser?"

"Ah, the Kaiser also wants to see the holy places."

"I see," said Fishel. "Our Kaiser is a pilgrim." He thought a while and then asked his brother-in-law. "And is it good for us?"

Yitzhak Haggis shrugged. "I don't know, but it can't be too bad."

Fishel sighed. "We will see, I'm afraid."

Actually, the news was both bad and good, depending on one's politics and place of residence.

On a pilgrimage for the betterment of his soul, Kaiser Wilhelm was also in need of some worldly profit. The Prussians, the most powerful military force in Europe, had been losing ground in the international arena. The French were in Lebanon; the British had their sphere of influence in Egypt and controlled the Suez Canal; and the Russians were, as always, stirring up things in Eastern Europe and the Balkans. The Kaiser was coming courting, hoping for a political and military marriage with the Ottoman Empire.

Some Jewish leaders saw the Kaiser's visit as an opportunity to generate interest and sympathy for the idea of a Jewish national homeland in Palestine. Dr. Theodore Herzl, one of the founders and best known of the Zionists, made a point of visiting the Holy Land at the same time, and actually had a brief audience with the Kaiser on Jaffa Road. He asked that the Kaiser of imperial Prussia speak favorably to the sultan of the Turks about Jewish settlement in Palestine. There is no record of whether the Kaiser fulfilled Dr. Herzl's request or of the reaction, if any, of the sultan, but subsequent events allow one to guess as to the effectiveness of the meeting.

Preparations for the Kaiser's arrival foreshadowed his appearance. In order that the Prussians might march with appropriate military pomp, the road from the port of Jaffa to Jerusalem was reconstructed. Houses were torn down, olive groves uprooted. An army of Arab workers labored day and night, widening and paving the old, narrow roadway.

The impending visit stirred everyone in Jerusalem, including the Hasidic community, which normally did not pay much attention to external events of a political, secular nature. Everyone talked about the Kaiser. Who was he? What did he look like? What would happen when he met the sultan?

The consensus among all parties was that the Kaiser's visit might be good for the Jewish community, or might not. To begin with, things never had been that great for the Jews, so it was a question of where exactly the baseline was to be drawn. Whatever happened, one adjusted.

Attitude was all. But one thing was certain: rules always seem to work against the Jewish community. Whenever the world talked about fairness, it meant a Jew had to give something up. Thus, the status quo was viewed, usually, as a good thing, because however onerous the rules, one learned to work them in his or her favor, or at least lessen their ill effects. Any change, even in the rare instance when the change was for the better, upset this delicate balance and created new obstacles.

And always and forever, against all man-made evil, there was the antidote, baksheesh.

Everyone argued and discussed; the prevailing wisdom counseled patience.

Then, a week before the momentous day, as Fishel sat at his desk in the stationery store, studying, a loud boom startled him.

A second boom was followed by a loud, tumbling crash, and Fishel felt the earth shake.

Shouting a prayer acknowledging God's power in creating earthquakes, Fishel dashed out. A thick dust cloud obscured the Jaffa Gate. He ran toward the gate as another tumbling crash sent more dust billowing into the air.

Men filled the narrow street, pushing against each other.

Through the dust, Fishel saw workers with sledgehammers and iron bars.

"They are destroying the wall!"

"The wall! The wall!"

The workers were driving long iron chisels into the stones.

The crowd screamed at the workers. Fishel too was shouting. The wall of the Old City, a wall that had stood for thousands of years, was being torn down. A short, stocky Hasid picked up a stone, cocked his arm, took aim, and let it fly into the back of a worker. Another Hasid then launched a second stone, and soon everyone was throwing whatever they could put their hands on. The workers dropped their tools and ran for cover. In a matter of minutes furious Arabs and Jews surrounded the Jaffa Gate. Fishel pushed through the throng and into the gate. The crowd was shouting, screaming, cursing and throwing stones at the fleeing workmen. The horror of the destruction overwhelmed Fishel. The supporting stones at the bottom of the wall had been smashed, and a section of the wall had tumbled down, leaving a jagged, narrow breach in the ancient stones.

And then: BANG!

For a long moment, there was utter silence.

Then another bang sounded, sharp and loud.

The Turkish soldiers were shooting.

Everyone fled, pushing and screaming.

Fishel ran.

He might have spent most of his life in a synagogue, praying twice a day, or at a desk, studying, but as a full-time Hasid he also danced for hours every Friday night, and at holidays and weddings, and his legs were no strangers to sustained, energetic movement. With his right hand holding his yarmulke firmly in place and his left holding his long black caftan just above his knees, Fishel took off at a full clip down Yafo Road.

More gunshots rang out and screams filled the air. Fishel ran without stopping, his heart pounding. A few Hasidim passed him, all running with a quick, gliding motion, holding their yarmulkes down and their caftans up, not lifting their feet too high off the ground in order to reduce unnecessary vertical motion. They were all moving fast, the long fringes of their undergarments flying behind.

So that the Kaiser's gilded carriages, white stallions, and cavalry officers with plumed hats and shining swords might have a more glorious entry into the City of Gold, the Turks demolished about a hundred feet of the protective wall surrounding Jerusalem. In order to build a viewing stand from which government dignitaries and military leaders could watch the grand procession, they then filled the moat around David's citadel.

The community was furious. Only a despotic, ignorant authority would have dared destroy any part of the historic wall surrounding Old Jerusalem, but the Ottomans, corrupt and despotic, had no respect for the historical or cultural significance of the ageless wall. The demolition generated clouds of heavy stone dust, which made deliveries to and from Fishel's stationery store difficult and hazardous. Fishel had to hire more workers while the demolition continued—these men were perhaps the only people in Jerusalem who benefitted from the wall's destruction.

The day of the Kaiser's entry into the Old City was declared a holiday. Schools and stores closed, the streets were decorated with Turkish and German flags. Parents brought their schoolchildren to the parade route. The stationery store was packed with friends and relatives, Fishel included, all of whom, in spite of themselves, were eager to see a genuine Kaiser.

Finally, with great fanfare and rolling drums, preceded by Turkish soldiers in clean uniforms, the Kaiser appeared. He was dressed in brilliant white and blinding gold. His stallion, equally white, carried less gold than the Kaiser did. Man and horse passed within a few yards of Fishel and Yitzhak Haggis, and in keeping with tradition, both men uttered the special prayer reserved for just such an occasion.

Every day a pious Jew is required to offer at least one hundred prayers or blessings. The daily morning and evening services contain almost eighty, and the shortfall is made up with the standard blessings before, during, and after meals. Eating, drinking, and washing hands all require their own blessing. The remaining half dozen or so can easily be found here and there during the day. There is a blessing for rain and thunder and another for rainbows. Putting on a new garment calls for a blessing, as does the sight of a fruit tree in blossom. In the evening, should the pious Hasid find that he's a few blessings in deficit, he can nosh on an extra piece of fruit, drink a glass of water, step outside and gaze up at the moon, all the while uttering the appropriate words.

Thus, most blessings are fairly common, requiring just a little ingenuity on the part of the pious; others, however, are rare and are realized only by lucky chance.

There is, however, a special blessing recited upon seeing a king or other head of state for the first time. These were rare events and worthy of special note. However, Kaiser Wilhelm of Prussia was a man of war, full of pride and wearing enough gold to pay for another housing complex. At his command, part of the ancient wall of Jerusalem had been destroyed, and he was not known to be friendly to Jews. How was a pious Jew to utter a prayer in honor of such a man? Yet an occasion like this came along once in a lifetime, and no observant Hasid could squander the opportunity. When one comes across a potential mitzvah, the sages say, he should treat it like wine; don't wait for it to go sour. Further, in order to be genuine, the blessing must be must be uttered publically, and those who hear it are required to say, "Amen."

As the Kaiser rode through the ancient streets, there rose from the mouths of the religious a general murmur: "Blessed are Thou, Lord our God, King of the universe, who has given your glory to a mortal man." A hundred amens followed. Thus, to the Kaiser and his entourage, there seemed to be a whispering song following them through the narrow streets, and they could only wonder.

"Glory to a mortal man," intoned Fishel, yet he knew that the Kaiser's glory was temporary, his gold mere trappings.

Kaiser Wilhelm visits Jerusalem, 1898

The Kaiser's visit, however brief, was a harbinger of worldly events that, over the next two decades, would engulf all of Europe, and Palestine, in murderous conflagration.

Part of the Ottoman Empire—an empire that endured for four hundred years—Palestine was a roughly defined geographical area without any cohesive political structure or firm national identity. During the latter years of the nineteenth century, wishing to exploit Ottoman weakness, European powers were steadily encroaching on Turkish hegemony, and the stage was being set for confrontation.

Ottoman rule, by and large, was not centralized, and the Turks allowed local authorities to establish their own limited spheres of influence. Palestine, regarded as a backward area of little economic and military significance, was generally treated with malignant neglect. Maintaining a military presence in the area as insurance against local insurrection and foreign intruders, and insisting upon their tax revenues, the Ottomans were content to let local officials exercise day-to-day power. The Jewish communities of Palestine, familiar with self-rule, were allowed, within limits, to create their own political and economic institutions. In the Old City, the grand mufti of Jerusalem controlled most economic activity among Arabs. The local police captains, usually Arabs of Turkish decent, were responsible for public peace. The Turks kept a military garrison, but the soldiers were generally ignorant, underpaid conscripts who, like their police counterparts, dedicated their lives to extracting from the citizenry every last ounce of baksheesh.

In the overcrowded, congested Old City, bribery was rampant. No structure, however small, could be built, no property could change hands, and not a single kerosene lamp or ream of paper could be sold without one applying a quantity of grease to the palm of a local policeman or Ottoman official. While the Turks had not yet organized any pogroms in the Russian mode or institutionalized the anti-Semitism of Europe, Jewish stores and institutions were constant targets of extortionists and petty politicians looking to make life difficult and make a profit.

Thus, to the devout Hasidim on the day of the Kaiser's visit, Fishel Linder among them, though a genuine king was prancing through the streets on his beautiful stallion, Jerusalem remained a place of danger and discrimination, a city yearning for peace and security.

CHAPTER 14

A year after Haskel and Reizel were married, Haskel became embroiled in a controversy that almost wrecked their marriage. Religious in nature, the controversy pitted two different groups of Ashkenazi Jews—the Hasidim and the Mitnaggedim—against each other.

Both groups came from Eastern Europe and shared the same basic religious precepts, but the Mitnaggedim did not approach Judaism with the ecstatic intensity and soulful piety of the Hasid. The two groups attended different synagogues and used their own rabbinical courts. They also had separate slaughterhouses, bakeries, and mikvahs, or public baths. The Mitnaggedim were larger in numbers, their rabbis were more prominent, and their congregants were wealthier; hence, their political power was greater, as was, therefore, their share of available funding. The Hasidim, on the other hand, however passionate in prayer, were not as well organized; their numbers were spread among many smaller groups, each with its own charismatic rebbe.

Both Haskel and Reizel had been raised in Hasidic families, and their married life followed the traditions of their parents.

Rabbi David Biderman was one of the most prominent Hasidic leaders in Jerusalem at the time. An immigrant from Poland, he was looking for an apartment in Jerusalem so that he could bring his family to Palestine. He had struck up a friendship with Haskel Linder in the Yeshiva Chai Olam, where Haskel was now a Talmudic lecturer. Not making much progress in his real estate quest, Reb Dubchela—as Rabbi Biderman was called—asked young Haskel if he might board with him until he could get his affairs in order.

Haskel conferred with Reizel.

"He's a very great rebbe," said Haskel. "Thoughtful and wise."

"It would be an honor to have him in our home," Reizel said. "How long will he stay?"

"Only until he finds a place to live."

"Apartments are hard to find," she cautioned.

"For such a distinguished rebbe, a place will be found soon, I'm sure."

Reizel was not as confident as her husband, but she gave her approval. The next day, the rabbi moved into their kleine shtibl, the small front room. This was an entirely proper room for the rabbi to occupy, for he could close the door while Reizel was home and observe all rules pertaining to gender and modesty.

Before long, however, Reb Dubchela, involved as he was in the complex doings of the Hasidic community in Jerusalem, was receiving visitors and petitioners all day long.

Her household routine was disrupted, but Reizel kept her smile.

Exacerbating the matter, an unexpected controversy broke out between the Hasidim and Mitnaggedim. It was over the baking of Passover matzo, the unleavened bread eaten during the holiday. The entire operation, from storage of the flour to its handling, mixing, and baking, was governed by a set of detailed rules designed to preserve the purity of the finished product. For instance, one was forbidden to bake the matzo on the same day the wheat was milled, for the flour was warm from the grinding process and would begin to rise as soon as water was added. Also, it was forbidden to transport the flour on a beast of burden without a thick leather blanket protecting it from the warmth and perspiration of the animal. To the less observant, these strictures might have appeared onerous, but to the devout, they were a pure pleasure.

For centuries in Jerusalem, all preparation of the flour and the baking were done by hand; it was a slow process that required many workers. The price of Passover matzo, therefore, was prohibitively high, yet the Orthodox, wanting the most kosher products, reluctantly paid.

That year, however, one bakery introduced an innovation that improved efficiency and lowered costs. Instead of carrying the individual matzo to the oven by hand, the bakery employed an ingenious conveyor belt that whisked dozens at a time into the waiting ovens.

The Mitnaggedim, always more flexible, accepted this efficiency wholeheartedly, but the Hasidim rose in fierce opposition. It was inevitable, they argued, that a tiny bit of moist, unbaked dough would stick to the machinery and rise into leavened bread, thus contaminating the machine, the oven, and the bakery. The contamination would eventually render all of Jerusalem unfit. This was anathema to the Hasidim; lines had to be drawn.

Marxist intimations complicated the dispute, for the Hasidim depended upon the hand process for employment. With paying jobs in pitifully short supply, many young Orthodox men made good money in the matzo factory in the months leading up to Passover. Any labor-saving device reduced employment and shifted the balance of power to the capitalist owner. Yet with the price of hand-baked matzo so high, many Hasidic families were hard pressed to buy enough for the holiday, and the Mitnaggedim pointed out, rightly so, that a true socialist would seek to alleviate such injustice.

Reb Dubchela, the spokesman for the Hasidim in this matter, issued a formal letter condemning the mechanical conveyor. However, the camp of the Mitnaggedim had many prominent rabbis prepared to certify the opposite.

Haskel, deeply involved in the dispute, spoke against the new method. The confrontation escalated. The rival parties held meetings and demonstrations. Mutual denunciations were exchanged. The Mitnaggedim, with modernity and market forces on their side, were carrying the day. The matzo produced with the conveyor was every bit as good and much less expensive, and even some of the Hasidim were buying it. Marx, it seemed, had it right when he described man as an economic animal.

At the suggestion of Reb Dubchela, Haskel and one of his friends decided to infiltrate the new bakery. They applied for work and were hired on the spot. Once inside the bakery, they kept a sharp, observant eye out for infractions. Two weeks later, they quit, convinced that the new method, however efficient it might be, was most certainly not in accord with rabbinical law.

Based upon their findings, a new Hasidic offensive was launched. Posters were put up all over Jerusalem, and circulars were distributed, spreading the word that it was the personal conviction of two young rabbinical students, based on firsthand experience, that the matzo baked by machine was not fit to eat on Passover.

Uproar ensued.

With the publication of Haskel's testimonial, Reizel's home, already Reb Duchela's office of Hasidic affairs, became overnight a public meeting place. Bearded men in black caftans and streimels rushed in, discussing, arguing, and shouting at each other, and rushed out.

As the lead player in a public storm, Reb Dubchela demanded more attention. He gave orders to Reizel in a deep, quick voice, his mouth moving fast in his thick black beard. He needed his meals served promptly, his clothes laundered, his shoes shined. "And please see to it that my visitors wait patiently in line until I am ready to see them."

"The rebbe must go somewhere else," she said to Haskel.

"Soon." Haskel was surprised at his wife's anger. "Our house is honored by the rebbe's presence."

"Haskel, I'm ready to let someone else have the honor."

"We must be patient. He won't stay forever."

"I'm not worried about forever. It's now that I want him gone."

"I can't tell such a great rebbe to leave."

"Don't tell him." Reizel was upset. "Ask him, and if he's so great, he'll take the hint."

"Soon, soon he'll go on his own."

But the disruptions only grew worse. Reizel waited until the Passover holiday was over, and then, with Reb Dubchela still holding court in the kleine shtibl, she decided that *genug vas genug* (enough was enough). In the morning, after Haskel left for prayers, she packed her things and returned to her parents, who were living just a stone's throw away in Batei Warsaw.

By afternoon, the news of Reizel's desertion had spread throughout Batei Warsaw and the Mea Shearim.

What a scandal!

Bright and early the next morning, her father-in-law paid Reb Dubchela a surprise visit. In his quiet, persuasive way, Fishel enlightened the rebbe, who, knowing what was appropriate behavior, packed his bags and was gone even before morning services were over. That same night, when Haskel returned from his studies, Reizel was waiting for him.

After that, she loved Haskel even more. He hadn't been able to get the squat, bearded, fast-talking Reb Dubchela out of their house, but that was because he had been too considerate. It would have been an insult for someone of Haskel's youth and stature to ask such a prominent rebbe to leave. Clearly, the rebbe had taken advantage of them, but then her father-in-law had gotten him out within a few hours. Furthermore, in the matzo dispute, Haskel had shown initiative and daring, confronting the powerful Mitnaggedim with strength and maturity.

Soon Reizel, feeling safe and secure in her new home outside the Old City, was ready to explore life in Batei Warsaw. From her front yard, she looked with wonder at the flourmill on the high hill, its tall stacks emitting dark clouds of fragrant smoke. Sometimes the strong winds carried the billowing smoke over her house, bringing a scattering of heavy raindrops.

She spent her days by herself, cleaning the house and shopping and cooking, waiting for Haskel's return from the yeshiva. Often, they had visitors for supper; her younger brother came twice a week, and Haskel had two close friends, young Hasidim from the yeshiva, who joined them almost every night for supper, after which the three young scholars stayed at the table discussing—and, at times, arguing—the fine points of Talmudic law.

Reizel would stand just inside the door of the grosse shtub, the big room, listening to them. She had no idea what went on in a yeshiva, and for the first time, she began to understand what it meant to study Torah. As she stood there, questions popped up in her head, but she would never step into the room to interrupt. Women did not discuss and argue these things. Standing there, sometimes she smiled to herself; their talk seemed silly and childish. If they constantly argued and disputed, how did they ever reach a conclusion? She, for instance, went to the market every day and made many quick decisions; if she constantly questioned herself, there would no supper on the table. But it was fascinating to hear Haskel and his friends talk into the night. Books lay open the table, and the kerosene lantern hanging from the ceiling spread a soft golden light on the worn pages. Often, one of them would grab a book and read from it, making a point. She would have loved to know how to read.

One night, after his friends had gone and Haskel was in bed, Reizel sat up. She had questions. She had listened closely and remembered much, and her husband was surprised, and impressed. Not quite knowing how to talk to a woman about such things, Haskel first tried to minimize her questions as trivial and unimportant, but she persisted, and, to his amazement, he found himself talking, explaining, and then arguing with her as he had just done with his friends.

CHAPTER 15

They had been married two years, and still there were no children.

Haskel never said a word to her about it, but she knew he was silent because he loved her and did not want to cause her pain. She was twenty-two, time was running out. Neither family was happy with her failure to conceive. In all this time, Haskel's mother had visited only four times, never staying long enough even for a quick tea. Reizel had often seen Haskel's aunt passing her house on Mea Shearim Road, and never once had the woman come in.

Her own mother didn't treat her any better. She spent a lot of time in her other children's homes, and it was obvious why—Reizel's sister and her husband had given her seven grandchildren already, and they were planning for more.

Everyone was tense and unhappy, and her barrenness was to blame.

Her dear father-in-law, Fishel, was the exception. He stopped by in the early evening as he returned from his stationery store in the Old City, while his son was still in the yeshiva. He came in and sat at the table, and Reizel brought him a glass of tea and then stood at the other end of the table while he told her about the day's business and the doings in the Old City.

"I saw Simontov today," he would tell her. "He has a new shipment of silks, very fine. He asked about you." Or he might say, "Your brother came in for inks and pens. He sends his regards."

Then, having taken only a few sips of his steaming tea, Fishel would stand, bade her *guten abend* (good evening), and leave.

Every Thursday evening, he placed half a golden Napoleon under the tablecloth—his contribution to the household budget and their only source of income. She never touched the money; she waited for Haskel to return home so that he could lift the corner of the cloth and hand her the golden coin.

Early one morning, just after Haskel had left, Reizel heard a loud, angry barking. From the front window, she saw a wild dog chasing a cat through their front yard. Around and around the little cat ran, the dog in close pursuit. *Oh*, she thought, *the cat will be killed*, and she ran to the door and flung it open just in time for the frightened creature to race inside.

It was really a big kitten, orange and black, and for the last month it had been wandering in and out of the yards in Batei Warsaw. Reizel had been putting out a small dish of milk in the mornings, so the little creature had run to her for safety. Reizel looked around—there it was, sniffing around in the corner, the wild dog forgotten.

The little cat came to her, sniffed her shoes, and then looked up at her and meowed. It was hungry, but there was no milk in the house. Reizel gave the cat some water in a bowl; put on her shawl and scarf; and, carrying a small glass jar in her apron, went out.

When she returned with the milk, the cat was nowhere to be found. She searched everywhere. The windows were closed, and the door had been locked. She heard a soft meowing, and followed the cries until she found the cat under the bed. Reizel got on her hands and knees and looked. The cat whimpered and then snarled.

Reizel looked closely.

In the shadows under the bed were three tiny kittens.

Reizel stood, poured the milk into a bowl, put the bowl under the bed, and pushed it close to the little cat. Fearful but hungry, the cat hesitated and then went to the bowl and lapped greedily. It looked at her once, meowed, and then bent again to the bowl.

Reizel wanted so much to take care of the cat and its baby kittens, but no one in Batei Warsaw kept non-kosher animals in the house. She watched the kittens under the bed as the little blind things tried to find their mother's teats. It was contrary to Jewish thought to see such a thing as this as omen, but Reizel saw it as a reproach.

She got off the floor and wiped her dress. It was Thursday, the day when she went to the Old City to shop for the Sabbath, and she had her chores. The cats could stay under the bed until she returned.

It was a warm summer morning, dry and pleasant in the hills of Jerusalem, and she walked quickly up Mea Shearim Road, holding her siddur, the prayer book her father-in-law had brought from Warsaw and given her as a wedding gift. The siddur was in Hebrew and Yiddish, and like many women, though she couldn't read either language, she could recite the prayers perfectly by heart, having spoken them all her life.

At the Jaffa Gate she stopped first at the stationery store. Her father-in-law was negotiating a large order with one of the rabbis of the Mitnaggedim, and he looked up and nodded and smiled. She was pleased, for his look was always kindly. She walked through the souk toward the Kotel Ha'Maravi. She walked faster than usual, not stopping to look at the goods on display, hurrying through Spice Street. Thoughts of the little cat and its tiny blind kittens hastened her steps.

On that bright morning, the Kotel was more crowded than usual. There were more women than men, for Thursday was the day when women shopped in the Old City and the Western Wall was one of their stops. In keeping with the tradition of separation of the sexes, the women had their own small space off to the side, separated by a heavy rope.

Reizel loosened her scarf, covered her face, and opened the siddur. The prayer book was comparatively new, but the first page, the only page she ever looked at, was stained with tears. She had stood here many times, asking for a child. Now, once again, she stood before the ancient, massive stones, the cracks between them stuffed with scrolls of paper holding names and requests. Had she known how to write, she would have put her own scroll in one of them. Her face covered, she prayed. Soon she was weeping. *A poor little cat could have three children, and I have none.* Her face covered with the scarf, her eyes blind with tears, she lifted a hand and pressed her palm against a stone made smooth by hundreds of years of countless other hands. "Bless me with children," she murmured as her tears fell onto the page. "Do not leave me barren."

Reizel closed the siddur and wiped her face with her scarf. Praying at the Kotel isn't just talking to voiceless stones. The wall responds. The wall inspires. The wall generates hope. Uttering one last prayer of thanksgiving, she felt strangely comforted and lifted her scarf from her eyes. Leaving the Kotel, she walked slowly back through the *ba'trak*, as the souk was called in Hebrew, and left through the Jaffa Gate without shopping.

The cat was still under the bed with its kittens, and Reizel poured more milk into the bowl and carried it to the front yard, and put it on the stones just outside the door. Leaving the door open, she went to the Mea Shearim market and shopped for the three Sabbath meals. When she returned, the bowl was empty, and the cat and its kittens were gone.

The next week, she fainted at the cistern.

Jerusalem had rain only during the few winter months, and water was a precious commodity. The Warsaw Houses had two large and one small cistern attached to a system of gutters and pipes that caught the water from the rooftops and fed it into two lined concrete holding tanks. There were no formal regulations on water use; instead, everyone was careful not to waste the smallest thimbleful.

Women made daily trips to the cisterns, and Reizel, young and healthy, easily carried two large galvanized pails back and forth. That day, however, while lifting both pails, she felt slightly dizzy. She put down the pails, paused for a moment, tried again, and fell.

That morning, she had felt a touch of nausea when changing the bedding. Now she was certain. Recovering, she walked home slowly with the heavy pails of water, then left her home and took the long, dusty road to the Old City. There, at the Kotel, she covered her head once again and gave thanks that her prayer had been answered.

*

The next week, Reizel decided to do something she had wanted to do for a long time.

It was a long, hard climb; she had to throw a stone at a stray dog that ran at her, and she fell twice, but at last she made it to the top. From high on the hill, she looked down at Batei Warsaw. How small the houses were, how gray and plain. In her front yard was her kitchen of tin and wood, and she imagined herself standing near the clothesline, holding a little child.

At the poultry shop next to the flourmill, she bought two live pigeons. She carried them bound and clipped down the long hill to the market in the Mea Shearim, where the kosher butcher slaughtered them and removed their innards. In her yard, Reizel plucked them, pulling out the little pin feathers with a tweezers, and added the little birds to the Sabbath stew.

That Friday night, she served them for the Sabbath meal, much to Haskel's surprise.

After supper, she told Haskel.

He wept with joy.

Now, everything changed in her and around her. The sullen grumbles about her barren state suddenly ceased. Her own mother, and the previously aloof relatives, now visited her regularly, all offering thoughtful advice and helpful suggestions. Reizel listened silently, giving each woman a nod and a smile.

In due time, Reizel gave birth to a girl, Chaya Sara.

And the grumbling of her in-laws began again.

Fishel, her father-in-law, was an only child, and Haskel was an only son—was the Linder name to fade away?

Haskel said nothing. He too was disappointed, but more so for her, for he knew how much she wanted to please him and his family. Relatives visited less frequently, and the disapproving looks of her mother-in-law returned.

Reizel didn't care. The baby was beautiful. Her milk overflowed, and two of her infant nieces were brought to her to be nursed. When spring came, she sat in the yard in the sunshine, feeding her little girl and the other two infants, singing to them all the while, and she was content. Still, she wished her father-in-law could visit her, for he always gave her hope and support, but Fishel Linder was away in Poland again, collecting funds to build a new Hasidic synagogue in Batei Warsaw, and he would not return for months.

*

The Hasidic community needed more than just a synagogue.

When my oldest sister was born at the end of 1899, the Jewish community in Jerusalem was struggling in an ever-deepening poverty. Here and there were pockets of relative wealth, but the general standard of living remained very low. The kolels did what they could, but were unable to keep up with the furious pace of immigration. Despite all efforts to raise the economic level, hunger and deprivation were often the rule, and much of the population lived with an overwhelming sense of futility.

Haskel and his fellow students shared some of the blame. Supported by the relatively few who worked, they spent their days and nights disputing the fine points of Talmudic law while the world around them fell into disrepair.

A great, heart-wrenching concern in Jerusalem was the growing number of orphans. The sudden influx of immigrants led to tremendous overcrowding, and infectious diseases, particularly tuberculosis, were common. The water supply, unprotected and uncertain, led to outbreaks of cholera and other bacterial infections. The food supply was equally precarious, and malnutrition contributed to the poor health of the community. Infant mortality began to climb, as did the mortality rates of the infants' parents. Regular outbreaks of influenza were particularly devastating to the older population and, by 1900, the growing number of orphaned Jewish children, reached crisis levels.

And others had been paying them much attention. The church had discovered that Jewish orphans were fertile ground for the harvesting of young souls, and Christian missionaries had already established orphanages in Jerusalem that sought out Jewish children. With their greater resources, the missionaries were successfully competing against their Jewish neighbors, which resulted in much enmity and mounting tension.

The first Jewish orphanage was founded by the Mitnaggedim, whose organizational skills and resources were greater than those of the Hasidic community. But it was not enough.

"We must do better," said Yitzhak Haggis to his brother-in-law. He was in the stationery store, watching Fishel doing the monthly inventory.

"I know. We're losing our children to the missionaries."

"We must do something," repeated Yitzhak Haggis. "Look at the Mitnaggedim—they have built an orphanage themselves."

Fishel agreed. "We will do something bigger."

Thus, the internecine rivalry between the Mitnaggedim and the Hasidim became an impetus for a noble deed; unwilling to be bested in the mitzvah department, the Hasidic community formed a committee to establish an orphanage for girls of Jewish parenthood.

One learns, thought Fishel, *that the motive for a good deed need not be examined too closely.*

Once again, Fishel Linder was called upon, and he assumed leadership of the organizing committee. Six months later, with the help of donations from abroad, the orphanage opened its doors, taking in six young girls, all rescued from the well-meaning arms of Christian missionaries.

Chapter 16

Time passed in Batei Warsaw.

Reizel was content. She had married Haskel willingly and never had second thoughts. Now Chaya Sara was one year old, and Reizel was trying to wean her, but the little girl refused to give up her mother's comforting breast. She was a happy baby and as pretty as a little flower, and Reizel didn't insist.

And Haskel was already a scholar of some note; teaching and lecturing, he spent most of his day in the yeshiva and the remainder of the afternoon and evening leading Talmudic study groups in the synagogue. Striving for a deeper understanding of halachah, Jewish law and ethics, he often came home midnight to find his wife already sleeping, their daughter in bed next to her.

Reizel wished that Haskel wouldn't spend so much time on his studies. But her husband was a true scholar, loving knowledge for its own sake. Their financial insecurity troubled her. They were entirely dependent on her father-in-law's generosity, which, though it was never failing, they couldn't count upon forever. She and Haskel had to earn their own way.

One night, she stayed up, surprising him when he walked in after midnight.

"Yes?" He spoke softly, not wanting to wake their little girl. Something was on her mind.

"We need more than your father's gold Napoleon," she said.

"I know, but for now, that's all we have." He spoke gently.

"I'm sure your father or uncle can find work for you in the store."

"There is no higher calling than the study of Torah," Haskel replied. "Torah encompasses all."

"That is true, but there must be a higher position than just a lecturer."

"That is not study. That is the business of study."

"Business is not so bad. You can become a judge in the Beth Din and sit with the other judges. And look at your father. He manages the stationery store and studies at the same time."

"I am not my father."

"But you are his son."

Haskel, tired and ready for sleep, said nothing.

Reizel didn't pursue him, for she knew that Haskel was really his mother's son, and knew that her true love of Torah had given Haskel an intense passion for holy words, in part to please her. He who wore the crown of holy knowledge was truly a king among men. Haskel was content; his studies had brought him the respect and admiration of the Hasidic community and the adoring praises of his mother.

Reizel wanted more for him—and for herself, their daughter, and their children yet to be born. Haskel had shown courage and initiative when he challenged the Mitnaggedim in the matzo dispute, and she wanted him to use some of that initiative for worldly achievement. She knew what she must do; she would get her father-in-law on her side.

*

According to halachah, Talmudic law, specific rules applied when men and women socialized. Whenever Reizel was in the house alone, the front door was left wide open so that her home was open to all passers by. When her father-in-law or any man was present, Reizel remained standing while the man sat. If Reizel was holding her baby when Fishel arrived, she did not pass Chaya Sara directly into his arms but placed the child in the cradle and let her father-in-law lift her from there. When he left, he put the child back into the cradle.

Early one morning, Reizel saw her father-in-law entering the gate. He was on his way to the store and was coming by, as usual, to hold and play with Chaya Sara. Reizel immediately went to the cradle and took the little girl into her arms. Fishel entered, and they greeted each other, and as usual, Fishel went directly to the cradle, but this time, Reizel held the baby tightly.

She apologized for not placing the child in the cradle; the baby was teething, she explained, and cranky.

"She's been up all night. Haskel and two students were talking until the morning."

The little girl was smiling and holding out a hand to her father-in-law, but Reizel kept her close. Fishel knew something was amiss.

Now, holding the baby, she spoke bluntly. "Isn't Haskel educated enough? Isn't he competent and honest? Why shouldn't he step out into the world?" Fishel pulled out his pocket watch. "Ach, I am late for the store. I'm sorry; I have to go so quickly. I'll come back later when Chaya Sara's rested."

Reizel watched him leave through the yard and immediately opened her siddur.

In early evening, Fishel again came in through the open door. The baby was sleeping. He sat, and Reizel served him tea, then stood at the other end of the table. Fishel had come prepared and, clearing his throat, delivered an effusive speech on the worthiness of study and teaching. He quoted from various sources. In particular, he had found a long passage from chapter 6 of *Ethics of the Fathers*, and he recited it.

> Rabbi Meir said: whoever occupies himself with the study of Torah for its own sake merits many things; nay, more, the whole world is open for his sake. He is called friend, beloved. He loves the Eternal One and he loves mankind; he pleases mankind. The Torah invests him with humility and reverence; it enables him to become righteous, godly, upright and faithful; it keeps him far from sin and draws him near to virtue. He who studies Torah is given the ability to judge. He is like a fountain that ever gathers force, and an ever-flowing stream. He becomes modest, patient and forgiving of insults. The Torah makes him great and raises him above all creatures."

Finished, and very satisfied, Fishel reached for his tea. It was hot and refreshing, and he smacked his lips. Reizel now opened her siddur and pretended to read, though she had spent all afternoon memorizing the lines from the Yiddish. It was also from Ethics of the Fathers:

Study is not the most important thing, but practice. All Torah study which is not combined with some trade must at length fail and occasion sin. Where there is no Torah, there is no bread; where there is no bread there is no Torah.

Reizel closed the siddur. She wanted to say more, but it was contrary to tradition for a woman to display such knowledge, and more importantly, she did not dare try to prove herself equal in Torah to her father-in-law. She remained silent and standing as Fishel finished his tea and said a few words about the day and its weather. Then he stood, his expression sad, put the gold Napoleon under the tablecloth, and, wishing her good night, left.

Reizel stood at the cradle and looked down at their sleeping daughter. She had many thoughts. Haskel could not change his ways; she would never ask him to give up his studies. Her father-in-law knew that, and that was why he was sad. Haskel had to live his life a certain way, but she too would live hers a certain way. Now that Chaya Sara was eighteen months old and could be left alone for a few hours every day, Reizel knew the time was right. She felt better already and bent down to kiss her little girl's forehead. Their lives were going to change.

*

The next morning, after Haskel had left for the yeshiva, Reizel carried their little girl to her mother's house, nursed her, and then left for the Old City. Nervous and excited, she passed through the Jaffa Gate without visiting her father-in-law in the stationery store. Nor did she linger in Spice Street. She walked quickly through the teeming market to the Kotel Ha'Maravi. The women's section was almost empty, and she stood close to the wall, breathing in the ancient dust. She didn't need her siddur, and she covered her head and face with her shawl and spoke her own personal prayers. Finished, she walked back through the souk and entered the fabric store of her old Sephardic neighbor and friend, Shlomo Simontov.

"Ah, Reizel," he said, his face lighting up.

Reizel, very excited, revealed why she had come.

*

During the first decade of the twentieth century, the New Jerusalem rising on the hills outside the Old City was becoming a small city in its own right. Housing projects, schools, hospitals, and markets dotted the barren hills. New roads, some of them merely wide beaten paths, connected one small enclave to another. The new immigrants, many of whom had never lived in the Old City, did not have the passionate attachment to the ancient stones that the earlier arrivals possessed; on the contrary, they preferred to live in a more modern setting.

In this, Reizel saw commercial opportunity. The walk from the Warsaw Houses to the Old City was long and dusty, the return with heavy packages even longer. The women complained all the time. They wanted to shop closer to home and avoid the crowds, the dirt of the old souk, and the Arabs, who, with each new wave of Jewish immigration tilting the political and financial balance against them, were becoming more and overtly hostile.

With only their one small child, their apartment in Batei Warsaw had more than enough space. They used the small room in the back as a storage room for odds and ends; Reizel wanted to put it to better, more profitable use.

That morning, after listening to Reizel, Shlomo Simontov showed her his overstocked fabrics that, for one reason or another, had failed to sell. From among the best of the remainders, she selected the most appealing patterns and colors. Simontov gave her the merchandise at rock-bottom prices; furthermore, she could pay him after she sold the fabrics.

She bought as much as she could carry home, and Simontov folded and wrapped each fabric in heavy brown paper, tied the packages with hemp cord, and then made two neat bundles, attaching handles to the cord. He also gave her, free of charge, a steel yardstick and an old pair of scissors.

"These are inducement gifts," he said with a smile, "so that you will come back and buy more."

The scissors, old and of high quality, was made especially for fabrics, with long blades and a big, open handle.

Carrying her heavy bundles, one in each hand, Reizel walked home as quickly as she could. She was full of excitement as she entered the gate of her front yard. She had told no one her plan, not even her mother. Later, she would pick up her baby, but now she had to prepare for her grand opening. The small room had a wall closet with four shelves, and she put the fabrics on the top two shelves, covering them with a tablecloth. She hid the yardstick outside in the kitchen, fitting it tightly between two pieces of wood. The scissors she put in a drawer under a dress. She had thought about everything and was certain it would work. Even Shlomo Simontov thought it was a good idea, but now, with her dream about to come true, she wasn't sure she could run a fabric store out of her house in Batei Warsaw. She went over her plan again; yes, it was going to work. After checking her hiding places, and satisfied that everything was in place, she went to her mother, picked up Chaya Sara, then returned home and prepared supper for Haskel.

The next morning, after Haskel left, she had her official Grand Opening. She went door to door in Batei Warsaw and announced to the women that she had fabrics for sale, all good merchandise and at competitive discount prices. She went home, took out the yardstick and scissors, and waited. She didn't have to wait long. With word of mouth spreading the news, by early afternoon of that day, Reizel sold out her entire stock.

The next day, she returned to Simontov's store, paid for the goods, and bought more, this time a larger selection of silks, velvets, satins, woolens, and cottons. It was too much to carry, so Simontov had his assistant load one of his donkeys and deliver Reizel's order that afternoon.

For three weeks, Reizel kept the store a secret. She did business four hours a day, two in the morning and two in the early afternoon, and still had time for household chores. Chaya Sara was no problem; the little girl was sweet tempered and played alone. Haskel, hardly home and ready for sleep as soon he walked in, never opened the door to the small back room.

Commercial success, however, brought difficulties. Reizel sold most of her goods on credit, and for a while she was able to memorize all the transactions, but as business increased, she couldn't keep track of who bought and owed what. Often, the women made partial payments, taking more fabric at the same time. Soon the numbers became too confusing to keep in her head. She had taught herself how to recognize and write simple numbers but didn't know even the simplest arithmetic; she could not add or subtract, and multiplication and division were completely foreign to her.

Needing Haskel's help and eager to show her husband the store, she planned a surprise.

The following week, when the store had been open for almost a month, she prepared a special supper. It was Monday, and Haskel was surprised to have pigeon and noodle kugel, not to mention a tomato and a hard-boiled egg, extravagances usually reserved for the Sabbath or a special holiday.

When the lavish meal was done, Reizel took her husband through their long, narrow main room and opened the door to the small room. She went in and lit the ceiling lantern. Haskel blinked. Her store had outgrown the little closet, and the bolts of fabric and sheets of colorful cloth filled the room.

Haskel stood in the doorway, astonished.

Reizel held her breath. Would he be angry that she had opened a store in their home and had women coming and going all day? Or would he be resentful that she had done it in total secrecy? He might condemn her, the young wife of a pious Hasid, for bringing the world of money and commerce into their home. Or would he be hurt that his father's gold Napoleon was not enough to live on?

He stood in the door in the dim light of the lantern.

Then his mouth moved into the tiniest of smiles.

Her relief was deep and immediate. He was true to himself, never demonstrative, and his little smile was a true display of acceptance. She relied upon his thoughtful, quiet manner, good heart and cool head—qualities he exhibited around the table at night while talking with his friends under the kerosene lamp. She admired and loved him for his gentleness, and now, watching his tiny smile increase just a fraction, she loved him even more.

Silently, he stepped into her store and looked around, smiling still. He walked around the small room, touching the bolts of cloth and feeling the silks and satins between his fingers. He said without looking at her, "you will need more shelves for all this material."

She should have been pleased, but the way he said "you" instead of "we" angered her. She was doing this for both of them and for their child.

"Look," she said. From beneath a piece of red silk, she took a small metal can. She took off the lid. Inside was a small fortune of coins and bills.

"You have a good business head." His smile was bigger.

"I need your help in keeping records. I have too many customers."

"I'll show you. And soon you'll learn to do it yourself."

He looked at her then, and in his eyes was a happy gleam. All her anger left her. He knew she couldn't read, write, or do arithmetic, and he didn't want to embarrass her.

"But now I'm very tired and have to sleep."

The next day, for the first time in months, he returned promptly from evening prayers, alone. He carried a small parcel that contained pens, ink, two small bound notebooks, and a file box, all from his father's stationery store. For the first time in almost a year, they sat side by side at the table, very close, almost touching.

"These books are for keeping records. You see, each page has a line down the center. On the right will be a list of things you buy from Simontov, and on the left, we will list what you sell. You don't have to write anything too complicated; you can even draw a picture of the fabric. Or, you see, you can use the first letter of every fabric as a code."

He moved even closer, and Reizel, a rapt pupil, leaned into his side.

"See? This is how you write a different letter for silk or for cotton, and then you can add a letter for the color. I'll do it right now—raish for red, bet for blue. It's not hard at all. They're easy to copy. We'll use this notebook for the customers on credit. All customers will have a separate page with what they bought, how much it cost, and how much they pay every week."

Reizel marveled. It was all so simple when he explained it.

"Don't worry about names with too many letters or long numbers. It's very easy; you just have to use a couple of letters of the aleph-bet— nothing more. You can make up your own code. And the numbers are very simple. I'll be your unpaid assistant, and every month I'll add everything up, and you'll know how much you're making."

She loved him more than ever, and had she known how to initiate lovemaking, she would have done so, but he was busy writing out a code for colors, and she pressed close and watched his nimble fingers moving the pen over the paper.

She didn't learn arithmetic until much later, but for now, the system worked well, and she was able to track her expenses and her credit accounts. It was amazing how easy it was to make money. Soon Haskel did more than the monthly bookkeeping. Now that their daughter was walking and getting into everything, Reizel found it difficult to get to the Old City to buy goods, so instead, once a week, Haskel made up a written list from her instructions and dropped it off at Simontov's store on his way to the yeshiva. The next day, the donkeys came to their gate, laden with goods, and that afternoon, she would go into the souk to pay Simontov.

As expected, her mother-in-law did not approve of a store in her son's home. The mixing of the scholarly with the commercial was unacceptable. Reizel didn't care as long as her father-in-law approved, and was nervous when, at his son's suggestion, he came by to see things for himself.

"Well, well," he said, standing there with the same little smile of his son.

She breathed a sigh of relief.

"All beginnings," he told her, offering her a bit of Talmudic encouragement, "are difficult. Do not be discouraged."

At first, Reizel's customers were friends and neighbors, and she charged higher prices for those who could afford it and lower prices for those who couldn't, sometimes even selling the material at cost. For poor brides in need of a wardrobe, she gave the material for free.

For her rich customers, she took samples of the expensive fabrics to their homes. The Berman family was one such customer. Mr. Berman, an immigrant from Odessa, Russia, had built a new bakery in the Mea Shearim, so naturally, he was known as the Odessa Baker. Mrs. Berman had a taste for velvet and silk, and Reizel went to her home every other week with heavy bolts of rich fabrics. She returned not only with money but also with a large corn bread or a round, warm pumpernickel, the dark color coming from the rich cocoa worked into the flour.

One of her favorite customers, for me anyway, was Ba'kir, the Arab charcoal merchant.

Kerosene came into fashion later, but charcoal was the usual fuel for heating and cooking. Ba'kir was more than a merchant; he was a professional charcoal maker. Once I went into the hills and saw his production method: he arranged long planks of fresh wood in a pyramid around a central fire in such a way that little air reached the interior of the stack, so the wood burned slow, without a flame. Remaining were charred black planks—carbonized cellulose—which Ba'kir sold to the women of Jerusalem, who broke the planks into irregular pieces of charcoal to use in their outdoor stoves and ovens.

Thursday was the busiest day of the week for housewives and their daughters, for that was the day of shopping, cleaning, and cooking for the Sabbath. It was also the day Ba'kir drove his laden camels into the square in front of my mother's gate in Batei Warsaw. He clanged his bell, shouted his presence, and waited for the women to gather round.

Ba'kir was rich by Arab standards. He owned a small parcel of land, four camels, and a horse. He got his raw lumber from Lebanon, and thus spoke a little French. He had the maximum of four wives allowed by Islamic law, the youngest about fifteen years old. His wives traveled with him, riding in small tents on top of his camels, the big sacks of charcoal hanging on either side. In keeping with his status, Ba'kir had a beautiful black horse with a bright silver bridle that glinted in the sun. He wore a black-and-white kaffiyeh, and his beard was black and pointed. Stuck into his belt next to his long dagger was a big pistol.

146

When the camels stopped, Ba'kir made them sit, and his wives stepped down. They were covered from head to foot with long veils that flowed over their faces and down their torsos, with rectangular eye slits in their head coverings.

Tempted by the beautiful fabrics other women were carrying out of my mother's door, Ba'kir's wives become her best customers. In the back room, they took off their veils, revealing their naked breasts covered with chains of silver and gold coins. Ba'kir bought something for every wife but spent most on his youngest, choosing the finest silks and brightest colors.

He trusted my mother, leaving his scales and measures in our basement, in appreciation of which he always gave her a special discount on his charcoal.

Ba'kir, and other Arab merchants and farmers in the villages around Jerusalem, found the Jewish settlements to be profitable markets, and every day before the sun rose long lines of farmers on horses, donkeys, and camels streamed out of the distant hills to the Mea Shearim, which had the largest open-air market outside the Old City. Many continued on into Jerusalem's souk and sold their produce to middlemen. The men rode horses, and their wives walked behind, their children strapped to their backs, with heavy baskets of fruits and vegetables, or sometimes a wire cage jammed with three or four chickens, on their heads.

As housing expanding outside the Old City and Jewish immigrants from Europe and Africa swelled the population, Arab laborers were employed as masons, stonecutters, and carpenters. Flowing in from Jordan, Egypt, and Syria, thousands of Arabs came in search of a better life, and soon became a second, growing immigrant presence.

*

One of the most powerful forces in the Jewish communities both inside and outside the Old City was tradition. Traditions, to those who follow them, appear to be eternal and God given, but in reality they vary with time and place. The arrival of great numbers of Jewish immigrants in the last decade of the nineteenth century and the first of the twentieth produced a great deal of turmoil in Jerusalem.

The ultra-Orthodox Ashkenazi communities in the Old City, unwilling to compromise on most religious matters, were constantly engaged in religious disputes, most often with those less doctrinaire but at times battling those in their own Orthodox community. To an outsider, some of the issues might have appeared petty or even ridiculous, but to the true believer the fight was always in the name of heaven, touching on the eternal. The Warsaw Houses, occupied almost equally between the Hasidim and the less rigid but observant Mitnaggedim, had their full share of heavenly disputes, the famous matzo fight being one of them.

Soon another arose in the Hungarian houses on the other side of Mea Shearim Road. In Batei Hungary, the population was almost 100 percent Hasidic; one would have thought that this demographic uniformity promoted harmony, but in the usual contrary manner they produced endless contention.

One bitter dispute involved the use of the shofar, the ram's horn, on Rosh Hashanah.

Celebrated in the autumn, Rosh Hashanah is the first of a series of holy days that begins the ten days of contemplation that culminates in Yom Kippur—literally, the head day—a twenty-four-hour period of fasting and prayer that constitutes a personal and communal cleansing and confession. The shofar is the instrument that the ancient Israelites used for communication and proclamation. Its sound is a haunting echo of the past and a call to the future. During prayer services on Rosh Hashanah, the shofar is sounded three times. The blower, the *baal tekiah*, practices many days in advance, for it is a singular honor, a privilege, and an obligation to sound the shofar, and he aims for perfection, not merely for the musical aesthetic but also as a demonstration of reverence. One honors the Name by doing one's best.

However, when Rosh Hashanah falls on the Sabbath, as it does from time to time, conflicts arise.

Halachah, traditional law, has strict guidelines for Sabbath observance. On that day, one is not permitted to carry any article—book, item of clothing, comb, or key, anything—from one's private domain to a public place or vice versa. Though it's an obligation, and a privilege, to hear the shofar on Rosh Hashanah, the holy Sabbath takes precedence over the holiday. In order that the baal tekiah, the sounder of the shofar, not be tempted to carry the ram's horn from his house to the synagogue, the sounding of the shofar is prohibited when the two holy days coincide.

Now, it was said that in Batei Hungary there were more shepherds than sheep—more rabbis than congregants—so it was to be expected that the war of the Sabbath shofar should be fought there.

Seeking to introduce a touch of rationality into their Rosh Hashanah observance, a group of more liberal rabbis from the Hungarian Houses challenged the prohibition. They suggested that the baal tekiah should bring the ram's horn to the synagogue on Friday morning, or that it be kept in the synagogue with the Torah scrolls, prayer books, and other sacred objects. In that way, the shofar might be heard on the Sabbath without violating any rules. This made a great deal of sense to many, but a number of the ultra-Observant rose in immediate opposition. The ban, they insisted, must be maintained; the prohibition against hearing the shofar on the Sabbath was a Syag L'Torah, a protective fence around the Torah. Given human nature, they argued, the slightest breach in the wall of tradition would be followed by the floodwaters of desecration.

That year, of course, Rosh Hashanah fell on a Saturday. True to timeless custom—actually, not so timeless, for the ban on carrying the shofar, according to the scholars, was a mere hundred years old—the shofar was not heard in any synagogue in Jerusalem, whether within the old walls or without. In Batei Hungary too, services in the main synagogue were conducted accordingly. The synagogue was packed, and tensions between the two factions, which had been simmering for weeks, actually lessened as the day wore on. By the afternoon the service was concluding, and the cantor, the lead singer, began chanting the supplementary prayers that are a tradition of Rosh Hashanah.

Up leaped a young rabbi, one of the modernists. Covered from head to foot with a long, flowing shawl of white wool, he climbed onto a chair.

The cantor stopped in mid song.

The young rabbi raised his hand. His voice was deep and thunderous. "I proclaim the power of this day!"

With that, he lifted his shawl and pulled out a long, gleaming ram's horn.

There were startled gasps and furious shouts, but before anyone could grab the shofar the young rabbi put it to his lips.

The trumpeting blast filled the synagogue and shook its windows.

It was the end of the world!

For a moment, there was a stunned, terrible silence, and then pandemonium broke out. In their fine holiday caftans and beautiful fur-trimmed streimels, the Hasidim flung insults and screamed curses at each other. Fists and feet flew. They fought like demons. They threw chairs, overturned tables, and flung siddurim about, smashed windows. While half the congregants pummeled each other the other half ran pell-mell for the doors. Between the stampede and the violence, half a dozen worshippers were fatally injured. The young rabbi was beaten to within an inch of his life. Outside, where the sound of the shofar had echoed through the streets of Batei Hungary, crowds of Hasidim raced in from Batei Warsaw and the Mea Shearim. Within minutes, word had spread to the Old City, and the devout came charging out of the gates, arriving in Batei Hungary huffing and puffing. Finally, the Turkish police showed up and, swinging their clubs and firing in the air, stopped the riot. They arrested as many Hasidim as they could put their hands on, while the bloodied and injured, their clothing torn and limbs broken, fended for themselves.

This dispute continued for many years, and though it was never resolved, it remained confined to the study halls of the yeshivas. Never again was the ram's horn heard on the Sabbath of Rosh Hashanah.

Chapter 17

The tale of Shukri, the police captain, and his treatment of Yichya, the poor Yemenite Jew, is a tale of how the weak can sometimes triumph over the strong, with a little help from their friends.

Shukri, a member of a prominent Arab family in Jerusalem—this family connection was his prime and only qualification for the job of police captain—was infamous throughout the Old City. The streets of Jerusalem were, for him and his officers, a gold mine of baksheesh. His visits to the souk were frequent and costly; his fat little hand, always open, with his fat little fingers waggling the air, was viewed with disgust and dread by the merchants, Arab and Jew. Shukri knew his limits, however, and stayed away from Yitzhak Haggis, whose stationery store supplied many of the central government offices in Jerusalem, both Turkish and Arab, as well as some of the Christian and Muslim institutions.

In addition to his illustrious ancestry, the police captain possessed two additional distinguishing assets.

One of them was his huge belly, which he was careful to feed with hourly infusions of the rich foods with which the owners of the souk's stalls plied him—all gratis, of course, for they wished to show the illustrious captain their utmost admiration and gratitude. Shukri's great weight, because of his diminutive stature, gave him the appearance of a big brown teapot. His weight was a status symbol, for girth of that magnificence implied both wealth and prestige.

Even more formidable, however, was Shukri's mustache. In keeping with his high position as police captain. Truly magnificent, it was long, waxed, and pointy, with a dip in the middle like a bow. More like a polished iron sculpture welded to his upper lip, its tremendous span covered both of Shukri's fat cheeks, with a little extra wingspan on either side.

Shukri strutted about like a sultan, for body size and facial hair were much prized among Arab men. Orthodox Hasidim had much facial hair too, but that was in keeping with a biblical prohibition, and they displayed little vanity regarding their beards. Shukri, on the other hand, regarded his mustache as a mark of imperial distinction, and he tolerated no mustache greater than his own. Making his daily rounds with an escort of two police officers, one of whom carried a small hand mirror and the other a pair of sharp scissors, Shukri kept an eye out for any man foolish enough to challenge his hirsute primacy. A longer mustache, or one with a more elaborate curl, was cause for great wrath, and the two police escorts soon reduced the offending hair to a humbler size, administering in the process a vigorous beating to the unlucky man on whose face the hairs had been found.

Shukri knew his limits, of course, and high officials or distinguished religious leaders could have mustaches as big as they wished.

One afternoon, while returning to the precinct house just inside the Jaffa Gate—in fact, the police station was located on the upper floor of the same building where my grandfather had his stationery store—Shukri stopped dead in his tracks.

"Who is that man?" he demanded of his two escorts.

"Why, he's Yichya, the sachlib seller," replied one.

"Yes, yes, I see he sells sachlib, but who is he?"

"He's a poor Yemenite Jew who lives on Mea Shearim Road in the Yemenite houses."

"Yes, yes, I see!" Shukri knew all this with one quick glance and kicked the stupid policeman in the shin.

Clearly, the man was a vendor of tea and sachlib, a sweet drink concocted of water, cornstarch, sugar, and cinnamon, for strapped to his back was his apparatus of metal and leather with the two thin, curved spouts sticking out on either end. When he poured the tea or sachlib, he would bend over on one side, depending on which beverage the customer wanted, let a thin stream of liquid arc into his cup, and present it to his customer.

Also, clearly, Shukri saw the vendor's colorful caftan, and his distinctive, colorful headwear, the fashion of a religious Yemenite Jew. He was poor too, because no one but a poor, desperate, unskilled man sold sachlib. And where else would he live but on Mea Shearim Road with the other poor Yemenites who had made that poor stretch of road their home?

The chief of police stood in the street, a small mountain of brown, and watched as the man bent and sent a stream of sweet sachlib into his cup.

The Yemenite's mustache was truly and without question a thing of wonder.

Yichya was a small, frail man with sun-dark skin and coal-black hair. Everything else about him was dark. His long, curled ear locks were black spirals down to his shoulders. From his chin sprouted a long, narrow beard, a goatee that almost touched his chest, equally black. His eyes were as close to black as eyes could be, and they shone in his gaunt, pinched face like bright onyx moons.

But it was his mustache that drew Shukri's wrath.

Of long, thick, lustrous black hair, it was impossibly wide, and totally out of proportion to Yichya's diminutive physique and thin face. It rose from his upper lip as the wings of a soaring hawk rose in full flight to the heavens.

Unlike Shukri, who tended his mustache with the loving regard of a gardener for his roses, Yichya paid no attention to his own naturally curved, powerful mustache. What did the poor sachlib vendor care for such things? He had more important things to worry about—namely, selling as much tea and sachlib as he could so that he might bring home a few pennies for his two wives and nine children.

Yichya's mustache filled the entire world of the police captain.

How dare this poor vendor of sachlib, this uneducated Yemenite scum, challenge the great Shukri? How dare he!

Furious, Shukri turned and, without a word, waddled off, his escorts following.

Yichya—the *ch* is pronounced with a guttural sound similar to clearing one's throat—had no idea his mustache was violating Jerusalem's unwritten laws. He had come from far away Yemen with his wives and children, a poor, pious Jew with too many mouths to feed, and before long, he had earned enough at odd jobs to buy the leather-and-metal apparatus required to sell hot tea and sachlib. He had gone into business for himself, a franchise of one. Like many other Yemenites, he was hardworking and religious, but not in the ways of the Hasid. He was illiterate and had no time to study and argue the fine points of religious law, so his piety consisted of obeying the commandants, eating only kosher food, sanctifying the Sabbath through prayer and rest, and, with his two wives, being as fruitful as possible on a limited income. The only multiplication Yichya knew was the production of children. His wives, like other Yemenite women, worked as laundresses, or at work they called *shpanza*, cleaning floors and windows.

Yichya lived with his family on Mea Shearim Road in a group of apartment houses built by the Yemenite Jews themselves. Dwelling with his large family were three small turtles that kept the house free of insects. Yichya loaned out the largest of the turtles, Haman, to people for three or four days at a time as an animal exterminator. His two wives supplemented their laundry and shpanza work by collecting horse and donkey droppings from the streets and drying them for fuel to be used for cooking or warmth. Needless to say, both food and house had a complex and interesting aroma.

There were perhaps a half dozen sachlib sellers in all Jerusalem, each with his own route. In the early morning, Yichya worked the Mea Shearim, whose open market, teeming with women and children clamoring for a sweet, was a gold mine. Later in the morning, he brewed more tea and made more sachlib and went into the Old City, where he sold to pedestrians and shopkeepers around the Jaffa Gate. For those who didn't have a cup, he had his own. The customer would drink from it, and Yichya would wipe it clean for the next customer with a quick swipe of the left side of his apron; he kept the right for his personal use. In the afternoon, with his supply running low, he made his rounds at his favorite yeshivas, Etz Chaim (the Tree of Life) and Chai Olam (Eternal Life), where the Hasidim looked forward to a quick pick-me-up before they hit the books for afternoon study. There Yichya rested awhile, dozing in the cool, soft light, lulled to sleep by the voices discoursing on God and Man.

*

A busy man about town, Yitzhak Haggis looked forward to his daily session of Talmud study. He looked forward too to his afternoon tea. Yitzhak, the rich businessman, and Yichya, the poor vendor, had become friends, a most improbable companionship, and often sat and talked in the synagogue in the Old City. Yitzhak wanted to pay more for the tea than the few pennies Yichya asked, but the Yemenite refused. He had only one price, which was, to Yitzhak's business sense, too low to turn a decent profit. But it also was a relief, for Jerusalem was not only a city of holiness but also a place where the price of a single pistachio became a source of eternal haggling. The energy that people put into these relentless negotiations, Yitzhak Haggis often thought, could have ruled an empire.

On that particular afternoon, Yichya had just left the synagogue, and Yitzhak Haggis had just opened his book, when outside in the street, there was angry shouting in Arabic, followed by a yelp of fear and then a wailing cry for mercy. Yitzhak Haggis rushed to the window.

In the narrow alley below was an ugly, confused scene. Two big policemen—Shukri's escorts—held Yichya with his hands tied behind his back while the fat chief waved his scissors in front of the Yemenite's terrified face. A crowd of Arabs was laughing and shouting encouragement. On the dirty stones lay Yichya's apparatus, with tea spilling out of its broken tap. As Yitzhak Haggis looked down, fat Shukri cut Yichya's mustache. The poor Yemenite twisted and squirmed, but the policemen held him fast. Blood spurted from Yichya's lip as Shukri clipped away. The crowd laughed and cheered. *Snip! Snip!* One side of the mustache was gone. The crowd roared. Yichya struggled desperately, twisting his head this way and that, but with another snip, the goatee was gone. The crowd yelled for more, but the police captain was satisfied. With half of his mustache gone, insult had been added to injury. Yichya looked ridiculous. Shukri signaled his policemen to release the bleeding sachlib peddler, who, once free, fled like a frightened rabbit, his hands still tied behind his back.

Yitzhak Haggis was filled with disgust and rage. He ran out of the synagogue, but the crowd had already left. Fat Shukri was waddling away with his police escorts. The Yemenite's blood was on the stones.

Yitzhak Haggis picked up the broken apparatus. The copper tubing was bent, a spigot was broken, and one leather strap was torn. All the tea and sachlib had run out. Watching the three policemen walk away, Yitzhak Haggis spat on the stones. "*Geh in dred,*" he muttered after them. "Drop dead."

"This isn't the first time that fat *momsa*, bastard, has hurt us," Yitzhak Haggis said to his brother-in-law later that day.

In the stationery store, Fishel listened to the tale of abuse. On Fishel's usually calm face was a look of contempt. He had bought tea from Yichya many times.

"He is a beast," said Yitzhak Haggis.

"Do not insult the beasts."

"Let him rot in hell."

"Sha, sha, let's think of Yichya and his family," Fishel said. "We must repair Yichya's apparatus and reimburse him for medical expenses."

"Yes, we have to," said Yitzhak Haggis.

Fishel added, "And we must compensate him for the humiliation."

The sanctity of men and women, and, thus, the dignity of the individual, were the cornerstones upon which the Jewish code of ethics was built, and any violation or diminishment of that dignity was considered not only a violation of a person's God-given sanctity but a serious breach of rabbinical law, therefore deserving of compensation.

"But how? With money?"

"Money never hurts." Fishel thought for a moment. "Leave it to me."

That evening, Yitzhak Haggis went to Yichya's apartment on Mea Shearim Road. Frightened, his nine children stood in a tight circle around their father, the younger ones crying. The poor tea seller's upper lip was swollen and bandaged. His wives had cut off the other side of his mustache and trimmed the goatee to give his face more balance, but the little, skinny man was still shaking, not merely from the physical abuse. Without his big, flowing mustache and goatee, Yichya's face looked even thinner and more pinched, his eyes huge, dark, frightened balls of dull black. He had been shamed in public, which, in Jewish ethics, was the equivalent to being physically wounded. He could not look at Yitzhak

Haggis. But his eyes brightened immediately when he saw his apparatus in Yitzhak Haggis's hand.

"We had it repaired, and it's as good as new."

The poor little Yemenite stared at him.

"Tomorrow we will go to the hospital. You need a few stitches and some ointment. The mustache and beard will grow back."

Yichya closed his eyes, moved his face side-to-side, and moaned. "Shukri will find me."

Yitzhak Haggis shook his head. "Shukri won't bother you again."

The trembling Yemenite looked up at him.

"Trust me, Yichya. You will be safe." Yitzhak Haggis put an envelope on the table. "This is compensation for loss of income."

Yichya looked at the envelope, dumbfounded.

"Rest now, and in a few days, you will be working again."

Yitzhak Haggis left, looking back as he went out the door, and saw Yichya holding the repaired apparatus, smiling, with his children and wives gathered around him.

Fishel Linder had many connections with influential government officials, including those in the Turkish administration. In addition, my grandfather was the mukhtar, the official representative of Kolel Warsaw. Within a week, fat Shukri and his immediate family were gone. It was rumored he had been transferred to a small village in Syria, but since no one ever saw or heard of him again, that rumor was never confirmed.

*

That year, Reizel's sister died. Golda Leah had been in poor health for a long time, and then, suddenly, one day, she was dying.

In search of a cure, her mother, Nechama, visited a famous Sephardic *baal moifes*, a miracle man, and returned with an amulet that my grandmother fastened around her daughter's neck. Reizel went to the Kotel every day to pray for her older sister. Standing before the ancient stones, she asked that her dear sister be given more time in this world.

A group of women went to their synagogue and opened the doors to the Holy Ark. When the ark is opened, so too are the gates of heaven. With heads covered and bowed, the women stood in front of the Torah and wept their prayers for Golda Leah's recovery.

A crier went through the streets, calling the young students of the Mea Shearim's Talmud Torah to gather in the yeshiva's auditorium. Children streamed from their houses and made their barefoot way over the rough stones. The voices of innocent children are known to penetrate deeper into heaven. Inside the big hall, they chanted psalms. At the request of Netanel Reisman, Golda Leah's father, a special delegation of three pious Hasidim left for Safed and Tiberias, where they prayed at the holy shrines of the Kabbalah Rebbe and of Rabbi Meir Baal Ha'Nes. Still another delegation of Hasidim went to Bethlehem, to the tomb of Mother Rachel, which is on the road to Hebron. There they entwined ribbons of white and blue around Rachel's tomb, and then, after returning to Jerusalem, they wrapped the same ribbons around Golda Leah as she lay dying.

There is a lesson in the Talmud about a Tanna, an important rabbi, who lay dying. His disciples were so overcome with the impending loss that they decided to save him. Praying night and day, they argued with the angels that their rabbi was needed on earth so he could continue his pious deeds. The angels wouldn't listen. The disciples persisted; after all, they pointed out to the angels, there were already so many rabbis in heaven that another wouldn't make much difference. The angels weren't impressed with that line of argument. Undeterred, the disciples continued praying with such insistent passion that finally, the Eternal One, who agreed to arbitrate between them and the angels, heard them.

The Talmud says "that the angels in heaven and the children of earth presented their arguments to the Great Judge, and the angels won."

The disciples returned to their beloved Tanna, only to discover that he had already ascended to heaven.

The miracle man with his amulet, the three pious Hasidim, the delegates to Rachel's tomb, all the prayers and chants of the children of the Talmud Torah, the supplications of the women before the open ark, and even the prayers of Reizel at the Kotel Ha'Maravi could not keep Golda Leah on earth. The angels won, and Reizel's sister ascended to heaven.

Her four sons carried her to the Mount of Olives and there, over her bed of earth, chanted the Kaddish.

Among many, the Kaddish's haunting melody is thought to be a prayer for the dead, but the Kaddish is not that at all. *Kaddish* means "sanctification," and its song is a song of the glory of this world and of the wondrous power that brought it into being.

> Glorified and sanctified be God's great name throughout the world, which has been created according to His will. May He establish His reign in your lifetime and in your days, and within the life of the entire house of Israel, speedily and soon.
>
> May The Name be blessed forever and through all eternity.
>
> Blessed and praised, glorified and exalted, extolled and honored, adored and lauded is the Name of the Holy One, beyond all the blessings and hymns, praises and commendations that are ever uttered in this world;
>
> May the praises and the supplications of the entire House of Israel be accepted by heaven;
>
> May there be abundant peace from Heaven, and Life, for us and for all Israel.
>
> He who created peace in the celestial heights, may He create peace for us and for all Israel;
>
> We say, Amen.

After the burial, Golda Leah's children left the Mount of Olives and returned to the house of their father, Netanel Reisman, to begin sitting shivah (*shivah* means "seven"), the weeklong period of mourning observed by Jews when a close relative dies.

CHAPTER 18

When Chaya Sara was three years old, Reizel gave birth to a second child, a son.

Hospital births were unheard of, and so my brother entered the world in our house, with a midwife and a gathering of bustling women attending my mother.

Happiness abounded. For almost a hundred years, the Linder family had had only one son each generation, and the birth of my older brother was greeted with great joy.

My grandmother was present at the birth, and she told Reizel that when the baby emerged, she saw bright lights in the corners of the room. According to legend, such lights appeared when a man destined for greatness comes into the world.

Haskel chose the name for their son. The tradition is to honor the past by naming the child after a dead relative, and given the many ancestors of both families deserving of such honor, Haskel was besieged with so many appeals, requests, and demands that to satisfy a fraction of them, he would have had to attach a dozen names to the tiny infant. After much discussion with Reizel and entirely too much input from his mother, they chose five names, and their son was called Moshe Menachem Mendel Elezar Yossef. Haskel had no idea who those people were but was assured they were all important ancestors whose immortality, at least in memory, would now be preserved. At Reizel's suggestion, they called their boy Moshe, or Moses. In Hebrew, the name Moshe means "to draw forth" or "to draw out" and refers to the infant Moses being lifted from the bull rushes of the Nile by Pharaoh's daughter.

Two years later, Reizel gave birth to another girl. They named her Yechevod. With her arrival, more grumbles from her mother-in-law were heard—the family, she pointed out, had more than enough girls.

"Yes," Reizel reminded her sweetly, "and you have two of them."

Their first child, Chaya Sara, now six, was old enough to help with the housework and childcare and was learning how to bake bread and challah and wash clothing—of which there was little, given the paucity of everyone's wardrobe. Sometimes she went to the cisterns and returned slowly with a heavy pail in each hand. She wasn't enrolled in school, not even for religious instruction. It was unfortunate, for many girls wanted to learn, and their abilities were simply wasted, their lives made smaller.

In contrast, her younger brother Moshe, at three and a half years old, was in Talmud Torah the entire day. He walked with a group of other boys or by himself from our house in Batei Warsaw to the school in the Mea Shearim. The route was safe. Motorized vehicles did not then exist in Jerusalem, and even the donkey drivers, walking behind their animals, set a slow, careful pace.

During those early years of the twentieth century, life was very circumscribed in Jerusalem, and all of Batei Warsaw and the Mea Shearim knew that the child Moshe, the handsome little boy with the large brown eyes, was the only son of Haskel Linder, the Talmudic scholar, and Reizel Linder, the woman who had the fabric store in Batei Warsaw.

There was a commonality of purpose and activity that made Batei Warsaw a self-contained village, especially for children. Their mothers always accompanied little girls, and on every day except the Sabbath, from early morning until late afternoon, when cheder, or elementary school, let out, the streets were empty of all young boys. Adults would have been alarmed to see a child, or a group of children, walking about unsupervised, and immediate inquiries would have been made, followed by appropriate action.

A year after Moshe's birth, Reizel gave birth to her fourth child, a second boy. He was named Hersh Leib, Hersh being the Yiddish equivalent of Tzvi, a stag, for he was named after of his great-grandfather Tzvi Yehuda Lederberg, the leather merchant from Poland who had died a year earlier, in 1903, and who was buried on the Mount of Olives, his bones awaiting the coming of the Messiah.

Sadly, Hersh Leib died when he was three years old. His sudden death stunned the entire family; no explanations were ever given. Many stories of his short life remain, and though I never knew him or saw his image—there are no photographs of him or of any of my older siblings as children—I, now a man of more than eighty years, see him to this day in my mind's eye, for I have been told often what a bright, beautiful child he was. My mother spoke his name on all occasions. She'd say, "By now, Hersh Leib would have learned Torah," or "At your age, Hersh Leib would have been four feet tall, maybe a little taller."

Not speaking or thinking of the dead kills them over and over, so by constant loving allusion, her infant child remained alive for my mother all the days of her life.

CHAPTER 19

In 1907, a year after my brother died, I was born.

I was named Chaim, which means "life."

In a family of mostly girls, I was a cherished addition, but I came the day before Pesach, Passover, when my mother had been rushing around preparing for the Seder, trying to fit in a hundred different chores. She had assumed that I would appreciate the importance of the holiday and delay my appearance for at least one day. My birth on the fourteenth day of Nisan in the year 5667 of the Jewish calendar was a big disturbance in the household, and instead of participating in the Seder, my mother stayed in bed, attended by a midwife who was equally annoyed.

Every Seder night thereafter, she chided me on my untimely appearance.

"You couldn't wait another day or two, could you, Chaim-le?"

Even as a child, I recognized the injustice of this accusation.

By the way, my name, Chaim, has two syllables. The first, *chi*, is said by making a small guttural sound in the throat and adding a long *i* sound: thus, *Chi*. The second syllable sounds like a quick, soft *im*, almost lost in the upper palette. Put the two together, and you get *Chi'm*.

As a baby, I lacked the beauty and charm of my older brother Moshe, but I compensated for that deficiency, my mother told me, with a good disposition, by which she meant I didn't require much attention, a true blessing in a crowded household. But with my two sisters and grandmothers hovering about, I got a lot of attention anyway.

Chapter 20

Now, as an old man in New York, I look back to my childhood in Jerusalem and marvel at the smooth flow of those years. How sweet were the days, their honeyed hours so full that I wonder still at the sweet surfeit of my youth. We lived as one--my brothers and sisters my father, mother, and grandparents, my many aunts, uncles, and cousins—ah, so much life in so small a place and so brief a span of time.

When I think of that world, I realize now that there really weren't any children or adults in Batei Warsaw; in Batei Warsaw, no one was too old or too young to be anything but, simply, a member of a great community.

Every prayer and blessing my mother recited was whispered into my ear, and her soft voice was the first and last sound I heard when waking and sleeping. When I was an infant and she put a drop of milk into my mouth, she touched my lips and said, "Blessed art thou, O Lord our God, King of the universe, by whose word all things exist." Putting me to sleep, my mother prayed, "Blessed art thou, O Lord our God, King of the universe, who makes the hands of sleep fall upon my eyes and slumber upon my eyelids." Sometimes she said more: "Cause us, O Lord our God, to lie down in peace and rise up to life."

When I was one year old, a skullcap, or kippur, was put on my head, never to be taken off, not even when I went to bed, and for all the days of my youth, I never walked bareheaded.

When I was two years old and started dressing myself, I put on a tallit katan, a small garment of woolen cloth with trailing fringes on its four corners, which I wore all my waking hours.

In our house, we always had guests for supper—relatives, friends, travelers from Europe and other parts of Palestine—and everyone sat around the table, speaking in Yiddish, words pouring forth in a tumble. There were no differences in how one talked to others, whether adults or children, men or women. We simply talked; familiarity did not preclude respect. I stayed up as late as I wanted and listened to the conversation around the table, contributing when I could, and my words were treated with the same respect as those of my elders, for the questions of a child were regarded as a special form of wisdom. Many times, I fell asleep at the table and woke up in bed as my mother whispered a prayer in my ear.

I loved sitting at the supper table for hours and hours, listening to everyone talking about everything, and I learned that the adult world had many difficulties, great and small, most of them the inevitable consequence of people living with one another.

I had great sympathy for everyone, and I learned from my father that a peacemaker is truly a wonderful person.

I had two different beds. In summer, I slept on the stone floor of the big room in a place of my choosing, which was always near the corner, next to my older brother; a single blanket, arranged and puffed properly, served as my mattress, pillow, and cover. In winter, I had a made-to-order bed that my mother built every night. She lifted a closet door from its hinges and arranged it on two chairs to keep it off the cold stone floor, and I wrapped myself in the same blanket of my summer bed and climbed on top.

I slept soundly always, never waking in the night.

I ate the same food the adults did and observed Shabbat and all the holidays with them.

Boys followed their fathers, and girls followed their mothers.

Children and adults were one group, one age, one category—we were, simply, Jews, proud and pious.

I started walking when I was eleven months old, and though I was confined to the house and the front yard, with an occasional, impetuous rush into the alley, a new world opened for me. Wanting to get on top of things, I moved chairs to climb on tables and moved tables to get to windows. When I was older, I got to the roof of the kitchen and then to the roof of the house, and I would run across the tops of all the houses in Batei Warsaw. Sometimes I went with my mother to the Mea Shearim market to buy wheat or corn, and then we brought it to the mill to be ground into flour. There she sometimes bought two or three pigeons for the Sabbath meal; returning home, she carried the heavy bags of meal and the pigeons, and I held on to her long dress, walking in back of her down the steep hill.

The time of my life when I was truly free, freer than I have ever been since, was the year between my third and fourth birthday. I was young enough to have no responsibilities and just old enough to do whatever I wanted. I ran and climbed, slept during the day, and ate when I wanted, coaxing from my mother and the many adults we visited or who visited us, cakes and hard candies, pieces of dried fruits, and chunks of challah with smears of honey.

As I approached four, before full-time school loomed, I had wheedled permission to leave the yard entirely, and early every morning I'd open the gate and rush up the seven steps that brought me to the flat, grassy area just in front of the big hill. Other boys were always there, all my age, and we chased each other in the wild grass and searched for small lizards and grasshoppers. In the tall bushes and low trees were birds' nests, often with eggs in them.

When I returned home, hungry, I simply went to the outdoor kitchen and ate whatever I found—bread that I dipped in sesame oil flavored with garlic, hard cheese, halvah and pickled herring, or a piece of cinnamon strudel left over from the Sabbath.

If my mother had customers in the back room, I went in and waited for them to say nice things about me, which they always did, often giving me a smile and sometimes a pat on the head.

Friday was the best day of the week.

My mother stayed home all day and prepared for the Sabbath. The challah and cake baking in the outside oven filled our house with warm, yeasty aromas laced with cinnamon. I made it a point to hover about in the yard, where there was always something to taste. I loved to be with my father when he ground the fish for gefilte fish and the meat for meatballs. To the ground fish he added small bits of carrots, fried onions, and dry challah crumbs. In the meat he stirred finely chopped fried chicken livers and coarsely chopped fried onions. There were no free samples of the gefilte fish, but if I hung around the kitchen, my mother would give me a sizzling hot meatball—just to taste, she said—and I balanced it on a dry piece of bread and took it inside to a corner in the big room, where I ate it with small, thoughtful bites, hoping to get a piece of the chicken liver on my tongue.

Even more exciting were the times when I went with my father and older brother, Moshe, to the mikvah, or bathhouse, late Friday afternoon for our Shabbos bath. The first few times, I was frightened—I remember it vividly, seeing so many naked men, young and old, thin and fat. I cried, but my father coaxed me into the water. The water frightened me too, for it was the biggest pool of water I had ever been in. We had no bathtubs in our house, and sometimes we would pour water into a large galvanized tub to bathe, but that took so many trips to the cistern that it happened rarely. Soon the mikvah became fun; the water was warm and soothing. When I got older, I was not able to feel comfortable unless I was able to bathe, and I looked forward to the weekly mikvah even more.

After our bath, our father, Moshe, and I went to the Hasidic shul in Batei Warsaw. My grandfather Fishel was always there, along with some of my uncles and cousins, of whom I had many, but since everyone went to his shul of preference, the many members of my extended family were rarely all in one place. The men prayed, sang, and danced, and I always fell asleep and had to be carried home by my father.

I was one of Grandmother Esther's favorite grandchildren, or perhaps all her many grandchildren thought they were. When I was old enough, my sisters and I would walk to her house almost every day, drawn in part by the expectation of goodies. She didn't give us candy or sweet drinks; instead, she put out plates of fruit, mostly Jaffa oranges from the groves of my uncle Yitzhak Haggis, and sometimes grapefruit, which she would peel and slice and, smiling at us all the time, watch us eat section by section.

She told us the same tales over and over, but they were always new and exciting. She told us about what it was like to live in Poland and about the endless forests our great-grandfather worked in and how the big trees came crashing down, with the birds flying about in fear and amazement.

"When he was a little boy, your own grandfather loved to spend the summer in the forest. And then he went to study in Warsaw. But he always wanted to come to Jerusalem. That is where we belong."

She told us how they left Poland and had to walk for weeks through the cold and the dark and how they were always cold and frightened and hungry. Then she told us how they had to wait for a boat to take them to Palestine.

"Your father, Haskel, was once a little boy just like you, Chaim," she told me over and over.

When I was a child, my imagination could not reach that far back. My father as a child? It was not possible.

She added, "And you are like him, calm and thoughtful."

One of the tales my grandmother Esther told us was about the miracle that happened to her when she was born. This was in Poland, in Plotsk, a faraway and vivid land I have never seen other than in my grandmother's words, but I have lived there all the same. Her mother had just given birth to twin girls.

"My sister and I were two months early, and we were very tiny, no bigger than two little kittens. And the midwife was clumsy and dropped both of us on the floor. One of the little babies died instantly, a terrible tragedy, but the other wasn't hurt, not the slightest scratch. And that little girl grew up to be me, and you should be glad, because otherwise, you wouldn't have such sweet fruits to eat."

My own mother explained the moral of this story, but I didn't understand it until I was older: what happens to you is a matter of chance, and a little bit of luck always helps.

When I was older and saw the world differently, I realized that destiny rules and that the hand of God is in all things.

*

There are no photographs of my grandparents and parents as children, nor are there any of me. Cameras were big, cumbersome instruments to be used for special occasions. There was not a single camera in all of the Mea Shearim or Batei Warsaw, and for official documents, such as visas, passports, and government work applications, we went to the

Old City. Our lives had no visual record; our history existed only in the memories that our parents and other family members gave us and in the acts of others that left imprints on our lives.

In Batei Warsaw, a camera was a frightening thing. A photograph, not quite as sinful as a carved statue, was close enough to a graven image to come under the ban of idol worship. The first photograph of me was taken when I was a teenager, about sixteen years old. I don't remember the occasion, but there I stand with my two younger brothers, Netanel and Fishel, looking into the alien glass eye. We are dressed as Hasidic children, for that is what we are, each according to our age. When I look at it, I marvel that I could have been so young and was once a boy running through the streets of Jerusalem or over the rooftops of Batei Warsaw, hurrying home to beg a lick of jam from my mother's finger.

CHAPTER 21

When I was about four, I started school full-time at the Talmud Torah in Batei Warsaw.

My first teacher was Reb Mordchale, whom we called Der Kleiner Rebbele (the Small Rebbe). His name was double-edged, for he taught the youngest, smallest boys, and he himself was a midget. His wife was also a midget, and we called her the Kleine Rebbitzin. Little children, we were as tall as both. They had no children themselves, and every day the Kleine Rebbitzin brought home-baked cakes and cookies to the class and smiled as we gobbled every crumb. I had a wonderful, happy year with Der Kleiner Rebbele, and then our entire class was promoted to the class of Reb Yeshaya, better known as the Der Roiter Rebbe (the Red Rebbe).

Der Roiter Rebbe loved us, and we loved him.

He was tall and had a big, curly red beard and small, even white teeth. He was informal, and had us push the benches and tables against the walls while he sat in the center of the room on the stone floor. We sat on the floor around him in a wide circle. He never raised his voice and always had candy for crying boys, some of who cried just to get the candy.

A habitual heavy smoker, the Roiter Rebbe would cough and cough until his cheeks blew up like happy red tomatoes.

Tobacco was expensive, and a rebbe's salary was small, so he collected cigarette butts from the street and asked that we do so on our walk to heder (class). The first thing we did each morning was sit in a big circle, unload our pockets, peel off the paper, and put the tobacco in a big jar in the center of the circle. He rolled his own cigarettes with pieces of newspaper and then smoked and coughed, and when he began one of his coughing fits, we coughed along with him, filling the classroom with a symphony of loud, childish hacking.

We were supposed to learn reading and then memorize Genesis, but the Roiter Rebbe made us put away our books and gather close around him to listen to the tales of the Torah.

We were terrified by the Akedah, the Binding of Isaac, the story of how Abraham took his son, Isaac, up the mountain to be sacrificed, binding him as he would bind a ram: "Take now your son, your only son, whom you love, even Isaac, and get you into the land of Moriah, and offer him there for a burnt-offering upon one of the mountains which I will tell you of."

The Roiter Rebbe told us how Abraham and Isaac marched up into the hills, carrying wood for the sacrifice.

"Imagine how you would feel if you were that poor little boy," the Roiter Rebbe said to us. "Imagine."

We did, and we were terrified.

"And then Isaac said, 'Abba, I see the wood for the fire, but where is the ram we will offer?'"

The Roiter Rebbe told us that Abraham built an altar, put the wood on it, and then bound his son and put him on the wood.

"And then," said the Roiter Rebbe, "Abraham took the knife and raised his hand, about to kill his son. He came this close. The knife was almost touching the skin of Isaac's neck." The Roiter Rebbe paused and looked around in befuddlement. "Where is my jar of tobacco?"

"Tell us! Tell us!" we demanded, but the rebbe was building suspense.

"Bring me my jar."

Two boys rushed to the front of the room and brought the jar. The Roiter Rebbe carefully rolled a fresh cigarette from his butt shreds, and only after he slowly smoked it to the end, coughing and coughing as his cheeks blew up as bright as tomatoes, did he continue.

"At the very last second, the very, very last instant, when Abraham was about to cut the throat of his dear little boy, Isaac, an angel came rushing down from heaven and called to him: 'Abraham! Abraham!' And Abraham answered, 'Here am I.'"

We held our breaths, ready for anything.

"And the angel delivered a heaven-sent command: 'Do not lay your hand on the boy, and do nothing to him.'"

We all cheered like crazy, but the Roiter Rebbe held up his hand for silence.

"'Do nothing to him, for I know now that you revere God, seeing that you have not withheld your son, your only son, from Me.'"

We cheered even more loudly, happy that the little boy had been spared.

I asked, for I was a concerned child, "But, Rebbe, what if the angel was late?"

"Ah, Chaim." The Roiter Rebbe smiled and wagged a finger. "Chaim, you should know that angels always come on time."

An Angel Stays Abraham's Hand The Binding of Isaac Genesis 22

By then, I was four, and I went with my father twice a day every day to shul, as we called the synagogue, for morning and evening services. After shul in the morning, I rushed to the Talmud Torah for study, and then I returned to the synagogue for the second service, after which I waited for my father to finish his Talmudic lecture so we could walk together through the dark streets with the other little boys and their fathers, and their fathers, all returning home from prayer, study, holy songs, and dances.

The next year, my class moved up a grade, and we had a new rebbe, Reb Shlomo, whose style was the opposite of the Kleiner Rebbele and the Roiter Rebbe. Reb Shlomo ruled the class with an iron first—no cookies, cakes, or happy stories and no collecting cigarette butts. This was a major calamity for us; childhood was over. Reb Shlomo insisted there be no memorizing of the text. Instead, we had to open our books and read out loud, but since the Roiter Rebbe hadn't bothered to teach us, the words were a meaningless jumble.

Reb Shlomo was disgusted. He told us that it would be a waste of his scholarly skills to teach us how to read, so instead, we spent a great part of our day keeping the classroom clean. Every day different groups of students were assigned to clean the floor, walls, tables, and chairs. At twelve o'clock, Reb Shlomo inspected everything and, satisfied with our efforts, closed the doors tightly, and all of us, including the rebbe, put our heads on the tables and napped until two.

Reb Shlomo also kept a box with shoe polish and brushes in his desk, and while we cleaned the classroom, he polished his black shoes, holding them up now and then to measure their gleam.

"See?" he told us as we went about our sweeping and dusting. "Like a mirror!"

One of the lessons I learned from Reb Shlomo was the importance of shoes.

"A man's shoes are the first thing other people notice. Shiny shoes get respect."

Most of the other students and I solved the problem of dirty shoes a different way: too poor to own any footwear, we walked about barefoot.

One time, during the winter, Reb Shlomo didn't come to class for three days in a row. We were told that our rebbe was ill. Showing our respect and performing a collective mitzvah at the same time, for it is commanded that one must visit the sick, our entire class walked to the rebbe's house. However, his wife informed us that the rebbe was sound asleep. Not wanting to waste an opportunity for an additional mitzvah, the rebbetzin put us to work cleaning the floors, walls, and windows of their house, assigning two of us to play with their five children so that the sick rebbe would not be disturbed during his curative nap.

The next year, our class was promoted to the class of Reb Chaim. He was a good rebbe.

Reb Chaim meant business. He tested us for reading skills and then divided us into groups according to ability. Of the three groups, I was in the first, the best group.

Without any dramatic stories or cleaning chores, the year went fast, and the next year, we began studying in earnest. Reb Yossef was our teacher. We started with the Gemara, our first real contact with Talmudic study, and it was difficult for the entire class. Luckily, my father was an expert Talmudist, and he and I studied together every Saturday afternoon. That year, the personality of the rebbe was less important than the material we were studying, and the year went even faster.

Our next teacher was Reb Motel, who didn't show up half the time.

"You're all big boys and know what to do," he told us the first day, "so do it."

When he did appear, he would explain a difficult passage of the Talmud, but most of the time, he told us jokes about the poor quality of the rebbes in the lower grades.

"When I was young boy in Jerusalem, we used to have too many donkeys but few rebbes, and we thought we needed more rebbes. But now the opposite is true, and we have too few donkeys. And do you know why? When donkeys get old, they become rebbes."

We laughed at Reb Motel's jokes, but many of us were disturbed. We had been taught to honor and respect our teachers as much as we honored and respected our parents. Furthermore, it is forbidden in Jewish ethics to speak harshly of another person. But Reb Motel had a point. Rebbes were not certified, nor did anyone ever evaluate them. Often, the older students became teachers in their own schools, and once you became a rebbe, you were a rebbe for life. The goal of the school was, of course, to educate us to become devout and devoted Jews who followed as closely as possible the traditions of our ancestors. We were expected to be honest, respectful, and, most importantly, law abiding. That meant obeying both kinds of law, Torah and civil. It was understood that these virtues had to be taught and explained until they became an integral part of one's life.

It was taken as a great truth that in a lawful and peaceful land, where men and women followed the word of God and the law of a just government, every person would eventually find their place in the world.

Chapter 22

The years of my childhood were full and busy. The day was never long enough, and the night, to my impatient eagerness to be out and about, never short enough; I jumped out of bed as the sun came up, ready for anything and everything. Jerusalem, both the Old City and New Jerusalem beyond its walls, was full of wonders—Turks, Arabs, and Jews arguing and talking, selling and buying. In my large family, someone was always getting married or giving birth; others were dying and mourning. And always people arrived from one place and left for another.

For instance, out of the blue, a brother of my grandmother Nechama showed up. He was named Naftali and came from Poland. A widower with no children, he was very poor. No one talked about his past in Warsaw, but it was whispered that he had been a *damsker schneider*, a woman's tailor.

Of all the trades and skills in the world that a religious man might choose, why a damsker schneider? No wonder it was kept a secret. Sewing women's clothing was work only for Arabs or Yemenites, not a pious Hasid, no less a brother of our grandmother.

Naftali was given a one-room basement apartment below the Mitnaggedim synagogue in Batei Warsaw. It was not quite a proper place for a man of his Orthodox habits, but it was the only apartment available. My cousin Yitzhak and I visited often. Uncle Naftali was poor but always had a smile, often a little sad. He was also ready with his needle and thread and would sew a loose button on our jackets or make a quick patch on a torn seam, of which, given our rough-and-tumble play, we had many.

Then my cousin Esther, my mother's niece, became deathly ill. She was only fourteen and pretty, and my aunt Nechama and uncle Netanel had already started saving for her dowry. My mother had given them many expensive fabrics for her married woman's wardrobe. Her illness was sudden and had no origin. The doctors did not know. My family

176

and all the Hasidic community rose in prayer to save her, but nothing sufficed. Again, the angels won the argument, and my cousin was taken up into heaven.

What tears there were and what bitter lamentation!

My aunt and uncle were never happy again.

*

I had so many cousins I could hardly count them, and my favorites soon became the five Reisman boys, with whom my older brother, Moshe, and I spent most of our free time. Because of our different ages and styles, Moshe and the two middle older boys went off on their own, and Cousin Yitzhak and I formed a happy little army of two.

I could never understand why Moshe was friendly with Zalman and Avraham. My older brother was polite, well behaved, and, like my father, calm—traits I shared. Zalman and Avraham, on the other hand, were terrors. They walked around in their skullcaps and fringed garments with pocketknives and slingshots, shooting stones at cats and birds, acting tough, and being rude.

Once, the two of them decided to teach themselves watch making and proceeded to practice on our wall clock. I told them not to, but they ignored me, and while I watched with growing anger, they took our precious, expensive clock off the wall and began to take it apart. Fortunately, my mother came in and stopped them, but my father had to take the clock to the Old City to be repaired.

Another time, they pulled the mezuzah, the little box holding the parchment on which the She'ma is written, from the doorpost of my grandparents' house—they just pulled it right off. Without the protective power of those holy words, my grandmother Nechama, a woman pious to the point of superstition, refused to cross her threshold. She stood in her yard, shaking and praying, while my cousins hid in an alley, sniggering. One of her neighbors rushed off to the synagogue, and soon my uncle Netanel came running into the yard, waving a hammer and a new mezuzah, which he promptly attached to the doorpost.

Another of their mischievous games was to take a pair of their father's pants into their yard—and he didn't have many pairs to spare. Zalman would put his left leg into one of the pant legs, and Avraham would put his right leg into the same pant leg, and then they would jump around like a screaming, laughing grasshopper, falling everywhere. When the seams of the pants burst, they laughed even more. Moshe, calm and collected, would just watch and smile.

My cousin Yitzhak and I went to different schools; I stayed close to home, studying in the Mea Shearim, while he went to a school called Pre Etz Chaim, the Tree of Life, in one of the newer outlying sections of Jerusalem. After school, we met in my house in Batei Warsaw and ate whatever we could find. Then we went out to see what was happening on the streets of Jerusalem, contributing whatever we could to the general activity, until, hungry again, we went to Grandmother Nechama's house, where there was always cake, cookies, and candy.

We didn't stay long, for that was the time of day when Mohamed came down from the mountain, and at the first sound of his flutes and bells, we began running full speed back to my mother's house.

Mohamed was an effendi, a landowner, and his fortune came from goats and sheep. Six times a week, with the exception of Shabbos and other holy days, when no commerce could take place, Mohamed came down from his village near Jerusalem with a small herd of goats and sheep. In the Jewish neighborhoods outside the Old City, he sold his portable milk supply directly to the consumer.

We could count on Mohamed showing up in our square just before sunset. He was well off, but not wealthy, and had only two wives, who, fully veiled, walked single file behind his beautiful white horse. An enormous ox, with milking stools and pails hanging from its sides and a big iron bell clanging from its neck, strutted close behind, followed by his two shepherds, who played a high, light melody on wooden flutes, leading Mohamed's goats and sheep, their udders so full of milk they could barely walk. Bringing up the rear was a ragtag parade of children marching along for the fun of it, led by Crazy Shimola, a homeless man wearing a fur hat and carrying a lantern in one hand and a broom in another, jumping up and down and spinning circles while yelling at the sky. Pausing at the foot of the hill in front of Batei Warsaw, the goats and sheep would relieve themselves, their hot streams of urine soaking the earth, before continuing on around the hill.

Running as quickly as we could, Cousin Yitzhak and I arrived just as the long milk caravan pulled up at the north gate. My mother and the other women were already waiting with their pots and bottles, and the shepherds immediately set up their milk stools, grabbed the udders, and began milking.

While this was going on, Cousin Yitzhak, the other children, and I tried to ride the goats, which was almost impossible, since goats detest being ridden and refuse to let anyone get on them. Meantime, the bargaining between Mohamed and the women was ferocious. The confrontation was simple and basic: the women always wanted more milk at lower prices, and Mohamed wanted the opposite. Some of the women were eager to buy and get back to their houses, but most employed a tactical patience, for they knew the goats had to be milked daily, and whatever Mohamed could not sell would have to be squeezed out onto the earth. As the dusk deepened, Mohamed threatened to leave, jumping on his horse and waving his hands.

"It's getting dark and cold," he yelled, "and I don't like to ride at night when it's cold!" He turned to his shepherds. "Stop milking! Pack up. These women don't want to buy."

Still, the women held back. Supply and demand were about equal, so it was a test of wills, and eventually, classic market dynamics produced a happy result for all. In the meantime, Mohamed's two wives were in my mother's store, looking at fabrics. Mohamed was proud of his horse, his goats and sheep, and especially his wives and never refused them anything, nor, as befitting his status as an effendi with a beautiful white horse, did he ever bargain.

"My little Reizel," he said, "what shall I pay for this?"

She always raised the price just enough, a few pennies perhaps, so that he might demonstrate his wealth.

Then, as suddenly as they had appeared, Mohamed and his traveling circus were gone. Mohamed sat on his horse, and his wives walked behind with the packages of fabric balanced gracefully on their heads. The huge ox followed, its bell ringing sadly in the growing darkness and a glowing lantern on a stick swaying over its back. The shepherds came next, their flutes leading the goats and sheep, which, much lighter, walked with a buoyant step. Soon, with the bell and flutes fading with the bleating of the goats, they disappeared into the dark.

At our gate, I would beg some of the warm, frothy milk from my mother, and she always gave me two long swallows. She gave the same to Cousin Yitzhak, who then ran home before it got too dark, and I would go inside, hungry and ready for supper.

Cousin Yitzhak and I shared all our secrets.

We knew where my mother hid her jars of homemade tzimmes, the sweet, thick jam she kept for special guests. It was behind the dishes on the top shelf of a wall closet in the large room, and we had to use a chair to reach the dizzying height. It was never profitable to start up with my mother, and we took only small portions of the jam and were careful not to break any dishes. One time, she caught us in the act. I was on the chair, holding the jar, and Yitzhak was standing. We were both licking our fingers. I was so frightened that I dropped the jar, but Yitzhak quickly caught it before it smashed on the stone floor.

My mother surprised me with her calm.

"At least did you say the proper blessing before you stuck your fingers in your mouths?"

Yitzhak and I looked at each other and then at her, our silence a confession.

"Say the blessing," she said, "and then put the tzimmes back when you're finished."

There should have been a blessing for those times when you got caught doing something you shouldn't. It would have been one of the most popular.

*

Our lives were simple. Our house in Batei Warsaw was new and spacious and was approximately four hundred square feet in total area. The front yard and the lean-to kitchen added another hundred or so square feet. Nine people—my parents, my three sisters and three brothers, and I—lived in this space. My mother also used the back room for her fabric store. As my brothers and I got older, we were out of the house most of the time, and when we were all home, the house was crowded, but we managed to find our own corners. We also put up overnight visitors, sometimes two or three of them, for days at a time. We knew nothing else, and besides, everyone lived that way, so everything was as it should be.

Our house had hardly any furniture. We possessed only the most essential items: dishes and utensils, which we kept on open shelves; a table and a number of chairs; a sofa; two real beds, the others makeshift; kerosene lanterns; and a few other items.

My parents had separate beds. My mother usually had the youngest child sleep with her until the next came along, usually in three-year intervals. My sister Chaya Sara, the oldest, slept on a wooden sofa in the small back room, where the walls were lined with shelves of my mother's fabrics. My other brothers and sisters and I slept on the floor in the large room or, if it was winter, on closet doors laid chair to chair. We had few linens, so our blankets, bundled, folded, or crimped, served as our sheets and pillows.

We had two valuable pieces of furniture: a wall clock and a wall mirror. They weren't really worth much, but they seemed valuable to me. The mirror hung high on the wall, close to the ceiling, and at first, I couldn't use it unless I moved a chair, so maybe that was what it made it special.

However, the wall clock, I believe, was genuinely expensive. I loved its musical chimes. I couldn't read the Latin numbers, but I counted the hours easily and was able to anticipate the quarter-hour chime.

The truly valuable items in our home were my father's seforim, or study books, many of which were part of the dowry my mother had brought. They were arranged in a beautiful bookcase with glass doors, which had the only locks in our home. My father took them out at night to study at the table, but they never left the house.

Each of us had a special holiday wardrobe consisting of a jacket, a shirt, and, when I got older, a pair of shoes. We didn't have many changes of underwear, shirts, or pants, and we washed every item constantly. We wore everything to the point of unwearability and then a little beyond.

Our family's income was the sum of my father's monthly salary from the Yeshiva Chai Olam, where he lectured and taught Talmud classes, and my mother's fabric store in the small back room. We paid no rent, for Kolel Warsaw absorbed the expense, and Moshe's and my education was also free, as it would be for my brothers when they were older.

Yet we lived in much greater austerity than other families who had less. We could have afforded more, but it was my father's desire to live as simply as possible.

Or perhaps my sense of our household economics was inaccurate.

My grandparents, my father's mother and father, lived the same way, and their house was as sparse as ours. My grandmother Esther was proud of her thrifty ways and often boasted that most of the clothing she now wore had been brought from Plotsk many years ago. My grandfather Fishel worked for a few charitable institutions and was the president of Kolel Warsaw, all nonpaying positions. His income came from Yitzhak Haggis's huge stationery store near the Jaffa Gate, where he was the manager.

His salary was more than adequate, but he kept only what he and my grandmother needed to maintain their modest ways. He donated most of his money to Jerusalem's many charitable institutions. At home, he dressed simply, wearing black pants, a plain white shirt without any adornment, and a plain black yarmulke. In the house, he wore soft, old slippers. Visitors often expressed surprise that one of Jerusalem's most prominent religious and social leaders lived so plainly.

In public, however, he was impressive, his wardrobe befitting his high position in the community. His black shoes shone like a mirror. His earlocks and pure white beard were neatly trimmed, and his complexion, very fair, gave his face a vital radiance.

He had a beautiful walking cane that had belonged to his grandfather in Poland. It was carved of shiny black wood and had a handle of pure silver that was shaped like the head of a fish, with eyes made of two shiny green stones. In public, he wore a large, beautiful fur-trimmed streimel, and when he walked down the stones of the narrow streets of Jerusalem with his two assistants trailing him on either side, even the Arabs would bow.

My other grandfather, my mother's father, Netanel Reisman, was genuinely poor. He visited us rarely. We loved him because whenever he came, he brought joy and laughter into our house. He was an optimist, manufacturing hope out of the air; one of his favorite sayings was, "Mark my words, it's going to be good!"

Although he wasn't academically accomplished and hadn't studied in yeshiva, my grandfather Netanel was still highly respected. He was one of the few Hasidim in the Warsaw Houses who worked for his bread—not, however, as a laborer or, God forbid, a women's tailor-- but as a clerk in two charitable institutions. He made money as a scribe as well, because he knew how to write Latin, as English was often called, and wrote letters and addressed envelopes for those who could not.

He loved to dance and sing and was welcomed at all synagogues and ceremonies, where his beautiful voice would fill the room with happiness.

Yet he seemed always sad. My mother told me he missed Poland. He would never return to Poland, of course, for he loved Jerusalem with all his heart and soul. He had bought two burial plots on the Mount of Olives, one for himself and one for his Nechama, which he would not need, with God's help, until his allotted 120 years were up. But even a devoted Hasid is a human being, and he longed to be in Gur with his beloved rebbe and his Hasidic friends. He often saw himself there, he told me, dancing and singing in praise of the Holy Name. If he were to go back—just for a visit, of course—he would take with him a large box of earth from the Mount of Olives and give bags of the precious gift to his long-lost friends in Gur.

"They will appreciate it more than gold and diamonds, believe me," he told us.

"Ach." He would sigh, thinking of how wonderful it would be, and then he'd smile.

"Mark my words, it's going to be good!"

*

My favorite uncle was my mother's younger brother. His name was Yisrael Yitzhak. I don't know why I liked him so much, but I did. He had experienced a great misfortune in his life: his wife had died after they had been married a year. My mother didn't know the exact date but the sad event was fixed precisely in her mental calendar, for the woman had died the same night the flourmill burned down. After a year of mourning, my uncle Yisrael Yitzhak remarried and gradually regained his zest for life.

He came to our house every evening to study with my father, and the two of them sat at our long table, the lantern throwing a golden light on the seforim. I would often sit on Uncle Yisrael Yitzhak's lap and turn the pages for him, and after every three pages, he would take a piece of candy out of his pocket and press it into my hand. Once, he complimented me.

"This boy has brains," he said to my father.

"Of course," my father replied.

I don't know on what evidence they spoke, but it was pleasant to get such a high compliment, for in my father's and uncle's world of books and words, having brains was important.

Before Uncle Yisrael Yitzhak left around midnight, he gave me another piece of candy from the inexhaustible supply in his pocket.

*

On the day of my grandfather Netanel's death in 1913, the town crier walked through Batei Warsaw, the Mea Shearim, and Batei Hungary, crying the sad news.

"*Geit tzu die levayah!*" (Go to the funeral!).

Doors and windows were flung open, and people stuck their heads out.

"Who died?"

The town crier called, "Reb Netanel Reisman! *Geit tzu die levayah!*"

He was fifty-eight, give or take a year or two.

Until the day of his death, he had never complained of fatigue or illness. His optimism might have created a false sense of his health in others, or perhaps he was marking his own words, thinking it would all come out well.

My grandfather Netanel died a poor man.

In Poland, his wife's inn had provided a good living, but the expense of the long journey over land and sea and the costs of settlement in Jerusalem had eaten much of their small fortune. He'd spent the remainder on the dowries, however small, for his daughters. Whatever extra he had went to his favorite shtiblech, or small synagogue, where he sang and danced every night in prayer.

His one legacy was a small purse of silver coins that he gave to his oldest son with the instructions that it be used to provide a feast every Saturday night in his synagogue. The Sabbath is thought of as a queen, and there is a special service for her departure at sunset. It's a festive, song-filled celebration that lasts long into the night, for, being a gracious and appreciative monarch, she will not leave until the dancing and singing are over.

At the service, Netanel's son, the cantor with the voice like the roar of the lion, sang his father's favorite melody.

> He who marks the holy from the profane,
> May He also pardon our transgressions;
> May He multiply our seed as the sand,
> And as the stars that appear in the night.
>
> The day has fallen like the shade of a palm.
> I call upon God who fills all my needs.
> The watchman-prophet has said: Morning comes,
> Bright morning comes after gloomy night.

My grandfather's bequest, the purse full of silver, was never opened, and we never knew how much money it contained. An accurate guess was that it probably didn't have enough for even one meal.

My grandfather Netanel rests on the Mount of Olives, waiting for his share of the world to come, though I know he'd rather be in Gur with his beloved rebbe and dancing Hasidim.

*

The dates of many events, even births and deaths, were approximate, positioned relative to other events and not to any abstract calendar. Significant singular occurrences created their own markers in time. My grandparents, for instance, regarded their arrival in Jerusalem thirty years earlier as the beginning of a new calendar and positioned other events accordingly. They couldn't tell me the exact year they immigrated without giving it a lot of thought. Sometimes the marker was a commonly known event, such as the visit of the Kaiser in 1898, which corresponded to the Jewish year of 5754. However, the actual year was unimportant, for its significance was taken for granted by all who experienced it and, eventually, through constant reference by those who had not. Thus, events existed in the general flow of time, subject to repositioning as other events of greater significance overtook them. My grandfather Netanel's age, therefore, was only an approximation, because an individual's birthday was not, of itself, sufficiently significant to create its own marker, and passed without notice—except mine, of course, for I had been born on the Seder night of Passover, but the notoriety came from the holiday and not the other way around.

Many people had their own personal markers. One of my mother's was the night the big flourmill on the hill burned down.

She used that catastrophe to date later events, such as accidents, births, deaths, marriages, illnesses, and even World War I. It was a cornerstone on which she built a framework of time, adding other happenings to complete the construction. She never referred to the month or year of anything; it was always before or after the mill burned down.

Many in Batei Warsaw and the Mea Shearim used the fire as a marker too. Visible from most areas of the city, the mill was one of Jerusalem's landmarks. As children, my cousins and I viewed it as our fixed star and used it to position ourselves as we navigated the streets of Jerusalem. The mill was a symbol of ancient Jerusalem's entry into a modern era; the dark clouds from its smokestack were towers of biblical smoke, a live weather vane.

The mill attracted Arabs from villages near and far. The trails leading up to the mill had lines of peasants, with their camels and donkeys carrying sacks of wheat and corn. The farmers came with their wives and children and pitched their tents on the sloping hillside. They stayed for days, sometimes weeks, waiting their turn to grind their grain. On the top of the hill was a large grassy area that was a vast bazaar of vendors selling food and all sorts of merchandise. Mainly Arabs went there, and much local business was conducted—animals and merchandise were bought and sold or exchanged, including women. One day a man sold his daughter for a number of breeding goats, though the exact rate of exchange was never revealed.

The great fire erupted on Friday night.

The owners and workers at the mill were all Jewish, so the mill was closed for the Sabbath and sat dark and deserted.

The entire Jewish community of Jerusalem was at rest. Evening services were over, the men were home from shul, and families were finishing the Sabbath meal. One by one, the windows of Batei Warsaw grew dark, the four entry gates of Batei Warsaw were locked, and a quiet serenity settled upon the houses.

The streets had no lights, nor were any on the high hill. Without moonlight, the sky was black, and the mill was almost invisible, a dark shape outlined by thousands of glittering stars. A distant whining and barking of stray dogs and coyotes could be heard in the black night. Suddenly, shattering the peace, I heard a shout in the courtyard just outside our yard.

"Fire! Fire!"

My father ran to the window and flung it open.

"Fire! Fire!"

Moshe ran out the door in his blanket, I right behind with my father.

"Fire! Fire!"

People burst from their houses, women ran out without their wigs, their shorn hair ragged and wild.

"Fire! Fire!"

We stood transfixed. The flames lit the faces of my mother and father with orange waves, and the sky seemed on fire. On top of the hill, horses, donkeys, and camels were running everywhere, their loads of grain on fire. Racing in wild circles, the terrified creatures began running down to our houses, fire in their manes and on their backs, sparks and cinders flying behind. A horse fell, rolled down the hill, tried to get up but stumbled and fell again, fire in its hair and tail. Animals screamed in terror and pain, dying of shock as they tumbled to the bottom of the hill. My father, always calm, was holding on to my mother, who was crying and praying at the same time. Around us, people were wailing out their terror. Others shouted out praises to God for his mercy in the hope that the fire would cease.

But there was no heavenly mercy that night. Fanned by the winds blowing across the high hill, the fire raged unabated. Swallows and pigeons filled the night sky, feathers burning as they circled wildly in the red sky, and fell to earth in a tumble of flame.

As I watched in terror, unable to cry, the tents of the Arab vendors burst into flame. In a panic, the Arabs tore full speed down the hill, their wives bare breasted and without veils as they carried and dragged their screaming children. Shouting to Allah, they raced past our houses and disappeared into the night. On the hill, the screams of the animals continued, and the smell of burning flesh and singed feathers blew over the houses of Batei Warsaw.

The fire smoldered for many days, and no attempt was made to salvage any of the mill. It had been the only mill in Jerusalem, and now it was a heap of smoking charcoal. A small group of Turkish soldiers with shovels and pitchforks appeared the third day and buried the dead animals, then left, nothing to be done.

Quickly, a number of new smaller mills were built. A Russian Jew, Gadalya, built a mill just north of Batei Warsaw, and it was called Gadalya's Mill. My mother and aunts and most of Batei Warsaw were soon going there; it was much more convenient and safe, and the pigeons were cheaper.

CHAPTER 23

The Talmud tells us that the B'nai Israel, the Children of Israel, dwelt in Egypt for a hundred generations yet were able to preserve their distinct national character by observing three traditions: they wore their traditional clothing, spoke their original language, and retained their Canaanite names.

Guided by this ancient example, my own ancestors abided by the same three precepts. Of course, their notion of these traditions—dress, language, and nomenclature—was a part of their own unique heritage, and they struggled mightily to keep their customs intact. For the most part, they succeeded, though sometimes at the cost of progress.

Once in Jerusalem, however, their days of wandering over, many immigrants were ready to discard the reminders of a dead and bitter past. One often changed his or her name to reflect the immigrant's status as a citizen of a different world. At times, the change was a practical one. Thus, after a few years, because my family had come from Plotsk, the name Plotsker was added. Since human nature seeks the most economical form, soon the middle name, Linder, was dropped, and my grandparents were called simply the Plotskers. Names were changed to indicate place of origin. There was Moshe Warshever, who came from Warsaw; Ya'akov Budapester, or David Pinsker, originally from Pinsk; and Mordecai Minsker, who came from Minsk. Over a short span of time, the name Linder was almost erased entirely.

But my grandfather Fishel Linder Plotsker was determined to keep our family name. Having at last realized his dream of returning to Jerusalem, he always retained in some measure the mental outlook of the exile—and with good reason. Jerusalem was not quite the pure Jewish land he had yearned for or expected. The ancient stones of the Western Wall did cast their powerful spell upon the Old City, but over the centuries, Muslims and Christians had destroyed and defaced many of the Jewish sites, and Turks and Arabs were a strong cultural and military presence. Plotsker was not a Jewish name. It referred to the past, the place of his exile, and he didn't wish to be reminded of the land from which he had fled. Refusing to be known as Plotsker, he insisted our family retain its traditional name.

My grandparents and, in turn, my own parents kept more than just a name. They did their best to follow their traditional language and mode of dress. We knew Hebrew but spoke only Yiddish, for Hebrew was considered the sacred tongue of prayer and not to be used for daily intercourse. Our wardrobe was that of the Polish Hasid: black pants, a white shirt, a long black caftan, and a black yarmulke, or skullcap (*kippur* in Hebrew), the head covering no observant Jew is ever without. No sartorial adornments were permitted—no ties, fancy fabrics, or touches of jewelry.

There was, of course, an unresolved contradiction in all of this, for our choice of language and wardrobe was dictated by the customs of our family's life in Diaspora Poland and not based upon anything remotely biblical. Consistency, I have learned, takes many forms, not all of them rational.

However, these rules served my ancestors well and kept their Jewish roots alive and growing through a thousand years of wandering. These roots were old and tough and had been pulled from the earth many times, but now, planted at long last in Jerusalem, my grandparents hoped the earth of the Holy Land would prove fertile and sustaining.

But as the twentieth century began, men and women were already leaving Jerusalem.

A new and wonderful world, a world of dreams, beckoned: America.

It was a strange and fearful world as well, and only the young and adventuresome and the desperate, and the foolish, dared go. Some went as collectors, seeking to tap the wealth of the small but successful American Jewish community and, at the same time, earn enough money through their salaries to support their families back in Jerusalem.

One of my cousins, Mordecai, went to America without even the pretext of doing charitable work. Mordecai, always a problem, had refused to attend the Orthodox Hasidic Yeshiva and instead had gone to a more liberal school. Shortly thereafter, he announced his intention to relocate to Jaffa, or Yafo. His parents argued strenuously against this rash, impious move, but he was determined to go.

Jaffa is far from Jerusalem, a wagon ride of twelve hours. As a symbol of the new life he was to live, Mordecai traveled by train, a whirlwind trip of three hours. A crowd of family and friends were at the railroad station to bid him farewell. His parents wept at their parting. Jaffa was a secular city, hardly fit for a Hasid.

Mordecai assured them he would remain an Orthodox Jew but in a new world. In Jaffa, which later became Tel Aviv, he could speak Hebrew rather than Yiddish and dress in a more European style. He trimmed his earlocks and beard—but not completely: he merely gave them a modern flair. He also acquired a secular education, studying history, literature, mathematics, and English. French and German were more useful in Jerusalem, but his goal was America.

Part of that new world was a more open attitude to women. His family was upset but not totally surprised when, shortly after moving to Jaffa, Mordecai announced that he had married a distant relative of their family in Poland.

"What's his hurry?" people asked. Why couldn't Mordecai have consulted his family? The long negotiations over the shidduch, the proposed marriage contract, of a child were important. Did this woman or her family have secrets?

Shortly thereafter, Mordecai and his new wife returned to Jerusalem to announce their imminent departure for the United States. He had all the documents—visas, medical papers, certificates of birth—and the boat tickets. They were leaving in two weeks. The family was stunned. His father asked him the name of the charity for which he would be collecting donations, but Mordecai didn't lie.

"Abba, I'm going to live there permanently."

"I see. And just what will you do in America?"

"I'll be a rabbi. They need Orthodox rabbis there."

"I see. Are things so secular in America that they have to import rabbis?"

"The American Jewish community is growing."

"And what about Jerusalem?"

"Abba, I'll always have Jerusalem in my heart."

With heavy hearts and tears, his parents gave him their blessing. He would not be back. Few who went to America returned.

A short time later, Mordecai's brother left Jerusalem also, but he didn't go as far. He married a young woman from Hebron, a six- or seven-hour wagon ride from Jerusalem. That was hardly next door, but compared to America—well, there was no comparison. Still, he left Jerusalem.

That year, one of my many cousins, Wolfe, with a wife and four children, left for the United States. He had no specific plans, he told me, other than to be a success.

"A success?" I asked. "At what?"

"I don't know," Wolfe replied, "but in America, you can do anything if you're ambitious."

It was inconceivable to me that anyone would leave Jerusalem and travel so far to a strange land. How could anyone leave his home? Israel was the center of the world, and Jerusalem was the center of Israel, which made Jerusalem the center of all existence. At least, it was the center of my world and the world of my brothers and sisters, and I knew with absolute certainty that I would never leave the place of my birth.

CHAPTER 24

When my mother gave birth to another boy, she named him Netanel after her dead father, my grandfather Netanel. She had been in an unacknowledged race with her older sister to see who would give birth to a son, and my mother was gratified that she was the first in her family to have the honor of continuing my grandfather's name.

I had mixed feelings about my younger brother. I had to give up certain pleasant privileges, but at least I was no longer referred to as the baby.

Once the war began, it didn't really matter.

Chapter 25

It began in a place so far away from Batei Warsaw that it really didn't exist. Germany was fighting Britain. On Germany's side were Austria-Hungary and the Ottoman Empire, while Britain had France, Russia, and Italy as allies. I had little idea where these countries were or what they were fighting about, but the Turks weren't our friends, so neither were the Germans, which meant that England and her allies had better win.

Palestine was far removed from the bloody battlegrounds of Europe, but we felt the effects of the war immediately.

The Turkish authorities divided the population into two groups: friends and enemies. People who had Turkish, German, or Austria-Hungarian passports or identification papers were friends. Those who held passports from Britain, France, or Russian were branded enemies.

Neither category was much of a bargain.

Enemies had to leave the country, but friends were drafted immediately into the Turkish army.

Service in the Turkish army, however, was a fate that many of the friends tried to avoid at all costs.

Arabs were considered friends. Many of them had migrated to Palestine from other Arab countries, arriving later than their Jewish counterparts, but had been given immediate Turkish citizenship because the territories had been part of the Ottoman Empire. A small number of Sephardic Jews had Turkish passports, and they were rounded up quickly and forced into military service. Many tried to hide, which was risky, for the Turks and their Arab allies were diligent in ferreting out the reluctant, and the consequences of discovery were severe. Deserters and draft dodgers were executed by hanging in public squares, usually at the Jaffa Gate.

My grandfather Fishel, sixty years old, was much too old for military service, but he possessed a Russian passport—the only one among us with any official papers—so my parents and all of us were considered to be Russian citizens, or enemies, and had to leave the country. My grandfather and parents could not bear such a tragic fate. After so many struggles to return home to Jerusalem, they were once again being forced into exile. They decided to stay. Others left for Egypt, which was then under the sphere of influence of Great Britain and thought to be a more hospitable country where they might wait out the war. My father, then forty years old, faced an impossible dilemma. He could retain his Russian identity card and be forced to flee Jerusalem, or with the liberal use of baksheesh, he could acquire Turkish papers and stay. However, if he stayed, even at his age, he would have to serve in the Ottoman army.

After much agonizing, he decided to leave and take us with him.

He was prepared to go to Egypt, but then a rumor reached us that the United States of America was opening its gates to Jews forced out of Palestine. Several boats flying the American flag were reported to be anchored in Jaffa, waiting to take us to America.

My grandfather would have none of this.

"You cannot leave Eretz Yisrael," he insisted. "We are here, and here you must stay."

"We cannot stay," my father said.

We were in our house, packing our things in old, beaten suitcases.

"Where are you going?"

"To America," my father said.

"There are no boats waiting in Jaffa. That is a rumor put out by the Turks to catch people like you and put them in the army."

"But I have Russian papers."

"They don't care what papers you have. They want men to carry guns."

"Then we will go to Egypt."

"You cannot return to Egypt. It is the land of our bondage."

"Abba," my father said sadly, "I cannot serve in the Turkish army."

"There must be a third option." My grandfather spoke in his calm and reasonable manner, but even I knew there was no way out.

"There are no angels coming to save us," my father said, and we continued packing.

The rumors of the American boats in Jaffa were not false, and quickly, with my father's contacts, we had all the official documents required to take the eight of us to the United States. On our last day in Jerusalem, my mother left in the morning, not saying where she was going. She returned two hours later, her cheeks streaked with tears. She had been to the Kotel, asking for forgiveness and promising to return.

Angels, however, always unexpected, tend to come at the last minute, making them even more welcome. My grandfather and his brother-in-law, Yitzhak Haggis, had connections with influential government officials who, moved by our plight and with hearts opened by enormous bribes, agreed to provide us passports of any country, even China or Japan.

A rented wagon had already pulled up at our gate in the Warsaw Houses, and my brother Moshe and I were helping our father load it, when my grandfather came rushing into the courtyard in his fancy public clothing, waving his silver-headed cane.

"Thank God! Thank God!" he cried triumphantly. In his other hand were papers. "You don't have to leave!" He waved the papers wildly. "Thank God! You will stay right here in Jerusalem!"

He had managed to get Austria-Hungarian passports for himself and my father, which meant we were friends and could stay in Palestine. Furthermore, with an extra touch of baksheesh, he had gotten my father a draft exemption based on a nonexistent heart condition. Since my brother Moshe and I and everyone else were too young to serve and the war would be over before Moshe was old enough, we were all safe. My grandfather was smiling through his tears. He had come all the way across Europe and the sea to settle in Jerusalem, and he was not about to let his family flee the Holy City for a distant and alien land. He pressed the documents into my father's hand, uttered a quick prayer of thanks, and then, applying his cane to the earth with vigor, hurried off on other urgent business.

My father slipped his new Austria-Hungarian passport into his vest pocket.

"Moshe, Chaim," he said, "help your mother unload the wagon."

Then he looked up at the sky and shook his head. "A *ganza metziah*"

(A real bargain). "We are now the loyal subjects of Kaiser Franz Yossef. I'll have to start speaking German."

Moshe and I looked at each other and smiled; it wasn't often that our father employed sarcasm.

Unfortunately, his sarcasm was well founded. The bargain was not to our advantage. Overnight, Jerusalem changed, and the first of many hard, bitter years began.

The Prussians wanted to weaken the French and British war effort in Europe by undermining their influence in Egypt, Syria, and Lebanon, at the same time keeping a watchful eye on the Ottomans, their weak and unreliable ally. Suddenly, the Germans arrived, thousands of them—civil advisers, military personnel in tight, well-tailored uniforms with pistols at their sides, and men in dark suits with oiled hair. Overnight, Jerusalem became a military command center. Civil rule, such as it was under the Ottomans, was replaced by martial law, with all its attendant dangers and indignities.

Much more disciplined than the Turks, and much harsher, the Germans cast a pall over Jerusalem. They were better educated and higher paid, and difficult to bribe; baksheesh became much more expensive.

We were, in our own way, eternal optimists; accustomed to our impoverished lives before the war, we thought we could deal with the new, harsher realities of military rule, but we soon learned that we had been living in comparative paradise.

Food became even scarcer, and all civilian goods disappeared from the stores.

We had no bread, fruits, vegetables, or meat. An egg was precious, and a chicken was a gold mine. Soap could not be found. Water was rationed, and bathing became impossible.

Many were not as fortunate as my family and, lacking either the connections or the resources, couldn't change their passports or acquire the right papers. People spent enormous sums in baksheesh for a stamp of blue, red, or green ink and the signature of a German officer.

We thought ourselves fortunate to have found a way to stay in Jerusalem, but soon we weren't so sure.

I thought often of my uncle Netanel and his happy smile. "Mark my words," he had said, "it's going to be good!"

It wasn't good at all.

Palestine is a desert land with few natural resources and is completely dependent on imports for most of its raw materials and finished goods. Despite these difficulties, Jewish immigrants had managed over the years to create a viable, if subsistence, economy of many small manufactures and commercial interests, all, however, dependent on import and export. With the outbreak of war in Europe and the disruption of the usual trade routes, these businesses were forced to shut down for lack of raw materials and retail goods. Skilled workers were in short supply, for those not drafted into the Turkish army had fled to Europe or were in hiding.

The Orthodox communities of Jerusalem, dependent upon donations from abroad but with their major source of funds cut off, were confronted with the most dire and devastating poverty. The Germans did not respect earlocks or long beards and did not grant the Orthodox Jewish community some of the basic amenities that the more tolerant, lazy Turks had allowed, such as letting us pray peacefully in our synagogues on Friday nights. Instead, the Germans sent their patrols through Batei Warsaw and the Mea Shearim, searching for conscripts. People locked their doors and talked in whispers. No longer did we have friends and relatives to our home to study and sing; instead, we stayed home in the dark, conserving the little kerosene we had, and ate our meager portions of holiday foods. Almost overnight, the narrow streets and twisting alleys of Jerusalem where I once played and ran with my friends became avenues of fear and danger.

As conditions worsened, people grasped at straws. Some thought that service in the Turkish army would be better than starvation, but that option was quickly abandoned. A short walk from Batei Warsaw were Turkish army barracks, where my cousin Yitzhak and I went to watch the soldiers train. We saw the men whipped or held down naked and beaten with canes. A few of the soldiers were neighbors with whom we had prayed in synagogue; now we watched them marching and running in the hot sun, falling, and being kicked and made to run again.

It was a great tragedy for Hasidic boys to be drafted into the Turkish army. Degradation and depression followed. Beards and earlocks were shorn; prayers were not allowed. The Holy Sabbath and all the other holidays and fast days ceased to exist. They went hungry because they could not bring themselves to eat the non-kosher food—meat from horses or camels cooked in greasy fat. They grew weak and, falling all the time, were beaten by the officers. Unable to escape, weak in body and sick of heart, they lost their will to live and died within months. In a final, wrenching indignity, the Turks buried them in the sand, uncleansed and unmourned, leaving behind the bitter tears of their families.

For those exempt from military service, there were the work brigades. There was no escape from serving in these brigades. Elderly men scarcely able to walk were put to work building army barracks and roads, digging up fields, cleaning streets, caring for the cavalry horses, and cleaning out stables. They lived in tents in the hills around Jerusalem and were led to work in large groups guarded by Turkish soldiers, themselves guarded by German officers. Work gangs were sometimes sent to other towns, where they slept in open fields and ate a single meal a day of dry bread and rotten horsemeat.

My uncle Chaim Shaia tried to hide, but he was caught and assigned to a work brigade building a new road between Jerusalem and Hebron. Not strong enough for heavy digging, he was brought back to Jerusalem to sweep the narrow streets. Every day at dawn, my uncle, his ankles chained to another worker, was led by soldiers through the Old City. Every morning I stood with the women and children on the streets, looking for our relatives. We called to them and tried to pass them food when the soldiers weren't looking. Some people held out baksheesh for the guards to get their relatives unchained, but that didn't work. My uncle could hardly walk. Sick of spirit, he cried when he saw me. I threw him a potato, but he couldn't catch it, and another prisoner quickly snatched it from the gutter. Finally, our family managed to give a large bribe to two high officials, and my uncle was released from the brigade.

"No more chances," my grandfather Fishel said, and Uncle Chaya went into deep hiding in a small, dark basement in the Yemenite section, sharing the cramped space with two other Hasidim.

I had been seven years old when the war started, and now I was eight.

My happy Jerusalem had become a sad ghost town.

Gone were the crowds that had thronged the marketplace; its stalls were now empty, its shelves bare. Soldiers patrolled the streets, stopping every boy over the age of twelve and demanding papers. My grandfather continued managing the stationery store, one of the only places still doing business. The inventory was under strict control, and my grandfather and Yitzhak Haggis had to report all transactions to the military governor.

With nothing to buy, currency soon lost its value. The black market flourished. Our mother had seen what was coming and, at the outbreak of war, had bought large quantities of fabrics, which she hid by distributing them throughout the house as if they were ordinary household linens—sheets, pillowcases, towels, and the like. She had a small, select group of customers she could trust. No money exchanged hands. Cash was still good for baksheesh, but money had no purchasing power on the street. Instead, she bartered her precious fabrics for goods and services.

Mr. Berman, the owner of the Odessa Bakery, was one of my mother's best customers, and she traded some of her cloth for additional rations of bread. His bakery was going full steam, literally, supplying bread to both the civilian and the military populations. The Turkish army requisitioned much of the bread—soldiers in the bakery watched everything—and the little remaining was strictly rationed. The war had reduced the amount and quality of the flour and yeast, and the bread was dry and tasteless, though to my starving mouth it was sweet manna. At the start of the war, the Odessa Bakery received donations from Mr. Berman's contacts in the United States, and he distributed the bread to the Jewish population in Jerusalem. Our mother's store was one of the distribution centers, and every morning, two donkeys brought big hampers of baked goods into Batei Warsaw. My mother, sisters, brother, and I gave out the round, heavy loaves; each family received a share according to the number of children in the household.

Our mother also gave some of her precious fabrics to the

orphanage home for girls in Jerusalem, which another of my uncles, David Weingarten, had helped found and where he was now the director. She could have sold the fabric at a high profit to some of her rich customers, but we all agreed that the poor girls must be taken care of first.

Every day we hoped and prayed that the war would soon be over. We asked ourselves how much worse it could get. How much longer could the nations continue fighting? Where were all the British, French, and Russian soldiers who were going to beat up the Turks and Germans? After the Germans came, nothing dramatic happened. Instead, every day we had to swallow another dose of bad medicine, each dose small enough to get down without too much pain, so we were able to pretend things weren't that bad. Nevertheless, the taste was bitter.

Then the news reached us that the British had sent their fleet into the Mediterranean Sea to blockade the coast of Palestine. For me, who had never seen the sea or a naval vessel, the news was both exciting and meaningless. The papers printed nothing but Turkish propaganda, so no one believed that anything had changed. Indeed, the blockade took some time to be effective, and the shortages of food and merchandise were not felt until later.

Ever resilient, the older Jewish population called upon the lessons and skills we had learned in the past. My grandparents and parents had lived with oppressive governments all their lives, and they knew how to cope with mindless authority; accustomed to scarcity, they taught us how to make little bits of food sit in the mouth and small pieces of soap last forever.

Then I was nine years old, and the war was still going on.

I had one pair of shoes, which I wore on Shabbat and holidays, and then only when I went to the synagogue for services. The rest of the time, day after day, winter and summer, rain or shine, I walked, ran, played, and climbed barefoot.

Most other children, and many adults, did the same. My one and only pair of shoes was repaired over and over. When my feet grew too big, the leather in front and on the sides was cut and patched, and the shoe was made to fit, however imperfectly. We protected our shoes as if they were living parts of our bodies.

A shoemaker was a true king, and we were lucky to have a good shoe repairer, Der Odessa Shuster (the Shoe Man from Odessa). Only a few people knew his real name, Yisrael. He rented a store near Mr. Berman's Odessa Bakery, and many people thought that because they were both from Odessa, Yisrael and Mr. Berman were brothers. They looked nothing alike, but such was the power of names and proximity. At first, I went to his store when I had to repair my worn and torn shoes, but soon we became friends, and I visited him twice a week.

With the scarcity of imported goods and the British blockade, the Odessa Shuster was unable to purchase new leather and instead recycled old, discarded footwear; he stuffed hundreds of shoes, boots, and slippers in a variety of colors and styles into the shelves of his tiny store.

"I will show you an ultra secret," he said to me one day. "Come."

He moved aside a table and then a small rug and pulled open a floor hatch.

"Come." He put his finger to his closed mouth and then bent it, beckoning.

With the Odessa Schuster holding a lantern, I followed him down the creaky wooden steps into his dark cellar.

"I have enough leather here to last through the war—at the most, another year."

I looked around, and to my eye, he probably had enough to last ten years. On the floor, on shelves, and hanging from the ceiling were hundreds and hundreds of pairs of shoes and boots.

"You must never tell a soul, Chaim."

"I won't."

"Not even your older brother, Moshe, or your cousin Yitzhak."

"I won't."

Then, beckoning me closer and lowering his voice even more, the Odessa Shuster revealed to me a greater secret.

"When I repair your shoes, I use only French leather."

I didn't know what to say.

"Chaim, I tell you this trade secret because I like you. French leather is the best leather in the world."

"Thank you," I told him.

"You're very welcome," he replied, and we went back upstairs.

In his shop, I watched him work. He would cut the old shoes, remove the torn or worn pieces; and then sew, glue, and nail the spare parts into place. I liked the smell of the leather and the glue and the quiet, deliberate way Yisrael used his knife and needle. With a quick wipe of his cloth, he'd put on a lick of dye to blend everything in and then add a smear of polish to make everything look new. While he worked, he told me stories and gave me pieces of candy, of which he had as many as his old shoes.

I always wondered how he got the French leather and candy when the British blockade made everything impossible to get, but I never asked. Yisrael was a bachelor, young and healthy, and I also wondered why he wasn't in the army. This too I did not ask. In my house, we talked about him, and my mother said that Der Odessa Shuster had seen the war coming many years ago and, believing that the less the government knew about you the better, had never registered with any official agencies. Without any documents or papers, he didn't even exist.

His store was in a long, dark, narrow alley and was divided into a small front area—where he worked and kept his old, precious shoes and other discarded items, such as handbags and valises—and the rear, separated by a curtain. The back area was a much bigger room, the Odessa Shuster's living quarters. Every night, he put two doors in front of the curtain, creating a light-proof barrier, and he retreated into his living space to cook his food on his little kerosene stove and enjoy a quiet meal before going to bed. I asked him once if he was afraid of the police, and he smiled and said that the police didn't even know he was alive

Still, I feared for him. The police were everywhere. Special groups of military police made surprise searches of houses, looking for deserters and draft dodgers. The soldiers wore green bands on their arms, and we called them Die Gruen Bunde (the Green Bands). They were fierce Ottoman nationalists, spoke only Turkish, and couldn't be bought off with baksheesh. Without warning, they rushed into Batei Warsaw or the Mea Shearim, sealed off a section of houses, churches and syna-gogues, smashed down doors and dragged men away.

One day the Green Bands sealed off the alley where Yisrael lived. He knew what was happening. Quickly, he put his two doors up and barricaded himself in the rear, but the Green Band soldiers must have known he was there and they smashed down his doors and found him under his bed.

It was noon, and I was walking home from heder for lunch, when from a distance I heard people screaming and wailing. I walked faster, and there was my Der Odessa Shuster in chains, with two Green Band soldiers dragging him over the stones through the Mea Shearim. I pushed to the front of the crowd. He had put up a fierce fight; his clothes were torn, and his head was bleeding. He looked dead, but suddenly he twisted free, jumped to his feet, and kicked one of the soldiers. The soldier tripped him and kicked him hard on his chest.

I was crying and yelling. "Stop! Stop! He's our best shoemaker!"

The big soldier kicked Yisrael again and blood spurted out of his mouth.

I didn't have my slingshot, but I picked up a stone and took aim. I was about to let it fly, when suddenly a hand grasped my wrist. I was too startled to react. I was picked up from behind and carried backward. I didn't know who the man was, but he was strong, and he carried me quickly into a side street and put me down. He stood in back of me, and I couldn't see him.

"*Yingele*" (Young boy), he said, "the Green Bands have no mercy. Remember that, and don't go back. Now, quick, run home."

Without turning, I ran home through the alleys, taking a few extra turns so that I wouldn't meet up with the Green Band soldiers. When I got home, I told my mother what had happened. She pried the stone out of my hand and told me to lie down in her bed. Then she sat with me and listened again to my story.

"Chaim," she said, "I know who that man was."

"An angel?"

"I am certain he was not an angel or anyone we know. He was Elijah the prophet."

Der Odessa Shuster was never seen again, and we found another shoe repairer. But he was not as good as Yisrael and had no secret supply of French leather.

*

As the war went on, the Green Band soldiers became more and more ferocious, bursting into houses like wild animals, sparing no one. One day they tried to catch my uncle Yisrael Yitzhak.

Ever since my grandfather Netanel died, I visited my grandmother Nechama more often. She always had a piece of candy for me, though now it was cut in half and rewrapped. Her apartment had two small rooms; in her yard was a small kitchen that she shared with her neighbor, a woman named Yetta, whose tiny one-room apartment next to my grandmother's. Yetta was as old as my grandmother and had no children. Before the war, she ran a small grocery store out of her single room. Actually, it wasn't a store at all, as her merchandise barely took up two shelves of a little bookcase. When Yetta went shopping or to the Kotel to pray, she left her front door unlocked, and whoever wanted to buy something would come in, take what they needed, and leave the money on a small table near the door. Now, with the British blockade in full effect, Yetta had nothing to sell and sometimes, my grandmother told me, nothing to eat. When I left my grandmother's house, I knocked on Yetta's door, and if she wasn't home, I went inside and put my piece of half candy on the small table. I didn't want her to know I was giving her charity, but whenever Yetta saw me in the street, she touched my head with a trembling hand and gave me a blessing.

One afternoon, I was in my grandmother Nechama's house, when my favorite uncle, Yisrael Yitzhak, dropped by. I sat and listened to them talk, holding my half candy. Outside in the street, children were playing. My grandmother and uncle talked about the war, as always. Suddenly, both of them fell silent. There were loud noises in the street just beyond the courtyard. During the war, all noises were loud and frightening, but now people were rushing through the courtyard and into their gates, slamming doors and closing windows. My uncle looked up as heavy footsteps ran across our roof. People were trying to escape. Then, suddenly, there was silence everywhere; the courtyard was completely empty.

"*Geh zuch*, Chaim," my grandmother said. "*Schnell.*"

I ran into the yard, saw nothing, ran out the gate and down an alley, and stopped in my tracks. A large group of Green Band soldiers had surrounded Batei Warsaw. One of them saw me and shouted, but I ran back another way and burst into the house.

"They're coming!"

My uncle turned pale. His papers said he was a rabbi and exempt from military service, but his documents had been bought, and the Green Band soldiers wouldn't care if the Kaiser himself stamped his papers in gold. They would drag him away and keep him in jail until he either proved himself innocent, which cost a small fortune, or was sent away to the army, never to be seen again.

Outside, we heard the Green Band soldiers coming.

My uncle was sweating, his mouth tight. My grandmother stood and almost fell over with faintness but grabbed the chair and managed to sit. Her older son was already in hiding, sick of body and broken in spirit, and now her other child was about to be beaten and dragged away. My uncle stood and looked around with wild eyes. I wanted to cry, but I was too frightened.

Suddenly, old Yetta rushed in.

"*Kommen Sie. Kommen Sie*," she beckoned. "*Schnell! Schnell!*" (Quick! Quick!).

The Green Band soldiers were just outside our courtyard, and one of them was shouting in clumsy Yiddish to open the gates.

"*Ofnen Sie das Tur!*" (Open the door!).

Every second counted.

Yetta rushed out, and my uncle followed and, bending low, took three big steps across the yard and dived through Yetta's door. In a flash, she slammed it shut and rushed back into my grandmother's house.

We were shaking. Our door was flung open. Three soldiers stomped in. In broken Yiddish, they ordered my grandmother, Yetta, and me to stand and face the wall. "Don't move," one told us. "Say nothing." My grandmother had two small rooms and just a few pieces of furniture, but they turned over the bed, threw the table and chairs against the wall, opened the two closets, and tossed out everything. They ordered us outside and looked in the kitchen, even into the brick oven, which was too small for anyone but a small child.

"Who lives here?" A tall Green Band was staring at Yetta's door.

Yetta had put her small lock on the door latch.

"Who lives here?"

My grandmother and Yetta shrugged. The soldier looked at me. I didn't move.

"Who lives here?"

My grandmother said, "An old lady is a tenant, but she left this morning, and we don't know where she is."

Two soldiers peered into the single window, first high and then low, and saw only a thin mattress on a narrow bed, a small table with two chairs, and her bookcase with a small half-rotten onion.

Impatient, an officer in the courtyard shouted a command, and the soldiers left without even trying to break the small lock.

We stayed inside for an hour while the Green Bands searched all the houses in our courtyard. To the cries and shrieks of their families, two men were dragged away through the gates. At last, after I followed the Green Band soldiers to be certain they had gone, Yetta unlocked her door. My uncle was lying flat on the floor under the window, pressed tightly against the wall. He stood, dusted off his clothing, and straightened his skullcap.

"God gives us a blessing," he said. "Evil people are often dumb."

"Baruch HaShem," replied my grandmother.

My uncle thanked Yetta for her quick thinking.

"Whom did they take?" he asked.

My grandmother told him, and my uncle shook his head and sighed. He waited until dark and then left, I walking ahead as his scout.

A week later, my friend Aaron, who lived in one of the new, beautiful houses on the hill where the mill had burned, came running into our house.

"Chaim! Chaim! Come on!"

I stood in the open door. Aaron was excited.

"Come quick—to the Jaffa Gate!"

"What's there?"

"Come on. You won't be sorry."

"Sure," I said, "let's go."

We hurried down Mea Shearim Road toward the Old City. I was barefoot, and Aaron wore shoes, but I easily kept pace with him. The bottoms of my feet were as hard as leather, and I could run over stones without feeling a thing. Aaron's family was rich, and even during the war, for the first two years anyway, they had plenty of food and nice clothing, but when the blockade really tightened, they suffered as everyone else did. We hurried along, passing soldiers and police patrols without a thought—nine-year-old boys could go anywhere.

I could see a big crowd around the Jaffa Gate. A horrible noise filled the air.

"Come on," said Aaron, and we walked faster.

There were no men in the crowd, only women and children. Wailing and screaming filled the air. The Arab women were hitting their chests and foreheads with their fists. A Yemenite Jewish woman was on her back on the stones, shrieking when she found the breath and then rolling back and forth, gasping for air till she could shriek again.

"Now you'll see." Aaron pushed through the throng, and I followed, and then stopped.

Twelve men were hanging in front of the Jaffa Gate.

"The Green Band found them," said Aaron.

Four of them were Yemenite Jews.

The women were shrieking, beating their breasts and rolling in the gutter while the children cried and wailed.

I couldn't look away from the Yemenite Jews. They hung by thin ropes, their necks bent and beards resting on their chests. The long fringes of their tallit katans were black with blood that dripped onto the earth under their feet as their frail bodies swayed gently in the wind.

I couldn't breath, and I turned away and pushed through the crowd and went home, crying all the way. My sisters and mother weren't home, and I lay down on the floor of the big room and rolled myself in my blanket. Soon my mother came in, my sisters with her, and when she saw me on the floor, she knew where I had been, and she tried to comfort me, but I couldn't stop crying.

The bodies were taken down the next day, and the Turks said it would happen again if people refused to serve in their army. For a long time, I had dreams of the men hanging by the ropes and the black blood dripping from the strings of their garments.

"This is what happens," my mother told me, "when evil men rule. Be grateful that it didn't happen to your uncle."

Yetta had saved him from the cruel Green Bands. Had she not been as quick as she was, Uncle Yisrael Yitzhak would have been hanging at the Jaffa Gate like the Yemenites.

My mother told me, "Now, go out and play with your cousin, and don't worry. It won't happen to us." She added under her breath, "God willing."

*

During the course of World War I, we were afflicted with almost every one of the ten plagues that had been visited upon the ancient Egyptians, as well as a few they hadn't experienced. Among the ultra-Orthodox, this was a depressing thought, for to the religious mind that sees the finger of God in all things, such unrelenting, cumulative adversity implies a high degree of heavenly disfavor. Others, including my grandfather, pointed out that it was not just the Jews who suffered; the hunger, cold, and discomfort fell on everyone alike—Jew, Christian, and Muslim; innocent and guilty; young and old.

This provided some comfort on the theological side but only minor relief on the temporal.

Palestine was stricken with the plague of blood, shed at the hands of the Turkish regime. There was the plague of darkness because we had no fuel for our lanterns, or candles to read by. Without soap and with little spare water, we suffered from the plague of lice. There were other afflictions not mentioned in the Torah—plagues of cold and endless hunger, of insult and fear, of diseases born of dirt and malnutrition, and of deep despair.

A most bitter plague was the plague of locusts.

They came on a bright, sunny summer day. I was going home from school on the Mea Shearim Road when suddenly a ferocious wind was roaring around me, and in a split moment the air was filled with giant flying insects. I batted at them with hands and fists, ducked and spun around, and then ran, flapping my arms, hoping to get out of the swarm, but they were everywhere, millions of them, making a horrible whirring noise that did not stop. I couldn't see where I was going, and I cried out in fear and flailed about. The noise was loud and whirring and the insects attacked my hands, face, and feet, biting and biting.

The locusts came in a heavy cloud that blocked the sun and destroyed everything that was alive and green. In an hour, every tree was naked and bare, every bush devoured, every flower, bud, and young fruit was gone in a minute. By nightfall, the hills and valleys around Jerusalem were a naked, dry desert, and a strange, terrifying winter descended on us in the middle of a hot summer.

The next day, a thick carpet of crawling, chattering insects covered Jerusalem. They were dark green, almost black, and their slick, shiny bodies were on the trees and the stones, the rooftops and the alleys. The first day they arrived, I had to walk home as they descended from the sky, and it was impossible not to step on them. In my bare feet, I felt as if I were walking on soft clay that, strangely, made a crackling sound like nuts being crushed.

The swarm stayed for three days and ate everything imaginable. We barricaded ourselves inside our homes, sealing the doors and windows with towels and blankets. When my parents went out to look for food or when I went to the public toilet, we covered our entire bodies with layers of clothing, buttoning tightly, and when that didn't keep the locusts out, we wrapped ourselves in sheets and hobbled about like lame ghosts. The locusts attacked hair and beards, and we had to wrap our heads and faces. Birds tried to escape but couldn't, and the locusts ate them alive. The horses, donkeys, and camels caught in the open were driven crazy by the voracious insects that bit at every exposed surface of their unprotected bodies, including eyes, ears, and nostrils. The poor creatures, defenseless, were bitten to death or died from shock.

The locusts were of different colors and varieties, small and large, and had different smells. The Sephardic Jews, who, in their great hunger, fried and ate them, considered a few types kosher.

Desperate and powerless, we looked to the heavens for deliverance, hoping a divine beneficence would cause the locusts to disappear. That first day, my father insisted upon going to evening prayer services but came back after making it only halfway. During the swarm, my mother stood guard at the front door with her broom, and Moshe and I stood at the rear windows with sticks, killing any invaders.

On the morning of the fourth day, the locusts departed as suddenly as they'd come, a thick black cloud vanishing into the sky with a mighty whirr and chatter. In the synagogue that evening, we offered joyous and relieved prayers of thanks for our deliverance. That night, we opened our doors and windows to let the cool night wind blow through our stifling house.

However, the aftermath of the plague was as bad as the plague itself. Coming in search of food, the locusts, like a well-trained and disciplined force, had eaten everything, and then flown on, leaving behind an invisible occupation force just as aggressive as their conquering army.

Over the next two hot days, their eggs hatched, and within a day, millions of tiny green worms invaded Jerusalem. They covered the earth, stones, and buildings with a thick layer of living green paint. The streets and alleys were green rivers, and the mighty stones of the Kotel were a quivering wall of green. We resealed our doors and windows and locked ourselves in. The stifling heat drove us crazy. The water supply, polluted, was declared unsanitary, and all of Jerusalem was desperate with thirst.

The authorities told us that though the worms would become insects and soon fly away, they would leave their own eggs, and the cycle would repeat.

We were terrified. The Turkish soldiers were in hiding, and even the Germans were desperate. People began to panic. My mother prayed night and day; men stood at the Kotel and implored the heavens. There was no escape from the insects and their eggs. Our food supplies were full of vermin and eggs; our houses were besieged. Starvation, disease, and death had descended over the land. It was the end of days, and there was no hope.

In a final attempt to stave off disaster, the Turkish military appealed to the public. Their own soldiers were dying, and civil authority was deteriorating. At this last desperate call to arms, everyone joined forces against our common enemy.

Early the next morning, at dawn, all the inhabitants of Jerusalem poured forth into the streets. Young and old, religious Jews and devout Muslims, police and civilians--all formed work brigades to attack and destroy the insects with every means at our disposal. My grandfather organized a special strike force of Hasidim from the Mea Shearim, Batei Warsaw, and Batei Hungary. Moshe and I, wrapped head to toe in sheets, our bare feet wrapped in rags and tied with cord, joined them. It was all out war. We took up brooms and shovels, swept the eggs and caterpillars into giant heaps, doused them with kerosene provided by the Turkish army, and set them afire. By nightfall, all of Jerusalem was enveloped in a heavy, malodorous cloud of burning insects and their eggs. Yet the next morning, the mountain winds had cleansed the air, and the sun shone brightly.

We had conquered.

"Baruch HaShem," my mother said.

The locust plague, together with the British sea blockade, which was now entering its third year and was becoming more and more effective with each passing month, brought Jerusalem to the edge of utter disaster. The adults were depressed and frightened and walked about with anxious eyes and sagging shoulders. My father tried to find comfort in his beloved books, but there was no light to read at night, and he barely had strength in his body to sit upright. I watched him as he sat at the table for hours with his head in his hands and stared at the pages. My mother had fabrics to sell or barter, but no one had money or anything to trade.

Adding to our misery, yet another plague struck. A severe typhus epidemic broke out. Spread by lice and driven by a lack of elementary sanitation, the infection caused irritating rashes and deadly fatigue.

Without antibiotics or any organized medical response, people lay in the streets, shaking with fever, unable to move a muscle. Every morning in Batei Warsaw, the black wagons were at our gates to carry away the corpses of those who had died during the night. Entire families were wiped out, and the body cleaners and cemetery workers were unable to keep pace with the avalanche of dead.

My aunt Yehudith died. Her husband, Uncle Chaim, was still hiding from the Turks, and now their four sons were alone in the world. Our grandmother Nechama took in two of them, but when she became infected with typhus, my mother took the two boys into our house and, feeding them only boiled water and a thin starch soup, kept them alive. In addition to the eight of us in my family, we now had eight more mouths to feed: my mother's mother, my other grandparents, my uncle in hiding, and his four sons. There wasn't enough food. One day my mother took some of the best silks from her hoard, hid them under her dress, and went to the Old City. She returned an hour later with three loaves of fresh bread and six eggs, on which we feasted for two days.

Every day she left home in the late morning to visit her sick mother and then went to the homes of others infected with typhus. We told her not to go, but she believed herself invulnerable.

"Heaven has to spare someone, Chaim-le," she told me, "so that someone can take care of the sick people."

But there were fewer and fewer of the living able to. At the outbreak of the war in August 1914, the Jewish population in Jerusalem numbered fifty thousand; two and a half years later, there were only half that, all starving, frightened souls.

After years of inadequate housing, many apartments in the Warsaw Houses were now vacant. The streets of Jerusalem were deserted; the synagogues empty. Death, disease, and the violence of war were taking their toll. Only old men and young boys were seen on the streets. Young and middle-aged men were either in the army, lost forever, or hiding in dark, cold places. Women took on many tasks once reserved for men, conducting most public activities.

In all of Jerusalem, there was neither song and dance nor voice lifted in happy prayer.

Many days, I didn't go to school. The Talmud Torah in the Mea Shearim still held classes, but there were only a handful of rebbes left, and the few students who did show up slept in their chairs, too depressed and hungry to pay attention. My father tried to tutor me at night, but we had no kerosene or candles. Besides, he was weak, his voice too low for me to hear. He smoked cigarettes—all his life, I must say—and now he rolled his own in squares of old newspapers using old, stale tobacco. The smell was terrible. We didn't like it, and he'd go outside and stood in the dark to smoke his once-a-day cigarette.

I always stood with him.

"Abba," I asked him once, "why are you still smoking?"

He sighed and patted my head. "It takes away my hunger."

Contradictions abounded; how strange that in this time of depravation and destruction, there were still people smiling, and walking about with full stomachs and clean clothes.

We were not those smiling people. My grandfather Fishel wasn't sick, just tired and depressed. He was losing weight, and for days at a time he didn't go to the stationery store but stayed inside his bare, simple home, dozing on and off.

I wanted him to put on his fine black caftan and pick up his cane with the silver fish and jeweled eyes, but he told me that he was too tired. He always had been ready to help others, and now he was a helpless man himself.

My grandfather had a cousin, a recent arrival from Germany. We called him Herr Kahn. *Herr* is German for "gentleman" or "sir." Herr Kahn's parents had left Plotsk when my grandparents had, but they had gone west to Germany. After the Kaiser's visit in 1898, when Germany formed an alliance with the Ottomans, German Jews began migrating to Jerusalem; it was then that Herr Kahn and his wife, Frau Kahn, showed up.

The Kahns were not Orthodox, and our families' paths did not cross often, but Herr Kahn had a civilian position in the German office that liaised with the Turkish military authority, and my grandfather and Herr Kahn met now and then. Soon, Frau Kahn, always interested in a fine piece of silk or velvet, became one of my mother's best customers.

During the war, my mother never took money; she always bartered, sometimes for favors, but most often food.

Seeing my grandfather so weak and depressed, my mother went to her hidden store of fabrics and selected a bolt of special silk that she had been saving for emergencies. I watched from the window as she left the house at a brisk pace. I thought she was going to Frau Kahn, but she took off in the opposite direction toward the Old City. Two hours later, she came back with a long, heavy package of brown paper. I locked the door, and she unwrapped it on the floor.

"Nu, Chaim?"

It was an Arabian carpet of soft wool, rich and colorful.

"It's beautiful," I said.

Satisfied with my response, she rolled it back into the paper and tied it tightly.

The next morning she left with the carpet. I helped her carry it partway and then watched her climb the hill to Zichron Moshe, the new housing development where the Kahns lived.

Frau Kahn herself opened the door, glanced at the package, and shook her head.

"I'm sorry, Giveret Linder. But I'm not in the market for anything today."

"I would like you just to look." My mother gently pushed past Frau Kahn and into the living room. "Maybe one of your friends would like something beautiful."

Frau Kahn shook her head. "My son isn't feeling well, Giverit Linder, and I just can't think about anything right now."

My mother had already rolled the rug out on the floor.

"Ah!" Frau Kahn stared down at it. "Zehr shoen!" *Very beautiful.*

"I knew you would appreciate it, Frau Kahn. It's very special."

"It is indeed."

While Frau Kahn admired the carpet, my mother pondered. She looked at the table near the window. On it was a platter of pastries, teacups and bowls of milk and sugar.

"How much is the rug?"

"I want no money for it, Frau Kahn."

"But I must give you something!"

"Frau Kahn, my father-in-law is not feeling well. He's unable to leave the house, even to go to the synagogue. It's been months since he's had even a taste of sugar. I give you this carpet as an act of kindness, in God's name, so that my father-in-law may get stronger."

Frau Kahn's eyes filled.

"Of course," she said. She left the room and returned with a parcel wrapped tightly in white paper and shaped like a pyramid. In silence, Frau Kahn gave it to my mother and, with it, an envelope. My mother covered the package with her apron, left the house. From the bottom of the hill, I saw her hurrying down the hill, her apron against her chest, the envelope in her hand.

I ran to meet her. "Imma, what do you have?"

"Shhh." I fell in step beside her. She was pleased. "You'll see when we get home."

As soon as we got home, my mother opened her apron. I looked at the parcel.

With a single glance, by its color and shape, I knew. Egyptian sugar.

"It's at least two kilos," my mother said.

This was a treasure beyond value.

"Chaim, close the door and windows."

In times like these, even neighbors couldn't be trusted. My mother unwrapped the white paper, and we both tore off the dark, blue wax paper. In the dim light, the pyramid had a silver glint, sparkling with hundreds of tiny stars.

"Chaim, bring a clean towel." I got one from the shelf and spread it on our floor.

"Now, Chaim, use your muscles." She handed me the heavy brass pestle.

I knelt on the cold stone, held the pestle with both hands, and whacked the pyramid into big chunks, kept hitting until they broke into chips.

"This one." She pointed out a chunk that needed another smash. "And this."

I whacked away until she was satisfied. I helped her pack the bigger chunks into a small box for my Grandfather Fishel. We kept a small amount of the sweet treasure for my father's tea.

"And this is for you, Chaim."

"All of it?" I took the towel from her hand.

"Don't tell your sisters or brothers."

I was overjoyed. My mother knew I had a sweet tooth. I picked off just a few of the bigger shards of glittering sweetness, then folded the towel and hid it under my holiday clothing in the back room. I went to it every day for a week, savoring the crumbs one by sweet one.

*

During the war, there were so many dangers in Jerusalem—both those we knew of and those we did not—that we walked about with a sense of dread. Indeed, about a week after the sugar surprise, my mother and I were outside in our front yard, when she suddenly leaped up.

"Chaim, look there!"

I looked to the top of the hill where my mother was pointing, and my heart stopped.

A Green Band officer had my father by the arm. We held our breath as the soldier raised his club high over his head and pulled my father closer. We could see my father reaching with his free hand into his jacket.

"Show him the passport," my mother whispered to herself.

That was exactly what my father did. We saw the little dark book in his hand and watched the officer lower his club and take the passport. We held our breath while the soldier opened it, turned a page. Then he gave it back, motioning with his club that my father could go. Without any haste, my father walked slowly down the hill toward us. He came into the yard very pale, but he had his little smile.

"A close call," he said. "He threatened me with arrest or at least a couple of blows."

My father knew enough Arabic to explain to the soldier that it would be to his benefit to see his passport first.

"He couldn't read, but he understood the language of money."

As the war dragged on, passports and other documents, all easily forged, lost their value, and the ever-reliable system of baksheesh was once again in force. Even the incorruptible Green Bands were not immune to picking up a little extra on the side. The war would end, and one had to make money while the bullets were flying. My father used a hairpin to attach a Napoleon to his Austria-Hungarian passport, and the glint of gold had blinded the officer to my father's transgression, whatever it was. Pocketing the Napoleon, he had sent my father on his way with only an insult. My father thought it was profitable exchange.

Through the war years, my mother's stock of fabrics held out, and she was able to replenish her inventory with discreet visits to Simontov's warehouse. She knew the wholesalers in Jerusalem who stocked dry goods—beans, flour, or sometimes powdered milk—and she had a good tongue for bargaining. The Arab landowners still came to our house for cloth for their large families and wives, and they always had farm produce to offer. She had a good relationship also with Mr. Berman, the baker, and visited the bakery every two weeks with a few pieces of choice fabric. She'd return with two of his large, heavy round loaves hidden in a big, soft pillow, which she carried in her apron. It was too risky, and insulting to others' hunger, she said, to carry such loaves through the streets when many people were starving. Once behind our locked door, she cut the bread into small portions for our family of eight, my three grandparents, and the four children of her brother, who was in hiding and for whom she set aside a special portion.

A loaf fed the sixteen of us for two days. In the morning, she handed me my portion, and a stern warning: "Chaim, remember, this is your share for the entire day. You may eat it all at once, or you may eat it in crumbs all day long, or you may feed the birds with it, but don't ask for more until tomorrow morning."

As the war dragged on, my mother was out most of the day, competing with all the women in Jerusalem for food. My three sisters—Chaya Sara, Yehoved, and Hinda—kept the house spotless, went to the cisterns for our ever-diminishing rations of water, and prepared whatever my mother brought home. Her secret supply of fabrics, though dwindling, kept us from outright starvation. I knew, however, listening to men the talking in the synagogue, that if the war continued much longer, not even a bolt of fancy, expensive silk would save us.

I was not eleven years old, and here I was, living from one day to the next, from one piece of dry, stale bread to another.

Because everyone thought the war would be over quickly, conservation efforts did not begin until it was too late, and now we had not a drop of kerosene or a single candle. At night, we poured a tablespoon of olive oil from our precious supply into a small cup, twisted a piece of cotton from an old, torn shirt into a wick, attached it to a button, and used the light from its sputtering flame. A box of matches was worth its weight in gold. Quickly, the oil became a luxury we could afford only on Friday night, when our mother lit the lonely cup for the Sabbath blessing. All other nights we sat in darkness.

We had no milk. Mohamed, with his two shepherds with their flutes, his flock of goats and sheep, and his veiled wives, no longer came to Batei Warsaw. Lying on my blanket on the stone floor, I pretended that my saliva was warm, frothy milk, and I fell asleep counting the chimes of our wall clock.

Gone also were Ba'kir and his camels loaded with charcoal. Scraps of wood were the only fuel we had, but the rocky, arid hills around Jerusalem were soon stripped of anything that could burn. People dismantled their houses, using closet doors and pieces of furniture to cook or heat water for bathing. Hot water was a true luxury, and with the public baths no longer functioning, we were dirty and full of smells. Our parents, even my mother, were as helpless as children, and my brother and my sisters and I became much older than we should have.

Sephardic Jews ate the few grasshoppers they caught in the barren fields around Jerusalem. I made a slingshot and killed birds for food, but there weren't many birds left. I climbed roofs in search of nests and eggs but never found any.

I missed my grandfather Netanel because I wanted to mark his words about how good it was going to be.

Not only were food and goods unavailable, but so was information. Jerusalem was in a corner of the world without a single newspaper in any language, and only bits and pieces about the war reached us. There was no shortage of rumors, however, and everyone had an opinion on the progress, duration, and eventual outcome of the conflict. Optimists insisted that a decisive victory for one side or another was just around the corner; pessimists predicted a long and difficult war.

Most of the discussions took place in the synagogue before, during, and after evening prayers. We were a distorted congregation, demographically speaking. Without the young and middle-aged men, congregants were the very young, such as my brother Moshe and me; the old and the weak; and a few others, such as my father, who had special passports.

In the synagogue, we sat at a long table in the dark and cold and shivered as we tried to make sense of things. We didn't sit still, because we were so infested with lice that we were in constant motion, scratching and picking at the little bugs, which feasted on the blood from our scrawny bodies. There was no way to cleanse ourselves; on the rare occasions the Friday afternoon mikvah was open, the water was so covered with a layer of dead lice that many refused to bathe, including me.

Everyone told what he thought he knew. One or two men had seen a newspaper, albeit briefly, from the outside world, while others had spoken with someone who had read it. Or a man had overheard a conversation between a German and a Turk or between two Germans, or had heard what an Arab on horse had said to a German on foot.

Listening, I learned that the war was being fought mainly in Western and Eastern Europe. The antagonistic parties, Great Britain and her allies, and Germany and hers, were approximately equal in strength. Both sides claimed advances and victories, but there weren't any clear prospects for either party.

"Unless," said a middle-aged man with a bad limp who, because of his knowledgeable manner and his limp, had become our military strategist at the synagogue, "the United States enters the war. Then Britain will win."

This was hotly debated; some said the United States would not enter the war, and others said the United States would ally with Germany. One faction held that unless US involvement happened soon, it wouldn't make any difference for us.

Later, reading newspaper accounts and a few secular books, I learned that World War I was a war of trenches and attrition, of machine guns and chemicals. The airplane had not yet been developed, and there weren't any modern tanks, so the foot soldiers did the fighting and killing in the fields, and the civilian population died of hunger and epidemics.

Soon even the pessimists in the Ohel Schmuel synagogue in Batei Warsaw had to admit that Britain and her allies were slowly gaining the upper hand, and that, indeed, a conclusion to hostilities might be approaching.

The military strategist with the bad limp informed us that his sources had revealed that England was about to begin a major offensive in Palestine against the Ottomans. The truth of this, the optimists pointed out with a touch of unintended irony, could be seen in the more brutal and restrictive rule of the Turks in Jerusalem. The pessimists, with the sarcasm that gives pessimism its biting edge, agreed that the Turks had indeed become more brutal.

Everyone agreed that if the war continued much longer, the Turks were going to drive themselves and us crazy.

Things were already crazy enough. Every day the military authorities issued new restrictions and threatened more severe punishments. One day it was announced that Jews were not allowed to walk on the right side of any street. No reason was given, though both the pessimists and optimists traded much trenchant humor over the proclamation. Then it was decreed that all healthy animals must be registered, upon penalty of confiscation. Naturally, everyone assumed the reason for registration was eventual confiscation of all animals by the military either for transport or food, so of course, no one was foolish enough to register a single animal, not even a chicken. A special force of Turkish police was deployed to find the animals, and overnight all creatures vanished. Whatever animals were found were quickly redeemed by appropriate applications of baksheesh.

Then the Ottomans made a special appeal to the "traditionally charitable Jewish people" for donations of pillows, blankets, and other bedding to be brought to specified locations in Jerusalem on a certain date, in return for which "a certified receipt" would be given to the "noble donor." The blankets and pillows, the appeal said, would be used "for the warmth and comfort of the heroic Islamic defenders of Jerusalem against the Christian marauders."

This appeal was greeted with much hilarity and sarcasm in the synagogue and, needless to say, did not produce the outpouring of household linens the Turks had expected.

The day after the appeal expired, however, the soldiers went on a rampage. Without warning, Green Band brigades and military police cordoned off Jewish neighborhoods. They beat people and ransacked homes. They took the few cooking utensils my mother had been unable to hide, as well as our blankets and pillows. They stripped our house to the bare walls and left us with two old, half-torn straw mattresses. Knowing something bad was going to happen, our mother had put all her fabrics on the roof, where none of the Turkish soldiers thought to look. After all, who sleeps on the roof? We used some of my mother's fabrics to make new blankets and sheets, but as for our furniture and pillows, we simply did without.

CHAPTER 26

Just as our military strategist had predicted, the British assault against the Turks commenced in March 1917, and quickly stalled in the Sinai Desert.

"The British have failed twice," the strategist informed us. "The Germans have built a fortified line in Gaza, and the British can't break it without heavy artillery."

"America will help," said the optimists, their eyes bright.

"Ach," said the pessimists, pulling their mouths down. "America is not prepared."

"The British will bring in General Allenby," the strategist predicted.

Indeed, General Edmund Allenby was given command of the Allied forces in Egypt. A devout Christian, Allenby was determined to bring the sacred sites of Christianity under the rule of the British Empire. Hoping to win their freedom from the oppressive Ottomans, many of the Arab-Muslim countries became enthusiastic, if temporary, allies of Great Britain.

Despite strict Turkish censorship and a total news blackout in Palestine, our own military strategist in the Ohel Shmuel synagogue in Batei Warsaw knew every detail of the campaign. Every day, before and after evening services, the Hasidim sat in their skullcaps and fringed garments, scratching at the lice while hugging themselves against the cold, and discussed and debated the moves of Allenby and the counter-moves of the Turkish army and their German advisers.

We had occasional visits from two other Hasidim from another syn-agogue, real specialists. Berrel Heller, who held an Austria-Hungarian passport, was the German military expert, and Fishel Munkatcher, without any credentials other than a knowing and calm manner, was our British military specialist.

Berrel Heller had no confidence in the Turks, but his admiration for the Prussians knew no bounds.

"Nobody can defeat the Kaiser," he insisted. "Not even the Americans."

Fishel Munkatcher, smoking a long pipe filled with tobacco that smelled like donkey manure, countered with a shake of his head and a knowing smile. He spoke softly and wisely, a true diplomat. "Wait and see."

"No, no," insisted Heller. "The Americans are children. They think they're going to a party."

We wrinkled our noses as Munkatcher puffed on his pipe. "Time will tell."

"They'll never break through at Gaza. The Germans have too much artillery."

"Wait. We shall see."

Our own military strategist with the limp said, "Allenby has been ordered to capture Jerusalem by December. He'll use his horse cavalry and a special force of camel riders."

Heller shook his head, convinced his Germans were invincible. "He might break through, but he won't be able to advance."

"Allenby won't bother with Gaza," countered our strategist, of whom we in the Ohel Shmuel Synagogue were proud. "He's going to go around the Germans and attack through Beersheba, and then he'll come up the Judean hills and take Jerusalem from the south."

Neither the optimists nor the pessimists had any comment, and both Heller and Munkatcher fell silent before the strategist's greater knowledge.

I listened to the old men talk, not knowing what was going to happen.

*

British reconnaissance airplanes were flying low over Jerusalem every day. They were small single-engine planes with double wings, and they came from the west; circled the Old City in a big, slow turn; and then flew away to the south. Finally, the Germans installed antiaircraft guns in the hills around the Old City. One battery was not far from our house, and they caught the British pilots by surprise. The noise was terrific, sharp and loud, with a deep, ugly rumble afterward: *CRACK-kaboom. CRACK-kaboom.* They shot down one of the British airplanes, and I watched it glide to the earth, a trail of gray smoke coming from its engine. I heard it crash with a little explosion. I ran barefoot with the other boys, passing the women and the old men hobbling on their canes as fast as they could. I joined the crowd looking at the dead pilot and his shattered plane. He wore a leather helmet, and his face, blackened and twisted, looked up at the sky. The plane was still smoking, and there was a smell of kerosene and burning oil. It was the first time I had seen an airplane on the ground and the first time I had seen a British officer. There was something different about his death that made it less horrible. The plane and the pilot had come from far away and had fallen from the sky. It was impersonal, not like seeing the Odessa Shuster beaten or the poor Yemenite Jews hanging from ropes at the Jaffa Gate. As we stood around looking and talking, a squad of German soldiers arrived and pushed us away. They roped off the crash site and then stood guard so that nothing was stolen from the pilot or his plane.

A week later, events seemed to be moving forward. I was a true believer in the military strategist in Batei Warsaw and was thrilled to learn that even as we prayed, General Allenby's pilots were flying over the Turkish army in the desert and dropping chocolate, candy, and cigarettes, humanitarian gifts from the people of Great Britain. It was the end of October 1917. With a knowing smile, the strategist told us that the goodies contained opium, and later that night, around midnight, when the British army opened their offensive, the entire Turkish army would be sound asleep.

That night, for the first time in years, all of Batei Warsaw was laughing.

The next day, we knew something exciting had happened. The Turks and their German advisers were racing about Jerusalem, mobilizing their forces.

That evening, our strategist informed us unequivocally that Allenby had broken through at Gaza.

"Now he has the water he needs. He'll regroup, and be in Jerusalem in a month."

"You see now," said Munkatcher, smoking his pipe and smiling, his faith in Britain's military prowess confirmed. "You see."

Heller pursed his lips and frowned. His dear, invincible Germans were running around the streets of Jerusalem like frightened children.

The pessimists could not be certain that the British offensive was good for the Jews.

"The Turks will be angry and take it out on us," they argued.

"No, no, they'll be too busy saving themselves," the optimists countered.

This time, the optimists were correct. Burdened with their own military problems, the Turks and Germans left the civilian population alone.

Everyone—the optimists, the pessimists, British and German advocates, and the military strategist—agreed that the end was in sight.

Overnight, Jerusalem became a silent, wary city. Sensing correctly that it was only a matter of weeks until the battered Turkish army would be driven from Jerusalem, every man and women, young and old, took extraordinary precautions to avoid even the most minor injury. It would be terrible to have lived through the entire war only to be killed just when it ended. The most effective way of avoiding mishap was to stay home. Not a soul stirred. When we had to go out, we walked close to the walls and spoke in whispers. At the sight of the Turkish police or a German soldier, my friends and I ducked into a door or ran down an alley. My mother and father stayed close to the house, going out only for essentials, such as water or prayers.

The German military advisers were the first to leave, retreating north to escape the British advance. Turkish soldiers, ordered to stem Allenby's advance, clogged the roads with ammunition wagons and light artillery pulled by tired mules.

Exercising realistic precautions, all shops in Jerusalem's Old City, and those in the market of the Mea Shearim, closed their doors against last minute looting by the retreating Turks. Only Mr. Berman's Odessa Bakery continued operating, turning out small amounts of low-quality bread, which my mother brought to us wrapped in her apron and which my brothers and sisters and I devoured.

It was the first week of December, and long winter nights gripped Jerusalem. A deep, silent anticipation reigned even as fear descended over the ancient stones. We were confined to our dark, cold homes and didn't dare walk even the short distance to visit our grandparents.

In the synagogue, we rushed through the prayers to get to the main business of military analysis. All the experts agreed: General Allenby would conquer Jerusalem in a few days.

"Mark my words," I heard my dead grandfather Netanel say, "it's going to be good."

There were still a few bitter pills to swallow, though we knew they were part of the cure.

As they advanced toward Jerusalem, the British army brought up their artillery and began shelling the Turkish positions. Though they avoided any direct bombardment of Jerusalem, sometimes bombs fell on the Old City. A number of civilians were injured; a few were killed.

The weather continued cold and cloudy. That Friday night was very cold. We had a small quantity of olive oil left, barely enough for my mother to say the Sabbath blessings. My father, Moshe, and I didn't go to synagogue to welcome the Sabbath queen; instead, we sat in darkness around an empty table as my mother pulled apart a loaf of stale challah and gave us our portions. We chewed the cold, wet bread slowly and then, chilled to the bone and too depressed to stay awake, went to our beds on the freezing stone floor and tried to sleep.

In the morning, my father, Moshe, and I went to the synagogue for Sabbath services. We walked in silence. I wasn't allowed to go barefoot to the synagogue, but I had no socks, and my shoes, too small and full of holes, rubbed against my skin and gave me blisters.

We began our service with the opening prayer, but suddenly, the earth and sky were torn apart with deafening explosions. We didn't need the military strategist to tell us this was the final assault. The artillery was miles away, and their shells were landing in the hills, but it seemed the bombs were falling on the roof of the synagogue.

We walked home in a thin, cold rain. The house was dark and damp and chilly. For supper we shared the two last slices of wet, cold bread. Two of my cousins came to spend Saturday night with us. Hungry and cold, none of us could sleep, and we sat around the table in the dark. One of my cousins was confident that everything was going to be just fine.

"*Der verstunkene* Turks," (The stinking Turks), he said.

Utterly exhausted from the days and nights of cold and hunger and from the years of having no light, heat, or soap and water and suddenly possessed of a sense that nothing mattered anymore, we started joking about the lousy Turks, who were now running away like frightened mice, and the Germans, who were running with them.

Even my father laughed.

Just then, Berrel Heller, the German patriot with the Austria-Hungarian passport, came in with his wife, Sarah. He sat at the table, while his wife joined the women in the side room.

Berrel Heller was well fed. He wore a new jacket and shirt. He had color in his face, and he was picking his teeth with a toothpick, apparently just having dined on some meat. In the dim light of our sad olive cup, his expensive leather boots shone like new.

Staring at his well-fed face, my brother Moshe, usually reserved, spoke with his smooth, golden voice. "I tell all of you. Tonight we are still Turks. But soon, after four hundred years of imprisonment, no more lousy, stinking Turks. Tomorrow morning, we will be Englanders!"

"God willing," said my father.

Berrel Heller shook his head. "Nonsense. The Germans and Turks are making a strategic retreat to fool the English. They'll take up positions on Mount Scopus, regroup, and mount a powerful counteroffensive in the morning."

"How can they fight," asked one of my cousins, "when they are running so fast they have to shit in their pants?"

"I have this on reliable sources." Berrel Heller puffed himself up.

All the women were standing in the doorway, listening.

"The Germans," Berrel Heller continued, "have just developed a new powerful cannon. It uses shells that are highly explosive and will flatten and destroy everything." He pushed aside the cup of olive oil with its tiny flame, moved the two seforim (prayer books) to the side, and raised his hand. "Just like this!" He slammed his hand flat and hard on the table. The flame trembled and the table shook. "Bam! Everything in its path will be as flat as this table!"

No one spoke. Just then, a loud explosion burst over the house.

My father, lost in his own thoughts, thought the noise was thunder and instinctively murmured the appropriate prayer. Instinctively, we all said, "Amen." Then there was a second explosion, followed by a third. It was the British bombardment, even closer. My father frowned. One must not invoke the name of God in vain.

"Is there an appropriate blessing to welcome the British cannons?" my brother asked.

We all laughed, except Berrel Heller.

As the ferocious bombardment continued, my cousin said to Berrel Heller, "I suppose the Germans will start using their new weapon very soon."

Without a word, Berrel stood and signaled to his wife, who walked out behind him.

"Let them go with their Germans," said my cousin.

The last of the olive oil was gone, and we sat in deep darkness. The bombardment continued. No one tried to sleep. We feared that in the last hours of their crumbling empire, the retreating Turks would take out their anger on us by destroying our homes and killing as many of us as they could. From time to time, I checked the door to make sure it was bolted and then looked at the ceiling, which shook every time the British cannons erupted.

We sat in silence as the cold winter rain fell.

Hearing noises, I went to the window in the back room, pulled aside the curtain, and saw columns of soldiers and horses on the Mea Shearim Road, dark shadows in the night.

"The Turks are in full retreat," I reported.

"They're going to their fortified positions on Mount Scopus," one of my cousins said.

We didn't know what to think. Maybe Berrel Heller had been right.

Maybe the Germans had a secret weapon that would destroy Allenby and the British army, and then the Turks would return and destroy us.

The rain continued all night, the cannons boomed furiously, lighting up the horizon.

We lay in bed, eyes open, listening and shivering.

At dawn, the bombardment suddenly ended, and a total silence descended.

It was Sunday. On the Jewish calendar, it was the twenty-fourth day of Kislev in the year 5677—December 9, 1917.

I was ten years old, going on eleven.

The Sabbath was over, and I got out of bed, took off my cold, wet shoes and wrapped my blistered feet in a thin, cotton blanket.

The rain had stopped, but our house was cold and damp. We stayed barricaded inside, afraid to leave. I looked out the back window. In the weak morning light, the street was empty. I joined my brother Moshe at the front window.

"What do you see?" my younger brother Netanel asked.

"There's no one there," I told him.

My father looked out, sighed, and turned away.

An airplane flew low over the house, its engine roaring hoarsely. I ran to the back window as the plane disappeared to the north.

"They're dropping paper!"

White leaves floated in the air, a few of them fell on the hill in front of our house. Moshe and the others joined me at the window. What could this portend? Moshe, ever the one for action, rushed out. No one dared join him. We watched from the window. He left the yard, ran back laughing and shouting and waving one of the papers.

"No more Turks! No more Turks! We are Englanders!"

The flyer was printed in Hebrew, Yiddish, English, and Arabic, informing us in the name of the newly appointed military governor of Jerusalem that all inhabitants of the city were now free of Turkish bondage. We would soon be given free medical assistance and food.

The streets of the Mea Shearim and Batei Warsaw were suddenly full of people. Streaming from barricaded houses and hiding places, we raced about on the cold stones. On everyone's lips were the traditional greetings of happy times: "Mazel tov" (Good luck) and "*Shalom ale-ichem*" (Peace upon you). People ran from house to house. "A miracle! Blessed be the Name!' What a great miracle it was that so many were still alive and healthy. The relief was like sunshine. I was so happy to see the grown-ups happy that I wept.

Everyone told jokes about the dumb Turks, laughing at our oppressors.

"Why, I was hiding right under their noses, and they couldn't find me!"

"God takes the brains of evil men!"

"Look at them run from the Englanders!"

The uncle of one of my schoolboy friends came rushing into our front yard. I had brought food to him during his years of hiding, and now he was laughing and weeping, and hugging me.

Then my grandfather, dressed in his public finery and waving his black cane in the air, walked into our yard. Everyone stopped talking.

His eyes were full.

"Baruch HaShem," he said.

A few men began clapping—not in applause but in a dancing rhythm—and soon others joined in. My grandfather held out his cane, and my father grasped its other end, and they started dancing around each other on the cold earth, one arm lifted, and singing. Then the women started clapping, and the men formed a dancing circle around my father and grandfather, moving in the opposite direction. From other yards came the sound of singing, voices in the morning damp, and we snaked into the big courtyard and formed one big circle, hands on each other's shoulders. We began a chant as the women clapped and sang, and my father and grandfather held the cane and turned around each other, smiling and singing, while all the Hasidim danced round and round, their caftans flapping and their earlocks bouncing, singing in praise of heaven's blessings, their voices lifting in the air, their joyous song rising to meet the sun.

British soldiers entering Jerusalem

CHAPTER 27

During the night the Turkish army had fled, taking with them the Turkish nationals who ran the municipal government. The British did not arrive officially until later that afternoon, and for a brief interval Jerusalem was without any governing force. Chaos reigned. An angry mob of Arabs and Jews ransacked the municipal offices near the Damascus Gate. The looting spread to all government buildings. My two wild cousins brought home brand-new Turkish officers' uniforms complete with long steel swords, and strutted around Batei Warsaw and the Mea Shearim, challenging other boys to duels and chasing a few frightened cats through the alleys. When my mother saw them carrying on, she ran out of the house to scold them.

"Shame on you! People are frightened enough, and you'll only hurt yourselves."

Brandishing their swords, my cousins rushed off to find new conquests.

About three o'clock, when there were still no signs of the British army, a dozen local dignitaries formed an ad hoc committee to find the Englanders and escort them to the Old City. The Balfour Declaration had fired the hopes of many, and the Jewish leaders were especially eager to meet the new rulers of Palestine. Dressed in their finest clothing, which after four years of war was not quite up to the standards of international diplomacy, the delegation set out on foot on the old Jaffa Road, keeping an eye out for British dignitaries. About two miles west of the Jaffa Gate, they came across two officers, cavalry scouts. After much discussion in a number of languages, the officers reluctantly accepted the unauthorized surrender of Jerusalem, and the delegation walked back to the Old City to await the rest of the mighty British army.

In the meantime, I was bored. My friend Baruch Weinstock was also bored. From the roof of my house in Batei Warsaw, we watched the roads, but there were no Englanders to be seen. Down in the courtyard, people were telling each other the same old stories about their miraculous survival and the same old jokes about the Turks and Germans.

"Let's get out of here," Baruch said. Instead of going to the Old City, we walked east, up the steep hill of Zichron Moshe and through the narrow streets, coming out on Jaffa Road at the police station. There we saw for the first time the Englanders. We stopped and stared. There were thousands of them. They were standing and sitting on the sidewalks and in the gutters in their desert uniforms with rifles and heavy packs and weapons hanging from their belts. Horses and mules pulled heavy cannons, and motorcycles, jeeps, and trucks were everywhere. This was our first exposure to motor vehicles of this sort—the Turkish army used mules and horses—and we didn't know war terms, so we called them, all, machines: two-wheel machines, four-wheel machines, or "the big machine with the box with the gun on top."

"Very interesting," said Baruch.

I agreed. "Very."

There was only so much looking at the Englanders and their machines we could do before it got boring, so we walked on past the Dr. Wallach Hospital and past the home for the aged. We continued on up the steep slope that led to Lifta, an Arab village that, in more prosperous times, had supplied Jerusalem with fruits and vegetables; to our left was a high hill with a narrow path leading to Givat Shaul, an area of big, open fields and barren hills.

We sat down by the side of the road to rest.

"You know, Chaim," said Baruch, "I don't feel hungry. What about you?"

"Not me either. That's because we don't have any food. If we found some, we'd be hungry like bears."

We didn't know anything about bears, but my reference to that exotic animal enhanced the uniqueness of the moment.

Baruch looked around, stood up, and pointed. "Chaim, look!"

There were wires running along the side of the road as it rose up the hill and curved down the other side toward Jerusalem.

"Yeah, I see. Wires. So what?"

"You're really dumb. This wire makes a perfect laundry rope."

He was right. Batei Warsaw and the Mea Shearim were one big spider web of laundry lines. Sometimes there were so many clothes hanging you couldn't walk without dragging down someone's wet underwear. On windy days, the old, frayed ropes broke, and the wet laundry fell into the mud, occasioning much lamentation. Wire would be perfect.

"The problem is," said Baruch as he and I crouched down examining the wire, "how can we cut it?"

"Now you're being dumb," I said. "We'll use sharp rocks."

"That's pretty smart."

Within seconds, we found a couple of sharp stones as big as our fists, got on our knees, and hammered at the black wire.

"Interesting," said Baruch. Inside the black rubber coating were two shiny red wires wrapped with red and white rubber.

"Yes," I agreed, "very interesting."

After the first cuts, we followed the wire along the side of the road and made our second cuts, cutting enough for each of us to have one long laundry line. Baruch, taller and stronger, walked on and cut a second length for himself. We pulled the wires into a heap and only then realized how heavy and bulky they were.

"How can we carry it home?" Baruch said.

"I have an idea. Let's roll it around our waists."

"Chaim, you're a genius."

I helped Baruch wrap the wire around his chest, he did the same for me, and we started back to Batei Warsaw. He had twice the length I did, but he was stronger, and we walked side by side down the hill, talking about how we were going to surprise all of Batei Warsaw with our discovery. Why, we might even go back for more and sell the wires to our friends.

Suddenly, in back of us, there was a loud, angry shout. We turned and froze. From the top of the hill, two big Englander soldiers were pointing and shouting. We couldn't understand them, but it was clear they weren't happy, and when they unslung their rifles and started running toward us Baruch and I didn't wait for the translation. We ran too, holding the wire around our waists with both hands, our fringes flying behind. Our yarmulkes were pinned to our hair or they would have fallen off. The soldiers had a lot of heavy equipment, but they kept pace, shouting at us, "Halt! Halt!" and other English words that were clearly military in purpose.

At first, the soldiers, good runners, gained on us, but soon, even running barefoot, we began to pull away. Baruch was in front, his wire coils bouncing up and down, his fringes flying behind and his earlocks trailing. Years of poor eating had taken the edge off my speed, and I was panting hard. The soldiers were no longer shouting; they were saving their breath for the race. I glanced over my shoulder. They were maintaining distance. I lifted the roll of wire over my head and threw it on the road. I picked up speed and sped pass Baruch. Baruch threw away one of his rolls. In back of us, the soldiers' boots pounded on the earth.

"*Sh'ma Yisrael!*" Baruch shouted, *hear oh Israel!*, and we really began to move. We flew past Batei Warsaw and into the Mea Shearim. The soldiers weren't giving up. I pointed to the left and we took the corner full tilt, made a quick second turn, ran past the shoe repairer's house, and turned again into a narrow alley. The soldiers had already lost their way. We ran in and out of the narrow streets and came out the other side of the Mea Shearim. We stopped to catch our breath, and I started laughing. Baruch laughed so hard he fell on his coil of wire.

Home, I told my older brother, Moshe, what we'd done, and he laughed too.

"Chaim, do you know what that wire was?"

"It was black wire."

"That's a telephone line for the Englanders."

"I know." I paused. "What's a telephone?"

"A telephone is a device that connects the army in the hills with an office in Jerusalem. You can talk through the wire."

"You mean your words travel along the wire?"

"That's right. You talk in one end, and the person hears you on the other. But you need the wire."

"How is that possible?"

"I don't know. It works with a battery."

"Of course." I didn't know what a battery was either.

"But anyway, you ran faster than the soldiers."

"They had on boots and knapsacks."

"What happened to the wire?"

"I had to throw it away or they would have caught me."

"Too bad. It would have been a good clothesline."

I had had no choice, but I was sorry; that evening was the first night of Hanukkah, and the wire would have been a useful gift for my mother.

*

Quickly, the Englander army arrived in full force. Thousands and thousands of soldiers marched down Mea Shearim Road; others rode in their big machines. There were lines of cavalry officers too—tall, fierce men with swords and rifles on big horses.

My mother quickly grasped the commercial potential of an occupying army and, not wasting any time, sent Moshe and me into our little cellar to bring out her big black pot, which we hung from an iron tripod on the side of the road. In our kitchen was some wood from an old door and, while my brother and I filled the pot with buckets of water and built a fire under it, our mother raced off to the Old City.

Never had I seen such an endless stream of marching men. They sang and waved to us, and we waved back. I was happy with all this friendliness. Soon our mother hurried back, holding two little pigeons that had been slaughtered, cleaned, and plucked. During the last two years of the war, there hadn't been a single chicken or pigeon in all Jerusalem, and now, amazingly, she had two. The pot was simmering. In went the two little pigeons. While they boiled, my mother sent me to the basement to get her secret emergency supply of flour—three kilos—and a small container of olive oil.

She had been planning to make latkes for Hanukkah, but the appearance of the mighty Englanders changed everything.

"The war is over," she said, "and now it's business before pleasure."

While my mother prepared the batter in the kitchen, and the pigeons cooked in the pot, Moshe and I stood on Mea Shearim Road and watched the soldiers march by. The two golden birds bobbed up and down in the boiling water, sending up clouds of perfume.

Two cavalry officers on big brown horses rode past. I waved to them. One of them waved back, glanced down at the pot, and rode on. Then he turned his horse quickly and trotted back.

Moshe stood on one side of the pot, and I on the other.

The officer said something in English. We shook our heads and said nothing. The snorting horse stomped the earth. The officer spoke again, and again we shook our heads. The horse was big and terrifying, the officer a giant man with a pale face and a big golden mustache. The pigeons were swimming in the boiling water.

The horse was snorting and stomping, and the officer jerked its reins. Then he pulled out his sword and brought his horse sideways to the pot. He aimed his sword.

"No!" I shouted.

He stabbed one of the pigeons hard, and the tip of the sword came out the other side. Before I could shout again, he did the same to the other pigeon and then lifted his sword, the tiny pigeons stuck through.

"Don't take our pigeons!"

The big horse nervously turned around on the earth, its rear legs stomping hard, and the cavalry officer worked hard with one hand to control him.

Moshe was frightened and said nothing.

"Give us back our pigeons!"

The officer said something in English, and with the hand holding the reins, he reached into his coat, and suddenly, a golden shower fell at our feet.

With the two pigeons on his sword, the cavalry officer galloped away, and Moshe and I scrambled to pick up the coins.

Neither my brother nor I knew the value of Englander currency, nor did our mother, but she knew we hadn't been cheated.

"A fortune!" she exclaimed when we brought her the money. "A fortune! Now we must earn some more."

What was a better treat for hungry soldiers who'd spent long months eating cold desert food than hot fried latkes? We carried away the pot, my mother arranged some bricks around the fire and put the frying pan on, and soon she was spooning batter into hot olive oil.

"We're doing a mitzvah for the Englanders," she explained. After all, latkes were the traditional Hanukkah food with which the holiday was properly celebrated. Between the smell of frying batter and my mother's shouts in Yiddish, the soldiers were quickly breaking ranks to line up at the frying pan, and my mother called to my sisters to make another batch of dough. Another cavalry officer bought a dozen latkes, holding out his sword so we could stick them on the blade. He pulled one off, gave it to his horse, and then, taking a small whiskey bottle from his saddlebag and raising it to our mother, toasted her in excellent Yiddish.

"*L'Chaim, L'Chaim, mir sind im Yerushalayim!*" (To life, to life, I am in Jerusalem!).

Our mother exclaimed, "a true pleasure! A Jewish soldier! God bless you!"

He drank from the bottle and reached into a purse hanging from his sword belt. His horse reared, snorting, and the officer flung a handful of coins to the earth in front of our fire.

"Be careful, *Mom-ele*, this is still a battle zone. The Turks will try to counterattack."

With that warning, he rode off, biting a latke off his sword.

Just before dusk, my mother stopped cooking, and we went inside our house, where our father was waiting to light the first Hanukkah candle. He had cleaned and polished our menorah. A tinsmith especially for my father had made it, and though it wasn't expensive, it was unique and beautiful. Made of tin and glass, the menorah had nine small glass bowls, the ninth bowl on the end higher than the others. The bowls held olive oil, and each bowl had a tin ring that fit over its rim to hold the cotton wick. The menorah was in a glass box that had two sliding glass doors in front and two windows in back so that it could be put outside without the wind blowing out the flames. It's hard to imagine how it really looked, but it was delicate and beautiful, and I loved to sit inside our house and watch it on the eighth day, when all nine flames were dancing, and the glass and tin were mirrors that caught the light.

We stood around the Hanukkah lamp—my father and mother;

my sisters Chaya, Yehoved, and Hinda; my brothers Moshe and little Netanel; and me. We were pale, weak, and undernourished, but alive.

Using a precious match from his tin supply, our father lit the wick in the shamus, the tall caretaker lamp, and, with a trembling voice, recited the three blessings of Hanukkah.

"Blessed are you, Lord our God, Sovereign of the universe, who has sanctified us with your commandments and commands us to light the candles of Hanukkah.

"Blessed are you, Lord our God, Sovereign of the universe, who performed miracles for our people in the days of old.

"Blessed are you, Lord our God, Sovereign of the universe, who has granted us life and sustenance and brought us through the year to this season."

We all sang "Ma O'tzor": "Rock of Ages, let our song praise your saving power."

In order to fulfill the blessing of the menorah, the lamp must burn for at least thirty minutes. During that time, we stood around the two flickering lights and recited with our father a psalm of David, Psalm 91: "O, he who dwells in the shelf of the most high and abides in the shadow of the Almighty ..."

We recited the psalm seven times, and as the two flames flickered, the eight of us stood in silence, grateful to be alive.

*

The cavalry officer's warning proved correct, and the next night the Turks counterattacked. A heavy winter rain was falling in the Jerusalem hills. As expected, the attack came from Mount Scopus, where the Turks and Germans had retreated to fortified positions. By the morning, however, the British infantry had surrounded them. Rather than launch a bloody frontal assault, Allenby brought up an artillery battery and shelled the Germans and Turks unmercifully. The British bombardment went on for two weeks, night and day, and the incessant booming made our lives miserable. We had to shout to make ourselves heard, and at night we covered our heads with our thin pillows and prayed for the bombardment to end. At the request of the community leaders, the British refrained from shelling for a few hours Friday night and Saturday morning, giving us a chance to celebrate the Sabbath in relative peace and quiet.

On December 11, 1917, two days after the first British troops entered Jerusalem, Sir Edmund Allenby finally appeared. At the head of a long line of vehicles and cavalry, the general made his way along Jaffa Road up the high hills to Jerusalem. My grandfather Fishel Linder was a member of the welcoming delegation. For this historical occasion, he put on his holiday clothes and his polished shoes and carried his beautiful cane with the silver head of a fish and the jeweled eyes. The roads around Jerusalem, rutted by the army vehicles and muddy, were difficult to navigate, and my grandfather, weak and tired, walked to the Jaffa Gate while I, dressed also in my special wardrobe and wearing my patched and pinching shoes, walked on his left side so that he could use my shoulder for support. We stood just inside the gate and waited for the mighty general to show. Finally, a great shout went up as Allenby approached the Old City.

Preceding him was the most amazing sound I had ever heard. I could hardly describe it then, and I can't even now. It was music, but the music was strange and beautiful. It got louder and louder as it approached the gate, and then, suddenly, it filled the air with a swirling, whistling sound punctuated by rapid, booming drums. Then I saw it. Giant men made the music on amazing instruments of bags and pipes in plaid skirts and long stockings. A dozen drummers twirling their drumsticks in the air as they struck their drums followed them. A Goliath in a long skirt who had a long marching stick that he moved up and down across his body led them. I stood with my mouth open as they marched by, my skin tingling. How the Turks and Germans must have run from them!

General Allenby came through the Jaffa Gate on a dark horse. Some people shouted, some clapped, and then everyone fell silent. He got off his horse, walked through the crowd to the Citadel, and turned to face us. He spoke in English, so I didn't understand, but my grandfather told me later that he spoke on behalf of His Majesty the king of Great

Britain, the British Empire, and the British people. He said he was there to establish a working government so that all the peoples of Jerusalem could begin to rebuild their lives in freedom and prosperity.

General Allenby enters Jerusalem, December 1917

My grandfather and I then returned home. He leaned on my shoulder as we walked through the muddy streets. Later, my grandfather and a group of Jewish delegates met with General Allenby in a large tent. Tea and cakes were served. The discussion, my grandfather reported to my father and a large group of Hasidim, was hopeful.

Soon after their entry into Jerusalem, the British lifted their naval blockade, and our lives quickly returned to normal—which meant that nothing was going to stay the same for long.

242

CHAPTER 28

Having perfected the art of colonization over hundreds of years, the Englanders immediately went about forming a public administration, albeit with the combination of efficiency and condescension unique to British imperial authority. By the fourth day, Jerusalem municipal offices began to reopen, ushering in an entirely new order in Jerusalem, Palestine, and, eventually, all of the Middle East.

The war continued in Europe and the region, but General Allenby easily beat back the ineffective attempts by the Turks and the Germans to retake Jerusalem. The fighting lasted another year, until Allenby defeated the Turks in a decisive battle at Megiddo. In recognition of his services, the general was appointed the British high commissioner of Egypt.

Approximately seventy-five thousand British and Allied soldiers were stationed in and around Jerusalem, most of them living in tent cities in the open fields near our home in Batei Warsaw or camping under the stars along Mea Shearim Road.

Knowing that young soldiers away from home were willing to pay good money for a home-cooked meal, my mother, with my father's approval, opened a small restaurant in our cellar on Mea Shearim Road. I call it a cellar because it was under the floor of our house, but we were on a steep hill, and the cellar's door opened to the street. We set up a small wood stove just outside the door, and within a day, there were lines of hungry young soldiers waiting for my mother's latkes.

While my sisters Chaya Sara, Yehoved, and Hinda prepared the batter in our outdoor kitchen, my mother stood over her portable stove in back of the house and did the frying. Moshe and I went to the Mea Shearim market for flour, sugar, and olive oil. My father, quick with sums, was in charge of the cash box.

Soon we enlarged our menu to include other fried goodies, baked sesame bagels, strudels, and fresh rolls. Never did my parents have so much money. We were rolling in gold and silver coins, but even with the lifting of the embargo, there wasn't much we could buy. That was just as well, my mother said, because soon, she predicted, the soldiers would be gone.

She was right. Our commercial success ended three weeks later, when most of the troops were redeployed to northern Palestine to fight the Turks. Those who stayed moved into army barracks outside the city limits. We closed the restaurant, but my mother continued cooking, and my father and Moshe carried the food to the barracks and sold it to the soldiers there.

A month later, my mother opened a small restaurant in Batei Ha'bocharim, where the British had their military headquarters. Our new restaurant was on the ground floor of a small building between the officers' new headquarters and the tent city where their aides lived. Adjusting her menu to the higher status of her customers, my mother expanded into blintzes, sweet-and-sour borscht, with potatoes, fried fish, and vegetable dumplings. She continued turning out her staples of latkes and strudel. The soldiers liked her home-style cooking, and the officers made sure her supply of raw materials continued uninterrupted.

Predominantly English, the occupation army was from all parts of the British Empire—Canada, Australia, New Zealand, and India. They lived in separate camps, and my friends and I became adept at recognizing their accents and uniforms. The soldiers from Scotland, with their kilts and long socks, amused us.

We looked high and low for Americans but found none.

Once, four fair and happy Scot soldiers came into our restaurant, took their rifles off, and sat at a table. Our mother knew a few words of English, not enough for a conversation, and the soldiers came to the counter and pointed at the foods. I sat in a corner, observing. They were about eighteen or nineteen, a few years older than I, and with their kilts and smiles, they were like happy children. They ate with great appetite, laughing and joking. When they left, my mother turned to me.

"See how young they are, and how they have to carry guns." She shook her head. "And from these young kilters the mighty armies of the Kaiser and the Turks ran away! Shame on them; they deserve it."

Of the many different soldiers, we disliked the Australians the most.

They were cruel and ill mannered. Late one afternoon, my mother and I were walking home from our restaurant in Batei Ha'bocharim, which is in the hills north of Batei Warsaw. On the empty road, we met an Arab shepherd boy driving his few young sheep. We moved to the side so he and his pitiful herd could pass. Then I turned at the sound of running horses. Two mounted Australian officers were galloping toward us across a low hill.

"Quickly, Chaim," my mother said.

They had already unsheathed their swords and were charging fast and furious.

We ran off the dirt road and into the shallow wadi alongside.

The Australians galloped down the hill at full speed, their swords held low and straight. With frantic cries, the shepherd boy drove his sheep toward the protection of a clump of bushes. One of the Australians gave a loud, terrible shout. Their horses panting, their hooves pounding, the two officers leaned low and sideways in their saddles as the sheep scattered.

There was a loud thud, followed by a terrible bleating cry.

My mother shouted curses. The shepherd screamed as they galloped off without slowing, each with a bleating, kicking sheep on his sword—their supper.

My mother and I stepped around the thick streaks of blood on the road as the shepherd boy wept and chased after what was left of his flock.

*

Within a month of Allenby's arrival, the yeshivas and Talmud Torahs reopened, and we returned full-time to school. My mother and father worked in our restaurant during the day, and my father went back to his evening position in the upper yeshiva. As before, my sisters stayed home and cleaned, cooked, and shopped in the Mea Shearim market. Thanks to the British, who wished to demonstrate their kind intentions, all the students in my school received a free lunch of soup, bread, and butter; it was strictly kosher, and we could ask for seconds.

One evening, returning home with my father from synagogue, I found my older cousin at our table. Mendel, who'd been in hiding for the last two years, now was a free man in more ways than one. Even before the war, he had strayed from the strict life of the Hasid, shaving his earlocks and wearing, instead of the long caftan, a short overcoat—a seemingly minor departure from traditional dress code but a significant act of sartorial rebellion. He also had begun to teach himself secular subjects. In spite of his rebellious ways, my father respected him; he still prayed twice a day in synagogue and always observed the Sabbath.

Mendel had come to speak with my father.

"Uncle Haskel, I've decided to join the Jewish Legion."

I had never heard of the Jewish Legion.

"Ah," said my father. "So now you are a follower of Jabotinsky."

"Zeev Jabotinsky is a freedom fighter. The Legion fought against the Turks."

"Yes, yes, and who will they fight against now?"

"We will fight anyone who denies us our rights."

"Ah, so now you will fight the Englander?"

"If we have to."

My father frowned but said nothing. Jabotinsky, I was to learn, was a Russian-born journalist who organized Russian Jews to fight against the pogroms. He was not a religious man, which was a big strike against him in the Hasidic community, but he believed that the only way Jews would survive was to have a nation of their own and that the first step toward that goal was to show they would take up arms in their own defense. He had been a reporter on the western front in 1914 and had gone to London to argue for a special Jewish unit in the British army. The British had finally agreed, and Jabotinsky, whose Russian name was Vladimir, had changed his name to the Hebrew Zeev, and came to Jerusalem to organize the Jewish Legion. Orthodox Hasidim, such as my father, did not know what to make of this man. A Jew with a gun was a different species. The very idea was anathema; wars didn't stop on the Sabbath or on the Holy Days, and some of the pious thought it was impossible to be both a soldier and an observant Jew. My father was not against fighting, mind you, because sometimes you had to fight; he was against the idea of Jews going out and looking for a fight. King David was a warrior and brilliant military strategist, but my father and the Orthodox community remained unconvinced of the efficacy of violence. However, Jabotinsky found his recruits and armed and trained them with the help of the British. The Legion fought the Turks at the Jordan River crossings, allowing the British to attack the Ottoman flank.

Later, the British would come to regret their decision to arm and train Jews, but for now, the Jewish Legion was a legitimate army unit.

My father asked Mendel, "Do you believe we will have a country?"

"The British agreed to a homeland."

My brother Moshe said, "They have given us the Balfour Declaration."

My father replied in his mild way, "Ah, the Englander agrees to many things when he has to."

"If they don't give us what belongs to us," Mendel said, "we will take it."

My father shook his head. To my cousin Mendel, England was the enemy, but my father disagreed. The Englanders had chased away the oppressive Ottomans and were now bringing peace to the land along with food and medicines. People like Jabotinsky and the other hard-headed Zionists did not appreciate the good acts of the Englanders. I sided with my father, of course. I liked the Englanders for the same reason he did, and they made life in Batei Warsaw more interesting, which, for a boy of eleven, was a big plus.

Mendel was standing. "You will see. One day we will have to drive the Englanders out."

"They do good for us, Mendel."

"I know. But history shows, Uncle Haskel, that once the British come, they stay forever."

My cousin left. Moshe and I watched our father, who remained silent and thoughtful.

*

At last, almost a year after the British liberated Jerusalem, peace finally came. On November 11, 1918, an armistice was signed, and all hostilities ceased.

By then, my father had returned full-time to his position in the Chai Olam Yeshiva to teach rabbinical law and Talmud, and my mother had closed her restaurant and reopened her fabric store in the back room of our house—but not for long. A month after the armistice, she had an announcement of her own.

"I have decided," she told us one night at supper, "to close the store in the back room."

We were stunned. Like the soldiers, the store made life more interesting, and it provided a big part of our family's income.

However, conditions, she told us, had changed drastically. Now that the war was truly over, there was no shortage of fabrics, and her little store could not meet the competition of the open-air markets in the Mea Shearim and the Old City.

I asked, "But what will we do for money?"

My mother paused and then smiled. "I'm going to open a bigger store in the souk."

We stared at her.

"I have already rented a space in the Ba'trak. It will open next week."

All of us, including my father, were even more stunned. The Ba'trak was the busiest street in Old Jerusalem.

Our father was looking at our mother with a little smile. He saw the value of a centrally located store. She would be close to the customers, and there would be more of them. Though his approval wasn't required, he gave it, as he always did when something involved our mother.

Her store was an immediate success. My father arranged his schedule to spend time at the counter and help her with the bookkeeping. The store was a short walk from the yeshiva, and when he showed up at two o'clock, my mother went home to oversee our household. My father closed the store in the early evening, about five or six, and returned to Batei Warsaw for evening prayers. On Fridays, my mother stayed home, and my father opened the store in the morning but came home in the early afternoon to do his Friday chores: grinding meat for meatballs and fish for gefilte fish. As always, I helped, and got the first taste from my mother's frying pan.

Friday was our best day. Friday was the Muslim holy day, and many Arabs came down from the hills to the mosques in the Old City. After morning prayers, they shopped in the souk. In dealing with them, my father was patient and tolerant, and they respected him.

My mother kept the little store in our back room for a few of her special customers. She also continued to supply material to the home for orphaned girls, which was managed by my uncle David. One of my jobs was to deliver the fabrics and collect the past-due bills.

"Uncle David," I would say, "my mother needs some money."

"Tell Reizel she doesn't have to remind me! There are more important matters here than her bills."

My uncle's orphanage was extremely overcrowded; during the war, the population of orphans had increased dramatically, and now, even with the lifting of the blockade and better medical care, many parents were still too sick or depressed to care for their children.

That was the case with my uncle Chaim Reisman, the *shagas ha'ari chazon* (the cantor with the roar of a lion), whom we had rescued from the work brigade and who, now out of hiding, was sick of heart and confined to bed in my grandmother Nechama's house. Two of his four sons lived with us, but our house was much too small, and my parents had to send them, reluctantly, to the Diskin Orphanage Home for Boys. I visited often, bringing my best friend and cousin Yitzhak cookies and rolls my mother baked. I was always upset when I saw them living in a big room full of cots. Once, my cousin looked at my sad face and smiled.

"Chaim, don't worry about me," he said. "I'm fine."

I said nothing.

"I promise you, Chaim. We have a lot of fun here, really."

I couldn't imagine how orphans ever had fun.

Immediately after the war, my cousin Mordecai, who was much older than I, returned from America to visit his sick father, my uncle Chaim. He traveled on a steamship; the voyage from New York to Jaffa lasted six weeks. He was now an Orthodox rabbi in Lakewood, New Jersey, a place as far away as the moon. News of his return spread like a trumpet blast, and he found himself the wonder of orthodox community. Doors and windows opened as he walked by, crowds gathered round the successful Amerikaner rebbe. He spent most of his time with his weak, sick father, who was now living with us. Wealthy, he brought in a specialist from the American Medical School in Beirut, but the famous doctor offered no hope, and my older cousin returned to America and to his new, successful life, and did not see his father again.

During the High Holy Days later that year, my uncle Chaim, too weak to go to synagogue, asked for a minion, and it being a great mitzvah to help a dying man pray, our house was soon filled with Hasidim. It was Yom Kippur, our most solemn day, so performing this act of *chesed* (loving-kindness) was even a greater mitzvah. After the bedside prayer service, the minyan left, and my uncle settled back in his pillows and dozed off. I was sitting by his side, when suddenly he opened his eyes.

"I wish to sit up," he said.

I called my mother, and we lifted him and put a pillow behind his back.

"Where is my tallit?"

My mother and I put the prayer shawl over his head and shoulders. There was new color in his face, and his eyes were alert. He sat up even straighter, cleared his throat, and started singing a psalm.

"The earth and its entire contents," my uncle sang, "belong to the Lord, the world and its inhabitants."

His voice was clear and strong, as one would expect of a professional singer.

"Who may ascend to the Lord's mountain? Who may stand within his holy place? He who has clean hands and a clean, pure heart, he who strives not after vanity and swears not deceitfully … raise your heads, O gates, raise yourselves, you ancient doors, that the glorious King may come in."

With the last note, he fell back and closed his eyes. He never regained consciousness, and three weeks later, after another visit by the doctor from Beirut, my uncle died.

"You see, Chaim," my mother said, "when your uncle sang, 'Raise your head, O gates,' he was heard, and the gates of heaven remained open until his soul was lifted into them."

During the seven-day shivah, our large extended family came and went day and night. Everyone marveled over the Yom Kippur episode, when my uncle had sung with such power.

Another of my many uncles explained it this way: "It is written that the light of God is the soul of man. You see, all of you, that when the light of a candle is about to expire, it gives a sharp flash of light before it disappears. Chaim's soul was such a light, and it gave a final, strong flash of light before it left his body."

So the generations passed.

My grandfather's brother-in-law, Yitzhak Haggis, with whom my grandfather Fishel had spent many good years and done many good deeds, the man who was full of energy and enterprise and whom my grandfather loved dearly, died in the spring of 1919.

He left a considerable fortune, including his big stationery store, which was thriving again now that the war was over. My grandfather Fishel was named the executor of his will; for his legal work, my grandfather received sixty pounds British sterling, a magnificent sum.

The death of his dear brother-in-law was a sad blow to my grandfather. They had left their homes in Poland in the 1870s and for forty years had shared in the struggles and triumphs of their beloved Jerusalem, where they had walked arm in arm in its ancient streets. They had been two living cornerstones upon which the Jewish community had built itself.

A year later, in the spring of 1920, my grandfather Fishel died.

I was thirteen years old, a student in the fourth grade in the Mea Shearim Talmud Torah. That afternoon, my sister Hinda was waiting outside the school to tell me, and we walked in silence to our grandfather's house. A hundred people were in the yard, dozens in the apartment.

The crowd parted so that I could pass through, for children and grandchildren are relatives of the first degree. My grandfather was lying on the floor, covered with a white bed sheet, his feet toward the door. Around him on the stone floor were lit candles. My uncles and cousins and men from the Hasidic synagogues stood and whispered prayers. He had died at two o'clock that morning, and he had been cleansed and wrapped in his white tallit. In keeping with the custom of prompt burial, we left the house at ten that night, carrying his body on a wide, flat plank of wood. Holding lanterns, a hundred people walked behind the bearers to the Mount of Olives, passing through the alleys and narrow streets where my grandfather had walked every day of his life to the Kotel. In keeping with tradition, the graveside ceremony was simple, and he was lowered into the earth at midnight.

Moshe and I walked silently through the streets. The spring night was already giving way to dawn. My older brother and I climbed to the roof of our house in Batei Warsaw and stood together in silence and watched the light rise in the east to touch my grandfather's new grave on the Mount of Olives.

*

My grandfather Fishel Linder was a pioneer in the wilderness of Palestine and a builder of a New Jerusalem. He strove to be as good a Jew as he could be, and from that, he believed all other good would flow. He was convinced that only in Jerusalem could he, his children, and their children live a life built upon the pillars of our religion, faith in God, and a belief in the sanctity of all life.

A few days before his death, he had given my mother the sixty pounds British sterling he had received as the executor of his dear brother-in-law's will.

It was the only money he had ever kept for personal use, and he wanted my mother, the dear wife of his only son, to have it.

He gave his silver cane with the silver fish head to his son, Haskel, my father.

We calculated that at the time of his death, my grandfather was sixty-three years old.

I wished—oh, how I wished it—that he had lived forever.

CHAPTER 29

At long last, my oldest sister, Chaya Sara, was married. She was almost twenty and by all standards an old maid, but the war had delayed many a shidduch, and now the matchmakers were making up for lost time. Quickly, a marriage contract was signed between my family, the Linders, and the Eisenbach-Pesters. The Eisenbachs had migrated from Budapest, Hungary, so Pester had been added to their name. Her fiancé, Yossef, did not use the name Pester, and my sister's name was simply Chaya Sara Eisenbach.

The wedding lasted the standard week. My two cousins in the orphanage were our special guests, and we spent most of the time running through the twisting alleys and scrambling over the roofs of Batei Warsaw. The saddest part of the wedding took place on the third day, Sunday afternoon, when the older women cut off my sister's hair. In Orthodox Hasidic households, a bride cuts her hair as a sign of her new status and will, for the rest of her life, wear a kerchief or a wig. My cousins and I watched as the older women gathered round my sister and cut her hair almost to the scalp. She had the most beautiful hair in Batei Warsaw, perhaps even in all Jerusalem, and I had played with it when I was a little boy, lifting it and letting it fall in thick ropes of soft brown. Now her head looked like a naked field of stubble. I couldn't look at her, and I couldn't look away.

After the wedding, she and Yossef went to live with my grandmother Esther until they could get an apartment in Batei Hungary, where the groom's family lived. A year later, my sister gave birth to a baby girl, and they named her Shifro.

Two weeks after that, my mother had another child, her last, a boy named Yechiel Fishel.

My mother was forty-two years old.

War, hunger, and time had not diminished her health. During the entire pregnancy, she worked in her fabric store in the Old City with my father. The day of the birth, she came home early, sent for the midwife, and then retreated to the small rear room. The midwife came quickly, and then, a little after midnight, as our wall clock chimed the quarter hour, my father woke me as I lay wrapped in my blanket in my corner of the floor.

"Chaim, you have a new brother."

We knew he would be named after my grandfather. My mother had almost worshipped him. He had welcomed her when she, a young woman from a poor family, had married my father. Even when I was a child, I knew that my mother was a free spirit, and my grandfather, with his generous, wise heart, admired her special qualities and defended her against all gossip.

She had seen my grandfather's early death as an opportunity for a last, loving gesture, for she knew, she told me, knew her unborn child would be a son she could name after him.

My youngest brother was the last child she would bear.

We called him Fishel.

*

Shortly after Fishel's birth, my parents lost their fabric store.

It happened in a strange way.

The store was doing well, and my father wanted to expand by adding a wholesale line; after secret talks with our mother, he announced one evening after supper that he was going to Alexandria, Egypt, to purchase fabrics.

We were all excited, especially my older brother, Moshe, who had his own dreams of traveling. My father was excited too; this would be his first journey since his three-month trip from Plotsk as a child many years ago.

The rail trip to Alexandria would take twenty-six hours. My grandmother Esther was against it; she didn't want her only son leaving Jerusalem, if only for three weeks. But he couldn't be stopped. Our entire family—dozens of uncles, aunts, and cousins—along with his friends, business associates, and fellow Hasidim, went to the station to bid him farewell. He carried not only clothing and money but also a supply of kosher food: dried meats and dates, crackers, and assorted jams and preserves. Before he boarded, the Hasidim danced around him in a circle while we all clapped and sang.

As the train pulled out, we all yelled and cheered. My mother held baby Fishel and waved his fat little hand at the train. Our grandmother burst into tears and shouted prayers at the retreating cars.

We went home to await his return.

At that time, Alexandria had a flourishing, if small, Jewish community, and my father stayed with a Hasid whose son-in-law was one of his students in Jerusalem. Such extended connections were common and a great facilitator in business matters.

His journey was a success, and on his return he told us his adventures. The first evening in Alexandria, he went to a synagogue to give thanks for his safe arrival. The rabbi there introduced him to congregants who were fabric wholesalers. My father knew enough Arabic to communicate with those who didn't speak Yiddish or Hebrew. During the war, a good number of Jews had found safe harbor in Egypt, and they were honored to have a visitor from Jerusalem. My father was impressed by the peace and harmony between the Jewish community in Alexandria and their Muslim neighbors. He was surprised too, he said, that by and large, the Jewish community in Alexandria was engaged in worldly endeavors without any apparent loss of piety. This, he told us, gave him a broader understanding of life.

With the fabrics from Alexandria due to arrive in Jerusalem, he and my mother now needed a source of cash. They were stretched to their limits—and not just financially. The new baby needed my mother's attention, and my father's teaching position in the Olam Yeshiva was his first priority. My father put out the word that they wanted a business partner, and quickly, they found one. One of the members of Kolel Warsaw had just married off his daughter. The groom was a full-time yeshiva student who had spent his entire young life poring over religious texts. It was past time for the young man, his new father-in-law insisted, to get off his tuchus—that part of the anatomy upon which full-time scholars spend most of their lives—and out into the world. A deal was proposed: The groom would use the substantial dowry to become my parents' partner, and would work full-time in the store for a fair salary, thus freeing my mother and father to pursue other interests.

The arrangement didn't work out. The groom knew nothing about business and wasn't interested in learning. His customer skills were minimal, and he had no initiative. Soon my mother was working again, and my father, forced to do the bookkeeping and customer contact, couldn't return to the teaching that he loved. Then the young groom insisted that the deal was not to his liking. He hadn't realized that full-time employment would prevent him from studying. My father offered to return his investment and cancel the deal, but Shlomo refused. With the parties unable to compromise, the dispute was brought before the Beth Din, the rabbinical court. A *toyion*, a rabbinical lawyer, represented the groom, and my father represented himself.

A Beth Din is a court that decides cases on the basis of rabbinical law, many of whose precepts form the basis of English and American common law. In such contractual disputes, the court is instructed, as a matter of legal principle, to settle the case on its merits. Compromise, once the case reaches the court, is not recommended. The notion is that the contract is itself a negotiated compromise between the parties and should be implemented by the courts as closely as possible to its original intent. To do otherwise would reward the more aggressive party, making all contracts mere starting points for endless revisions and negotiations.

As was customary in dealings between members of the Orthodox community, the agreement between my parents and the young groom was an oral one based on mutual trust. There was no written contract, and no witnesses had been present during negotiations.

The Beth Din appreciated the merits of my father's case and indicated they would rule in his favor, but without a written document, they asked that he give his testimony under oath. He refused. He had spoken truthfully but was unwilling to swear an oath, even to the rabbinical court. His stand put him at a distinct disadvantage, and the Beth Din granted him a two-week stay during which he might decide on his course of action.

That night, I sat at our long table with him.

"Abba, you're telling the truth. I remember what you told us about the contract."

"Yes, Chaim, those are the terms we agreed to."

"Why don't you swear to it?"

"Because, Chaim, I will not invoke God's name for secular profit."

"But the Beth Din is asking you to do it."

"Yes, and I am choosing to do what I think is right."

"Will we lose the store?"

"I don't know, Chaim. That's in God's hands."

My brother Moshe and I wanted our father to do as the Beth Din requested. We thought our mother would convince our father to take the oath, but she wouldn't argue with him.

A few days later, one of my father's friends approached us as we were walking home from morning prayers.

"Reb Haskel, may I speak with you on an important matter?"

"Certainly," my father said, and he invited him to come home with us.

The man was Yitzhak Yoffe. Some given names, such as Yitzhak, were popular, so most people were called by their full family name. Yitzhak Yoffe was a rabbi and a legal expert.

We sat at the table while my mother served breakfast.

"I heard about your case, Reb Haskel. I'm willing to represent you without fee."

"I have already represented myself."

"The court is sympathetic, but according to law, it will require your oath."

"I'm not willing to give it."

After a pause, Yitzhak Yoffe took a clever, more dialectical tack.

"You're absolutely certain you are telling the truth?"

My father was offended but answered calmly. "Of course."

"And you agree that the truth is the highest expression of ethical behavior?"

My father agreed.

"Aha! So swearing to it is just as ethical!"

"That is true, but I will not use the name of God to enrich myself."

"Ah! But, Reb Haskel, you are merely retaining what is legally yours."

That was a good argument, but my father shook his head.

"Though I am concerned about the legal and economic aspects, Reb Yoffe, I am not going to sacrifice my religious principles."

"Are you ready to lose all your savings?"

My father said nothing.

"Are you willing to let your partner take the entire store? Are you willing to let the wrong triumph over the right? Do you not have an obligation to the community to prevent a dishonest man from feasting on the fruits of his lies? And what about your family? Are they not dependent upon the store for their sustenance?"

My father said nothing. Reb Yoffe peppered him with more questions and arguments, but in the end, my father remained true to his principles and did not swear before the Beth Din.

The rabbinical court issued its decision, and we lost the case and our store.

The groom was now the sole owner of the fabric store—but not for long. Incompetent and lazy, he lost money and customers, and within a year, the store went bankrupt and closed. He returned to the yeshiva and spent his days bent over holy books, once again supported by his father-in-law.

I thought my father was overly fastidious. Reb Yoffe had made a strong case against my father's position, particularly the point that wrong must not be allowed to triumph on a technicality, but my father did not view his stand as a mere technicality. He would not invoke the name of God in pursuit of any worldly gain.

I was surprised how calmly my mother took this turn of events.

"You will see, Chaim," she told me. "Everything will work out for the best."

Her prediction came true. The Old City was no longer as safe for us as it had been; the Arabs, seeing many more immigrants from Europe and Russia and facing more sophisticated competition both politically and economically, were becoming increasingly hostile. Vandalism against Jewish property increased and personal attacks became more frequent, especially at night. The British authorities were unable to stop the Arab aggression; some cynics suggested they did not want to. Many Jewish merchants were moving out of the Old City and setting up shop in the growing communities outside.

Within a month, my mother reopened her store in the small back room of our house, and with my youngest brother now able to fend for himself, was soon doing a brisk business. My father was freed at last from the burdens of commerce, and returned to teaching and lecturing full-time and was much happier.

For the first time in a long time, things were working out better than I expected.

CHAPTER 30

Judah Ben Tema, said: At five years the age is reached for the study of Torah; at age ten for the study of Mishna; at thirteen for the fulfillment of the commandments; at fifteen for the study of Talmud; and at eighteen, for marriage.

—Ethics of the Fathers 5:24

Until the age of thirteen, my older brother, Moshe, had followed the path laid down by the Ethics of the Fathers and seemed well on his way to becoming a pious Hasid. With the war, however, life had come to a halt: the Talmud Torahs closed; the rebbes went into the army or into hiding; and the students, hungry and sick, stayed away. When the war was over, Moshe was eighteen, neither ready for marriage nor willing to return to school.

Nor did the Spartan ways of our grandfather or father appeal to him; at an early age, my brother displayed a taste for the good life.

After his bar mitzvah, Moshe worked in a matzo factory. His job lasted four weeks, from Purim to Pesach, and he worked six days a week, fourteen hours a day. The factory had a small synagogue attached to it so the workers could pray in the morning and evening. Twice a day, I carried food to the factory for Moshe's breakfast and supper. His wages were low, but he had no expenses other than the few pennies he gave to our mother, and he spent the rest on a well-preserved, secondhand pair of shiny black shoes.

During the war, the matzo factory cut back production, and Moshe was laid off. He spent most of his time avoiding the Green Band soldiers and trying to earn a penny here and there, not usually succeeding. When the Englanders drove the Turks out of Jerusalem, Moshe made good money selling my mother's cooking to the soldiers in their barracks. Her fried chicken and cinnamon strudel roll were her best sellers.

He gave most of the money back to my mother, of course, but she let him keep 20 percent of the profits.

Once the armistice was signed and the British army left, Moshe was determined to earn some money. He decided to become a sopher, a holy writer, a trade that one of our brothers-in-law, Yoshke, was willing to teach him. A sopher transcribes passages from the Bible onto small pieces of parchment, which are then inserted into tefillin (phylacteries) and mezuzahs, the little boxes nailed to the doorjambs of homes. Before the war, many of those items were produced in Poland and Romania, but the conflict brought a halt to all European production. With peace, the pent-up demand made the work profitable, and Moshe, a fast learner, was soon busy night and day filling orders for Americans willing to pay for sacred parchments from the Holy Land.

With his newfound wealth, Moshe's own pent-up demand for worldly goods found expression, and soon he was buying imported delicacies from expensive shops in the Old City and fitting himself with new, fancy clothing. This was unheard of in our modest, pious home. As soon as our eldest sister moved out, Moshe took possession of the small back room. He redecorated it—rather, he decorated it for the first time—by bringing in a table, which faced the window, a desk chair, and a new kerosene lamp. He spent a good part of the night writing on parchment with quill and ink. Moshe kept his equipment safe and secure in the little wall closet, where he also kept his expensive imported foods. He bought a little metal lock and fitted it to the closet, and he carried the key with him at all times.

This occasioned much family discussion.

"Since when do we have locks on our closet doors?" my father asked, more in surprise than alarm.

"Even our front door is never locked," my mother added.

One might point out, as I did, that we didn't have anything worth securing behind locked doors, but it was the principle of having a lock-free house that was at stake.

Nevertheless, no one interfered with Moshe.

His surprises followed one after another.

He began to wear beautiful neckties, a sure sign of latent secular yearnings.

Our mother was alarmed, but our father, curiously, wasn't.

"Aha!" my mother exclaimed. "A Daitch!"

"Don't make a big tummel out of this," my father told my mother. "Let him play around a little; he'll grow out of it."

Our mother called in her younger brother Yisrael Yitzhak, my favorite uncle, a deeply pious and knowledgeable Hasid, now a rabbi of the court, who sat Moshe down for a discussion.

"Moshele, you don't need all these fancy Shmatas." (*Shmatas* is Polish for "rags.") "People are going to think that you're becoming Daitch." That is, Deutsch, or German—a snob.

"Ties are an important addition to a gentleman's wardrobe," Moshe explained.

Uncle Yisrael Yitzhak was genuinely puzzled. "How can anyone who scribes the holy words onto parchment use his holy earnings to buy Shmatas?"

Moshe took offense at the pejorative; stylish haberdashery was not rags.

"Being well dressed is not incompatible with holiness," replied Moshe, thus daring our mother's brother to a debate on philosophy and ethics—never a good idea with Uncle Yisrael Yitzhak, who was very quick and well versed in Talmudic wisdom.

"Nor does it lead to piety," replied our uncle. "And what does not lead to Torah leads away from Torah."

This was classical logic and indisputable. Moshe listened, said nothing, and continued his flirtation with the secular. I too was interested in this aspect of life. While my older brother sat in the small room with his fancy ties, writing the sacred words, I delivered his finished parchments to various shops. He called me Der Kleiner Shamus'l (the Little Sexton), a shamus being the caretaker, or sexton, of a synagogue. Racing through the streets of Jerusalem, I always made the deliveries ahead of schedule and sped back with cash in hand. Money was new to my brother, and though later he became a generous man, he was then quite tightfisted. I was constantly bargaining for higher pay.

"Chaim, you're taking all my profits."

"Then get someone else to do your deliveries."

"Do you know the cost of parchment? And ink? Quills don't grow on trees, you know."

"If you want me to be your Shamus'l, you have to pay me more."

"You're squeezing me." He sighed.

In a week, he upped my salary, and I was pleased. However, rather than the few pennies he begrudged me, I wanted some of the delicacies he kept under lock and key. I knew exactly what he was eating—chocolates from Switzerland, dried apricots from Morocco, sweet sparkling waters from Italy—because I shopped in the market for him and carried home his goodies in a cloth bag. Then, because he preferred to eat in private, he closed the door and hooked it from inside. I stood outside his room, drooling, and my nose against the door to catch the wonderful aromas of imported sardines and fragrant cheeses.

One day, after I had made half a dozen deliveries, he sent me to the big market in the Mea Shearim to buy fresh bread and pistachio halvah.

"Chaim, just wait," he said. "You're going to have a meal that will be a totally new experience."

When I returned, there was a strong odor of pepper and garlic in the room. Moshe had unlocked his secret hoard and set the table, cutting open a big paper bag to use as a tablecloth. He had a long, round salami, something I hadn't bought. He must have gotten it from Meshulem Kishkemacher (Meshulem the Sausage Maker), who walked through the Mea Shearim with salamis hanging from a long pole across his shoulder, calling out his wares like the town crier—not that anyone could mistake the strong odors of garlic.

Moshe picked up the salami.

"This is the Tam gan Eden" (the Taste of Paradise). "And you're going to see what heaven is like." With a sharp knife, he took a thin slice off the end and held it out on the point of the blade. "Go ahead. Taste."

I took the slice, quickly said the required blessing, and popped it into my mouth.

"Good, eh?"

More than good, it was wonderful, sweet and strong at the same time, soft and chewy.

We sat and ate dried apricots and halvah, sardines drenched in olive oil, and the Tam gan Eden, washing everything down with glasses of sparkling soda water.

"Well, Chaim," Moshe asked after every morsel, "what do you say? Delicious, eh?"

Rather than another raise, this was my bonus.

*

My brother brought the outside world into our house.

We had little entertainment in our lives. Chess and checkers were the only games played in Batei Warsaw and probably in the entire Hasidic community. Cards were forbidden, gambling unheard of. Secular books were not found in anyone's house, and of course, there was no radio or television.

Moshe was a good chess player. He belonged to a chess club, and every Saturday afternoon, after services, the members gathered in some-one's home and spent the rest of the day and sometimes the night over the board. Our parents didn't like it, because Moshe often missed the Sabbath farewell ceremony in our synagogue in the evening.

One Saturday night, he was out much later than usual, and our father, concerned, went searching. At the house where the club had supposedly met, our father discovered, that everyone had gone instead to see a Purim play. Based on the book of Esther, which tells how the Jews of Persia were saved from the evil Haman, the drama was per-formed at one of the more modern synagogues to a full house. Such entertainments were rare in the Orthodox community.

My father and mother were disturbed.

Moshe, knowing he had transgressed, slept away that night.

My father made inquiries. Much to his relief, he learned Hasidic men, with earlocks and beards, had played all the roles, including, I assumed, Esther, who must have appeared a strange creature. Still, it was a dangerous departure from tradition and decorum to attend a play, regardless of its religious content. It smacked too much of idolatry. One thing always leading to another, inevitably the actors would soon playing Abraham, Isaac, and Jacob. Then Moses and maybe even, forbid the thought, God. That would be a desecration most sinful. It blurred the lines between the human and divine. People would associate the actor with the role and assume God was, in some form, a man. Assigning human traits to God would corrupt the idea of the Supreme Being, whose attributes were so beyond our grasp that we referred to him, it, or her as Ha Shem (the Name), ineffable, unutterable, and unknowable in its unimaginable magnificence.

God, of course, would not be diminished; it would be humanity that lost.

At any rate, Moshe didn't come home for three days, by which time my father and mother welcomed him with open arms.

That taught me a lesson: not all problems have to be solved immediately, and sometimes, but not always, a little extra time changes everyone's perspective.

Moshe continued his scribe work, but seeing how lucrative holy writing was, many men took up the trade. The competition undercut the value of the product, and his parchment prosperity was over.

Moshe sold his equipment and his route and, casting about for another profession, he decided to try his hand, literally, at becoming a shochet, a ritual slaughterer. This was a highly respected and well-paying job in the Jewish community. Certification required knowledge and experience. For the theory, Moshe went to my father and one of our uncles, both of whom taught him the halachah of kashruth, the kosher laws. He learned the basic principles of the slaughtering trade: animals had to be clean and free of disease, and glatt, smooth, meaning free of lesions; the creature had to be killed quickly and in a way that it lost consciousness quickly, thus minimizing pain and suffering; knives, therefore, had to be extremely sharp and without nicks.

To get his license, Moshe had to have worked in a slaughterhouse. This was more a stumbling block than he had anticipated; the Jewish community in Jerusalem was still, after the war, too impoverished, and neither of the slaughterhouses for cows, goats and sheep, would take my brother as an apprentice. Poultry, however, was in demand, so Moshe had to train on chickens, pigeons, and the occasional duck.

Meanwhile, matchmakers were banging on our door.

Our parents weren't in any rush. A young man like Moshe—handsome, healthy, industrious, and from a pious Hasidic family—was a good catch. True, he wasn't frum, ultra Orthodox, but our family's reputation was more than sufficient. I heard my parents talking between themselves; Moshe would command a good dowry.

At the end of his eighteenth year, Moshe became engaged. Dvorah Schwartz was the oldest of seven sisters and the first, therefore, to wed. Dvorah's family was wealthy, but after the other six sisters were matched the family wouldn't be as rich, so my brother was lucky to get in on the ground floor, so to speak. The wedding was held in the bride's home, as was customary. It began Friday afternoon and was to continue for seven days, but early Saturday morning the grandmother of the bride died unexpectedly. Though life is always favored, in this case, death took precedence; the ceremony went ahead, but the celebrations were canceled so that the burial and shivah could be given their proper due.

It was not an auspicious beginning.

Unable to afford an apartment of their own, Moshe and his wife moved into Dvorah's parents' home in the Old City. It was a small apartment, and they had to share it with Dvorah's six sisters. Having developed a taste for commerce, Moshe used the dowry money to open a fabric store. A year later, his wife gave birth to a boy, whom they named Shevach. At about that time, my oldest sister, Chaya Sara, and her husband, moved out of our grandmother's apartment to Batei Hungary, and seizing the opportunity, Moshe convinced his wife to leave her parents and six sisters in the Old City and move in with our grandmother.

During the war, there had been no new home construction, and now, as the business of marriage and childbirth picked up, people were forced to share small apartments with their relatives. These intergenerational arrangements did have a positive aspect, and from an early age, people learned social skills and perfected the art of close living. However, those skills took one only so far. Space was minimal, privacy was unheard of, and the tensions proved many and deep. Patience and compromise were encouraged, but personality clashes were inevitable, and power struggles between children and their parents and in-laws were constant. There was a great deal of moving around from one relative to another in search of peace or, at the least, less strife.

More, primitive conditions made our lives difficult. Without indoor plumbing of any sort, household chores were time consuming and strenuous. Women spent most of their day in manual labor. Without any privacy, opportunities for intimacy, whether emotional or physical, were few and far between. Sexual activity was primarily reproductive in purpose, and erotic exploration was minimal. Not that sex was immoral or to be avoided; Judaism is not prudish. Indeed, the Talmud is quite straightforward about a man's sexual duties toward his wife and gives guidelines as to the frequency of intercourse expected by men in different vocations. Thus, a laborer or a camel driver, whose job requires hard physical labor, is not required to have relations with his wife as often as a scholar, whose sedentary lifestyle leaves him with greater reserves of energy, which may be called upon by the wife for her satisfaction.

At any rate, my brother was able to escape the crowded conditions of his wife's household for the relative spaciousness of my grandmother's tiny apartment, and my grandmother was eager to have a grandchild, especially Moshe, come live with her.

*

My life in Jerusalem went on as before.

During the war, I had continued my studies, however sporadically, in the Talmud Torah in the Mea Shearim. I was always a good student and was one of the few boys my age studying the Gemara, which is one of the bodies of commentary, among others, that comprise the Talmud. I attended classes six days a week and two hours on the Sabbath. Ironically, the day of rest was my busiest day. I was in shul, synagogue, until noon, then raced home for our weekly feast of noodle pudding; chopped eggs with onions; cholent, a beef stew that simmered from Friday afternoon until noon on Shabbos; and tzimmes, a sweet carrot and potato compote. Then I hastened back to school for a two-hour lesson; went home to study again with my father; and returned yet again to the shul with him and my other brother, Moshe, for the second service in the late afternoon. Incidentally, the word for Saturday, *Sabbath*, has two slightly different Hebrew forms: *Shabbos*, the Ashkenazi pronunciation, or *Shabbat*, the Modern Hebrew.

My father and I were a good match; he was eager to teach, and I was ready to learn. He was a gifted teacher. He spoke plainly, did not dramatize or use elaborate explanations, and was patient. I can't remember him ever showing irritation or impatience if I failed to grasp a complicated point of Talmudic interpretation, and he treated my every question, no matter how foolish, worthy of a thoughtful answer. After our midday Shabbos meal, he and I sat at the table and went over my Gemara lesson for the coming week. I sat on his right, my mother his left, both of us pressed close against him and concentrating on the book between us.

One of the disappointments of my childhood was my bar mitzvah. I was born on the fourteenth day of the month of Nisan, the day before Passover, when everyone is busy with holiday preparations. Though we don't fuss over birthdays, a bar mitzvah merits a display of some sort, but my coming of age was anticlimactic. After the morning service, during which I chanted a portion of the Torah and gave a little lecture on a point of religious law, there was barely enough time to serve cake and wine before everyone rushed home to burn the hametz, leavened bread, the final act in the Passover cleansing.

After the war, I resumed my studies. My school had frequent visitors from America, men and women who had migrated to the United States from Europe, and now wanted to see the land of their dreams and the golden city of Jerusalem. They wanted to visit a Talmud Torah that reminded them of the schools of their youth in Eastern Europe. They sat in our classrooms, had tea with our teachers, and told us about their own childhoods. Since our school depended in large part upon their generosity, we made the Americans feel especially welcome.

One day our rosh, or principal, came to our classroom. A rich visitor was coming from South Africa the next day, he told us, and he wanted our class to make a special effort. We immediately closed our books and swept the classroom and washed the windows.

After our rebbe inspected our work, he gave us more instructions.

"Wear your Shabbos clothes, put on whatever shoes you have, and remember, be on your best behavior."

The next day, Der Afrikaner arrived on schedule. Born in Jerusalem, he had attended our school as a child, and now, returning as a wealthy middle-aged man, he went from room to room, looking for memories. I was in Reb Chaim's class, and it was exciting to see the Afrikaner walk in and recognize my rebbe. They hugged each other and talked quietly in front of us. We could see their lips move but could not hear their words. Then Der Afrikaner sat on a rear bench and listened to the lesson. When I looked, tears were streaming down his cheeks.

Before he left the class, he gave each student a silver coin, a South African half dollar, and then turned to our rebbe.

"Reb Chaim, I would like you to select your four best students, the very best. I want them to visit me in my hotel tomorrow morning." He smiled. "For a very special treat."

He left, and our rebbe stood in front of the class and looked us up and down. To my great surprise, Reb Chaim chose me as one of the four.

My parents were happy for me, and that night, after polishing my shoes, I got into bed. I couldn't sleep. I rose at first light, polished my shoes again, and put on my long Shabbos caftan. Similarly attired, the other three lucky students met me at the door of our school, and the four us walked at full speed to the Hotel Amdurski. The weather, unfortunately, was not cooperating, and a driving rain lashed our faces with sharp, cold needles. We arrived at the Amdurski completely drenched. But, for the first time in my life, I was about to enter a real hotel. We were shy and respectful, and the porters, expecting us, took us into a large room. We walked across the thick green carpet with water squishing from our shoes. At a long, narrow table, we sat without moving a muscle or saying a word. The thick green carpet was slowly darkening with the water dripping from our clothing. A beautiful kerosene lamp hung from the ceiling and spread a golden light. After a short wait, Der Afrikaner entered and beamed at us.

"*Meine yungele buchers!*" (My young students!).

He took the chair at the head of the table and signaled the waiters. It was the third day of Hanukkah, and the waiters rolled in tables laden with holiday latkes, cake, and sweet drinks. We four young scholars wanted to make pigs of ourselves, but the awe-inspiring surroundings restrained us, and we picked at the treats. Our Afrikaner host, smiling at our excessive good manners, exhorted us in Yiddish.

"Go on, *kindele*" (children). "Eat as much as you want! I'm not taking it back with me!"

We looked at each other and then started grabbing and stuffing ourselves like starving animals. The Afrikaner encouraged us with smiles and full eyes. He saw himself in us, a young, poor Jewish boy studying Talmud. And now here he was, a rich old man from South Africa, home again. When we finished licking our fingers, he told us to go to a small table in the corner of the room. My shoes pinching, I crossed the thick carpet with awkward steps. On the table were four small plates covered with snow-white napkins.

We stood around the table in silence.

"Are you ready, kindele?"

We said nothing.

"Now, one at a time," Der Afrikaner told us, wanting to savor our reactions. "Lift the napkin from the plate in front of you."

I went first.

I stared in wonder.

On my plate was a pocket watch attached to a silver chain.

I couldn't believe it.

"The watches are made of silver, and they come from America."

I was afraid to pick it up.

"Take it. It's a Hanukkah gift to the four best students in my rebbe's class."

Never had I dreamed of such a Hanukkah gift!

I had never studied geography, and I had no idea where South Africa was, and now there I was, holding a beautiful, expensive watch from Der Afrikaner.

I had an overwhelming impulse to hug the rich, old man, for I knew that was what he wanted, and then I immediately had a second impulse to run out of the Amdurski Hotel to show off my watch to everyone. The old Afrikaner was crying, and I did neither; I only stood still and stared at the beautiful silver watch in my hand.

By the next day, all of Batei Warsaw, and half of Jerusalem, knew about the rich Afrikaner's generosity. Our neighbors came by to see my silver pocket watch. For a week, I couldn't walk on the street without a kibitzer demanding, "Hey, Chaim, the exact time, please!"

The watch was beautiful, and I was going to keep it forever, but in my wanderings over the years it managed somehow to get left behind in one of my many furnished rooms in America. But the lesson of that watch remained with me forever. I had not thought of myself as being particularly bright, but I realized I'd been underestimating myself. I had thought of myself as quiet and unappreciated, but others had recognized my skills and intelligence. Henceforth, I saw myself in a much different, brighter light. After the first week, I left the precious watch at home but carried its meaning with me all the time, and returning to school with more confidence, I soon became one of the best students in the entire yeshiva.

CHAPTER 31

Jerusalem is built on the top of the Judean Ridge, a series of low mountains that run from the Dead Sea north to the Jezreel Valley. Jerusalem's summers are mild, except when the hamsin blows in from the western desert and drives the temperature into the high nineties. This doesn't happen often, but when it does, we complain unendingly about the unusual heat and humidity and retreat inside our cool stone houses. The winter is short and mild, with infrequent rains, and seldom does the temperature fall below freezing. Yet the cold season is unpleasant, for the thick stonewalls of Batei Warsaw do not retain warmth, nor are their cold stone floors kind to our bare feet. Snow is an exception, and until the winter of 1921, not a single snowflake had fallen on my head since my birth fourteen years earlier.

The snow began falling Monday morning and continued into the night, and I woke to a strange and beautiful sight. The city was painted white. Fascinated, I stood upon our roof in the falling snow and watched Jerusalem disappear hour by hour under a curtain of crystals. By night, however, as the snow showed no sign of stopping, I was terrified.

In the morning, with the snow still falling, our yard was filled with two feet of heavy, soft, cold snow. We had to push hard on the door to open it, and once outside, walls of white imprisoned us. The streets of Batei Warsaw were cold white mountains. We had no shovels, boots, gloves, scarves, or winter clothing. Accustomed to running barefoot, and not about to wear my Shabbos shoes, I was unable to leave the house.

Our father was amused, likening our plight to the people of ancient Jericho, who were "straightly shut up; none went out, none came in." By evening of the second day, however, with the snow still falling, he was no longer smiling.

Having lived all our lives without refrigeration, no one had food supplies beyond a day or two, and with the streets impassable, we suddenly had nothing to eat. Horse carts got stuck, and donkeys refused to step into the cold snow. With heroic effort, my mother slogged her way to the Mea Shearim. She returned after an hour, wet, cold, exhausted, and empty-handed.

"*Nicht,*" she said, "*und gornicht*" (Nothing with nothing).

We were suddenly threatened, as in the war, with hunger, but now our suffering was at the hands of heaven. On Tuesday night, with the snow still falling in thick white flakes, a public kitchen was opened in the Mea Shearim Talmud Torah. However, no one would brave the high snowdrifts. My father volunteered as a food distributor and, carrying two large pails of steaming soup and a half dozen loaves of bread in a sack on his back, was wrapped in so many layers of clothing and blankets that he resembled a fat white dybbuk.

By early Wednesday morning, the roofs of Jerusalem began caving in. Both my grandmothers had to be evacuated when their roofs collapsed. In Grandmother Nechama's house were three visitors from Hebron, while in Grandmother Esther's, my sister, her husband, and their new baby had to be evacuated. The eight refugees trudged through the drifts to our house, and by Wednesday night, we had seventeen assorted adults, children, and infants camping out in our small three-room apartment. Every item of furniture—tables, chairs, doors, and dresser drawers—was converted into some kind of sleeping device. It was impossible to use the public toilet on the hill, so that complicated things further.

So there we were, a small army of people in a tiny house, cold, wet, and hungry.

My mother stood in the large room and clapped her hands for attention.

We looked at her.

"I'm going to tell you this once and only once: no one is to waste their breath complaining; it won't do any good."

We said nothing.

By late Wednesday night, the snow began to taper off. Except for Moshe and me, everyone else had fallen into a fitful sleep, and our house was a symphony of cacophonous snoring. I lay awake, counting the chimes of our wall clock. Just after two in the morning, as I was about to doze off, there was a timid but distinct knock on our door. I sat bolt upright. Moshe jumped to his feet. We heard another knock, just as timid but distinct.

My father stepped over the sleeping bodies.

"Who is it?"

"It's us." We could barely hear the low, frightened voice.

"Who's us?"

"Us—the orphans."

My father opened the door, and there stood my cousins from the orphanage, Yitzhak and Moshe Aaron, wrapped from the crowns of their heads to the bottoms of their soles in assorted shmatas. It had taken them three hours to walk from the orphanage near the Russian compound to our house in Batei Warsaw. They stood in the door, their rags covered with snow and ice, half frozen and trembling, unable to move. My father and Moshe pulled them inside.

"We were lonely," said Cousin Yitzhak, reviving in the relative warmth. Moshe Aaron was shy and let his brother do the talking. "And there was no food left."

My mother, half asleep, pushed aside two sleeping bodies for the orphans.

In the morning, at last, the sun was shining, and a warm wind was blowing. I went out into our yard, climbed up the kitchen wall and onto our roof, and was greeted with the sight of Jerusalem blinking and shimmering in the morning sun—a wonderful city of sparkling white. Within an hour, Batei Warsaw came back to life. People came out of their houses like animals leaving their dens. By midmorning, British soldiers with shovels and brooms had opened narrow paths in the snow. My parents went to the free kitchen in the Mea Shearim and brought back soup and bread. Moshe and our little brother Netanel, our cousins, and I went out and had a snowball fight, the first and only one of our lives. Without shoes and gloves, and with no knowledge of snowball production or fighting tactics, the experience was a disappointment.

By afternoon, with the bright sun and warm winds, the snow was melting fast. Water ran off roofs and down the alleys—first in drips, then in trickles, and soon in a steady stream. I was on our roof with Cousin Yitzhak, when I heard a familiar and dangerous sound. Roaring down the big hill in front of our house was a wild river. Below in the courtyard, people were shouting and running as the torrent poured through the gates of Batei Warsaw. My cousin and I climbed down and got inside just as the water swept into our front yard.

So there we were, trapped again.

The water was lapping at our front door.

"We are in Noah's ark," said my cousin Yitzhak.

My father laughed. "Except that our ark is fast to the earth."

"And we don't have any animals," said my little brother Netanel.

"I'm hungry," said my other cousin.

We all were. My father rolled up his pants; my mother wrapped pillowcases around her shoes; and stepping out bravely into the rushing waters, made another trip to the free kitchen. In the house, my two grandmothers began complaining of the cold and damp. Soon the two babies were crying. My cousins whined about being bored and started punching and kicking each other. Covering every inch of the floor were our makeshift beds and blankets and the clothing we had wrapped ourselves in. My brother Moshe and my two uncles tried to impose some order, telling everyone to be quiet and clean up the house, but the complaining, crying, and fighting continued. My parents returned, but they were empty-handed; the kitchen had run out of food. By late afternoon, confined to the house, hungry and dirty, we were all fed up with each other.

Desperate, my father went out again, and very soon came back with three violins that had been stored in my grandmother Nechama's house.

"Here," he said, handing my two uncles and my older cousin the fiddles. "Play and sing."

Then he and my mother left again on a search for food, and we sang songs while my uncles played the violins.

Suddenly, my cousin Moshe Aaron began to sob, and we stopped singing.

"I'm hungry," he wailed.

I had no sympathy whatsoever; hunger was a familiar state of being in my life.

"We're all hungry," I said, "so don't complain."

"I'm hungry!"

"Too bad. Just be quiet."

His brother, Cousin Yitzhak, looked at me with slitted eyes. "Where does Aunt Reizel hide the jam?"

"There's no jam in the house," I said.

"Come on. Where does Aunt Reizel hide the jam? I know you know."

Moshe and I did know, but we didn't say a word, or the two jars of apricot jam would vanish in seconds.

"I'm hungry!"

"So what?" I said.

"Where's the jam, Chaim? Tell me."

"I'm not going to."

"Tell me."

Before I could respond, my uncle Shneior spoke. "Everyone, be quiet."

He had a soft, gentle voice that got people's attention. He turned to my cousins.

"In the orphanage home, they sp-spoil you. They f-f-feed you three big meals a day—eggs, f-fish, s-soup, meat, cake." His mild stammer was a result of wartime typhus. "Here at Aunt Reizel's h-house, there's l-less. If y-you don't like it here, very well. Y-you may go back t-to the orphanage right now. We aren't forcing y-you to stay. Remember that."

There was a long pause, and then my cousin took a deep breath and let out a long wail.

Uncle Shneior tried again. "T-think of the A-Arab shepherd and his flock of sheep and g-goats. W-where are they now in this storm? Aren't y-you better off?"

An empty stomach isn't filled with arguments, and my cousin continued wailing.

Soon the two babies joined in, while from the small back room came my grandmothers' deep, rumbling snores.

By the late evening, however, as the sun warmed the hills, the snow disappeared and the waters subsided, our refugees gathered their belongings and melted out of our house. By afternoon of the next day, the roofs of our grandmothers' houses had been repaired, and they too were able to return home.

Chapter 32

Then my father went to America—not by choice, however; he had to.

Now that my oldest sister and older brother had been successfully matched, my parents turned their attention to my two other sisters. Given our family's piety and scholarship, their husbands would have to be from an observant Hasidic family.

However, with every boatload of secular Jews arriving in Palestine, this sort of boy was a rare and expensive commodity. Few yeshiva boys had any marketable skills, nor did they have an inclination to acquire any. But they all expected to marry a beautiful, rich young woman whose parents would pay for a lavish wedding, find an apartment for them, fill it with nice furniture, and then support him and whatever children followed with a few years of kest, the monthly stipend allowing him to study untroubled by financial concerns.

My parents' resources would not cover even a fraction of such a dowry. The windfall profits of our early postwar restaurant business were gone. There were nine in our family, and my grandparents and various cousins, aunts, and uncles, received financial assistance from my parents. Even when we had our fabric store in the Old City, we were just meeting expenses, and now our finances were at a low point.

Yehoved and Hinda Dvorah could have found quick and inexpensive matches with non-Hasidic boys who would have paid a reverse dowry to marry into our family. The matchmakers proposed a few such shidduchs, but my mother and father categorically rejected them. Such a marriage would have been a sad break in our long and honorable Hasidic tradition.

My parents' financial quandary was not uncommon in the Orthodox community, and the war and its aftermath only deepened the problem. Not only were there fewer Hasidic boys, but also, the donations from Europe that helped defray the dowry costs had dried up. From the little I read, I knew that Europe was sinking into an economic depression. Some families, desperate to marry their daughters, borrowed large sums at high rates and spent the rest of their lives in debt. Other families got money from relatives in America. Some fathers did the next best thing: they went to America themselves to work as collectors. Earning much more than they could in Jerusalem, they usually stayed two years, sending money home every month. Some never returned and instead brought their families across the ocean to the golden shore.

However, we knew our father would never leave Eretz Israel, the center of his world, much less Jerusalem, not even for a brief sojourn in America. So we were all astonished, even our mother, when one day at supper, he told us he was going to the United States.

We were so astonished that none of us took him seriously.

Moshe even kidded him, which only Moshe could get away with. "In America, Abba, you'll have to wear one of my ties."

That was a funny image, our father with one of my brother's fancy silk neckties, but it seemed his trip to exotic Alexandria had given him a taste for travel, so when he told us he had already made arrangements to go to America as a collector for the Chai Olam Yeshiva—all expenses paid, plus a salary—we knew he meant business.

A month later, on a Friday morning in August 1925, my father sailed for America.

The day before I had gone with him, as I always did, to daven (pray) in the Ohel Shmuel synagogue. From there, we went to the house of his mother, my grandmother Esther. He had kept the news a secret, and she almost collapsed when he told her he was leaving for America.

"When?"

"Tomorrow morning," he told her.

She burst into tears and clutched at his sleeve. "No, no! *Mein kleiner kinder*" (my little boy). "Don't leave! Don't leave!"

He tried to explain why he had to go and assure her he would return, but she kept telling him not to go, and, finally, we left grandmother in her chair, weeping.

Our family and friends gathered for a farewell party, and my mother served her special dishes, the tastes of which she hoped my father would carry with him during his sojourn in America. A bus was waiting to take our father to Jaffa, from where his boat was to sail early the next morning. I stayed behind while my mother and Moshe, wishing to see my father off properly, got on the bus. We waved until the bus disappeared on Mea Shearim Road.

They returned the next day, both of them quiet. In the evening, I took my young brother Netanel to the Mea Shearim synagogue for Sabbath services, as my father had taken me. Many of the congregants asked about my father, and I gave them the basic facts. When I returned home that night with my brother, it was clear that I, not my older brother, Moshe, who was in the middle of yet another of his many career changes, would have to take over for my father. I was eighteen years old.

That Friday night, I sat upright in my chair, held my wine goblet in my right hand, and recited the Kiddush, the sanctification. I led the table in singing the ancient melodies, just as my father had done. Between courses, I read from his sofer and tried to engage my brothers and sisters in conversation about Jewish law and tradition, as my father had done.

Supper over, we went to bed, thinking our own thoughts about what had come to pass.

My father's chair at the head of the table sat vacant for seven years. I missed him immensely.

He and I were closer than any of my brothers and sisters, and we had spent much time praying together in synagogue and studying at our table. We had sat side by side, looking at the book between us, our fingers sometimes touching on the soft, worn page. He often told me he hoped I would become an educated man. I knew he meant that he wanted me to be knowledgeable not just in religion but also in secular areas.

Before leaving for America, he had helped me gain admission to the Yeshiva Torah Emet, an academy run by the Lubavitchers. First, they had given me a series of tests and interviews. Apparently, I met their high standards, for just before my father left, I was admitted to their program. This was a singular distinction for someone barely a teenager, and gave me much prestige. I was to begin my new academic career in six months.

The Lubavitcher yeshiva was located in the Mea Shearim, a short distance from our house, and I looked forward to the day when I would enter its doors, as did my mother. Her little fabric store in our back room was not doing well, and the monthly stipend the Lubavitchers promised me would go a long way toward improving our family finances.

CHAPTER 33

Letters—my mother called them a paper bridge.

Ten long weeks passed before we received my father's first letter from America. We had expected the long delay, for the voyage itself took five weeks, but it seemed an eternity.

My father wrote in Hebrew, a mark of his liberalism and education, and when I read his letters to my mother, I translated them into Yiddish as I went along. I had to repeat them three or four times, without the slightest variation, so that she could commit them to memory. After that, she didn't care what happened to the letters. "The heart," she said, "is the safest place to keep anything."

Reading and translating his letters took some skill. His style was that of Loshen Ha'kodesh, the Holy Tongue, and used the syntax, penmanship, and abbreviations of sacred script. More difficult, however, was composing a reply. As a yeshiva scholar, I could read Hebrew, but strange as it may seem, I had never been taught the written word of any language.

My mother's first letters, therefore, were scribed by her younger brother, my uncle Yisrael Yitzhak. He too used the Holy Tongue, which did not please my mother. It was too fancy, she said. She insisted that her letters be written in Yiddish and in her precise words. This became a big problem. Her brother was an important rabbi and community leader and simply couldn't write three letters a week, the minimum number my mother considered essential for proper communication. He wrote one, and insisted upon the more ornate biblical Hebrew.

After two weeks, my mother gave me a short, sharp lecture.

"You, Chaim, a student in the last year of yeshiva and about to study with the Lubavitchers, should know how to write a simple letter! Look how many words you know in Yiddish! And what is so difficult about it? How much writing do you have to know to write a simple letter? Who taught your father and uncles how to write? And you're smarter than your uncles."

"We didn't learn how to write yet, Imma. That comes next month."

"Next month! Tell them to teach you now."

Uncle Yisrael Yitzhak, looking for an escape route, took me aside.

"A yeshiva student of your caliber should know how to write a letter."

"We haven't learned writing yet."

"Oh, well, that's interesting. Hmm. You really haven't been taught to write?"

"No."

"Well, I see."

"Besides, Imma wants Yiddish."

"Hmm. She wants Daitch?"

He meant Deutsch, or German, as Yiddish was sometimes referred to.

"That's right, Uncle. She wants me to write in German."

Giving this some thought, he was even less sympathetic. "Chaim, what kind of yeshiva student doesn't know how to write a little Daitch?"

"But, Uncle, I told you—we haven't been taught it!"

"Nu, nu, so do it anyway."

Minimizing a problem, or denying that one existed, was standard in Batei Warsaw.

The next month, my class began writing and arithmetic. We learned addition and subtraction and then division and multiplication. I loved multiplication and practiced it a lot in my head. We had four lessons a week in writing. First, we learned to shape the letters by placing tracing paper over a printed sheet of the aleph-bet. Then we copied words and sentences from a stack of newspapers in the library. The papers were old, and I learned some illuminating things about World War I. The next lesson gave us some basic vocabulary, and from there, Reb Chaim exhorted us to construct our own simple sentences.

Standing over my shoulder as I practiced at our table, watching me progress in the literary arts, my mother insisted I be her scribe.

As the Talmud points out, all beginnings are difficult, and indeed, my first attempts were time consuming and frustrating for both my mother and me. She insisted I take her dictation precisely. She knew every word she wanted and would accept no substitutes. Then she changed my style and the order of the words, even when I told her she was incorrect.

"It doesn't matter if it's perfect," she told me, "as long as it comes from the heart."

She wanted my father to hear her voice.

Her letters required three or four drafts before she gave her qualified approval.

"Nu, Chaim, it's good enough. Send it to America."

Just as my father had taught me Gemara and Talmud with repetition and patience, my mother taught me how to write Yiddish with much more of the former than the latter. But I soon learned her style, and the writing went much faster. After the sixth letter, my mother gave me an honor certificate written in florid Hebrew by Uncle Yisrael Yitzhak, certifying me as a Writer of Letters par excellence.

In America, my father lived in New York. He was a boarder in the home of a son of our friend Berrel Heller, the German patriot who had insisted that the Kaiser would beat the British. The son was a slaughterer in a kosher meatpacking company in New York, and he had a big house in Harlem, where my father rented a small room. Every week, we got a letter from America, and upon my return from classes, my mother made me sit, read it to her, take her dictation, address the envelope, and post it immediately.

I bought supplies in the Old City—paper, ink, and an expensive fountain pen. Soon the word of my literary prowess spread throughout Batei Warsaw and the Mea Shearim, and within a month, the women were at our door. Every morning and again in the afternoon, I set up shop at the desk in the back room, where Moshe had produced his holy parchments, and transcribed the women's hearts and problems onto paper. I wrote in either Yiddish or Hebrew and often a pidgin combination of both. I didn't ask for money and even refused offers of payment, but most left a few coins on the table, just enough to cover the cost of my supplies.

The letters were sad and full of questions and uncertainty. Often, their husbands had not written for many months, nor had they sent the money they had promised. America was a big, rich country full of many temptations, and the women feared that their men wouldn't return. They poured their hearts out, often weeping, and there were times when I could not make out their words, but I wrote what was in their tears. I learned about love, marriage, fear, and jealousy and how difficult the adult world was. I learned how men went forth on adventures and how women stayed home and hoped for their return. They were frightened for themselves and their children, and I tried to comfort them, assuring them their husbands would come home. I don't know if they believed me, but they saw their feelings take shape on the page, and I saw that they believed in the magic of my pen, and for those brief moments, they were reassured.

Never once did my mother or I doubt that my father would return.

*

The houses of Batei Warsaw might have been made of stonewalls, but we were really living in open tents. There were no secrets, big or small. It was often said in Batei Warsaw, "you can count the noodles in my pudding, but I'll count the beans in your soup."

Before my father left for America, not a single shadchan came within knocking distance of our door. The matchmakers knew every family's income to the shekel—or, now, pound sterling—and they knew that my parents could not afford high-class, scholarly Hasidic boys for my sisters Yehoved and Hinda. We were a pious and respected family, but that counted for little when the true count was made. My sisters' good looks might tempt the young men, but a pretty face did not balance an overdrawn bankbook.

My sister Yehoved was especially attractive; even I, her brother—and sometimes family members do not really see their siblings—knew she was unusually lovely. She had big dark eyes, and her mouth was like my brother Moshe's, finely shaped like a bow, but with a woman's cast. Even after I returned to Jerusalem after many years away and she stood before me as an elderly woman, I was struck once again by her beauty.

However, neither her looks nor her pleasant disposition mattered; if our parents couldn't pay the dowry, why waste everyone's time?

After my father had been in America for two months, attitudes changed dramatically. When my mother cashed the first hundred-dollar check drawn against a New York bank, Batei Warsaw knew of the transaction within an hour. When the next month she did the same, the status of the Linder girls rose immediately, and kept rising with each check. A hundred dollars American was the equivalent of twenty pounds British sterling, a small fortune.

"Hey, Chaim," they called to me, "the rich American."

With the matchmakers now banging on our door, Yechevod was soon married.

*

The Lubavitcher yeshiva where I now studied had students of all ages. There were older, more advanced students, a few them already married, a few ordained rabbis. They studied by themselves and came and went as they pleased. I was part of a younger contingent supervised by a rebbe, and we had a strict schedule of classes. We were assigned tables in the auditorium of the Habad Lubavitch Academy, a big, open space filled with rows of movable study tables.

Each table sat four. My table was near the entrance, in the corner close to the big brick stove that warmed us in winter. The front doors were kept open in warm weather, so I also had the cool breezes in summer. I was glad not to be in the crowded center, where a large group of older students were always engaged in noisy, excited argument.

I sat with two other students, an elderly blind man and a young scholar my age. The man we called Saggi Nohoir (Rich in Light), a common euphemism for the blind. Saggi Nohoir was sitting when I arrived in the morning and stayed after I left. He didn't read, of course, but sat still and alert, listening to the voices around him. He and I became good friends. I knew little about his life, but by his demeanor and education I knew that he had been an active, productive man. It was rumored that he was wealthy and had donated large sums to the yeshiva.

The other student at our table was Baruch Ashlagg, already an ordained rabbi and one of the best students in the yeshiva. He came two days a week and stayed only an hour or so. He spoke little to us. His silence was a kind of arrogance, and Saggi Nohoir and I ignored him. Yet there was something dignified about him. Slightly smaller than average height—shorter than I—he appeared tall because he held himself erect and walked with short, quick steps. His wardrobe was Hasidic but better tailored and obviously expensive. His shoes always had a mirror shine. I assumed his father was the well-known Rabbi Yehuda Ashlagg, a prominent rabbi in Warsaw, Poland, who had immigrated to Jerusalem at about the same time as my grandparents. He was a kabbalist, and an established authority among young Hasidim. After I had been at the yeshiva a few months, Baruch Ashlagg did not show for two weeks. I commented on his absence to the Saggi Nohoir, who said he had heard that Baruch Ashlagg had left the yeshiva.

Later that night, walking home with other Habad Lubavitcher students, I ran into my uncle Yisrael Yitzhak on Mea Shearim Road. He was returning from a lecture. We walked together in the dark, my uncle making small talk until he asked, out of the blue, "Well, Chaim, can I trust you with a secret?"

I smiled, for he sometimes called me Chaim Shoisek (Silent Chaim)—not because I wasn't a conversationalist, but because I knew how to keep my mouth shut.

"Of course, Uncle." I had no idea what special tidbit he was about to divulge.

"Nu, Chaim, soon we'll drink a l'chaim" (a toast to life). With God's help, you're going to have a second brother-in-law."

"Oh, well!"

I was surprised. It was impossible to keep such things a secret, especially if it involved my family. The Linder sisters were prime catches. We walked in the dark street while I digested this news. Pleased that my uncle had entrusted me with a genuine revelation, I was annoyed at my mother; I assumed I'd be included in important decisions. But I really had no say in my sisters' marriages. I would hardly have a say in mine.

Uncle Yitzhak continued. "The shidduch is still in preliminary discussion, but he's a very fine young man, so I've heard."

"I assume the match is for Yehoved?"

"Of course." She was older than Hinda and next in line. Uncle Yisrael Yitzhak clicked his tongue. "But it will be very expensive for your parents."

"Does my father know?"

"It just happened a few days ago, so we have to proceed without him."

Again, I was hurt that my mother would sooner confide in her younger brother than in me. "I should correspond with my father and ask his opinion," I said.

"You should, but it will take a few months. And it's best to move quickly with such a catch. We can trust Reizel."

I asked, "Do you know the prospective groom?"

"Not personally, but I know his father, Rabbi Yehuda Ashlagg."

It was a pitch-black night, and my uncle couldn't see the surprise on my face. I thanked him for telling me and then changed the subject. We walked home together, my thoughts in a tumble. *Baruch Ashlagg! Quite a catch.* I wasn't certain I liked him. Perhaps, knowing who I was, he was staying away from our study table.

That night, my mother asked me to send another letter over the paper bridge to America, and I carried my paper, pen, and ink into our big room and sat at our table and took her dictation. In the morning, I brought the letter to the post office in the Old City. In due course, a few months later, with my father's approval, the marriage contract was signed, and my lovely sister Yehoved became engaged to Baruch Ashlagg. My father, a Hasid with a lifelong interest in the kabbalah, sent a formal letter committing to the dowry, including three years of kest, the living allowance that would permit Baruch Ashlagg to continue his studies without interruption.

The wedding was a major event in Jerusalem's Orthodox Hasidic community. There were guests from Europe and America. Yehoved and her husband moved into the Old City, the better to be closer to the center of the universe. Every week, our mother gave them one-pound British sterling, a fairly large sum.

A year after the wedding, with our father still in New York, Yehoved gave birth to a girl, Yehudith (Judith).

It was about that time that the Arabs, angered by British policies they interpreted as pro-Jewish and instigated by their own anti-Jewish agitators, began a series of attacks against the Jewish population of the Old City, and my sister, with her husband and infant, along with many of the residents of the Jewish quarter, had to leave their homes.

It wasn't the first time Arabs had attacked Jews, and it wouldn't be the last.

Chapter 34

For a while after the war, things had been looking up for us.

Earlier in 1916, the British, French, and Russians had signed the Sykes-Picot Agreement, proposing to partition the Middle East into different zones, or spheres, of influence. Palestine was to be administered jointly by the three signatories. The agreement angered the Arabs, for it nullified earlier British promises of Arab independence that they had given when courting Arab support in their war against the Turks.

The Balfour Declaration of 1917 further eroded Arab trust in British commitments. They believed that we had snared the English in a carefully spun web of Jewish power and wealth. Walking barefoot through the cold wet Jerusalem winter and eating my soggy piece of cold bread, with my aunts, uncles, and cousins shivering in rags, I could not imagine us possessing either power or wealth.

On its face, the Balfour Declaration of 1917 was a true miracle. For the first time in two thousand years, redemption seemed possible. Great Britain had declared that "his Majesty's Government views with favor the Establishment in Palestine of a historical home for the Jewish People, and will use their endeavors to facilitate the achievement of this object."

Four years after the armistice, in 1922, the newly created League of Nations approved the terms of the British mandate, entrusting Great Britain to exercise a just and equitable governance over Palestine.

The Jewish communities viewed this as another promising omen and were even more encouraged when the British government sent a Jew, Herbert Samuels, to be the first high commissioner of Palestine.

The day of his arrival was declared a national holiday. We said prayers for him in my synagogue, and many Jewish stores and schools were closed. Classes ended early, and my fellow scholars and I, and the faculty, waved British flags at the high commissioner as he rode through the streets of Jerusalem.

The holiday mood did not last long.

"What does one expect?" the skeptics asked. The mandate, which at first seemed to promise a new era in Palestine, was, said the political realists, an attempt to substitute one imperial power for another. They shook their heads and smiled with rue. We got rid of the Turks only to be burdened with the British, who were more clever. Furthermore, was not the Great War, the socialists pointed out, really a power struggle among old enemies, with Britain, France, Germany, and Turkey killing each other for the right to exploit the rest of the world?

Viewed in this cynical light, the Balfour Declaration was seen by conspiracy theorists to be merely another in a long series of diplomatic ploys whereby the British sought to enlist the aid of the international Jewish order in their fight against the Germans and the Ottoman Turks. Using public statements modified by private understandings based on secret treaties, Great Britain held together an impossible coalition of antagonistic parties. Promises were made in the belief that they would not have to be kept or, if forced to deliver, would be negotiated down.

A close reading of the record will show that British policy was, indeed, driven by conflicting, contradictory views within its own government. Early military reversals at the hands of the Turks convinced the British of the need for concessions to potential Arab allies, and in a series of quiet, delicate negotiations, the British promised the Arabs a sympathetic ear in their struggle for independence. Similar promises were made to Jewish emissaries. There were many in the British government who hated Jews and loved Arabs, and there were many whose hatreds and loves went the other way. Some hated both but placed their bets on who might better serve Britain's interests. Thus, in the first year of the war, the British government, led by the liberal Herbert Asquith, insisted that the Arabs were the key to British success in the region. In 1915, however, the new Tory government of Lloyd George, with his foreign secretary, Arthur James Balfour, took the opposite tack, hoping that a pro-Jewish posture would bring America into the war more quickly. And also keep Russia, wracked by the Bolshevik Revolution, actively fighting against the common enemies, Germany and Turkey.

In addition, Lloyd George, a student of the Bible, believed that the Jews were entitled as a matter of God and scripture to their ancient homeland. The efforts of Theodor Herzl and other Zionists were in part responsible for England's shift. Needless to say, the Arabs denounced the Balfour Declaration as contrary to their interests and which they saw, along with the Sykes-Picot Agreement, as just another British betrayal.

Perfidious Albion, as the British were sometimes called, was up to its old tricks.

The mandate giving Great Britain administrative control over Palestine recognized the geopolitical realties of the postwar world. Without changing the basic structures of colonial imperialism, the Great War had shifted the balance of power. The Ottoman Empire had been destroyed, and the lands of the Middle East were now accessible to the victorious Allies. The invincible Prussian military was humbled at last, and Germany was stripped of its colonies. Czarist Russia was no more, and the Communists were too busy fighting the aristocracy, and themselves, to be a serious threat to Great Britain and France.

While granting the British broad powers in Palestine, the League of Nations recognized the emerging nationalism among the region's peoples. The League's mandate required Great Britain to use its powers "to secure establishment of the Jewish National Home." Further, Britain was exhorted to recognize and work with "an appropriate Jewish Agency" in furtherance of such a home. To that end, timetables were proposed for increased Jewish immigration, with the understanding that "other sections of the population would not be prejudiced."

Neither Britain's Balfour Declaration nor the League's mandate proved to be the generous promise it first seemed. The British were not as eager for a Jewish homeland as they had first indicated, and they offered qualified support, at best, to the Jewish communities of Palestine. High Commissioner Herbert Samuels found it impossible to reconcile the contradictory political aspirations of two diverse populations. The Arabs, unwilling to give legitimacy to Jewish claims, refused to participate in any joint projects.

Indeed, even before Britain began to exercise its mandatory powers, the Arabs, pressing Great Britain to repudiate the Balfour Declaration, took their cause to the streets. With the British occupation forces standing by as neutral observers, the unarmed, unprepared Jewish population soon found themselves at the mercy of an implacable, well-armed foe.

The first organized Arab riots began in the spring of 1920. Previous outbursts of violence were sporadic and predictable. The end of Ramadan, the month-long holiday of daily fasting and nightly feasting, was often marked by angry Muslims spilling from their mosques. Rampaging through the streets of Jerusalem, the mob shouted anti-Jewish epithets, broke a few windows, and delivered a few kicks to any unfortunate Jew caught in the open. We were well aware of the potential for violence and celebrated Ramadan in our own way by closing our shops and staying indoors. Before the war, the Turkish military police had kept the violence under tight control.

The British, either out of incompetence or policy, did not.

Arab hatred of the British was fed by a rabid provocateur by the name of Haj Amin al-Husseini, a charismatic leader who had sided with the Germans in World War I. He expected that a victorious Germany would quickly expel the British from Egypt and Syria, paving the way for eradication of the Jewish presence in all of Palestine. His dream was derailed by Germany's defeat, but his hopes for an exclusive Arab Jerusalem lived on.

In the spring of that year, the three major holidays of Passover, Easter, and Ramadan fell on the same day: April 4, 1920. The streets of Jerusalem were jammed with celebrants and pilgrims. Streaming into Jerusalem from their villages in the surrounding hills, Arabs gathered in the Old City to pray at their mosques. In the late afternoon, with prayers over, they marched en masse to the tomb of Nabu Mussah, the prophet Moses, whose burial place they claim to have identified. This is contrary to the Torah, which explicitly states that Moses was not allowed to enter the Promised Land and that his grave site, at least to Jews, remains unknown. The Arabs gathered at the Jaffa Gate, where local agitators led by Haj Amin al-Husseini, stirred them up with furious denunciations of Jews and Zionists. In his royal residence on Mount Scopus a few miles away, High Commissioner Herbert Samuel received periodic field reports of the situation. Within a short time, the streets around the Jaffa Gate were full of angry, Arab mobs. A squad of British policemen arrived at the gate, but under orders from the military command not to inflame the situation by too prominent a presence, they kept a discreet distance.

In Batei Warsaw, all was quiet. It was the second day of Passover, a day of rest and study. My brother Moshe and his friends were going to Hebron on a three-day vacation to enjoy the cool of the mountains. My brother had hired an Arab driver and was already walking to the Old City to meet the driver with his donkey cart.

I was napping quite pleasantly when one of my cousins burst through our door.

"They're killing Jews!" he shrieked. "They're killing Jews!"

Too frightened to stay, he raced out.

"Moshe!" my mother cried. "He's going to the Jaffa Gate!"

My brother had left ten minutes earlier, but he would walk slowly to keep his fancy clothes neat and clean. There was still time.

"Chaim!"

At my mother's sharp command, I was through the door in a flash and running barefoot out of Batei Warsaw. I raced through the back alleys of the Mea Shearim, lost my skullcap and ran back for it, said a prayer, jammed it in my pocket and ran bareheaded. It was the first time in ten years I was without a head covering but I was running like the wind. I knew Moshe would have to pass the Italian hospital, and I was going to get there ahead of him. I did, but there was no sign of Moshe. I knew my brother—he was walking slowly to keep the dust off his polished shoes. I waited half a minute to catch my breath and then ran to the Old City.

At the new gate, I heard the piercing, wailing shriek of an Arab war cry, and I ran even faster. I should have seen Moshe by now. The cries were louder and mixed with shouts and screams. I think I was crying, but it didn't matter. People, mostly Hasidic Jews, were running in the opposite direction, one or two with blood on their faces, their clothing torn. I was at the Jaffa Gate. A mob of Arab men were holding knives in one hand and shooting rifles in the air with the other. Two Hasidim were dragging a third away from the gate; blood ran down his face.

Everyone was running and screaming, and suddenly I was caught by the wild crowd and carried toward the gate. I tried to turn around, but I was in a wild storm. I pushed and fought, got to the side, and looked around for my brother. An armored car with British soldiers stood just outside the gate, the soldiers sitting there with their guns across their laps.

Behind me a small, sharp explosion went off—I had heard enough gunfire in the war to know what it was—and then there was a terrible silence as everyone, including the Arabs, froze. A voice shouted in Hebrew and two more shots rang out. An Arab fell to the ground. Everybody started running in all directions.

"Chaim!"

I turned and saw my cousin Mendel holding a rifle. He had a blue band on his arm. He was with three men, all with rifles and blue bands.

"I'm looking for my brother!"

"He's not here!" Mendel was breathing hard, his face pale. "Go home, Chaim—now!"

Around the other side of the Jaffa Gate three more men with rifles and blue bands were running toward us—the Jewish Legion. Another shot rang out inside the gate.

The British soldiers leaped from their jeep.

My cousin grabbed me by my shirt and spun me around.

"Chaim, go home!"

He was on one knee, taking aim, and I ran as fast as I could back to Batei Warsaw.

"No Moshe!" I shouted to my mother as I burst into our yard.

"Baruch HaShem. You're safe. Now, put on your yarmulke."

A little later, my father walked in with Moshe.

Moshe and his friends had just gotten into the donkey cart when the riot began, and their Arab driver had thrown a big blanket over them and maneuvered his cart through the mob. My father had found him in the Mea Shearim, in the house of one of his friends.

"Mendel was there." I told them what I had seen.

My father spoke. "Yes, Jabotinsky was there too."

"Good for him," my mother said. "He gave them what they deserved."

"Mendel's in the Jewish Legion," I said.

"It's not called the Jewish Legion anymore." Moshe was undoing his necktie. "Now it's the Haganah."

Haganah means "the protector."

For many years after, the second day of Passover in our house was celebrated as the day my brother was saved by an Arab mule driver.

*

Paradoxically, at a time when many Jews who had been born in Jerusalem were leaving for the United States, others from Western Europe were making their way to Palestine.

These postwar immigrants were different than my grandparents' generation. The Linders and the Reismans had left their homes in Russia and Poland in search of religious fulfillment and had little interest in creating a Jewish national state. They had lived for centuries in the Diaspora, subject to discrimination, humiliation, and murderous pogroms. They yearned to live in Eretz Israel, even if it meant more of the same oppression by the Turks and Arabs, for at least in Jerusalem they were closer to their holy places.

Those who came later were more educated and worldly, professionals and highly skilled workers. Idealists eager to build, their Zionism was not the product of religious fervor but of the passionate desire to create a new national identity. Their notions of what that identity might eventually be were the subject of much heated debate, but they had one driving impulse: a fierce determination to claim their place among the peoples of the world.

They sought not continuity, but a break with the past, for they were embarking upon another voyage—one of self-realization. They wanted to partake of the new millennium, become citizens of a free world. And this was their moment.

Their secularism was frightening to the older immigrants. Fears of assimilation and loss of identity always produced great anxiety in the Orthodox community, and the newcomers to the Holy City seemed determined to destroy their traditional way of life.

The very language became a battleground. The linguistic analysis that modern scholars used as interpretive tools in Bible studies were anathema to the ultra-Orthodox, who believed that the holiness of the Torah could not be parsed into its constituent linguistic parts. To the pious Hasid, Hebrew was the Loshon Ha'kodesh (the Holy Tongue), distinguished from all other languages by virtue of its divine origins. Yiddish, both spoken and written, was the lingua franca in Batei Warsaw and other Hasidic enclaves. Except for the everyday prayers, which they had memorized, many religious Hasidim had no knowledge of Hebrew, nor did they need it, for all religious writings had been transliterated into Yiddish.

The new immigrants detested Yiddish. It was the language of exile, the tongue of oppression. Hebrew was the Holy Tongue but also the voice of a free people, and they insisted on using it anywhere and everywhere.

On this point, as on many others, the Orthodox and secular communities found themselves in smoldering conflict, which burst into open conflagration when the British, in keeping with their mandatory obligations, asked the Jewish communities to form their own governing councils. The councils were given authority on various aspects of civil law governing marriage and divorce, education, burial practices, and the myriad of other activities that are part of an intricate, urban existence. These councils were funded by the British, and were given the authority to distribute the necessary money as they saw fit.

The religious factions were soon fighting tooth and nail over the spoils. Remaining true to their historic customs, the ultra-Orthodox wanted a strict Sabbath observance written into the law; they were against voting rights for women and against competitive sports. They wanted to continue the prohibition against public display of secular art, which, in their eyes, was the first step toward idolatry. The Orthodox were relatively few in Jerusalem, but had considerably more institutional power than the less observant immigrants, and they refused to join any council that seated secular Jews.

Some of the more politically astute and less doctrinaire among the Orthodox searched for compromise, hoping that by joining in common purpose they might slow the drift toward the extreme secularism advocated by antireligious, socialist thinkers who viewed the Russian Revolution as the harbinger of a brave new world. Playing off one faction against another, Britain's high commissioner, Herbert Samuels, employed Britain's time-tested imperial policy of divide and rule. They granted the Orthodox faction the right to organize their own councils in opposition to the secularists, thus assuring constant confrontation, rancor, and ultimate stalemate.

The ultra-Orthodox community, of which my family and I proudly considered ourselves members, was concentrated in the triangle formed by the Mea Shearim, Batei Hungary, and Batei Warsaw. These cauldrons of devout Hasidism produced a great deal of overheated argument without generating much light. One of our neighbors, an extreme religious fanatic, joined with a few of my relatives to publish a pamphlet, which, unfortunately, contained a number of libelous accusations against one of the chief rabbis of Israel, a religious moderate. The chief rabbi sued in high rabbinical court. The charges were defamation and lies, serious offenses in the Jewish code of law, for words are considered to be as powerful as any physical force and, at times, even more injurious. The defendants refused to appear in religious court so were sued in British civil court. They were found guilty of malicious slander and imprisoned for three months. This act of chutzpah on the part of the chief rabbi further inflamed the ultra-Orthodox and led to much bitter, internecine feuding.

On this particular issue, my family was divided down its teeming middle, with aunts, uncles, and cousins choosing sides between the ultra-Orthodox, who would have nothing to do with the secularists, and the moderates, who were convinced the world must be acknowledged and, with diligent and intelligent application, shaped to one's needs.

My father remained publically neutral, using all his temperance and skill to keep both sides of our family on speaking terms. For the most part, he succeeded, though not at all times was the conversation pleasant.

Much to my gratification, he secretly tended toward the moderate.

*

My cousin Mendel, born into a devout Hasidic family, was one of the eager converts to the new way of thinking. He had joined the Jewish Legion, a small army unit commissioned by the British in 1917. The instigating force for the Jewish Legion was a Russian Jew, Zeev Vladimir Jabotinsky, born in Odessa in 1880. After studying law in Italy and Switzerland, Jabotinsky became a journalist for Russian newspapers. The pogroms of the early twentieth century inspired him to take up the Zionist banner, and moving from words to action, he organized paramilitary groups for Jewish self-defense. When war erupted in 1914, he took up his pen again and became a war correspondent on the eastern front in Africa. History had taught him nations had to defend themselves; the Great War was an opportunity to learn how to fight.

Jabotinsky approached the British, whose war efforts at the time were not going well. Welcoming any help they could get, the British created an auxiliary unit of Jewish fighters, but with an eye to the future, Jabotinsky insisted upon a full-status unit with its own command structure and equipment. Out of desperation, the British army finally agreed, and the Jewish Legion came into being. My cousin Mendel was drawn to it immediately. "Give up your books for bullets," they said. "Fight for your life." The Legion fought the Turks at the Jordan River crossings and, with British army units, overran the Ottomans at Es Salt.

The Legion was decommissioned at the end of the war, but growing Arab violence and infamous British neutrality convinced many of the new immigrants, who were trying to establish collective farms, the yishuvs, outside the major cities, that a defense force was necessary. The fighters regrouped, but the British declared the Legion illegal. Jabotinsky and many of his fighters went underground, renaming themselves the Haganah. When Arab violence exploded during Passover in the spring of 1920, Jabotinsky and the Haganah stood at the Jaffa Gate. For his efforts, he was tried by the British and sentenced to fifteen years of hard labor.

"You see, Chaim," said my mother, "the British are different from the Turks. The Turks didn't care who was guilty; they hung both the

Jew and the Arab. But the British are interested in justice. They first have a trial, and then they hang the Jew."

Within a month, however, public demonstrations and international pressure, mostly from the United States, forced the British to free Jabotinsky. In June of that year, the Haganah publically declared themselves the protectors of the Jewish people in Palestine, and my cousin Mendel became an officer and went into hiding.

*

However oppressive their rule, the British were experts at public works, and began construction of a much-needed central sewer system for Jerusalem. The cynics among us—and there were many, though they preferred to call themselves realists—suggested this was a bad sign, for it meant the British intended to stay awhile.

"I tell you, Chaim," one of my uncles told me, "the Englanders don't want to smell their own shit."

The project was ambitious, ringing the Old City of Jerusalem with a complex system of drainage pipes. Jerusalem is built on rocky hills, so the work was slow and difficult. Soon, without warning, loud dynamite explosions rattled our windows and doors, making everyone jump with thoughts of bombs.

The sewer lines ran alongside Mea Shearim Road, and I passed the workers every day on my travels to and from the Old City. Arab laborers broke the shattered rock with sledgehammers and picks and, the hillside being too steep and dangerous for donkeys, hauled the debris away in small wheelbarrows. They worked twelve hours a day, from sunrise to sunset, six days a week. The British wanted them to work seven, but we insisted that no work be done on the Sabbath, at least not in our neighborhoods, so the workers had one day of rest, even if it was forced.

"Shame on the British," my father said. "They treat them like slaves in Egypt."

The project was financed by taxes collected from the various kolels, but the British contracted the work to rich Arab effendis, who paid their peasant workers subsistence wages and pocketed the rest as baksheesh.

But anything was better than nothing, and as word of employment spread, Arab families flocked into Jerusalem. They slept in tents around the city, and at night I saw their campfires in the fields around Batei Warsaw and smelled their cooking.

The plan was simple and elegant: big sewer pipes circled the Old City, with smaller lines radiating outward like spokes on a wheel. When that phase was finished the Arab workers were fired. The outlying communities had to build their own local systems at their own expense and connect them to the central sewer lines. The kolels hired Jewish workers, who, in anticipation, had already formed a union with a set of demands on wages and conditions.

Early one morning, a small work gang of Sephardic Jews with long dark beards and colorful clothing showed up in front of our house with shovels and picks, and began digging outside our yard. My mother, sympathetic, invited them in for breakfast, expecting them to abide by proper ritual and blessings—washing their hands, sprinkling salt on the bread, and uttering the appropriate blessings over the various foods. However, they jumped on the food without ceremony and, worse, ate without skullcaps and, when finished, left without a single word of the after-dinner blessing.

"What, these are Jewish workers?" She had squandered sympathy on ingrates. "They are fressers!" People *ess*—that is, eat—but animals *fress*. "Never again will they be invited into my house! Never!"

Hearing of these violations, my father shook his head in disappointment.

"You see," he explained to us, "the blessings aren't for God; they're for us. Men are always hungry and thirsty—that is what flesh is. Animals devour their food without thought or ceremony. But we cook and prepare our meal and then sit down and eat. We slow our appetites just a little while we say the blessing, and we become something more than animals. Besides, believe me, the food tastes better if it cools a little."

*

Before our new sewers were put in, the thirty-six apartments in Batei Warsaw had only six public toilets on the hill. Cold, dark, and malodorous, they were unsafe, and the inhabitants were constantly making sarcastic jokes about their neighbors' digestive systems. Now that the main pipes were in place, Kolel Warsaw raised more funds to build private exterior toilets for each and every house in Batei Warsaw

They were wonders.

The little brick bathrooms, with their amazing flushing toilets, were built next to the kitchens in the front yards. Their drainpipes ran underground to the larger sewer pipes in the street. Our new neighbor, Leibush Gladstone, was hired to do the work. The Gladstones had emigrated from Warsaw just after the war, moving into the vacant apartment right next to us. Leibush was a general contractor in partnership with his nephew, Zalman Leib Levi, whose parents had emigrated from Vladislav, Russia, in 1889. The Levis were longtime residents, and had been in Batei Warsaw for more than twenty-five years.

Leibush was a Hasid like us, and I sometimes sat next to him at my study table in our synagogue. He was a tall blond man with broad shoulders and the big, strong hands of a worker. When we sat together, I always kept my hands, those of a child, in my lap. His nephew, Zalman Leib, lived a few houses down from us, next to my uncle Yisrael Yitzhak.

I tell these tales about Zalman Leib Levi because he was destined to play a role in my life much larger and more significant than I could possibly have imagined at the time.

Leibush had taught his nephew, Zalman Leib, construction work, and the two men, the big strong uncle and the smaller but equally strong younger man, labored side by side in our yard. It was summer, and they worked in their shirts and suspenders with sleeves rolled up and skullcaps pinned. Watching them was interesting and somewhat strange; most of my life, I had seen Jews studying and discussing, not digging in the earth, and now these two religious, observant Jews were mixing concrete and laying bricks, their earlocks damp and dark.

I was apprehensive too, for my previous dealings with Zalman Leib had not been as cordial as I would have liked.

Years earlier, when I was full of mischief, my friends and I would climb the roofs and run from house to house, making a nuisance of ourselves. One of our most amusing misdeeds took place during the feast of Sukkoth, when families in Batei Warsaw built a hut, or sukkah, in their yard, usually against one of the stonewalls of their house. It's a mitzvah, a worthy deed, to eat meals in the sukkah and an even greater mitzvah to sleep in it overnight, imitating the ancient Israelites. One of my favorite activities was to sneak along the rooftops with a bucket of water, find a sukkah, and pour water through the roof onto the unsuspecting Hasid. Once or twice, I almost fell off the roof laughing. But we only did it to other Hasidim. We left the Mitnaggedim alone; their sense of humor was not as developed. Once, I poured water—by mistake, I should add—upon the head of Zalman Leib, a Mitnaggedim. Zalman Leib had a quick temper, and he charged out of his sukkah to dispense justice on the miscreant, but, running like a mountain goat across the roofs and through the alleys, I escaped his wrath.

"Shame on you! Shame on you!" he shouted ran after me. "It's a sin to foul a mitzvah!"

But I was laughing too much to care.

He shook his fist at me. "I'll inform your parents and your rebbe!"

Zalman Leib was a Mitnagged, more modern in his outlook than my ultra-Orthodox family. For instance, the Mitnaggedim sent their children to secular schools as well as yeshivas, and were not as strict in their observance—not that they were impious; they simply did not approach religion with the extreme regard for the letter of the law that drives a good Hasid. The Mitnaggedim generally built their synagogues on a grander, more expensive scale. They were more formal too, for unlike my shul, where you sat anywhere you wanted, everyone in a Mitnaggedim synagogue had his assigned seat.

I had a number of confrontations with Zalman Leib, one of them over a tree.

As a child, I was perfectly happy in Batei Warsaw and had no reason to complain, for I knew of no better place, but I must mention a minor, if significant, lack: Batei Warsaw, built on rocky, barren soil, had few trees of any significant size.

There was, however, a tree near Zalman Leib's house—a beautiful eucalyptus tree, tall, green, and fully branched.

It was the pride of Batei Warsaw, and I loved to climb it.

Zalman Leib kept a watchful eye on his beloved eucalyptus tree, chasing away any child who approached. God forbid a single branch be broken or a leaf torn.

It wasn't difficult, however, to climb the tree; I ran along the rooftops until I came to Zalman Leib's house and then took a short leap of about three feet to the low branches, and up I'd go. One day Zalman Leib, hearing my footsteps on his roof, ran out just as I jumped.

"I'll get you!" he shouted, and he rushed up the ladder he kept against his house. Once on the roof, however, he dared not make the leap to the tree. I was out of his reach, sitting comfortably in the high branches.

He shook his finger at me. "I have all day to wait!" he shouted. "All day!" Glaring at me, he crossed his arms and planted his feet. "I warn you—I have all day!"

But I knew he did not; though a Mitnagged, Zalman Leib was very observant, with many ceremonial time constraints. As the afternoon darkened into early evening he threatened me again, demanding that I climb down from his beloved eucalyptus tree, or I would be sorry.

"Don't you have to go to synagogue?" I called to him.

"Don't tell me what I have to do, you little *schneke!*"

"But they need you for a minyan!"

"There will be a minyan without me!" he shouted, angry but beginning to waver. He and I both knew that the Mitnaggedim, unlike the ultra-Orthodox Hasidim who overflowed every synagogue, were sometimes short a man or two.

"Come down, you little schneke!"

"Only after you go to services!"

"Come down now!"

"Go to services! They need you for a minyan!"

"And you, from such a pious home, you have to go to shul too!"

"No I don't. I'm not bar mitzvah!"

"You come down right now!"

"Go to synagogue and doven."

Frankly, I didn't care if I missed evening prayers, but Zalman Leib did, and soon he climbed down and hurried off to the Mitnaggedim synagogue. I shimmied down the tree, leaped to the roof, and ran home.

*

We prayed in the Ohel Shmuel Shul, where my grandfather was president until he died; the Mitnaggedim had the Ohel Yitzhak Synagogue, where Zalman Leib's father, Shmuel Yaakov, was the sexton.

The Mitnaggedim synagogue was a more modern building than our old shul. It was decorated with fine filigree scrollwork and was kept clean and sparkling. Every member had an assigned seat, and young boys were expected to sit with their fathers and be quiet. A leader and a cantor conducted the services. Everyone kept his voice down, the prayers finished on time, and the congregants filed out, leaving the synagogue empty until the next service.

In contrast, my Hasidic shul was devoid of decoration and in constant need of repair. Until we were ten or eleven, we roamed about and sat anywhere we wanted, as did all the congregants. Services were conducted in a free-for-all manner, and often, one, two, or half a dozen men would burst into song, and the rest joined in. If the spirit moved us, the services continued into the night. Almost every day some sort of community or religious event took place after services, and a large assortment of refreshments was served, after which there was a great deal of singing and even more dancing. The singing was important, but it was the dancing that really mattered.

Not that the Mitnaggedim couldn't dance. On one occasion, I saw Zalman Leib dance, and adjusting for my critical Hasidic eye, I have to admit he was a dancer without peer, even when measured against the dancers in my shul, and we had some of the best dancers.

When I talk about dancing, I do not mean ballroom dancing or what happens today. I mean a certain kind of dancing that comes from a pious heart so filled with spirit that the body, bones, muscles, and sinew simply rise up in celebration of the Name.

That time I saw Zalman Leib dance was during a special event.

A wealthy family had donated a new Sofer Torah (Holy Scroll) to the Mitnaggedim synagogue in Batei Warsaw. A new Torah is an expensive and precious item. A scribe works for years with quill, ink, and parchment, laboring night and day with determined fervor. All of Batei Warsaw was following the progress of the scribe, and on the day the Torah was to be completed, a crowd of Mitnaggedim gathered in the Mea Shearim, where the scribe was working. The crowd grew larger and more festive as the day progressed. When the scribe was on last paragraph, the singing began. At last, Zalman Leib's father, Shmuel Yaakov, came to the door of the school with the Torah in his arms. A tremendous shout of joy filled the air. The Torah was wrapped in a beautiful silk mantle decorated with gold, silver, and jewels. The scroll would be carried under a canopy through the streets of Jerusalem to the synagogue of the Mitnaggedim, there to be placed in its permanent dwelling place in the synagogue's ark, never to leave.

All of Mea Shearim and Batei Warsaw were in a holiday mood; the streets were festooned, the stores were closed, and all children had been excused from school. The procession began when Chaim Shishi, the only Orthodox musician in Jerusalem, put his clarinet to his lips and blew the first note of a lilting melody. With Shishi leading, the procession made its way through the streets. A young man carried the Torah under the canopy while Zalman Leib and Shmuel Yaakov Levi, son and father, danced arm in arm upon the stones. We all sang, clapped, and stamped our feet. Shishi played his clarinet as if calling the Messiah. When Shmuel Yaakov tired, as fathers were wont to do, Zalman Leib continued dancing solo, leaping, spinning, and clapping his hands over his head just behind Shishi. The two of them, flute player and joyous dancer, led the procession to the synagogue of the Mitnaggedim.

Everyone, even my father, marveled. Who could have thought that a Mitnagged had such dancing in him?

Zalman Leib danced like David before the ark, like a young boy flying a kite, like a mountain that skipped like a ram. He did not falter upon the steps of the synagogue. He danced the holy scrolls into the synagogue while Shishi played his heart out, and once inside, Zalman

Leib continued dancing in front of the Holy Ark, his body and soul offered in praise of Ha Shem, the Name.

*

I had other encounters with Zalman Leib, one of them over Elijah's chair.

My Hasidic shul was the center of all our community events. One of the happiest of these events is the Brit Milah, the circumcision rite for a male child, which takes place when the infant is eight days old. Legend has it that the prophet Elijah is present at every bris, no matter where it takes place, though, of course, Jerusalem is his favorite place. As an honored guest, and in order to add some realism to the miracle of his appearance, Elijah has a special chair, which doubles as the chair in which the sandek—the male relative honored to hold the infant boy while the mohel performs the circumcision—sits.

My Ohel Shmuel Shul had bought an expensive, beautiful chair with a back and seat fully upholstered in the finest silk and velvet and decorated with needlework and semiprecious stones. We called the chair, appropriately, Elijah's Chair.

In order to maintain the chair's special status, keep it clean, and be certain that tired Hasidim did not sneak a quick nap on its comfortable velvet cushions, we kept it in the house of Zalman Leib Levi. A Mitnagged and therefore a staunch opponent of our more doctrinaire ways, Zalman Leib was respected as an honest, pious man, and he was pleased to be given the opportunity to perform a mitzvah of this sort. He also lived close by. Whenever there was a bris at our shul, two lucky congregants would be given the honor of fetching the chair from the house of Zalman Leib, and two other lucky Hasidim would take it back when the ceremony and festivities were over,

One day a bris was scheduled to take place after morning prayers, and my friend Baruch, who had helped me cut up the Englanders' telephone wires, and I were given the honor of bringing the chair to our shul.

We went quickly, and importantly, to the house of Zalman Leib

Levi. Entering, we found him, to our shock, sleeping in Elijah's Chair. There he lounged on the soft cushion, his legs stretched before him, chin on his chest and hands laced across his stomach, snoring away.

We pondered. We were two young boys. It was contrary to all etiquette to wake an elder from his sleep, even from a nap, which was considered one of life's true blessings.

Our needs, however, were pressing, and after Baruch and I discussed the situation in tense whispers, I approached the chair with measured steps.

"Reb Zalman Leib." I spoke in soft, respectful tones. "Reb Zalman Leib."

Reb Zalman Leib continued to snore.

Baruch whispered, "Talk louder."

"Reb Zalman Leib! Reb Zalman Leib!"

After a quick snort and a hand brushing at the disturbance, the snoring resumed.

Time being of the essence and needing to fulfill our holy mission, Baruch and I began to panic. Zalman Leib had a reputation for a temper.

"Okay, here goes," said Baruch. He stood on the other side of the chair, and on the count of three, we each shouted into Zalman Leib's ear.

"We must have the chair! We must have the chair!"

Zalman Leib shot up.

We leaped back.

"What! What?" Confused and angry, he looked around wildly. "You schnekes! How dare you disturb my sleep? Get out of here this instant!"

Zalman Leib jumped out of the chair, but I moved fast and his hand slapped empty air.

We stood just outside his door and turned to face him.

"We're not schnekes!" Baruch yelled. "A bris is taking place in the shul right now. The prophet Elijah and a hundred Hasidim are waiting!"

I yelled, "My uncle Yisrael Yitzhak is the gabbai of our shul! The chair belongs to him!"

Now fully awake, Zalman Leib immediately calmed down and apologized to us, even though we were children.

"Come. I will help you," he said, and the three of us carried the beautifully upholstered heavy chair to the door of my shul. Zalman Leib, however, refrained from entering, as any respectful Mitnagged would.

All these encounters with Zalman Leib Levi happened when I was a mere boy, yet still, it was with some nervousness that I greeted Zalman Leib and his uncle when my mother invited them in for breakfast the day they began building the toilet in our front yard. I said hello and then went about my business, realizing quickly that Zalman Leib had no idea I was the boy who had poured water on his head while he slept in his sukkah and wakened him from his much-needed nap. After all, I was now a young teenager, and my appearance was much altered, as were my voice and manner.

Soon, as we were both conversationalists, Zalman Leib and I were talking as I watched him and his uncle mix mortar and lay bricks. It was unusual for a man such as Zalman Leib Levi to engage in manual labor of this kind, but he had a large and growing family of many daughters and was consequently in need of money and, therefore, took whatever job he could find.

Watching Zalman Leib and his uncle, it was obvious that bricklaying wasn't difficult. I could do it myself. In fact, I knew I could build my mother her new brick stove for Passover. We always demolished the old stove, which had been used for cooking non-Passover foods all year and was contaminated with leavened bread, and built a completely new one for the holiday. While Zalman Leib and his uncle took a lunch break, I went into our outdoor kitchen and counted the bricks. Mulling how to phrase my request, I finally got the courage to approach them, deciding I would ask the uncle.

"Leibush Gladstone," I asked, "could I have some bricks from your stack in our yard?"

He smiled, didn't say a word, and continued mixing mortar.

"I think I need thirty-two bricks, if that's all right."

Zalman Leib, a brick in one hand and a trowel in the other, looked at me. "Why does a yeshiva bucher need bricks?"

"I'll save the bricks until Pesach and then build a new stove."

Zalman Leib gave me a stern look. "I don't understand. You, a Hasidic boy, want your mother to accept stolen bricks to build a kosher stove for Passover?"

"But I'm not stealing the bricks. I'm asking you to give them to me."

"That's true." Zalman Leib, his temper rising, waved his trowel at me. "You yourself aren't stealing them, but the bricks don't belong to me. They were bought by the kolel to build these toilets, and you're asking me to steal them for you instead of doing it yourself!"

Feeling my face getting red, I walked away. He was right. I, a yeshiva student studying Torah and Talmud, the foundation of all ethical behavior, should have known better. I was embarrassed also for what I had done to my father and mother, for I was sure Zalman Leib was wondering what sort of parents had raised a son with such a larcenous heart. In Jewish ethics, persuading someone else to commit a crime is a greater sin than committing it yourself.

*

One day, soon after the war, and the British were in firm control, my entire class was taken to another classroom to be examined by eye doctors. We had no choice in the matter, and I was one of four young teenagers diagnosed with trachoma.

Trachoma, I learned later from a medical handbook in Jerusalem's Central Library, is a chronic infection of the conjunctiva of the eye— the cornea and surrounding areas—and if untreated, as it often was in Jerusalem in those days, results in scarring, deformity of the eyelid, impaired vision, and, finally, blindness. The infection is contagious in its early stages and is transmitted by contact with infected clothing, flies, and other people. The disease is common in dry, hot climates with poor sanitation and untreated water, which made Jerusalem a prime breeding ground. Indeed, trachoma was widespread in Palestine and a major cause of blindness in the Jewish community.

In response, shortly after the war ended, the Hadassah Organization in America had sent a medical team to Palestine with the specific goal of eradicating trachoma. That morning, as we bent over our books, nurses in bright green uniforms invaded our classroom. Our rebbe ordered us to obey all commands, so we had no choice but to submit. The plan had been arranged, in secret, with the principal of the Talmud Torah. In haste and stealth, the doctors had set up a temporary clinic in the auditorium. Had they known, our parents, unfamiliar with medical treatments and afraid of doctors, would have kept us out of school that day.

In the auditorium, an eye doctor examined me.

"Another one," said the doctor, and I was taken immediately to a field hospital in a big tent outside the school.

Everything moved so quickly I didn't have time to be afraid. A nurse speaking Yiddish helped me put on a long white shirt double my size, and then tied it closed. She told me to sit down in a chair. Before I knew what was happening, she'd tied my hands behind my back, but so gently that I wasn't afraid. The nurse explained in Yiddish that any head movement would make it difficult for the doctor to work. Then a doctor in a clean white uniform stood over me—in a place where water was scarce, the bright, fresh cleanliness of his clothing was impressive—and suddenly, with a quick hand motion, he sprayed liquid into my eyes. I cried out in surprise and pain, but in a moment, all sensation vanished.

"You see? Not so bad," said the nurse. Her Yiddish was perfect, but even stranger was that she was a grown woman on an equal footing with the doctor. Her manner was unlike that of other women in Batei Warsaw. The doctor worked quickly, using an instrument on the inside of my lids, and then applied a warm, thick ointment.

"*Avar,*" (Perfect), he said in Hebrew.

Through my blurred vision, I saw the nurse smile at me. "All done. All's well."

With my hands still tied and a blindfold over my eyes, I was led to another room full of other students who had just been treated. After about two hours, the blindfold was taken off. A different nurse, equally adept in Yiddish, gave me a small jar of ointment and told me to apply it to my eyes once a day for a month.

"*Vershteshed?*" (Do you understand?).

"I do."

"*Gut.*"

With three other boys who lived in Batei Warsaw, I was sent home. Eyes still tearing and our vision blurred, single file and holding hands, we walked slowly on Mea Shearim Road, stumbling like blind people.

Alerted by Batei Warsaw's well-oiled rumor mill that something unholy was going on in the Talmud Torah, my mother was standing watch at the rear of our house, and when she saw us making our lame way down the road, she flew down the street.

"Chaim! Chaim! *Vas ist das?*" (What is this?).

"Doctors operated on me."

"What! Doctors? An operation?"

"It's for trachoma. I have medicine."

"No! No operations!"

"Imma, the nurse spoke Yiddish."

Not interested in the American nurses who spoke Yiddish and the doctor who spoke Hebrew, my mother was already racing to the school.

She wasn't the only person running. Entire families rushed by—aunts, uncles, cousins, brothers, sisters, neighbors, and friends. All of Batei Warsaw was determined to see the American doctors and their nurses and the hospital that had been set up overnight in the Talmud Torah. There was genuine excitement in the air. Life in the Orthodox community tended toward a certain dull, reassuring sameness, and novelty exerted a powerful drawing power. In my mother's rush, however, she completely forgot the patient, and I, eyes watering, was left to grope my way into the house, feeling along the wall for a chair, there to wait for my mother's return.

When she walked in, she was happy. The American doctor had explained that it wasn't really an operation, just scraping and swabbing, and had impressed upon her the miraculous nature of the entire proceeding. It was a miracle they had caught my trachoma in time, for if we had waited another year, I might have gone blind.

"God forbid!" the doctor had added.

The doctor not only spoke Hebrew but also used a clean, elegant

Yiddish that added to the power of his explanation. The cleanliness of his uniform was equally impressive. He wore a yarmulke, and my mother of course noted that he recited the proper blessing before drinking a glass of water. My mother was thoroughly convinced of the correctness of the surgical procedure to which I had been subjected, and her opinion of all doctors, especially those from the United States, was greatly enhanced.

Of the nurses, however, she was still wary; women like that, whether Jewish or not, were still beyond her comprehension.

On a return visit to the clinic the next week, I learned that the doctor who had treated me was named Dr. Ticheu, and I followed his career through the grapevine of commentary that was an indispensable source of information in Batei Warsaw. Upon his death at the hands of an Arab terrorist a few years later, I read in his obituary in *Doar Hayom* that he was a well-known eye doctor who had devoted his life to philanthropic work for Hadassah, and had organized and opened half a dozen clinics in Palestine and Africa.

CHAPTER 35

With my father in America and my older brother, Moshe, and two of my sisters married and living elsewhere, we had so much extra room that at my request, my cousin Yitzhak moved in. He was now working as an administrator in the orphanage he had left, and between his salary and the modest financial assistance he received from his three brothers in America, he was able to contribute to our household expenses, and still have money for himself.

I had no such wealth. I was still a full-time student, and my only income was the small monthly stipend from the Lubavitcher yeshiva, most of which I gave to my mother. What was left could hardly buy a piece of bread.

My cousin's presence was wonderful. Like all the Reismans, my mother's side of the family was more relaxed about religion, and his conversation was full of laughter. After all, his father had told us to mark his words, and we all knew how good it was going to be.

Cousin Yitzhak had studied English—the orphanage gave him a better, more secular education than I got—and I, eager to learn this most useful language, asked him to get some English textbooks from his brothers in America. After a few months, a small package of grammar texts and a dictionary arrived. They proved, however, too advanced for me, and I tucked them away under my clothing for future reference.

Like the Reismans, my cousin was musically inclined. He sang well and, even better, played a violin. In exchange for his fiddling, I read him books. His favorite was a collection of tales about famous Hasidic rebbes and their wonderful miracles. The stories were written in Hebrew, which he couldn't read. Often, my mother and her mother, my grandmother Nechama, joined us at the table as I read out loud. I used appropriate and impressive tones to heighten the sense of the miraculous. My mother and grandmother marveled at the wonderful miracles the rebbes performed. Through my words, they saw every deed with their own eyes.

My cousin Yitzhak was considerably more skeptical. He had a tendency to ridicule some of the miracles and once interrupted my narrative about a rebbe transporting himself through the air during a snowstorm.

"Chaim, do you really believe this stuff?"

"It's written in black and white." I held up the book.

"But tell me—who wrote it?"

"I don't know." I looked at the title page. "The author isn't given."

"Aha! It could have been written by the rebbe himself to make himself more important."

"They wouldn't write any lies."

"Can any of our rebbes fly?"

"Of course not."

"Has anyone you know ever seen a rebbe fly?"

"No."

"So?"

"But that's the point," I said, trying to explain. "What makes it a miracle is its rarity. Besides, there are different categories of miracles."

"Okay, but how do you know these stories aren't lies?"

I had to admit I didn't.

Later, after much internal ruminations, I realized it didn't really matter if the miracles had actually happened. The stories were about hope and aspiration, about spirits that soared and souls that yearned, and the truth of such things, as my mother pointed out, lay in one's heart.

Besides, when I began reading more secular books, I found a story by Franz Kafka that was almost exactly like the story about the flying rebbe: "A Country Doctor." It's about an old man, a doctor, who travels through the air on a cart with flying horses, also during a snowstorm; the notes in the introduction called it surreal.

Then my cousin Yitzhak told me that he had a girlfriend.

I was not surprised. Our house was without secrets, and I had found his small wardrobe of secular clothing—nothing as fancy as my brother's, just a couple of shirts and a more stylish hat, but clear indications of worldly behavior.

"Don't tell anyone," he cautioned me.

"I won't."

"I don't want Aunt Reizel pestering me."

"I know how to keep a secret."

A few days later, he suggested a double date.

"I'm going to visit my girlfriend. She wants me to bring you along."

It was Saturday, and we had finished the morning service in synagogue.

"She's going to have a friend there," he said.

"Oh? Okay, I'll go."

"But don't be nervous."

"Why should I be nervous?"

"Well, don't be. No one's going to find out."

Both of us nervous, with Cousin Yitzhak looking around furtively, we walked quickly through the streets. For a young man and young woman to see each other secretly, in private, was unheard of in my family. And what kind of girl would even agree to such a meeting?

My cousin's girlfriend was pretty, and so was her friend. Their house, in a new development some distance from the Old City, was furnished in a modern style. The girl's parents weren't home, which was a relief, and we sat and talked. Cousin Yitzhak knew how to joke and keep the conversation light. He and his girlfriend did not touch, but their looks said enough. Both girls wore long dresses to their ankles, sleeves to their wrists, and no makeup, of course. My girl was not quite as pretty as Yitzhak's, but her talk was so quick and easy that I wished I felt more comfortable.

When we left, my cousin did something extraordinary: he kissed his girlfriend on the cheek. I certainly wasn't going to kiss my girl and wondered if I should shake hands. She was uncertain too and kept her hands behind her back, so I said goodbye without doing anything.

"Well, any comments?"

We walked back slowly, not eager to be questioned by my mother.

"About those two girls? I think they're very nice."

"I mean my girlfriend. Do you like her?"

"She's very pretty."

"She is. What about her friend?"

"She's pretty too."

"Did you enjoy yourself?"

"Me? Of course I enjoyed myself."

"So why were you curling your earlocks so much?"

"I wasn't curling my earlocks."

"Yes you were. All the time curling them around your finger."

I didn't know I had been doing that, and I felt my face getting red. "Well, it was my first time on a date."

My cousin said nothing, and we picked up our pace; we didn't want to be late for the afternoon Sabbath service. As we got closer to Batei Warsaw, my cousin reminded me about keeping it a secret.

"Of course," I said. The last person I wanted to know about potential girlfriends was my mother, who would tell my uncles, particularly Uncle Yisrael Yitzhak.

But nothing more transpired. A few weeks later, my cousin told me that his girlfriend had entered into a shidduch with a young Hasidic boy, and her girlfriend, the one who had such an appealing way of talking, was about to get engaged too.

I thought about her a lot and dreamed about her once, and that was the extent of my first date. No other opportunities to spend time alone with a young girl presented themselves. By seventeen or eighteen, Hasidic boys and girls were usually married. Though I was completely unattached at the age of seventeen, that was becoming more common. The war, the British occupation, and America, were changing many things, and though the direction of the changes was as yet unclear, I sensed my life was going to be different.

Most fervently, I hoped it would be.

I had been a student in the Lubavitcher yeshiva for more than two years, yet was without goal or purpose. My studies were routine and boring: Talmud and Gemara for most of the day and an hour for the more philosophical and interesting Sefer ha'Tanya, which delved into the deeper, mysterious aspects of existence.

I saw little point to any of it.

The world outside was beckoning, and I had only the faintest intimations of what such a world held.

I was enclosed in a wall of tradition and conformity, and I saw no door through it.

However, an unseen hand was directing events.

One afternoon, my Talmud teacher, Rabbi Shapiro, passed my table, turned back, and bent over me.

"Yes, Rebbe?"

"Ah, Chaim." He kept his voice low. "Come by this afternoon for a little talk."

He hadn't had a smile on his face, and entering his office after lunch, I approached his desk with some wariness.

Rabbi Shapiro had a gentle, soft voice much like my father's.

"I want to compliment you, Chaim, on your record in the yeshiva. I'm going to recommend that your monthly stipend be increased. Not very much, but a little extra."

"Thank you very much, Reb Shapiro."

He looked at me for a long moment and cleared his throat. "May I ask, Chaim, where is your beard?"

I took a deep breath. Other students had warned me about the beard problem. I had my response prepared.

"My beard? I remove my beard with scissors."

Rabbi Shapiro smiled, not too warmly, and gave me his standard rejoinder.

"I'm sure you use scissors, Chaim. None of our yeshiva students would ever use a razor. But still, Chaim, I wonder."

I disliked his sarcastic smile as well as his cat-and-mouse game, and I answered with the certainty of a clever teenager.

"The Torah," I said, quoting verbatim from the commentaries, "forbids one to take off the earlocks with any tool. But with regard to a beard, the Torah forbids the use of a razor only. It's not a mitzvah to have a beard, so all means other than a razor are permitted to touch the hair of the face."

"This is true, Chaim. And we expect our students to know rabbinical law, as you obviously do. I'm not accusing you of shaving with a razor. But I am puzzled, I must admit, with your beard's on-again, off-again behavior. It's quite a miracle for one so young."

Again, his sarcasm was provocative, but I held my tongue.

Rabbi Shapiro spoke in his low, soft voice. "Chaim, I shall start from the beginning. Before your father went to America, he came to me and pleaded that I take you into the yeshiva. 'I must go to America,' he said. 'Take my son, and let him study with you.' I did as he requested because he is a maggid, a lecturer, in the Chai Olam Yeshiva. And you've been a good student, as you see by the increase in your stipend. But we have strict rules here. All our students must have beards. We are concerned not just for ourselves but also for others who do not know the law as well as you. They don't know that scissors are permitted to remove beards. Instead, they will look at the students without beards and say, 'Aha! We are allowed to take off our beards,' and they will use a razor. We don't want our students to be the cause of this violation."

The rebbe didn't have to tell me my choices. It was either grow a beard or leave.

"I have to think about this," I told him. "I'll give you an answer in a few days."

After a long pause, he replied, "We sincerely hope you will stay with us."

Walking out into the sunshine, I knew what I would do. I had already decided to leave the Lubavitcher yeshiva, and my decision had nothing to do with my beard, though I must admit I liked my face without one. My studies, once so stimulating, had become a burden. I had been studying the Torah, the Midrash, and the Talmud since I was four, and I needed a change.

Saggi Nohoir, my blind study partner, was sad when I told him.

"Ah, Chaim, when are you leaving?"

"Tomorrow."

"So soon?" He reached up with his right hand and touched my face with his gentle fingers. "Ah, I see. Yes, you have to go."

He lowered his hand, and I shook it farewell.

"Baruch HaShem," he said.

My mother was mildly disappointed but, as always, accepted my decision.

"What will you do, my Chaim-le?"

319

"I don't know."

"Well, don't take too long to decide. You have to do something with yourself."

A week later, I read a short ad in the *Doar Hayom*, my favorite daily Hebrew newspaper:

> Students wanted for a new American-style yeshiva in Givat Shaul. All prospective students must apply in person.

Perfect, I thought, and I set out immediately for Givat Shaul, a hilly, barren area west of Jerusalem. It was a brisk walk of about two and a half miles from Batei Warsaw. I got there in the afternoon, and the rosh, the principal, interviewed me then and there and accepted me on the spot. Classes were to begin the next week. Each student was to receive a monthly stipend of three pounds sterling—three times the amount I'd received from the Lubavitcher yeshiva.

Talk about miracles.

My mother was impressed, but she had a question.

"Tell me, Chaim—what is meant exactly by 'American style'?"

"I'm not sure myself, but I'll find out next week."

I asked around and learned that the yeshiva was founded and financed by a rich American, Mr. Andrew. He had owned a number of hotels in Lakewood, New Jersey, a popular resort. Mr. Andrew had developed glaucoma and, in spite of the best treatment, lost his sight. He sold his hotels and moved to Jerusalem with his wife, and lived in Givat Shaul. Devoting his life and considerable fortune to philanthropic causes, he founded a yeshiva in Givat Shaul.

The new yeshiva had eight students and one teacher, Rabbi Stein, who was also the principal and chief administrator. The nine of us, together with Mr. Andrew, comprised a minyan—ten men over the age of thirteen, a formal religious quorum.

At our first meeting, we lucky eight met with Rabbi Stein, who sat at his desk with a little metal box in front of him.

"Some of you might want to know what an American-style yeshiva is," Rabbi Stein said, "and I must confess I don't really know myself." He pushed the metal box to the side and folded his hands. "Mr. Andrew never really told me. Mr. Andrew, albeit blind, is very energetic. But he's somewhat limited physically and also somewhat lonely. So he founded this yeshiva to keep himself busy and involved. He likes the company of young, intelligent students, and you can expect to see a lot of him. The course of study here will be very progressive. You will be in class six days a week, from ten in the morning until six at night. Every day two of you will visit Mr. Andrew in his home, where you will read out loud a newspaper, book, or magazine of his choosing. You will discuss local events and general politics. Allow Mr. Andrew to talk about anything he wants. Do not interrupt him. Listen to his boasting about his great financial success in America. Don't challenge his opinions or any statements of fact, even when you know them to be false. Above all, let him have the last word in any discussion. Do you have any questions?"

The eight of us looked at each other. This was the first time in our lives that anyone as full of authority as a principal had asked for questions, and we were too surprised to take advantage of the opportunity. *This must be part of the American style*, I thought.

Rabbi Stein continued. "Every evening, the minyan will gather in the synagogue for services, and after prayers, we'll have supper with Mr. Andrew and discuss the Bible and Talmud. Otherwise, the rest of the time, you will be on your own. Any questions?"

Grasping the American style, I asked, "When you say 'on our own,' what do you mean?"

"I mean exactly that. Free."

"Free to do what?"

"If you're not required in Mr. Andrew's home or in synagogue for services, you can do whatever you want."

"And what will you do while we do whatever we want?" I asked, liking this style.

"Well, hmm, I don't really know. But I'm sure we'll all learn a great deal."

Another student took courage. "And for this we get the three pounds sterling?"

"Every month. In fact, Mr. Andrew has directed me to give you the first month's stipend in advance."

He moved the metal box in front of him and opened it. My fellow yeshiva buchers—buch means book in Yiddish, so a bucher is a book-ster, or student--and I looked at each other in amazement as Rabbi Stein took out a stack of silver coins and began counting.

A miracle!

Based on Rabbi Stein's description, I had expected Mr. Andrew to be a boring, difficult gentleman, but I enjoyed his company very much. Open-minded and intelligent, he spoke Hebrew, Yiddish, and English. He received a great deal of mail from New York—journals, magazines, and newspapers, including three Yiddish dailies: *Der Taggeblatt*, the *Jewish Morning Journal*, and the *Forward*. I was the only student who read Yiddish with any fluency, and soon became Mr. Andrew's favorite conversationalist.

He had many questions about my family and life in Jerusalem, and I told him about my grandparents and their lives in Poland and how they came to Palestine in the nineteenth century, my father's work in America, and my sisters and brothers. When I mentioned the name of one of my cousins who lived in Lake Wood, New Jersey, Mr. Andrew became excited.

"What! You mean Mordecai Reisman, the chief rabbi of Lakewood? Your cousin? What a small world!"

He kept repeating that phrase, shaking his head all the time, until, getting over his profound wonder of the world's smallness, he said, "you know, Chaim, your cousin was a very strict rabbi. He was exceptionally careful that my hotels served only the most kosher meat. Yes, yes, a very strict and honest man."

From then on, Mr. Andrew referred to me as his son.

"You know, Chaim," he said, "you must write about your family. History is important."

"My family is very ordinary."

"Chaim, even the histories of ordinary men and women are important. Think about it."

I did think about it, but not seriously. My days were too full with so many things that I didn't have time to do anything but live.

I had a wonderful time in Mr. Andrew's American-style yeshiva.

Other than completing the minyan in the synagogue, our principal, Rabbi Stein, was neither seen nor heard. Apparently, this was in keeping with the American style. I spent more and more time in Mr. Andrew's home. He had a well-stocked library, and I began reading secular Hebrew books, translations of English and French books, some of them novels. Soon I was consuming almost two books a day. Mr. Andrew didn't mind; after an hour of conversation, he fell asleep in a big reclining chair while I sat at a table over an open book. He enjoyed falling asleep, he said, to the sound of pages turning. I read the stories of Guy de Maupassant; I liked "The Necklace" and told the story to Cousin Yitzhak, who reacted with cynical humor.

"Chaim, how can you believe that such coincidences really happen?"

"The author is making a point about life."

"But it's only a story."

"No, no, it's fiction."

"Just another word for lies."

I explained that even an imaginary story could be real, but Cousin Yitzhak didn't appreciate the concept.

The other students in our American-style yeshiva had their own interests. Two of them were brothers, immigrants from Poland, and had been living on a kibbutz for three years until, disillusioned and impoverished, they saw the ad for Mr. Andrew's yeshiva and decided to give it a try. They were university graduates, and the older brother, Pesach, was a foreign correspondent for a Yiddish daily in Riga, Latvia. We soon became a close family, and Mr. Andrew called us, "my boys."

Alter Hamberger was the only one who did not appreciate the yeshiva. It was too American for him, meaning, I suppose, too much fun. Alter was very religious and wanted us to pay more attention to our studies. He complained that our rosh was spending less and less time with us. My fellow students and I considered this a positive development. Alter was also upset that I read so many secular books, not to mention those newspapers from America.

"Look, Chaim," he argued, "you're not going to learn anything new there. It's always the same again and again. If you want real news, study the Torah. It's like a newspaper from an earlier time. Different men doing the same things to each other."

Alter was also a big eater, and one day the eight of us had an eating contest. I lost easily. Alter won big. He ate fourteen hard-boiled eggs, three large herrings, a loaf of rye bread, and an assortment of vegetables and fruits. After, we didn't see him for three days. Mr. Andrew didn't notice, and Rabbi Stein, hardly there, never took attendance anyway.

With all our free time, we explored the hills and valleys around Givat Shaul, an ancient area of Jerusalem cited in the Bible. We discovered a farm in one of the valleys, and to my surprise, it was owned by a man who once lived in Batei Warsaw. The world, at least our part of it, was indeed small. The man was a widower and lived on the farm with his five daughters. We called it the English Farm because the man was from England, and we renamed him Mr. Englander. He had lived in Batei Warsaw for two years and moved when his wife died. Mr. Englander and his five daughters were all tall and redheaded, a rarity in Jerusalem. He went to the Old City every day while his daughters tended their few goats and sheep. There was a small swimming pool, a hole lined with cement, fed by an underground well.

Whenever we approached the farm, their two large dogs rushed out, barking and snarling, which was the signal for the five sisters to appear. Naked, they ran out of the house and jumped into the pool, laughing and splashing.

"We dare you to come in! We dare you!"

They laughed and teased us, splashing water when we got too close.

"Come in and get wet!" they shouted, but only the brothers from Poland, the kibbutzniks, had the nerve. They jumped in with their clothes as the girls shrieked with laughter. The rest of us backed away so that our skullcaps and caftans wouldn't get wet.

One of my solitary walks in Givat Shaul was to a stonecutting quarry about a mile from the yeshiva. The echoing boom of dynamite guided me over the hills. In a field near the quarry, the stonemasons worked on long, low benches beneath wooden roofs that protected them from flying debris. Nearby, in the shade of a wooden hut, three camels on their haunches waited to be loaded with stones for the Old City. These quarries had been used for a thousand years, and they would be used for another thousand. Most of the masons were Arab, with a few Yemenite Jews sprinkled here and there.

Twice a week, I walked to the quarry and spent an hour watching the masons cut and shape the stones. After the second week, I stood near one of the Yemenites and waited.

He looked up. "Chaim," I said, putting my hand on my chest.

He smiled, nodded, and tapped his chest with his chisel. "Akivah."

I stepped closer, and we began talking in Yiddish, telling each other about ourselves. One day Akivah asked if I wanted to try cutting a stone, and I said, yes. It looked easy. You held the chisel in one hand and the hammer in the other and after a few light taps pieces of stone fell away, and there it was—a well-shaped brick to be stacked with the other bricks. Akivah was as skinny as I was, and he held the hammer and chisel without strain, and I held out my hands. The chisel was heavy, but I managed to place it against the stone. The hammer was much heavier than it looked, but I lifted it and let it fall. It bounced off the chisel, which flew out of my hand and onto the ground. Akivah smiled.

"Not so easy, eh?"

"No. I only lift books."

"Books are heavy in their own way," Akivah said.

I was about to agree, but there was shuddering under us, followed by a sharp *crack* deep in the earth. I froze. A moment passed, and nothing happened. It might have been a shock from a distant dynamite blast, but when I looked at Akivah, he was frozen and pale. There was a deep, strange silence. I looked around. All the stonecutters were absolutely still. After a few moments, when nothing more happened, the masons lifted their hammers and went back to work.

Then, without warning, there was a tremendous rumbling in the earth like the galloping of a thousand wild horses. The stones bounced, and the huts trembled and shook.

"Earthquake!" Akivah had thrown down his tools and was running down the hill.

The other masons followed. "Allah Akbar!" they screamed.

Holding my yarmulke, I ran too, shouting with Akivah, "*Sh'ma Yisrael!*"

The earth was floating, and my feet couldn't hold the ground. I fell, tumbled, got up, and ran down the hill after Akivah. The earth lifted itself again and then fell. Nauseated, I kept running, my feet confused, arms flailing, and raced into the wadi where the stonecutters had gathered. They were shouting, "Earthquake! Earthquake!" and shouting in Arabic and Hebrew.

In a minute, even less, it was over. The silence was profound. The masons were pale and shaking, and some of them were vomiting. Akivah sat down, shaking, and muttered the Sh'ma: "Hear O Israel, the Lord is God, the Lord is One."

When the earth had been still for ten minutes, I straightened my clothing, walked quickly back to Givat Shaul, and found Mr. Andrew and his wife outside their house with the other students. Mr. Andrew hugged me. "My dear son," he said. He had been terrified. The only certainty a blind man has is the firmness of the earth under his feet, and that had been taken from him. Finally, Rabbi Stein showed up, looking sleepy and well fed, and he convinced the Andrews that it was safe to go in.

In Batei Warsaw, it was the same. No one would go into their house unless someone—the British, a rabbinical authority, an angel with a sign—told them it was safe. I convinced my mother, and we found only a few minor cracks in the corners. Our expensive mirror had survived, and our clock on the wall was chiming the three o'clock hour. The stonewalls of Batei Warsaw and Mea Shearim had withstood the mighty forces of inner earth.

"Stone and mortar," my mother said and added, for stone and mortar are man-made things, "Baruch HaShem."

Chapter 36

As I read my father's letters to my mother, my eye, running ahead, made me stop.

"Yes, Chaim. What?"

"Abba wants earth from Jerusalem."

My mother sat silently.

I continued reading, but without pleasure, and my mother was no longer listening.

That night, I couldn't sleep. I was certain my father would return to Jerusalem. I was certain too, though I had no evidence of it, that he was not ill. But my mother's silence was troubling. Did she know something she was afraid to tell me? I had not the faintest idea what America was like, but as I lay in the dark, my imagination conjured vivid images of my father in New York. In his black caftan and fur-trimmed hat, I saw him walking the streets of the city, a small man with a long beard, his soft brown eyes looking at the world with a lonely stare as he made his rounds from door to door, begging for funds, his heart pining for Jerusalem. Now he wanted earth from the Mount of Olives. I lay in the dark on the cold stone floor and wept.

In the morning, my mother rose before dawn. I lay very still, listening to her recite the morning prayers with great fervor:

> You shall love the Lord your God with all your mind, with all your strength, with all your heart, with all your being. Set these words, which I command you this day, upon your heart. Teach them faithfully to your children; speak of them in your home and on your way, when you lie down and when you rise up. Bind them as a sign upon your hand; let them be a symbol before your eyes; inscribe them on the doorposts of your house and on your gates.

She left without making morning coffee, and I watched from the door. Sometimes she turned left to the Ohel Schmuel synagogue for morning prayers, but now she turned right, to the Old City, most likely to the Kotel to talk to God and perhaps ask for a favor, just one, an ordinary everyday miracle. But it was too early to go to the wall. From our back window I saw her in her Sabbath dress, clutching her worn prayer book in one hand and a piece of white fabric in the other, walking briskly down Mea Shearim Road.

The day had begun cool, but by midmorning, it was hot and humid, with a wind blowing from the south. Late in the afternoon, standing sentinel on our roof, I saw her returning. She walked slowly with the prayer book and a small bundle of the white fabric. I scrambled down and went inside just as she came in. She was breathing heavily, her lips dry and pale, and she sat at our long table, put the cloth down, and closed her eyes.

"Imma, where did you go?"

"I am very tired, Chaim. Such a terrible, hot day. I walked to the Mount of Olives and prayed at the graves of your grandparents and Chaim Shaya, Yehudith, and Golda Leah. All my dead. I should have taken a big spoon to dig with, but I used a sharp stone."

She opened her eyes and looked down at her hands. Her nails were dirty, and two fingers were still bleeding.

"Are you all right, Imma?"

"I'm just very tired."

She stood, went to the side room, and lay on her bed.

I left the white bundle untouched on the table, and when my brothers came home from heder, they looked at it and said nothing.

The next afternoon, she went to the market in the Old City and returned with a small, tin box. She washed her hands, spread a white towel on the table, put the bundle on the towel, and unwrapped it. The mound of earth was full of small stones. Using her baking sieve, she sifted the earth onto the white towel. Murmuring prayers, she repeated this a second and then a third time, until all traces of stone, weeds, and other debris where sifted out. The earth shone with a soft gleam, each grain a gem. From her fabrics, she cut a piece of silk the color of evening sky.

"Chaim, give me the tin box."

I brought her the box, and she fitted the silk into the bottom and then lifted the towel and carefully poured the earth in. She shook the towel to get every last grain and then folded the silk over the top and put the cover on. I helped her wrap it with two layers of paper, the first one old newsprint and the second the heavy brown paper she used for expensive fabrics. I tied strong white cord around the package and then wrote my father's address on the outside.

> Haskel Linder
> 49 Attorney Street
> New York, New York
> The United States of America

She sat for a minute, staring at the package, and then stood and left, carrying the box with the earth from the Mount of Olives to the post office on Mea Shearim Road, where it would begin its slow ocean voyage to my father in New York.

CHAPTER 37

Paradise on earth doesn't last forever.

After two years studying in Givat Shaul, Mr. Andrew died unexpectedly, and his American-style yeshiva ceased to exist.

I had to make a decision: Should I enroll in another yeshiva and become a religious Hasid or get a job and step out into the world?

The question held its own answer. One doesn't decide to be a Hasid; one simply is such a man.

Though I was a good student and enjoyed reading and discussing the fine points of halachah, it was more for the intellectual stimulation than the spiritual content. Sometimes one may lead to the other, but not for me.

I saw that piety had no end. It is recommended, for instance, that a pious Jew say one hundred blessings a day. I had uncles and cousins who were members of the Hundred Club, and they kept a strict account of their blessing quotient. One of my older cousins prided himself on meeting the quota every day for the last twenty years; he was constantly muttering to himself, and whenever I was with him, I too had to mutter in response. As a child of ten, I had tried to meet the quota, but after a few days of going around the house blessing everything, my mother suggested I stop before I drove everyone crazy.

An address in Batei Warsaw was an address for life.

Seemingly a small place to live, Batei Warsaw was, for the pious man, just the opposite, for within its tight gates, within this circle of prayer and learning, one lived beyond boundaries, traveling between heaven and earth, visiting God and returning, when one wished, to the here and now.

My favorite uncle, Yisrael Yitzhak, came to Jerusalem from Poland when he was a young boy with, as he often said, fewer years than the days found in the week. He dwelled in the ancient city all the days of his life, leaving only to visit the holy cities of Safed, Tiberias, and Hebron. Within walking distance in Old and New Jerusalem, Uncle Yisrael

Yitzhak had his houses of prayer and learning; his favorite bathhouses and matzo factories; the Beth Din, or rabbinical court, where he served as a dayon, or judge; the Kotel Ha'Maravi; and the cemetery on the Mount of Olives. Thus he lived in the world of Torah and good deeds, in the presence of the Eternal.

One summer, I stayed in his house for two months and had a chance to observe my uncle in his private and public life.

I learned once again how contradictory is human nature.

He went to bed every night at nine thirty and rose at midnight for the special prayer that mourns the destruction of the two temples of Jerusalem, the first by the Babylonians and the second by the Romans in AD 70. Then he studied the Zohar until three in the morning, when he returned to bed for more sleep. Rising again at six, he went to the mikvah for a ritual bath and then to the Ohel Shmuel Shul for morning prayers, where I joined him. We returned to his home for a breakfast considerably more lavish than the morning meal in my own home. Unlike many ultra-Orthodox Hasidim who took every opportunity to deny themselves physical pleasure, my uncle never indulged in deprivation.

During the day, we visited our relatives and stopped in at different synagogues and yeshivas. We ended our day in the Hasidic shul with the evening service, after which he delivered a closing lecture in Talmud. We then returned home for an ample supper before getting into bed at his regular hour, to rise again at the stroke of midnight.

My uncle Yisrael Yitzhak was one of the guardians of Torah and tradition. He had a naturally kind heart, which, combined with our charitable traditions, reinforced his desire to alleviate the plight of the poor and the downtrodden.

Yet contradictions abounded.

As gabbai, or president, of his shul, he was uncompromising in his Orthodoxy. On the Sabbath and other Holy Days, he stood upon the bema and extended aliyot to the congregants, calling only those of obvious piety and ignoring any man who had trimmed his beard or shortened his earlocks. Any decorative element of clothing, such as the ties my brother Moshe fancied, was a disqualifying demerit.

In all systems of belief, there is the potential for obsession; indeed, carrying things to a logical extreme appears to be part of the human condition. The ultra observant Hasidim of the Mea Shearim, including my uncle, were on the constant lookout for even the minute cracks in the wall of Orthodoxy. To them, the world held many temptations that hardly seemed dangerous when indulged in one by one, but were an avalanche of secularism when enjoyed sequentially.

The Romanian circus was one such temptation. Flyers had been distributed throughout Jerusalem, advertising the arrival of a traveling circus. The show boasted lions, tigers, elephants, fire-eating men, two-headed ladies, animals that talked, and other wonders, both human and otherwise.

The religious community had a genuine dilemma. On one hand, the Romanian circus would bring something new, different, and exciting to the humdrum lives of Jerusalem's inhabitants. On the other, it was something new, different, and exciting, and dangerous.

My friends and I wanted to see the lions, tigers, and fire-eaters.

"You, Chaim," Uncle Yisrael Yitzhak said with backhanded praise, "of all young men. I expect more of you."

The arguments pro and con were many and, in the final analysis, inconclusive. Animals and birds are divided into two categories: kosher and non-kosher. Cats and dogs, non-kosher, are not usually found in religious homes. The more exotic non-kosher animals, such as lions and tigers, the reasoning goes, do not belong in any home, and is not Jerusalem our holy home? The counterargument was potent. Did not Almighty God create all things, including the beasts and the birds? How can they be considered evil and dangerous? And didn't Noah himself have a circus in his ark, so to speak?

My uncle was not against jungle animals—he himself would have loved to see a tiger, for instance—but he was against clowns and acrobats. He disliked the parading of deformed people for entertainment. The historical precedents were instructive; theater and circuses originated in Greece and Rome, from where idolatry and gladiators spread. The Romans were a cruel people, torturing men and beasts for pleasure. Many people of the ancient world, including Jews, fought against these abominations, and rightly so. I knew the laws concerning the treatment of animals. "It is forbidden to hurt any living creature. It is, on the contrary, one's duty to save any living creature from pain. Nevertheless, should animals injure a man or woman, or if they are needed for medical purpose or sustenance, it is permitted to kill them."

Uncle Yisrael Yitzhak also had a quote handy: "Blessed is the man who walks not in the counsel of the ungodly … nor sits in the tent of the scornful." The religious community organized boycotts and demonstrations, and I never got a chance to sit in the tent of the Romanian circus with its lions, tigers, and elephants.

Also suspect were organized sports, for they too originated in the pagan cultures of Greece and Rome. Much hostility followed after the British built an athletic field behind Batei Hungary. Men, and often women, could be seen in various states of undress, throwing and kicking balls, running, and leaping. Upsetting too were the soccer games played on Shabbos. The Young Agudath Israel, an organization of Hasidic youth, was categorically against such desecrations. Thousands of the Orthodox, I among them, gathered on Shabbos afternoon around the athletic field to heap imprecations and insults upon the athletes and spectators. Fistfights and rock throwing were common, and the police began patrolling Mea Shearim Road on Saturday afternoons, watching for Hasidim heading for the stadium. My mother was a good friend with the mother of the police captain, David Tidhor, who would wag a warning finger at me when I walked to Batei Hungary.

"Chaim, no stones!"

Thus, ironically, the Sabbath, our sacred day of rest, when all should have been peaceful, was often a day of contention, and the busiest day for our police department.

On one such Saturday, while my mother was out, two of my young nephews visited, and I, as the oldest cousin on site, was assigned to supervise them. They were always well behaved, so I left them to their own devices while I took the obligatory Shabbos nap.

Later, I pieced together the sequence of events. The younger boy, named Fishel after our deceased grandfather, needed a bathroom and, without telling anyone, went to the back room and urinated out the window.

This was not as rare or as bizarre as it might seem. Our rear window, which looked out over Mea Shearim Road, was about ten feet or so off the ground, and it was not uncommon for small children, and sometimes even grown men, to use the window as a time saver, especially before our front yard toilets were installed. Old habits die hard, however, and even with the new plumbing, there were times when a call of nature was heeded without regard to propriety.

Life is never perfect. Young Fishel's lapse would have passed unnoticed, and I would have enjoyed a longer nap, had not Captain Tidhor and his sergeant been on patrol.

Angry shouts woke me. I ran through the house, passing my terrified nephew racing in the opposite direction. I stuck my head out the window just in time to see Captain Tidhor and his sergeant running full speed into the entrance to Batei Warsaw.

I ran back to our front door, slammed it shut, and threw the bolt.

My nephew was scrambling under the bed.

The sergeant's nightstick rapped sharply on our door.

"Open this instant!"

I backed away from the door.

"We know you're in there!"

"Linder! Linder!" Captain Tidhor bellowed. "Open immediately!"

Everyone knew who lived where.

My other nephew was trying to squeeze under the bed, but his brother kicked him away.

The sergeant's blows were sharp and heavy. "Open up, or we'll break it down!"

"Linder!" Captain Tidhor was furious. "Linder! Open immediately!"

Bang! Bang!

Such a scene draws an appreciative audience, and indeed, we soon had a crowd of the curious in our front yard. People were shouting advice, some telling me to open the door and others advising me to sit tight, for it was the Sabbath, and the police had no right to arrest anyone on the day of rest—a novel legal theory that Captain Tidhor hotly disputed. Under the bed, my two nephews stuck out their heads, interested in how this was developing.

Then my mother's voice came through the door.

"Dov, why are you trying to break my door down?"

"Reizel! Look at me! This is urine from your grandson! What kind of *vilde hyahs*"—wild animals—"are living in your house?"

"Chaim!" my mother shouted. "Open the door."

When my nephews heard her, they squeezed themselves as far under the bed as possible.

"Chaim, open the door."

I slid the bolt and opened the door. With a tiny smile on her mouth, my mother fetched towels for the captain and his sergeant and then ordered my two nephews out and ordered them to apologize. Captain Tidhor shook his finger and lectured the little boys without mercy, and then, with his sergeant wiping his hat on his sleeve, the two walked away through the crowd of laughing Hasidim with as much dignity as they could muster.

My mother shook her own finger sternly at her grandsons, and then asked if they wanted some sweet apple strudel, which, of course, they did.

*

In addition to protecting the Sabbath against pagan athletics, the Agudath Israel actively campaigned against the rising tide of Zionist encroachments. Their antagonism was deep and fundamental and, for many Hasidim, irreconcilable. Some of the extremely Orthodox believed that only God could bring Israel into existence, and any attempt to force the issue through political means was doomed to failure. So strong was their antipathy, that some allied themselves with anti-Zionist elements in England, as well as with moderate Arabs in Jerusalem.

The British wasted no time in exploiting these differences, playing off one group against another and all of us against the Arabs. This constant conflict created a sense of turmoil and anxiety, adding to Jerusalem's discontents.

Unlike the Turks, who could be bought off with a smear of gold across their open palms, the British were not interested in easy money. Building their empire over hundreds of years, they were long-term investors in foreign real estate. The League of Nations' mandate gave them temporary administrative authority over the region, but they knew that with their usual skill and determination, they would eventually, one way or another, claim all of Palestine, a prelude to establishing a hold over the entire Middle East. They were professionals. With their army of civil servants arriving on the heels of conquest, the British moved in and held on.

They knew how to give a gloss of benevolence to their essentially acquisitive nature. They funded public works, opened schools, and staffed hospitals. The pound sterling set the standard for the region's currency.

My cousin Mendel did not like the British.

"You will see, Chaim."

In hiding most of the time, Mendel was in our house for a rare visit.

"You will see. Once the British come in, they stay until you throw them out."

"But they're doing some good in spite of everything."

My cousin made a face. "And a lot of bad in spite of that."

"You have to take some bad to get the good."

"When the bad destroys, of what use is the good?"

We yeshiva students knew how to argue.

"They have split Palestine into two unequal parts," my cousin said. "The Arabs have their own territory, and they're bringing in their fighters."

He meant Transjordan, the area east of the Jordan River, which the British had created with their cartographers and surveyors. We were not allowed to buy land there, though the area has been part of biblical Israel for thousands of years.

"They won't let us arm ourselves," he added, "but the Arabs get all the guns they want."

He was right; the streets of Jerusalem were full of armed British soldiers and Arabs with knives and pistols. On the roads and hillsides, the Arabs on horseback carried rifles. Rumors claimed they were hiding cannons in their villages. Only the Jews were not allowed to have weapons. But what would a Hasid do with a gun?

Reading my thoughts, Mendel said, "We have to train ourselves. The Arabs are getting bolder. They're raiding our farms and villages during the night."

He took my silence as a challenge.

"What will you do, Chaim, if the Arabs attack Batei Warsaw and the Mea Shearim?"

The idea was unthinkable. There was nothing we could do.

"The British would stop it," I said.

"The British?" Mendel's scorn was a rebuke.

Then my mother came in, and we stopped talking about guns and fighting.

*

Then my cousin Yitzhak moved out. I knew he was planning to leave.

"Chaim," he told me, "I'm getting tired of Aunt Reizel's gefilte fish."

With the wages from his full-time job at the Diskin Orphanage Home for Boys, he rented a small apartment in the one of the newer housing complexes.

My mother was sarcastic. "Ah, you want to live like one of the Amerikaner bluffers," meaning without responsibility.

Actually, yes, he wanted some freedom, and with money he was able to buy it.

Indeed, money was eating away at the Hasidic community. Children depended upon their parents for all things; girls stayed at home, waiting for matchmakers, and the young men studied Torah. When they married, their parents continued supporting them. The dowry, an important element in the religious community, provided social and religious continuity. The lack of housing was part of this mix, for it meant people had to share apartments, and the watchful eyes of the elder generation kept the younger in line. With housing so scarce, the kolels that built and administered the housing projects gave married couples and families top priority, and single people stayed put in their parents' homes. A young man with his own apartment was rare, and an unmarried young woman living alone was unheard of.

The mandate changed everything. With the British came soldiers, officers, and administrators. They came with cars, trucks, and motorcycles. They brought their own mechanics, but they hired people to build houses and garages and provide clerical and other services. They taught the locals new skills. Wherever the British went, the French, Germans, and Italians were sure to follow, and they too had their needs.

People like Yitzhak had marketable skills. He did not have to get married in order to live, and now he was living on his own—not like a king but better than I, coming and going as he pleased, going out on dates, seeing movies. He didn't have to get anyone's approval or offer any explanations. That was what money bought: independence.

I wanted independence too, but I had no source of income, and to be candid, I wasn't ready to leave the safety of my parents' home. I did not tell myself this, but I knew it.

In addition to the problems of the British, the Arabs, and the wave of secular immigrants who were threatening the religious community of which I was a part, I had another enemy.

That enemy was myself.

I had grown in physical stature and intellectual capacity as well, but I was only a child in a bigger body. I was still dependent upon my parents and the greater community financially and emotionally. Now it was time for me to step out into the world.

But how?

Uncle Yisrael Yitzhak wanted me to become a pious Hasid, and follow in his footsteps.

"You're smart and thoughtful, Chaim," he told me. "Don't waste your talents."

A compliment like that from my uncle was tempting, but when the American-style yeshiva shut its doors, I knew I wasn't going back to books, at least not religious ones.

I had to find work of some kind, but what could I do?

I cast about, measuring my talents against the available jobs, and saw that my studies had prepared me only for more study.

*

"Chaim, I'm going to America," Moshe told me one day.

"You are?" I had a dozen questions to ask but managed only one. "But when?"

"As soon as I get my ticket."

"Does Imma know?"

"Of course. Abba too."

"Is Dvorah going with you?"

"Not now. Maybe later."

I was stunned and did not know what to think, but when I thought about it later, America seemed the most logical place, the only place for my older brother to go. His many attempts at gainful employment had failed, not for want of trying. His holy scribing career was foiled by market conditions; the dowry money he had put into his fabric store was lost when the war and its aftermath changed the economic land-scape. When slaughtering didn't work out, he returned to the matzo factory but was injured while lifting a hundred-pound sack of flour and was fired. A week after that, his wife gave birth to another boy, whom they named Fishel. The child joined the growing army of young boys carrying the name of our grandfather.

My brother was an independent soul with a taste for the good life, but he had grown despondent. Dvorah's parents offered him a monthly study allowance, but the life of a rabbinical student wasn't for him. One of our uncles got him a clerical position in the Diskin Orphanage, but Moshe lasted a week; the work was tedious and without a future.

As always, once decided, Moshe moved fast. Responding to my brother, our father in New York mailed back an affidavit and enough money for Moshe's transatlantic ticket.

Our mother was ambivalent. She didn't want another member of our family fleeing to the New World, but she could not deny the sad economic reality of Moshe's situation. Dvorah wanted him to stay in Jerusalem, but she understood that he had no choice.

Two weeks after he dropped his bombshell, Moshe and a dozen other young Hasidim holding tickets and affidavits boarded a bus on

Mea Shearim Road. Traveling in style, my brother had packed his fancy clothes and neckties, and as I said goodbye to him, he presented me with one of his favorites: a tie of pale blue silk with sprinkles of yellow stars.

"Put this tie on, Chaim, and they'll think you're a real *macher*" (a man of substance).

Our mother held him tightly and kissed him on his forehead, and Moshe got on the bus.

From the moment he left, I missed him. I was now a young man of some eighteen years, but that night, I wept, though my tears for my brother were different from those I had shed when my father had left for America.

I knew Moshe wasn't coming back.

With my brother in America and my cousin Yitzhak living on his own, my days were less interesting but the house was much more spacious. My sisters were married and gone, and my two younger brothers, Netanel and Fishel, were in school. My mother's errands kept her out of the house most of the day. For the first time in my life, I had plenty of time and privacy to do a few things I had always wanted to.

I obtained a card for the Central Jerusalem Library, roamed among the stacks, and brought home books to read in my empty, quiet house—books that would have attracted too much attention in a house of curious people. I read the Hebrew translations of novels and short stories by French, Russian, and British authors. In the library I read Hebrew magazines and newspapers. I found a Hebrew anthology of the great poets of the world; each poet had a picture, a short biography, and a few excerpts. I snatched the book off the shelf, carried it home, and, getting comfortable on our small upholstered sofa, started reading.

I should have closed the door, indicating no one was home, for when I at last looked up, my uncle Yisrael Yitzhak was staring at me with hard, unblinking eyes.

I jumped.

"So, Chaim," my uncle said, "just what are you so absorbed in?"

He pulled at his beard, waiting for me to speak. The week before, he had seen me going into the Central Library and waited to accost me, but I, spotting him from the window and knowing he always had someplace important to go, had simply outwaited him; however, I had been too nervous to take out any books and had rushed home empty-handed, afraid he was lurking around one of Batei Warsaw's many dark corners. But Uncle Yisrael Yitzhak wasn't fooled. Knowing what I was up to, he had come in quietly to catch me red-handed.

My uncle was, as I have said, a powerful member of the Hasidic community. He was a dayon, a rabbinical judge, and a member of the high court; strictly observant and ascetic in his personal life, he never carried money and never entered a store to buy anything, even on credit. Unlike many Hasidim, he did not smoke cigarettes. His only vice, which was actually not a vice at all but the gentle expression of a truly loving heart, was the pocketful of candy he accepted from my grandmother Nechama every morning, which he distributed to his countless nephews and nieces during the course of the day.

Stroking his beard, Uncle Yisrael Yitzhak stood over me as I lay on the sofa with my poetry anthology. Showing respect, I stood, still holding the book, and waited until he sat at our long table. I sat on the edge of the table and gave him the book, opened to the page I had been reading. He looked at it, put it on the table, and, saying nothing, reached into his pocket. He fumbled around and pulled out a piece of soft taffy. I was too old for candy, but this was a proffer of intimacy, and I took it.

A long silence followed during which I unwrapped the taffy, popped it into my mouth.

He lifted the book, turned it over to its cover, turned it back. The writing was in Hebrew—not good. Better to have been in Yiddish. With a long finger, he pointed to the picture on the page. "Who is this man?"

"Alexander Pushkin, a famous Russian poet."

"Why is he dressed so fancy?"

"That was the style poets dressed in in those days."

Closing his eyes, my uncle digested this information in silence. He opened his eyes, nodded at the picture. "Tell me more about this poet, whatever his name may be."

I gave him the few facts I had just read and then added,

"Unfortunately, while he was a young man, he was killed in a duel. He could have written many more valuable literary works."

"Chaim, just what is a duel? Is it an animal or disease that kills poets?"

I wasn't much of an expert in the art of dueling, and I tried to explain. "It's a prearranged shoot-out between two antagonists on a point of honor. Pushkin died in a duel in which he fought against another person in defense of his wife's good name."

"Ah, he was killed for honor?"

"A man had offended Pushkin's wife, and Pushkin challenged him to a duel, and there was a shoot-out and—"

"A shoot out—just a simple fight with pistols?"

"It's a little more complicated. Pushkin and the other man went to a forest, accompanied by their friends and one neutral party. It's done according to rules and regulations. The two duelists stood a certain distance apart with their loaded pistols aimed at each other. They waited for the signal to fire, which was given by the neutral party. They both fired, gun shots echoed in the forest, and Pushkin fell dead to the earth."

That was a direct quote from the biography.

My uncle's face was pale. "You know so much about these things—a woman's honor, worldly poets, duels, and killing."

"I just learned it from this book."

"Ah, Chaim, you mentioned that the duel was done according to rules and regulations. But there aren't any rules and regulations about murder. The man who offended Pushkin's wife's honor—and what exactly goes on with Russian poets that they are insulting other men's wives?—had a little more luck than your idiot Pushkin. He pulled the trigger faster, and his hand didn't shake, and Pushkin was killed. Does his death mean that the wife deserved to be insulted? And if this Pushkin had been luckier, the other man would have fallen dead to the earth." My uncle waved his hand, disgusted. "Regardless, the unlucky Pushkin had planned in advance to kill another person and is himself guilty of murder."

"Uncle, in those days, people looked at such incidents entirely differently."

I began to explain, but my favorite uncle would have nothing to do with it.

"What do you mean, Chaim, 'in those days'? Pushkin lived thousands of years after the Ten Commandments were given on Mount Sinai. There are prohibitions against such behavior. That's why we have a Beth Din—to decide these things without this illegal bloodshed. We know that words can hurt like knives, and public insults are illegal. We would have fined and rebuked the man who insulted Pushkin's wife."

My uncle stood and handed me the book. "Read more, and then tell me, Chaim—if the poets and teachers are killing each other, what can we expect from their students?"

*

At about that time, I realized my eyesight was getting worse. At first, I thought the printing was poor and the letters blurred, or the ink had smeared before it dried, but then, upon conducting a few experiments suggested by my cousin Yitzhak, it was clear I needed glasses.

Jerusalem's only optometrist was a German Jew who had a store near the central post office on Jaffa Road. I needed three visits before I found a pair of glasses that helped. I say *found* because the optometrist didn't make glasses to a customer's specific needs; instead, when I walked in, he directed me to a cabinet against the wall.

"There. Go look in the top drawer, and see what you can find."

I tried one pair after another without much improvement.

"Come back next week," he told me. "Another shipment is coming in."

He bought his glasses new and used from Europe and England, with an occasional shipment from America.

"America," he assured me, "has very good glasses. But the best come from Germany."

I returned the next week and still found nothing. However, the third time, I found a pair that clarified everything. After adjustments to the frames, he said, "Come. Let's try them out."

He handed me a book of short stories written in Hebrew. I opened it at random, and the pages fell open to a story titled "The Monkey with Eyeglasses."

I read the first paragraph without any problem, paid him his half-pound sterling, and left with my new glasses. They were from Germany, and their frames were thin black wires that held the lenses, and extended to fit snugly over my ears. With these modern spectacles, I looked forward to great strides in my reading career.

Chaim and his younger brothers, Fishel and Netanel

Fishel Linder

Reizel Linder

CHAPTER 38

With so many new immigrants arriving in Jerusalem, the available housing had to be redistributed. The original system had been based on need, but over the years, the first tenants, still living rent free, had come to regard their quarters as their own. Desperate for a place to live, the new arrivals wanted housing to be distributed more fairly. A raffle system was proposed.

As with every new idea in Batei Warsaw, this one produced endless argument and recrimination. My grandfather Fishel, still alive at the time, was not against raffles, for he thought an element of chance often produced a measure of fairness. He wanted the kolel to exempt the old and needy, many of whom had suffered through years of deprivation and war; he believed they had earned the right to stay in their homes now that conditions were improving. He pointed out, too, in a blind raffle, some of the winners would be wealthier than the tenants they dispossessed.

His suggestions fell on deaf ears, however, for Batei Warsaw, forever contentious, had a political dynamic that did not favor compromise. Some objected to the compromise proposed by my grandfather. But he didn't want the truly needy subjected to cruel chance, and used his political powers to stop the raffle. When he died, however, the new immigrants amended the kolel's charter to give themselves significant advantages. My uncle David Weingarten became the council's head, and under intense pressure, lacking the stature of my grandfather, he was forced to implement the raffle system.

Matters simmered and then came to a head when the poor water carrier, Yaakov, and his wife and five children lost their tiny basement apartment in the first drawing. Yaakov was a tall, strong man with a profound lack of skills. He earned his living, such as it was, by carrying water from the public spigots to people's homes for two shekels a bucket—a pittance for such heavy loads. His wife, an amateur matchmaker who never made any matches, was given a few coins here and there, more out of pity than performance.

Delivering water to my mother's house one morning, Yaakov put down the two pails and burst into tears. After hearing his sad tale, that night, my mother, with me escorting her through the dark, empty streets, barged in unannounced as my uncle David was sitting down to his supper.

"Ah, Reizel." He sighed and put down his fork. He knew why we had come.

Without preamble, my mother attacked.

"David, why did you pick the poorest family to evict from Batei Warsaw?"

"They weren't picked. It was an honest raffle, and everyone had the same chance."

"And who picked the names to be raffled?"

My uncle glanced at his plate. His supper was getting cold. "Reizel, please! What do you want from me? The new people are the majority in Batei Warsaw. They know how to get their people on the council. And the others, the Hasidim, have their own agenda too. Both sides vote in a solid block. They voted to put the water carrier's apartment in the raffle. If I didn't cooperate, they'd vote me out."

My uncle had begun with a belligerent tone, but he finished closed to tears.

My mother said nothing. After all, reality could not be denied.

My uncle spoke again, lowering his voice. "I should tell you, Reizel. Some want your apartment to be raffled. I fought them off, but next time, they might win. Just so you know."

My mother backed away from the table and spoke.

"Our father-in-law, Fishel Linder, of blessed memory, twice left Jerusalem to wander alone in Poland to raise money for Kolel Warsaw to build our houses." She was angrier than I had ever seen her. "He raised the money to build thirty-six houses and was given the honor of putting two golden Napoleons under the cornerstone of the first house, and now you and your newcomers have the chutzpah to put the name of his son, Haskel, in a raffle and evict him from his apartment? Shame on all of you!"

We left my uncle sitting still and staring down at his supper.

Three days later, the water carrier and his family were evicted.

We demonstrated in front of his house by shouting imprecations and throwing small stones, the weapon of choice in Batei Warsaw. The men carrying out Yaakov's few pitiful pieces of furniture shouted back but did nothing more, themselves not pleased. Besides, we threw the stones to miss. My mother organized a collection, and the same day, the water carrier and his wife and five children found an apartment in a new housing project not far from the Old City.

"Ah, Chaim," my mother said that night, "so many changes."

Three years later, while my father was in the United States, my mother lost our apartment in the raffle.

*

In keeping with their theory of colonial governance that local problems should be handled by the local citizenry, the British organized a municipal police force, recruiting and training the staff, including the chief officers, from area residents. They drew the precincts so that Jewish police patrolled Jewish neighborhoods, and Arab police patrolled Arab. This had obvious benefits for us and also for the British, for it meant we would have to mete out justice to our friends and neighbors, while they could sit back and stay above the fray.

The British, however, wishing the power to fine and sentence, kept control of the judicial system, imposing needed reforms in both the criminal and civil courts and eliminating most, if not all, Ottoman corruption.

In a clever move, they also allowed the rabbinical court to maintain its jurisdiction within the religious community, and the Beth Din continued to adjudicate cases involving libel, slander, and divorce, as well as a limited range of commercial disputes involving breach of contract.

At any time, however, secular Jews could, if they preferred, take their grievances to the civil courts run by the Englanders. The unintended consequence of this dual system was an even greater increase in fractiousness among the different religious factions, a development perhaps not unwelcome to the British.

However, the many and various disputes between the religious zealots and the more secular Jews were not amenable to either rabbinical or civil jurisprudence. Whether the dispute was over the Romanian circus or athletic events on the Sabbath, the factions fought it out in the streets with loud, angry words, often followed by stones and fists. Then the police would rush in, swinging their nightsticks, make arrests, and try the offenders in British criminal court. My mother complained that the Jewish police were harsher on the religious Jews; the secular Jews insisted it was the opposite.

One source of constant friction was the immodest dress of the secular Jewish women, who, from time to time, found themselves in the Mea Shearim and other bastions of Orthodoxy. Women with short dresses or short-sleeved shirts were viewed as willful provocateurs, drawing harsh comments and sometimes a stone or two. On Shabbos and other holidays, the roads into Mea Shearim were cordoned off so that intruders, either by foot or vehicle, would not desecrate the sanctity of the day. An occasional stone was also thrown at those who violated the peace of our Sabbath streets.

CHAPTER 39

From America, my father's checks arrived punctually every month, and my mother continued to sell fabric out of our small back room, but we were supporting three families: our own and those of my sisters Yechevod and Hinda, whose large dowries required that my parents maintain the monthly scholarship stipends. However, the income from the store was dwindling as the British imported more and more goods, bringing up the supply and bringing down the prices. At the same time, prices for other goods, especially foodstuffs, were going up. And I was no longer bringing in the three-pound sterling from the defunct American-style yeshiva.

In spite of everything, my mother remained optimistic.

"God will provide," she said to me every night.

In Batei Warsaw, a generous providence was an indispensable ingredient of our economic health.

But I read in the newspapers that Europe's economies were in poor shape. Inflation was increasing, people were out of work, socialists were instigating violent labor demonstrations, and the capitalists were fighting back. At least America was still rich, though my father's checks were getting smaller with each passing month. Donors were harder to find, he wrote, and their donations less generous. However, he was glad that at least our family's personal finances were, if not wonderful, satisfactory.

They weren't, but my mother's weekly dictation remained inappropriately optimistic. Perhaps she was unaware of how bad things were. As her bookkeeper, I was duty bound to point out the imbalances in her accounts, but she had, once again, a simple response.

"Chaim," she said every night, "we will overcome our difficulties with the help of God."

The entire Orthodox community was confident of divine intervention, and my mother was no exception. But we needed so many miracles that heaven's entire supply would have to be allocated just to us, and even then, we would most likely just break even. Eventually, my mother's books got so out of balance that I stopped keeping records.

Still, I shared some of her optimism. Overcoming the impossible difficulties of the war years, I too believed that a benign Presence was watching over us. As my dear grandfather Netanel always said, it was going to be good.

However, I discovered just how bad things were when, one evening, two of my uncles came by. They sat at the table with somber faces while my mother made tea. Uncle David took out a snuffbox and treated himself to three giant sneezes, while Uncle Yisrael Yitzhak relaxed in his chair and, not wasting one unnecessary moment on secular matters, hummed a Hasidic melody as the water boiled. His presence alarmed me, for he usually ignored matters of commerce. This was serious.

Ready at last, my mother sat down.

Her younger brother, Uncle Yisrael Yitzhak, spoke first.

"Reizel, we have learned that you have been taking out loans at very high interest."

"Nu?"

"I have one simple question. Exactly how much do you owe?"

As her bookkeeper, I knew she didn't know, and I listened as she responded with a question of her own.

"Why do you have to know the exact amount of my debts?"

Her brother rolled his eyes but kept his temper. "Then an approximation."

"Approximately? More or less, approximately six hundred pounds sterling."

We were stunned. This was a staggering sum.

Both uncles were speechless for a long time.

Finally, her brother spoke.

"Reizel, how did this happen?"

My mother sighed and said nothing, but my uncles knew: the interest rates on her loans were sometimes close to 50 percent, but she had no sense of how this multiplied the debt.

My mother sat quietly without a trace of concern; perhaps God would give her a long-term interest-free loan to cover her debts.

Uncle Yisrael Yitzhak, uncomfortable with money, drummed his fingers on the table.

Uncle David, disturbed, took an extra large pinch of snuff and delivered a mighty sneeze across the table that almost blew out the kerosene lamp.

My mother finally spoke.

"Right now, I must pay a debt of twenty pounds."

"When is 'right now'?" Uncle David asked.

"Tomorrow."

Uncle Yisrael Yitzhak sighed. "Reizel, Reizel."

Shaking their heads, my uncles stood and, after Uncle David promised to satisfy the twenty-pound debt personally, left, looking depressed.

My mother glanced at my sad face.

"Chaim, don't worry. God will provide."

Two days later, while I was reading in our empty house, my mother walked in, and I closed my book and stood.

"I have been in court today," she said.

"I didn't know you had to be in court."

"The judge told me to return tomorrow with a lawyer."

"Why court?" I demanded. "Why a lawyer?"

"All will be fine with the help of God."

"Are there more debts than the twenty pounds?"

"All will be fine with the help of God."

To every question, I received the same reply, and I stopped asking and tried to read, while my mother went about her business in our kitchen with nary a worry.

The next day, she came home late. She had been in court, she said, with a lawyer.

I peppered her with questions, but she gave no answers and offered no details.

That Thursday morning, I came home after morning services and found my sisters Yehoved and Hinda in the house, as usual, helping my mother bake challah and cake for the Sabbath. We were eating breakfast when a police officer walked through the open door and stopped just inside the threshold.

He was formal. "Is Giverit Reizel Linder present?"

Our mother stood, equally formal. "I am Giverit Reizel Linder."

He stood to the side. "Please come with me, Mrs. Linder."

I felt an ominous twinge, but our mother didn't show any concern. She turned to us.

"Don't worry, children. I'll be home soon. With the help of God."

My sisters and I watched the police officer escort my mother to the street.

"Chaim," asked Hinda, "what are we going to do?"

Yehoved was on the verge of tears.

I left my breakfast unfinished and rushed to the Old City and caught Uncle Yisrael Yitzhak as he was about to enter his yeshiva. I apologized for intruding, and then told him what had happened. He listened, reached into his pocket and handed me a piece of orange candy.

"After my lecture, we'll see what's going on."

I waited outside his classroom and then hurried him along to our house. Yehoved and Hinda were weeping quietly. There was no word about our mother. My uncle stayed to comfort my sisters, and I rushed to the local police precinct near the market and was directed to the police station at the Jaffa Gate in the Old City. There, a clerk at a small desk sent me to central police headquarters. It wasn't far, and I ran. At headquarters, a British clerk in a suit and tie looked at a typewritten list and, speaking Yiddish with a British accent, gave me the terrible news.

"Mrs. Reizel Linder has been imprisoned for a three-month term."

I was stunned. "But why?"

The clerk made an impatient face, stood, went into another room, and returned with a file. "Mrs. Linder defaulted on a debt of twelve pounds and failed to appear in court."

"Twelve pounds? Not twenty?"

"Twelve pounds."

"I was under the impression," I replied, "that she had been in court as requested."

"Not according to the record."

"Where is she now?"

"At the main prison in Jerusalem."

"Where is that?"

The man looked at me with curiosity. "Are you her son?"

I asked again where the prison was.

"Near the Russian compound," he said. "You can't miss it."

"Thank you," I replied, and I was about to run off, when he spoke.

"Young man, it's after four o'clock. The prison gates are closed, and there's nothing you can do for your mother until tomorrow morning. I suggest you use the time to procure the funds necessary for her release."

"Thank you," I said, both for his advice and the kindness of his tone.

Trying not to weep, I raced home. *My mother is in prison! Something must be done, or she will spend Shabbos in a cage like an animal!*

I arrived home, panting. Uncle Yisrael Yitzhak was sitting at the table, and my two sisters were standing at the opposite end. I gave them the news. Uncle Yisrael Yitzhak stood, took three pieces of candy from his caftan pocket, put them on the table, and left without a word.

Why waste breath when action was required?

That Friday morning, after morning prayers, my uncle Yisrael Yitzhak, my sister Hinda and her husband, and I went to the courthouse. Hinda's husband held the envelope with the money. We waited half an hour for the clerk and then paid the twelve pounds and other administrative expenses. Then we waited again before receiving a stamped order stating that the judgment in Mrs. Reizel Linder's court order had been satisfied and that prisoner Reizel Linder was to be released forthwith.

It was already past noon, the Friday sun would soon be setting. My uncle Yisrael Yitzhak walked faster than I had ever seen him. He swept the crowded street clean with his cane, and my brother-in-law, caftan open and flapping, followed half a step behind. I, showing proper respect for my elders, kept an additional half step to the rear, and my weeping sister Hinda brought up the rear. We raced single file to the central prison near the Russian compound.

With a formal gesture, my uncle presented the order of release to a British guard. He took the paper, looked us up and down, told us to wait, and disappeared inside.

We waited and waited. My sister could not stop weeping, even though her husband assured her that everything would be fine. My uncle calmly hummed a Hasidic melody to himself. Action had been taken; the rest was in God's hands.

We waited.

Pacing back and forth, I looked at the sky and checked the shadows.

At last, at three thirty, a door opened on the other side of the prison yard. Our mother appeared. She looked around, confused.

"Imma!" I called out, and she looked up.

She was smiling.

She walked tall and steadily across the bright, sunny yard, not a trace of stress on her face. The guard stood at attention, opened the gate for her, and closed it with a clang.

She hugged my sister.

"I was about to put on the prison uniform," she said, "and they told me, 'you don't have to. You can go home.' Thank God for that. It was too big. Baruch HaShem."

I thought, *yes, it's fine to praise the Name, but without my running back and forth across Jerusalem and Uncle Yisrael Yitzhak's connections, you'd still be in prison.*

At home, my mother said she was tired, and everyone left. My two younger brothers were back from class, and we rushed about, cleaning the house for Shabbos while our mother went into the kitchen, and within half an hour, everything was ready for the Friday night meal. Before she lit the candles, she showed us the palm of her right hand.

"See?" she said. "The name of the warden."

He had written his name in red so that she could pass through the gates and checkpoints.

"I'll wash it off after I light the Shabbos candles," she said.

CHAPTER 40

Spurred on by this last episode, and knowing it wouldn't be the last, I began to search for an escape from Batei Warsaw. I was tired of misery and stagnation, poverty and conflict. In the face of so much need and want, I had no means to help anyone, even myself.

I resolved to change my life.

The very thought filled me with hope. Yes, I had a goal! Yes, I would act! I had no idea what I might do, but I knew that in the same way I had mastered my studies, I would master my fate. I walked the streets of Jerusalem in a fever, my eye casting about for opportunity. Surely a young man such as myself, a young man full of hope and ability, would find purpose. My mother expected the help of God, and though I didn't share her blind confidence, I did hope for some attention at least.

Sure enough, walking on Jaffa Road one morning, I saw a sign on a store window:

Goldman's
Jewelry
and
Watch Repair.
Boy wanted.

I had never thought of a career in gems, but now that it was presented to me in such a light, I was ready to spend a life dealing in pearls, diamond rings, and gold watches.

Without hesitation, I went in.

The man I presumed to be Mr. Goldman was sitting at a little table, peering through a magnifying glass at the innards of a pocket watch. He looked up.

"I'm interested in learning about jewelry," I said.

He stood and looked me up and down. "Well, I don't need anyone for gold and jewels. I need someone for watch repair."

That's not as exciting, I thought, but still a timely opportunity.

After much discussion, he and I came to an agreement. One, I would pay him a hundred dollars in advance as an apprenticeship fee. Two, I'd work in his store for a year without pay. Three, after that year, Mr. Goldman would not be obligated to employ me any further.

I immediately wrote to my father, and at the end of the month, a check for a hundred dollars arrived.

"Jewelry and watch repair," he wrote in formal Hebrew, "is a good trade. People will always need this service. I know that your endeavors with meet with all success, and you will soon be able to earn your own living. Remember too, my dear son, all beginnings are difficult. Never be discouraged."

When I brought the money to Mr. Goldman, he had changed his mind. Pointing to my black-framed German eyeglasses, he shook his head.

"The work will make your eyesight worse, and you'll be unable to continue. Trust me, Chaim. I don't want to take your money in exchange for false hope."

I was disappointed, but Mr. Goldman's honesty softened the rejection. But I was optimistic for I knew that another opportunity would appear—and it did, right under my nose.

One of the little treats I gave myself was *Doar Hayom*, the Hebrew newspaper. It was a daily extravagance I could not have afforded had I not had two reading partners. Baruch Weinstock bought the paper early in the morning, kept it until noon, and then brought it to the synagogue, where I read it after morning services. I kept the treasure until the early evening, reading every story at least twice, and then brought it to the home of Chaim Zuckerman, who had it for keeps. We often joked that with patronage such as ours, the paper stood on chicken legs.

Chaim Zuckerman and his father owned a small print shop that turned out all sorts of circulars, pamphlets, small books, and announcements. His father, who was very talkative, insisted I linger whenever I visited, and usually I acquiesced, knowing that an invitation to supper was inevitable.

"So, Chaim, what's new?" he'd ask, and we'd start talking about everything.

The same day that Mr. Goldman rejected me, I brought the *Doar Hayom* to my friend's house, as usual; Mr. Zuckerman asked his usual question, and when I told him what had happened, he looked up from his soup.

"Ah, you know, I didn't think you'd be cut out for watch repair. Come see me tomorrow at my shop, Chaim, and we'll see what you can do."

The next day, Mr. Zuckerman gave me a tour of his print shop, proud of his three-foot presses and even prouder of his modern two-man cylinder press. The press, Mr. Zuckerman explained, turned out two hundred impressions an hour, more or less, depending on the strength of the men turning the wheels.

"Take your time, Chaim, and look around," said Mr. Zuckerman.

The shop was a big, square room filled with cases of gleaming hand type and long steel tables. Four kerosene lamps spread a soft golden light. His son was printing invitations on one of the smaller foot presses, and he stopped to demonstrate the machine's complexity.

"Nu, Chaim, what do you think?"

Mr. Zuckerman had been watching me.

"Very interesting," I replied.

He handed me a long apron. "So tie it on. There's no harm in trying."

Right there, I began working. His son taught me type composition, not a difficult skill, and another worker showed me how to redistribute the dead type into its case. The work wasn't difficult, and I soon learned the layout of the case and how to position the type.

At quitting time, I gave the apron back to Mr. Zuckerman.

"Nu, will I see you tomorrow?"

I had only a moment's hesitation. "Yes," I said.

"Good. Be here after morning prayers."

The next day, I learned more about typesetting, which is simply the technique of pulling individual pieces of type from the case and arranging them one by one in a handheld form. There were a few tricks to it, such as the use of space bars and how to adjust the punctuation. With Mr. Zuckerman and his workers helping, I learned the process quickly, and by the end of the day I was well on my way to becoming a semiprofessional hand compositor.

The work was steady, the wages were not high but fair, and I was glad to have my first job in the real world. However, I was a fast reader, skipping words and sentences to get to the essence. Setting type by hand was much different. I had to pause over every word and letter and hand-pick each period and comma. Worse, the print shop was a windowless dark room, with the smoky kerosene lamps providing the only light. I thought often about the American-style yeshiva in Givat Shaul; the open, sunny library full of books and magazines I read for hours every day, the hills and valleys I explored, and the swimming pool with the five naked, red-haired girls splashing and laughing.

But this job was my door to another world, and I slowly and steadily accumulated wealth.

I had the hundred dollars my father had sent for my watch-repair apprenticeship, which Uncle Yisrael Yitzhak was holding in trust against the day I got married. Out of my modest wages from the print shop, I gave half to my mother and, exercising great thrift, squirreled away a few piasters every week.

I kept this a secret from even my best and most trusted friend, my cousin Yitzhak. I wrapped the coins and bills in a piece of blue silk, and hid my treasure in our big room, behind the small chest.

I exercised strict control over any extravagant impulses. My needs were modest, my expenses low. There was my one-third partnership in the *Doar Hayom* reading club, a mandatory investment in my secular education. Not smoking cigarettes was, of course, a great savings, though my sweet tooth drove me to the occasional soda and ice cream, and a very infrequent morsel of sweet chocolate.

Exposed to English in the Zuckerman print shop, I began a serious study of this most necessary language. Supplementing the textbooks cousin Yitzhak's brothers had sent from America, I bought the first edition, from 1898, of the *Yiddish-English/English-Yiddish Concise and Complete Dictionary* by Alexander Harkavy. All entries in the dictionary began with a capital letter, giving the most inconsequential words a semblance of majesty. I paid eighty-five piasters for it—a huge sum of money for me.

My mother soon discovered my English studies.

"So, Chaim," she said, "you want to learn Latin?"

"It's an important tool for success, Imma."

"Nu, you don't have to do it alone."

To my surprise, she hired a private tutor for my sister Hinda and me. The three of us kept it a secret, for Batei Warsaw wouldn't look kindly upon such secular aspirations. The tutor was a young man from New York, and he wanted to teach us modern usage.

One day he asked us to memorize the word *wave*. My mother knew what a wave was, but neither Hinda nor I did, and the tutor tried everything, from hand motions to a description of the ocean. However, we had never seen an ocean or a river. Only once had we gone by bus to the Jordan and the Dead Sea, and the waves there weren't much to get excited about. Our tutor, however, was a poet.

"A wave. You can see waves not far from here. When you walk behind Batei Warsaw on Mea Shearim Road, you see fields of wheat and corn, and when the wind blows, you can see silver and golden waves."

I knew exactly what he meant, because unlike my sister, who had been tethered to the house, I had played in the fields when I was a boy.

*

The work in the print shop was easy; finished by midafternoon, I often spent the rest of the day with a book in hand, walking through the fields where I wandered as a child. After the war, Batei Warsaw lost a great deal of its simple, bucolic charms. A second floor of apartments was built on top of the original houses, the massive stone and cement walls bearing the weight without protest. An exterior staircase was built so that the upper tenants had unfettered access. A long, narrow balcony was built for the upper floors, cutting off a few hours of our light. We soon had to share our bathroom and yard with another family, though the inconvenience was tolerable. However, the streets and yards were noisier and more crowded, and the additional clotheslines choked our yards with fluttering wash, adding to the congestion. At the same time, new houses were erected on the hill facing our front yard, and suddenly the sun was gone during the day, the stars and moon obscured at night.

Some wilderness remained, however. Behind the Warsaw Houses and to the north were open fields of wheat and corn and then, beyond the beautiful houses of Batei Ha'Bucharim, were fields of lonely trees and singing birds, of sun and wind, and silence. It was to these rolling hills that I carried my Yiddish–English dictionary to sit and hope, dreaming of another life of which I yet knew nothing.

However, now these open fields were not as empty as before. On the dusty, narrow paths Arab peasants went from village to village, the men on donkeys, their wives and daughters toting small children and household goods. On market days, the roads were crowded with Arab farmers laden with vegetables and fruits, heading toward Jerusalem. How little fear they had to travel among us, yet we had much fear of them. But the Arabs always carried knives and guns, and we were not allowed.

Leaving the dim, airless print shop and the teeming streets of Batei Warsaw, I escaped into these remote hills. I needed solitude and a place to sit and watch the sky. Higher and higher I walked, passing a goat-herd driving his flock of skinny goats over the hillside. Here, women never were seen alone, and when they walked they walked in groups, and quickly.

A long time ago, on one of my childhood adventures for which my mother had scolded me, I had found a fig tree on this high hill, and growing with me over the years, this little blossoming tree had become my tower of solitude. In spring and summer, sitting in the crook of two low boughs, I was invisible, and through the bright green of its branches, I gazed upon the hills, spying out the land and all its creatures.

About half a mile away was a garrison of British soldiers, and from my leafy hiding place, I watched them going about their duties. They lived in tents and huts, their vehicles parked nearby. Arab women in full veil went with the soldiers into the high grasses around the camp, and the soldiers emerged shortly, hitching their pants. One morning, while I was walking to my fig tree, deeply absorbed in a book, an Arab girl stepped out from behind low bushes. Facing me, she stopped and unhooked her veil. I dropped my book, snatched it up, and, confused, ran away, her ringing laughter chasing after me.

Another time, on a warm afternoon, ready to leave my fig tree, I saw a group of British soldiers. They sat in a little dip of the hill, drinking and playing cards. Off to the side, movement caught my eye—an Arab girl was on the other side of the hill, unaware of the soldiers. I stood up in the tree to warn her, but one of the soldiers spotted her. Quickly, he and the others became a hunting pack, with two running down the hill to cut off her escape while the others formed a semicircle in front of her. She ran, saw she was trapped, and hurled stones and clumps of earth, but they pulled her down and dragged her behind the hill.

I climbed down from my tree and left quickly.

*

After six months, I quit the print shop. Mr. Zuckerman offered me a pay raise—he couldn't afford very much, he said, but I was a good worker—but I wasn't ready to make typesetting my career. The work was boring. Without ventilation, the shop stank of ink and alcohol. Every morning, walking into the dim kerosene light of the windowless shop, I left the sun behind, and was always grateful to find it still shining when I emerged in the afternoon. I thanked Mr. Zuckerman for the opportunity and said goodbye to the other workers, and went home.

*

After a week of idle reading and long midday naps, I returned to the yeshiva Chai Olam.

I was welcomed back with great kindness and enthusiasm and then left alone. No one asked where I had been. No one had to. Everyone in Batei Warsaw knew I had left the Lubavitchers and why. They knew I had spent two years at the American-style yeshiva in Givat Shaul. They knew too of my attempt to apprentice myself to Mr. Goldman and of my work in the Zuckerman print shop.

In Batei Warsaw, everyone knew everything.

Now I sat at the same table in the corner near the stove and opened the same books I had opened years ago. My eyes glanced over the pages I had studied years earlier. I sat quietly, staring at the page or out the window, my heart heavy and my eyes not seeing the words.

I knew that a good measure of what attracted me to study was the intellectual stimulation, not necessarily the material itself. It was my father I loved, not the words. Rather, I loved the words because he loved them, and I loved him. We had sat side by side in his yeshiva or at our long table in our house, the glow of the kerosene lantern lighting the pages. His soft, patient voice was a love between us, the word the medium through which that love passed. But he was in America, and without him, only the content remained, now repetitious and cold. I had nothing else, and I sat at the table with the books open before me and tried not to despair.

A week later, walking home from morning prayers, I ran into my uncle Shlomo. In Batei Warsaw, an uncle or cousin is usually just around every corner, so our meeting was no surprise.

Everyone in the Orthodox community over the age of five is always busy, but even by our hectic standards, my uncle Shlomo was an exceedingly busy man, rushing here and there for literary and social events and, in between, rushing to various synagogues for prayers, so I was surprised and moved when he stopped to chat, for it was rare that he had more than a few moments to spare between rushes. I always liked to talk to Uncle Shlomo; he had a good sense of humor and a quick turn of phrase and, most appealingly, usually took my side in all matters, defending me, for instance, against my mother's charges that I read too many secular books. He had said, "Not by Talmud alone does a man live," but he spoke with a smile and a twist so that even my mother wasn't angry.

Uncle Shlomo fell into step with me.

"Nu, Chaim, nu." He looked into my face. "You don't look so happy these days."

His unexpected sympathy filled my heart, and I couldn't speak.

Watching me intently, he said, "Let's go to the Kotel." He smiled. "I feel like I want to talk to the stones a little."

We walked silently to the Jaffa Gate, made our way through the narrow streets of the Old City, passed through the narrow stone arch, and stood in front of the ancient stones. I wasn't in the mood to pray and said nothing, but my uncle closed his eyes and, stepping close to the wall, murmured a short prayer. He then stood silently for a few long moments before turning, ready to go. "Nothing fancy," as my father always said. "A good prayer is short and simple." Many need only a few words, sometimes a touch, and they are sustained.

Jerusalem, The Kotel
The Western Wall 1929

We returned along the same route. The stones of the Kotel had opened my heart. Uncle Shlomo listened as I unburdened myself. I spoke of many things: my father's absence, the stress of our household, and my cramped life and seemingly hopeless future. My uncle said nothing until I told him about our financial problems, including my mother's loans and her day in jail.

"Really? I had no idea that smart Reizel is in so much trouble." He thought for a while. "Chaim, I have some advice. It's time for you to move out of the house. There are too many problems there that aren't yours and that you cannot solve."

"I know. But where could I go? America?"

I had thought of America often but had been afraid to say it out loud, even to myself.

"Maybe. But why go so far if all you have to do is walk out the door?"

"Because sometimes the farther away the better."

"Ah, Chaim, that's right, but why not just leave Jerusalem? A day's journey is as good as a month's. You have a good head on your shoulders, and you shouldn't waste your talents. Yerushalayim is a wonderful place, but not everyone's happy here—believe me. The yeshivas in Petah Tikva and Hebron are very good. A student like you could get free room and board and maybe even a little spending money. With a little freedom, you'll see; you'll feel much better."

His words lifted my heart. He was right. I had to leave Jerusalem, but I wasn't ready for America. Hebron had a new yeshiva, which was reputed to be top notch. Two of my cousins were enrolled, and I had heard many good things about the living conditions.

Now, there in the street, under the warm, sympathetic gaze of my uncle, I made two quick decisions: the first, to leave Jerusalem, and the second, not to go to America.

I said, "I think the yeshiva in Hebron would be perfect."

Uncle Shlomo's smile was like the sun. "Well, Chaim, that settles that!"

When I saw how happy he was, I realized that our meeting had not been entirely by chance. We parted at the little green wooden gate on Mea Shearim Road, and I continued on with a lighter step, going home to the place I had just decided to leave.

By coincidence, as I contemplated a special trip to Hebron to apply to the yeshiva—I knew I would be admitted without problem—my cousin Yitzhak invited me to join him on a trip to Safed for the Lag b'Omer holiday. Two busloads of yeshiva students from Hebron were going to pass through Jerusalem on their way to Safed, and we could hitch a ride with them. Cousin Yitzhak was excited about the excursion. He was going with a girlfriend, and he wanted me to meet her. My two other cousins from the Hebron yeshiva would be there with their wives.

"Come on, Chaim. You can spend time with your fellow scholars. We'll all have a good time. It's Lag b'Omer."

Lag b'Omer is a special holiday, the thirty-third day of the Omer period, the seven weeks between Passover and the holiday of Shavuot. Those seven weeks are a sad period full of memories of Roman persecution and crusader violence visited upon the Jews of Europe, but Lag b'Omer is the opposite. Known as the Scholars' Festival, all sorrows and lamentations are put aside for a day, and the holiday is celebrated with high and happy spirit, for even in the midst of sorrow, one must create joy. Marriages are performed, and parties are given. On that day too, many Jews both religious and secular undertake a pilgrimage to the tomb of Rabbi Simeon ben Yohai, who died in the second century; he was the author of the Zohar and the founder of kabbalah, the intense movement that sees the Torah, and all life, as a mystical, wonderful creation.

"Well, Chaim, will you come or not? There'll be some pretty girls there."

"Of course."

So I went with my cousin Yitzhak and his girlfriend to Hebron, where we met up with two of my other numerous cousins, Yaakov and Moshe Aaron, and their wives and children. We went up into the hills of Galilee to celebrate Lag b'Omer.

It was a wonderful week, the happiest of my life. It was spring in Upper Galilee; the days were warm, the nights were cool, and the air was scented with the perfume of blossoming apricot trees. Thousands of us walked to the tomb of Simeon ben Yohai to pray and give thanks and then returned to our tents. A shochet slaughtered goats and sheep, and we roasted them over open fire pits. We built huge bonfires, and on every hill as far as the eye could see, fountains of flames threw sparks into the windy night. Everyone had a musical instrument—my cousin had his violin—and we ate, drank, sang, and danced around the fires.

I was free, happy, and glad to be alive.

The morning of Lag b'Omer is special too, for it is the day when many Jewish boys get their hair cut for the first time. As it is written in Leviticus, "You shall not clip the edges of the hair at the temples or near the edges of your beard." In an observant family, a boy's hair is first cut when he is three years old, and from that day he will wear his earlocks until he dies. For this special occasion, the boys are brought to Meron, near the tomb of Simeon ben Yohai. A blessing is said, and the cutting commences. Refreshments are served as the adults sing and dance, and everyone is happy, except for the little boys, who usually cry. Watching them weep in childish fear, I remembered how I too had cried at the approach of the barber. I saw myself standing there, the fearful scissors hovering, and my hand went instinctively to one of my earlocks and pulled at it. *Until I die,* I thought, and I smiled at the little children.

My trip to Safed lasted from Monday to Thursday evening; it was the longest period I had been away from Batei Warsaw. I made friends with some of the students at the Hebron yeshiva, and I looked forward to joining them after the High Holy Days in autumn, for a new season of studies and a new life.

It was not to be.

CHAPTER 41

The summer of 1929 was a time of great unrest in Jerusalem. Friday, August 23 of that year, was the last day of the Muslim holiday of Ramadan, and large numbers of Arabs were in Jerusalem. Throughout that day, Arab agitators spread rumors that Jews were preparing to destroy the Mosque of the Golden Dome. The mosque—sometimes called the Dome of the Rock, for it is believed that therein sits the large stone from which Muhammad rose to heaven—had been built on the Temple Mount, the site of Solomon's Temple, and the word in the souk was that once the mosque was destroyed, we were planning to erect a new temple on the site. During the morning, an Arab mob rampaged through the streets of the Old City. They killed three, and the Haganah shot an equal number of Arabs.

We retreated to our houses and kept watch from the rooftops. We weren't strangers to Arab violence, but these riots were more frightening than ever. Professional agitators were spreading the word that armed Hasidic Jews were killing Muslims in their mosques. But we were hiding in our houses, hoping for God's help.

By early Friday afternoon, the British finally exerted their police powers and a semblance of calm returned to Jerusalem. In the Old City and outside its gates, throughout all Palestine and in Safed and Hebron, we were preparing to celebrate our Sabbath, our day of rest—a day of peace.

My mother was in our outdoor kitchen, stoking the fire, and I was inside.

Suddenly, people were running down Mea Shearim Road.

"They're coming! They're coming!"

I ran to the rear window but saw nothing.

"The Arabs have guns!"

I ran to the front yard. The central courtyard had a crowd of confused, frightened people. Just outside our gate, a group of men were arguing about what was happening. A Hasid in his Shabbos finery ran

368

by and stopped to shriek at them: "Why are you idiots standing here and fighting with each other? The Arabs are already in the Mea Shearim!"

Terrified, he ran on, his caftan flapping.

My mother shouted at me to stay inside, but I was out the yard, through the gate, and in the Mea Shearim in half a minute. No Arabs were there. The marketplace was empty and the stores were shuttered, as expected at this late Friday hour. I went on, feeling calmer. Men were standing at their gates and in front of the synagogues. Many held canes and bats, others had iron bars or stones. I was told of injured Jews and rioting Arabs, but no one had seen anything firsthand.

I left the Mea Shearim and hurried to the Italian hospital. King George Road was full of men in their Shabbos clothing, milling about. Pushing through, I came face-to-face with a contingent of British soldiers standing in single file across the road. They lowered their rifles, not letting me pass. I asked them questions, first in Yiddish and then in broken English, but they remained mute and impassive. Finally, their officer gave me a push.

"*Kleine Yiddle, geh vek.*" (Little Jew, get lost).

I turned around and questioned the Hasidim in the road. From the few who had actually seen something, I pieced together what had happened.

Half an hour earlier, a mob of about five hundred Arabs—that being the average of the widely differing numbers from a dozen sources— had gathered outside the Old City. With cries of "Allah Akbar! God is great!" agitators exhorted the mob to storm the Mea Shearim and wreak vengeance on the alien Zionist Orthodox infidel Jews. A Jewish police captain first begged the British soldiers and then demanded that they do something, but their commanding officer refused. His majesty's solders had been ordered to remain neutral and await instructions.

Just when the mob reached a murderous fever pitch, another of our miracles occurred. From nowhere, an old jeep appeared. Out leaped two soldiers from the Haganah. One of them had a revolver. He took careful aim at the shrieking leader, and brought him down with a single shot. The entire mob scattered in all directions.

Before the British soldiers could exercise their neutrality, the men sped away.

Now the shadows were lengthening, the Sabbath was soon to commence. I left the British soldiers to stand guard across the road and await further instructions, and hurried home.

In Batei Warsaw, the fear had eased somewhat, and I went to the synagogue for evening prayers. We tried to muster some of the customary joy, but the service was cut short when a Hasid stuck his head in the door and warned us of a possible attack.

Home, I found my sister Hinda and her husband in our house; they had come, as usual, to spend a happy Friday night with us. My mother lit the Shabbos candles. I sang the Kiddush, and we sat down to supper. But the streets outside were full of uncommon activity. People had gathered to talk and ague, while from doors and windows others were shouting at them to shut up and observe the Sabbath. My mother served supper. I knew that the food was delicious, but it was dust and straw on my tongue.

Just after darkness, we heard unusual noises on Mea Shearim Road. Two old buses with Haganah soldiers were rumbling toward Batei Hungary, where it was rumored the Arabs would attack. My brother-in-law and I left to check things out, and after an hour of investigation, we learned, according to the most reliable sources, the Arabs, under threat of retaliation by the Haganah, were leaving Jerusalem and returning to their villages in the hills.

But the rumors were many. Someone told us that a hundred Jews had been killed; others put the number at a dozen. A man whose brother-in-law was a policeman said that only a handful had been injured. As we talked, a British army truck pulled up, and a dozen soldiers jumped out. Their officer ordered us in loud, broken Yiddish to return home immediately or be shot.

"By order of the high commissioner," he bellowed, "Jerusalem is now under martial law. A twelve-hour curfew is in effect."

With rifles level, the soldiers moved among the crowd, forcing us to disperse.

"Are we not permitted to pray?" a man demanded.

"Medical exemptions are allowed. There are none for the fulfillment of religious duties."

The man said something in English, and a soldier immediately swung his rifle. The man fell to the ground. People started shouting. A stone was thrown—I admit it came from my hand. My brother-in-law restrained me. The soldiers moved into a battle line, and we saw the wisdom in retreat.

I had lived through the cruel, fearful years of World War I and had heard firsthand accounts of bloody pogroms, but that Friday night I was beset with an anxiety more unremitting than any I had ever experienced. The deep darkness of the Jerusalem summer night was electric with fear. No one slept. My sister and her family were curled quietly in a corner; my two younger brothers lay on the floor on their blankets with their eyes open. In her chair, my mother sat in the dark and looked at me as I stood at the front window.

All of Batei Warsaw was awake.

When our wall clock struck eleven, a vehicle drove down Mea Shearim Road and stopped just under our rear window. I ran to the back and saw only the dark outline of an old army truck. There were quick footsteps in our yard, followed by a knock on the door. Terrified, my mother put her finger to her mouth. I held my ear to the door. A second knock, but friendly.

It was my cousin Mendel, a pistol in his hand. He stood in the dark.

"Chaim, tell your mother and sister not to worry."

"What's going on?"

"The Arabs are regrouping. But we have our people here, and nothing will happen in Jerusalem. I give you my word."

He left, and I bolted the door.

Outside, there were motor vehicles racing on the road and figures in the black shadows. It was the first hours of the holy, peaceful Sabbath, and men with guns and cars should not have been in Batei Warsaw or on Mea Shearim Road. However, the preservation of life takes precedence over all other obligations, and no one raised any objections.

"It is written," I told everyone, "that when you know someone is coming to do you harm in the night, you have the right—more, the duty—to take up arms and strike first."

Exhausted, I fell into a chair, pulled a thin blanket over my head, and dozed off.

In the morning, the curfew had been lifted, and the synagogue was especially crowded. Horror stories were circulating, but no reliable information was available. The curfew had kept everyone indoors since early last evening, and our usual sources—the curious, the concerned, and the busybodies—had been unable to gather any data. Jerusalem had no radio station, nor, for that matter, did we have any radios. Newspapers were not published on Saturday, and even if they had been, no one in the religious community would have bought or read one. The lack of information only increased our fears.

But the Haganah was on full alert.

You had to know whom to look for and where to look, but everywhere I turned, I saw our protectors, some of them in disguise in alleys and others, bolder, holding rifles on rooftops.

My cousin Mendel was just inside the green door in Batei Hungary. Jerusalem was safe.

But Hebron was not. Eight hundred Jews lived in Hebron, with a hundred more yeshiva students in dormitories nearby—the continuation of a Jewish presence that had existed in Hebron for almost two thousand years. Relations between the Jews of Hebron and their Arab neighbors were unusually cordial, and relying upon that long history of mutual respect and friendship, the Jewish leaders there had refused the Haganah's offer of protection. My cousins who lived in Hebron often had Arab guests in their homes; Yaako, the ritual slaughterer, also performed circumcisions on Jewish infants, as he did for the local Arab boys, who underwent the ritual when they were thirteen years old.

However, hate is contagious, and violence knows no bounds. The Haganah warned the community in Hebron that events were spinning out of control, but their words fell on ears made deaf by hope. Rabbi Yaakov Slonim, the leader of the Hebron community, was not afraid. Even during the ten years of British rule in Palestine, when there had been riots and killings in other cities, there had never been problems in Hebron.

Two days earlier, on Thursday, the community leaders had turned away two buses of Haganah soldiers, fearing that the presence of armed Jews might inflame the Arabs. In addition, responding to the riots in Jerusalem, the British army had stationed a small unit just outside the city limits. The Haganah officers pleaded, but in the end, they had no choice but to turn their buses around and depart.

On Friday night, the Arabs who had attempted to storm the Jewish enclaves in Jerusalem retreated back to their hillside villages. Inflamed, they marched on Hebron.

All through the night, the Jews of Hebron heard the Arabs gathering. Shooting rifles in the air and ululating their war cries, they filled the darkness with terror. Without arms of any kind, defended only by hope, the Jewish community huddled and prayed.

The small unit of His Majesty's soldiers remained on the outskirts of the city, steadfastly neutral and awaiting further instructions.

*

Early the next morning all of Batei Warsaw poured out into the street. There was no news. Trying once again to kindle the Sabbath spirit, we went to morning prayers. By Saturday afternoon, rumors of terrible things in Hebron were circulating. Our synagogue, always full of song and dance, held only low, tense talk. Again, the British had cordoned off Jerusalem and imposed a six o'clock curfew. Nothing could be verified. Armed British soldiers patrolled our streets, and we were ordered into our homes and told to wait for morning.

In my house, the tension was unbearable. No one spoke. There was no word of my two cousins and their families in Hebron. Fear and hope raged in our breasts. My mother sat through the night, neither moving nor speaking. At dawn on Sunday, we rushed out into the streets to join the crowd from the Mea Shearim, but the British had sealed off the roads to Hebron, and no one had gotten through yet. We knew little but the rumors, which we found impossible to believe.

At noon, word came.

The horrors were true.

*

The British administration had given the chief rabbi of Jerusalem the names of those killed and injured.

My mother and I rushed to the residence of the chief rabbi. The streets and courtyard were crowded with men and women, some trying to get in and others wailing and shrieking. Two police guards stood at the gate.

"Go in, Chaim," my mother said.

I stated my name and my family connection to the Hebron residents and was allowed in. I stood in line outside the rabbi's door. We went in one by one. I watched the faces coming out. My heart was full of terrible foreboding and endless hope. Then it was my turn. My mouth was trembling, and my heart was beating heavily in my chest. I went in. The rabbi stood at his desk. His face was gray, and his beard was streaked with tears.

On the wall in back of me were two lists: one of the injured and one of the others not as fortunate. The names were in alphabetical order, with the injured listed first. My cousins were not among them. Then, on the list of those killed, I went immediately to the R's:

> Reisman, Moshe Aaron
> Reisman, Yaakov Zeev

Oh, the horror!

Woe, woe, and more woe.

My mother kept stumbling, and with her arm around me for support, we made our way slowly up Jaffa Road to Batei Warsaw, stopping every few yards so she could catch her breath.

Our poor little house was crowded with people.

My cousin Mendel was there. He had tried to protect our family in

Hebron but had been turned away. He knew about the massacre before we did and had come as soon as he could get through the British lines.

He nodded at me and then at my mother. His face was ashen. He sat quietly on a chair, lowered his head, and put his arms on his knees, and stayed like that for the afternoon.

My uncle Yisrael Yitzhak came in, stood in the center of our big room, looked slowly at the walls and ceiling, and then left without saying a word to anyone. We did not see him for many days.

On Monday, the survivors were evacuated from Hebron and brought to Jerusalem in British army vehicles. My dead cousin Yaakov Zeev's children and his wife were alive and uninjured, and were also brought to Jerusalem.

With the evacuation, the Jewish presence in Hebron came to an end after two millennia.

The British justified the evacuation on the grounds of security concerns.

We knew better. The British—the civilized, educated, neutral British—were playing their own particular brand of ugly politics, using the pretext of the massacre to give the Arabs the city of Hebron, free of Jews.

"The British," someone said.

"May they rot in hell," responded one of my uncles.

*

Over the next few days, the *Doar Hayom* published the details.

Early Saturday morning, at first light, the Arabs began their massacre.

The first attack was against the yeshiva. Many of the students had left for synagogue, and only twenty-seven young men were in the dormitories. The Arabs tortured and killed them, cut off their heads, stuck them on sharpened sticks, and carried them through the streets to the insane jubilation of wild Arab mobs.

The news had raced like bitter fire through Hebron, and many Jews fled to the house of Yoel Slonim, the rabbi's son, whose family had lived in Hebron for generations. His house was a fortress of heavy stone and iron gates and protected by goodwill and years of peace.

The Arabs stormed the gates. Thirty-seven more Jews were killed. Men and women, young and old, children and infants, were tortured and beheaded, as was the rabbi's son.

The torture, rape, and pillage continued into Saturday afternoon, until the British soldiers, finally receiving their instructions, entered Hebron and fired a warning volley into the air, scattering the Arabs into the hills. My cousin Moshe Aaron was killed on Saturday morning in the yeshiva auditorium, along with the twenty-six other students who had gathered for Sabbath prayers.

My other cousin, Yaakov Zeev, was killed at home when he returned from synagogue.

Both suffered the same ugly fate at the hands of the wild Arabs: their heads were cut off and carried on spikes through the streets of Hebron.

The rioting lasted six hours, the news reports said. Observers stated that the local police, consisting entirely of Arabs, had been unable to prevent the violence. The British claimed, so the newspapers stated, that their soldiers had been unaware of the massacre, but when apprised of the situation, they took forceful action by firing into the air.

On Thursday, four days after the killings, the British administration informed us that a convoy of trucks would convey relatives and friends of the victims to Hebron, and we would be able to retrieve whatever property could be found. The convoy would travel under the protection of His Majesty's armed forces.

My mother asked me to go.

I was one of many. We sat in a big, open army truck, gripping the sides as we bounced along the mountain roads. There were four trucks, and in front and back of the convoy were armed escorts.

The convoy parked in the village square and the soldiers helped us out. We walked to the Jewish quarter, soldiers in front and back. It was a beautiful summer day, sunny and breezy. The streets were empty, birds were singing. The soldiers' boots clacked on the hard earth. It was impossible to believe that anything evil had happened here.

We walked to the yeshiva. Twenty-seven students had been killed there. It was a slaughterhouse. Blood was everywhere. Books were torn and burned, tables and chairs broken. Windows were smashed, and glass littered the floor.

Just weeks earlier, I had been here for Lag b'Omer. I had sat with my cousins at these long tables. We had studied side by side. When we prayed, his slender frame had swayed like a reed in the wind as we chanted the ancient melodies.

"When will you start your studies?" he had asked.

"In the fall, with the new year."

"You will like it here, Chaim," he said.

The soldiers led us to the home of Rabbi Slonim. The iron gates were twisted and torn, and the interior doors had been ripped from their hinges. Everything that had not been looted was covered with blood. A curl of blond hair and a few feathers from a pillow lay on the floor, stuck together with clotted blood.

I turned at a sound; a British officer was crying.

In the Jewish quarter, the soldiers stood outside, their rifles unslung, while we went in.

In my cousin Yaakov Zeev's house, nothing had been touched or taken. In the kitchen were the special knives he'd used to slaughter animals for kosher meat. As required, they were exceptionally clean and sharp. The long, wide mahogany table where Yaakov and his Arab neighbors had sat, drank tea, and listened to music, was set for a meal. In the backyard a few chickens pecked the earth.

There was a noise at the door. A British soldier was gesturing; the convoy was leaving.

A few weeks later, furniture and household items from Hebron's Jewish quarter were brought to Jerusalem and given to the relatives of the dead. I took two of my cousin's prayer books for my mother.

On that terrible day in Hebron, sixty-seven Jewish lives were extinguished.

Together with those killed in Jerusalem, the total was 133.

The wounded numbered 339.

My mother was brought to the edge of despair. My cousins' deaths were hideous beyond comprehension. There had been no ritual burial, and all the dead had been cast into a single pit dug from the rocky earth.

My poor mother went about her daily routine numb and weary, unable to smile.

She did not curse or condemn.

"The barbaric Muslim killers," she said, "and the false English guardians are exactly who they are. It is expected. I am angry with God. He was my friend."

I had no wisdom or solace to offer, nor had her brother.

Sad, mournful weeks passed, and one day my mother came to me.

"Chaim, I want you to read from the Midrash for me."

The Midrash is the body of work that explains and interprets the themes of the Torah, revealing God's love and justice. It is many volumes long and contains passages of great beauty.

"Imma, what do you want to hear?"

"That part, Chaim, where God is asked questions."

She sat and waited, her eyes closed.

I knew the passage by heart. It was in Hebrew, and rather than read and translate it, I recited it in Yiddish: "'The Assembly of Israel asked of God: Your Torah forbids us to slaughter a cow and her young baby-calf in the same day because of the tender feelings of the mother for her baby calf. Why were You silent when the enemy slaughtered our mothers with their children in the same day? We are obliged to sacrifice our lives for Your Name, but Heaven remains silent when we are annihilated.'"

My mother sat still and silent.

I looked at her for a while and then left the room.

Where was the angel who could have stayed the hand of the executioner?

British Transport, Hebron 1929

Hebron, a Ransacked Jewish Home

CHAPTER 42

With the end of my Hebron dream, America became my Promised Land.

Unacknowledged to even myself, it had always been.

I corresponded with my father and my brother Moshe in New York, and they wrote back promptly, promising to help in every way.

Surprisingly, my mother was enthusiastic about my America adventure, as she called it. At last, she was able to admit that the life of a yeshiva scholar was not for me. Matchmakers had been talking to her, but she knew that I was not ready for a family and had rejected all proposals, not even bothering to inform me.

My American adventure also served her own interests. America was a *goldene medina*, a country of gold, and she assumed I would make my fortune in the United States and then, unburdened by wife and children, lift her heavy burden of debt. She assumed too that my absence would be temporary and that, upon returning to Jerusalem after a reasonable interval, I would marry, have children, and live in Batei Warsaw.

However, I simply wanted to leave Batei Warsaw and get to America; after that, my life was a blank page.

News traveled fast in Batei Warsaw, and one morning my favorite uncle, Yisrael Yitzhak, arriving for his morning coffee, gave me an unusual sharp look.

"So, Chaim," he said, sitting down at the table, "what's your hurry to leave Jerusalem?"

It wasn't a question as much as an invitation to argue, emphasizing not the positive aspect of going to America but the negative of leaving Jerusalem. Knowing that any discussion would require me to defend every aspect of my life, I did not respond.

A person determined to prove his or her point will find something wrong with everything.

Besides, I knew Batei Warsaw: the least little change provoked endless outcry.

My plans quickly took shape.

My father sent affidavits and other papers needed for my visa. I provided two photographs, a statement from the police attesting to my lawfulness, and a letter from an ordained rabbi affirming my high moral character. I could have provided a dozen such letters, but they only wanted one.

With these official papers transformed by the bureaucratic alchemy of colored stamps and seals into higher forms of documentation, I was ready to purchase passage to the New World. The booking agent required still more papers. I needed, first, a formal letter from a doctor that I was in perfect health and, second, another letter from an oph-thalmologist that I was free of all infectious eye diseases, including trachoma. The agent was insistent; the steamship companies were accepting too many sick and half-blind passengers, burdening the United States government with the expense of sending them back to their native lands. A law had just been passed in America, the agent explained, that made the companies responsible for the cost of return, so travel agents now insisted that passengers comply with American health codes.

"You see, Chaim," my mother said, "the American eye doctor knew what he was doing."

Baruch HaShem.

My file complete, I was ready to buy a ticket.

Travel agents are like matchmakers, preferring to deal with the best, for that was where the biggest commission lay.

First class was the only way for a young scholar such as myself to travel.

"The best," they insisted, "is what you want, young man. A cabin on an upper deck with a window—that's the way to go."

I made inquiries, did some hard bargaining, and booked accommo-dations that my mother, with a sarcastic smile, described as "the best of the worst."

I wasn't upset. After all, the boat and I were entering into a brief marriage of convenience, and I wasn't going to squander my meager funds on luxuries of which I knew little and would not miss. I was concerned only with the price of the ticket, and was too inexperienced to ask about the size of the boat, its condition, the length of the voyage, the number of ports of call, the size of my cabin or the number of passengers in it, nor the deck where the cabin was located. The ticket agent knew he had an amateur.

"Young man," he assured me, knowing he would never see me again, "for your money, you're getting the absolute best."

I had a choice of two sailing dates. The agent advised sailing early, in mid-October, when the notoriously stormy Atlantic would be calmer. I decided on the November date, so I would be in Jerusalem for the last of the high holy days.

"My son shouldn't be sailing on the ocean," my mother said, "during the Sukkoth holiday without a family and a sukkah to eat in."

My ticket to America cost $110.

The voyage would take thirty-one days.

The ship was the *Alesia*. It was to sail from Jaffa on Thursday, November 15, 1929.

I was advised to take at least fifty dollars for incidentals; I had no idea what incidentals I could possibly require in the middle of an ocean.

I had a hundred dollars held in trust by Uncle Yisrael Yitzhak, which my father had sent from America for my short-lived apprenticeship in watch repair. My uncle gave me the money without comment, though his eyes spoke his sadness. The secret savings from my various yeshiva stipends, principally from Mr. Andrew's American-style yeshiva, yielded another thirty dollars. Without hesitation, my mother offered to make up the balance. She expected that my sojourn in America would produce immediate financial rewards for her, and my credit rating in Jerusalem was climbing to new heights as news of my departure spread.

With ticket and documents in hand, my future beckoned. In mid-October I began an intensive study of English. I read as many newspapers as possible, my dictionary open on the table. Without a partner to practice with, I had to imagine the pronunciation. Many English words have a German origin, and on some, I came close. *Water* and *wasser*, for instance, are not that far apart. *Come* and *kommen* are obvious. However, the silent letters and the diphthongs were problematic. *Enough*, for instance, I pronounced *enug*, which was close to the

Yiddish *genug*. I had trouble with *schedule*, which I thought should sound like she-doo-lee. I thought about my English tutor and the word *wave*. I would soon be seeing real waves.

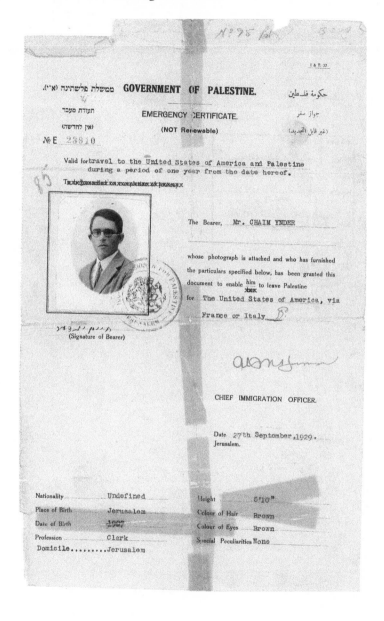

Mr Chaim Ynder

is free from Trachoma and any

other eye - defect, which could

prevent to earn a living.

——————

Ticho

OPHTHALMIC HOSPITAL – JERUSALEM

DR. A. TICHO בית מרפא

Out-Pat. Dep. 379
Phone Residence 561

№ 34.042

Dr. M. NEUMANN

Telephone 205.

Jerusalem 4 – 10 – 1929

I Dr. M. Neumann certify
that I have to-day examined
Mr. *Chaim Ynder*
and found him to be in good
health and in particular free
of leprosy, syphilis, plague.
tubercular affection of
any kind, body parasites
and their eggs, loathsome
or dangerous contagious
diseases, or mental defects
or physical disability.

F. Neumann

Dr. M. Neumann
Jerusalem

As summer ended and the High Holy Days began, the time I had left in Jerusalem dwindled with the falling light, and I began to make my farewell rounds.

On Friday, I went to the Mea Shearim Talmud Torah, where I had spent so much of my life from the time I was three until I turned fourteen. I went in the late afternoon, when the school was empty. I wanted to be alone with my childhood companions, who had scattered over the years to faraway places.

Ah, they were all in attendance, sitting at the long, narrow benches, talking and laughing in the gentle afternoon light

I was there too, a little boy in earlocks and bare feet.

The younger version of me seemed to sense my presence, for he looked around, curious, measuring the air, then returned to his book, a serious, quiet child.

I walked through the classrooms in the order of my years, smiling at my teachers, some of whom no longer walked the earth. They all recognized me and smiled back.

In one room, I sat in front of the Kleine Rebbe, the little man and his little wife. In another room, I sat on the cold stone floor around the Roiter Rebbe, listening to his stories about Abraham and Isaac and watching his cheeks puff up with the cigarettes made from the butts we found on the street, his face as red as a tomato as he coughed and coughed. Through the empty school I walked, slowly, looking about. What a soft and tender child I was, innocent and trusting. All through the war, through years of hunger and cold, fear and hope, even after the terrible blows in Hebron, I was still innocent. Would America take that from me? Friends and relatives kept warning me, and I had begun to doubt the wisdom of my journey. It was not too late. I could stay in the safety of these rooms and become a rebbe to successive generations of young boys. It was not too late. They would call me Reb Chaim, and I would be gentle with them, for I remembered how I had loved gentleness.

I would give them my father's advice not to take their studies too seriously.

"Chaim, you have studied enough," he often said. "Now it's time to play."

Time to play, I thought. *Time to live.*

My mother and I didn't talk about my upcoming journey

"The thing," my mother called it. "We will not talk about The Thing until we have to."

On the first day of November, two weeks before sailing, I bought a valise and put it on the floor in a corner of the grosse shtub. I left it open, a clear and unequivocal sign meant to convince everyone about the seriousness of my American adventure.

I wanted to convince myself as well.

My educated, witty uncle Shlomo Wertheimer came by a week before departure to bid me farewell. He told me of his travels on the high seas and talked at length about the great whales that inhabit the deep. Though he himself had not seen such creatures when he sailed the Mediterranean, he described them in some detail, citing commentaries on the story of Jonah.

"Their mouths are very wide and very long," he told me, "and their bodies are sized accordingly. They have an interesting color, and their eyes are able to see in almost total darkness. I am positively certain you will see them in the Atlantic."

"I certainly hope I will."

"Of course, there is nothing to fear from these mighty leviathans. Modern ocean going vessels are built to withstand such hazards."

"I have every confidence in my boat."

"And you must take a blanket, Chaim, for warmth. The ocean in winter is very cold."

My valise was small, but I assured him I would give the blanket consideration.

"And this too." He held out a large jar doubly sealed with a screw cap and wax paper. "It's mish-mish for my son, Wolfe, in Philadelphia."

I took the jar; it was heavy.

"I made it myself yesterday from apricots just outside Jerusalem," said Uncle Shlomo. "You know how your cousin loves jam. I made this extra sweet, the way he likes it. But only if you can, Chaim. I don't want to give you an extra burden."

For my educated, witty uncle Shlomo, of course! I put the jar in the open valise.

With departure imminent, a steady stream of family and friends came to say goodbye, all with advice and warnings. I took my daily walk through the streets of Jerusalem, but my mother admonished me to stay close, lest someone miss me.

Saying goodbye to people is easy; you sit at home, and they come to you. To part with places, however, requires perambulation, and I spent my last two days in Jerusalem visiting the streets of my childhood.

My last visit to the Kotel Ha'Maravi was hard. I stood before the wall for only a few minutes, explaining why I was leaving Jerusalem, my true and only home. I pressed my lips to a warm stone, said goodby, and left.

In the Old City, I kept an eye out for the child running on the dusty streets with his cousins, and here and there, in his favorite alleys and in a few of his secret hiding places, I saw young Chaim barefoot and laughing. But the boy ignored me, for he was not interested in spending time with the stranger I had become. Besides, he had to be home for supper. So did I, or my fretful mother would scold me. I left the Old City and hurried through the Jaffa Gate.

I visited the Talmud Torah on last time. I went from classroom to classroom, stopping at last in the big auditorium. Two men were at the study tables. Leib Matmid (the Diligent Learner) called me over; we had last seen each other five years ago.

"Chaim, what brings you to our yeshiva today?"

"I'm leaving for America tomorrow."

He stared at me.

"Yes, tomorrow," I said. "I wanted to say goodbye."

He turned away and said nothing.

At another table near the window, in his usual place, sat Moshe Soisek, or Moshe the Silent One. He did not speak, he had told us, because he had learned that most talk led to lies and gossip, and he wanted to use his mouth and tongue only for prayers and study. True to himself, he did not ask why I was there, but I told him anyway, and his silence spoke his displeasure.

I walked to the Lubavitcher yeshiva, where I had studied for three years. It was the time of day when the scholars had left and the classrooms were empty. In the big study hall I sat at my assigned seat at the table near the door. There I had sat with the aloof young rabbinical scholar who had married my sister, and with my blind friend, the elderly Saggi Nohoir, rich in light. We had talked of many things, including what was and what might be. Though blind, he had many memories of his youth of golden sight, his cornerstones of sight upon which, during his decades of blindness, he had built towers of bright, wonderful visions.

Nothing on earth is ever lost. My old blind friend had died years ago, but now, as I sat in my seat, his voice was alive across the table. Before blindness had overtaken him, he had been a scientist, and in his house he had a phonograph. I had been amazed at the music coming from the strange device. He had a vision that one day in the future, science would invent an instrument that would retrieve all the lost voices of the world. "All songs and melodies will be collected," he'd told me, "and we shall hear the voices of the prophets, of Isaiah and of Moses, and perhaps even the voice of God speaking to the children of Israel on Mount Sinai."

"Ah," I'd said, "and perhaps science will also invent instruments that will let the blind see, and you will walk again with the sun in the day and with the stars at night."

Tears had flowed from his sightless eyes. "Yes, Chaim, someday that will happen."

I gave the walls a last look, spoke a silent promise to return, and walked out.

Not ready to go home, I retraced my steps and wandered aimlessly through the streets of Jerusalem, the center of my universe. There would be no more yeshivas, no more books, and no more sounds and smells of the marketplace.

Tomorrow at this very hour, I will be on the road to Jaffa. Yet how strange—I am here for the first time. Everything is new. See these stone buildings and the men in their long black caftans. I, a child, stand among them while they sway before the wall, prayer books open, mouths moving in praise of HaShem.

Late in the afternoon, I finally returned home. My mother gave me a chiding look; where had I been all afternoon? Lately, whenever I went out, she cautioned me about getting lost. I knew what she meant. But how could I be lost, for I was finding myself.

Now she was bent over my valise, fussing with it yet again. I was traveling for thirty days to a faraway land, and my valise was half empty, a testament to the poverty of our lives. I had packed a winter coat of wool and felt and cotton, which my mother had sewn from her collection of fabrics; one pair of pants; some underwear and socks; three shirts; and a cap—not a hat. Watching her rearrange my clothing with her nervous hands, I wanted my journey to America—The Thing, as she called it—to be done.

Fearing that the boat might run out of food on such a long voyage, my mother had baked all sorts of cakes and breads. My sisters had made my favorite Friday night strudel and two jars of pickled herring. I packed everything, and the apricot jam for my cousin Wolfe in Philadelphia, in a big tin box that fit snugly in the bottom of my valise. On the advice of Uncle Shlomo, who not only was an expert on whales but also knew much about ocean travel, my mother added a dozen lemons, for seasickness. One of my aunts had contributed a big chunk of halvah, not for any medicinal value but simply because I liked it. I put every thing in my tin can. My peripatetic larder was now heavier than my valise.

At dusk, after my last evening service in Jerusalem, I visited Moshe's wife, Dvorah. My older brother had been gone for five years, and she hoped that when I saw Moshe in New York, I would convince him to return to Jerusalem and renew their marriage. Dvorah gave me two photographs: one of their two children and the other of herself in a more modern dress and what looked like a touch of lipstick.

"Be certain Moshe gets them," she told me.

"I will give them to him the moment I see him."

Home, visitors were waiting. Some gave me names and addresses of friends and relatives in the United States. Others gave me letters and asked me to address them in Latin letters and to mail them as soon as I arrived in America. The stream of visitors continued till midnight, their advice and gifts easily filling another valise. My mother would not go to bed.

"I can sleep when you're gone," she said. "Now I'll stay up so you don't get lost."

Early in the morning, I went one last time to the Hasidic synagogue, where the *baal tefilah*, or the leader of the prayers, raced through the service so that the day laborers could leave promptly for their jobs. That morning, the baal tefilah was Meir Ackerman, known as the Express Cantor, who, despite his speed, never missed a precious word.

"Chaim," he said, "I wanted to finish quickly and say goodbye. Do not forget us."

At home, my grandmother Nechama gave me her formal blessing, placing her hands on my shoulders and asking that I be given courage, strength, and faith. I hurried off to my grandmother Esther. Talking with her was always a delight, for she spoke in quotes from the Bible. When asked her name, for instance, she did not respond directly but said, "So thou have learned, whoever reports a thing in the name that said it brings deliverance into the world; as it is said, 'and Esther told the king in the name of Mordecai.'"

That morning, she spoke without reference or quote. "Chaim, your names means 'life.' It means also 'wise,' for if you add all the letters of your name, the sum is sixty-eight, as is the word for 'wise': *chochom*. And that is a double blessing."

Returning home, I checked my valise, added a few items to the tin box, and told my mother I had to go out for an hour.

"The bus for Jaffa leaves exactly at three o'clock," she reminded me for the tenth time that morning. "And it won't wait for you. Don't get lost."

Unable to stay away from the synagogue, I went there again, expecting it to be empty. There was one solitary congregant in the cold building.

"Ah, Chaim, back so soon from America?"

He studied me as I looked around.

"What is here to see," he finally asked, "that you haven't seen many times before?"

The walls were in place, and the ark stood in the dim light on the bema. I stood in the cool silence of the synagogue, and every tefilah I had ever spoken filled the air with its chanting melody and echoed in my heart, never to be lost.

Home, I had lunch with one of my sisters and her husband. We ate in silence at our long table. My mother put my tefillin (phylacteries) and a siddur (prayer book) into my valise. At the chime of three, the bus blew its horn on Mea Shearim Road. I walked through a long line of neighbors wishing me luck, success, and return.

The driver threw my valise onto the roof of the bus, where his helper arranged it so that it had a fighting chance of not falling off. My mother, my two brothers, and I found seats in the rear of the crowded bus. It was three months after the recent Arab attacks, and the windows were protected with hanging sandbags. I told my mother to sit on the aisle. Soon the twisting streets of Batei Warsaw were behind us. We picked up a few passengers, and soon were on the road to Jaffa. We sped down the long, open highway to the Mediterranean. My mother opened her prayer book and murmured from memory.

We stayed that night with relatives of my grandfather Fishel. They too had emigrated from Poland, had settled in the secular city of Jaffa. Thursday morning, they served an abundant breakfast.

"Take, take," my cousin kept saying. "Take all you want. You'll see, Chaim, what it means to go to America. You think this breakfast in Jaffa is big? Wait till you get to America!"

Suddenly, it was late, and we rushed through the streets of Jaffa to the dock, only to be told that I could not board until the ship's doctor examined me. While my brothers and cousin guarded my valise, my mother and I rushed to the medical office.

My mother sat in the waiting room. The Thing was about to happen. My brother had left and would probably not return to Eretz Yisrael; my father had planned to return after two years but had been gone almost five. Now I was going to America. She had given me her blessing, but if my departure could be delayed even briefly, she would be pleased. She sat in the waiting room, eyes fixed on the door. When I emerged, she knew by my smile that all hope was gone.

We walked very slowly, arm in arm. It was a foggy autumn morning, and the clouds were low and thick. A cold wind was blowing. She stopped.

"Look at you, Chaim."

I had not buttoned the top two buttons of my shirt, and now she lifted her hands to my chest. Her trembling fingers fumbled over my heart.

"Chaim, don't forget to button your shirt and coat in America. Don't go without supper. Take care of yourself. Chaim, promise me."

"Of course. Cold doesn't bother me."

"It's colder in New York than in Jerusalem."

We walked very slowly to the port, my mother stretching the moments. On the dock my brothers and cousin were still standing close guard over my valise.

Then I saw it.

The fog, slowly lifting, had opened the sky, and there in the middle of a bright patch of water sat the *Alesia*. It was the first time I had seen the sea or a boat.

It was to be the first of many others.

BOOK 3

The United States of America

There's a place for you in this world.

CHAPTER 43

In 1929, my father was a young man of twenty-two when he left his home in Jerusalem to immigrate to the United States. Like his father before him, who had left Poland half a century earlier and was to marry a young woman and start a new life in Jerusalem, my father was to meet, quite by chance, a woman who had also immigrated from Palestine, with whom he would make a life in New York.

In my possession is the small portfolio of thin blue fabric in which my father carried his precious documents, among them an inspection card that allowed him to board the *Alesia*. This card indicated that he was in third class, the lowest level on the ship. He was listed on the ship's manifest, number thirty-eight, as passenger twenty-seven.

My father left Jerusalem in search of a better, more productive life, and he always joked about his poor timing. He arrived in the New World barely two months after the stock market crash of October 1929, when the land of gold was about to become a realm of dross. But he had experienced great and prolonged deprivation, and the Great Depression held no terrors. No matter how little he had, he told my brothers and me, it was more than what he'd had in Jerusalem. He lived for a while on the Lower East Side of Manhattan, on Rivington Street, as well as in furnished rooms in various parts of Manhattan and Brooklyn. While attending night school, he sold neckties in bars, restaurants, and barbershops. Then he learned printing, and began a life long career--

But I am getting ahead of my father's story. His sea voyage to America proved to be quite interesting, and he'll tell you about it himself.

Chapter 44

In 1929, Palestine didn't have a port deep enough for boats of the *Alesia* class, so I descended from the dock to a small platform, and into a small rowboat powered by two young Arabs.

It was the first time I was on water. Huge waves lifted the tiny boat high and dropped it with a heavy smack. The two Arabs spat into the sea and cursed the waves, the sky, and all people who made boats. Every three strokes, one of them scooped the water swirling around our feet into a pail and threw it overboard. I balanced the valise on my knees, the heavy tin on top of the valise. The Arabs cursed, spat, rowed, and bailed as the rowboat rocked and swayed, plunged and rose. I took my cue from the Arabs, who were more angry than frightened. We rose and fell to a rhythm of Arabic curses. At last, I was experiencing a real wave. I held the side of the boat with one hand, my tin with the other, and tried to suppress my growing nausea.

From shore, the *Alesia* had looked small, but now it was a towering cliff of dirty black steel. I saw no gangplank or steps. Maneuvering closer and closer, the Arabs cursed, spat, and rowed furiously. One of them saw me looking around, and he pointed, grinning, to a ladder made of wood and rope against the side of the ship. As one Arab worked his oar, the other reached out, grasped a guide rope, and pulled the ladder close.

"*Geh*! *Geh*!" (Go! Go!), he shouted in accented Yiddish.

This was another first—a seemingly impossible one. I left the valise in the rowboat, put the heavy tin box under my arm, stood, and reached for the ladder with my left hand. The rowboat rose and fell, and the ladder, held in position by the two Arabs clutching the guide ropes, swayed in and out. I fell back into the rowboat.

"Geh!"

I stood. One of the young Arabs put his hand under my arm. I put my right foot on the ladder, reached with my free hand for a higher rung, pressed my tin box to my chest, and tried for the next rung. I had run over rooftops in Batei Warsaw, scrambled up trees, and dashed through the alleys of Jerusalem, but this rope ladder was an altogether different animal. Slowly, carefully, clumsily, and propelled by curses of encouragement, I crawled halfway up the ladder. I had to rest. I looked down at the sea and the Arabs gesturing in the tiny, bouncing rowboat. I marveled at myself—a thin Hasidic young man in caftan, yarmulke, and new shoes, working his way up the side of a huge ship in a heaving sea. I started up again, but my slow progress was unacceptable, and a sailor slid down the guide ropes and held out his hand.

"*Gib mir.*" (Give me), he said in German.

He wanted my tin box, and without hesitation I surrendered my precious larder. He scrambled up the ladder like a monkey. I, freed from my burden, climbed the rest of the way without difficulty, followed by one of the Arabs with my luggage strapped to his back. I should have given him a few piasters for his help, but I didn't know anything about tipping, and baksheesh didn't seem appropriate.

I stood on the deck of the *Alesia*, wet, cold, and thoroughly confused.

A command in Yiddish, delivered with a distinct English accent, clarified matters. Four British soldiers with strapped rifles stood behind a long table. The officer who had shouted at me sat in the only chair. He beckoned. Valise in hand, I placed my documents one by one on the table. Without a glance, the officer pushed them back.

"*Genug.*" (Enough). His Majesty's Royal Government wasn't going to prevent a Jew from leaving Palestine.

"*Geh recht,*" he said.

I went right, and stood at another table. Two sailors in black berets sat behind it, an officer stood between them. He asked for my ticket in Yiddish heavily accented with French. He glanced at it, pulled his mouth down, and snapped an order. The sailor on his right reached into a box and handed me my room key. Another order, and a sailor from a long line picked up my valise and food tin.

"*Komst du.*"

I was in the lowest deck, so he didn't bother to use the polite form.

I ran after him as he hurried down a metal staircase to a lower deck, took a quick turn to a second flight, followed by another quick turn and yet another flight. Down we went, each staircase narrower, each corridor tighter, and each ceiling lower, until we could go no lower. I followed closely as we made a number of turns in narrow corridors until, at last, we stood in front of a door. The sailor took my key, opened it, and motioned me into the cabin. In a moment, he was gone, the key still in the lock. Having observed a few passengers, I would have given him some baksheesh had he not been so fast, but he must have thought I was a poor prospect.

I looked around.

It was a small, windowless cabin with a loud exhaust fan above the door. In the ceiling, a covered bulb threw soft light around the room, much brighter than a kerosene lantern. Two sets of double bunks were on opposite walls, with barely enough room between for a tiny wall sink with two faucets. A small mirror was over the sink. My cabin mates had claimed three of the four bunks, so I took the last bed, the lower one on the right, and put my valise on the mattress and the tin box on the floor.

This was my home for the next month. I stood in the center of the room beneath the covered bulb. The fan was humming loudly and would hum night and day for the entire voyage. There was a faint odor of oil and salt water, nothing unpleasant. The sink produced a thin but steady stream of cold and, most impressive, hot water that was considerably warmer than any water I'd had in my life up to then.

In the mirror, I saw myself smiling. I had only three other people in the room, hot and cold running water, an electric light for reading, a fan for ventilation, my own mattress off the floor, two sheets and a blanket, and a dining room where I would eat three meals a day.

The travel agent had been truthful. This was luxury!

Relieved and content, I locked the cabin door and, retracing my descent, found the stairs, and walked up one flight after another until I reached the boarding deck. I found a place at the rail and observed the proceedings. A steady stream of passengers ascended the rope ladder, followed by young Arab porters with their burden of luggage. A group of young women in modern clothes, their hair in curls to their shoulders, were at the rail, watching too. Suddenly, a voice called my name: "Reb Chaim!" A man was waving from the ladder. It was none other than Ezriel, my neighbor in Batei Warsaw. Filled with unexpected joy,

I waved to him as if he were a long-lost friend, though it was only two days ago that we had passed each other in the street, with neither of us mentioning our journey to America. I waved to him again, and then strolled along the deck, already feeling more of a sea traveler than the new passengers struggling up the rope ladder. Soon the pace of arrivals slowed to a trickle, and by three o'clock the little rowboats were fleeing back to shore. The British soldiers closed up shop and clambered down the ladder. The French sailors then hoisted the ladder up and swung in the rail gate.

"Chaim."

It was my neighbor Ezriel.

"Too busy looking at the girls, eh? For a moment, I thought you would refuse to recognize me."

Not having begun the process of Americanization and taking everything too literally, I apologized for the unintended slight.

"Reb Ezriel, I'm sorry. I would have waved to you sooner, but the young women were blocking my view. I couldn't ask them to leave. The boat doesn't belong to me."

"But you could have turned your head away couldn't you?"

Ah, he was joking; I began to see what America was all about. It was going to be good.

"I saw your mother and brothers onshore," he said. "They send their wishes for a good voyage. They're waiting until we sail."

I was suddenly consumed with an intense longing to see them one last time. But I was on the wrong side of the ship. I excused myself, raced along the deck, up a staircase, found myself in a corridor with open cabins on either side. My desire to see my family overcame my manners, and I entered a cabin at random. The room was large and had two wide beds on opposite walls. A passenger was lying fully clothed on one bed, napping. Another man stood at one of the two windows. I went to the other, but all I saw was the broad, bright sea. The man at the window was staring at me with an angry expression.

"Hey you! You don't belong here! This is first class, you little schneke!"

It was Zalman Leib Levi!

I should have said hello and explained myself, but he wasn't in the mood to socialize.

"Get out!" His habitually short temper was in full display. He didn't recognize me. "You shouldn't even be on this deck! Get out, you schneke!"

In shame, I fled. I got to a lower deck and walked to the other side of the boat. It wasn't surprising that Zalman Leib was going to America. He had a large family of seven children, six of them girls, the oldest still a teenager, and his odd jobs around Batei Warsaw didn't pay enough for any dowry. America was the last recourse. But how could he afford a first-class ticket?

With a hundred other passengers, I stood at the rail and looked intently at the distant shore. Jaffa was golden in the setting sun; the people on the dock were tiny, faceless sticks. We waved as the boat rocked gently. A loud, harsh blast from the smokestack broke the evening peace. Passengers shouted prayers and blessings. I stood against the rail and waved.

The *Alesia* was suddenly alive. The deck trembled, and dark smoke came out of the stack. Sailors raced up ladders, pulled ropes and hoisted flags. Slowly and heavily, our great ship moved away from the shore. The passengers wept as the beloved land sank into the sea, perhaps never to be seen again. We continued waving as the Alesia gathered speed and swept out into the vast, churning Mediterranean.

*

Two generations earlier, at this same Jaffa port, my parents had entered Eretz Yisrael.

They were little children then, and now I, a young man, their child, was leaving the land they loved.

I stood upon the deck of the *Alesia* and watched the shore recede into the darkness of an autumn night. During the last two years, from the moment the possibility of America had sprung into my consciousness to the moment just a few hours ago when I'd stepped out of the little rowboat and placed my right foot upon the rope ladder of the

Alesia, I knew I was destined to go to America. Telling no one, not even my closest friend or my mother, I had bided my time.

Yet I had overheard my mother say to her younger brother, my uncle Yisrael Yitzhak, "You should see how Chaim plans his trip to America. Look at how calm and self-assured he is. Nothing will stop him."

I didn't think she knew.

I was surprised too at my own fierce determination. I had been so integral a part of my family in Batei Warsaw, so at one with the religious community, that leaving should have been unthinkable.

In Jerusalem, I was near God.

For all the days of my life, from morning to night, year in and year out, I was never alone. Always there were my parents, sisters, brothers, grandparents, aunts, uncles, cousins, relatives twice and thrice removed, friends, neighbors, rebbes, playmates, and fellow students. People were always and everywhere around and near me, helping, praising, scolding, teaching, and blessing me.

In Batei Warsaw, I was close to heaven.

In Jerusalem, heaven was everywhere—in the synagogues and Talmud Torahs, in the yeshivas and classrooms, in my home, on the street, in the ancient bricks, and in the cool, sweet air. In the silver moonlight and the golden rays of sunset, in the dark ink of night and the thousand points of stars, there was the Name. From the very stones of the Western Wall, the voice of the Shechinah rose with its promise of return, as I now upon this darkening sea promised myself.

On this mighty boat upon a sea whose limit I could not imagine, beneath a dome of bright stars, I sailed from home in search of a new world, and a place for myself.

Chapter 45

The *Alesia* was a ship of the French Fabre Line, a hybrid vessel half-passenger, half-cargo. At fifteen thousand tons, it was small by today's oceangoing standards, but in 1929 the *Alesia* was a major ocean-going ship of its day. When I purchased my ticket, I was told the voyage would take twenty-eight days, but two storms in the Mediterranean—one before we reached Constanta, Romania, and the other as we approached Lisbon, Portugal—extended the voyage to thirty-two. By the end of the first week, it was apparent that the *Alesia* was in no hurry to go anywhere.

Most of the sailors and officers were French, with a sprinkling of Germans and Poles in the lower ranks. The French, always haughty, made us bend to their tongue—a beautiful, if incomprehensible, language. Yiddish and German being so similar, the German sailors were cordial to me and the other Jewish passengers.

That first day, once land was no longer visible, I returned to my luxurious cabin in the bowels of the ship and found my three cabin brothers, worldly young men, sitting on one of the lower bunks, playing cards. We introduced ourselves, and I discovered I was traveling with three pious Hasidim. They were David, Daniel, and Shimon, all in their mid twenties; I was the youngest, but not by much.

Just then, the dinner bell rang in the corridor, and we filed out immediately, trudging up four flights behind a long line of passengers pressing upward. The *Alesia's* dining room had a kosher table, which cost an extra twenty dollars. More curious than hungry even though I hadn't eaten anything since breakfast, I was eager for my first meal.

The kosher table was in the middle of the third-class dining room, a large open space with a low ceiling and many small, glowing electric lights. This was another first for me, for all homes, synagogues, and shops in Batei Warsaw, large or small, were lit by kerosene. I was not impressed by the menu's variety, but its quantity and quality were more than adequate. Our first supper consisted of fresh rolls, breads, and biscuits; butter and jam; sardines and onions; and tea and coffee. Wanting to meet people, all of us chattered incessantly. I made a friend immediately: Avram Gandzel. He was a Hasid my age, twenty-two, and we were happy to find each other. After dinner we went out to explore our new oceangoing home.

The sky was cloudy, and a hard wind was blowing, but fortified with a good supper and three glasses of hot tea, I was awake and excited. Avram and I toured the deck, marveling at the massiveness and power of our vessel, and then joined our kosher-table friends at the stern. The wake of the *Alesia* churned a shining white path to the land of Israel. A passenger started playing a harmonica, another had a flute, and soon a dozen of us were singing Hebrew songs. From the upper decks, people came to the rails and joined in.

"Hear me, my friends!" a man shouted into the night, and a sudden hush fell over us. "We are a hundred miles from Jerusalem!"

The thought of this great distance filled my heart with such deep longing that I could not contain myself. I wept quietly. *A hundred miles! An eternity of distance!* Never had I been so far from the center of the world, from home, and from those I loved.

Avram's voice rose in song, his clear, bright tenor bursting forth: "O," he sang, "beautiful are the nights in Canaan."

His voice filled the night, and we sang with him as the flute led the melody, while from the upper deck, another voice joined in and then another, and soon everyone was singing.

"Beautiful are the nights in Canaan."

At two in the morning, the night pitch black and the sky filled with stars, I walked down, down, down to my cabin. The exhaust fan was humming, and the dim light in the corridor cast the faintest of shadows on the beds. My three cabin partners were sleeping soundly. Exhausted, I took off my new shoes and my coat, crawled into my bunk, and fell asleep immediately.

A few hours later, a loud rattling woke me. It was the two bunk beds. I couldn't make out what was happening. The *Alesia* seemed to be rolling from side to side and going up and down at the same time. I tried to stand but fell back into the mattress. This was like the horrible earthquake in Givat Shaul, but it wasn't stopping. Up I floated, then down, and up again. Soon the breakfast bell rang in the corridor. My three cabin partners left while I stayed in bed and sucked a lemon, which, unfortunately, had the opposite effect I had been told to expect by my educated, witty uncle Shlomo. I lurched to the sink just in time, lay down again and closed my eyes, but opened them immediately. The bunks were shaking and rattling. The light was flickering. I tried to sleep but could not and eventually gave in to my nausea. I lay groaning and pressing my hands against my face, letting the great, dark, unseen waves lift me higher and higher, only to drop me into a bottomless pit.

When I woke, the rattling was gone, and the ship was running flat. I looked around, sat up, stood. My legs were sturdy; all trace of dizziness gone. I checked my pocket watch. It was late afternoon. I went up to the third-class deck and found my new friend, Avram, standing at the rail. The waves were high and rolling, but the storm was over, and the sky was clear.

"Let's sit in the center of the boat," Avram said.

We found deck chairs in the middle of the deck, where the effect of the high sea was less severe. I sat bundled in my coat and cap, my earlocks turned over and around my ears. I wasn't hungry in the least and could have gone without supper, but then I realized with a shock that it was Friday night. This was the first time in my life that I had been away from Batei Warsaw on Erev Shabbos. I hadn't been to synagogue, nor had I said any of the blessings or drunk a single drop of sacramental wine.

The cold wind made me shiver, and I stood. The dinner bell rang, and Avram left for the dining room. The thought of eating nauseated me, but I did not want to return to my windowless cabin either. Instead, I went to the third-class lounge, where passengers were drinking liquor and playing cards. I found a big, soft chair in a corner and observed, for the first time in my life, these secular activities, which were even worldlier for taking place on Erev Shabbos.

Early the next morning, Avram and I went to the small synagogue on the first-class deck. Ezriel, our neighbor, officiated.

After the service, I spoke with him.

"How is Zalman Leib Levi?"

"Ah, yes, he's traveling in first class with the other aristocrats." Ezriel shook his head. "Poor man," he said. "He's been seasick for three days."

Not all first-class passengers were rich people; on the contrary, some of them were quite poor, as was Zalman Leib. It was well known that the immigration officials regarded first-class ticket holders as healthier than the poorer passengers, such as myself, and did not examine the aristocrats as closely as they otherwise might have. Zalman Leib Levi had so many mouths to feed he would pay any price to get to America, and indeed, the price was steep. I learned later that he still had traces of trachoma, and he hoped that a first-class ticket would get him into America without travail.

By the time morning services were finished, Avram and I had missed breakfast.

"Now we have to wait until noon," he fretted.

There was hunger in his eyes, but for me, waiting three hours for the lunch bell after years of near starvation was not at all difficult, and I could have easily fasted until dinner.

The *Alesia* did not go directly to America. We sailed north for two days and nights until, early Monday morning, having passed through the Dardanelles and the Bosporus during the night, with much careful maneuvering, horn blowing, and black smoke pouring from her four mighty stacks, the *Alesia* docked in Constanta, Romania.

The wind was biting, and I dressed as warmly as I could and went on deck before breakfast. As soon as a gangplank was attached, a line of uniformed policemen marched across, conferred with a French officer, and disappeared inside. Fifteen minutes later, they marched off with a young woman in handcuffs. She stumbled, and was carried off the boat. No one had the slightest idea who she was or what she had done. Her name was Miriam. She had sat at the kosher table, eating quietly, and then joined our singing group on deck, but never sung, only listened with wide, shining eyes. Often, she walked barefoot on the cold deck, her bare arms wrapped around her thin body, not speaking to anyone. Some of the young men approached her, but she turned away without a word, and they quickly learned to leave her alone.

Now, from the rail, I watched as she was put into a bus and driven away.

In the meantime, a dozen or so passengers bound for Romania left the *Alesia*, among them my neighbor Ezriel. Constanta was a major port in the Black Sea, and a long line of passengers with bags and valises strode up the gangplank, eager to begin their voyage to the United States. The crew loaded cargo and supplies. I was wrapped in my new winter coat, which my mother had sewn from an assortment of her best woolens, but the cold wind was fierce, and I wished I had taken Uncle Shlomo's advice about bringing a blanket.

I stood at the rail with Avram. A solitary Romanian soldier with a rifle stood on the dock guarding the gangplank. Barefoot and wearing a long khaki overcoat almost twice his size, he shivered in the bitter cold. Passengers wishing to leave the boat had to show the soldier a special pass, and though I was interested in achieving yet another first by stepping upon the earth of a major European metropolis, the barefoot soldier in his threadbare coat wasn't the best advertisement for Romania.

Standing near the soldier and shouting up to the passengers was a man wearing a fur coat and a skullcap. He had a tripod and camera and held a big black dog by a leash.

"Romania," he shouted in Yiddish, "is a proud and ancient country! Have your portrait taken next to the boat!"

The photographer caught our eye.

"Young men, come down for your portraits! Record your passage to America!"

I smiled and shook my head.

"Have a history of your voyage! It's only a penny!"

One of the passengers said to me, "why not go down and have him take your picture?"

"The soldier is standing guard," I replied. "I don't have a pass."

"Ach, you don't need anything. Throw him a coin."

Of course, baksheesh. "How much do you think it would take?"

"Oh please, it doesn't matter. Look at the poor man."

The soldier was unshaven, his overcoat splattered with mud. He hopped slowly on his bare feet while trying to keep his rifle on his shoulder and his hands in his pockets.

Avram dug into his pocket and came up with a penny. He waved it at the soldier and threw it over the rail. The soldier hobbled slowly to the edge of pier and picked it up. He held it in his palm, studied it, closed his hand, and looked up at the rail. Avram and I waved and gestured. The soldier gestured feebly, and we ran down the gangplank.

"Ah, two Yiddlich"—young Jewish boys—"on their way to the New World," the photographer said. "Would you like a very special photograph?"

Avram and I looked at each other. Why not?

He charged us an extra penny to be photographed with his big black dog, which sat between Avram and me and wagged its tail ferociously. The photographer ran off with the plate to his little hut at the end of the pier, and we stared at the dog and the soldier, both of whom stared back with unblinking eyes. The dog, its tail wagging, seemed happier in our company. The photographer returned with two photographs, and Avram and I, having experienced as much of Romania as we cared to, retreated up the gangplank.

Dockside in Constanta, Romania, November 1929
Chaim, right, and his shipmate, Avram

Shortly before four o'clock, the *Alesia* left Constanta, and I went to the third-class lounge and joined the crowd awaiting the ship's bulletin. Typewritten in three languages—French, English, and German—the bulletin listed onboard activities as well as a few lines about events in the world at large. At the touch of the hour, an officer tacked a single sheet to the board.

> Miriam Eisen, a Communist agitator, is now in custody. A convicted criminal and an escapee from jail, she will stand trial in her native land, Romania, for crimes against the state.

*

Returning to the Aegean, the *Alesia* sailed west through the Dardanelles, and I gazed upon the mighty fortresses the Turks had built, and marveled that the British, who, despite their trucks and cannons, did not, to my knowledge, possess such magnificent pediments, had defeated such a powerful people. Ecclesiastes taught that the battle goes neither to the strong nor the race to the swift but that time and chance happen to all. It wasn't chance or fate, however, which had brought victory to the British. Will, purpose, courage, and intelligence had determined the outcome of the war. Staring at these mighty works from the deck of the *Alesia*, I took courage; a shy and skinny young man such as myself, possessing little secular education and no financial resources, might, against all odds, succeed in the New World.

Indeed, I was already walking the third-class deck with a jaunty air, looking at the new passengers with a smug superiority tinged with pity. They had much to learn. They would have to make friends with the waiters, time their bathroom visits, and secure the sunniest and least windy locations on deck.

I made a major effort to become friends with my three cabin partners, with little success. They were young secular Jews from Jaffa, full of quick jokes and many opinions, and regarded me, I am sure, with my Hasidic wardrobe and earlocks and my quiet ways, as a strange creature.

However, my cabin partners didn't wait for a friendship pact before partaking of the edibles in my tin box. As early as the second day, after I left for prayer services in the *Alesia*'s small synagogue, they began treating themselves to generous portions of sesame cake and pickled herring. I knew immediately that my inventory was being depletion. Believing their thievery undetected, they continued raiding my larder the next day. Their appetites, driven no doubt by Marxist theory, which insisted that all property was held in common, knew no bounds. Or were they simply ill mannered? Whatever the case, their chutzpah was intolerable.

The next morning, I left at my usual hour for prayer service, but pausing at the staircase, I returned to the cabin without warning.

The three of them were standing over my tin box, which was open on the floor. Shimon's hand was in the jar of herring, trying to pull out a piece. He kept chewing while he stared at me. Daniel had been about to pop a chunk of halvah into his open mouth, and not knowing what to do with it, he simply held it in front of his face. David, with a huge piece of cake in his hand, had crumbs on his shirt.

"Nu?" I said. "So?"

Finally, Shimon the herring man, spoke.

"We were hungry," he said, "for some homemade food."

"I see that," I replied, "and I would gladly share my food with any-one who is, but you are required to ask before you take."

The three of them stood in embarrassed silence, finished chewing, and, wiping their faces on their sleeves and their hands on their shirts, left the cabin.

Daniel came to me later that day and apologized, and I accepted without fuss. It was more important to get along with my three partners for our month of enforced togetherness than to stuff myself with cake and herring. My mother and sister, who'd provided the food, would have concurred. For the rest of the voyage, they left the tin can alone. Fortunately, I was much thinner and less stylish than they, so my cloth-ing was not a temptation. Our relationship, however, was strained; they blamed me for my trickery and, refusing to accept the consequences of their own acts, saw me as the cause of their discomfort. However, they soon found young women and often were gone all evening, sometimes not returning until morning.

Avram Gandzel and I became dedicated walkers, logging many circuits on the *Alesia*'s deck. We talked about our old lives and our plans in America. I soon became friendly with two young Hasidim at the kosher table, and they the four of us went round and round as the *Alesia* sailed on a straight line into the setting sun.

Most of us at the kosher table had tiny cabins on the fourth deck, the most dark and cramped on the boat. The *Alesia* was a French ship, and the first-class passengers were eating like kings, while below we were served only the basics. Some passengers complained about the portions, but I was never hungry, which, in my world, was a new experience.

For all the time and attention we spent on food, our true obsession lay on the other side of the Atlantic. While walking the decks and sitting in the lounge and at the kosher table, we discussed and debated the unknowns of the New World.

My father, who'd entered through Ellis Island in New York, had written, "It wasn't pleasant. Be brave and courageous, and with God's help, you will enter America."

It was a sobering thought that even in the United States, God's help was indispensable.

My brother Moshe was much more reassuring, but he was always an optimist.

"Have no fears at all. Remember, you are smart enough and healthy enough to be admitted without a problem. But above all, Chaim," he cautioned, "do not attempt to give the authorities any baksheesh. America is a rich country, and such things are not done."

A passenger at the kosher table knew someone who had been examined by three different doctors on Ellis Island, one of whom had made him crawl around a table and then stand on one leg just to prove he was coordinated.

Much more worrisome than physical endurance and agility were rumors of the mental tests we'd have to pass. Reliable witnesses at the kosher table knew someone—unspecified relatives and friends—whose knowledge of these matters was incontrovertible. One passenger's brother had been asked trick questions: How many legs does an American cat have? From what country did American Indians immigrate to the United States?

A woman at our table shook her head in dismay. "I don't know what I would have said!"

Adding to our anxiety were the tales told by another passenger, an actual American returning from a trip to Jerusalem. We knew him as, Jack.

A wealthy man, Jack was traveling first class, but he liked coming down to the lower decks. He enjoyed watching us devour the food at the kosher table. Laughing, he warned about dire conditions ahead.

"Eat up, boys! Eat up! This is your chance to fatten yourselves, because in America, you're going to starve!"

Looking at Jack loosening his belt and wiping his chin after each meal, I wasn't convinced that in the United States people were going hungry.

There were recurrent lice infestations, usually after the *Alesia* picked up passengers at different ports. These little creatures spread fear and panic in the lower decks. I was well acquainted with lice. During the war, lice plagues had been a persistent, maddening problem in Jerusalem. By some miracle, our house in Batei Warsaw had never been infested, but I'd often seen people combing their hair and throwing handfuls of the tiny insects into pit fires in their yards. Lice spread fast, and we feared that anyone infested would be barred from entering the United States. The ship's medical staff conducted periodic examinations of the lower-class passengers and quarantined the infested to separate cabins. Two of those passengers, a woman and her young daughter, were regulars at our table.

Regardless of our personal concerns, the *Alesia* sailed on without a thought, bringing us closer and closer to the day of reckoning. Heading south, we docked in Smyrna (Izmir in Turkish). There, among others, four pious young Hasids in long black caftans and curling earlocks come on board. They huddled together on the deck, bewildered and fearful, until a German sailor spoke to them in Yiddish and led them to their cabin deep in the *Alesia*'s hold.

We left Smyrna and sailed through the Greek islands, passing south of Sicily. At every port, the crew unloaded and loaded cargo; a few passengers left, and many more came on.

All were going to America.

*

After we left Smyrna, the four pious Hasidim were reassigned to one of the small, windowless cabins on my deck. They were from Batei Hungary, near the Mea Shearim, and extremely observant. Not trusting the kosher table, they had brought their own food, and I often saw them through their open door at a tiny table in their tiny room, sharing a meal. Their food supply seemed minimal, but fasting was second nature to them. On the first day in their new cabin, they attached a big mezuzah to the doorpost, using a hammer and nails they had brought along for just such a purpose; the righteous always come equipped. The chambermaid, who wore a big cross around her neck, took one look at the strange object and, suspecting it of powerful and unchristian forces, ran to the deck officer. He came down to our lowly floor to observe the offending amulet. A report was issued, which slowly made its way up the chain of command until it reached the captain. A consultation was held with the supervisor of kosher affairs, and after some pondering, the captain, representing the *Alesia*'s highest authority, bowed to an even higher one and allowed the four pious Hasids to keep their mezuzah.

*

As Columbus discovered a new world while sailing the Atlantic, I, a passenger on the *Alesia*, found a new universe as well.

In Batei Warsaw, I was shielded from the outside world. Constructed with religion, faith, traditions, and indestructible family ties, the shield was broad and strong. My world was limited, but the rewards were many. As a member of a large and cohesive community, I was proud of my heritage and walked the streets of Jerusalem with a strong heart, knowing my actions contributed to the well being and continuity of my people. As a member of the Hasidic community, I was doubly blessed, first to be chosen to be a Jew and then to be a member of a special self-chosen group among our own people.

> And You, O God, have chosen us from all people; You
> have loved us and taken pleasure in us, and have exalted
> us above all tongues. You have sanctified us by Your
> commandments, and brought us near You into Your service,
> You our King, and have blessed us by Your great and holy Name.

However, my father and all my teachers had cautioned us not to see ourselves as a people with special privileges. We were not chosen for wealth or prestige or to rule over other nations, for we were few in number and scattered over the face of the earth. Rather, we were told, we had been chosen for service.

This, then, was our lot: to obey the commandments and to serve.

In Batei Warsaw, I had dedicated myself to learning Torah, the better to know what was required of me. We were taught that the world depended on doing God's work. Life was short, and one must take every opportunity to do good deeds, and thus heal the world.

On the *Alesia*, I saw other young men, French and German sailors, doing other kinds of work. They were disciplined and had their own rules and codes. They went about their business without prayers and blessings. They too served a higher purpose, for without them, the boat would not have sailed, and we travelers, holy and not, would not have been carried across the seas. These sailors and officers too had been chosen, and given the privilege and dignity of labor.

My mother would have looked upon these sailors and given them her blessing. She had once argued with my grandfather that my father should do more to earn money.

"Where there is no Torah," she had quoted, "there is no bread; where there is no bread, there is no Torah."

Sailing to Portugal, we passed through the Straits of Gibraltar at night and ran headlong into a ferocious storm. For three long days, the *Alesia* fought towering waves and fierce winds, making little headway as the ship pitched and rolled. I lay in my cabin, moaning and writhing. I'd occasionally stumble to the sink to vomit and then lurch back to my mattress. The decks were deserted; the dining room was empty. Even the sailors were reeling. On the morning of the third day, the storm finally abated, and the *Alesia*, with its sick, grateful passengers, finally entered the port of Lisbon. All of us, including the lower classes, were given three hours of shore time.

Avram and I strolled through the streets of Lisbon, marveling at its cosmopolitan wonders. There was a sense of joy among its inhabitants; in contrast to the cramped streets of Jerusalem, Lisbon's open plazas and boulevards lent a high grace to the city. The eye could roam. Men and women walked about, and commerce flourished.

On a side street near the docks, we passed a small shop.

414

Avram and I looked inside.

"A barbershop," Avram said.

We looked at each other.

"What do you think?" I asked. "Do I need a haircut?"

"I think so. What about me?"

"We could both use a trim," I assured him.

The barber, a short man with a dark mustache waxed to two fine points, sat me down. He asked me to take off my skullcap. I put my head into his professional hands. Snipping away, shaping my hair to a more modern look, he accidentally cut off my sidelocks.

Avram, with some hesitation, took the chair, removed his skullcap, and closed his eyes.

Outside, we looked at each other. We said nothing about our suddenly secular heads, and walked slowly back to the *Alesia*.

Of all the places in the world, it had to happen in a barbershop in Lisbon, Portugal.

The *Alesia* anchored in Lisbon for three days. A few passengers left, and many more came on; freight was unloaded, other goods were taken on. Every morning, a pack of local peddlers rushed the gangplank to set up shop in a special area on deck. They sold clothing, gloves, and leather products, and food. Crew and passengers bought as they wished. One morning, a peddler arrived with the strangest fruit I had ever seen. A throng of sailors and officers surrounded the man immediately. Curious, I studied these marvelous objects. The fruit was large, oblong, and seemingly heavy. It had a gold and greenish color, was coarsely textured, and had spiky green leaves sprouting from its head. The sailors and officers pushed and fought, and within half a minute, each magnificent fruit was gone.

"Ah, yes, of course," said our rich, first-class American, Jack. "Those are pineapples. You can buy them in America, but you won't earn enough."

*

Contrary to the dire predictions of Batei Warsaw's many experts, we had a smooth crossing. The German sailors said it was the calmest winter of the last ten years. The crossing from Lisbon to Providence, Rhode Island, took eleven days. The weather was spring like, the sun low but warm, and I walked the decks all day, circling my own little world of the *Alesia*, wrapped loosely in my home-sewn winter coat.

Our kosher table was now the main attraction in the dining room. We had a number of professional entertainers at the table, and we clapped and used our utensils to set a rhythm for the singers. Every evening, after supper, we gathered on the open decks and sang to the stars while the musicians played their violins and flutes, returning to our cabins only when the night winds, blowing stronger and colder as we approached the United States, drove us inside.

On Friday, the thirtieth day of our voyage, at precisely 4:00 p.m., the *Alesia's* last news bulletin was posted in the third-class dining room.

> Attention, All Passengers:
> Tomorrow, Saturday, December 14, the *Alesia*
> will dock at Providence, Rhode Island. Final preparations
> for disembarkation must be completed by 6:00 p.m. today.

Excited, I went down to my cabin. My tin box had been depleted some time ago, and had I not hidden the jar of mish-mish, my cabin mates would have made short work of it.

Tomorrow we would be going through American immigration, and I wanted to be prepared for the medical examination. On the fourth deck was a small bathroom where, for twenty-five cents, one could take a warm bath with soap. By Jerusalem standards, twenty-five cents was a huge sum of money for hot water, even with soap, and I stayed in the bath for twenty minutes before the attendant banged loudly on the door.

"There are people waiting!" she shouted.

In the corridor, a line of passengers glared at me; everyone wanted to be clean and ready.

In my cabin, I checked my papers, and counted what remained of my money. Of the ten extra dollars I began with in Jaffa, I now had exactly five left—not bad for a month of living.

I tallied my costs: one photograph with my friend Avram Gandzel on the pier in Constanta, Romania—an extra coin for the photograph with the photographer's big black dog; a haircut in Lisbon, Portugal— no extra charge for removing my earlocks; one warm bath; and three bottles of sparkling water to alleviate my nausea during two ocean storms.

In Batei Warsaw, I had been taught how to preserve my wealth.

That Friday night, our last night on the *Alesia*, we celebrated with a lavish Shabbos dinner. The tables were covered with white decorative tablecloths and set with fine dishes and silverware. The meal was the best of the voyage: wine, challah, gefilte fish, chicken soup, large portions of brisket and roast chicken, and a variety of cakes and desserts. We sang and played music, then sang and played on the deck until midnight.

I tried to contain my excitement and get some sleep. I wanted to be fresh for tomorrow's unknowns. I knew how to do well on examinations, but these would give me entry into the United States or send me back across the Atlantic. I lay still and stared at the mattress above. My cabin partners could not sleep either, and the four of us turned and twisted, sighed and prayed. I dozed off and woke an hour before the breakfast bell. I finished the light meal quickly, walked one last time around the *Alesia*, and, very tense, returned to my cabin. My three cabin partners and their belongings were gone. I opened my valise and checked its contents. Everything was in place. I put the apricot jam into the valise and went through my papers yet again: visa from America, letters from doctors attesting to my good health, a vaccination card from the *Alesia*'s physician. After one last look around my windowless home, complete with electricity and hot and cold running water, I walked down the long corridor with my uncle's mish-mish rolling back and forth in my half-empty valise.

With Avram Gandzel at my side, I watched the coast of Rhode Island rise from the sea. Our rich first-class American, Jack, was puffing on a cigar.

"Well, kids, I see you had a good time on the boat." He looked us up and down. "Gained some weight, eh?" He took a few deep puffs. "Well, I'm glad you enjoyed yourselves, but now you're going to starve!" He walked away, chuckling to himself.

As the *Alesia* drew closer to shore, I made out the skyline of Providence, and then, as tugboats came out to meet us, I saw a mass of people on the dock, waving and cheering.

Chapter 46

By midafternoon, the A*lesia* was almost empty, but I was still at the rail. American citizens had disembarked first, followed by first and second class. Avram and I, and more than a hundred third-class passengers, had yet to be called.

I stood with Avram at the rail, cold, nervous, and excited. We joked, pretending to a confidence we did not feel. We thought of all sorts of depressing possibilities, none of which we dared speak of. I wanted to get it over with, one way or another.

At last, our names were called, and I walked off the *Alesia* with my valise tightly in hand, coat buttoned, collar up, and cap pulled down over my ears. I hadn't been on land since Lisbon, and I walked with a slight roll. On the pier, men were separated from women and children. We walked down a rope path into a vast auditorium. Uniformed men directed me to one of the many narrow wooden benches. I sat up straight and did not move. My anxiety was acute. For the tenth time that morning, I checked my papers. Avram sat at my side, as still and nervous as I. A man in a blue uniform held a long list and called out names at two-minute intervals. We sat in utter silence, not even daring to move, lest our clothing rustle. The room buzzed with fear. When called, the passenger stood and walked to the front to be examined by two doctors in long white uniforms. The doctors moved fast, using stethoscopes and touching different parts of the body, including the jaw, the armpits, and sometimes the groin. A few examinations took longer than others. When the doctors finished, the passenger was directed to one of two doors. Only a few passengers were sent to the right. The quicker the examination, the more likely the passenger went to the left. Avram pushed his knee against mine, and I looked at him. He made a face; we knew which door we wanted.

At last, my name was called. Valise in one hand and papers in the other, I walked as calmly as I could down the path. With a quick nod from one and a tight smile from the other, the doctors began. One looked at my eyes, mouth, and ears, and the other listened to my heart. Then one put his hand on my groin and instructed me to cough. I coughed. He nodded and removed his hand. The entire examination took less than two minutes. The doctor nodded toward a guard, who pointed to the left.

On the other side of the door was a corridor, at the end of which was yet another door with another guard waving me forward. I walked quickly, surprised by the man's urgency, for in Jerusalem, guards and officials did not care about time. The jar of mish-mish rolled back and forth in my valise. On the other side of door was another large auditorium, and yet another guard directed me to another narrow wooden bench. A minute later, Avram sat down next to me.

We looked at each and tried not to smile. I sat quietly, head erect, and carefully looked around.

We faced a long wall. In front of the wall were six massive desks, and at each desk were three officials: one sitting and two, in uniform, standing. In front of the desks was a low wooden railing where the passengers stood. One of the men in uniform took the passenger's documents and brought them to the desk to be examined by the sitting official, a representative, I assumed, of the United States of America. I remembered what my brother had written about baksheesh, and watching the proceedings, I began to understand what he meant. America was a land of high civilization and encoded law where officials were dignified and professional, and where the extra piece of gold in your pocket made no difference.

To the right of the desk area was a wide, double door. I could see, as the passengers went through it, a vast, open space with soft lights, upholstered furniture, and men and women lounging about. I could only catch a glimpse of it before the doors swung closed.

My breathing was shallow with excitement. The hardest part was over, and I wanted to lean toward Avram and tell him we had made it, but I was getting closer and closer to that double door, beyond which lay America, and I wasn't going to utter a single unnecessary word.

On the wall behind the desks was a big, round clock with long black hands: 3:30 p.m.

The minutes went by.

The only voices were the officials asking questions and the passengers answering as best as they could in broken English. I began a mental review of the few English words I knew.

At 4:12, my name was called loudly.

"Linder! Linder!"

Valise in hand, I walked to the wooden railing. A guard took my papers to the desk. The middle-aged official examined my documents without a single glance in my direction.

To my right, on my side of the railing, stood an elderly man. He caught my eye and bent toward me.

"I'm Mr. Cohen."

He spoke Yiddish, and I realized that even without my earlocks, I looked exactly who I was.

"I represent HAIAS, and if you don't know any English, I'll translate for you." Mr. Cohen kept his voice low in keeping with the quiet solemnity of the occasion. I didn't know then that HAIAS was a philanthropic organization that helped Jewish immigrants.

"Thank you," I said.

Now my fears had returned. My body had passed inspection, but what if my papers did not? At the desk, the official was going over my documents, checking the official stamps. Why so much attention? His expression was unreadable. At last, he looked up at my face and then down to my photograph. He did it again.

I was tense. I was who I was, neither more nor less—a young, trembling immigrant yearning to step through the last door into the soft lights and upholstered chairs.

The official was holding out a typewritten form in one hand and a pen in the other. I took both and, preparing to sign, turned to Mr. Cohen.

"Should I sign in Yiddish or English?"

"It doesn't matter. However you want."

I wanted to sign in English, but my hand of its own wrote in Yiddish.

The official checked my signature against those on my documents.

Then he stood and, without a word, gestured. I hesitated, uncertain, but I had watched the procedure, and I lifted my valise over the wooden rail.

There weren't many items to inspect. He pushed aside my clothes, a few books, and my religious articles. He picked up the jar of Uncle Shlomo's jam. He looked at it low, held it high against the light, lifted it to his ear, and shook it several times. He examined the tight cover and its wax-paper seal. He frowned.

He spoke to Mr. Cohen.

Mr. Cohen turned to me and spoke in Yiddish. "What's in the jar?"

I had a vocabulary of a few hundred English words, but *apricot* wasn't one of them. Besides, in Jerusalem, this was mish-mish.

Wanting to assure the official of my absolute innocence, I said to Mr. Cohen, "there's nothing in it that's unhealthy or dangerous. The jar contains mish-mish, which my Uncle Shlomo Wertheimer asked me to bring to his son, Wolfe, in Philadelphia."

"Very interesting, and I'm sure you trust your uncle Shlomo," replied Mr. Cohen. "But the United States government is concerned that any fruit that may contain insects or diseases not be brought into the country. Please, young man, describe exactly what the sealed jar contains."

Mr. Cohen and the official waited.

"I told you exactly what it contains. The jar is full of mish-mish jam. My mother often makes it during the summer in Jerusalem, and we eat it during the winter. But this particular jam was made by my uncle Shlomo for his son—"

"Never mind your mother, your uncle Shlomo, and his son Wolfe!" Mr. Cohen was impatient. Then he smiled. "Ah, I understand. You mean that this is a mishmash of different fruits, which you call mish-mish."

"No, it's not a mishmash of different fruits. It's a single fruit—mish-mish."

"All right, I believe you." Mr. Cohen was both irritated and amused. "Now, tell us what sort of fruit it is before your mother and your uncle make it into jam."

I hesitated.

"Describe it as best as you can," said Mr. Cohen more kindly.

"It grows on small trees. It's about the size of a walnut, is yellowish orange, and has a pit in the center. We pick it in the early fall, and it's sweet and tart at the same—"

Mr. Cohen's face lit up like a lantern. "Oh, for heaven's sake, apricots! Why didn't you say so in the first place?"

Okay, let it be apricots! I loved mish-mish in Yiddish, and I was sure it was even more delicious in English.

The official looked from me to Mr. Cohen.

"It's apricot," Mr. Cohen told him.

"Ah, why didn't he just tell us?"

With the mish-mish problem solved, the blond official smiled for the first time.

"Young man, you may go."

I understood—*go* was similar to *geh*—but to be absolutely certain, I turned to Mr. Cohen, who repeated the instruction in Yiddish.

"*Gehen Sie.*"

"Thank you. Where?"

"Through that door."

"And then?"

"Anywhere you want!"

Ah, of course! America!

I quickly closed my valise, jammed my papers in my wallet, and walked away as quickly as I could without breaking into a run.

Who knows? They might change their minds

At last, I was in the big hall with soft lights and large, comfortable chairs. Tables and lamps were arranged in pleasant ways. *Aha, this is a waiting room in the American style.* I peered about and saw through a wide window people walking on the sidewalks in the growing dark. I knew they were Americans.

I sat in one of the comfortable chairs and smiled to myself. Avram and I had agreed that who ever finished first would wait for the other.

For the first time in more than a month, I felt at ease. Since leaving Jerusalem thirty-one days ago, I had not relaxed for a moment. The sea journey had been rich with new experiences and jammed with anticipation, and I had been in a constant state of excitement. In my sleep, the pounding of the *Alesia*'s engines bringing us closer to the American shore had filled my dreams, and when I'd walked the *Alesia*'s deck, I'd dreamed of walking the streets of the Lower East Side.

Now, at last, I was here.

How good it was to be alone, even for a few minutes. All my life, I could not escape the crowds of humanity. Even on the boat, I'd eaten in a crowded dining room, shared a windowless cabin with three strangers, and walked the deck with hundreds of others. I sat in the soft chair in the big, quiet hall lit by soft electric lights that glowed on the pale blue walls, while outside in the cold winter night, Americans walked the streets onto which I would soon step in my new shoes.

I was smiling, yet strangely, there were tears in my eyes.

I would never be barefoot again.

There were many challenges ahead, but now, for the first time in years, if only for a brief interval, I was at long last, free.

I was in America.

I put my valise under my legs, closed my eyes, and slept.

When Avram woke me, it was five o'clock.

"Come, Chaim. My father's waiting."

Outside, it was cold, and the night sky was dark, but the streets were brilliantly lit with electric lamps. Cars whizzed by in opposite directions. I held tightly to my valise, fearing that all this speed and light would pull it from my hands. A man was smiling at me.

"Ah, so you are Chaim!" Avram's father hugged me and kissed me on my cheek. "*Eine Kuss*. From your father, until he sees you."

"How is Abba?"

"Very good and very happy that you are here. He couldn't travel on the Sabbath. I am very pleased to deliver you to him."

He led us to the railroad station and bought three express tickets to New York.

"We have two hours," said Avram's father. "Are you hungry?"

We hadn't eaten since early morning, and the anxiety of our arrival had suppressed our hunger. His question triggered a rush of appetite, and suddenly, I was starving. Avram's father took us to a cafeteria. The restaurant was brightly lit and full of men and women sitting together and talking. Avram and I devoured a basket of rolls and then, to the smiling amazement of the waitress, did the same to the second.

"Can we have more?" asked Avram.

"Go ahead. They're free of charge," said Avram's father.

Knowing that the American style permitted questions, I asked for a third basket and more butter.

Who said people were starving in America?

On the express train racing to New York, we reclined in soft uphol-stered chairs. The train was bright and warm. Outside, the dark winter night raced by in a blur. In the seat opposite Avram and I, sat another passenger, who, overhearing our Yiddish, spoke.

"And how old are you two young men?"

We told him.

"Ah, and where are you from?"

We told him that too.

"Ach, you remind me of myself when I came to the United States many years ago. I went to New York right away. It was the only place I wanted to be. I look at you, and I see—yes, I see ..." He shook his head and breathed a long sigh. "It was more years ago than the ages of both of you."

A food cart came down the aisle, and he bought four bottles of Coca-Cola and insisted we drink the full eight ounces.

"Go ahead! For the first taste, one sip is not enough."

After we wished one another "L'chaim" (To life), I tasted the siz-zling, sweet drink for the first time in my life—another of many steps on the way to becoming an American.

At three o'clock on Sunday morning, we arrived in Grand Central Station in Manhattan. One of Avram's uncles—everyone from Jerusalem had uncles everywhere—drove us to our final destinations. Without any idea what was happening or where I was going, I got into the backseat and held on to my valise. There was no traffic, and we sped through the bright, cold streets as the jar of mish-mish rolled back and forth in my valise. Avram sat next to me, his father in front. The uncle drove with determined ferocity, hurtling over the streets at fantastic speeds. From the rear window, I saw things I had never seen before: green and red traffic signals, neon signs glowing in store windows, an overhead train that roared like thunder and rattled like a hundred empty pots, and tall buildings whose tops I could not see.

"We're going to the Lower East Side!" the uncle shouted over the roar of the car. "Your father has a room there close to Avram and his father."

Soon the car stopped.

"Here you are," said the uncle. "Attorney Street is on the right."

I got out, and the car sped away. Shivering and confused, I held on to my valise with an iron grip. The street was dark and empty; streetlights cast long shadows. I looked around. I was on the corner of Attorney and Broome. I walked down Attorney, and there it was: a three-story building. On the front door was the number 49. How many times I had written that very address on my mother's letters, and there it was, in red paint!

After thirty-one days and thousands of miles of ocean, I stood on an American sidewalk.

Stores were on the ground floor, their windows dark and doors locked. I opened the center door. A dim bulb lighted the stairwell. My father had written that he was on the second floor, and I went up the creaking, narrow steps. There were four doors, two on each side of the hall. I did not know the apartment number, and I knocked on the closest door. I had in some way also touched an electric bell, and there was a loud buzzing inside the apartment. What had I done? Before I could retreat, the door opened, and an elderly man smiled broadly.

"It's you—Haskel's son! Your father is my friend." He spoke in a torrent of Yiddish. "My name is Furman. Your father and brother have been waiting all night. They've been very concerned, but you're here safe and sound. Good, good, though you do look a little tired. And so thin—ah, America will fatten you up! But how are you? Did you have a safe ocean trip? Was it cold in Providence? How did you get to New York?"

"Mr. Furman, could you please tell me where my father and brother are?"

"Yes, yes, they live in the other apartment. Come. This way."

I followed Mr. Furman to the end of the hall, where he rang a bell, producing the same loud buzzing; in America, everything was fast and loud, even in the middle of the night. Another elderly man opened the door. I wanted so much to see my father that in the dim light, I thought it was he and moved to embrace him. He pushed me away.

"No, no! I'm not your father. Your brother Moshe left, and your father went to sleep. Come in."

I stepped inside.

"There," he said, pointing to a closed door. "That's your father's room."

I knocked once and then again. A voice full of sleep spoke. "Come in."

My father, fully dressed, was rising from the bed, tucking in his shirt. He turned on a small bedside lamp and looked at me for a long time.

"At last, my dear son, I see your face again."

He put his arms around me, pressed me close. We stood together in silence.

I hadn't seen my father in seven years—a lifetime.

At the time, I had no idea how much time was to pass—much more time than I thought the world could hold—before I saw my mother again.

In the kitchen, my father introduced me to the elderly gentleman, Eleazar, with whom he shared the apartment. From across the hall, Mr. Furman returned to join us at the table to drink tea and coffee and help us eat the cake they'd bought to celebrate my arrival.

It was five o'clock in the morning; the long winter night was not yet over.

"Moshe will come later," my father said, "and take you to his furnished room. For tonight, you can sleep in Mr. Furman's apartment."

Mr. Furman smiled and wagged his finger. "And you'll have your own room."

Everyone in America had his own room.

I followed Mr. Furman down the hall and went into the small bedroom. What a long day it had been. I was too tired to even look around, and I lay down on the bed fully clothed. Resting my head on the cool white pillow, I smiled again. This was the first time in my life that I would sleep in a room of my own. "*Gut nacht*," Mr. Furman said, and I fell asleep immediately.

*

"Come on," Moshe commanded. "You're going to have your first American breakfast."

It was ten o'clock, and I was in my father's apartment with Moshe. It was Sunday, the best day to catch donors at home, and my father, a collector for his yeshiva in Jerusalem, had already left.

"Come on," my brother repeated. "And put on something warm."

I put on my Jerusalem coat and followed Moshe. Outside, the sky was bright, the air blisteringly cold. I saw everything with a fresh and happy eye. I had addressed letters to Attorney Street, but the actual bricks and mortar of the buildings were nothing I had imagined. It was a dream come true. Moshe pointed out the mighty Williamsburg Bridge.

"See? It cuts right across Attorney Street. No nonsense. You can walk to Brooklyn over the river. That's a real bridge."

I marveled at the girders of steel, and at the vehicles racing up and down its roadway.

"Nothing like this in Jerusalem, eh?"

On Delancey and Clinton Streets, Moshe explained the system of traffic lights. We waited on the corner on red, and then crossed at the green.

"You see, Chaim." My brother waved his hands at everything, "New York is not Jerusalem."

I nodded, too cold to talk. New York was definitely not Jerusalem. The wind cut through my coat and tore at my throat like a wild animal. By the time we got to Borden's Dairy Restaurant, my fingers were icy sausages, and my face was stiff. My brother led me to a table in the crowded restaurant.

"Sit down, Chaim, and warm up. I'm going to order just an average breakfast, and I want to see if you can finish it."

Moshe lifted his hand, and immediately, a young waitress came to our table.

"How are you, Sweet Little Rose?"

"Just fine."

"Rose is my steady waitress."

"I certainly am."

"And she knows what we want."

"I certainly do."

Sweet Little Rose came back with two glasses of fresh-squeezed orange juice and a basket of rolls and butter. A minute later, she brought scrambled eggs, french-fried potatoes, and more rolls, and then brought a plate of herring and sweet pickles.

"From Abe," she said, "special for you."

"Who's Abe?" I asked my brother.

"Don't ask. You'll see."

I ate everything, but Sweet Little Rose brought cinnamon cake and coffee and cream. Moshe encouraged me to keep pace with the food.

I did but, lifting my second slice of cake, finally asked, "Why so much food?"

He shook his head, dismissing the question with a phrase he was to use often in the coming weeks: "Chaim, please don't ask questions. This is America!"

Sweet Little Rose kept filling my cup with coffee. Then a big man with a cook's apron and a yarmulke came to our table and beamed at me.

"You are in America now! Mazel tov!"

"Thank you."

"When did you arrive?"

"Just yesterday."

"Ah, a greenhorn. Mazel tov! Your brother will show you how things are done here. Was the breakfast good?"

"Delicious, and so much food."

He beamed.

429

Moshe reached into his pocket, but the man shook his head vigorously.

"No, no! This is your younger brother's first meal in America. It's on the house!"

The man, who I assumed was Abe, returned to the kitchen, and I asked, "What exactly is 'on the house'?"

"No charge. Free." Moshe shook his finger at me. "Don't ask questions. This is America."

We left the table stuffed like goats. Moshe took out some bills, rolled them into a tight bundle, and tucked them quickly into Sweet Little Rose's apron pocket. She gave my brother a big smile.

"Chaim, it's very important," Moshe said as we walked out. "In America, you tip."

I didn't dare ask why.

Outside, Moshe said, "Now we'll have a treat."

I was afraid I would have to eat more food, but instead, we went for a ride on the Delancey Street trolley. We rode down the middle of the street with cars and trucks on either side; people were everywhere. This was quite a modern way to travel. As the trolley crossed the Bowery, there was a thunderous, deafening noise above. I cringed, and then looked up. Moshe laughed.

I had been too busy looking at the street scene to notice the tracks.

"I know that America is a land of machines," I said, "but I never thought trains would run overhead."

"That's what it means to be in America."

We walked on Orchard Street, and at last, I feasted my eyes on something familiar: pushcarts and tables of merchandise on the street, clothing on open display.

"Like the Mea Shearim market," I said.

"The Lower East Side," Moshe corrected me sternly, "is not Batei Warsaw."

"I know, but certain things are similar."

"Wait until you've been here a while before you start making comparisons. Now, I want to show you where I work."

We walked quickly now. The regular American breakfast had

fortified me and I didn't feel as cold. At Rivington and Suffolk Streets—at my brother's suggestion, I paid close attention to the street names—we entered the Sommers Photo Studio. Moshe introduced me to Noah Sommers, his boss, and his boss's wife and two young boys.

"Ah, so this is the young greenhorn," said Mr. Sommers.

Ruth, his wife, looked me up and down. "Moe says you don't have a place to stay."

I'd assumed a bed would appear on someone's floor, as in Batei Warsaw.

"I expected to stay with Father."

"No, no," said Moshe, "this is New York. You have to stay someplace more modern."

"Why not stay with us?" said Ruth. Her husband seconded her offer. Obviously, they had discussed my living arrangements. Moshe was an apprentice photographer for Noah Summers, but the pay was very low, and the Sommers were giving my brother room and board.

"The bed in Moe's room is big enough for two," Ruth said. "Especially brothers."

"What would I have to pay?"

Ruth laughed. "For now, nothing."

It wasn't my own room, but sharing a large American-style bed with my brother in his private room was better than anything Batei Warsaw had to offer—and it was free.

"Of course," I replied. "Thank you for your generosity."

"Oh, it's nothing," she said. "A little more water in the soup."

That settled, Moshe had work to do in the darkroom, whatever such a room was, and he suggested I go back to our father's house, rest a while, then return to the photo studio in the afternoon.

I was tempted to ask directions, but knowing how Moshe disliked questions, I refrained. If I was to be an inhabitant of this new land, I had better learn to navigate its streets. Besides, unlike the twisting streets and dead-end alleys of Jerusalem, I could see that the streets of Manhattan were laid out in easy squares. Most importantly, they had names, a modern system yet to be implemented in Batei Warsaw and the Mea Shearim.

I remember my first morning in New York as if it were yesterday. I stood alone on the sidewalk. The sun was bright, and the air was no longer cold. Cars and trucks rushed by. This was my new life. The signs were in English, but I had a good memory and a basic vocabulary, and I got my bearings and walked one block to Delancey, waited for the green light, crossed over and walked two blocks, and there it was: 49 Attorney Street.

My father was on his rounds. I didn't have a key and rang Mr. Furman's bell. To my surprise, a young woman opened the door. She looked me up and down and smiled.

"You must be Chaim." She spoke Yiddish.

"I am Chaim."

"I'm Pearl. Come in. My grandfather isn't home, but you can wait here."

We sat in the kitchen, drinking tea. Pearl was talkative, her Yiddish heavily accented with Polish. Her grandparents, the Furmans, she told me, had brought her to America four years ago. Two years after, her grandmother had died, and now she and her grandfather lived together. She didn't behave at all like a young girl from a small town in Poland; she smoked cigarettes and played loud dance music on her radio.

"Do you have any work yet?" she asked me.

"No. I don't know what I'm going to do, but I'll find something."

"I work in a dress shop. The pay isn't bad."

I wanted to ask what she meant by "not bad," but I remembered my brother's caution about questions. Later, I would discard that advice. There was another question I did not ask: How could a young woman sit with a young man alone in a house and talk so easily and smoke cigarettes while the radio played? This could never happen in Batei Warsaw.

Someone was at the door.

"That's my grandfather," Pearl said.

"Ah, Chaim." Mr. Furman smiled. He was unconcerned that his granddaughter had been entertaining a young man. "So how is your first day in America? Is it too cold for you? The forecast is for more cold. Has my granddaughter given you any lunch? Do you need a sweater or gloves?"

Pearl smiled and lit another cigarette.

*

At the Sommers Photo Studio, I found only Ruth and her two young boys; my brother and his boss had a bar mitzvah and a wedding to shoot, as Ruth called it, and had already left for the Bronx.

"Come home with us now," she said. "You'll see where we live."

Their apartment was on Broome Street at the corner of Suffolk. I knew the system, and I waited at the corner for the light to turn green. It finally did.

"Let's walk fast before the light changes," she suggested. I held the hand of her five-year-old son; she carried the two year old. We made it across just in time.

The Sommers lived in a two-bedroom apartment on the third floor of an old tenement. The halls were dark and narrow; the steps steep and equally narrow. The four Sommers slept in one bedroom, and my brother had the other.

"Come see Moe's room." She took me to the back of the apartment. "See? The room might be small, but the bed certainly is big enough for two of you."

"This is perfect."

"Good. I was afraid you'd think it was too small."

The room was as big as my cabin on the *Alesia*, and, even more impressive, had a small window that looked out on an airshaft.

"It's perfect. May I ask—do you have a pen and paper? I would like to write a letter."

"Of course."

I rolled up my sleeve and sat at the kitchen table. I wrote in Yiddish in the open, free style that my mother had taught me. I didn't have to think about my first sentence: "Imma, this is the beginning of a paper bridge between us."

When I finished, the winter sun was setting, and I went into Moshe's room—our room now—and took off my shoes and stretched out on the wide bed. Warm and content, without a single thought, I fell asleep.

433

*

We went to our father's apartment for supper, interrupting him in the middle of dinner preparations. I was surprised to see him do kitchen work. I offered to cook, but he refused.

"This is our first meal together in your new life, Chaim," he told me, "and I want to make it special."

He moved about the kitchen, stirring pots on the tiny gas stove and going to the window to take food from the sill. In Jerusalem, he made gefilte fish and ground meat for Shabbos meatballs, but never did any housework. Here in New York, he not only cooked and washed dishes but swept the house and did his own laundry.

When everything was ready, he didn't portion out the food on our plates but put everything on the table and let us take what we wanted.

He had become an American, like my brother, Moshe.

Some things were different about my father and brother, while some were the same.

My father hadn't changed much during his seven years in America. His white beard was neatly trimmed and brushed, and his earlocks were still long and full, though now he rolled them behind his ears in the American style. He still wore Hasidic clothing, and his black yarmulke sat in the same place on his head. He spoke Yiddish to us, with the same accent, and his eyes had the same open, kind look they'd had in Jerusalem

In contrast, Moshe had changed a great deal. Without his beard and earlocks, he looked young. I almost hadn't recognized him. His style of dress, not quite Hasidic even in Jerusalem, was even more modern now. He peppered his Yiddish with as much English as he thought I would understand, and to my ear, his Yiddish had a different rhythm. My father and I called him Moshe, but the Sommers and his Sweet Little Rose at Borden's Restaurant had called him Moe.

What really surprised me, however, was that Moshe went bare-headed in our father's presence, and wore neither hat nor yarmulke.

But then, our father hadn't commented on my missing earlocks.

Chapter 47

Some things, of course, never change. Whether in Jerusalem or New York, I had to have a routine, and within a week, my days began to take shape.

Weekdays were the same. Every morning, Moshe and Noah Sommers left the house at seven thirty, and began their workday. I rose half an hour later, ate breakfast with Ruth and her two children and then retreated to my room while Ruth put the house in order, then left with her children and went to the studio.

I left the house a few minutes later, remembering to take my keys, another new experience. Batei Warsaw did not lock its doors, and no one carried a key, but by the third day in New York, I had two—one for my father's house and the other for the Sommers house—and I carried them always.

That first Monday morning, after a long walk on the west side of Manhattan, I went to my father's house for lunch. There were two newspapers on the kitchen table. It had been more than five weeks since I had left Jerusalem, and I devoured the two Yiddish dailies from front to back. I was especially interested in stories about Jerusalem, as well as news about the stock market crash and its effects on the American economy.

Every day, I took long walks. It was cold, but the trick was to keep moving, and I developed a sense of traffic and stop lights to avoid unnecessary delays at the street corners. From my brother, I borrowed a white woolen scarf and a pair of gloves, and soon I was out and about in even the bitterest weather.

On Monday, my first Monday in America, I stood on the corner of Delancey and Suffolk and looked longingly at the Williamsburg Bridge, but I did not have the courage to walk across it. Instead, I turned south to Chinatown and then, wanting to see the center of American commerce, continued to Wall Street. I was at home in the maze of narrow streets and lanes. The massiveness and reach of the architecture was astounding. Unlike Jerusalem, where buildings were jammed together, Manhattan soared. I went into a tall building just to ride an elevator and was rewarded with a touch of dizziness when the operator, who identified me immediately as a tourist, brought the car to a sudden stop.

I returned to Orchard Street at lunchtime, and as I walked among the pushcarts, I heard my name called.

"Chaim?"

The peddler was selling fancy fruits from a pushcart.

"*Bist du* Chaim?" (Are you Chaim?).

Never had I seen the man, but the man knew me.

"I'm sorry," I said, "but who are you?"

"My father," he replied, "shares an apartment with your father."

I stared at him.

"At 49 Attorney Street. I've seen your photograph many times—the one with your two younger brothers."

"But I look much different now." My earlocks were gone, as was my long caftan.

"Oh, I can recognize a new arrival from Jerusalem just like that." He snapped his fingers.

Was my immigrant status that obvious?

He gave me a shiny red apple from his stock, a welcoming gift, and we said goodbye.

New York was a vast, new world, but a small one, after all.

I was impatient to become an American—and not just any American, but a New Yorker. At the newsstand on the corner of Delancey and the Bowery I bought my first *New York Times*. It cost three cents—three times more than any newspaper in Jerusalem. I was familiar with *The Times,* if second hand. Papers in Jerusalem, such as *Doar Hayom,* often quoted it.

Back at Attorney Street, I opened the paper on the kitchen table and, much to my surprise, saw that the headlines and subheads were almost identical to the Yiddish my father read. I knew some English, compared the Yiddish, written in Hebrew characters, with the English words, which sounded the same. As I went from one paper to the other, I made an extraordinary discovery: the Yiddish papers simply reprinted many of the stories word for English word, rendering the English word phonetically in Yiddish. Sometimes a sentence was rearranged or a few words were changed, but the vocabulary was essentially equivalent.

The revelation was inspiring; with careful textual comparison, a technique my Talmudic studies had taught me, I could acquire a high-level English vocabulary on my own.

My father and brother walked in in the middle of my literary endeavors. Each had a bag of groceries. My father cooked supper, and the three of us ate. My father's roommate, Eleazar, arrived as we finished, and immediately wanted to know what I thought of America.

"How can he think anything," Moshe responded, "when he's just off the boat?"

My brother had a question of his own.

"Chaim, what else do you have from Jerusalem in your valise?"

"I have something from Dvorah."

I went into the bedroom and returned with the photographs of Moshe's wife and two sons. My brother stared at the photographs for a long while and, without a word, turned them down on the table.

"So, Chaim," he said, "what else are you hiding?"

"I have a jar of jam from Uncle Shlomo for his son, Wolfe, in Philadelphia."

"Bring it out so we can see it."

My father and Eleazar were smiling.

I retrieved it and placed it on the table.

Moshe looked at the jar intently. "What kind of jam is it?"

"It's mish-mish."

The three burst out laughing. I should have known to call it apricot.

Moshe wagged his finger. "You see, Chaim, how people laugh? Don't be a greenhorn. Now, what are you going to do with the jam?"

Moshe held the jar against the light and studied its color.

"Do? I'm not going to do anything with the jam. It belongs to our cousin Wolfe in Philadelphia."

"And just how is this jar of mish-mish going to get there?"

"The same way it reached New York from Jerusalem."

"What, you're going to Philadelphia?" Moshe lifted his eyebrows in surprise. "Do you have any idea how far Philadelphia is from the Lower East Side?"

I was silent.

"Almost as far as Jerusalem is from Haifa. So you understand what I'm getting at?"

"Yes, first, it is far, but I traveled much farther when I came to the United States from Jerusalem. And second, I know exactly what you're getting at."

Our father, quiet until now, said, "The jam can be mailed to him."

"That's too much work." Moshe shook his head. "Besides, the postage for this heavy jar will cost twice as much as what the jam is worth." He hefted the jar. "Twice as much, maybe more. I know what postage is."

I took the jar out of his hand. "Uncle Shlomo asked me to bring this jam to his son, Wolfe, our cousin."

"What, apricot jam for our dear cousin in a distant city is now your major concern?" My older brother, who liked to get his way in all things, waxed sarcastic. "I'm sure Wolfe is spending sleepless nights wondering when his mish-mish will arrive. Chaim, Wolfe is practically a millionaire—that's right, a millionaire. Do you know what that means in terms of how much jam he can buy if he really wants jam?"

"I'm sure Uncle Shlomo knows that. It's not because his son can't afford jam that he asked me to carry it to America. It's so that his heart can have a taste."

That stopped my brother cold and made my father smile.

Eleazar had a suggestion.

"Look, Chaim, we don't know if the jam is still good. We should taste it just to be sure."

"That was going to be my next suggestion." Moshe held out his hand. "It's the smartest thing to do."

I held on to the jar. "I know you like tasty foods, but we're not going to open it."

"Okay, Chaim, if that's what you want. It's not for myself that I want to open the jar. Go ahead—spend a small fortune to mail Cousin Wolfe his jar of mish-mish. But just remember, it's been traveling on the high seas for a month in a hot, windowless cabin, and what do you think that's going to do to it? Think how disappointed our cousin would be if you sent him some rotten apricot jam."

Then our father spoke. "Chaim is right. The jar has to be delivered to Cousin Wolfe in Philadelphia. It's not our place to argue if the jam is good or bad or how much it will cost to send it. But, Chaim, it's an expensive package to mail and a long trip to deliver it yourself. Write to your cousin, and see what he wants to do."

That settled the matter, and I returned the mish-mish to the valise.

*

On my third day in New York, I made a significant discovery: the Sommers had a magic box.

I had seen a radio only once in my life, in Jerusalem, when a student in the yeshiva dashed into class shouting about a fantastic talking box. It was in a restaurant in the Old City, and though he himself had not seen it with his own eyes, a rebbe of some repute, standing in the crowd outside the restaurant waiting his turn to see this marvel, had told him of the box's existence, and the student was positive that the thing was so. The next day, a group of us went to the restaurant, paid our quarter penny, and went inside. A big wooden box with a glowing glass window and many knobs and dials stood against the wall. We were allowed to listen for five minutes. Palestine had no broadcasting system of its own, and what we heard, we were told, came from faraway Rome. The words were blurred, and the music was scratchy; for we all knew, it could have come from China. In Batei Warsaw, my reportage was greeted with skepticism.

My uncle Yisrael Yitzhak in particular was disappointed in me, his smart nephew.

"How is it possible that a box can talk?"

"But it did!"

"How can you believe in such nonsense, Chaim?"

"But I saw it with my own eyes!"

"Ah, but did you see inside the box?"

439

I said nothing.

"They tricked you. There was a small man in the box, holding a lantern and making funny noises. They only wanted your money. Use your common sense."

But this morning, here was a real, genuine talking box that I could listen to anytime I wanted. I had to use earphones and turn the radio at a precise angle, but the sound was clear. I knew exactly where to go on the band to find the Yiddish station in Jerusalem.

That evening, as usual, Moshe and I ate supper with our father. My brother was excited and kept encouraging me to hurry up and finish. Finally, Moshe put down his knife and fork.

"Chaim, we have to go."

"What's the rush?" my father asked. "He's still eating."

"We're going to school. And you, Chaim, are going to register for evening class."

But how could I register in an American school? I wasn't a citizen, I didn't know English, and other than basic arithmetic, I had studied only Torah and Talmud, not exactly American subjects.

"Come on, Chaim. Let's go."

"What's the rush?" my father repeated. "He's been here three days. Let him rest some more."

Moshe had his coat on and was holding mine. "The sooner he becomes an American the better. Come on. Registration closes at eight."

We hurried through the cold night to East First Street. The school was completely different from the heders of Jerusalem. It had many small rooms with desks attached to the floor, blackboards on the walls, and pictures and posters everywhere.

At the registration desk, the clerk asked for my last name, and I said in English, "Linder."

"First name, please," said the clerk.

"Chaim."

Moshe spoke. "Not Chaim. It's Herman, please."

I gave my brother a look, *Herman?* Moshe ignored me.

"Take this to the class," the clerk said. I looked at the registration card. I was now officially Herman Linder. "Hurry up. The class is about to start."

We raced down a long corridor

"Why Herman?" I asked.

"Don't ask questions. I'll tell you later. Look, the class is meeting. Go in."

I opened the door and took a seat at one of the desks. Our class, the teacher explained, would give us the equivalent of an American elementary school education. We'd meet for two hours, four evenings a week, Monday through Thursday.

"So, let us begin," he said.

He was a middle-aged man and, based upon my many experiences with rebbes, an excellent teacher, educated and sincere. That night we had our first lesson in arithmetic. Half the class was sleeping when we finished at nine thirty. As we left, he handed out four textbooks: Basic English, mathematics, American history, and geography.

At the Sommers house, I walked into a surprise party.

"Mazel tov!"

"Congratulations on becoming a student!"

Ruth had a prophecy. "You'll all see. Hymie will reach high places!"

Moshe frowned. "Ruth, please, no more Chaim. My brother is officially registered in school as Herman. It's finished and done."

I spoke up. "What's wrong with Chaim?"

"What's wrong with Chaim?" Moshe rolled his eyes. "This isn't Batei Warsaw, where Chaim is always Chaim. In New York, Chaim is Hymie. See how Ruth called you that? The streets of the East Side are filled with Hymies. Shout out, 'Hymie!' and half the men turn around and say, 'Who? Me?' That's what's wrong with Chaim."

"He has a point," said Noah Sommers.

"That's right. I do. And let me show you something else." From the index finger of his left hand, he pulled a ring. I had noticed it before and hadn't said anything. The idea that a man could wear a decorative ring or any other piece of jewelry was unheard of, but this was America, and I wasn't about to ask another of my greenhorn questions.

Moshe held the ring in front of my face. "What does it say?" he said.

"Maurice. What's that?"

"It isn't a *that*; it's my name. Maurice."

I was astonished.

"I use Maurice in my signature." He held the ring up to the light. "In conversation, I prefer to be called Moe. I didn't mind that you called me Moshe for the first few days, especially in front of Abba. But now you can start calling me Moe."

Manhattan's Lower East Side

CHAPTER 48

Uncle Moe was what my brothers and I called our father's older brother. He lived in the Bronx, a long way from our house on Avenue X in Brooklyn. He was a professional photographer specializing in portraits, and I loved going into his darkroom and watching him slip the blank paper into the developer. I stood in the dim, red glow and watched an image rise beneath the liquid. Holding the print with tongs, he'd slip it into the shortstop bath made of vinegar, hold it under for a second or two, and place it into the last tray, the fixer.

In the war, Uncle Moe had been a military photographer in New Guinea. Something of a renaissance man, creative and practical, he designed a camera that was used for high-altitude photography, an invention for which he received a medal. He returned from the Pacific with boxes of photographs. There were pictures of him with other airmen outside their tents. This was a real, unretouched jungle—little men with crude bows and arrows and penis sheaths—and I could feel the heat and dampness, and see on the men's faces that this wasn't much fun.

Uncle Moe always had the latest piece of equipment. For instance, he had a phonograph that flipped the record automatically. When the needle touched the broad inner circle, the arm lifted and swung back, and two long arms with pincers swung into place and grasped the record on its outer circumference. The pincers lifted the record high, rotated it over, and gently lowered and centered it on the turntable. The arms swung away, the needle arm moved in and dropped, and the music started again. It was a complicated and completely unnecessary piece of equipment that always fascinated me.

Uncle Moe also had the most advanced home movie equipment. Our mother's home movies were silent reels of eight-millimeter film, but Uncle Moe shot in sixteen, and in sound. One of the required activities of every visit was viewing a short jungle documentary. Uncle Moe hadn't actually shot the footage himself, but that didn't matter. The movie showed a fight between a black jaguar and a python, with music and a narrator. I never tired of it, but I forgot whether the snake or the jaguar won.

Uncle Moe was an adventurer. One day, deciding he had had enough of photography, he sold his studio in the Bronx and went out to Chattanooga, Tennessee and bought a grocery store in a run-down part of the city. Our father was only slightly amazed. Uncle Moe spoke glowingly of the opportunities in Chattanooga, but our mother insisted that we first see what life was like out there. Our father had no vacation time left, so my three brothers, our mother, and I went without him. As usual, the trip to see Uncle Moe involved a long train ride.

At any rate, Chattanooga was not to anyone's liking. I helped Uncle Moe for an afternoon in his grocery store, stocking the shelves with cans of soup and boxes of cereal. He stood at the register and rang up the sales, checking the prices and hitting the keys hard on the old cash register. He made change, and then bagged the groceries. His customers were poor black men and women. I watched my uncle's face as he bagged the groceries. He was not happy.

We returned to Brooklyn after a week. Our father asked us how we liked it, and we said we didn't. Later that night, I heard my parents talking quietly in their bedroom. They were speaking in Yiddish, and I understood most of it. We did not move to Chattanooga.

Nor was it the life my uncle wanted. A year after our visit, he left Chattanooga and moved to Chicago, and opened a portrait studio and became, very quickly, quite successful.

As a teenager, I knew he really liked me, and I can say with certainty, and much pleasure, that he and I had a special relationship.

I miss him, and I know my father does too.

CHAPTER 49

The apartment at 49 Attorney Street rented for twenty-two dollars a month. Eleazar and his wife had lived there for years, and after she'd died, Eleazar invited my father to move in with him. The building had been built as a cold-water tenement without heat or hot water, but a short time before I arrived in 1929, a central heating system had been installed, and now each apartment had radiators and hot water.

The building had five floors, and four apartments on each floor—two to a side and front and back. My father's apartment, in the rear, had three large rooms. The center room was a combination kitchen, dining room, and sitting area. The big room in front was Eleazar's bedroom. My father had the smaller bedroom in back, for which he paid ten dollars a month. For the larger room, Eleazar paid twelve. Every apartment at 49 Attorney Street had a bathtub in the kitchen, and a hot bath filled the entire apartment with steam. The toilets were in the hall, two to a floor; the tenants on the right shared one toilet, those on the left the other.

The larger front room had two windows on Attorney Street and let in the afternoon sun. In the back, where my father slept, there was a solid brick wall about seven feet away. The wall was the back of the Clinton Street Movie Theater; the screen was against that wall, along with the sound equipment, so the soundtrack of every movie could be heard inside his bedroom, even with the windows closed. When a western was playing, the guns of the cowboys and their galloping horses echoed through the apartment. It was an amusing irony that my father, who was mindful not to sit in the seat of the scornful and did not attend plays or go to movie houses, was now able to enjoy endless movies, their sound tracks at least, in his own bedroom. The show went on every day, noon till midnight, with a midnight show on Saturday, all free of charge.

"Not much of a bargain," he commented.

*

Every morning for a week, after I had breakfast with Ruth and her children, I stepped out and strode up Delancey Street with Moshe's scarf and gloves. I wanted to familiarize myself with the sights and sounds of America, and by the end of first week I was striding the streets of Manhattan as if I belonged there.

But I didn't belong anywhere. The streets were full of people, cars, and trucks rushing everywhere; everyone had a place to go and something to do, except me.

I had not thought things out. I was a professional student, and I had assumed that once in America, I would enroll in a yeshiva and become an ordained rabbi. But almost immediately, I knew it wasn't going to happen. My father did not possess the financial means to support me for the years of schooling a rabbinical degree would require, nor did he intend to remain much longer in America. As for Moshe—or Moe, as he wished to be called—his wages barely covered his own expenses. Even if Moe had any money, he was against any further religious training.

"Herman," he said, "rabbis in America are a dime a dozen."

As I walked the streets on the Lower East Side, I saw that I was in the same predicament as in Jerusalem: I was not qualified for any work.

There was so much I had to learn. I could tease out a sentence from the *New York Times*, but my English was primitive. My evening classes helped, but it would take a long time for me to learn what I had to, and the world wasn't going to wait for me to catch up. Ordinary Americans were doing things I couldn't do. For all that my life had changed, I could have stayed in Batei Warsaw and walked the alleys in the Old City. At least I wouldn't have frozen in Jerusalem.

And America was entering hard times. The headlines screamed of layoffs and bankruptcies. Hopelessness and poverty clouded the horizon. If American citizens couldn't find work, what hope was there for an immigrant yeshiva boy from the Holy Land talking about mish-mish and unable to do anything but open a holy book?

*

One night in midwinter, I found the classroom decorated with color-ful balloons and small electric lights. In Jerusalem, we all knew that Christmas was an important Christian holiday, but its impact on the Hasidic community was minimal. The few Christians in Palestine usu-ally kept to themselves. Easter was more visible. The Christians paraded through the streets, some of them carrying wooden crosses through the twisting alleys, wailing and praying. Once, we'd seen a man, naked except for a loincloth and a crown of cactus thorns, carrying a heavy wooden cross on his back. He whipped himself with a chain and bled from his back and legs. I had asked my father what it meant, and he had shaken his head, not understanding it himself. My cousin Yitzhak, however, possessed an abundance of information.

"The gentiles say that this man is a god and that he died on a cross, and they pretend they are him. They say too that he's Jewish."

We both thought that was quite extraordinary.

In America, Christmas was celebrated everywhere. Stores were dec-orated; holiday music spilled out into the street. On many street corners, men in red-and-white costumes and thick white beards rang bells for charity. That night, the teacher dismissed our class early; classes, he told us, would resume after New Year's. I was confused. New Year's was in the month of Tishri, half a year away, not ten days. My brother Moshe explained that January first was the start of the secular calendar, and there would be big parties all night long and a lot of drinking as people counted down, second by second, the arrival of the New Year.

Whatever its source, I welcomed the vacation. I had missed the first two months of classes and needed the time to catch up on my studies.

*

On Friday morning, my first in America, I was in the kitchen of my father's apartment reading the *Morning Journal* and eating my breakfast. Eleazar was sweeping his room; my father was dusting in his. I could not help but notice a small smile on my father's mouth. This meant good news, though of what sort I could not say. I knew my father; he was savoring something. I picked up the *Forward*, lay it next to the *Times*, and began my textual comparison. From time to time, I glanced up and noted my father still smiling.

Finally, his Sabbath preparations finished, he stood at the table in his apron. His earlocks hung down, his skullcap was high on the back of his head. I looked up from the newspapers.

"Yes, Abba?"

"Chaim, I found a job for you."

"A job?"

"Come. Follow me."

He led me into the front room and pushed aside the curtain.

"Look. Do you see the store on the corner, on the right-hand side?"

"The one with the big window?"

"Yes, that one."

On the store's window, in a semicircle of big gold letters, was a sign: Silver's Delicatessen. Under it, in smaller gold letters, in Hebrew, was the word *Kosher*.

"Go there right now. I spoke with the owner, and he's expecting you. You'll be able to start working immediately."

I started to speak, but my father smiled and patted me on the shoulder.

"Ask your questions there. Mazel tov."

It was too early for Silver's Delicatessen to be serving, but the door was open, and I walked in and looked around. A tall elderly man with a well-trimmed beard and a dark felt hat looked up from the cash register. He greeted me in Yiddish. I introduced myself, and his face lit up with a big smile.

"Ah, Haskel's son. Yes, yes, I told him I had work for you." He looked me up and down. "Sit down. Get warm."

He disappeared into the back and returned a minute later with two glasses of tea.

"Hot tea on a cold morning." He smacked his lips. "Good, isn't it?"

"Yes. Do you have a little sugar?"

"Of course."

He reached behind and produced sugar and a spoon.

"I enjoyed talking with your father. A very good, very honest man."

"Thank you."

"So. We need a young man but not here in the restaurant. You see, we make our own meats, and we need a worker in our meat department."

"I'll take any kind of work."

He was looking at my hands cupped around the glass.

"You have to be strong. This isn't about reading books, you understand."

"Of course, though some books are very heavy."

He looked at me for a long moment before laughing. "Yes, yes, of course. When I went to school, some books were too heavy for me!" He drank more tea and smacked his lips.

"My father said I would start immediately."

"As soon as you can. We observe the Sabbath, so we're going to close early today. You'll start work on Sunday morning." He wagged his finger. "Seven o'clock—no later."

"Of course."

"*Ganz gut.*" (Very good).

Mr. Silver stood, so did I.

"Thank you very much," I said.

"Wait a minute, Chaim."

He disappeared again into the back room and returned promptly with a long wrapped package. I knew immediately what it was.

"Gut Shabbos to you and to your father, from me."

Outside, I looked up. My father was watching from behind the curtain in Eleazar's window. I waved the package in the air and raced across the street.

"Yes, yes," my father kept repeating when I told him what Mr. Silver had said. "Yes, yes, *zehr gut*. And what are the conditions and wages?"

My mouth dropped; in the excitement of getting my first job in America, I hadn't asked.

"Whatever he pays you," my father said as he unwrapped the salami, "you're going to have plenty to eat."

That Friday, my father and I went to a small synagogue on Attorney Street. What a contrast to my little shul in Batei Warsaw, with its dark walls and long, low benches, and peripatetic congregants saying hello to each other as they murmured their prayers. Here, people sat quietly in rows of comfortable chairs and paid attention. The synagogue was freshly painted and decorated with fine ink drawings of Jerusalem. However, like my shul at home, the congregation was poor and had no regular rabbi, so my father sat in the rabbi's chair. At the proper time he stood to offer some words—a sermon, they called it—on a point of Jewish law.

At home, my father had decorated the table with a beautiful tablecloth. Moshe joined us, and my father lit the Shabbos candles. It was the first time in my life that my mother had not lit them for us. He said Kiddush, then the blessing over bread. Moshe and I joined in. In silence, for no words should come between the blessing and the completion of the act, my father cut the challah and gave us each a slice. In silence, we sprinkled salt on our bread. Then each of us, with our own long thoughts, partook of the warm, sweet challah.

In Batei Warsaw, and in all of Jerusalem, the spirit of Shabbos was in our homes, and the synagogues, and the streets. All activity ceased, and peace descended upon the ancient city.

At 49 Attorney Street, we did our best to welcome the Sabbath queen, but the extra dimension of serenity was missing. Traffic continued to roar, people rushed back and forth on the sidewalks, and stores conducted business as usual.

As Moshe said, "This is America."

*

At the Sommers home, where news of my employment had circulated, Moshe and I walked into a noisy, enthusiastic welcome.

"Mazel tov!"

"Good luck!"

"A great achievement—one week in the United States, and he's in school!"

"Not to mention gainful employment! Mazel tov!"

Noah Sommers poured wine for everyone. "L'chaim."

I lifted the glass of wine and drank—and then gagged and spat it back into my tumbler. I had never tasted unsweetened wine, and it was strong, sour, and biting.

Everyone laughed.

"Still a greenhorn!"

"You'll get used to the finer things in life, like your brother Moe!"

Basking in praise and admiration, I got to bed late and enjoyed a deep, restful sleep.

Early in the morning, Moshe and I had breakfast at Borden's Dairy Restaurant. Sweet Sweet Little Rose brought two extra slices of French toast. It was the Sabbath, so no money changed hands; Moshe had paid the day before, a common arrangement among observant Jews.

After our regular American breakfast, Moe suggested a leisurely walk.

Slowly but surely, I was calling him Moe.

This was America.

"Chaim," my brother said, "ten more days, and there's going to be a new year, 1930. It's not like Rosh Hashanah. In Jerusalem, we pray; here in New York, people play. No one fasts—they eat and get drunk. You'll see. With some extra money, you can really have a good time."

I knew immediately that my older brother was after something. He was always instructive, preaching about America, but now he was nervous. And he was calling me Chaim.

"So tell me more about this New Year's playing."

"As you know, I'm just starting to learn photography, and it's going to be a profitable line of business. Of course, my wages are still very low, barely enough to cover my daily expenses. I don't have to tell you that I'm very hard pressed financially."

His appeals to my pity were a variant of his usual aggressive approach.

"I know," I replied. "Abba said something about it. Besides, I can see that you're spending too much money."

He was wearing a new tie of yellow silk with little blue squares.

"This is America, Chaim. You have to keep up appearances."

We walked on Delancey Street in the cold morning sunlight, and then Moe spoke again.

"I owe Abba so much that I can't ask for any more. Next year, I'll be on top of things, and I'll pay him back. And of course, you have a job. Considering conditions, a miracle! The New Year costs money. May I ask, Chaim—did you bring anything from Jerusalem?"

"Not much. Five dollars."

Moe's face brightened. "Not much? You're as rich as Rothschild!"

After a quick negotiation, I loaned him three dollars.

A month later, with New Year's behind us, he treated me to another American breakfast and paid it all back.

CHAPTER 50

On Sunday morning, the first day of my first job in the United States, I woke at six, washed and dressed quietly. Moshe stirred but didn't wake. The morning was very cold, the streets dark and empty.

The Silver Kosher Delicatessen was closed. I tapped on the window. An elderly lady with a broom shook her head and walked away. I tapped again, and she waved her broom in my face.

"It's too early for business!" she shouted in Yiddish through the glass. "Come back later!"

Shivering and hopping from one foot to the other, I shouted back, "I'm not here to buy! I'm here to work!"

The Yiddish did the trick, and she held up a finger and left. In a minute, a young man opened the door.

"*Gut morgen.* Come in."

His hands and white apron were stained with blood. He asked me to wait and hurried off. He came back few minutes later with clean hands and a clean apron, a sign of respect that made me like him immediately.

"Excuse me," he said. "I was cutting meat inside. A messy business. My name is David Silver. You must be Chaim. My father told me about you. Let's have some tea."

We sat at the same table where I had had tea with his father.

"We produce and sell strictly kosher meat products," David explained, "and we always need reliable workers who know kashruth and who aren't afraid to get their hands dirty."

I looked at his hands; he had scrubbed them hard.

He smiled. "Yes, very dirty."

I spoke Yiddish to him, and explained that I had studied all aspects of Jewish law in Jerusalem and was very familiar with kashruth, the Jewish dietary laws. Moreover, I was reliable—look how early I had come.

"There's plenty of dirt in Jerusalem, and it never bothered me."

"Good," he said. "You'll work six days a week—you get a day off on

Shabbos, from late Friday to Sunday morning. You'll work ten hours a day, from seven o'clock to six o'clock, with an hour off from noon to one. You'll get all the Jewish holidays off, thirteen days maximum—your choice as to which—with pay, plus one week paid vacation in the summer, when business is slow. Your workday will be split half and half between the shop in the morning and deliveries in the afternoon. Your wages will be twelve dollars a week."

"I accept the job."

"Very good." We stood and shook hands. "Now, let's start."

We went through a door and he introduced me to the foreman.

"This is Louie," said David. "We call him the Boss."

Louie was a short, stocky young man with a long gray rubber apron and gray rubber boots that came to his knees. The apron and his hands were streaked with blood.

"So you're Chaim."

"I am."

"Louie, show the young man around."

Louie turned and waved his bloody hand. "Come on, Hymie. Time to learn the business."

The Silver Delicatessen Store had three distinct areas. In the front was the restaurant. To the side was the cold storage section, where the finished meats were cut, wrapped, and stored. The third area, a large open space in the rear of the building, was the work area where the raw meat was processed into the Silver product line: garlic rings, salamis, frankfurters and sausages, pastrami and corned beef, and tongue. This area had a cement floor, steel walls, long metal sinks against the wall, and long metal cutting tables in the middle of the room.

After a quick tour, no questions allowed, Louie led me to the factory area.

"Okay, Chaim, this is where you'll start."

From a hook on the wall, he took a gray rubber apron; I tied it around my waist. He handed me gray boots, and I put them on over my shoes.

"You'll have to wear these too."

He handed me gray rubber gloves.

I put them on, my hands lost inside.

"Okay, now bring those into the factory."

He pointed to six barrels against the wall. There were as high as my waist and full of big pieces of dark, raw, half-frozen meat and whole beef tongues, thick and wet.

"These?"

"Yeah, those. And now."

Louie waited without smiles.

I grasped the top of the barrel rim with both hands, planted my feet solidly, braced myself, and pulled. The barrel didn't budge. I tried again, pushing this time. The barrel did not move the slightest fraction.

"Don't be a schmo!" Louie was disgusted. "Roll them!"

I had never seen a barrel rolled, so I tried to push them over on their sides and roll them that way. Louie watched me try to tip one over. He was more amazed than angry.

"On their bottoms, schmo! They're round, see, so you roll them on their bottoms."

"But how do you do that?"

He looked at me for a long moment. "Okay."

He showed me how to rock the barrel so that it lifted off the floor and then how to use my arms to rotate it and get it moving. Very soon, with a bit of muscle and a lot of cleverness, I moved the heavy barrel across the floor.

"Okay, the yeshiva boy learns fast."

One by one, Louie watching, I rolled the six barrels into the factory room.

"Okay, pretty good. Now take the meat out of the barrels, and put it on the tables."

I reached in with one hand, pulled out a chunk of cold, wet meat, and placed it on the long steel table. With the same hand, I took out another piece and put that on the table.

"Okay, okay!" Louie stepped between the barrel and me. "This a shop where you're paid to work with both hands. If you use one hand, you'll get half pay, or you'll have to work twice as long. So you tell me—how do you want to do this?"

This made a lot of sense, and I dug in with both hands. But the meat and the tongues were frozen together. Even with the gloves, my fingers were numb in an instant, and the meat stayed stuck together.

Louie spoke more gently. "Chaim, look, use one of the small water hoses." He pointed to the wall. "You'll see how everything melts like butter."

He was right. I dug in with both hands, pulling out heavy, cold chunks of meat and half thawed tongues, and when I looked around, Louie was gone.

When I had finished all six barrels, I went to Louie's little office.

"Okay," he said. "Finished?"

"I'm ready for more."

"How do you feel?"

"Fine." My arms were aching and my hands were numb. "But the apron's a little too tight, and the boots are too big."

"I see. And the gloves?"

"The gloves are just right."

Louie stood and patted me on my back. "On Friday, when you get paid, you can buy yourself a custom tailored apron and made-to-order rubber boots."

His sarcasm was educational.

My next chore was to sweep the factory floor.

"Get a broom from Esther," Louie said. "She's the lady you saw this morning. Don't let her give you any orders. You work in the factory for me and not anyone else. Okay?"

"Okay."

"When you find her, don't say, 'I want the broom.' She won't give it to you. Say, 'Louie wants the broom.' Okay?"

I found Esther in the restaurant and got the broom using Louie's code. Louie watched me for a minute and, satisfied with my sweeping abilities, went to his office.

Next, I washed the blood from the walls and floors of the meat-cutting room. Louie showed me how to use the special high-pressure hose so it didn't fly out of my hands, and how to aim the water into the corners.

"It's important. Everything has to be hosed clean; no blood or uncooked meat can sit for even a minute. Okay?"

Okay, but the water was extremely cold, and I had to double up on the gloves.

"You'll have to get used to ice water. That's all we use here. Hot is too expensive. And it's also illegal, because hot water might cook the meat. Okay?"

"Okay," I said, and then, before I knew it, it was time for lunch. I was about to leave, when Louie, holding a loosely wrapped package, caught me at the door.

"This is part of the pay. Eat all of it," he advised, "and you'll have plenty of strength for the afternoon."

"Do I have to eat it here?"

Louie smiled. "Anywhere you want. Just be back in one hour."

I was at my father's apartment in less than a minute. Louie's package held an enormous club sandwich, half pastrami and half corned beef, still warm from the steam box. With it were a large sour pickle and a tall bottle of ginger ale. I managed to eat half, and then put the leftovers in the icebox and rested on the sofa for half an hour before returning to the shop precisely at 1:00 p.m.

It was lunchtime, and the place was packed. Mr. Silver and his wife, Esther, and two of their daughters, were behind the counter and waiting on customers.

"Keep your coat on, Chaim," Mr. Silver told me. "You have deliveries to make."

The Silvers had two other restaurants on the Lower East Side; they also sold to a number of high-class kosher hotels and catering halls in Lower Manhattan.

Mr. Silver handed me a package for the Broadway Central Hotel.

"Take the bus," Mr. Silver advised.

Returning quickly, they gave me another order for their restaurant on Rivington Street, on the corner of Pitt. That took about forty-five minutes, and when I walked in, Louie waved me into his little office.

"Okay, Chaim, you're finished. You can go home now."

It was only four o'clock.

"Am I being fired?"

"Of course not. Don't look a gift horse in the mouth."

"I won't." I didn't know such a creature, but I thanked him.

At Attorney Street, my father was very interested in the workings of a delicatessen, and we talked for more than an hour. When he saw the half sandwich in the icebox, he was suitably impressed, but he refused any of it.

"Take it to Moshe," he suggested. "Your brother likes good food."

That was true, especially when it was free.

Moe's eyes lit up when he saw the sandwich.

"Mmm, good stuff," he said as he gobbled it down in short order. "Very good stuff."

Then, as a special treat, Moe said that he and I were going to Brighton Beach to visit one of our cousins.

"It's going to be your first time on a subway," Moe said. "Come on. It's a long ride."

It was amazing. We went in Delancey Street station, pushing through heavy wood turnstiles. While we waited, two trains roared by on the express line in opposite directions. The noise was terrific, even louder than the overhead trains on the Bowery. Moe smiled. "This is America!"

We rode to Canal Street, then took the Brighton Beach Express. Here was a different world entirely. The massive steel beams and the heavy concrete vaults were like underground cities. I heard and felt other trains rushing by above us, the powerful machines sending forth a unique smell of oil and earth, the odors of an advanced civilization.

It was Sunday, but the train was crowded, and Moe and I squeezed together in the car. We moved slowly along the underground tracks until, suddenly, we emerged into the open.

We were on a bridge!

Moe spoke into my ear. "The Manhattan Bridge. It crosses the East River into Brooklyn."

I pushed my way to the door and looked out on the bright skyscrapers

458

and the waterfront below. After the bridge, we went underground again. In the dark tunnels the roar was tremendous and the lights rushed by in streaks. Then we reemerged into open air and raced along a long trench with houses on either side. Soon we rose onto an elevated track way. Now our train was almost empty, and Moe explained what was happening.

"We're on an express. See how we pass the other stations, where passengers are waiting for trains? They have to wait for the local."

I grasped the system immediately and was impressed.

Moe was watching me. "So what do you think?"

"Very interesting. But I'm wondering where the locomotive is."

"Follow me." He went to the front of the car and slid open the door. "Come on. Step through."

I refused. A few thin chains held the cars together. Below were the rushing tracks. The noise was even harsher, the wind terrific. Without a word, Moe stepped out of the car, crossed the tiny, swaying platform; and slid open the door of the other car. I took a deep breath and followed, and we walked through four cars that way until we got to the front of the train.

"In there is the conductor." Moe pointed to a small closet. The door was half open, and inside was a motorman in uniform, sitting on a round stool and holding a sticklike mechanism.

"The subway runs on electricity," Moe explained. "Look out the front window, and you'll see the rail on the side. There are no locomotives. No coal or oil. What do you think would happen if a steam engine tried to go through a tunnel? The smoke would be impossible!"

From the window, I could see the tracks flying by, the third rail higher than the tracks.

"So what do you think?"

"It's quite a wonder."

"Of course. What did you expect in America?"

*

Seven o'clock Monday morning, I walked into the delicatessen with a new self-assurance.

Louie was there. "Feeling rested, Chaim?"

"I feel fine."

"Good. Put on your apron and boots. Today we're making sausages."

Louie led me into the meat-processing room to a big hand-operated meat grinder.

"This is very simple, Chaim," he said. "It's all about speed. You turn the handle either faster or slower, depending on what we're making."

"How will I know what we're making?"

"I'll tell you."

We took up position. Louie stood at the hopper on a step stool—he was short, and the machine was tall—and I stood with one hand at the crank, ready.

"Okay, Chaim, let's go!"

Louie dropped meat into the hopper and added spices, and as I turned the crank, he ran to the front of the machine and attached sausage casings to the machine's mouth. I cranked away, the casings filled, and Louie tied them off with a quick twist of his hand and placed them neatly on a large metal tray, which I carried to the baking room, where David, one of the Silver sons, slid it into the oven.

For the next three hours, without stopping, I cranked the meat chopper and then carried the heavy trays of raw sausage to David.

Mind you, I'm no Hercules. I am about five feet ten inches tall and have never weighed more than 150 pounds. Having spent most of my life on benches, reading sacred books, the work that morning was taxing. Everything had to be ready for the lunch rush in the restaurant, and deliveries had to reach the hotel kitchens in timely fashion. Louie exhorted me to move ever faster. Throwing various cuts of meat and spices into the hopper, he shouted out commands.

"Salami! Slow it down!"

I cranked slower.

"Perfect! Now we're making a garlic bratwurst, so give me some speed!"

I gave him speed.

"Here come the frankfurters, Chaim! Crank it up!"

I gave him even more speed.

"Now for the bologna! Slow it down!"

I took some speed off.

"Not so slow!"

I cranked harder.

"Slow! Fast! Okay! Take a little off, Chaim! Put a little on! Give me some wrist action!"

Just when I thought my arm would fall off, Louie signaled me to stop.

Mr. Silver had come in.

"How are things going, Louie?"

"We're doing very well, thank you, Mr. Silver."

"And our new worker?"

"He's doing a very good job."

Mr. Silver looked at me. "Well, young man, I see they're putting you to work."

Glad for the brief rest, I said nothing.

"Louie, I'd like to talk to Chaim for a few minutes."

"Yes, sir, of course. Chaim, you're finished here."

I followed Mr. Silver into the restaurant and sat at a table while he made tea for us. The lunch hour had not begun and the restaurant was empty.

"I observed, Chaim," Mr. Silver said, "that you were reading my *Morning Journal* this morning. I thought that a yeshiva student from Jerusalem avoids such secular material."

I remained silent; he was leading somewhere.

"Can I ask you, Chaim—do you know how to wash and salt meat according to the law?"

"I've studied the *dinim*"—laws—"of kashruth, but we never had enough meat in my house that my mother needed an assistant."

Mr. Silver smiled. "I've been thinking about you, and I'd like you to do the koshering for us. Don't worry about not having experience. I can see that you'll learn it very fast. Come."

I followed Mr. Silver into the processing room, and started salting meat right there and then. The rules of kashruth are complicated, and preparing freshly slaughtered meat is time consuming. As a rebuke to ancient rites of human sacrifice in which pagans drank the blood of humans and animals, the blood of any creature is forbidden. Thus, meat is salted as a means of drawing out the excess blood. Before salt is applied, however, the meat must be cleansed of all visible traces of blood and then submerged in water for half an hour. The meat is removed, and the water is allowed to drip off so that when the salt is applied, the meat is not so wet that the salt is dissolved, nor should the meat be allowed to dry before salt is applied, for then the salt loses much of its drawing effect. The salt can be neither too fine nor too coarse but should be of medium grain. It must have no additives, such as iodine or anticaking chemicals. Hence, there is a special brand of salt known as kosher salt, coarse grained and pure. The salt is sprinkled on all sides of the meat, and the meat is arranged in an oblique position in order that the blood may freely flow onto a nonporous surface, hence the steel tables. The salt stays on for an hour, and then the meat must be thoroughly washed in cold running water three times.

Mr. Silver watched me clean, wash, and salt a barrel of meat, and, satisfied, left the room. The work wasn't as difficult as grinding out sausages, and time flew by. At lunchtime, Louie gave me another meat sandwich wrapped in thick wax paper.

"Okay," he said, "Mr. Silver likes you. I do too. You're entitled to a sandwich every day. Be smart, and don't wait for the Messiah to feed you. Go to the counter and make your sandwich exactly the way you want it. Use as much meat as you want. Promise me."

"If you say it's okay."

"Of course it's okay. And look, why wait for lunchtime?" He looked at my thin arms and chest. "Eat as much meat as you want. You need the strength."

Never in my life had I eaten as much meat as I had in the last few days.

When I returned from lunch, the wursts, salamis, and frankfurters I had made in the morning were ready for delivery. I loaded everything onto a pushcart and set out along Delancey Street. The pushcart, laden with meats and accompaniments—big jars of sour pickles, pickled tomatoes, and coleslaw; containers of mustard and mayonnaise; and baskets of rye breads, thick Italian bread, and rolls—was heavy and unwieldy, and it took all my strength and then some to get it over the high curbs and down the bumpy cobblestones. The whole time, I was dodging the hectic, angry traffic. But it was a welcome change from the drudgery of working with the raw meat. For the next week, the days went fast.

Adding to my pleasure was the long Christmas holiday from school. During the day, I stuffed myself with meat and salad, then returned home to the warm comfort of the Sommers family's apartment. By eight, the children were in bed, and I opened my textbooks and dictionary and studied undisturbed while listening to the magic box, and was in bed before my brother and Noah returned from the studio.

Life was much better. I had dreaded the cold winters in Jerusalem, where, without heat of any kind, the cold and damp built up in the heavy stonewalls until the house was an icebox. In my bedroom in America, the radiator hissed and clanked and threw off soft, fragrant heat. The radio brought music to my ears, and under the unwavering electric lights I was able to catch up on my schoolwork. My yeshiva experience served me well; I had no trouble sitting for hours at a time in full and easy concentration. The schoolwork, compared to Talmudic analysis, was easy; the only stumbling block was my lack of English, which would, with time and determination, be corrected.

On Friday morning, the end of my first week of work, Louie took me aside

"Chaim, I'm going to give you the complete story."

Again, I asked if I was about to be fired, but he laughed and told me not to worry.

Because of the short winter day, he explained, and an early Shabbos, the store would close at two thirty in the afternoon. To make up those lost hours, everyone was expected to come in Saturday night, after the Sabbath, to work.

"We make sandwiches and go out on deliveries."

"I wasn't told that when I was hired. I thought Shabbos was our day off."

"It is, Chaim. But look, I'm going to explain the philosophy of the Silver Delicatessen."

I waited.

"This is a family business, okay? You, Yoel the butcher, and I, are the only nonfamily people here. David and his mother start at five in the morning. Mr. Silver comes in after morning services and stays all day. His two daughters are college students, but they come in whenever they can. Even their younger son—who's a lawyer, by the way—comes in on Saturday night. Sometimes he doesn't go home and sleeps on one of the tables, but he's a workhorse. On Saturday night, we make thousands of sandwiches and deliver them to parties and restaurants. It's a big part of the business. The way we do things here is we work as long as we have to, and then we go home. Last Sunday, you left two hours early. In the winter, we work hard, but in the summer, you'll see—there are only a few hours of work a day. You come in the morning and say hello, and you're out by eleven. Besides, you get a vacation and paid Jewish holidays. So don't be too upset about working Saturday night. It's not the end of the world."

Louie's presentation perked me up; he was right—the Silvers were treating me well. My father gave me some of his usual helpful advice.

"Chaim, go in Saturday night with a smile. It makes it easier for everyone—you too."

*

Louie had lived in New York all his life. He had been working in the Silver Delicatessen for twelve years and earned thirty-five dollars a week, not including the vast quantities of meat he consumed during the day and the occasional salami or slab of corned beef he took home. He even had a girlfriend who came to the store once a week for a free sandwich.

"I'm going to marry her," Louie said. "What do you think? Cute, isn't she?"

"She's very cute. Mazel tov," I told him.

Louie always called me Chaim, not Herman.

"That's a ridiculous name. In private, you can call me by my Yiddish name, Leibl" (pronounced "Label"). "We outsiders," he said, "have to stick together."

I really liked Leibl.

Mr. Silver, the owner, stood at the cash register and watched everything with a hard but fair eye. He had a good philosophy of life: what he couldn't control, he ignored; when confronted with defeat, he compromised with a minimum of stress.

Whenever business slowed, he sat at a table with a glass of hot tea, a slice of lemon on the side and a lump of sugar in his mouth, and read the *Morning Journal*. His peace, however, was precarious, for Mrs. Silver, with apron and broom, would immediately start sweeping under and around his table. Without a word, Mr. Silver picked up his tea and paper and moved to another table. Hot on his trail, Mrs. Silver moved her sweeping operation. These maneuvers continued until Mr. Silver made a complete circuit around the dining room, finishing his tea and newspaper at the last table before returning to the cash register behind the counter.

He left at five, when his youngest daughter, Sarah, came to take over at the register. Sarah was fast with money calculations and comfortable with the customers. I could tell she was a good student—she kept her books open under the counter, and at every break in the action, she gave the page her full, if quick, attention.

That Friday, we closed at three, for the Sabbath would be upon us by four o'clock. Mr. Silver sat at a table and counted out the weekly wages in single dollar bills for the nonfamily employees. Louie got thirty-five dollars, Yoel the butcher got twenty-eight, and I got my promised twelve. I also got an entire salami wrapped in white paper.

"Thank you, and gut Shabbos," I said.

Mr. Silver smiled and shook my hand. "Gut Shabbos to you and your father."

*

"I have to decide what to do with the money."

Wearing his apron and holding his feather duster, my father sat opposite me at the table. My twelve dollars sat in a proud, short stack between us, the long salami next to it.

"First," said my father, "you should give four dollars to Avram Gandzel's father to pay for your train ticket from Providence."

It had been only two weeks ago that I had gotten off the *Alesia* in Rhode Island, and I had completely forgotten. Life in America had kept me busy. Avram lived with his father on East Broadway, and I should have visited him sooner.

"And second, Chaim, you should not be a free boarder in the Sommers house. You see how they live. They aren't rich people. What do you think would be a fair rent?"

I did a quick calculation based on the little I knew of rents and American finances and said, "Twelve dollars a month. That's three dollars a week."

"That sounds very fair."

Actually, it was probably high compared to what my father got for ten, but Ruth Sommers did all the cooking and cleaning.

My father went about his Sabbath preparations while I sat and contemplated my little stack of dollars. As a Talmudic student in the Lubavitcher yeshiva in Jerusalem, never in a million years could I have imagined myself rolling barrels of raw meat in America and salting beef tongue on a table, but here I was in New York, earning twelve dollars a week, a magnificent sum by Batei Warsaw standards. After meeting all my obligations, I still had five dollars left. It was not a fortune, but considering the times and my circumstances, it was not a small sun either.

*

Six thirty Saturday night, I joined the large group on the sandwich-production line at the Silver Delicatessen. Louie and Yoel the butcher sliced the meat and passed it to the lawyer, who arranged it on a slice of rye, piling the meat in the center so that the cut sandwich would be high and full. The mother, with her apron but minus her broom, and her two daughters, applied the mustard and closed the sandwich. I stood at the end of the line, inserting each sandwich into a small paper bag, along a small bag containing a green tomato and a slice of sour pickle.

"Don't press so hard, Chaim." Mrs. Silver had a sharp eye. "The sandwiches have to look nice and full."

Two hours later, at eight thirty, Sarah and I were in her Studebaker driving over the Williamsburg Bridge. In Brooklyn we delivered trays of sandwiches to half a dozen synagogues and catering halls. In one hall, people were dancing and singing.

Sarah stopped to watch. "We have time before we have to go back. Let's dance."

I declined.

"Are you sure? We don't have to rush back."

"I'm sorry," I said. I wished I knew how to dance.

We drove back to the Lower East Side in her gray Studebaker and picked up more sandwiches for deliveries in the Bronx.

Besides, I had just left Batei Warsaw, and it was much too soon to dance with a young woman.

I got home after midnight. Moe, Noah and Ruth Sommers, and another couple were talking and laughing. They wanted me to join them, but I had to be at the Silver Delicatessen at seven the next morning. I go into bed and lay awake for a while

To dance with a young woman!

At seven the next morning Mrs. Silver opened the front door, brandished her broom at me, and the week began.

In contrast to my job, with its religious days off and paid vacations, Moe was a slave to his work. The Photo Studio was open seven days a week, and he often was in the darkroom until midnight. The same was true for Noah Sommers, and Ruth was always complaining that her husband had no time for her or the children.

One evening, as we ate supper in our father's apartment, Moe suggested I take Ruth out to see a movie.

My fork stopped in midair.

"Don't look so amazed," Moe said. "It's a simple social event."

"I work at the delicatessen, and I have night classes. I have to study afterward."

"You can find the time. Besides, there's a holiday next week."

I had forgot; we had a day off to mark the birthday of the first American president.

"Herman, you're a wage earner now, so spend some money on a good time."

I glanced at my father, who, listening with a little smile, wasn't about to get involved. For a single man to take a married woman to a movie was a violation of so many Hasidic laws and customs that he probably didn't know where to even begin. But this was America.

I asked, "What movie should we go to?"

Moe smiled. "Just ask Ruth."

I saw that Moe had been plotting, and the next week Ruth and I went to the Loew's Theater on Delancey Street.

My cinema experience in Jerusalem had been limited to two brief silent movies, and this was my first talkie. It was also my first date with a woman—and a married one at that.

The first part of the program consisted of two features, a long newsreel, two cartoons, a sport short, and three coming attractions. This smorgasbord of visual delights prompted our hunger, and during the intermission we each had an ice cream cup and an entire bottle of soda.

Back in our seats, we were treated to seven acts of live vaudeville--dancing, singing, jokes, and acrobatics.

The entire show lasted four and a half hours.

It cost thirty-five cents apiece, and I paid for both of us, including the ice cream and sodas.

The first movie was a love story, and though I couldn't follow the dialogue and so lost some of the fine turns of the plot, it was about a failed romance and its attendant sorrows. Norma Shearer played the leading woman's role. Ruth was moved and kept asking me during the film, "Isn't she beautiful? Isn't she beautiful?" She was, but the emotional aspects were overdone and repetitious, and I was not enthralled. The second movie was a cowboy adventure, and though the characters were not as romantically engaged or as high-strung, the storyline was precise and easy to follow. There was little dialogue and much action, plenty of flying fists and galloping horses. The gunfights were fast and to the point. Adding to my satisfaction, good was easily distinguished from evil, and eventually, good won.

CHAPTER 51

Home is where I was born.

One day, I found my father at the kitchen table. He looked up, and I could see that something was wrong.

He spoke. "A letter came from home."

My uncle Yisrael Yitzhak in his formal, florid Hebrew wrote it. It had little of my mother, but at least it was a letter. My mother feared that my departure would leave her bereft of her personal scribe, letting the paper bridge to her husband and children fall into the sea.

"Chaim knows exactly how I feel and how I think," she told my uncle Yitzhak before I left. "Where will I get another Chaim?"

My uncle might not have been Chaim, but he was the only scribe she had, and after penning his standard greeting full of "God willings" and blessings of the Name, he told us about my mother's dire financial problems and expressed his "sincere hope" that Chaim, "fresh from Jerusalem, will make it crystal clear that help must be sent immediately."

My father sighed.

Was I never to escape?

I looked at the letter's date; it had been written while I was on the *Alesia*.

Moe came in at midnight, and woke me with a gentle shake.

"What do they write from home?"

He listened, and said nothing.

Two weeks later, another letter arrived, also written by Uncle Yisrael Yitzhak.

"We offer thanks that Chaim has crossed the mighty ocean in good health," he began.

This was an assumption on his part, for he'd written the letter a few days before my arrival in Providence.

This second letter had some of my mother's more emotional, natural style, the gist of it being that financial help was needed urgently.

"We all have great hopes that you and your two sons will find great wealth in America and send some of it back to rescue your family in Jerusalem from their impossible and ever increasing debts."

I had known, however, when I saw my father at 49 Attorney Street in his dark, sunless room with the loud music and galloping horses from the Clinton Street Theater echoing in his sleep, that my mother's pitiful hopes would not be realized.

My father had come to America to earn dowry money for my sisters Yehoved and Hinda Dvorah. As a collector for the Chai Olam Yeshiva in Jerusalem, my dear father had traveled long hours on bus and train; slept in many cities, small and large; walked up many steps; and knocked on many doors. He had endured long waits in outer offices and been subject to refusal and insult. He was a stranger in a strange land, far from the land he loved and the people who loved him. Always, he carried himself with dignity and purpose, and had been one of the most successful collectors in the history of the Chai Olam Yeshiva. Still, it wasn't enough.

After my uncle's second letter, my father and I talked.

"Chaim, I am very tired these days." We were at the kitchen table with the supper dishes between us. "I must return to Ha Eretz. Your sisters are married. My work in America is done."

"Abba, things are very bad in Jerusalem."

I told him how our mother struggled night and day against a rising sea of debt. I did not tell him about her time in debtor's prison or how my uncles had begged the money to get her released before the Sabbath.

"We must all try to send her more money," I said, "so that she can pay what she owes."

My father's only response was a sad silence. He would not speak bitterly, complain, or make excuses. He could do only what he could. He stood and cleared the table, and the way he bent to place the dishes in the sink made him look old to me for the first time.

The letters from Uncle Yitzhak arrived regularly, all hammering on a single theme: "Reizel desperately needs help. We pray to God for aid, but you must be the messenger."

"Abba," I said, "I'm going to send Imma one hundred dollars."

"Have you saved so much already?"

"Only fifty dollars."

In addition to my wages, I earned three dollars in tips from the wealthy families on the East Side. I spent nothing on food, and often brought home dinner for my father and brother.

My father was against it. "I don't want you to use your money for our family's expenses in Jerusalem. You must keep your money here. The times are getting more difficult."

His wealthy, dependable donors were cutting back on their donations, and some were unable to give anything.

"And you must remember too, Chaim, that you are a noncitizen in a strange land, and you must always have some money saved."

I had been warned in Providence that, as an alien, I would face deportation if I should ever apply for government assistance or become a burden to society.

"The money isn't a gift, Abba," I told him. "I'm repaying the hundred dollars you gave me for my apprenticeship with the watchmaker. I used it to buy my ticket to the United States. It's only what I owe you and Imma."

Presented this way, my hundred-dollar offer was accepted, with smiles.

*

My brother's is a true American tale, and the trajectory of his life was a living example of the power of possibility. Full of energy and ready to try all things new and different, Moe lived a full and free life. Handsome and possessing great charm and social skill, he thrived, adapting quickly to the American style of dress and carriage, taking on, too, the distinct hue of the optimist.

He had looked for work as a rabbi, but his studies in Jerusalem did not meet the standards for American certification, nor was his English good enough for congregational duties. Desperate for work, he answered an ad in the Jewish *Morning Journal* and talked his way into a job as the kosher slaughterer in a hotel in New Jersey. His work with poultry in Jerusalem had given him some rudimentary skills, and he taught himself the rest on the job. He worked three days a week and, by his own accounts, made good money. He had a facility with language, and spoke fluent Yiddish, Hebrew, German, and Arabic. He was determined to master English, and soon spoke it without accent.

My brother wrote regularly to his wife and children in Jerusalem and sent them as much money as he could. The amount was small by American standards, but a great deal in war-ravaged Jerusalem. America was Moe's golden land of freedom and opportunity, and he wanted his wife and children to share its riches. Despite all his entreaties, Dvorah didn't want to leave Batei Warsaw, and responded with pleas of her own for his return to Jerusalem.

Moe continued as a reluctant shochet in New Jersey. He didn't like the work; after all, who enjoys killing animals? Then he got a lucky break. There was a special fund-raising banquet sponsored by the Jewish community of Bradley Beach. The featured speaker, an elderly rabbi, had taken to his bed with a bad cold. The rabbi had met Moe and, taken with this handsome young shochet from Jerusalem, suggested that he stand in. Moe jumped at the chance. Wearing his new suit bought for this very purpose, gleaming shoes, and beautiful tie, he made quite an appearance at the podium. Then, mixing his newly acquired English with Talmudic Hebrew and high Yiddish, he delivered a speech that brought the audience to their feet—and brought in more than $3,000, a huge sum of money in those Depression days. The rabbi, in poor health, elderly, and thinking of retirement, was so impressed that he took Moe under his wing as his heir apparent. When, shortly thereafter, the elderly rabbi retired, Moe quit his slaughter's job and became the full-time rabbi in the wealthy New Jersey synagogue. He was soon respected and admired by the congregation, especially the women.

Moe earned a high salary and spent lavishly. His was the American dream realized. On his days off, usually Monday, he visited my father and me and his many friends. Rather than camp out in other people's bedrooms, Moe usually stayed in one of the Lower East Side's more opulent hotels, the Libby. While strolling about Lower Manhattan, Moe stumbled across the Sommers Photo Studio, and he stepped in to have his portrait taken, then sent the photographs to us in Jerusalem.

My brother's good fortune did not last long. Nascent grumblings about his marital status grew. According to Jewish tradition, a rabbi should have a family, for a wife and children are not only the mark of maturity but also a moral anchor in a world full of transient temptations.

Then there were rumors about his involvement with a certain woman of the congregation, followed quickly by whispers about his secret family in Jerusalem. He admitted later that he should have revealed the existence of a wife and two children, but at the time it seemed to him an inconsequential detail. Inquiries were made, and his past was uncovered. Moe resigned, and gave up all thought of a religious vocation. Just as well, he said, for the religious life was not for him.

The American ideal of self-sufficiency was one Moe's guiding principles; valuing personal freedom above all else, he was determined to have his own business. With one thing leading to another, as happens when one is guided by will and purpose, his visit to the Sommers Photo Studio led to a friendship with Noah Sommers. Moe soon had a new love: photography. It was a love made even more intense by stirring the latent artist in him--as a young boy, Moshe had a good hand for drawing, but in our deeply observant household, his creative impulses were not encouraged. Now, in America, he could develop his talent and achieve, finally, financial security; independence of spirit would follow.

All this happened before I immigrated to the United States. When I showed up, Moe had been Noah Sommers's apprentice for almost a year. He had another year to go before striking out on his own.

"That's when I'll start making real American money."

He hadn't planned on the Great Depression.

Looking at my brother, one would never have suspected that he teetered so close to poverty. He dressed in high style and wore expensive jewelry—at least it looked expensive to me. He ate in fine restaurants. Now and then, he borrowed a few coins for a newspaper or trolley. There was my three-dollar loan for his night on the town on New Year's Eve. He always paid me back promptly and to the penny. We both understood that his lack of funds was temporary, and very soon, as my grandfather Netanel Reisman had foretold, it was going to be good.

I had many adventures with my older brother. During his

apprenticeship, Moe was always on the lookout for any and all kinds of freelance work, and one evening, when I came by the studio to help in the darkroom, Moe was packing up a lot of gear.

"I need an assistant," he said. "It's going to be interesting. And profitable for you."

"What is it?"

"A big assignment. They want a lot of photographs, and I need someone to handle the camera and the lights and carry some equipment."

"I'm interested."

"First, Herman, I should warn you. We're going to photograph a dead person."

That seemed strange; in Jerusalem, the dead were buried quickly without photographs or parties, but I was interested.

"I'm ready," I said.

"Good. Let's go. It's in Brooklyn."

It was a dark and rainy night, and the ride to Brooklyn was a trip to a forbidden land. Passing through many neighborhoods, rich and poor and in between, we finally pulled up at a brightly lit house. It seemed a mansion. A butler let us in.

"Gentlemen," he said, and left.

We stood in a large foyer with our heavy equipment and waited. To the left was a big room with chandeliers and ornate furniture. In the center was a long buffet table with a lavish spread of many foods. A bartender poured drinks on the side. A big group of men and women were having a party.

A man in a suit and tie approached. "Ah, at last. Follow me, gentlemen."

He led us up a winding staircase, down a long corridor, and into a spacious bedroom.

"Over there, gentlemen."

On a wide four-poster bed decorated with a canopy of flowers lay a young woman.

We went closer. She was dressed in a silvery-white evening gown. There were diamonds and pearls in her hair, and around her neck, wrists, and fingers were necklaces, bracelets, and rings. Her face was powdered pink, and her lips were a deep red.

I was shocked.

The man suddenly looked tired.

"There she is," he said. "My daughter. She is beautiful, is she not? Please take many pictures." His mouth trembled. "Thank you."

I wept silently while we set up the equipment. I positioned the tripod and adjusted the lights as Moe took photograph after photograph of the beautiful, dead girl.

Another time, Moe took me along as his assistant to a New Year's Eve party, again in Brooklyn.

We took a lot of equipment, jamming it into a taxi. We rode over the Williamsburg Bridge and into the heart of downtown Brooklyn. As we bumped and bounced over the cobblestones and trolley tracks, Moe warned me.

"Herman, brace yourself. We're going to photograph a stag party."

"What's a stag party?"

"A party exclusively for men."

That wasn't anything unusual. In Orthodox circles, men did not mingle with women, even at social functions. I suspected by his tone that we weren't going to a religious function.

"So what's so special about this kind of stag party?"

"There will be women there—but only to entertain the men."

"I see." I really didn't, but Moe didn't go into any details.

The party was in the showroom of a furniture company. They were celebrating a profitable year. There were about thirty men and about half as many women in different states of undress. There were tables of food and liquor but no bartenders or waiters. Everyone was having a good time.

I was fascinated and repelled. I knew nothing of this sort of blatant display of flesh, as Orthodoxy did not encourage, to put it mildly, overt expressions of sexuality. The voices were loud and harsh, the laughter crude. The sensuality of the women and the coarse quality of the exchanges between them and the men were disconcerting.

Despite his worldliness, Moe wore a tight smile. We unpacked the equipment and got the camera ready. A man holding a bottle of whiskey approached.

"Have a drink," he said to me.

"I would like to," I said, "but I'm here to work."

The man waved the bottle at me. "No sober bastards allowed here!"

I continued setting up the tripod.

"Whatsa matter? You don't wanna drink with me?"

"I'm sorry, but I can't while I'm working."

"Pictures over here!" A man was shouting from a sofa. "I want pictures!"

Two naked women were sitting on the man's lap.

"Pictures! Goddamn pictures over here."

Moe said, "Gentlemen, we won't photograph any nude people."

"What?"

"No photographs of nude people," he repeated.

"Goddamn bastards, what did you think you were hired for?"

"He won't shoot naked women!"

"I'll break your goddamn camera!"

"Everyone has to drink!"

Moe leaned close and said in Hebrew, "Chaim, we're getting out of here. Get ready."

I nodded.

"Pictures! Pictures!"

"Break his goddamn camera!"

"You first," whispered Moe. "Now!"

Case in one hand and half-open tripod in the other, I bolted for the door. With his camera and flash attachment, Moe was on my heels, pounding hard. The men cursed and threatened, but they were too drunk and undressed to give chase.

"Crazy people," Moe said as we stood on the corner and looked for a taxi.

Both assignments, the dead woman and the stag party, were disturbing, though the image of the beautiful young woman in her gown and sparkling jewels stayed with me long after the images of the stag party faded.

Moe told me it was nothing out of the ordinary. "Believe me, Herman, when you're a photographer, you see everything."

*

My first winter in New York was bitter with a cold I had never experienced. I was always shivering, my frozen hands barely able to grip the handles of my cart as I pushed the meats and condiments through the streets of the Lower East Side. My coat was worthless; the wind tore through with hardly a thought. Seeing my coat for the first time, Moe cast a disparaging eye upon our mother's handiwork. She had tailored it from the remnants of her fabric store.

"Do not dare to wear that shmata in my presence," Moe told me.

It wasn't his style certainly, but it had a style of its own.

Moe's smile held a sarcastic line. "It hangs on you like a sack."

At last, spring came.

Spring on the Lower East Side of Manhattan, with the massive steel of the Williamsburg Bridge cutting Attorney Street in the middle and the overhead train tracks cutting off the sun, was not the glorious spring in Jerusalem. There, the olive trees uncurled their small leaves of delicate green, and apricot and almond blossoms sweetened the air. Nevertheless, it was spring; my back no longer ached, and my fingers lost the blue tint they'd acquired from washing and salting barrels of cold meat at the Silver Delicatessen.

And 49 Attorney Street was made ready for Pesach.

As my mother had done in Batei Warsaw, my father worked assiduously, washing and scrubbing. He used a new feather duster to deep clean the corners of the kitchen and get every last tiny crumb of bread. Eleazar went to his son's house for the eight days of Passover, and Moe and I joined our father for the Seder. Traditionally, Jews living in the Diaspora, outside of the land of Israel, hold a Seder on the second night too, but because our father intended to return to Jerusalem, we had only one.

He led the ritual, and Moe and I joined in reading the Haggadah, the book of the Seder. Our father had a soft, clear voice and sang the

Hebrew songs in his Polish Hasidic accent, Moe and I singing with him. He smiled at us often, but his clear gray eyes shone with sadness. Then I, the youngest at the table, asked the four questions.

"Why," I sang, "is this night different from all other nights?"

The four answers are presented in the Haggadah, and I read them with feeling.

"Because we were slaves in Egypt," I sang, and my brother and father joined in.

However, there was another answer to that question, which I did not utter. This night was different from all the other Seder nights of our lives, more different than we could ever have imagined. Glancing at Abba as his eyes filled with tears, I knew he wasn't here with us in New York, sitting at a small kitchen table beneath a dim electric light. He was far away in Jerusalem.

*

The Silver Delicatessen was closed for the holiday and I had a paid vacation, which, with the two Saturdays on either end of the holiday, lasted a full ten days. Over the last few months, I had managed to save a substantial amount of money, and I took advantage of the time off and the good weather to buy a new holiday wardrobe.

I splurged on the following items: a navy-blue Crawford suit for $17.00; a pair of black Thom McAnn shoes for $2.75; a gray felt Adam's fedora for $2.25; and two shirts bought from the Orchard Street open market for $2.50 total (if purchased separately, they would have been $1.50 each).

Moe praised my good taste and threw in two classy, if slightly out-of-style, ties.

Ruth Sommers looked me up and down. "It's about time."

In my new attire, I visited my friend and fellow seafarer Avram Gandzel. Avram, who worked at the Manischewitz Matzo factory in New Jersey, was also on vacation and, like me, wore his spanking-new Passover clothes. We decided to visit the Rosenfelds, a family we had met on the *Alesia*; they lived in Brooklyn not far from the Williamsburg

Bridge. We could have easily afforded the three-cent trolley over the bridge, but being stylish sports, Avram and I strolled across the East River in our new clothes, feeling wealthy and totally New York.

While living it up during my first vacation in America, I spent an evening at the Clinton Street Theater, the movie theater that blocked the sun from my father's bedroom and provided him with a free soundtrack. I wanted to see for myself just what went on in there.

There was a double feature that night, both cowboy movies.

I enjoyed them thoroughly.

In the first movie, a young bachelor sheriff employed his strong fists and a long revolver to rescue a poor but beautiful orphan girl from the clutches of a gang of bad guys. Waging a just battle against these evil men, the noble sheriff not only gunned down the villains but also shot himself straight into the heart of the beautiful orphan.

My improved command of English allowed me to grasp some of the finer points of the plot, which were not that complicated to begin with, and I was able to appreciate the interplay of dialogue and story line.

The second movie, with a few minor variations, was of the same theme and caliber.

Pleased with myself and satisfied with the two happy endings, I stood up and reached for my hat—but where was it?

I had put it on the wire shelf under my seat, a shelf made especially for men's hats, and now I couldn't find it. It was the gray Adam's fedora I had just purchased. I found an usher with a flashlight, and we searched high and low but found nothing.

I spoke with the theater manager, who apologized and took my name and address.

"Should we find your hat, Mr. Linder, we'll let you know immediately."

"Thank you."

Then the manager, a thin man with a thin black mustache, had a question.

"Are you sure, Mr. Linder, that you came to the theater with a hat?"

That was an odd question.

"If not a hat, what other covering would I wear on my head?"

Everyone wore some kind of hat.

"Well, perhaps you were bareheaded. Many young men like you are not wearing any hats at all. The styles have changed."

He was insinuating, of course, that I was lying about my hat so that I could get some money out of him.

"May I ask you then," I replied with undeniable logic, "if hats aren't valued anymore, why was mine stolen?"

At the Sommers Photo Studio, Moe downplayed the incident.

"It happens, Herman," he said.

He and Noah Sommers agreed with the manager, however, on the subject of style. Hatless, said Moe, was the modern way. I knew what my brother was driving at, but that day, I went out and bought a new hat, the same gray Adam's fedora at the same price of $2.25.

I wasn't ready to walk around bareheaded. My father was very gentle, and reluctant to impose his views on anyone. He wouldn't have said anything, but would have been sad to see me without a head covering of any sort. It wasn't just my father, however. The owners of the Silver Delicatessen all wore either a yarmulke (*kippur* in Hebrew), or a cap of some kind. I had been hired, in part, because the Silvers were comfortable with my religious background. They treated me well, and though I might have been ready to go bareheaded, I didn't want to put the Silvers, or my father, through unnecessary and avoidable discomfort. Furthermore, contrary to the theater manager's and my brother's assessments of urban fashion trends, hats were still in style.

And there was the principle: I had paid $2.25 for the gray Adam's hat, which was a perfect match for my new navy-blue Crawford suit, and no thief was going to deprive me of the pleasure of wearing it.

*

My brother Moe was determined to Americanize me as rapidly as possible. It was important, he insisted repeatedly, that I recognize the differences between America and Batei Warsaw; a student of the Talmud himself, Moe was always prepared with a topic of discussion.

Once, while I was helping him in Noah Sommers's darkroom, he told me that a number of our relatives in American were rich and that one or two might even be millionaires.

I knew the concept of wealth but was not familiar with the notion of a millionaire.

"What exactly is a millionaire?"

Moe laughed at my question and, as he did when he wanted to argue, asked another.

"Tell me, Herman—are you a millionaire?"

I wasn't going to be trapped, and I returned fire. "Do I look like a millionaire?"

"What do you think a millionaire looks like?"

"I don't know, but would I keep it a secret from you and the rest of the family?"

Angry now, Moe took the photograph out of the developer and slipped it into the shortstop bath. "Look, Chaim, don't argue like a yeshiva student from Batei Warsaw, answering one question with another." When he was irritated with my naïveté, he referred to me as Chaim and made references to Batei Warsaw. "Right now, I want a clear answer to my question, as clear as this photograph. Are you a millionaire, or are you not?"

"No, I'm not a millionaire."

"And why not?"

"Because I don't have a million dollars."

"Now you're talking sense. You have to have a million dollars to be a millionaire. Okay, now you can ask a question."

"Is our cousin Wolfe a millionaire?"

"Not yet, but he's getting there."

"What about Cousin Mordecai? I heard he gets ten times more in New Jersey as a rabbi than Uncle Yitzhak gets in the Old City. Is that true?"

"Mordecai makes a hundred times as much as Uncle Yitzhak."

"Mordecai gets a thousand dollars a week?"

"Chaim, the trouble with you is that you're still using Batei Warsaw as a standard. Mordecai gets a salary, but the real *kessef*"—silver—"comes from bar mitzvahs, weddings, funerals, and unveilings. He issues certificates of kashruth to hotels and butcher shops. He makes a lot on the side, just like I do."

Moe picked up side cash, as he called it, doing darkroom work for other studios.

We now had half a dozen enlarged photos in the fixer bath, and it was time to rinse and squeegee them and then hang them up to dry.

But Moe had more to say about millionaires and rich people in general.

"You see, Herman, in Batei Warsaw and the Mea Shearim, everyone is poor, so they make a big deal about a rich man. Mind you, just how rich can you be in Batei Warsaw? But here in New York or in New Jersey—all over America—rich people walk the streets just like you and me and nobody pays attention. You see the way I dress? People think I'm rich. Soon, if you keep buying the right clothes, you'll look rich too. Remember, no one counts your money. In America, it's what they think you have that matters."

Another time in the darkroom late at night, I was helping him develop photographs of a wedding he had shot over the weekend. Moe told me of an embarrassing episode.

"How was I supposed to know that you don't pronounce the letter *k* in front of an *n*?"

He had been invited to a cousin for supper. Two other couples and a young woman were at the table. Moe had a rule of speaking English only, and asked the hostess for a knife, pronouncing the *k* with a distinct flare, as is done in Yiddish and German.

"May I have a k-nife?"

He was still mortified. "How was I to know that the *k* is silent? Why didn't they teach us these things in Batei Warsaw?"

This was just one of the hidden traps that could open beneath my brother on his journey through the wonderland that was America. I shared some of his fears, but most of my concerns were not about the pitfalls of Americanization.

I missed home; Batei Warsaw, the Mea Shearim market, my mother, my younger brothers, and my sisters and their children were in my thoughts constantly, as were all my uncles and aunts who were forever visiting and talking. What were they up to? I missed my uncle Yisrael Yitzhak, his love of all things holy, and the candies he dispensed from the pocket of his caftan, pressing them into my palm with a quick smile.

I missed the wind, the rain, the nights full of stars, and the morning sun on the hills of Jerusalem.

I missed the Western Wall, the ancient stones that comforted me with their warm, accepting silence.

I missed my best friend, Cousin Yitzhak.

He would have loved America, New York especially, and we would have done so many things together.

CHAPTER 52

The one thing upon which my father and brother agreed was that I should find a wife.

It wasn't practical, my father said more than once, not to be married. It wasn't an admonishment as much as his wish to see me secure. He had someone in mind, of course, and would make remarks about Pearl, who lived with her grandfather, Mr. Furman.

"She's a fine girl," my father reminded me often, mentioning in the same breath that her grandfather was a wealthy man in the business world. That my father suggested a match with a worldly non-Orthodox young woman showed either an open mind or anxiety about my future.

"Abba, I'm not ready to get married."

"You have to be practical," my father replied.

Moe, on the other hand, encouraged me to think not about acquiring a wife as much as getting a girlfriend. He had a standard lecture on dating American style, a subject on which my brother considered himself a full professor.

"You see, in Batei Warsaw, boys and girls don't date. Of course, you might meet accidently on the street, but the only way you can exist is to get married. And then you have to have children immediately. Here in America, boys and girls date. They don't have to get married right away. Now, Herman, be honest—which way do you prefer?"

Interpreting my silence as disagreement, Moe shook his finger to drive home the point. "I warn you, Herman: don't get trapped. If you date Pearl, she's going to belong to you very soon."

In furtherance of the American dating project, Moe asked me to go to the Bronx, to Goldman's Photo Studio, to pick up some negatives for a freelance retouching job. I demurred; the Bronx was a long ride.

"Come on, Herman. What do you have to lose?"

Indeed, I had nothing to lose at all, except two hours of my Sunday.

Inside Goldman's Photo Studio, Mr. Goldman looked me over as he shook my hand.

"You'll have to wait for Bayla," he said. "She has the negatives."

I assumed Bayla was why Moe had asked me to go; curious, I sat and waited. Other customers came in, and Mr. Goldman told them the same thing: "Wait for Bayla." Soon there were a half dozen of us waiting. Who was Bayla that everyone had to wait for her?

Bayla finally emerged from the back room. She was blonde and pretty. She greeted me with a big smile.

"So this is Moe's younger brother from Jerusalem."

Before I could speak, Bayla kissed me, on my mouth.

With a quick smile, she turned to the other customers. Finally, when we were the only ones left, Bayla handed me an envelope.

"I must have these back by Thursday evening," she said. She looked at me, smiled again, and returned to the back room. I thanked Mr. Goldman, and left.

"Well?" Moe asked.

We were sipping coffee in a cafeteria on East Tremont Avenue, a few blocks from the Goldman Photo Studio.

As often, my brother's one-word question required a long answer.

"It seems that Mr. Goldman doesn't know much about the business of photography."

"Never mind what Mr. Goldman knows. I'll ask again. Well?"

"It seems that Bayla manages the business by herself."

"I know that too. Why won't you answer my question?"

"What kind of answer can I give to a question like 'Well'?"

"Stop answering me with another question! A bright yeshiva student from Batei Warsaw knows exactly what 'Well?' means. It's a plain, simple question!"

Before I could respond with a plain, simple answer, Moe put down his coffee and delivered a variation of his lecture on dating American style.

"Now that you've seen Bayla, you can compare her to other girls, such as Mr. Furman's granddaughter, Pearl. Bayla was born and educated in America. She's a sophomore at City College. That means a lot. You can date her without complications. Bayla wants to have some fun. Pearl wants to get married."

The following week, with the Silver Delicatessen closed on Sunday, as it would be for the entire summer, Bayla and I met in the Bronx Botanical Gardens. Again, the outing marked a number of firsts for me. This was the first time I'd been in such a beautiful, natural setting. It was also the first genuine date of my life. I enjoyed everything about the afternoon. The rose garden was in full bloom, the air was sweet and warm, and Bayla and I walked slowly on the garden paths with the other couples and families. Bayla had taken a college course in botany and knew the names of most of the flowers and many of the birds.

"Look," she said, pointing to a low branch. "They're cardinals. The male is bright red, and the smaller, brown one is his mate."

"I thought the female would be more colorful."

"It's the reverse of the human world," Bayla said. "Usually, the males are flashy."

"Why?"

"Oh, it's because they want to attract the women."

As we walked, Bayla told me the names of the flowers.

"Knowing flowers helps in photography. When I go to a wedding, I sometimes suggest flowers for the bride. Even a plain bride can look beautiful with the right flower."

Later that night, I thought about Bayla; we had talked about many things, including ideas, people, and current events, a conversation that was impossible with the young women of Batei Warsaw, not that I ever had the opportunity.

Because her weekends were busy—Saturday night and Sunday were taken up with weddings and bar mitzvahs and then, later in May and June, graduation ceremonies—Bayla and I dated infrequently. Then I heard from Moe that she had gotten engaged to one of the darkroom assistants at the Goldman Photo Studio. Bayla didn't want to have that much fun after all.

*

487

That fall, Moe completed his two-year apprenticeship with Noah Sommers and immediately got a job in another studio, working shorter hours for higher pay.

Moe and I had never liked the sunless, noisy room where our father lived, and when his roommate, Eleazar, announced plans to remarry, we decided it was time for a change for the three of us. Moe and I still shared a bedroom in the Sommers apartment, and with our overlapping schedules, it was impossible to get a restful night's sleep.

With Moe's new job and my steady pay, my brother and I rented a large two-bedroom apartment at Pitt and Delancey Street. We gave our father the smaller bedroom, and Moe and I bought two beds for the second. The large kitchen was also our dining room. There wasn't any central heating, but the kitchen had a small, efficient coal stove that we used for cooking and general heating. We also had a private bathroom in the hall.

The apartment was sunny, airy, and quiet, and my father thanked us—and God, of course—for this wonderful upgrade in his living conditions.

As Moe said, "Listen, Herman, there's no reason for us to live like immigrants."

Chapter 53

Eighteen long—and often difficult—months had passed since I'd first stepped onto the soil of Providence, and now, at the end of my second spring in America, I graduated from night school. In keeping with the dignity of the occasion, we all wore suits and ties. The room was decorated, and refreshments were served. After a speech of praise and encouragement, our teacher presented us one by one with our diplomas. Each was embossed with the official blue stamp of the Board of Education of the City of New York.

During the reception, the teacher took me aside.

"So, Herman, what did you think of your school experience?"

"I learned a lot. English was the hardest subject."

"But you have achieved mastery. I suggest you go on to high school. It's time consuming, and you'll have to study harder, but you have a good head on your shoulders. Use it."

"I'm not sure I have the time for more studies," I said.

"Of course, a living comes first. Tell me—what did you do in your home country?"

I told him I had been a professional yeshiva student in Jerusalem, and, very curious, he asked about the curriculum and the method of study.

I answered, and he patted me on my shoulder and smiled. "Ah, so that explains it."

He said that I was much more disciplined than most students in night school; I read the assignments, did the homework, and never missed a class.

"If you can't go to high school," he continued, "don't let your education go to waste. Pick up a book just to read for the sake of reading. And write for the sake of writing."

"I'm looking forward to doing that in English."

He looked at me with a kind smile. "Do you have a wish?"

I didn't know what he meant.

"A wish—a secret desire to do something you always wanted to?"

I had never thought of that; there were no wishes or secrets in Batei Warsaw. One's life was ordered and arranged, and one spent one's days trying to survive. But caught off guard by the teacher's kindly smile and inquisitive eyes, I answered spontaneously.

"Yes," I said, "I would like to write books."

However, that was only a wish, a secret I had kept to myself until I uttered it to Mr. Berman. At seven the next morning, I tied on my apron, pulled on my boots, and began another day of salting and grinding meats, followed by an afternoon of wheeling my pushcart through the loud, frantic traffic of the Lower East Side.

Over the course of the year, my wages had increased from twelve to seventeen dollars a week, one single dollar at a time. My hours were exactly the same; the work was still dirty and exhausting. With the business in family hands, there was little chance this would ever change. I was ready to move on, but it was 1931, and the economy had gone from bad to worse. When I looked at the faces of the men waiting in long lines for a bowl of soup and a piece of bread, I thought this was like Batei Warsaw during the war, except back then, we'd had no soup. But I had a job, and a warm, sunny place to live. And every Friday afternoon, Mr. Silver counted out seventeen dollar bills in a neat stack on the table.

Later, thinking about my teacher's question, I realized I did indeed have a few wishes—nothing secret or grand or requiring heaven's intervention, just standard everyday wishes.

I wished for a better job and higher wages.

I wished my father would smile more often and return to Jerusalem soon.

I wished my brother Moshe would be reunited with his family and find happiness.

I wished my mother, brothers, and sisters in Batei Warsaw would not be hungry and cold.

I had other wishes too, for myself, but those would have to wait.

As for my first wish, once again, my father was able to arrange a minor miracle.

He knew the Orthodox rabbi who was the head mashgiah, the

supervisor of kashruth, at the Bronfman Meat Provision Company, then the largest kosher meat producer in the United States. It employed hundreds of workers, and its products were sold throughout America and Europe. Its factory was located just one block from where I worked. When my father told me he had spoken with the mashgiah, I wasn't interested.

"Abba, it's just going from one meatpacking job to another."

"Chaim, pay the rabbi a visit. What do you have to lose?"

On Sunday afternoon, after finishing work at the Silver Delicatessen, I crossed Delancey Street, walked a couple of short blocks, and paid the rabbi a visit. After some pleasant conversation, he told me he had good news and bad news. Since the entire company was unionized and I wasn't member of the union, there were no jobs available. However, the kashruth department, which was under his supervision, had an opening.

I was sufficiently Americanized to ask questions.

"What sort of work would it be?"

"Since you are a yeshiva student from Jerusalem and because you have eighteen months' experience at the Silver Delicatessen, I can offer you a job as a meat salter."

This was a tight knot of reasons, but I didn't care as long as I got a better job.

I asked for particulars, and they were good: I'd work six days a week for eight hours a day; earn thirty-five dollars a week, get all Jewish holidays and, because the plant was unionized, all American holidays. Plus, a week's vacation and all the meat I could stuff into my mouth.

I accepted the job on the spot, shook hands with the rabbi, and left. My father had been right; I had lost nothing and gained a great deal.

When Moe heard, he immediately bestowed upon me the exalted title of Mr. Meat Salter.

Mr. Silver was reluctant to see me leave but couldn't match the rabbi's offer, and the next day I began work in the Bronfman Meat Provision Company. The process at both companies was the same, but the Bronfman Company was more technologically advanced. The salting division was adjacent to the meat-cutting area. The other three salters had thick beards and black yarmulkes, and salted thick cuts of meat on long metal tables. Conveyor belts brought the meat from one section to another. When the meat reached my table, I used a long metal hook in my left hand to catch a chunk and pull it onto the table, and then used my right hand to rub the salt in. After the meat sat on my table for an hour, I washed and rinsed it with cold water and sent it on its way on another conveyor belt.

For eight hours a day, the belt never stopped. How many animals did they have to slaughter to produce this endless supply of meat? How could there be so much meat in a country that was sinking into economic depression? The first day, I salted enough meat to feed an army, and I did the same the next day and the day after. The use of gloves was contrary to ultra-Orthodox rules of meat preparation, and with my right hand always covered with salt, any sort of cut, even the slightest nick, became red and swollen.

We salters were careful not to put our hands in harm's way, for then we were not allowed to handle the meat.

The work was dull and routine, but I worked fewer hours for double the pay.

Lunch at the Bronfman Meat Provision Company was a Roman spectacle.

The cutters were the elite of the work force and treated themselves accordingly. They ate prime meat exclusively—thick steaks, which they broiled to perfection in their factory ovens. For lunch, the three other kosher salters and I joined the two dozen butchers at long tables piled with roasted and baked meats; green salads; rye bread; cold, foamy beer; and sweet soda.

And it was free!

On my first day, when I entered the lunchroom with the other salters, all of whom were big Hasidim with muscular shoulders and powerful hands, the butchers burst into laughter. The jokes about my thin arms and skinny chest flew furiously, and I was awarded yet another title: the Kosher Baby.

*

I was a rich man.

In these severe depression times, my salary of thirty-five dollars a week was a small fortune. Except for my father and my brother, no one knew how much I made. Every day I ate as much prime meat as I wanted—thick broiled slabs of meat with a crusty layer of sizzling fat, sausages dripping with juice, and sandwiches of spicy salami. I no longer had to watch my mother put tiny portions of meat on my plate just for the taste.

Moe gave his unqualified approval of my new and improved status.

"See, Chaim? This is what it means to live in America!"

But I had a long way to go before I was completely Americanized.

However, there was one American trait I acquired on my own: saving.

While working at the Silver Delicatessen, I had opened an account in a nearby bank, and now, with my large salary, I was making ever-larger weekly deposits. It would have been a mistake not to save while earning such good money, for I knew, given what I had lived through in Jerusalem, that times often got worse before they got better, if they got better at all.

Moreover, my father was planning to return to Jerusalem, and I wanted to help him reduce our family's impoverishment. Though my parents and my aunts and uncles in Jerusalem were rich in dignity, possessing piety beyond measure, their pockets were empty. No one saved even the smallest sum, because you couldn't put aside what you didn't have.

Working at Bronfman Meat Provision Company, I was able to save twenty-five dollars a week. Though Moe addressed me as Mr. Money Banks and asked his usual prying questions, I kept my balance a close secret; not even my father knew.

Yet, I kept my perspective; I was in no danger of becoming a millionaire. I watched every penny, and was always on the lookout for a bargain, sometimes paying dearly for it.

In the open market on Orchard Street, I bought a pair of shoes from the pushcart of Joseph the shoe man. The shoes were priced at $1.10, but for me, a young *macher,* a big shot, Joseph graciously allowed me to bargain him down to ninety-nine cents.

"Less than a dollar!" Joseph rejoiced at my good fortune. "How could you go wrong?"

Now, from youthful and extensive experiences regarding footwear, I knew that new shoes had to be worn for a certain time before they conformed to the foot, so I was not unduly concerned when my ninety-nine-cent bargain was initially tight across the arch. I persisted, walking the streets of the Lower East Side on pinched toes, but the shoes remained stubbornly, unaccountably tight. I complained to Joseph the shoe man, who shrugged.

"What do you expect for less than a dollar?"

"But they squeeze my toes, and they aren't worth a single penny if I can't wear them."

Joseph didn't see my problem, yet he gave me some advice, and it was free: "Go home, take a razor, and make a few cuts where it squeezes."

I should have known better than to complain to a pushcart merchant on Orchard Street.

My mother would have said, "Ah, Chaim, small problems, such as tight shoes, are what you have when you have no big problems."

I cannot remember a time in Batei Warsaw when I didn't have a problem of some sort, big and little. Shoes were a perennial source of problems. As a young child, I wore them so rarely that they were either too tight, too big, torn, without laces, or sometimes without heels. When I was older, during the later years of the war, my shoe problems were solved for good, for I had no shoes at all.

Once, I told my father that my left shoe had a hole in it and that water was coming in.

"Chaim," my father said, "that's a problem that can be solved easily. Make a hole on the other side, and let the water run out."

My father was both an optimist and a humorist, though it seemed the two traits, when applied simultaneously, produced a certain passivity.

I raised this point with my father, and he smiled.

"Can you show me a person who doesn't have any problems?" my father asked.

I thought and thought, and other than an angel, I couldn't think of anyone.

"Good. So if everyone has problems, why not ignore them?"

"I understand your reasoning, but why not look for a solution?"

"Of course. But not all problems can be solved, Chaim. And sometimes, when problems multiply, they fight among themselves and leave you in peace."

Then why, I wondered but did not ask, *do we have so little peace in Batei Warsaw? And even less in the wide world?*

*

Then Moe surprised us by announcing that he had just bought his own photo studio. We shouldn't have been surprised. My brother always did things lickety-split. He had already given the owner a small down payment, the rest to be paid in monthly installments. He took me to his new studio the next day. It was in Borough Park, Brooklyn, on a busy street. I went inside, and my heart sank. The place was old and run down.

"Well, Chaim?"

I had nothing positive to say, and instead quoted from the Talmud. "All beginnings are difficult."

"Yes, and this will be too."

We stood in the dim light and stared at the cracked, dingy walls.

"And if not now," Moe said, encouraging himself with a quote from Hillel, "when?"

A month later, I didn't recognize the place. Working night and day, plastering, painting, and cleaning, Moe turned the shabby space into a modern photography studio.

"I'm opening the business tomorrow," he told me.

"Mazel tov."

With Moe's unique combination of social charm and business skill, his studio took off from the start. Yet all beginnings are difficult. Unable to afford an assistant, who was essential in a photography studio, he worked long hours and slept many nights on a sofa in the studio, and was away from our apartment on Pitt Street for days at a time.

*

That winter, working at the Bronfman Meat Provision Company, I lived well. I bought two good pairs of shoes, a warm winter coat, two suits, and other assorted items of clothing essential to a well-dressed New Yorker. Moe was pleased with my sartorial upgrades and, always rotating his inventory, gave me three of his expensive ties. He suggested I look at his suits if I was willing to wear last year's style, but they were too big for me. "Too bad," he said, "because you'd look very good in them," meaning "very American." Every so often, now that he was making good money, Moe would buy a completely new wardrobe.

Meanwhile, my father was not pleased with my line of employment. He had helped me find both jobs in the kosher meat industry, but regarded them as way stations on the road to my true calling, whatever that might be. He knew I wasn't ready to return to full-time religious studies, so one night, over supper, he suggested that Moe might teach me photography, and we would become partners in his new studio.

Citing a number of reasons, Moe rejected the idea immediately.

I remained silent, giving him the burden of dashing my father's hopes, but I was not about to join my brother in a photography venture—or in any other business. Moe was a perfectionist. He knew everything, whether he knew it or not, and knew it better than anyone. A partnership consisting of an older know-it-all big brother and the younger kid brother was not the right mix for a successful business.

After listening to Moe, and my silence, my father didn't bring up the subject again.

CHAPTER 54

Once again, I learned that paradise on earth doesn't last forever.

After working at the Bronfman Meat Provision Company for ten months, I lost my job, as did a few hundred other workers.

It's a tale of how a good man can be brought low by the criminal acts of others. Mr. Bronfman was strictly observant and Orthodox, and he had built a company whose honesty and integrity were beyond reproach. A team of rabbis whose job was to certify that the many rules of kashruth were followed to the letter supervised the Bronfman Meat Provision Company.

A kind and pleasant gentleman, Mr. Bronfman walked through his factory, talking with the workers and inquiring about their health and their families. Twice a day, he visited the meat-salting department and chatted with me and the three other salters. When he learned that I came from Jerusalem, he was delighted.

"Is it as beautiful as I am told?"

"It's called the City of Gold, and the stones shine in the sunlight."

"Yes, yes," he said, "I must go there. I must."

Alas, while Mr. Bronfman's personal and business ethics were above reproach, those of his managers, some of whom were his relatives, were not. The production of kosher requires great care and expense from beginning to end. From the time the animal is born, raised, selected for slaughter, and finally killed, all things, great and small, must be done according to Jewish law. The cost of the raw product was high, as was the expense of processing, so the price of the finished product was usually double, and often triple that of non-kosher meat.

However, some of Mr. Bronfman's managers were turning a quick and illegal profit, and they brought disaster down on all our heads.

After it was over, I read about it in the newspapers.

One of the Orthodox butchers had his suspicions, but instead of going to Mr. Bronfman, he went to the local authorities. Shortly thereafter, the FBI quietly notified a rabbinical organization that they had reason to believe that the Bronfman Meat Provision Company was in violation of federal laws regarding the production of kosher meat. The FBI asked the rabbis to cooperate. The rabbis, alarmed and wanting to know for themselves, agreed. Acting on a tip, FBI set up a surveillance team.

On a dark and cold winter night, two Orthodox rabbis joined two agents in an unmarked government vehicle. After a long ride, they found themselves at a cattle farm in New Jersey. They shut the headlights and drove in pitch dark along a bumpy farm road until they came to a barn in the middle of the woods. With guns drawn, the two FBI agents, with the two rabbis in long caftans and beards, tiptoed through the trees, stumbling over exposed roots and tearing their clothing on thorny bushes. At the barn, they peered through cracks in the siding. What they saw was terrible: old, sick cattle being cut with long, dirty knives and bludgeoned with heavy hammers.

The two rabbis were horrified. The animals bellowed in terror and cried in pain. The men inside were coldhearted killers. The agents and rabbis watched as the butchered carcasses were loaded onto two dirty trucks and driven away.

Rushing back to the unmarked vehicle, the agents found they were stuck in the thick mud. The rabbis jumped out of the car and, with one of the agents, pushed until the car was free. They drove like mad to overtake the trucks. The rabbis held on tightly as they bounced along dirt roads and over hills covered with snow. Finally, the agents spotted one of the trucks, and, heaving sighs of relief, they followed it to New York, and soon came upon the second truck.

The little convoy arrived in Lower Manhattan in early morning and drove through the deserted streets. In the dim light of dawn, the trucks entered the Bronfman factory. To the rabbis growing fury and sadness, the rabbis—who, with the FBI agents, had entered through a back door—watched as the tainted meat was dumped into the vats of kosher meat waiting to be processed. With firm nods from the rabbis, the agents, guns and cuffs ready, moved in.

I learned all of this later. In the morning, when I showed up for work, the gates of the Bronfman Meat Provision Company were padlocked. Federal marshals and New York City police guarded all entrances.

Hundreds of workers milled around, uncertain and anxious. I stood among them, listening and wondering. Rumors abounded—there'd been a death in the family, someone had embezzled millions, there'd been a murder, or—most likely, most of us thought—there'd been a surprise sale of the business or even bankruptcy. At last, Mr. Bronfman's lawyer appeared and read a statement. A deep silence fell over the crowd. I was stunned. Men began to cry. Near the gate were my three fellow salters, gray with shock.

The pain in the Orthodox community was tremendous. Trying as best as they could to follow the laws and customs of Judaism, housewives now discovered that they and their families had been eating foul meat. It was not their fault, and therefore, no guilt accrued, but to be led into violation of Jewish law by a fellow Jew was a sad and terrible blow. The stores and butcher shops that sold Bronfman meats were affected. Great psychological and financial damage ensued, and with all trust lost, the Bronfman Meat Provision Company closed its doors forever. No one blamed Mr. Bronfman himself, but he quickly disappeared from public life, his charitable contributions coming to an abrupt end.

Hundreds of workers, I among them, lost their livelihoods. To be unemployed during this time of economic turmoil was terrifying; misery, hunger, and loss of dignity were sure to follow. Men stood in front of the locked gates and groaned to the heavens. I turned away and walked home.

Two years after arriving in America, I was back to square one—yet not quite. The realities of my new situation, though harsh, were not insurmountable.

No one depended upon me for food or shelter, so I'd be able to economize without harming anyone. I would never starve. I might miss a meal, but that was nothing new. I might have to share a bed, but I had slept on stone floors through dark, cold nights. My father and brother might have their own financial problems but they would always take me in without complaint or question. As Robert Frost wrote (one of my sons studying English literature read the poem to me many years later), home is where, when you have to go there, they have to take you in. In Batei Warsaw, in all of Jerusalem, the cold compulsion of Frost's poem was unheard of; when you showed up, you were welcomed, not all the time with open arms, but you stayed at long as you wanted. Unlike some of the men and women who lost their livelihood when the Bronfman Company shut down, I knew I would never find myself out on the street, cold and beaten.

While salting meat, I had been preparing myself for life in America. I was now enrolled at Seward Park High School in lower Manhattan. I had classes four nights a week, studying English, algebra, civics, and American history. As always, English was the most difficult. But I always got good grades in writing and composition; perhaps, with my accent giving away my obvious immigrant background, my teachers were being generous.

I hadn't told my brother or father, but I was planning to become a citizen as soon as possible.

I had managed to save almost a $1,000. Neither my father nor brother knew of this fortune. I would not refuse to help my family if necessary, but Batei Warsaw had taught me that everyone was always in need of money, even those who had it. I knew too that availability often bred need, and should people learn of my savings, many pleading hands would soon be stretched in my direction.

But with the end of my meat-salting career, my father once again began pushing me to renew my religious studies.

"You're not working now," he pointed out, "so try. It's a living. What do you have to lose?"

Not certain that I wanted more study, but indeed having nothing to lose, I went for an interview at a well-known yeshiva in Manhattan. Impressed with my record of studies in Jerusalem, the rabbi in the admissions office offered admittance on the spot. Without committing myself, I thanked him and left. Giving the matter much thought, I decided to decline. In Jerusalem, with my knowledge of Talmud and rabbinical law, I would have qualified for ordination, but in New York the road to accreditation was long and expensive, and the United States did not have the systems of financial support that had allowed me to study in Jerusalem.

Moreover, I would have had to commit myself to a certain way of life, and I wasn't certain that such a life was the one I wanted.

My father accepted my decision reluctantly. Disappointed that neither of his two older sons wished to pursue religious careers, he nevertheless understood my refusal to embark upon a long, expensive journey while I was so full of uncertainty.

He continued, however, to keep a watchful eye out for any possibilities. A few days after I turned down the offer from the yeshiva, my father showed me a letter from one of his many contacts, Rabbi Werner in Jerusalem. This rabbi was first cousin of the owner of the Manischevitz Matzo Bakery, one of the world's largest producers of matzo and kosher supermarket products. Obviously, my father had written to Rabbi Werner with me in mind, for inside was a letter of introduction to the mashgiah, the factory supervisor. With a little smile, my father handed me the letter.

"Nu, go. What do you have to lose?"

Times were rough, I needed a job, and New Jersey wasn't so far away.

The next day, I handed the letter to a receptionist and was ushered into the office of the mashgiah. He wore a stylish suit, but had the beard and hat of a Hasid. I took the chair in front of him. On his blotter was the letter of introduction.

"Reb Werner writes very highly of you, Chaim. Unfortunately, we're in a very slow time, and I have nothing to offer you."

"I understand," I said.

It was November, and business wouldn't pick up until the end of January, when the factory began their Passover baking.

"Of course, there might be something later." He lifted the letter. "But for a young man of your educational qualifications"—he shook his head—"its low-paying work which I'm afraid you'd find very boring."

Even low paying, boring work was better than nothing, but that was his way of saying goodbye, so I thanked him and stood. He lifted his right hand and patted the air twice. We had been speaking in English, and now he shifted into Yiddish.

"Sit, sit. What's the rush?"

Indeed, I was in no rush.

"Tell me, Chaim—how do you like New York?"

"I have mixed thoughts. On the one hand, it's a new world where one can survive; on the other hand, it takes a lot of effort."

He smiled. "Yes, yes, New York is not Jerusalem."

I agreed; it was not Jerusalem at all.

The mashgiah leaned across his desk. He looked from my small, black skullcap to my polished shoes; took in my stylish suit and tie, one of Moe's castoffs, and lowered his voice. "Why should an accomplished yeshiva student like you be interested in work in a matzo factory? Eh? Why don't you continue your studies?"

"I would like to, but it requires too many years of full-time schooling, and I just don't have the financial means to support myself."

He tapped the letter. "And your father, Reb Haskel?"

"My father wishes he could contribute to my studies, but he's in no position to do so."

The mashgiah smiled. "You and your father may not have the financial means, but there are many Orthodox parents who would be pleased to support a future son-in-law such as you—nice looking, intelligent, and from a good Jerusalem family. I am a good judge of character. You have what it takes."

Flattered and stunned, I remained glued to my seat while he pulled out a notebook from his breast pocket, thought a moment, turned a few pages, and wrote a few lines. He stood and handed me the paper.

"Give a ring. It may open up a new horizon for you." Walking me to the door, he added, "All good mazel"—luck—"to you."

I thanked him and put the paper in my pocket.

Outside, I took out the little piece of paper. On it were the names of a woman and her parents, their address, and their telephone number.

Upon hearing the report of the interview, my father offered his usual advice. "So give a ring. What do you have to lose?"

*

I did not give a ring. First, the modern age of telecommunications had not yet blanketed New York with its ubiquitous devices, and a telephone was hard to find.

Second, though at first I was inclined to call—after all, what did I have to lose? —the more I thought about it, the less I wanted to. As the mashgiah in New Jersey had said, New York wasn't Jerusalem, but in some ways, it could be, and that made me hesitate.

I had left Batei Warsaw in part because of the insular, claustrophobic culture of the Orthodox community. There was much of value there, certainly; an extended family and an established mode of living contribute to the well being of the individual, and sustained one through hard times. But I needed something more. Somewhat paradoxically, having gained strength and confidence from my large, caring family and the greater community, I was now confident enough to strike out on a different path. I had left Batei Warsaw reluctantly but willingly, and now, suddenly, I was being tempted back in. The little piece of note paper with the young woman's name and number was the key to the door of a world I had left behind. Were I to give a ring, I had no doubt I would initiate a series of events that would change my life.

I was tempted.

An education in America wasn't the same as one in a yeshiva in Jerusalem. I would be exposed to a higher level of secular education as well as a higher standard of living. Contrary to my brother's opinion, an American Orthodox rabbi with a Jerusalem pedigree commanded great respect and a high income.

I was tempted.

Soon, I would have to think about a wife. As my father had said, living alone was not practical. As with many blessings, independence was proving to be mixed. I did everything myself—buy and prepare food, clean the house, do my laundry. Everything little thing was my responsibility. I'd found the privacy I had craved. But the pleasures of solitude, great as they were, had to be balanced by someone other than myself.

If I was not for myself, who would be? And if I was only for myself, what was I?

Had I given a ring, I might have had an American wife and married into an established American family.

But I did not give a ring.

I had been teasing myself too long with the possibility of continuing my religious studies as a way of hiding from my own truth—that I was inclined toward the secular. I would always be bound to my heritage and take inspiration from the moral precepts and humanistic impulses of Judaic teaching. But I could not return to the world of the yeshiva student, a world subsumed in a greater universe of religious Orthodoxy.

I didn't tell my father any of this, but words weren't necessary; as always, he understood.

A few days later, I folded the piece of paper with its name, address, and telephone number, and put it with the pile of letters and bills to be thrown out with the week's accumulation of newspapers and magazines.

*

I'd been out of work for three months and watching every penny, yet my savings were dropping at an alarming rate. I was willing to try anything, so when Harry Cohen, a friend of Moe's, offered me a job in a dressmaking shop, I was ready, if not eager. Harry was a manager for a large apparel manufacturer and was always on the lookout for sewing machine operators.

"I got a high turnover," he said, "and I need dependable people."

I assured him I was dependable.

"You'll have a chance to learn how to use a machine, and once you learn how to sew, you'll never starve. Women are always wearing dresses."

That sounded right, and I asked him about the pay.

"Okay, I should warn you, Herman: it's piecework. You'll earn very little at first, but once you get the hang of it, you'll make a decent living."

I said I was ready to work.

"Good." Harry was pleased. "What do you have to lose? Come in Monday."

I was not totally unfamiliar with sewing machines. My mother owned one of the first Singer sewing machines in all of Batei Warsaw. It was a precious gift from my grandfather Fishel, brought back from his second trip to Poland as a collector for Kolel Warsaw. Big and solid, the machine was powered by a wide foot pedal. Like many such rare and expensive machines, the Singer was considered Batei Warsaw's community property, and all my sisters and assorted relatives used it on a first-come basis. My mother cherished and cared for that sewing machine as if it were a child.

"God's wonder," she called it. "And strong! You can't break it with a hammer!"

She had so much confidence in the machine's invincibility that she allowed me not only to operate it, which I did twice, but also to take it apart just so we could see how the wonder worked. It was easy for me, because the moving parts were few, their position and function easily identified.

The name of the machine was especially significant for my mother. "Listen to it when it sews—it sings."

Indeed, when the foot pedal was working up and down at full speed, the machine threw out a happy, competent hum.

I hadn't touched a sewing machine in years, and Ruth Sommers, cheering me on, let me practice on her brand-new electric Singer.

"You'll do very well," she assured me.

Early Monday morning, I met Harry at his shop on Twenty-Third Street and Seventh Avenue, the center of Manhattan's Garment District, and he led me to a table and chair in an open loft and pointed to a machine.

"There's your girl!"

Harry called his sewing machines babies, and sometimes girls, as in, "that girl is really stitching!"

I sat at my girl and looked around. The loft was long, wide, and high and had about a hundred women jammed close together at identical tables with identical machines. Overhead, large spools of different-colored threads fed into the sewing machines. All the women were leaning toward their babies, hands ready, waiting for Harry to give the signal. I counted about a dozen men, all of them much older than I.

"Okay, on your mark!" Harry stood in the middle of the room, holding his whistle. "Three, two, one!"

I was almost knocked out of my chair. The noise was like a roaring subway train. Ruth's Singer was a small, dainty girl compared to these heavy women screamers. The crazy whirring clamor made it impossible to concentrate. I had no idea what the word *piecework* meant until I saw the woman next to me finish two sleeves before I had even turned on my machine.

I sat paralyzed at my baby as she threw another sleeve into her basket.

Harry ran through the tables to my station.

"Relax, Herman. Relax!" He had to shout over the roaring hum. "Come on. I'll show you!" He sat on my chair, pushing me to the edge. "Look how simple it is. See? Feed the cloth slowly and steadily. The little girl will work by herself. Don't be nervous. Just let the material move away from you as the baby takes it. Now you try."

Harry stood, and I slowly and carefully sewed a sleeve to a second piece of fabric that I thought was the body of the dress. Harry frowned.

"Keep trying, Herman!" he shouted. "Good luck!"

I tried all morning, but under my trembling fingers, the fabric had a life of its own, as did my baby girl, who worked at her own speed while my fingers worked at mine. At precisely noon, Harry blew his whistle, and all activity ceased in an instant. The silence was heaven.

"Chaim," said Harry, "lunch," and I followed him to a cafeteria on Seventh Avenue.

"Not bad for a beginner. Not bad." Harry sprinkled his encouragement like sugar. "You'll see. You'll learn how to handle your girl, and then you'll be making money. The trick is not to fight her. Let the baby set her own pace. Put away your money, Chaim—my treat."

We returned to the shop at one. All the operators were at their machines, waiting for Harry's whistle. I held my breath as he counted down. When the roar began, I turned on my machine and fed my baby as fast as I could.

At the end of the day, when Harry counted my pieces, rejecting those with crooked seams or missed stitches, I had made fifteen cents.

Harry was being generous. The woman next to me had a small mountain that earned her $3.45.

The next morning, I met Harry at Delancey and the Bowery and told him I would not be going back to his shop.

"It gets easier, Herman. Trust me. It was your first day, and you didn't know how to handle your girl."

"Harry, it's not for me."

"You know, Chaim, you could always learn to knit."

I thanked him but declined. I wasn't going to return his good intentions by telling him that the work was dull and monotonous and would kill anyone's spirit, but I think he understood.

"What are you going to do for a living?" Harry asked.

"I don't know."

Harry wished me good luck and hurried to his shop; his girls were waiting.

*

My father, who had just bought his boat ticket for Jerusalem, asked me the same question: "What are you going to do for a living, Chaim?"

"Abba, I don't know."

In the meantime, my brother had just rented an apartment closer to his studio in Brooklyn and was moving out tomorrow. That would leave me alone and unemployed in a three-room apartment with a rent I couldn't pay.

Ironically, out of a job, I now had steady, unpaid employment trying to find one.

Every morning, I checked the want ads in the dailies, but found nothing.

Unable to stay home, I went out early for a long walk, setting the hour before which I would not return home, forcing myself to exercise at the same time that I kept my spirits up.

Having explored Lower Manhattan thoroughly, I now ventured into Brooklyn, walking over the Williamsburg Bridge, then walked on Bedford Avenue to Prospect Park, turned around at Grand Army Plaza, and returned to Manhattan via the Manhattan Bridge. For a change of scene, I walked in Manhattan, taking Fifth Avenue all the way past Macy's, and then farther north to Times Square. The Empire State Building was in its final stages of completion, and I sometimes stopped to watch the construction workers over Fifth Avenue.

Returning to my apartment in the afternoon, I did my homework before leaving for Seward Park High School. I had classes four nights a week for three hours a night, I got home a little after nine, ate supper with my father, and then helped him wash the dishes and clean the kitchen. Finished, I sat at the table with the *New York Times* and the *Forward*, comparing the various stories and writing down new and interesting words in my vocabulary notebook.

This was my daily routine for almost a month, until one day, on one of my uptown excursions, I stopped to read a plaque on a building: Baron de Hirsch Trade School.

I checked the street signs; I was at Third Avenue and East Sixty-Third Street.

I knew about Baron de Hirsch. He was a Jewish philanthropist known in Jerusalem for his support of Jewish institutions. I stared at the sign. It occurred to me that as a poor Jew in need of a vocation, I was certainly qualified to receive a small portion of the baron's immense wealth.

I went inside. The receptionist gave me a school catalog and advised me to register as soon as possible for the winter session.

"The classes are in high demand," she said, "and there aren't many seats left."

Heeding her warning, I opened the catalog right there in the office, perused the list of trades in which training was offered, and registered on the spot, without the least hesitation, for the printing course.

The receptionist smiled. "You got the last seat, Mr. Linder."

My father also smiled, but not with approval.

"To learn printing, you had to come all the way to America? You could have learned it just as well in Jerusalem."

"Abba," I replied, "one can learn anything anywhere. It's what happens after you learn it that makes America different from Jerusalem."

Admission required an English test, spoken and written, in which I scored in the top ten percent. The school doctor, who spoke Yiddish, also gave me a medical examination. When he learned I was born in Jerusalem, he was surprised.

"Where does a thin yeshiva student like you get so many muscles?"

"I was a meat salter at the Bronfman Meat Provision Company for almost a year."

"Ah, yes. A very sorry affair. Breathe deeply, please."

Formally enrolled, I now had to wait three months for classes to start in February. The printing course was six months long, after which the school would try to find me a job. When I looked at the balance in my account, I knew I wouldn't make it. My thousand dollars was almost gone; I had enough for two months at the most.

Then, as often happened in Batei Warsaw but less frequently on the streets of the Lower East Side, a miracle occurred—not exactly a miracle, but an opportunity.

Strolling on Allen Street, I stopped in front of the window of a men's haberdashery.

There it was, in black and white: Salesman Wanted.

I'd never been a salesman, had never thought of being one, but what did I have to lose?

I walked in. An elderly gentleman with a pleasant manner greeted me, listened, and shook his head. The sign was a come-on, he explained gently, to attract inquiries.

"We don't need any indoor salesmen." His kind manner implied that he wished it were otherwise. "We have more than we need of indoor people. We need outdoor vendors."

"Well, outdoors work is not so bad," I said.

His store, he said, was the retail outlet for a tie and haberdashery manufacturer, but in these times, few customers came in from the street. They needed roaming salesmen to find customers in bars, barbershops, and restaurants.

The elderly gentleman paused.

"What kind of commission would I earn?" I asked.

"No commission," he said. His company would sell me their ties at wholesale prices, which I would sell at whatever the market would bear. In addition, the company would provide a professional-quality portable display case that gave an especially classy look to the merchandise. I would have to put a security deposit on the case, which I'd receive back when I retired from the business and returned the case.

"At first, you'll have to pay for the ties cash up-front, but after you've established your honesty and ability, we'll put you on a credit basis."

Like Moe, I was quick to decide, and after giving it a few moments' thought, I agreed to become a vendor.

He gave me an application, and I wrote my name and address in good Standard English.

"Herman Linder," he read. He looked at me closely. "Ah, I spotted it immediately. You're an educated young man. Hard times, eh?"

"Yes, but not as hard as what I lived through in Jerusalem."

He looked at me more closely and put out his hand. "I'm Mr. Wise."

Mr. Wise, the owner of the store, had a psychological turn of mind, and had some good, practical tips on the art of peddling.

"Don't set up at busy intersections, because you'll block traffic, and the police will be after you, and you'll be in a pickle."

I understood; I was an alien and could be deported.

"And also, don't set a fixed price. Always bargain. Start high, because people like to think they're getting expensive merchandise at a discount. Use your head, and you'll make sales." With his forefinger, he tapped his temple. "Bars and restaurants are good places to sell; people are feeling good, and they have their wallets ready. Sometimes you have to sweet-talk the bartender or owner to let you in. Don't hesitate to give a free tie; they're cheap. Remember, a man likes to impress a woman, so look for couples at a table, and let the woman pick out a tie for the man; that way, she's on your side. The man will buy because he has hopes."

I left the store with a selection of ties and a classy, small valise, glad I had followed my impulse and confident I had found another source, albeit a temporary one, of income.

Expecting to be greeted with praise, for I had laid plans both for my long-term future and my immediate needs, I was taken aback when my brother expressed displeasure. He didn't see why I was planning to learn printing and sell neckties, of all things, in the interim.

With my father listening, Moe peppered me with objections.

"Where is this going to lead you, Chaim? After you graduate from printing school, is there going to be a printing job waiting for you? You think people can afford to buy books in these times? Clothing they always need. You should slug it out and learn piecework. Harry'll teach you to sew. Besides, what's there to learn about a Singer sewing machine?"

I refused to debate the issue, and Moe, goaded by my silence, continued his barrage.

"Don't worry about quality. Get some speed, and you'll be earning twenty-five or thirty dollars a week easily. Harry told me that. That way, you can graduate night school, and in three years you'll be in Brooklyn College. You'll see—it's straight into law school! Then there's nothing stopping you. Remember, this is America! And you want to sell ties? And just how will men buy your neckties when they don't have any jobs?"

"In the same way they buy ties to be photographed in your studio."

Moe grimaced; he didn't like to be challenged.

"Yeah, Chaim, but will they buy them from you?"

Monday morning at ten, I made my debut as a peddler. Earlier would be pointless, Mr. Wise explained, because there's no breakfast trade in neckwear. Outside, I saw immediately that I needed a marketing strategy. I knew from my experiences in Batei Warsaw that inventory was important, but location was crucial. Orchard and Ludlow streets, all the Lower East Side, were jammed with vendors fighting for customers; I decided to try my luck in Brooklyn.

I paid three cents and trolley'd across the Williamsburg Bridge to Brooklyn, and then crossed to Broadway, where the elevated Jamaica Line ran over a long commercial street. I had rushed out without breakfast, and I found a small diner, sat at the counter and, over a buttered roll and coffee, opened my valise and arranged my stock. The valise had three compartments, and I arranged the ties into three categories, ranging from ten cents to twenty-five. As I was about to leave, a man from a table approached and asked to see my selection. I opened the valise, and without any bargaining whatsoever, he bought six of my higher-priced ties for a total of $1.50.

It was a most auspicious beginning.

Walking down Broadway, I glanced into a small candy store. I saw a man reading a Yiddish newspaper at the soda fountain. I went in, and he looked up.

"Good morning." I showed him my valise. "Care to buy any neckties?"

"Neckties? So early in the morning? What's the hurry?"

I gave this a psychological reading, as Mr. Wise would have done, and suspected the man was amenable to engagement, the first step in negotiation.

"Distinguished reb," I said, addressing him in Yiddish, "does it really matter early, late, or just right on time? Do you care to buy a necktie now, or shall I come back later?"

My polite boldness caught him off guard. "Well," he said, "why not?"

I opened the valise, and he selected three middle-range ties for forty-five cents.

Again, he did no bargaining—a good omen. Had he negotiated, I would have given him the ties for thirty-five.

Seeing no need to leave my lucky street, I continued down Broadway beneath the elevated tracks. But my beginner's luck had run its course, and I made no sales in half a dozen stores. At Myrtle Avenue, where another elevated train joined the Jamaica Line, I went into a barbershop, remembering how Mr. Wise had recommended them. The place was clean and bright, with three barber chairs waiting for customers. No barber was in sight, and I turned to leave, when through a door came an older black man in a white uniform.

"Good morning," he said. His smile was gracious; he gestured with his right hand to a chair. "Haircut this morning?"

"Not this morning. I'm selling neckties, and I thought I would find a customer here."

The barber was disappointed. A quick glance around the shop revealed its wear and tear: the wall mirror was cracked, and the seat on one chair had been patched with tape. He needed customers too, but I could go out and find them, whereas he had to wait for his.

"Are you interested in buying? I have a fine, inexpensive black necktie that would go well with your uniform."

"I'm afraid not, young man."

For a few moments, we stared at each other, a young Jew selling neckties and a black man cutting hair, both on poverty's edge, and we laughed.

The man looked at my hair. "Son, you surely need a haircut."

He gestured to the first chair, and I got the haircut in exchange for three high-price ties.

I finished my first day of peddling with a half dozen sales and a long-overdue haircut.

*

I was familiar with barter trade.

In Batei Warsaw, in all of Jerusalem, bartering was a time-honored way of doing business. My mother traded fabrics for food, food for shoes, and sometimes shoes for cooking pots. Labor was a solid currency, and one could trade a certain number of hours of digging or painting for a certain amount of sugar or flour. I was gratified to see the ancient ways flourishing in America, even in Depression-era New York. Noah Sommers, for instance, traded a framed set of family portraits to the owner of the Borden Dairy Restaurant, Abe, for a week's worth of meals. Another time, the owner of the Shapiro Wine Company, whose store was next door to the studio, traded twenty gallons of sweet sacramental wine, kosher for Passover, in exchange for photographing the wedding of Mr. Shapiro's oldest daughter. It was too much wine for Noah, and he gave Moe and me a gallon each, which we gave to our father.

With my classy valise in hand, a new world of commerce beckoned.

The next morning, Tuesday, I returned to the tie shop and restocked. Mr. Wise was impressed; he hadn't expected Brooklyn to be such a gold mine. The ten-cent ties cost me two cents, the fifteen-cent ties cost me three, and the most expensive ties, the ones I sold for twenty-five cents, had a wholesale price of a nickel. I looked over Mr. Wise's selection, and at his suggestion, bought a combination of bright colors—to make people feel good—and darker ones, which he said were good for both business wear and funerals.

Before I started my rounds, however, I had other pressing needs. My shoes and my eyeglasses needed repair; they would be a good test of my bargaining skills.

In a shoe repair shop on Delancey and Essex, I offered the owner three neckties in exchange for full repair of my beaten shoes. He wore a heavy cloth apron and held a small hammer in his hand. He barely glanced at me, and then waved his hammer.

"Don't bother me," he said, and went back to work.

In a second shoe shop, the owner wore a skullcap and earlocks behind his ears. He looked at my valise and then at my shoes.

"Look, *boychik*," he said in Yiddish, "those things on your feet aren't worth half an onion. My advice—and I won't charge you for it—is to buy a new pair."

At last, in my third attempt, I got new soles and heels for five ties. I had to sit in the shop for two hours, but I kept my valise open and sold six ties to waiting customers.

Now I turned my attention to my eyeglasses. The wire frame on the right side was bent, and the image through the left lens was blurred, which no amount of cleaning would clarify. Having learned from the shoe experience, I looked for an optometrist's shop that wasn't too fancy or run down. My reasoning was that the fancy shop was doing well enough not to need my ties, and the poorer wasn't doing business because of low-quality work. I cased a number of shops before walking into an optometrist on Delancey Street. I offered him two ties for a frame adjustment. He took my glasses, studied them for a long time, and gave me the same long look.

"How old are these glasses?"

"They're my first pair," I said. "I got them many years ago."

"Ah, where did you buy them?"

"In Jerusalem."

"What do you use them for?"

The question caught me by surprise. "Why, to see."

"I mean, do you read a lot?"

"Yes, newspapers and books."

He put the glasses on his counter and shook his head. "I can't fix these. The frames are no good, and your eyes have changed. The lenses are wrong. I'm sorry."

"I'm sorry to hear that."

He looked at me for a long time. "For five ties, I'll give you a completely new pair."

He tested my vision in his back room, and within an hour he had constructed a new pair of glasses from frames and lenses he had in stock, and I walked out with a brighter, new look on life.

Not every day, however, was I so fortunate.

Once, walking on Broadway in Brooklyn under the elevated line, one of my most profitable routes, I passed a furniture factory—the same place Moe and I had gone two years earlier to photograph the New Year's Eve stag party. It was lunchtime, and workers were standing outside, eating and joking. *Aha*, I thought, *a business opportunity.* I joined them, opening my valise. They gathered round, looking at the ties. Suddenly, one of them grabbed a tie and ran. I immediately took off after him, but when I rounded the corner, he was gone. I looked around and, angry and disgusted, returned to discover my valise empty and the workers nowhere to be seen. Furious with all mankind and discouraged, I returned to Mr. Wise's shop to restock.

"Ah, the *gonifs*," said Mr. Wise. *Gonif* is Yiddish for "thief." "I should have warned you, Herman. A gang of bastards will surround you, and one of them will let you see him grab a necktie and run away." His kind, gentle manner was soothing; given human nature, this was to be expected. "Be smart, Herman, and don't chase anyone, because it's a trick to steal your goods. I'm going to give you a discount on the ties so that the pain and the insult will be lessened."

From then on, I was watchful, and it never happened again.

Bars and restaurants were ideal places to sell neckties.

Learning quickly from a few negative experiences, I never went into expensive establishments. The best places were small bars where I could sit at a table and order a sandwich and a glass of beer. I ate slowly, opened my valise, and made a show of folding and arranging my ties. Sometimes I would spread them out on the table and examine them for spots and wrinkles before putting them back into the valise. I usually sold half a dozen ties within an hour.

Drunks in bars were good customers. They usually were less picky, and they didn't have the skill, or desire, to bargain. In one of my regular bars, I saw a man sitting with two young women, all three obviously drunk. I ordered a small beer and did my usual act, holding up the ties to the light and folding them neatly on the table.

"Hey, you!"

I looked around with some puzzlement.

"Hey, you, I said."

"Me?"

"Yeah, you, with the ties! Come here!"

I carried my valise to his table. He had an arm around each young woman.

"Show me your ties."

I tilted the valise, and he studied my merchandise and then put both hands in and lifted a handful of my expensive neckties.

"You call these ties? They look more like shoelaces!"

The women giggled, and I sensed a good deal coming; I didn't say a word.

"How much do you want for your pile of lousy shoelaces?"

Actually, I was insulted; my ties might have been inexpensive, but they were quality merchandise. But I wasn't going to argue with a drunk, especially a potential customer.

"Come on. Gimme a price before I break your goddamn glasses!"

"For you," I said, "not a penny more than twenty dollars."

"Twenty lousy dollars for a bunch of lousy ties?" He stood, swaying back and forth, pulled out a roll of money, threw a twenty-dollar bill on the table. "Gimme my lousy ties."

I grabbed the twenty, scooped the ties from my valise, dropped them in a pile on his table, and ran out.

They had cost me about ninety-five cents wholesale, and I took the rest of the day off. I could have charged even more; the man was showing off to the young women, and he would have thrown me anything I asked.

But still, a 2,000 percent profit wasn't bad.

Chapter 55

In the summer of 1933, a few months before my father returned to Jerusalem, a telegram arrived informing him of his mother's death.

He took the news with great sadness. He had already bought his passage and was yearning to gaze upon the towers of Old Jerusalem, and stand once again before the Kotel Ha'Maravi and thank the ancient stones.

We got the news two days after my grandmother Esther died, and Moe and I stayed with our father for the next three days. He had missed his mother's burial, had been unable to recite the Kaddish at her gravesite and not sat shivah with his family, and this added much to his grief. For a week, he did not leave the apartment.

In our ultra-Orthodox Hasidic family, it was thought unlucky to count the age of one's parents or close relatives, and we didn't knew my grandmother's true age, but the consensus was that she was past ninety when she died, perhaps close to a hundred.

I was her favorite grandchild. Entering our house, her first question was "where's Chaim?" Alone, she always called me *leib*, meaning "darling," which is similar to the word *leben*, Yiddish for "life," which is also my name in Hebrew, Chaim. She said often that I reminded her of her father.

Her affection for my siblings and me did not lessen the antagonism she had for my mother. The two were never on good terms, and though my mother abided by the commandment to honor and respect her parents and in-laws, the tension between them was obvious.

She never said it publically, but there was never any doubt that my grandmother blamed my mother for my father's long sojourn in the strange, ungodly land of America. My grandmother, indifferent to worldly possessions, silently accused my mother of wanting too much. In a way, this was true, for my mother saw nothing noble in poverty or holy in deprivation. Our father went to the United States to secure the futures of my older sisters. He had been caught in a cultural anachronism, that of the dowry, without which my sisters would have remained unmarried, a truly bitter fate. At the same time, as a collector, he was supporting the Orthodox community of Jerusalem. But my grandmother blamed my mother for her son's long absence, just as she blamed her for Moshe's departure for America and then, in 1929, mine.

At the time of his mother's death, my father had been in the United States for more than ten years. For the last half year he had been ill, and Moe and I were supporting him. How sad it was that a man who had helped so many and refused to take charity himself was now dependent upon others for sustenance. He had met his goals, sending enough money home so that Yehoved and Hinda Dvorah could marry devout Hasidic husbands, and he had raised thousands of dollars in charitable contributions. And he knew that his two sons in America were secure.

Cornerstones had been laid.

Moe now had his own photo studio and had reduced his debts substantially. He was doing well enough, in fact, to buy a new car. My father went to the window to see who was making such a tumult with a car horn and was astounded to see his oldest son waving to him from the running board of an automobile. Against his better judgment, he allowed Moe to take him for a quick spin up to Times Square. They returned an hour later, my father impressed and somewhat relieved, offering the observation, in his low-key manner, that the car was certainly faster than any donkey he had ridden on Mea Shearim Road.

I was moving toward self-sufficiency too, though not as quickly as Moe. I would begin classes at the Baron de Hirsch Vocational School. I wasn't yet able to buy a new car, and my only source of income was peddling neckties out of a valise, but who, as my father pointed out, could predict the future?

Was not his life, varied and yet unfinished, testimony to the truth of that question?

Tired and longing for home, my father returned to Ha Eretz, the Land, in the fall of 1933.

The evening before he left, Eleazar, his former roommate and longtime friend, came to bid him farewell.

"God willing, a safe trip, Reb Linder."

"For you, God willing, next year in Jerusalem."

My father had not yet packed his bags. There was little to take—some clothes, a well-worn siddur, and some official papers. He left behind a few books for me and a necktie of blue silk Moshe had given him that he had never worn.

There was another item he was going to leave behind, and Eleazar waited while my father and I went into the bedroom. I knelt with one knee of the floor, reached under the bed, and drew out the small tin box.

In the kitchen, my father held it in both hands.

Eleazar's eyes did not leave the box.

No promises had been made, but it was understood that my father would give it to his dear friend.

It was done in silence.

Our father put the box on the kitchen table and took off the cover. In the electric light, the pure earth that my mother had gathered from the Mount of Olives and cleaned and sieved still shone with the same soft glow it had many years ago in the pale kerosene light of Batei Warsaw.

Eleazar bent over it, closed his eyes, and inhaled with a long, loving breath. He rose, took the cover from my father, and sealed the box. In silence, he wrapped it carefully in a white towel and hurried out the door.

I had been a young boy on that golden summer dawn in Jerusalem when my mother rushed from our house to the Mount of Olives, and now I was here on this autumn evening in New York when my father gave the precious earth to his friend.

Day and night, season-to-season, through all the years, the earth of Jerusalem filled my world with light.

The next day, Moe and I took our father to the boat.

We said goodbye on the pier and watched him walk up the gang-plank, a stooped man with two small valises and a hundred dollars in single dollar bills distributed among the pockets of his long, frayed black coat.

He left America as he had come.

He waved to us once from the deck and then, tired and needing rest, went to his cabin.

Moe and I walked off the pier arm in arm.

God willing, I will see his face again. And the face of my mother. And the faces of my brothers and sisters, Cousin Yitzhak, and all the aunts and uncles of my youth. God willing.

*

Two weeks later, I gave up our three-room apartment and moved into a furnished room on Suffolk Street, off Rivington. The apartment belonged to a middle-aged couple whose two grown children still lived at home. My room had its own entrance in the hall, so I had a good measure of privacy. Another family shared the toilet at the end of the hall. The bathtub, however, was in the kitchen, and I was more comfortable going to the public baths at Rivington and Eldridge Street. Occasionally, I was invited into the family's kitchen for coffee or tea, where their son and I had quite a few interesting conversations on politics and social issues. Their daughter worked long hours, and I saw little of her.

They did not have central heating; a coal stove in the kitchen supplied the apartment's warmth, little of which found its way into my distant room.

Waiting for my vocational classes to begin, I continued to sell neckties on the streets. Two evenings a week, I attended Seward Park High School and went often to the public library on East Broadway or to the Jewish Educational Alliance close by. Both had central heating and comfortable chairs, and there I did my homework, read, and, now and then, enjoyed a conversation with some of the other regulars.

I dreaded returning to my cold, damp room and my lumpy mattress. Walking in after dark, I crawled into bed fully clothed, shedding items one at a time as my warmth built.

Chapter 56

In February 1934, I began my printing course in the Baron de Hirsh Trade School. Classes met five days a week from 9:00 a.m. to 3:00. Our classroom was a reconstruction of a modern commercial print shop, our teacher's professional printers and typesetters, and we learned the trade by doing the actual work. The classroom had four presses: two small hand machines operated by foot pedal and two larger commercial presses with automatic features.

During the first two weeks, we alternated between composition in the morning and presswork in the afternoon. The instructors were knowledgeable and sympathetic. They hovered over us, assessing our skills and aptitudes, and at the end of the two-week period each student was directed to either typesetting or press production. Though some students enjoyed working on the larger presses, for big machines have their allure, I found the presswork boringly mechanical. Typesetting, with its focus on words and their arrangement, had more appeal. I found myself reading the material as I composed it, an added inducement. At my own suggestion and with the agreement of the teachers, I was assigned to typesetting and composition.

Combining business with business, I brought my valise to class and sold a few neckties to the students and instructors—at bargain prices, of course.

The Baron de Hirsh Trade School was located at Sixty-Third Street and Third Avenue; the Third Avenue elevated line ran above the avenue, a peddler's paradise of bars, restaurants, barbershops, and shoe stores. When class let out at three o'clock, I walked up and down the avenue with my valise, and I never lacked for customers.

With my father's departure and Moe in his new apartment, I was truly on my own for the first time in my life. At first, a certain amount of anxiety clouded my days. But I had survived some difficult times, and soon I was feeling proud and independent.

It was the spring of 1934, and I was twenty-seven years old.

*

Five months later, I graduated from the Baron de Hirsh Trade School. We had a small graduation ceremony, and friends and relatives came to the classroom for refreshments and a chance to see our work on display. Moe looked at my two printing compositions and smiled.

"You have a good eye," he said. Looking at the other work, he added, "I see that printing is a lot like photography."

The principal of the trade school, Mr. Green, offered comments and praises, and then our main instructor, Mr. Hanson, added his. They were not encouraging. We had finished the prescribed course of study and were certainly well trained, but we were not yet professional printers. This graduation, Mr. Hanson told us, was not an end but a beginning, and we were now about to confront our most challenging task.

We sat and listened intently, hope and fear at odds in our hearts. The economic situation was grim. I had already made inquiries at a handful of printing firms and knew that work of any sort was hard to find, if not impossible. If journeymen printers were unemployed for years, what hope did I, a recent, inexperienced graduate of a trade school, have of earning a living?

But I had my peddler's trade.

"Chaim, your credit is good. Believe me," said Mr. Wise.

He was willing to carry me for two months at a time.

"Take more, sell more, and don't worry," he told me every week. "Now that the weather is better, no more freezing your toes off. Remember," Mr. Wise said, indicating his own store, "jobs come and go, but everyone, even the unemployed, needs a tie." He waved his finger at me. "Neckties are a living."

He was right, and by working three or four hours a day in the right locations, I was soon selling enough to meet my expenses. I needed seven dollars a month for my rented room and about a dollar a day for two meals: a big breakfast of eggs, toast, and coffee for fifteen cents and a hearty supper at one of the many restaurants on the Lower East Side, usually no more than sixty cents. Dessert was a true luxury, but I had to satisfy my sweet tooth, and with no uncles and aunts around to push a piece of candy into my hand, I often bought myself a treat.

Every morning, I left my furnished room to buy the Yiddish and English papers at the corner newsstand and return home to read the want ads in my room. Finding nothing, I would pack my valise and leave on my peddling rounds. I registered at a number of employment agencies and heard the same bad news at all of them: there were no jobs available, especially in the printing trades. Besides, I didn't have a telephone in my room, nor did the Bronski's, my landlords, and without a telephone, how would prospective employers reach me? On my peddling rounds, I visited the agencies every week, always hoping but finding nothing.

One morning, there was a small box notice in the Jewish *Morning Journal*: the Young Israel of America, an Orthodox youth organization, had just opened a special employment office at 120 Wall Street. I put on my suit and tie and hurried down to register. The application requested a job preference, and I wrote, of course, printing. I thought for a moment and then added, "Will consider any other work."

The clerk behind the desk reviewed my application. "Try to show up every day," she said. "If something comes up, we'll call your name, so it's important to be here. You can stay until noon. There's free coffee and cake and a washroom."

The reception room was crowded with men and women of all ages desperately looking for any kind of work at any pay. I stayed for a while, enjoyed the free coffee and cake, and then returned home and got my valise, refreshed my stock, and went out to earn some money.

Graduation Class at Baron de Hirsh Trade School Chaim
on the bottom row, second from the right

Working on a linotype

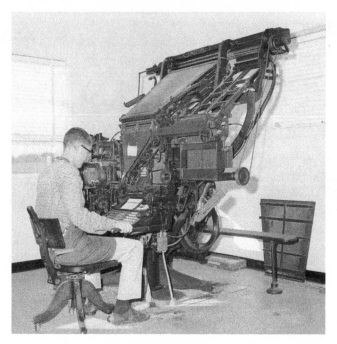

A Linotype

I went back to Wall Street the next day, the day after that, and every day for three weeks. People sat and read or just simply sat. Everyone was very quiet, listening for his or her name to be called. To keep us occupied, the center presented lectures and talks by rabbis and Jewish academics on various religious, philosophical, and literary subjects. Now that my printing classes were finished and Seward Park High School was closed for the summer, these mornings were a welcome change from my solitary existence in my furnished room. I listened to the lectures, sipped tea, and nibbled cake until the doors closed at twelve, and then walked the streets with my valise full of ties in the afternoon. I never opened my valise in the Young Israel office; it would have been an insult to try to sell ties to unemployed, desperate people. As the days went by, more and more people registered; we waited and waited, but few names were called.

Then mine was. It was the end of the third week. The clerk's voice was loud and clear.

"Mr. Herman Linder? Mr. Herman Linder?"

The room became silent. I rose from my chair. All eyes were upon me. I had been chosen—a miracle! I walked quickly to the front desk, afraid that the slightest delay would be fatal. The clerk had just gotten a telephone call requesting a worker with some experience in typesetting and a reading knowledge of Hebrew and Yiddish.

That was the perfect job for me. "I accept," I said. "When do I start?"

"But it's not a job yet," the woman explained. "You have to have an interview first. Here's the address. Go there as soon as you can."

I looked at the slip: the Berg Press on Ralph Avenue and St. Johns Place, Brooklyn. It was at least an hour away.

"Would you like carfare?" The woman held out two nickels.

I declined and walked through the deep, watchful silence as quickly as I could without displaying too much haste.

"Mazel tov!" a man called out to me.

Outside, holding my valise under my arm, I broke into a run, dodging pedestrians in the narrow sidewalks of the Financial District and dashing across streets against the light. At the Bowery, I slowed to a trot, saw the Ralph Avenue trolley leaving Delancey Street, and took off after it, caught it at the next light. I sat panting as we went over the Williamsburg Bridge. It was the longest ride I ever had. At St. Johns Place, I jumped off, chased the trolley for a block to retrieve my valise, turned round, and, pausing a few moments to catch my breath and straighten my tie, walked through the open door of the Berg Press.

A man—I assumed he was Mr. Berg, for there was no one else in the shop—glanced up from his small hand press, wiped his hands on his apron, and looked me up and down. There was a touch of amazement in his face.

"That was quick," he said.

I said nothing, for he knew how scarce jobs were; if I could have, I would have spread my arms and flown over the East River.

He introduced himself. He had a beard and a skullcap, so I used my Hebrew name.

"Take a seat, Chaim."

Mr. Berg pointed to a chair at the side of his desk. He took off his apron and washed his hands in a sink, returned to the desk.

"I told your organization that I needed only an apprentice. Did they tell you that?"

I remained silent, for the receptionist had told me nothing.

Taking that as a yes, he continued. "You will work six days a week for nine hours a day, just like me. No paid holidays or vacations, just like me."

Apparently, he was hiring me.

When I raised no objections, he continued.

"No work on Shabbos, of course."

Just like Mr. Berg.

"Your salary," he said, and then he stopped. He looked at me for a long time before he spoke. "Your salary will be ten dollars a week."

"I see," I said.

Mr. Berg waited.

I kept my expression unchanged. I earned more money selling ties out of my beaten valise, but I could not tell him that, for that would cheapen his offer and embarrass him. However, having looked around while Mr. Berg washed up, I knew I would accept the job under any conditions. His shop was clean and airy, and his presses, though small, were modern. I'd always been good at reading people and situations, and I knew that Mr. Berg was a kind and friendly man. Moreover, he not only wanted an apprentice—which he needed, for he was about my father's age and could clearly use some young muscle in his shop—but also, working alone, was in need of company and conversation. Ten dollars was meager, but judging by Mr. Berg's half-empty shelves and the few scattered papers on his desk, it was probably more than he could afford.

"I'll take it," I said. "When do you want me to start?"

"What's wrong with now?"

"Now is perfect."

Mr. Berg stood, and I began to get up, but he shook his head.

"Stay seated, Chaim," he said, his tone now that of the boss.

He left and came back with three thick, old telephone books. He put them on the desk and then handed me scissors.

"Sit in my chair. I want you to tear out the pages and cut them up in quarters."

I had already taken off my coat and rolled up my sleeves. It seemed an odd request, but Mr. Berg was the boss, and for the next hour and a half, while Mr. Berg moved about the shop setting type and working his hand press, I cut up a thousand pages of telephone listings into pieces of papers about four by five inches.

Finished, I found Mr. Berg at the press.

"Good. Let's see what it looks like."

On his desk were four stacks, each about seven or eight inches high.

"Good, good, Chaim. Very good."

"Where should I put them?"

Mr. Berg gave me a look: How could I not know?

"Put them in the bathroom, Chaim."

I did, placing the squares in a little box built expressly for the purpose, near the toilet.

*

The Brownsville neighborhood of Brooklyn, in which the Berg Press was located, had a large Jewish immigrant population with its own unique cultural, social, and financial institutions. The landsmanshaft, or home-fellowship group, was one of the most common clubs. Named after the country of origin, these landsmanshaften—or societies, as they were called, such as the Society Sons of the Land of Israel—were places where the lonely, anxious immigrant could meet others telling stories in a familiar language about the Old Country. Members paid quarterly dues and received in return, if needed, some form of aid or a free burial service or cemetery plot. In addition, societies would also give their unemployed members a stipend, usually between seven and ten dollars a week, for up to ten weeks.

These landsmanshaften gave Mr. Berg much of his business. Bulletins, newsletters, invitations to weddings and bar mitzvahs, death announcements, and notices of synagogue events kept the Berg Press busy the full nine hours a day that Mr. Berg had promised and were the source of my ten dollars a week.

I learned how to compose type in all configurations. Many of the institutions used mainly Yiddish or Hebrew, but they wanted their members to jump into America's waters headfirst and insisted that English be used whenever possible. My compositions were usually in two and sometimes three languages. I ran the columns side by side, and recalling how I'd learned English by textual comparisons, I composed the material so that the sentences matched English to Yiddish to Hebrew. Now that Mr. Berg had a young trilingual apprentice, he took on even more work, and soon both of us were working long, late hours. Wednesday and Thursday were especially hectic, as we rush-jobbed circulars in Yiddish and English for the many stores and groceries on the streets of Brownsville.

The trolley ride from Delancey Street in Manhattan to Ralph Avenue in Brooklyn took more than an hour, and soon my life consisted of an hour on the morning trolley; nine hours working nonstop, plus an hour for lunch, making it ten; and another hour of evening travel. I did this six days a week, and with neither the time nor the energy for study, I reluctantly gave up my night classes at Seward Park High School.

I thought of moving to Brooklyn, but the rents were much higher. The cheapest room I found was eighteen dollars a month, more than double the seven I was paying on Suffolk Street. I decided to stay, for the while, on the Lower East Side. There, I was a short walk from Orchard Street, where the open-air market reminded me of the souk in the Old City and the market in Mea Shearim—touches of my old life that were as necessary to me as light and air.

Every Sunday I went to Moe's studio in Brooklyn, worked with him in his darkroom, processing the week's negatives. Moe at last was doing well. However, he was working seven days a week, slaving from morning to night, often sleeping in his studio.

He complained bitterly. "My life is nothing but work, work, work. I can't even get enough sleep."

"That's the beauty of American democracy," I said.

"Oh, how is that, Herman?"

"You're rich, I'm poor, and we're both exhausted. The American economic system doesn't discriminate by income. Now, that's equality."

He laughed as I took a print from the shortstop bath and slipped it into the fixer.

"It's not America's fault." He loved our adopted country. "It's Batei Warsaw's."

"Oh, how is that, Maurice?"

"I'll tell you, Mr. Yeshiva Student. In Batei Warsaw, we did everything the hard way. We were taught that if you're good and pious and pray to God, everything would work out in the end. Miracles will happen, and angels will come down. We weren't taught secular subjects—literature or mathematics or history—and we didn't pay attention to the outside world. Look at yourself. You could have learned English in Jerusalem, but it was too secular for us."

"Our parents weren't afraid of the outside world," I reminded him. "Our mother had the fabric store and then the restaurant. Our father lived in America when he was a collector. And look at us—here we are."

"Our family was different. But we should have done more with ourselves. That's why I came to America. Look at how hard things are for you—night school to learn English, lousy neckties in the street, and now you work for Mr. Berg for slave wages!"

We were both silent for a while.

"Let's finish these negatives," said Moe, "and get supper. I know a good restaurant."

Moe liked to eat well, and Sunday supper was the best meal of my week. Sometimes he ordered a drink for both of us or a small bottle of wine. My brother knew how to spend money, whether he had it or not.

During one of those suppers, he suggested we should rent an apartment together in Brooklyn. I wasn't keen on this idea, but Moe persisted, and we rented a two-bedroom apartment on South Fourth Street, near the Williamsburg Bridge, for twenty-eight dollars a month. The apartment wasn't far from Moe's studio and was much closer to the Berg Press, cutting my travel time in half. As an inducement, Moe paid the full rent. He bought bookcases and a small desk for my bedroom.

Ruth Sommers came over once a week and cleaned for us. Often, we had company on the weekends, cousins and friends, some of who stayed overnight; in spite of my initial hesitation, the arrangement was working out well, and we were enjoying ourselves at last.

My brother was climbing the ladder of financial success.

Once, he took out a thick roll of bills and put it on the kitchen table. "Herman, how much do you think that is?"

I had never seen so much money so close. "I don't know."

"Come on. What's your estimate?"

"Three hundred."

"This is America, Herman. Seven hundred dollars."

"Why do you carry so much around?"

"What do you mean 'so much'? That's my weekly spending money."

Only four years ago, he had begged to borrow three dollars.

The next Sunday, when I went to his studio, Moe's smile vanished when he saw my face.

"There's very sad news." I handed him the telegram. "Abba died."

Moe read it standing and then sat and said nothing.

"He died in Jerusalem," I said, hardly able to speak.

Moe remained silent, and we both wept quietly, him sitting and me standing at his side.

My father had been a gentle man and had loved me in so many ways, and I was blessed that he had been my father.

I would never see his face again.

CHAPTER 57

Mr. Berg, resigned to a business that was small, inefficient, and barely profitable, encouraged me to think of a better future.

"I'm an old man," he often said, "but you're young. Printing is a wonderful thing. There will always be a need for the page. Composition by hand is old-fashioned. Focus on press work."

He was right about hand composition. In the United States, most composition was done by hand, one letter at a time, a tedious and tiring process that had been the mainstay of printing for hundreds of years.

Movable type, an idea that seems obvious, was a revolutionary breakthrough. It's usually credited to a Chinese printer, Pi Sheng, who, around the year 1045, used clay to make reusable individual pieces of each character. It was a good idea that was not fully realized; the Chinese language had too many characters to make the process efficient, but it was a start.

Books in Europe, however, were still handwritten, an expensive and laborious process that limited the reach and power of the written word. The early Renaissance, with its newfound desire for knowledge and learning, created a tremendous demand that could not be filled with the old methods of block printing and hand copying. In the middle of the fifteenth century, Johannes Gutenberg and his fellow printers began using individual pieces of raised metal type. The technology progressed rapidly, and soon printers were able to turn out three hundred pages a day. This was so impossible that the authorities, ever watchful, regarded it as the work of the devil, and books produced from Gutenberg's press, thought to possess evil powers, were burned in the hope that the flames would purge the page of evil.

This technique of composition—that is, of arranging individual pieces of type—once established, did not change for five hundred years. The process is straightforward: the compositor forms words, sentences, and paragraphs one character at a time. All letters, spaces, and punctuation marks are set in a form; when one line is completed, a space bar is inserted, and the compositor begins the next line, putting each character in place one by one. The compositor requires a certain amount of design talent, and soon typesetting was viewed as an art form. The finished composition is then locked up in a form and secured in a press. After printing, the type is redistributed in its case. A child's wood block and ink set uses the basic principles. Hand composition has many pluses—it can be done by anyone anywhere and requires a relatively small investment. It has a number of drawbacks, one of them being the limited number of typefaces, or fonts, that a small shop, such as the Berg Press, can carry. Sets of fonts, produced from high-quality steel in exact detail, are expensive, and each font requires its own case. Most small shops have a dozen fonts at the most, and some carry as few as three or four.

However, in the late 1800s, a new method of typesetting was invented. The Linotype machine, invented in 1884 in Baltimore, Maryland, revolutionized the printing trade. The Linotype is a self-contained little print shop that allows an operator to type in the copy—the words to be printed—and produce a composition line by line of cast lead. The machine does three functions: assembles brass matrices—the molds of each character, whether it be a letter, space, or punctuation mark—into a line; casts the line out of molten lead to create a slug; and then automatically redistributes the matrices to their places so they can be used again. The operator sits on a little swivel seat in front of a keyboard and types the copy. Various keys select the matrix and execute the different functions. The operator can also change the font by removing and inserting a different set of matrices.

It sounds complicated, and it is. The typical Linotype is as big as a small bathroom and has more moving parts than an automobile engine. It uses a gas flame beneath an iron pot to supply the molten lead. Lead is used because it is plentiful and cheap, melts at a relatively low temperature, flows easily, sets quickly, and holds detail. With so many moving parts, the operator has to be something of a gifted mechanic to keep the machine running.

During the first decades of use, the Linotype, which was patented by an inventor, Ottmar Mergenthaler, went through a number of improvements that soon made it the machine of choice for compositors. It held sway until the 1960's, when photocomposition began to replace the linotype, eventually becoming the dominant technology. Old Linotype machines, however, are almost as indestructible as my mother's old Singer sewing machine, and are still found in many less developed parts of the world, faithfully turning out slugs of lead.

At first, only large printing companies and newspapers could afford the Linotype. The machines were large, expensive, and difficult to maintain, and shops such as the Berg Press didn't have the volume that justified the expense. But the machine was so much more efficient than hand composition that a new service sprang up: typesetting for the trade. One shop with a few Linotype machines could do the composition for dozens of small printers, charging either by volume of type or, if the job was complicated and lengthy, by time.

A few blocks from the Berg Press, a new typesetting plant had opened; the plant had four Linotype machines and a large selection of fonts. Like many other small printers in Brooklyn, Mr. Berg started contracting out some of our composition work, and once a week, I went to the plant with a job or two. Seeing the machine's speed and versatility, I knew this machine was the future of printing, and I decided then and there to be part of it.

I made inquiries and learned that the Mergenthaler Linotype Company had its own training school in Manhattan. Classes were held during the day from nine to five. The course lasted ten weeks and cost $300.

Mr. Berg was sympathetic but could not afford to give me the time off, nor did I have $300. I finally found a free school, the Bushwick Evening Trade School in Brooklyn; it had three Linotype machines and offered classes at night.

I went there immediately after work and registered for the new term.

The Bushwick Trade School was far from ideal. The machines were often broken, and the instructor, who also taught full-time during the day and worked these extra night hours to support his large family, slept at his desk most of the time. We didn't have the heart to wake him. The seven of us formed a student team, and learned through trial and error the use of space bonds, line measures, accuracy of composition, hyphenation, how to pick and change fonts, elements of style, and, most important, the lubrication, cleaning, and general maintenance of this intricate piece of machinery. The broken machines and our sleeping teacher proved an advantage—one of life's serendipitous rewards.

It was a cold, long winter, and with my full-time day job and long night classes, I was tasked to my limits. In February, I came down with a bad cold that forced me into bed, and I paid four dollars for a doctor's home visit. My cold, the doctor told me, was just a symptom of generally poor health.

"You're anemic." He had just taken a blood count and was shaking his head. "You need more red blood cells. I suggest you eat more red meat and fresh vegetables."

I didn't need a doctor to tell me I was overworked and undernourished, and I thanked him for his time, pulled the covers over my head, and went back to sleep.

Only later did I realize I should have asked my brother for the tuition money at the Mergenthaler school; he gladly would have given it to me, and it would have made my life much easier. As Moe said, however, coming from Batei Warsaw, we did things the hard way.

*

The next Sunday, I was well enough to help Moe in his darkroom. I was at the developing tray, and I watched as pictures of my brother emerged. They looked like passport photos. Moe noticed my surprise.

"I'm leaving for Jerusalem next month."

"You are?"

"Chaim," he said, "I'm going back to my wife and children."

Over dinner, he told me more.

"I've been gone almost ten years. I miss my children. There were a few times I was planning to go back, but something always came up. A lot of nonsense, all my problems—when I had the money for a trip, I didn't have the time. When I had the time, I had no money. Now I have both." Moe sighed. "I don't want to go back. I have to."

The next morning, Moe slept late. That was unusual, and I was quiet as I made breakfast for myself and then left for work.

When I returned that evening, Moe was in the easy chair in his room, reading the *Forward*. The *New York Times* was scattered on the floor around him.

"Well, this is a change," I said. "Now you can tell me what's happening in the world."

He raised his head. "There are a bunch of anti-Semitic bastards in Europe."

"I know," I replied. "They've been around for a while."

"The bastards," Moe said, "especially this Hitler."

In the middle of my preparations for supper, Moe came into the kitchen.

"It smells good in here. I didn't know you were such a good cook."

After supper, we sat at the kitchen table and played a game of chess. It was the first time we played each other in years. Moe was a better player, and he let me come close before he moved a knight for a checkmate. We set up the board for a second game but let it sit there.

"How long do you plan to stay in Jerusalem?"

After a long pause, he said, "Maybe permanently."

I wouldn't have been surprised if he didn't return to New York. Moe loved his two children, Shevach and Fishel, but it was his wife, Dvorah, who brought out his maybe.

"I have to try," he said. "I once loved her."

Once my brother got an idea in his head, he didn't waste energy on doubt or delay.

"I'm leaving as soon as I get my papers," Moe said. "Tomorrow I want you to sign some bank papers. I'm putting my money into a joint account with you. In case something happens."

"What could possibly happen?"

"Don't ask questions! Nothing's going to happen. Just in case. You'll know what to do with the money."

"I won't know what to do."

"Yes, you will."

I couldn't speak.

"Chaim, I trust you with my life."

*

The news of Moshe Linder's return spread like wildfire through Batei Warsaw.

The orthodox community opened its collective arms to him. Dvorah and his children were ecstatic, and extremely tense.

However, good intentions and hope were not enough, and he returned deeply troubled by his failure to reestablish his family ties.

"She was trying so hard," he said, and shook his head and looked away.

I could picture the first meeting. There was my older brother, without a trace of a beard or earlocks, in his high-rolling suit, perfect tie, and shiny black shoes, facing his wife in her long holiday dress, her shorn head covered with a festive kerchief.

"I wanted it to work." My brother sighed. "We live in different worlds."

Without going into the sad details, Moe knew within a day that the marriage was over. He visited our father's grave and stayed long enough to get a rabbinical divorce, settle some of our mother's debts, and spend time with our brothers and sisters.

His youth in Jerusalem was now a closed book never to be reopened.

CHAPTER 58

When I returned to work after my illness, Mr. Berg gave me some sensational news: one of his customers had given him a major job that had to be done on Linotype, and would be jobbed-out to a shop on the Lower East Side.

Again, I found myself on the receiving end of a miracle, or maybe it was just a lucky chance, another form of the miraculous.

Before I left for Manhattan, mindful of the doctor's advice to get a little more fresh air and exercise, I went for a stroll on St. Johns Place, where, through an open door, I heard the distinct sound of a Linotype in operation.

It was music to my ears.

I peered in, stepped inside. A young man was working furiously at his keyboard. The clatter of the machine masked my entry. I took another step and then another. I peeked over his shoulder. It was bilingual keyboard of Yiddish and English.

"Excuse me," I said loudly.

Startled, he turned around. "Yes?"

I made a quick assumption and spoke in Yiddish. I told him I had been walking by, when I heard the sound of his machine, and I wanted to ask the boss a few questions.

Rising from the little operator's chair, he wiped his hands on his apron, held out his right hand, and spoke in high Yiddish, "I'm Isaac Moinester. Ask away. I'm the boss."

*

Back at the Berg Press, I told Mr. Berg of my discovery, which meant I wouldn't have to run back and forth into Manhattan; instead, over the few weeks I ran back and forth between the Berg Press and Isaac Moinester's Linotype shop.

Soon Isaac and I became friends.

A month later, I met his family.

The United States is a large country, and New York a major city, yet it's a small world. Isaac's father had emigrated from Jerusalem at the outbreak of World War I. He had studied at the Hasidic yeshiva with my uncle Yisrael Yitzhak, and they were still exchanging letters.

"Ah, Chaim," Isaac's father said, "why didn't we hear from you sooner?"

"Well," I replied, "but here I am."

His father had given Isaac the capital for his printing business, and now he wanted to help his son expand.

"He needs someone he can trust. Someone who's dependable. From what my son has told me, Chaim, I think you're that person."

I thanked him and waited for more.

"His machine is old. I'll buy a more advanced Linotype, if you will agree."

"What would I be agreeing to?"

"To work for my son."

*

Isaac closed his shop for three days while he and I searched New York City for a Linotype. We finally located a used Model 14. It had originally belonged to the *Morning Freiheit*, a Yiddish newspaper with a rigid Marxist slant; the *Freiheit* had published editorials in support of the Arab riots of 1929, in which my two poor cousins in Hebron had been beheaded. In an editorial, the *Freiheit* called the killing of my cousins "a just struggle against British-Zionist imperialism."

Within two days, the paper lost 40 percent of its readership; management was forced to reduce staff and sell assets. There were no takers for its Linotype. The machine was in storage and in excellent condition. Isaac was able to buy the Model 14, which had sold for more than $8,000 when new, for just $1,700.

After two months of delays and difficulties—the machine had to be dismantled in Manhattan and reassembled in Brooklyn—Isaac and I finally got it operational. Isaac had the new machine, while I used his older, less reliable Model 5. I knew the Model 5 from the Bushwick School, and I kept it functioning.

Mr. Berg was sad to see me go; but I was glad to leave. Technology had made hand composition obsolete, and my new skills in Linotype assured my future. I had learned valuable lessons at the Berg Press, most of them how not to run a business. Mr. Berg had a particularly bad habit of not paying his bills. He ignored bills for gas, telephone, and electric until the services were shut off, and I found myself running from one office to another, cash in hand, begging clerks to turn our heat and light back on.

Mr. Berg didn't seem to mind. "Why pay until you have to?"

He ran his business on a primitive, modified barter system. He never paid me directly; instead, he directed a customer to pay me out of the cost of the job, and then asked the customer to buy a money order from the remainder to pay a supplier. Sometimes he got the customer to give the money to his wife. Many times, Mr. Berg didn't pay his suppliers, so we ran out of ink and paper. This was not good for a print shop. It was extremely frustrating and unprofessional, but Mr. Berg remained unruffled.

"Keep the money in your pocket until you have to pay," he advised. "That way, you always have something."

Now that I was working for Isaac, I insisted that Mr. Berg pay us cash on delivery.

"Chaim," Mr. Berg would say, "what's the rush?"

"I must insist," I told him. "We need the money to pay our suppliers."

"But why pay until you have to?"

Indeed, why?

Then, one morning, delivering a small job to Mr. Berg, I found a policeman and a city marshal standing guard just inside the door.

Mr. Berg, pale and trembling, cried out to me.

"Chaim! My automatic press, Chaim! They're taking my automatic press!"

It was the only valuable piece of equipment he owned. Tears streaking his grey beard, Mr. Berg looked on in anguish as two workmen dismantled the machine.

"My automatic press! I'll starve without it! Chaim! My press!"

I should have turned and left, for this was Mr. Berg's just dessert, but I saw my mother on that Friday afternoon, walking through the gates of the prison in Jerusalem, and I had to stay.

"What's going on here?" I spoke loudly, putting some authority into my voice.

The auctioneer sneered. "Beat it, sonny. This is none of your business."

"Why are you taking the man's livelihood?"

The auctioneer pointed to the city marshal. He held out a judgment order. Mr. Berg owed one of his paper suppliers sixty-five dollars, and the supplier, losing patience after two years of excuses and empty promises, had gone to court.

Without thinking, the words came flying out of my mouth.

"I'll pay the sixty-five dollars."

The auctioneer shook his head. "Too late, sonny."

The workmen continued taking apart the press.

"My press! My press!"

I went to the marshal. "I'll pay the debt. Isn't that fair and legal? As long as he gets the money, does it matter who pays?"

After a long pause, the marshal agreed, and he and the auctioneer consulted. The auctioneer signaled the workmen to lay down their tools.

"Okay, if you want to pay." The auctioneer held out his hand. "Pay."

"I don't have that much cash on me. I have to go to the bank."

"What goddamn bank?"

"The Lincoln."

"I'll give you two hours, not a goddamn minute more."

I dashed out, leaving Mr. Berg wringing his hands, his tears streaking his beard.

Time was short, but I jumped on a trolley, got to the Lincoln and withdrew sixty-five dollars from Moe's account, and got back with a half hour to spare. Mr. Berg greeted me as if I were the Messiah. The auctioneer counted out his money and signed a few papers. He led his workman out, leaving the press parts scattered on the floor.

*

When Moe returned from Jerusalem, he was angry.

"Knowing you, Chaim, and your honesty, I cannot understand what was so urgent about that sixty-five dollars."

"Mr. Berg was about to lose his livelihood."

"I don't want to hear about Mr. Berg!"

"You have to hear about Mr. Berg if you want to understand why I did it."

"There is no explanation I will accept."

"Would it have made any difference if I had asked you first?"

The question caught him by surprise, and he said nothing.

I quoted the Talmud to the effect that a person who can help another without causing harm to himself and does not, has failed in his duty to perform a positive mitzvah, a good deed. Such a failure is considered an ethical failing.

My brother knew this as well as I.

"You lost nothing," I told him, "except a few months' interest on sixty-five dollars. And I'll pay you back everything."

Moe was insulted. "I am not going to take interest from my brother!"

"Okay, then just the sixty-five dollars."

"Herman, the money isn't important."

"So what is?"

He was silent.

I threw another bit of ethics at him. "One must not stand idly by the blood of one's neighbor."

My words were having an effect.

"It isn't the lousy few dollars that bothers me." His tone was softer. "You know how free I am with money. It's the unlimited trust I had in you."

His response didn't make any sense except on the primitive level of brotherly betrayal, but I accepted his limitations and did not press. He was free with money but only if he was spending it. He had a deep-rooted anxiety about money—understandable, considering our early impoverishment—that was part of his drive and success. Full of contradictions, he tipped as if he was a millionaire but begrudged the sixty-five dollars that had saved Mr. Berg.

A few months later, when I proffered the sixty-five dollars, he wouldn't take it, only shook his head and smiled. That was his way, I'm sure, of admitting that I was right.

*

Never one to sit still, within a week of his return from Jerusalem, Moe bought the Graff Photo Studio. It was located in Manhattan, in an area known as Hell's Kitchen. The studio was dilapidated and about to go under and went for a low price. Moe refurbished it and, with his charm and expertise, was soon turning a good profit.

Once again, however, my brother was working long, hard hours and, not wanting to commute from Brooklyn to Midtown Manhattan, he suggested we give up our joint apartment. Moe rented a small two-room apartment closer to the studio, and I found a room on Marcy Avenue. It was large and sunny, had its own private entrance, was convenient to work, and was a short subway ride away from the Lower East Side, where I liked to walk among the pushcarts and listen to the music of the endless haggling. The room was yet another of my dwelling places in the golden land of America.

Chapter 59

After working for Isaac Moinester on the Linotype Model 5 for almost a year and a half, I had mastered the art of typesetting, and was ready to sell my skills on the open market.

It was 1936, the height of the Depression, when experienced printers and typesetters were wandering the streets and haunting the hiring halls, yet I always had work and, going from one job to another, earned ever higher wages under better and better conditions.

New York City was then a publishing paradise, printing books, magazines, and dozens of newspapers, from the mighty *New York Times* to the more humble Jewish dailies. There were many journeymen printers, but the keys to my good fortune were my knowledge of Hebrew and Yiddish and my ability to translate one into the other and both into English.

Besides my steady jobs, I took on freelance composition jobs from many smaller print shops that couldn't afford their own full-time typesetter.

Soon I was earning forty dollars a week and, with overtime, often more.

I would never be rich like my entrepreneur brother, but I was doing extremely well.

Then, one day, while at work at Ginsberg Linotype, a top-of-the-line jobber in Lower Manhattan, I got a telephone call from the president of the Hebrew-American Typographical Union. It was important, the president said, that I come to his office as soon as possible.

Local 83 was a closed union that an outsider, such as myself, could not join. The president sounded eager, but I wasn't going to give up half a day's pay, and it wasn't until lunchtime the next day that I went to the union's office on Henry Street. In the waiting room were a dozen unemployed typesetters standing around and looking depressed. They looked at me with curiosity and some anxiety, for in my ink-stained work clothes, I was obviously a working printer. The receptionist took me in to see the president, who, wearing a spiffy suit and tie, greeted me warmly, offered me a seat, and asked after my health.

"Tea or coffee, Mr. Linder?"

"I'm on my lunch hour, so no, thank you."

"Yes, well. No doubt you noticed the men in the waiting room."

I said I had.

"Too bad, eh, Mr. Linder. We have many members and such little work. It's a shame."

I agreed that it was bad that good printers didn't have jobs; this was his way of telling me that he wasn't going to offer me membership in his union.

"But sometimes a good job turns up for the right Yiddish typesetter."

"Who exactly is a right Yiddish typesetter?"

"I mean an all-around man with the right qualifications. Not just a typesetter but also someone who knows all the phases of composition. I think, Mr. Linder, you're that typesetter."

"May I ask how you heard about me?"

"Word gets around, Mr. Linder. Any typesetter who works for Ginsberg Linotype is more than qualified." Without further preliminaries, the president got to the point. "There is a full-time position available at *Die Welt* in Cleveland."

I knew the paper; it was a Yiddish daily that covered local events, with the usual international material stolen shamelessly from the major newspapers.

"They need an experienced, qualified typesetter, and they're willing to pay." The president rolled out the salary and benefits in one long breath. "Six hours a day, thirty-six hours a week, double time for overtime, a half-hour lunch included, two dollars an hour, all Jewish holidays at full pay, and two weeks' paid vacation."

The offer was tempting, but I was perplexed. "You know that I'm not a union member."

"I know, Mr. Linder."

"And I assume that *Die Welt* is a union shop."

"*Die Welt* is a union shop. But it will be arranged so that you can work there."

"That means," I said, for I knew the process, "that I'll be given a temporary union card but would have no rights to claim union membership."

"Yes, exactly."

"So I am the right man for the job but not good enough for union membership."

The president said nothing.

The offer was too good to turn down. I did a few calculations, and accepted.

"Excellent, Mr. Linder."

"But I do have to ask you—in the waiting room, I counted eleven unemployed union men. Yet you're willing to give me a union card so that I can work in a closed shop. Why don't you send one of your own members to Cleveland?"

The president looked at his watch and shook his head, grimacing at what he saw on his wrist. "I wish we could discuss that point, Mr. Linder, but I have another appointment in ten minutes. But first, I'm going to call *Die Welt*."

He did so in my presence, informing them, "I'm sending one of my best, most experienced men, and you can expect him there within two days."

The president shook my hand, asked his secretary to give me more details, and left.

It was an even better offer than the president had made out; I was given my first week's pay of seventy-two dollars right there, and an advance to cover my travel expenses. Once I got to Cleveland, I'd get an allowance to cover the cost of relocation, and a temporary union card.

It was Wednesday, and I was expected in Cleveland by Friday. I returned to Ginsberg Linotype, finished my day, gave them notice, and went home to pack. The next day, Thursday, carrying the same valise I had used when I'd come to America seven years earlier, I went to Grand Central Station and bought a first-class ticket for the overnight express to Cleveland. With a few hours at my disposal, I dropped by Moe's new studio.

Glancing at my valise, Moe smiled.

"Going somewhere, Herman?"

Events had moved too rapidly to keep him informed, and I showed him the train ticket and the temporary union card.

Once again, Moe proclaimed the great virtues of our adopted country. "You see it yourself, Herman. Success follows hard work. This is America!"

He wanted to see me off at Grand Central, but first, he had darkroom work. I went to Ninth Avenue; bought two long Italian loaves, salami, and a few chocolate bars.

When I walked into the studio, Moe sniffed the air. "What's with all this food?"

"In case I'm hungry. Its five hundred miles."

"Still the same Chaim from Batei Warsaw!" He looked at me with pity, and amusement. "Nothing's changed, has it? On the boat, you were loaded down with pickled herring and Uncle Shlomo's mish-mish. Now you're schlepping salami sandwiches to Cleveland. Chaim, a union sends you to work and pays all your expenses, have some pride. Go in style."

Among Moe's many goals, going in style was at the top of his list.

"Okay, what would you do?"

His eyes lit; he loved giving me free advice, which usually cost me a great deal.

"For one thing, I wouldn't smell up the train with these salami sandwiches. I'd go to the dining car and have a good meal with a glass of wine, and then I'd relax at the table and read a newspaper over coffee."

In matters of style, he was often right; that was exactly what I was going to do.

At Grand Central, he helped me select a seat and then talked to the porter, slipping a fresh bill into his hand. I couldn't see the denomination, but it was most likely a twenty. My brother was always a big sport about tipping when it came to waiters, cabbies, and shoeshine boys.

Excitement kept me awake during the night, and at first breakfast call, I went to the dining car for rolls and coffee. I tipped well, as Moe had admonished. In Cleveland, I stood on the platform, looking around without the slightest idea whom to look for—the president's secretary had forgotten this essential detail.

"Mr. Linder?"

A young man with his hand extended was coming my way.

"I'm Chaim Eichenthal. Was your trip from New York restful, Mr. Linder?"

"Very good, thank you."

"I have a taxi waiting."

As we walked to the cab, I asked, "How did you spot me from the other passengers?"

Eichenthal smiled. "I used a little common sense. There aren't that many Yiddish typesetters around, and they have a special look."

Was it my immigrant's valise?

Eichenthal was holding the door of the cab. "Please, Mr. Linder, after you."

*

We pulled up in front of a dark building; inside, Eichenthal turned on the lights, and I looked around, surprised and disappointed. I was ready to work at a busy, bustling newspaper, but there wasn't a soul present, nor could I sense the least publishing activity.

Sensing my disquietude, Eichenthal said, "This is the editorial room. The shop is in the back."

Just then, another man entered and looked me up and down with great curiosity.

"This is Avraham," Eichenthal said. "Avraham's the best hand compositor from Vilna, Latvia."

The Latvian compositor led me into a big, bright production room. I put down my valise and took a quick inventory of the equipment. *Die Welt* had one rebuilt Linotype machine, six magazines of type matrices, two full barrels of lead slugs, one electric saw to cut them, two square metal lock-up tables, and two racks of hand type.

I was shocked and angry. This was not a professional setup. With

Avraham the Litvak following, I went back to the editorial room. Eichenthal was pecking away on an old typewriter.

He looked up, startled to see me with my valise and an angry face.

"That's not much of a production room. You don't have enough to turn out a daily newspaper. The Linotype is not in good shape. I really can't stay under these conditions."

Eichenthal stood, confused. "I'm only a reporter, Mr. Linder."

Avraham was wringing his hands.

"Where is the production manager?"

"We have no production manager, Mr. Linder."

"How can you run a newspaper without a production manager?"

There was a deep, rumbling cough off to the side. I looked. A man with thick, bushy ash-gray hair was sitting at a desk, reading the *New York Times*. After slowly folding the paper and placing it carefully in the middle of his desk, he swung around in his swivel chair and, with a slow, graceful movement, stood. He continued to stand until he reached his full height of six and a half distinguished, majestic, well dressed feet. Drawing himself up an extra half inch, he spoke with a voice as majestic as his appearance.

"I'm Leon Wisenfeld, your editor in chief and production manager. I believe you are our professional compositor from New York. I welcome you to Cleveland."

He extended his hand; his grip was strong and sincere. Not giving me a chance to speak, Mr. Wisenfeld continued in regal mode.

"For twenty long, productive years, I was the editor of *Die Welt*. Most sadly, those days are over. I will never go back, not if they beg me, but they do not even have the humility to do that. You are not in Cleveland, Mr. Linotyper from New York, to work for *Die Welt*. On the contrary, you are going to help me publish my own newspaper. We shall begin as a monthly, then a weekly, and very shortly, a daily. Be our compositor, and you will be amply rewarded."

Not convinced we could even turn out a monthly, and angry that I had been lured to Cleveland by promises that I would be working on a major Yiddish American newspaper only to find myself in the middle of a poorly planned vanity project, I was about to announce my immediate resignation. But seeing the fear and pleading in the eyes of the three men, I held my tongue. They waited. It was apparent that Mr. Wisenfeld's enterprise depended almost entirely on me. I admit I was impressed by Leon Wisenfeld's magnificent voice, which was like the rumbling from Sinai, not to mention the dignity of his silver hair and great height. Motivated too by the possibility of success, however remote, I made a spontaneous decision.

Wisenfeld was holding his breath.

"Okay, I'll see what I can do."

Eichenthal and Avraham burst into cheers. With Leon Wisenfeld looking upon us with kingly approval, the two of them took turns shaking my hand furiously, thanking me, and wishing the venture and all of us the best of luck.

What did I have to lose?

"And now, gentlemen of the press," intoned our editor in chief, "and I use that term in all its historic glory, though it is"—he checked his watch—"nine thirty in the morning, we shall have a toast."

From a desk drawer, Mr. Wisenfeld produced a half-empty bottle of Johnny Walker Black. He found three small glasses in another draw and doled out a small quantity of the precious liquid in each glass. Raising the bottle high over his head, our editor in chief offered a "L'chaim." We drank, he from the bottle.

"Ah. And now, staff, we have much to accomplish before we rest. Let us begin."

Avraham, the hand compositor from Latvia; Eichenthal, the writer from Cleveland; and I, the linotypist from New York via Jerusalem, placed our glasses on Mr. Wisenfeld's desk and hastened back to the production room.

When I looked, our editor in chief had his feet up on the desk, the *New York Times* on his lap, and the bottle in his hand.

*

We planned to publish our newspaper in two weeks; the pub date was set for Friday, the second-best day of the week for a daily. It would be twenty-four pages in full newspaper size. Wisenfeld wanted eighteen pages in Yiddish and six in English. The English copy had already been hand set by our Latvian. I was to get out the eighteen pages of Yiddish copy in time for publication.

To someone unfamiliar with newspaper publication in those days of Linotype and hand paste-up, this might not seem difficult, but the relatively low level of our production facilities made it almost impossible for a lone compositor, even one as experienced as I.

It was even more problematic when I discovered that our Linotype was broken and had not turned out a single slug since the day it was bought.

However, I was determined to get that newspaper out on its pub date.

*

All beginnings are difficult—and often dirty.

I put on an apron, rolled up my sleeves, and explored the innards of the Linotype. I ran a few tests. A number of minor maladjustments were throwing off the alignment of the matrices and short-circuiting the casting operation. A machinist was called, repairs were made, and by three o'clock, working nonstop at the keyboard, I had set up the first galley of Yiddish composition. Avraham the Latvian struck the first proof and, grabbing it from the press even before the ink was dry, he stuck the long, wet page on a broomstick, and with Eichenthal whooping like an Indian, the two danced around the tables, waving the galley like a flag. From the door, Mr. Wisenfeld and his wife watched the scene with glowing faces and brimming eyes.

I was their linotyper, the angel who had come from New York just in time.

I continued working. The afternoon flew by, and at five I remembered that I hadn't eaten anything since my breakfast on the train. I asked Mr. Wisenfeld where I could get a bite.

"A bite? Why only a bite?" His dignified baritone boomed forth. "Why not a full meal?" He turned. "Avraham!"

"Yes?"

"Mr. Linder requires sustenance!"

Money and whispers passed from Mr. Wisenfeld to Avraham, and the best hand typesetter from Latvia dashed out. He returned fifteen minutes later with a big shopping bag. In it were a boiled chicken, fried onions and carrots, thick slices of challah, and a compote of prunes, apricots, and raisins.

"Eat, eat!" boomed our editor in chief. "A Yiddish linotyper from New York deserves more than a bite!"

I worked until six and told Mr. Wisenfeld that I wouldn't work on the Sabbath.

"Of course." He reached into his pocket and from a roll of bills peeled off my full week's wages. "Come. You must stay with us tonight," he insisted. "You will not spend your first night in Cleveland in a lonely hotel."

In the morning a former advertising agent for *Die Welt* drove me around Cleveland in search of lodgings. I found a furnished room in a nice house owned by an elderly couple whose children had left many years ago. They were pleased to have a young boarder, and gave me a corner bedroom with a private bath.

The rent was twenty-five dollars a month, a great bargain even in those Depression years. They were not Jewish, and when Christmas came, they put up a pine tree and hung it with a few strings of lights and a handful of decorations. Though Jews have holidays that are less religious than others, such as Hanukkah and Purim, I was struck by how secular Christmas was.

*

Though New York City was the publishing center for Yiddish periodicals and literary journals, a number of other cities with sizeable Jewish populations had their own specialized publications. Chicago, for instance, published a Western edition of the New York *Forward* and had its own Yiddish daily as well, as did Philadelphia, St. Louis, and

Cleveland. In Cleveland, *Die Welt* (the *World*), published by a wealthy Jewish family, was a vanity publication barely covering its expenses.

Leon Wisenfeld, a respected journalist and reputable editor, was hired to breathe some life into *Die Welt*, and under his leadership, the paper increased its circulation dramatically. During the last year, however, a bitter feud broke out between Wisenfeld and the publishers. Larger than life and quite imperial, Wisenfeld was soon editorializing the news and personalizing the editorials. The publishers objected, and Wisenfeld was forced to resign.

He sought revenge. Waving his charismatic banner, he raised money from his supporters and admirers and then convinced Chaim Eichenthal and Avraham the Latvian to join his cause. Now, armed with pen and paper, the editor in chief and his two young warriors were determined to take on the *World*.

It is true, of course, that without writers and editors, a newspaper cannot exist, but speaking from the perspective of a professional compositor, it is the machinery of production, along with the skills of the typesetters and pressmen, that transmutes the word onto paper and puts it before the eyes of the reader.

For that they needed an experienced New York linotyper.

With a bachelor's degree in English and a master's in journalism, not to mention fluency in Yiddish, Chaim Eichenthal was assigned to compile articles from Yiddish newspapers and translate them into English. The young academic, however, was not aware that a good deal of the Yiddish in the articles was transliterated from Hebrew, a language with which Eichenthal was woefully unfamiliar. Stumbling constantly over the Hebrew vocabulary, he found himself coming to me every ten minutes with a list of words needing translation.

That first Sunday was the start of a critical week. I called a meeting, and we had a long, argumentative discussion in which I addressed the many technical obstacles preventing us from publishing on schedule. But when I learned that the pub date had already been postponed twice, I agreed to do whatever was necessary to meet the deadline. Technically, we had to abide by union work rules stipulating a six-hour day, five days a week, which left only sixty hours in which to do the job.

I wasted a precious hour explaining to Wisenfeld why he had to stretch the budget for overtime, and he agreed to institute a ten-hour day for the composing room.

Wisenfeld was writing most of the material. He was an experienced, professional journalist, and supplied me with good, clean typewritten copy. This was a welcome rarity in Yiddish composition, in which most copy was handwritten in a cramped, half-legible scrawl on whatever paper was available, leaving the compositor to make sense of it.

However, even the best writers make errors; my proofing eye, well trained, quickly picked these up. The bigger problem, however, was the editorial changes—the dozens of additions, subtractions, and corrections that every editor insists are absolutely necessary to improve an article. The initial submissions of Wisenfeld the writer were excellent, and with a few minor corrections, I set them quickly and then ran proofs.

That was where the difficulties began.

We did not have a proofing department—in fact, we did not have any writing staff other than Eichenthal and Wisenfeld—so Wisenfeld did all the editing and proofreading. There are standard proofreading marks and symbols—a technical written language that allows the editor and the typesetter to communicate quickly and clearly—but Wisenfeld did not know them. His corrected proofs were sloppy, and soon I was spending a great deal of precious time trying to decipher his corrections and tracking him down in the front room to get his long, convoluted explanations. One of his smaller articles, which was two galleys long, about forty column inches, had changes and corrections totaling three extra galleys. Working from a proofed galley takes considerably more time and effort than setting original copy, and by the fourth day, it was clear we would not make the pub date. I knew how to push the work along. I confronted Wisenfeld and gave him a hard deadline for submitting final proofs.

Wisenfeld was not appreciative.

"We are printing the truth," he insisted. "And the truth cannot be rushed."

Well, the truth might be long, but time was short. Book publication is more forgiving, but periodicals work to a deadline. We had a skeletal staff and one slow, barely functioning Linotype, and there was no time for Wisenfeld's endless changes and additions. He didn't understand that changing a word or phrase changed the other elements of spacing, punctuation, and pagination. How could a man living in a world of newspapers not know this?

I did my best to accommodate our great and tall editor in chief with his wonderful voice and waves of silver hair. Working ten-hour days, I had most of the Yiddish section set and paged by Wednesday morning.

Yet Wisenfeld was still writing the feature article. Spread over two center pages, it would put forth the injustice of his treatment and explain why he was publishing his own newspaper.

I saw, much to my alarm, that Wisenfeld was coming down with the dreaded disease of writer's circle. He wanted his article to be brilliant and convincing, passionate and literate, and could not rest until every word, phrase, and line of argument was perfect. The more he changed, added, subtracted, and clarified, the closer he came to his original text.

Finally, at noon on Thursday, two hours before my final composition had to go to press, Wisenfeld put his corrected pages on my copy table, each page block-stamped in big red letters "Final," and left for lunch.

Without a glance, I too left for a quick lunch. After returning a half hour later, I checked Wisenfeld's pages. I was pleasantly surprised. His proofed copies were clean, with only a few corrections here and there, nothing time consuming.

However, my pleasure turned to dismay when I got to Wisenfeld's justice and explanation piece. Our editor in chief had written a complex and convoluted article in which every idea was explained, displayed, and examined, every sentence full of clauses, pauses, commas, and semicolons. Marked in red ink with a big "Rush" in the margin of every page and riddled with blue proof marks, it resembled nothing less than a New York subway map.

Resetting it would require adjustments everywhere, and there wasn't enough time.

I consulted with Eichenthal and Avraham, and they were of common mind: I must do what I thought was professionally correct. I put

Wisenfeld's piece on the bottom of my work pile and began my final composition run.

Soon Wisenfeld entered the composition room and went directly to the worktables. When he didn't see his corrected article, he came to the Linotype. Looming like a dark angel, his deep silence demanded attention. I sat on my little swivel seat and kept my eyes on the copy-holder and my fingers on the keyboard. Wisenfeld went through the copy stack and saw his article on the very bottom. I glanced up at him. He had come in from a late lunch, and a white dusting of snow on his winter coat and hat gave him a wizened look.

He glared at me. "Chutzpah. Sheer chutzpah!"

I said nothing and returned my attention to my keyboard.

Wisenfeld stormed away, growling deeply, and then turned on his heels and stormed back. He yanked his article from the pile and slammed it down hard on the table.

"You shall work on these pages now!"

I continued typing.

Avraham and Eichenthal were crouched behind copy tables.

Wisenfeld's baritone rumbled forth. "Mr. Linotyper, you shall answer me!"

I shut off the Linotype and stood. He was a foot taller than I and had twice as much hair.

"There is only one way I can get our newspaper out on time. I must be allowed to do the work correctly and in the order I think best."

Wisenfeld's mouth opened, then shut. I braced for a thunderous outburst as his head reared back and his eyes tightened. I took a step back. With a supreme effort that contorted his face and lifted his hair in leonine fury, he turned around and strode from the composing room.

I sat on my little swivel seat, turned on my machine, and resumed work.

Avraham and Eichenthal came out of hiding.

Shortly, Wisenfeld reappeared and, without a word, took his proofs. An hour later, he slipped the article to the bottom of the pile and left. I stopped working and looked at it. He had marked many of his changes with a "Stet" and they no longer had to be retyped.

*

The first edition of Wisenfeld's newspaper hit the stands early Friday morning, on schedule. Marking this historic event, Wisenfeld treated us to a lavish lunch in the composition room, and offered a champagne toast.

"It is in this composition room," he intoned, "that our newspaper was born. Without our linotyper from New York, none of this would have been possible. To you, Chaim, we say thank you. L'Chaim, L'chaim" (To Chaim, To life).

"L'chaim," we responded, raising our glasses to the birth of a new Yiddish weekly.

The first edition was a great success; we printed eight thousand copies and sold every single one.

We increased the press run of the second issue to ten thousand but sold only six.

Working on the copy, I saw the problem. Wisenfeld was repeating his earlier mistake. He was personalizing the paper. He was both publisher and editor in chief, and by the third edition the paper had become a one-person editorial. Wisenfeld soon emptied his pen, and after eight editions the newspaper ceased to exist.

It had been an exciting and profitable experience in more ways than one. I got an unexpected taste of the good life. Chaim Eichenthal and I became good friends; we dined often, and he taught me billiards, at which I became quite proficient. As a freelance theater critic, Eichenthal got free passes to movies and plays, and I accompanied him often. *What a far cry*, I thought one evening as he and I dined in a restaurant, talking about a play we had just seen, *from my life in Batei Warsaw.*

Despite our numerous confrontations, Wisenfeld and I got along well. On my last day, as I was cleaning the Linotype for storage, he took me aside and suggested a partnership; he would upgrade the present plant, and we would open our own printing company, not just as jobbers but as publishers of our own books and periodicals. It was very tempting, but his ideas about print-worthiness were not in accord with mine. In addition, his rich, deep voice, flowing hair, and charismatic charm, after first exposure, were exhausting. I thanked him for the offer and wished him good luck.

I had earned about $250 a week, a tremendous amount of money in those Depression days, and I was able to save over $1,200. I acquired, too, something equally bankable: experience and confidence. I knew I could manage my own printing plant, and I was determined to have one.

As my brother had always insisted, this was America.

Back in New York, while preparing for my future, I returned to the Shulsinger Press in Brooklyn, where they welcomed me with open arms and a raise. I rented a large furnished room on Park Place. It cost twenty-two dollars a month, and had its own bath and, much to my pleasure, a rear garden with trees, flowers, and grass. Close by on Eastern Parkway were a number of good restaurants, and a few blocks farther, for a change of cuisine, was the Little Oriental Restaurant.

I found freelance work here and there at smaller printing shops that needed a few hours of Yiddish composition on an emergency basis.

One of them was the United Linotype Company on the Lower East Side; whenever they needed me, they'd leave a message at the Shulsinger switchboard that said, "Mr. Linder, the US needs you."

Mr. Hollander, the owner of United, paid well and always fed me a hefty deli sandwich from Katz's Delicatessen on Delancey Street. United had three Linotypes, and Mr. Hollander had his favorite. He named it the Boss. The Boss had a unique keyboard that combined English and Hebrew. He was a heavy smoker, and put anything in his mouth that he could light and inhale—cigarettes, cigars, pipes. When he finished working, the Boss's keyboard had a fine dusting of tobacco bits and ash. On the few occasions when I was given the honor of working on the Boss, he warned me not to even think of cleaning it.

"See how my dirty machine works like a happy devil?" Mr. Hollander would watch as I sat on the little swivel seat. "Look at the other two Linotypes—clean as a whistle, but you can't squeeze a single slug out of them. Remember, Herman, dirt is your friend!"

The Edelman Typesetting Company at Norfolk and Delancey was another shop where I free-lanced. The plant was in a long, narrow basement space, with an exhaust fan howling night and day, summer and winter. Lou Edelman, the owner, catered to my tastes, as multilingual linotypists were hard to find, and whenever I came to his shop, we first had to visit the corner candy store to get something nourishing. We both had a sweet tooth, but Mr. Edelman, quite overweight and always on a diet, used me as his excuse. I always wanted a Coke, and he always refused to let me have it.

"No, no, not a plain Coke! You need energy, Herman!" He shouted at the elderly woman behind the soda fountain. "Hey, Mama-le, make it a malted! Two scoops vanilla, and throw in a half scoop of strawberry. And do the same for me. I don't want to sit here taking up space without paying your rent. And do it today—we have work to do!"

Lou Edelman had bought a Ludlow typesetting machine, a simpler device than a Linotype, and he taught me how to use it.

"She's a good baby, not like the lousy Linotype, which is always breaking. She works like a fiddle. Look at her—one line, a second line, never stopping. A real pleasure!"

For years, Lou Edelman had worked at a Yiddish newspaper before opening his own shop in the dark, airless basement. In the small world of New York Jewish printing, he was known as Crazy Lou.

"He had it so good," everyone said. "Steady work, union wages, plenty of overtime. Now he works like a horse and takes home less. You say he has plenty of business? He'll never pay off the expensive machinery. That Lou is crazy!"

I wondered if they would call me crazy too when I gave up my good hourly wages to open my own printing plant.

Chapter 60

By the summer of 1939, it had been two years since I'd returned from Cleveland, and with economic conditions in the United States slowly improving, the time had come to act.

Moe had been urging me on, citing himself as the perfect example.

"Look at me, Herman. Owning your own business is the American way."

"I know. It's just a question of money."

"Don't let money stop you. It never stopped me."

"It's the lack of it that's an impediment."

"Come on, Herman. Just how much money does it take to open a printing plant?"

"Considerably more than it takes to open a photo studio."

"That's not so."

I pointed out that functioning studios were readily available, whereas there weren't any old Hebrew-Yiddish typesetting plants on the market, and a new one required more capital than I could ever accumulate.

"What are you talking about?" Moe countered. "Equipment is equipment."

I argued the contrary. I knew what was required for a studio: two good cameras, a darkroom with the basic equipment, a set of inexpensive lights and reflectors. The front room had to be pleasantly appointed and painted, with a few chairs and a decoration or two.

A typesetting plant, on the other hand, required at least one modern Linotype, many sets of font styles and sizes, a proofing press, electric saws, steel tables, and quantities of lead, which formed the basis for the castings. It would cost at least $20,000 to build a plant from scratch.

After a hard-edged analysis, I knew I needed a person who knew the trade and had more money than I. And he had to be honest, dependable, hardworking, and compatible.

Going through my inventory of friends and family, I came to the conclusion that I did not know such a person.

*

I owe many of my experiences, and a few successes, to my love of walking; at crucial junctures, a long, contemplative stroll undertaken with an alert eye has opened up a different path. Indeed, awareness of one's surroundings and a willingness to engage strangers are indispensable elements of a rich life, for then chance and circumstance are allowed to play their parts.

One Sabbath afternoon that summer of '39, strolling on Eastern Parkway, I noticed a man approaching. About my age, he looked vaguely familiar. We closed the distance, and I glanced more closely at him. We passed without a word.

Lost in his own thoughts, he hadn't paid me the slightest bit of attention.

I slowed and turned; did I know him?

I did, and I walked fast, caught up with him. I adjusted my pace so that I might pass him at a casual clip.

"Good Shabbos," I said.

He glanced at me without interest. "Good Shabbos."

I slowed and used a more intimate tone. "And how are you?"

"Sorry, but we haven't met."

I kept pace. "You are Joel Shapiro, aren't you?"

"Yes, I am."

"We met at the Geller Typesetting Company on Boerum Place in Brooklyn."

We stopped. He was puzzled.

"I came in looking for work," I said, "and you told me the boss was out for the day, and we talked a little more before I left."

"Oh yes! You said you were just walking by, saw three typesetting machines through the open door, and thought you'd come in for a look."

"Those days I was always on the lookout for work."

"Of course. Your brother had a photo studio on Manhattan Avenue. You're Chaim Linder."

We shook hands and found a bench on Eastern Parkway.

"Are you still working for Geller?" I asked.

"For the last seven years. It's the only place I've worked. I practically run the shop. What about you? Did you find steady work?"

"As much as I want, and then some. Since then, I've been in half a dozen shops."

"Really?"

"I learned a lot from each job, and I earned more money that way. I also worked in Cleveland, putting out a newspaper—a very interesting experience."

"I could imagine. Where are you now?"

"At Shulsinger. I pick up some freelance work when I can. The money and conditions are good, but I'm tired of working for someone else. I'm ready to open my own shop."

"I've thought of that myself," said Joel Shapiro. "But the investment in time and money is too much for one person."

We were both silent for a while, then resumed talking about the printing trade and its future. We sat on the bench in the afternoon sun, sizing the other up. Might this stranger be the right person? He was thinking the same thing. We talked for an hour, and then, because Shabbos was drawing to a close and we both had places to be, we exchanged particulars. Joel would not use a pen on the Sabbath, so we each memorized the other's address.

We lived about ten streets from each other, and were, in a sense, distant neighbors. Both of us walked often on Eastern Parkway, and on that Shabbos afternoon, driven by a casual destiny, we had finally met.

CHAPTER 61

During the summer of 1939, the newspapers were full of foreboding and evil. I read obsessively. The sky over Europe was dark with the threatening clouds of war. It had been coming for a long time. Europe loved strong, violent men who brought out the worst in people and convinced them that evil was good.

Jews were being beaten and humiliated in Germany. Some hoped the abuse would stop, but most of us knew it would not. It had been going on for years, and it would soon get much worse; we would be slaughtered by the millions.

And the world was doing nothing.

I read the papers and listened to the radio. Hitler had feasted on the Rhineland and Czechoslovakia and now, slowly digesting the rich meats of appeasement, was looking for his next meal. Poland would be devoured quickly. The statesmen of Europe, impotent and fearful, wrung their hands and closed their eyes. But there is never blood enough to quench the devil's thirst, nor fuel enough for the fires of hell.

Palestine, as it was still called, remained under British mandatory rule, and His Majesty's Government, terrified of the Nazi beast, sought an alliance with the grand mufti of Jerusalem. Not so secret promises were made that, should Britain prevail in the coming war, His Majesty's Government would look with less favor upon the establishment of a Jewish homeland and with considerably more upon the creation of a new Arab empire. However, when the war started, the Grand mufti openly sided with Nazi Germany.

After what I saw in Jerusalem during my youth and in August 1929, when the Arabs slaughtered the Jewish students in Hebron, beheading two of my cousins, I knew what the fate of my family in Jerusalem would be should German armies march into the Old City.

As for my friends and relatives in Palestine, they took up whatever arms they could find and prepared to defend themselves.

Yet, life goes on. On September 1, 1939, after months of discussion,

Joel Shapiro and I signed a formal partnership agreement and opened the Modern Linotype Company.

The same day, Nazi Germany invaded Poland, and World War II began—surely not an auspicious beginning.

Our shop was located on Eastern Parkway and St. Johns Place, not far from where Joel and I had met that Saturday afternoon in August.

I had wanted to locate the business in Manhattan, the center of New York's publishing and printing trade, but acquiesced to Joel's desire to remain in Brooklyn. Of the initial investment of $5,000, we spent $3,500 for a rebuilt Intertype typesetting machine, a better version of the original Linotype. The rest of our capital went toward a selection of Hebrew and English fonts, an electric saw and a hand press for proofing, and various other essentials, such as ink and paper. In contrast, my brother had bought the Graff Photo Studio, equipment included, for $1,200.

In the window of our new shop, we hung a small sign:

Modern Linotype Company
English ~ Hebrew ~ Yiddish

Our plan was to concentrate on books, periodicals, and a few weeklies—because of tight deadlines, newspapers had their own composition rooms—but in need of immediate income, we accepted work from Brooklyn's many small print shops. Working quickly and without stop, and only for cash, by the second week, Joel and I were able to draw wages, if only a token sum.

My partner worked the Linotype, and I did everything else—cutting and trimming; locking the slugs into quoins, or forms, so that they could be printed into galleys; proofing the galleys; and the dozen other assorted chores that keep a print shop and running. I was also the outside man, scouring Brooklyn and the Lower East Side for customers. Our ability to set type in three different languages was a big selling point; my Jerusalem connection was a significant factor in landing a number of jobs.

There was a great demand for our services, and we were soon

overwhelmed with work. We hired two part-timers, a high school student who came in three hours a day after class and ran errands and cleaned the shop. We also hired a young woman three days a week to do billing and inventory. But we lost a few customers when we failed to deliver on schedule. We needed more investment capital, but the banks were wary. Without a second Linotype, we were forced to put in extremely long hours for little pay.

But at last, I had my own business, and I knew that given time and an improving economy, my partner and I would succeed.

As my brother never tired of reminding me, this was America.

CHAPTER 62

Then, I went to a wedding.

My partner, the groom himself, had printed the invitation in our own shop.

It was Sunday evening at the end of August 1940 in the Broadway Mansion on the Lower East Side. The ceremony was Orthodox, the reception flavored with American modernity: men and women sat at the same tables, but danced separately, yet with equal fervor.

At my table were three young women, one of whom had been my neighbor in Jerusalem. She introduced me to her sister. I didn't quite catch the name of the other woman, because in the middle of our introduction the band started up, and, exclaiming her need to move her feet, she rushed to the dance floor.

Dancing was not one of my skills. As I talked with the two sisters, my eye was drawn to the dancers. The men were dancing Hasidic snake dances—long lines of rhythmic shuffling and jumping—and the women danced with women. Neither gender touched. The dancing girl was clearly one of the best. Her energy was abundant and her enjoyment more so. Then a hora began, fast and buoyant and merry, and for the first time in my life, I wished I was a dancer. The wedding dinner was served, and with each course the band rested, and the dancing girl returned to the table for a quick bite, only to jump up again as the band struck up.

At last, we were served wedding cake, and the musicians started packing up. The guests said their goodbyes. The dancing girl sat down for a few moments to catch her breath. I was ready to go.

"Oh, I didn't know it was this late!" She looked at her watch. Then she looked at me. "Would you care to take me home?"

She added, laughing, "I don't live far from here—near Yankee Stadium."

I smiled, but with a mix of relief and regret. Yankee Stadium was in the Bronx, at least an hour away by subway. It was 2:30, Monday morning. My partner was leaving for his honeymoon later this morning, and I couldn't possibly take the dancing girl home and get back to Brooklyn in time to open the shop at six. I said nothing; silence is not consent. The dancing girl smiled at me, gathered her sweater and purse, wished the bride and groom good luck, and left.

Outside, a chilly rain was falling. Standing at the corner and shivering under a small green umbrella was the dancing girl, waiting for the light. I was thinking about my workday. I had three composition jobs due in the afternoon, a delivery of a set of proofs to another shop, and a meeting with a potential customer on the Lower East Side. She was crossing the street, walking fast, her umbrella bouncing.

I caught up with her and took her arm.

"Hello," I said. "I decided I want to go to Yankee Stadium."

We walked to the Bowery to get the Third Avenue El, and waited on the platform in the blowing rain while I prayed silently, fervently, for an express. There were no miracles that night, however, and when the local pulled in we took it. We sat side by side on the wicker seat, the only two people in the car. At Thirty-Fourth Street, I glanced at my watch. It was 3:00 a.m. I looked at the dancing girl; her eyes were open but blank.

"You must be very tired," I said.

"Not really."

"You should be. You never stopped dancing."

"Why didn't you dance?"

"I wanted to talk to Sarah and her sister. When I saw her last, she was ten years old, and now, well, we had a lot to talk about. I'm not much of a dancer."

"That's too bad. I enjoy dancing."

"I could see that—you dance very well."

"I couldn't dance like I like to. The dance floor was small and slippery, and I didn't think the band was that good. And I had to dance with women. It's easier with a man."

Her English was very good, with the slightest hint of a British accent.

The train crawled through the dark tunnels, and we sat back in our seats, silent. Unconcerned for my needs, the train lingered at every station and then crawled to the next. I snuck a look at my watch, and despaired. It would be after five when I got home. The car's heat had come on, and my brown woolen suit was uncomfortably warm. I didn't care for the dancing girl's dress. It was plain and dark blue with long sleeves and was buttoned all the way to her chin like a soldier's uniform.

She turned her head to look at me. "Are you from Jerusalem?"

"I was born there."

"I thought you were—you called the two sisters 'my dear neighbors from Batei Warsaw.'"

We pulled into the station at 125th Street.

"Here we are," I said, and I carried her green umbrella as we walked through the deserted station to another platform to catch the Jerome Avenue train, which would take us cross-town to the Bronx. My hopes for a miracle remaining unfulfilled, we had to take another local.

We had the car to ourselves, and we sat side by side.

"What brought you to the wedding?" I asked.

"I wasn't supposed to go. I don't know the bride or groom, but my parents are friends of the bride's family. My parents live in Baltimore, and they come to New York every summer for two weeks. They were going to be here tonight, but just yesterday, my sister Shoshana had to be taken to the hospital for her appendix, and my parents had to go back to Baltimore. They asked me to represent them at the wedding. I didn't want to go—I wasn't in the mood to come all the way down-town for a wedding where I didn't know anyone. It was going to be a religious wedding with no mixed dancing. And I didn't have time to get my hair done, and I had nothing to wear. Look at this shmata. I borrowed it from one of my cousins. But my father really wanted me to go to celebrate, in their name." She smiled. "'You like parties,' my father said. 'Pretend that it's just another party, and you'll enjoy yourself. Go. What do you have to lose?'"

I smiled too; it was a familiar bit of advice easily given by the person who would incur no cost in following it.

"And why were you at the wedding?" she asked.

"Joel, the groom, and I are business partners."

"Oh, so you're a very important guest!"

"I didn't feel like one. I didn't know too many people there."

"You were talking to everyone at the table."

"While you danced. Are you always so full of energy?"

"Usually, especially when there's music. But now I'm suddenly tired."

"It's almost four o'clock."

The train crept along.

The dancing girl said, "If you don't mind, I'll put my head on your shoulder and close my eyes, and since you talk much more than you dance, you can tell me a story about Jerusalem."

She closed her eyes and rested her head lightly on my left shoulder. I culled my store of stories, and began a tale about my uncle Yisrael Yitzhak and one of his neighbors, Zalman Leib Levi. I didn't mention any names because, after all, the dancing girl had no idea who they were, and just wanted a voice to fall asleep to.

"The only thing my uncle and his neighbor had in common was a joint front yard. Otherwise, they were worlds apart. My uncle is a Hasid and very Orthodox, but the neighbor was a Mitnagged—observant but just the opposite of a Hasid. This caused more than a little friction. Not that they really quarreled, but they made it a point to mind their own business."

The dancing girl, her eyes still closed, murmured.

"Adding to the friction was the neighbor's temper—he had a large family, so many that everyone lost count, and all but one were girls, which added even more to his temper."

The dancing girl kept her eyes closed and smiled.

"Every Sukkoth holiday, a bit more friction was added to their relationship. My uncle built his sukkah a month before the holiday began. That's how Hasidim are, always *zrizim makdimim*— ahead of the time. They can't wait to do a mitzvah. My uncle is a dayon, a rabbinical judge, and very pious, and he could have attached his sukkah to one of the outside walls of his house, but of course, he built it freestanding because the fourth wall added an extra measure to the mitzvah. But the neighbor was too busy with odd jobs—his six daughters were expensive—and waited for the last minute to build his sukkah. Two days before the holiday he finally put it up. But he was pressed for time and materials, and attached it to one of the walls of my uncle's, so from the street, it looked like one big sukkah. And that's how the trouble began."

I paused. The dancing girl was still, and I turned my head carefully to see if she had fallen asleep, but on the contrary, her eyes were wide open and alert.

I continued. As she knew, I said, most of the men in Jerusalem slept in their sukkahs. It was a great mitzvah to spend at least one night in the little hut. "I've done it often, and it's very pleasant, like sleeping in a tent. The nights are very mild in Jerusalem that time of year, and it's the dry season too, so there's no chance of rain. I used to look through the roof at the moon and stars. Both my uncle and his neighbor would sleep in their respective sukkahs, side by side, separated by a thin wall."

I paused, and the dancing girl, her head still on my shoulder, nodded. I continued.

"Now, though I love and admire the Hasidim—after all, my entire family and I were Hasidim for many generations, though I obviously am no longer—there are many things about the Hasidim that are seemingly contrary to their holy ways. There's so much pressure to always be pious and thoughtful and do good deeds that every once in a while, even a devout Hasid needs a break from all his sincerity. On Sukkoth, for instance, many go around with pails of water, climb over the rooftops, and pour water on their fellow Hasidim sleeping in their sukkahs. It's hard to imagine, but it's true. They start on the first night of the holiday, which leads to an endless chain of revenge pourings and counter-revenge pourings for an entire week. Some nights, all of Batei Warsaw is full of giggling Hasidim carrying buckets and pails and climbing like burglars over the rooftops. But they usually pour water only on their fellow Hasidim, who react with anger and threats and, at the same time, with hearty laughter. You have to laugh at yourself, even if it means laughing when wet. It's part of the Yom Tov spirit, the holiday joy, in Batei Warsaw and the Mea Shearim. But the Hasidim don't pour water on the Mitnaggedim; there's too much tension there to begin with, and besides, the Mitnaggedim don't have a good sense of humor when it comes to getting wet."

This was prelude to my actual story, and the dancing girl was no longer resting her head on my shoulder. We had two more stops, and I picked up the pace of the narrative.

"I was one of the Hasidic children pouring water on people in their sukkahs. I climbed over the rooftops, ran along barefoot, found someone sleeping, and then poured water through the reeds. I was going to do it to my uncle Yisrael Yitzhak, one of my favorites, but because his neighbor had built his own sukkah against his and because it was dark and all I saw was the outline of a sleeping man, I poured a bucket of cold water on the head of my uncle's neighbor, Zalman Leib Levi. Judging by his snores, he had been sleeping very soundly, and the cold water hit him like a wet bomb. He jumped up and ran out into the yard, yelling for the police, but I ran away over the rooftops and jumped down into the alleys and got away."

The dancing girl was sitting up now and laughing very hard.

I laughed too, at the memory.

"If you think that's funny," she said as we pulled into our station, "what would you say if I told you that I know your uncle's neighbor very well?"

"I'd say it was a small world."

We stepped out onto the platform.

"Smaller than you think. You poured water on my father."

"Zalman Leib is your father? The man with all the daughters?"

"I'm his oldest!"

Standing on the platform as the train pulled out, we laughed and laughed.

The rain had stopped, and the sun was rising, and we went into a luncheonette for rolls and coffee.

"I must confess," I said, "my story made me sad. I reminded myself of home. I'm sure it's because I'm tired."

"I know. I feel sad too. I've been gone only three years, and I miss Jerusalem."

"I don't even know your first name."

"Yona."

"Oh? How interesting. Yona is a male name. There's the prophet Yona, and I knew a few boys named Yona."

"Hebrew is more modern now in Eretz Yisrael. We add and change words and names all the time. My original name in Yiddish is Taibl."

"A dove," I said.

"And in Hebrew, a dove is *yona*. I changed it before I came to America." She looked at her watch. "It's really late."

I walked her home and then turned around and walked back to Jerome Avenue. I took a series of trains to Eastern Parkway. It was close to opening time, and I went directly to my shop. It was just after eight in the morning. I went straight to the Linotype, sat in the little swivel chair, put my hands on the keyboard, and began composing. Within half an hour my eyes were closing, and my fingers couldn't find the keys. I shut down the machine, locked the front door, went into the back room, cleared off a worktable, and, using my folded coat as my pillow, stretched out and closed my eyes. The dancing girl and I had exchanged addresses and telephone numbers, and we were going to see each other next Saturday night. I dozed lightly on the hard, cold table. The phone rang every few minutes, and then, as I drifted off, a customer pounded on the front door. I didn't care. Destiny was beckoning.

At last, I wouldn't be alone.

CHAPTER 63

My father was thirty-three years old when he met my mother in the summer of 1940; my mother was twenty-three. Photographs show him to be a tallish young man. Official documents give his height as five foot ten and his weight about one hundred forty. His eyes were hazel, his hair brown.

Years later, my mother's sisters, my aunts, told me how surprised they were at their oldest sister's choice.

They were different in upbringing, temperament, turn of mind, and time of life. My father was ten years older than my mother, less physically robust, more intellectual and introspective. My mother, on the other hand, was an athlete and quick to act. She was impatient with delay, though her outbursts, if they even could be called that, held more flash than fire. She was much like her own father, my grandfather.

After he met my mother, his dancing girl, my father had a sense that destiny had taken him in hand.

He wrote,

> In my ultra religious Hasidic home in Batei Warsaw, I had been taught to think big: the universal God, the Holy Torah, the Jewish people, and the land of Israel, Jerusalem. Destiny was the butter on my daily bread.

And he wrote,

> The sudden and unexpected meeting with the dancing girl, who I knew now as Yona Levi, couldn't have been an accident. Thoughts of her and our meeting consumed my mind and heart. Was this the bigness that had been part of my life since I was a child? I looked for answers, for there must have been a reason why I

wanted to come to America and why the dancing girl had come too.

There was so much chance at work, that there must have been purpose too.

Why at the last moment did the dancing girl's sister have to be taken to the hospital by her parents, so that she was given the assignment of being the family representative at the wedding?

Why did I first reject her request to escort her home and then, when I saw her standing in the rain on the street corner, change my mind?

What was it about the way she stood that moved my heart?

And why, in response to her request for a story about Jerusalem, did I come up with the tale of the sukkah and my uncle's neighbor, who happened to be her father?

Why, though my family and the Levi family were such intimate neighbors in Batei Warsaw, did I not even know of her existence until we came to America?

Offering no explicit answers but suggesting, by posing these questions, that there was indeed a connection, however hidden, my father included the details of their initial courtship:

During that first week after our meeting, Yona and I spoke several times by telephone, and the following Saturday, we met and saw a movie on Broadway and then went to the Horn and Hardart Cafeteria, and from there, we walked up to Central Park. We had a great deal to talk about. And soon, seeing each other every week and talking about our own lives in Jerusalem, we began talking about a future together.

It was an unlikely match, yet it happened.

Perhaps neither of them wanted to be alone any longer.

One sees, in these, my father's tales, a tremendous sense of unity that was an integral part of his life. Given the crowded conditions and large families of the Orthodox community, this was, in part, a unity born of necessity. One was never alone. Solitude had to be sought, as my father did on his long walks in the hills around Jerusalem. In like fashion, in America, he relished his solitude, finding in those furnished rooms a measure of peace.

But he remained true to himself. After living for years in furnished rooms that were sometimes cold and damp and other times warm and pleasant, he had his fill of solitude. Before marrying his dancing girl he had been in America for eleven years, and was ready to have a family of his own.

I see my father very much as he portrayed himself. He buys his clothes, cleans and washes them, changes his bed linens, feeds himself, sweeps his room. There he is, walking quickly down Delancey Street with a newspaper, most likely the *New York Times*, folded in his hand. In his long gray work coat, he sits at his Linotype, his nimble fingers dancing over the keys. I see him too as a child in Jerusalem and, though he pays me no attention and does not even know of my existence, I run with him through the twisting alleys of the Old City and join him on his long solitary walks in the hills around Jerusalem.

His destiny was to have a wife and children and be a part of something greater than himself; when he met my mother, the dancing girl, he stepped gladly into his future.

It was a joy to find her.

And for her, too, there was joy; she was ready to start a new life.

*

In the spring of that year, a few months before he met my mother, my father became an American citizen. On the parlor floor of our brownstone in downtown Brooklyn, in a brass-and-glass frame, is his certificate of naturalization, dated May 6, 1940. His height is given as five foot ten and his weight as 135. His prior nationality is listed as Palestine-Great Britain.

My mother became a citizen on May 18, 1943 a year after my older brother was born.

Her former nationality is given as British, though that's a mistake of the United States District clerk. Whereas my father never had a passport and was simply issued an emergency travel visa in 1929 by the American consul in Jerusalem, by the time my mother emigrated, the British mandate had been well established, and my mother left Jerusalem in possession of British-Palestine passport number 83521, issued April 16, 1937. Her profession is listed as government officer—she was a clerk in a minor British office. Her height is listed as 168 centimeters (roughly five foot four), and her hair as brown. Her eye color is "greenish." The passport is in English, French, Hebrew, and Arabic and is valid for travel in Italy, France, and the USA.

She used the passport only once. It's stamps show that she was issued an emigration visa on July 19, 1937. She left Haifa two days later, docked in Cherbourg on July 28, then at Marseille for another official stamp:

> *Transmigrant*
> *n'est oas autorise a sejourner*
> *en France plus de quinze jours.*

An entry on the first page sheds light on the political currents of the time, currents that would roil the waters of the Middle East for generations:

> National Status:
> Palestinian Citizen by Naturalization. son/
> daughter of a Palestinian Citizen by
> Naturalization under Article five of the
> Palestinian Citizenship Order 1925.
> cit. cert. No 1822B of 10.1.28

Technically, she was a citizen of no country. Palestine was a mandate and, as such, had no authority to issue its own passports. Great Britain would certainly not have allowed this twenty-year-old Palestinian Jewish woman to claim British citizenship; indeed, her passport does not even give her the right to step onto English soil. Had they known of her affiliation with the Haganah, they might have arrested her instead.

Her passport is a sad geopolitical irony. A citizen of no country, she is probably one of the few people on earth—and a Jew no less—to possess a Palestinian passport, a worthless document arising from a series of legal fictions put forth by the League of Nations. Carrying this small brown passport, she was entitled to no rights or protections. My mother was traveling, in effect, as a noncitizen, belonging nowhere and having no country whose protection she could claim—except the United States of America.

CHAPTER 64

Moe was surprised at my choice.

"With all the women in New York, you had to date an import from Batei Warsaw?"

True, she was import, but her life in Jerusalem was so different that she could have been an American. The photographs themselves are testimony to our differences. Neither my family nor I have any such albums, nor did I have even a single photograph of my parents, brothers, and sisters together as a family.

But my dancing girl looked into the camera proudly and happily. There's a picture of her as a Girl Scout in uniform and one of her in a bathing suit. One was taken when she was in the Maccabee Sports Organization wearing shorts and blouse, yet another is of her in a tight, black cat costume getting ready for a Purim party. There are more photographs of her and her school girlfriends from the Evelina Rothschild School for Girls, where she learned to speak the King's English; upon graduation, she worked in the office of the British governor of Jerusalem.

On the last Sunday of November 1940, Yona and I visited her parents in Baltimore. We entered into a large kitchen, where a woman was tending two large pots.

Yona spoke in Hebrew. "Imma, we're here."

Imma turned, wiping her face with the corner of her apron. "Ah, Chaim! Yes, yes, Reizel's son! Very good, very good."

They talked in Hebrew; I glanced into the side room. A man with a skullcap sat at a long table, absorbed in a book. I took a deep breath and, with my youthful indiscretions preceding me, stepped into the room.

"*Shalom Aleichem*," I said.

Zalman Leib looked up from his book.

"I'm Chaim. You know my parents, Haskel and Reizel Linder in Batei Warsaw."

"*Aleichem shalom*," he responded.

Well, all beginnings might be difficult, and this was especially so.

Now Yona was at my side. "You disappeared so quickly from the kitchen! I wanted to introduce you to my father properly."

Zalman Leib flashed some of his notorious short temper, now tempered with a dash of irony. "Don't talk in such a manner to my neighbors' son! He's tired and thirsty from his trip. Bring him something to drink."

Zalman Leib also had a penchant for ordering everyone about.

Imma was already walking in with a tray of cake and tea.

Zalman Leib was standing now. "So, Chaim, this is my wife, my Rivka. Your Yona's mother." He tried to hug his wife, but she pushed him away.

"Leave me alone! I have too much to do in the kitchen. Come, Yona."

Zalman Leib and I sized each other up. I was that little schneke of a boy who had tried to borrow his bricks for my mother's new Passover oven (steal them, as he had put it), poured water down his nose when he slept in the sukkah, climbed his eucalyptus tree, not to mention a dozen other bits of Batei Warsaw mischief which I had visited upon him. Now I stood before him, unrepentant, his future son-in-law.

Zalman Leib, for his part, regarded me with a wary, evaluative eye. I came from an ultra-Orthodox family—the Linders were well known in Jerusalem—and perhaps, he might have thought, I disapproved of his more secular ways.

However, he had only to look at my American wardrobe and haircut to know I was quite a secular young man.

And after all, I was interested in his more modern daughter.

On the table were scattered newspapers, among them *Doar Hayom*. I commented on a headline about the United States' economy, Zalman Leib eagerly responded, and we found ourselves in a lively conversation about current events. The living room faced Asquith Street, where a trolley ran, and I took my cue from Zalman Leib and stopped talking whenever the cars clanked past. We conducted our discourse in quick bursts of conversation punctuated with long, rattling silences. We found ourselves talking about the war in Europe and the Nazi persecutions.

"Chaim," Zalman Leib said, "the world knows and does nothing. We must have our own guns and our own land, or they will kill us all."

I agreed, and he was pleased, for in Batei Warsaw many of the ultra-Orthodox did not think we needed modern weaponry or need stoop to armed combat; many insisted we must wait for the hand of God to free us from the grasp of evil. But Germany wasn't Egypt, nor was Hitler another Pharaoh.

A pretty young teenager entered, and Zalman Leib asked her if she had finished her schoolwork. She ignored the question, looked directly at me.

"I'm Pninah" (pronounced P'nee-nah).

Zalman Leib replied with two words of his own: "Number four."

Pninah is Hebrew for "pearl." I recognized her from Yona's photo albums. She was in high school and worked part-time in a beauty parlor.

We continued talking, and soon Yona's mother appeared in the doorway.

"Zalman," she said, "Yona and Chaim have made a special trip from New York to see us. Maybe they have something special to say, or ask."

Zalman Leib immediately fell silent.

"We don't have anything to ask," I replied, grateful for the lead-in, "but we did come to tell everyone that Yona and I have decided to marry."

Zalman Leib sat up, twiddling his fingers. "What! So suddenly? Getting married! But when? Where?"

"We haven't decided the time or place," I said.

Imma Rivka embraced me. "*Mit alle mein herz*" (With all my heart), she said. "Mazel tov."

Another teenage girl came in and gave me a look. "Are you the one?" Before I had a chance to respond, she walked up to me quickly and kissed me. "I love you."

"Number three," said Zalman Leib.

She was Shoshana, Yona's second younger sister.

Imma spoke to Zalman Leib. "Call the girls in for dinner!"

He opened a window. "Girls, that's enough playing! Time to come in!"

Entering, they got a scolding.

"Two big girls like you are still playing with the kittens? All day you play with the kittens! Wait until you grow up and get married, and then you'll have your own children to play with. Now, go wash up. Quick—the meal is ready."

Zalman Leib turned to me. "Six and seven."

I recognized them from Yona's albums as Miriam and Elisheva.

At last, with everyone seated, Abba served wine, which he had made himself in the basement, and we drank to life, and he recited the blessing over the bread.

My nervousness fed my hunger, and I ate with appetite. Watching me, and thinking perhaps of the days of near starvation in Jerusalem during the war, Abba urged me on to ever greater feats of indulgence with a running commentary on the tastiness of his Rivka's cooking, particularly her soup, which he pronounced in the Yiddish: *zoop*.

"Good zoop, Chaim. Very good zoop! Imma, give Yona's Chaim more zoop."

In the middle of our meal, a smiling teenage boy came in, and Abba introduced his son.

"This is Avraham."

Imma corrected him quickly. "Avraham Chaim."

"Number five," said Zalman Leib. "Imma, give Avraham some of your good zoop."

When the meal was over, Shoshana, Number Three, stood.

"Where are you going, my dear lady?" Zalman Leib asked.

"Where I always go—to exercise. I have to spread the food around inside my body."

"Why are you the only one who has to always spread the food around inside?"

"Because it's healthier."

"Whatever you do, don't stand on your head."

"But it's healthy, Abba."

"How many times do I have to tell you not to stand on your head after a big meal? The food has to go to all parts of you, from your stomach to your hands and feet and then up into your head. When you stand upside down, the food will roll down into your eyes and mouth and nose, and it won't be healthy."

"I know," said Shoshana, but needless to say, when I looked a minute later, Number Three was upside down in the living room in the corner, her head on the floor and her legs straight up, heels touching the wall.

Zalman Leib then spoke about another daughter.

"My beautiful daughter Miriam is a student of the French language. You see, Chaim," he said, singling me out as the only person at the table who might possibly agree with him, "I know of three beautiful languages: Hebrew, Yiddish, and English. I myself love to write Hebrew. My Rivka, your Yona's mother, is not that good in Hebrew, which we know is a difficult language to learn. But she's very good in English, better than me. Go ahead and talk to her in English; you'll see how much she knows. Those three languages are more than enough for anyone. My beautiful daughter Miriam also knows those three languages, so why should she learn a fourth? Now, French is a difficult language, so there must be a reason she wants to learn it. Maybe she wants to share secrets in French, because in French, everything sounds like a secret. But, Chaim, this is my question: Because no one else knows French, to whom will she reveal her secrets?"

*

Monday morning, I sat in the quiet of my shop and wrote to my mother. In due time, I received a reply expressing my family's joy that I was marrying a young woman, a former neighbor in Batei Warsaw, whose family was known to them for three generations.

"My dearest son Chaim," my mother had someone write, "at last you will be happy."

I thought how in November of 1929, I had left my home in Jerusalem and come to New York, a young man, a stranger in a strange land. Eleven years later, in November of 1940, I would start my own family in that land, no longer strange.

Home was a magic word to me; for many years, I'd been living in furnished rooms and eating in cafeterias and other people's kitchens. Now I would have a home of my own, and a wife to share it with.

And, if we were blessed, we would fill it with our children.

*

Yona was away for a week; every day I received a letter of eight or more pages. Her letters were like her picture albums, overflowing with images of her childhood and youth in Jerusalem.

I had once thought Batei Warsaw was where the unlocked doors and open windows were symbolic of our community's openness, a place without secrets. But after reading Yona's long letters, I saw that Batei Warsaw had many.

Though her parents were not wealthy—in fact, quite the contrary—Yona had attended one of the most expensive girls' schools in Jerusalem, the Evelina Rothschild School for Girls. There, classes were taught in English and Hebrew, a dangerous, secular approach. Even more scandalous, the school had extensive sports facilities. "I loved the sports," Yona wrote, "especially track and field."

When Zalman Leib went to America on the *Alesia*, one of the first things he sent back was a Kodak box camera and film. Such things, besides their prohibitive expense, were viewed as intrusions of a vain modernity.

"I love to photograph everything and love to be photographed by others."

She told me how her father had returned from the United States with special, American gifts for her, such as face powders and lipsticks and costume jewelry, luxuries that she had seen in the Jerusalem markets but could not afford.

She had joined the Girl Scouts and went on long three-day hikes into the hills of Jerusalem and even farther, into the Jordan Valley. When she was older, she joined the Maccabee Sports Organization. "I won medals for running and high jumping. In 1934, I could have gone to London to compete, but we didn't have the money. And even if we had, I was only seventeen. Anyway, I didn't have any professional coaches, and I wouldn't have won."

After high school, her English was so good that she worked in the British central government in Jerusalem as a clerk. Her income was three pounds sterling a month. "My father didn't make enough money in America to support us, and I gave everything to my mother. It was the right thing to do. But I resented it, just as I resented being the oldest. I always had to help in the house and take care of my younger sisters. It wasn't fair. My childhood was spent being a second mother."

Later, still working for the British government, she secretly joined the Haganah.

"I learned how to shoot a small gun and how to drive a motorcycle. But it was dangerous. Once, when I was riding a motorcycle downhill at full speed, I hit a bump, the motorcycle kicked up, and I fell off—luckily, I wasn't injured, just a few cuts and bruises."

She soon discovered movies and fell in love with them. My family regarded these activities as ancient Roman iniquities. She and her friends went to the movies twice or even three times a week: "All movies came from America, and my favorites were musicals. My friends and I had a special way of remembering the songs. I had the best sense of melody, so I was assigned to memorize the tune, and my girlfriends would remember the words, and when we got outside, we'd put them both together."

In that same letter, she wrote:

> You are the only one to whom I can tell this. After seeing so many movies, I had a fantasy—don't laugh at me—that I would go to America with Abba and somehow find my way to Hollywood and become a movie star. I could sing and dance well enough—you've seen me dance, but you don't know how well I can sing—and with the right makeup and hairstyling, I could be in pictures. And then my father wouldn't have to work so hard all the time doing so many different jobs, because I would have enough money for all of us.

My father has to struggle to feed us. After he returned to Jerusalem, he had to go back to America again, but this time, he stayed only two years, because he missed his family and Jerusalem so much. When he came home, he said he would never leave Ha Eretz again. But then he had to go back to the United States once again because conditions were so bad, and we didn't have any money. When he left Jerusalem for the third time, I went with him. Our plan was that I would work in the United States, and with our combined income, we would bring the rest of our family to America. I was very excited. America! I'd be able to buy beautiful things for myself and maybe even go to Hollywood.

We sailed on a big ocean liner for three weeks, stopping in Italy and France before crossing the Atlantic. In New York, we stayed in the house of my aunt Eva, my mother's youngest sister. They got me a job in an office that collected funds for a charity in Jerusalem. The pay was very low. My father didn't like the traveling and couldn't make that much money anyway. Instead, he looked for a position as a sexton in an Orthodox synagogue in New York.

I quit my job, and for three weeks, I was my father's secretary. As you saw for yourself, he can speak English, but it isn't the best. But he doesn't know how to write or read English, so I became his correspondence secretary. But there weren't any sexton positions in New York, and we traveled together to other cities in search of a job. Finally, we found an Orthodox synagogue in Baltimore that hired him. Once he had a job and a house to live in, I looked for work and took whatever I could get. Finally, we were making enough, and I helped him get the documents that brought Imma and my sisters and brother to the United States. I had very little free time to dream about a movie career in Hollywood.

The congregation paid Abba fifteen dollars a week, not enough to feed our family and buy clothing. Just the buses cost us three dollars a week. But we had a big house that was rent-free. We didn't need all the bedrooms and bathrooms, so my mother boarded collectors from Jerusalem and made extra money that way.

I was very happy that my father didn't have to work as a collector anymore. He never liked knocking on doors in strange cities and staying in the houses of people he didn't know. Abba was always such a hard worker. In Jerusalem, he picked oranges in the groves, worked in a flourmill and matzo bakeries, and worked as a mason and bricklayer. He always came home very tired, but of course our house was tiny and crowded, and so he never got enough sleep, and was very irritable.

Now his life is much easier. He has time to take a nap during the day. He likes to read his Hebrew and Yiddish newspapers and then write long letters—you can see where I get my inspiration—to his father and other relatives in Jerusalem. He's so afraid he will not see them again before they die, but he has to stay in America and work. He dreams of the day he'll return to Jerusalem forever.

Yona, on the far right, her Five Sisters, and her Brother, and Mother

Zalman Leib Levy

Rivka Levy

I read Yona's long letters at night in my furnished room, tired, like her father, from my long day's work. I left the letters open on my bedside table, and slept better.

They were our paper bridge.

One long letter told the story of her childhood in Jerusalem.

> You see, I was born with two "faults." I was the first child, and I was a girl.
>
> I had many aunts and uncles, and their children were mainly girls, so another girl was not much of a prize. And after I was born, Imma had three more girls very quickly, so I became a servant and did a lot of the housework. Until I was fourteen, my mother was either pregnant or nursing. When I was eight, I was already washing our stone floors. Barefoot in winter and summer, I mopped and dried the floors in our apartment.

I never was sick, which was good, but it meant that I never could lie in bed and sleep.

Our apartment in Batei Warsaw had three rooms, as you know, because they were the same rooms you had. Besides my parents and the seven of us, we also had two boarders for a few years, my aunt and uncle. We slept all over the house, each of us grabbing a corner and a blanket. We never had any privacy. But we were all healthy and strong, maybe because we kept the house very clean.

I loved school because for five or six hours, I didn't have to clean our house or take care of my younger sisters. I had friends my own age, and I could sit and read, run and play, and be a child.

I always knew, even when I was very young, that Imma and Abba gave up a lot so that they could send me to a private school. My parents were very poor, and my father had to go to America for us. But they paid my tuition every month. They had to, because the Rothschild School for Girls was very strict about their money.

I knew the courage it took to send Yona to private, secular schools. Batei Warsaw was surrounded with a wall of tradition, and deviations would be grounds for evicting tenants from their rent-free apartments. There were many rules, and each rule had sub-rules, all subject to interpretation and modification.

Indeed, for a number of years, my mother presided over a special morals committee, a semi official group that heard cases and levied punishment against women in Batei Warsaw accused of improper behavior. She might have talked a hard line, but in practice, my mother proved the liberal member of the committee. Interested in adult doings, I hung about quietly and listened to the proceedings in our house. Once, a young woman named Sara was accused of hiding her long blonde hair beneath a kerchief. Sara had a poor husband and four children and lived in a basement apartment in Batei Warsaw. She had been summoned to our house to stand before the morals committee. Sara stood before my mother and two other women. My mother asked her to remove her kerchief and unpin her hair. From my hiding place in the yard, I could see her thick blonde curls fall to her shoulders. This was the first time I had seen a married woman with such beautiful hair. I was amazed by its yellow glow. Sara made no excuses. One of the women took out scissors and wanted to cut Sara's hair right there, but my mother objected and asked the young woman to leave the room.

"Look how small and thin she is," my mother said. "The smallest wind will blow her away. She and her family are very poor and have no pleasures in their life. And in her dark basement, her hair gives a little extra light. It's the only charm she has, and if she has to cut it off, her face will look like a frog. Let her keep her hair and her husband."

The woman put away her scissors, and Sara was sent home unshorn.

*

In December of that year, we picked a date for our wedding; we chose Yona's birthday, February 14, only two months away. For financial reasons, we planned a small, informal wedding. In another financially motivated decision, we decided to rent an apartment in the Brownsville section of Brooklyn, near my typesetting shop.

Time was short, and much had to be done. Yona quit her job and went to Baltimore for two weeks to use her mother's sewing machine.

Finding a place to live was not at all difficult. Brooklyn, and all of New York, had an abundance of vacant apartments. The Depression kept economic activity down, and not many people could afford even the modest rents, so everyone was living with families and friends, much like my childhood in Batei Warsaw. We rented an apartment at 347 Saratoga Avenue, between St. Mark's Avenue and Bergen Street. The building had three stories, with two apartments to a floor. Reuben Kaslow, the landlord, ran a kosher butcher shop on the ground floor, and he and his wife lived in a small apartment in the rear.

Our apartment was on the top floor and had four small rooms. It was a railroad flat, with one room opening directly into the other. One entered into the kitchen—that way, one always knew immediately what supper was going to be. The kitchen had a small gas range, a narrow cast-iron sink on legs, and a small, old icebox. Electric refrigerators, rare and expensive appliances, often blew the fuses. The small private bathroom was off the kitchen. Behind the kitchen was a small room that we designated our living room. In back of that was the second bedroom. Yona called it the children's room.

The rearmost room, the smallest, looked out over the backyards and clotheslines; we claimed it as our bedroom.

The rent was eighteen dollars a month, and wanting to clinch the deal, Mr. Kaslow agreed to paint the apartment at his own expense.

Yona put up shades and curtains, decorated the rooms with pictures, and brought in plants. It was a month before our wedding, and we had no furniture of any kind, nor could we afford any. I was worried; the print shop wasn't enough, and Yona was looking for work.

One evening, standing in our empty apartment, Yona was smiling happily.

"Chaim, I have a secret, but I'm not supposed to tell you."

"I can wait, but if it's good news, let me enjoy it now."

"Abba and Imma promised to give us bedroom and kitchen furniture for a wedding present. But they want it to be a surprise."

It was indeed a wonderful surprise; now our home would be ready in time for our marriage.

One of Yona's friends knew a furniture salesman in Brooklyn.

"You'll get a bargain there," she promised.

"Ah, the newlyweds," said the salesman when the three of us walked in. "I'm going to personally give you the honeymoon special."

The friend beamed.

"I'm going to take twenty-five percent off, and throw in free delivery."

"We live on the top floor," I warned him.

"Free is free, Mr. Linder."

Knowing Zalman Leib's finances, I suggested furniture that was plain and sturdy.

"We don't need anything fancy," agreed Yona. "Children should be free to play in the house, and we don't want to worry about them breaking things."

Including free delivery to our fourth-floor apartment, we paid $207.20.

Three days later, the furniture arrived. I was elated. In the apartment, I walked from room to room. The sunlight lit our new furniture, lifting the cloud hanging over me. I could not have begun our married life in an empty house. It would have been too much like the barren, impoverished days of my youth, and I wanted my new life in America to be different.

*

We were married on Saturday night, February 14, 1941, Yona's twenty-fourth birthday. The ceremony took place in the Brooklyn home of family friends, our neighbors in Batei Warsaw. We signed the marriage contract according to Jewish law, and then a rabbi performed the ceremony beneath a chuppah, the canopy under which the bride and groom stand.

The rabbi recited the blessings and read from the Song of Songs:

> Set me as a seal upon thy heart,
> As a seal upon thy arm.
> For love is stronger than death.
> Many waters cannot quench love,
> Neither can the floods drown it.
> And thy love is better than wine.

Yona walked around me seven times, we drank the sacramental wine from the same goblet, and then I smashed the glass with a hard stamp of my foot.

She lifted her veil, and we kissed.

We were married.

Our guests sat at three long tables that ran the length of the narrow railroad flat. Imma had cooked a traditional holiday meal, and Zalman

Leib exhorted everyone to have seconds of her good zoop. At midnight, we pushed aside the tables and chairs and, clapping and singing, danced and danced.

At last, the guests gone, Abba Zalman Leib stood before us.

"So where are you two going now?"

"We're going home," I said. "To Saratoga Avenue."

"Who is taking you?"

"We're going by ourselves."

Impatient, Zalman Leib shot back, "How?"

"We'll decide when we get outside. We may walk or take a trolley."

"How can you walk on a cold night like this?" He pulled out his pocket watch. "Look at the time! It's one thirty in the morning!"

Yona spoke. "As Chaim told you, Abba, we're going to walk home. It should take about an hour. If it's too cold, we'll take a trolley. Chaim likes to ride the Ralph Avenue trolley, and that'll take us two blocks from Saratoga Avenue."

"And you agree to all this?"

"Of course. I like to walk too."

"Both of you are crazy!" He thrust his hands into his pockets, but he was wearing his Sabbath clothing and found no money. "Rivka!" He looked around. "Where's my Rivka?"

She was in the kitchen.

"Rivka! Give me five dollars!"

"Zalman Leib, why do you need five dollars?"

"You see, again, how she asks unnecessary questions! I want five dollars!"

Imma Rivka found a five in her purse, gave it to Abba Zalman Leib, who gave it to Yona.

"Both of you, no crazy walks and no happy trolley rides on Ralph Avenue. Take a taxi!"

It was a cold winter night, and Yona and I set out at a brisk pace through the empty streets. We were underdressed, and we found an all-night cafeteria and had hot coffee. Fortified, we stepped out into the cold and hurried down Broadway, only to dash into another cafeteria on Marcy Avenue for hot tea.

It was now two thirty in the morning.

At the counter, three taxi drivers were eating an early breakfast; one of them kept glancing our way, suspecting he might have a fare. His suspicion proved correct. I looked at Yona shivering and sipping tea. Zalman Leib had been right. This was crazy. I caught the cabbie's eye, and we were soon at our front door. The fare was $1.25, and having learned a lesson from Moe about tipping, I gave the cabbie a dollar extra. After all, it was Zalman Leib's gift, and it was a mitzvah to share one's wealth, especially in those hard times.

Holding hands, we walked up to our new home and our new life.

*

I woke at eight in the morning.

The radiators were hissing, and there was frost on the windows.

Yona was sleeping.

Outside, the sun was bright, and the wind was brisk. The Kaslow butcher store was open, and Mrs. Kaslow was on a chair, plucking a chicken. Outside, on St. Mark's Avenue, I ran into Mr. Kaslow returning from morning services at the local synagogue. He stopped.

"Young man, just where are you running to so early in the morning?" Before I had a chance to reply, he looked me up and down. "And where is your coat in this cold?"

"I'm going out to find something for breakfast."

He looked me up and down again and, deciding I was telling the truth, smiled. "Of course, one has to eat. And mazel tov!"

I hurried across the street. Racing about early in the morning without my coat, I must have given the impression of a man in desperate flight from his new wife, or perhaps he thought I was trying to skip out without paying rent.

I was on vacation, and we spent the week visiting our friends and relatives, eating in restaurants, and seeing movies in Times Square and plays on Second Avenue, known as the Yiddish Broadway.

A week later, Sunday, our honeymoon was over. I returned to the shop. It was midwinter, a busy time for the printing trade, and I was soon working ten-hour days to catch up on our backlog of composition work.

Yona returned to her job in Manhattan and soon was working six-hour days, five days a week.

Our life had a pleasant routine, and soon the snow and cold winds of winter gave way to a warm spring. In the backyard, the trees outside our bedroom were full of white blossoms, and when we opened the windows, their perfume blew through the house.

Yona's parents were letter writers, and we received weekly missives from Baltimore; Imma Rivka wrote only in Yiddish, while Abba, wanting to keep his language skills sharp, rotated through his three languages every week. Clearly, English gave him difficulty, but I was a typesetter, and knew how to get to his meaning. This was before the telephone was as common as it is now, and letters were the only way we communicated. They were tangibles, and Yona and I took turns reading them out loud.

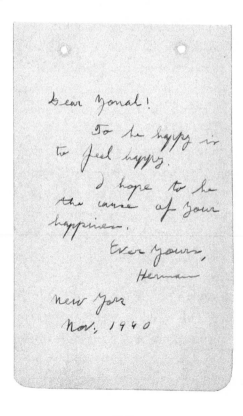

In the Adirondacks, New York

Yona in Flight School

P. F. No. 51.

CERTIFICATE OF SERVICE.

Name of Officer	Miss Yonah Levy
Position held and Department	Unclassified Typist (LP.6.000 per month)
	Department of Public Works
Period of Service — Date of commencement of engagement	15th March, 1936
Date of termination of service	18th July, 1937.
Cause of termination of engagement	Resignation.
Efficiency	Good.
General Conduct	Very good.

Fawcett Pudsey.

DIRECTOR OF PUBLIC WORKS.
Head of Department.

Date 19th July, 1937.

NOTE.—The date here given is that of the last day on which the Officer performed the duties of his post in the country. Any leave granted is not included in the period above.

D5.

N

Form 340 Rev. 6-1-39

PASSENGER CARRYING PROHIBITED

UNITED STATES OF AMERICA
CIVIL AERONAUTICS AUTHORITY
WASHINGTON, D. C.

THIS CERTIFICATE MUST BE CARRIED AT ALL TIMES WHILE PILOTING AIRCRAFT

This certifies that **STUDENT PILOT CERTIFICATE NO. S 106056**

YONA LEVY

(First Name)   (Middle)   (Surname)

is properly qualified and is physically able to perform the duties of a Student Pilot.

Address 611 AISQUITH STREET

BALTIMORE MARYLAND

WEIGHT	HEIGHT	DATE OF BIRTH	HAIR	EYES
140	5'4"	2-14-17	BROWN	HAZEL

DURATION

This certificate is of 60 days' duration and, unless the holder hereof is otherwise notified by the Authority within such period, shall continue in effect indefinitely thereafter, unless suspended or revoked by the Authority, except that it shall immediately expire (1) at the end of each 12 months period after the date of issuance hereof if the holder of this certificate fails to secure an endorsement by an authorized Medical Examiner or Inspector of the Authority within the last 45 days of each such period, or (2) at any time an authorized Inspector or Medical Examiner of the Authority shall refuse to endorse this certificate after inspection or examination.

The holder hereof is now physically qualified for no higher grade of pilot certificate than that of COMMERCIAL - CPT

Date of Issuance: OCTOBER 26 1939

By direction of the Authority: *C. Eldredge Acksony*

Medical Examiner of the Authority

CERTIFICATE ENDORSEMENTS
OR REFUSALS TO ENDORSE

MEDICAL EXAMINER'S OR INSPECTOR'S SIGNATURE	Physically Qualified	DATE

LIMITATIONS

Yona Levy

Signature of Student Pilot

Any alteration of this certificate is punishable by a fine of not exceeding $1,000 or imprisonment not exceeding three years, or both.   (over)

598

THE UNITED STATES OF AMERICA

ORIGINAL
TO BE GIVEN TO
THE PERSON NATURALIZED

CERTIFICATE OF NATURALIZATION

No. 4765209

Petition No. 342836

Personal description of holder as of date of naturalization: Age 29 *years; sex* male *color* white *complexion* medium *color of eyes* brown *color of hair* dkbrown *height* 5 *feet* 10 *inches; weight* 135 *pounds; visible distinctive marks* none

Marital status not married *former nationality* Palestine-Gt Britain

I certify that the description above given is true, and that the photograph affixed hereto is a likeness of me.

Herman Linder
(Complete and true signature of holder)

UNITED STATES OF AMERICA } *ss:*
SOUTHERN DISTRICT OF NEW YORK

Be it known that Herman Linder *then residing at* 714 9th St, New York, NY *having petitioned to be admitted a citizen of the United States of America, and at a term of the* District *Court of* The United States *held pursuant to law at* New York City *on* May 6, 1940 *the court having found that the petitioner intends to reside permanently in the United States, had in all respects complied with the Naturalization Laws of the United States in such case applicable, and was entitled to be so admitted, the court thereupon ordered that the petitioner be admitted as a citizen of the United States of America.*

In testimony whereof the seal of the court is hereunto affixed this 6th *day of* May *in the year of our Lord nineteen hundred and* 40 *and of our Independence the one hundred and* 64th

(SECURELY AND PERMANENTLY
EDGE OF THE PHOTOGRAPH)

Herman Linder

Seal

George J. H. Follmer
Clerk of the U. S. District *Court.*
By _____ *Deputy Clerk.*

DEPARTMENT OF LABOR

Series 1940–41

G. R.

The University of the State of New York

THE STATE EDUCATION DEPARTMENT

DUPLICATE Nº 184122

Be it Known that Herman Linder residing
(To be filled in by applicant in ink)
at 1755 St Johns Place having met the requirements
prescribed in Section 166 of the Election Law, and rules and regulations of the Regents of the State of New York, and having made the signature appearing above in the presence of the examiner, is herewith granted a CERTIFICATE OF LITERACY

Lillian V. Hedinger
Signature of examiner

Given at P. S. 144 Borough of Brooklyn
New York, N. Y.

this 10 day of October 1940

Harold G. Campbell
Superintendent of Schools

Principal _____ Teacher ✓
Position of examiner (Check one)

Ernest E. Cole
Commissioner of Education

NOTICE TO ELECTION INSPECTORS. This Duplicate Certificate of Literacy is not valid for registration. It is to be kept by the applicant as evidence of having fulfilled the literacy requirement for new voters.

Chaim, 1939

CHAPTER 65

In May of that year, 1941, Yona told me we were going to have a child.

"At the end of March, I thought I might be, but now I know I'm definitely pregnant."

We had not talked about children; both of us had assumed we would begin a family immediately. By Batei Warsaw standards, we were long overdue.

We prepared the small room, buying more furniture and linens. Then, at the end of September, Yona was fired from her job in the sweater factory.

The supervisor of the shipping department brought her into his office. "Mrs. Linder," he told her, "I've tolerated your condition long enough, but no more."

"What do you mean? What condition?"

"Look at you. You're sticking out like half a giant ball. It's not decent for the other girls in the shop."

"I'm legally married, and it's not illegal to be pregnant."

"Decent women don't show they're pregnant, especially in the presence of young unmarried girls."

She was furious, but there was nothing to be done. Her ten dollars a week was a big part of our income—I was drawing twenty to thirty dollars a week from our business—and we had to economize even further. We had been saving five dollars a week, but we reduced that to three. We also cut our food budget by another three dollars. Mrs. Kaslow wanted to know why we were eating less meat, and Yona made up a story that too much protein wasn't good for the baby. Of course, Mrs. Kaslow didn't believe that. Who had ever heard of too much meat?

CHAPTER 66

In early December of that year, 1941, one of my childhood friends came to New York. Baruch Weinstock, now calling himself Ben, and I had known each other since we were children. It was with Baruch that I had tried to steal the telephone wires from the British, though Baruch, stronger and faster, had been more successful.

Ben and his wife arrived on Thursday, planning to stay through Monday. It was good to see him again, and despite the cold of early December, we went for long walks on Eastern Parkway and up to Prospect Park. The lake was frozen over, and we took some old bread to feed the hungry ducks that waddled toward us over the ice. "What a life," I said to Ben, watching the ducks gobble down the chunks of dry challah. "I wish I had people bringing food to me."

That Sunday morning, a few friends, fellow immigrants, joined us, and we sat in the living room and talked of many things, including the bad economic times, the terrible war in Europe, Hitler, and Mussolini. We spoke also of happier times, of our childhoods in Jerusalem and the bright futures we expected in America. In the kitchen, preparing breakfast, Yona was listening to the radio; Ben and his wife were concerned about a snowstorm that was going to hit the city later that day, and Yona wanted to get the forecast.

Suddenly, Yona was in the living room.

"Be quiet, everyone! Listen!"

The radio blared from the kitchen.

"We repeat this breaking news: Japan has attacked Pearl Harbor! We repeat this breaking news: Japan has attacked Pearl Harbor!"

We stood.

"We repeat this breaking news: Japan has attacked Pearl Harbor!"

No one said anything.

The radio kept repeating the same words.

I looked at Ben. He was pale. When he looked at me, he shook his head and said nothing.

All of Europe was in flames, and now Japan had attacked us. Everywhere, the forces of evil were on the march. Should the Nazis ever reach Jerusalem, my family would be annihilated. Now even America was threatened.

Ben and his wife quickly packed.

"Chaim, we really have to get back," he said.

Our other guests were putting on their outerwear.

The radio kept repeating itself.

For the second time in my life, I stood before the dark abyss of a world war.

The pain of those terrible years in Jerusalem flooded through me— the hunger, lice, filth, disease, and executions in public squares, darkness, cold, and fear.

We were at war.

Chapter 67

Saturday evening, February 28, 1942, Yona came out of our little bathroom. I was in the kitchen, reading the *New York Times*.

"Chaim, I think—no, I'm sure."

"I'll call a taxi." I was heading for the door to use the Kaslow's telephone..

"Don't call a taxi. We can walk to the hospital."

She sat on a chair, closed her eyes, put her hand on her stomach, and was silent for a moment.

"Are you sure?" I asked.

"In the closet in the children's room, on the right side in the corner, is a small valise. Bring it to me."

*

In twenty minutes, we were at the Brooklyn Women's Jewish Hospital on Eastern Parkway. Valise in had, Yona followed a nurse through a door. An hour later, a hospital physician—we didn't have our own doctor—came out.

"Mr. Linder, it's going to be awhile. I suggest you go home."

"Is she going to be all right?"

"She'll be fine, but it'll take awhile."

"What time should I come back?"

"Not before tomorrow morning. Try eight o'clock, though I think it'll be longer."

In our apartment, I tried to read the paper but was unable to concentrate. I went into the baby's room, thinking I should get it ready, but it already was ready. The morning was too far away. I was cut off from Yona. I was very tense. It was different in Batei Warsaw, where women gave birth in their homes, and the midwife was a neighbor. People rushed in and out of the birthing room, and nothing was hidden. Here, Yona had disappeared through two swinging doors, and I had been sent home until the morning. I walked from room to room. Everything was quiet and still. I stood in the middle room, our child's room. Yona had painted it and hung pictures on the walls. I stood in the dark. How quiet it was. I went into the kitchen and looked at the front page of the *Times*. Armies were marching across the earth, and hell rained from the skies. What kind of world was our child going to be born into? I finally lay down in the bedroom, but did not sleep.

I arrived at the hospital at six o'clock in the morning.

A nurse greeted me.

"Mrs. Linder gave birth to a baby boy a half hour earlier, and your wife and son are doing well. Congratulations."

The birth was without complications, and Yona stayed in the hospital for nine days, as was customary. Today things are much different; one of my grandchildren, Samuel, for instance, was born in a birthing center in Upper Manhattan and was home the afternoon of the same day.

The following Sunday, when our son was eight days old, Imma and Abba came from Baltimore for his Brit Milah, the ceremonial circumcision. The event was held in the hospital in one of the large conference rooms and was attended by 150 guests.

We named our son Haskel Simcha after my dear father and my cousin Simcha, who had died recently.

On his birth certificate, our child was officially registered as Charles; we call him Chuck.

His first week home, Chuck lived in a dresser drawer, wrapped warmly in a blanket. Then my brother Moe arrived, carrying a crib.

"This is America," my brother reminded me. "We don't sleep on the floor, on tables, or in boxes."

How tiny our son looked on his ocean of mattress.

We were deluged with gifts; the war, however, had created shortages of certain goods and materials, so Chuck received no toys made of metal or plastic. Cotton, however, was in abundant supply, and our son was soon in possession of an extensive wardrobe of children's clothing.

CHAPTER 68

The war was fought two oceans away, but its effects on us were immediate and severe.

The streets were empty; the men were gone. The draft worked by a lottery system; those with low numbers were called up immediately, and the higher numbers were called later. My number was very high, and I was never called. Had I been, I would not have passed an induction physical. My eyesight was poor, and with every eye examination, I required new glasses. My hearing too was slowly getting worse, and my general health, due to the poor nutrition of my childhood, the endless hours I was putting in at our printing shop, and our need to reduce our food budget, was not the best.

America was still a land of plenty, comparatively speaking, but after Pearl Harbor and Roosevelt's declaration of war against Japan and the Nazis, a national rationing system was put into place, and suddenly, many basic food items were hard to get.

Overnight, meat products were strictly rationed.

Mr. Kaslow observed the rules of rationing as strictly as he observed the Sabbath, shaking his finger at any customer who tried to bribe or charm him.

"Show me the coupon or you get no chicken!"

Citing health needs, unexpected supper guests, and aged parents, people tried to squeeze out an extra hamburger or chicken wing, but Mr. Kaslow was not moved.

"No favors, please! This is a war against Satan! We must defeat the Nazi beasts!"

And the beast was at our door. Fear and anxiety abounded. In the early dark years, the Nazis were invincible. The Yiddish papers were full of horrors. The headlines of the *Times* screamed of blitzkrieg and of Allied losses all over Europe. Rommel was threatening Egypt, and no one had any illusions about Nazi designs on the Jewish population of Palestine. I read the newspapers and listened to the radio news with great anxiety, and disgust. Yona refused to read the newspapers and tuned the radio to a music station when the news came on.

The Germans were so mighty and full of evil purpose that we feared for our lives. Government officials assured us that the Nazis did not have the air power to reach America's shores, but we suspected they did. The nightly blackouts of New York only heightened our anxieties. The Germans had U-boats that could cross the Atlantic, and the Japanese might send their carriers to attack us again.

At night, I stood over our baby son sleeping in his crib, determined to protect him with my very body should the bombs fall.

A great patriotic wave swept the land. Those who had preached isolation were now silent. Parades were held in all cities, people were encouraged to donate clothing and plant war gardens. Defense bonds were sold in installments using twenty-five-cent coupons. Yona and I bought them for our son, and his future.

Yona had not lived through the starvation and misery of the First World War and did her best to reduce my anxiety, and gradually, as America's tremendous might began to take effect, I realized that my worst fears would not materialize. We would not starve or even go hungry; disease and filth would not engulf us; there would be no public hangings; and because this was America, there would be no pogroms.

And at last, we were turning the economic tide. The Great Depression was lifting. As the United States prepared to defeat the Japanese and the Nazis, industry came alive, and more and more people were finding work and earning more than ever before.

So despite the news of German victories and Japanese advances in the Pacific and despite the published lists of American dead and the news of battles lost, my spirits gradually lifted. There were going to be dark days ahead, but our little family would be safe. America was gathering will and purpose, building a war machine that would destroy Hitler and free the world.

*

With the birth of our son, my brother telephoned every day, leaving a message with Mrs. Kaslow in the butcher shop, and visited us every Sunday. Coming through the door with his camera, he immediately got down on the floor to take pictures of Chuck, getting him to smile and laugh by making faces and dangling a colorful toy in front of him.

One Sunday, after taking a few photographs, he put his equipment away and said he wanted to talk.

"I'm going to enlist."

I was surprised. Moe had a flourishing business and was leading a good, prosperous American life.

That was precisely his point.

"I'm an American citizen now. Why should I wait until I'm drafted? And even if there weren't a draft, would I stay here in New York while the Nazis destroy Europe? Do you read what's going on?"

"I read the papers and listen to the radio. I know what's happening."

"Hitler is exterminating the Jewish people." His voice broke. "He must be stopped."

He volunteered the next day, sold his Graff Photo Studio the next week, and gave his landlord notice that he would vacate by the end of the month. I helped him pack. He gave me his books and a few other valuables; handed me a box of his shirts, which were too big for me but which he wanted me to have anyway; and then, in a special presentation, offered me his ties.

"Herman, don't wear that tie with the red dots anymore."

"The politics of family life," I explained, "require that my father-in-law's tie be seen around my neck with appropriate frequency."

"All right," Moe said, "but not in public."

The night before he left for the army, a cold winter night, Moe was more at ease than I had ever seen him; for the first time in his life, he had no decisions to make or actions to take. His fate was in the hands of others. He embraced Yona and picked up our son and held him tightly.

"I'll see everyone again, when peace is on the face of the earth." He gave our little boy back to Yona. "I don't know when that will be, but I will come home then."

The city was in deep blackout, and the streets were dark and empty as we walked to the subway on Fulton Street.

"I don't want to be a hero," Moe said. "Some of my friends asked me, 'What are you trying to prove? That you're not afraid?' Chaim, truthfully, I am not afraid of war."

Arm in arm, we walked through the cold night.

"Funny, I'm afraid of the little things. I looked at a map yesterday, and I was thinking that tomorrow I could be sent anywhere in the United States. And after training, where? In Jerusalem, I was in hiding for almost a year, running away from the goddamn Turks. I remember thinking that I wouldn't fight to save the Ottoman Empire. Some of my friends remind me of that and ask me why I'm fighting now. They don't see the difference. I'm not a pacifist."

I knew that; neither was I. Sometimes not fighting is just as immoral as killing.

We embraced at the entrance of the Fulton Street subway station.

"Shalom, Chaim," he said, using my Hebrew name for the first time in years.

"Moshe, be safe."

I watched him walk down into the darkness of the station, the beginning of a long, unknown and dangerous voyage.

I returned through the black winter night to my wife and child. I was shivering with the cold, for as usual, I hadn't bothered to put on my overcoat.

*

We didn't hear from Moe for two months, and then a postcard arrived. It was two lines: "All is well. I will soon be shipped overseas." There was no return address, only a code of numbers and letters to which we should address our letters.

I wrote back immediately. Two more months went by, and then his next letter arrived. It was heavily censored, but I learned that he was with an army airborne unit in New Guinea, had the rank of staff sergeant, and was an aerial photographer.

I went to the library and looked in an atlas. New Guinea was far away.

Then the letters arrived with greater frequency. They contained photographs of the New Guinea natives, women with bare breasts and naked men with spears, bows, and arrows. He wrote little about the war itself, and whatever he did write was blacked out. He did write, however, about the horrible conditions and unbearable climate.

"This is worse than Jerusalem in the first war. At least we had some cool and dry weather. But here, insects and snakes are everywhere, and they crawl, bite, and sting. The food is full of bugs, and the heat and humidity drive you crazy. The Japanese are vicious."

My dear brother Moshe, I thought, *look at you now. The son of Hasidic parents in Jerusalem, themselves immigrants from Poland and Russia, how you struggled to come to America. You learned photography and had your own business and nice suits and expensive ties, and now you are flying in the skies over the Pacific, photographing Japanese war ships and their island fortifications, defending our freedom while slapping at insects and living in a tent.*

After the war, the United States Defense Department awarded my brother the Bronze Star.

Chapter 69

Our son was in no hurry to grow up.

He liked being carried, and we indulged him. He'd crawl from one adult to the other, hold out his hands and smile, and would soon be picked up.

When he was fourteen months old, his grandmother Imma Rivka visited from Baltimore, and his easy life was over.

He had crawled to her, lifted his hands expectantly with a big, hopeful smile.

"Why is my grandson still crawling on all fours?"

Yona spoke. "He'll walk when he's ready, Imma. We don't want to rush him."

"At fourteen months, all my children were running already, and here my grandson is not even walking. I don't like it. You shouldn't tolerate it."

"Imma, he'll walk when he's ready."

"He won't be ready until he has to be ready."

Exasperated, Yona said, "Okay, Imma, let's see if you can teach him."

Imma picked Chuck up, and he, sensing immediately that these hands were not indulgent, began to cry, his hands reaching out to me.

"Give him to me," I insisted.

"Sha, sha, don't worry." Imma soothed me. "Leave him to me."

With Chuck wailing now, she carried him to a wall, put him on the floor, and tried to get him to stand. When she pulled her hand away, he grabbed her other hand; when she freed both hands, he grabbed her dress and then her nose. At last, Imma managed to prop him up against the wall. She backed away, and he looked up at her, frightened. She held out both hands.

"Walk!" she commanded.

Chuck, obeying his grandmother's order, with his hands flapping and his knees lifting, took a step forward. He paused, then took another step, and, suddenly smiling, took one last step before falling into Imma's arms.

By the end of her visit, he was running through the house.

Later, in June, Yona told me that we would have another child next year, in the early spring of 1944.

That year was difficult in many ways.

The austerity of war took its toll on our small typesetting plant. With so many men in military service, it was impossible to hire any help. My partner and I worked longer and longer hours, doing everything from sweeping floors to delivering finished compositions.

The Linotype, an intricate piece of machinery, needed constant repair, but there weren't any parts or any machinists to do the work, and we had to resort to hand composition to meet some of our deadlines. Lead, the metal used in casting the slugs, deemed by the military to be necessary for the war effort, was in short supply, and we found ourselves delaying one job in order to melt down the slugs from another.

The weather that winter was bitterly cold and full of snow, so walking about was difficult. I did not feel strong and soon was losing weight. Yona, six months pregnant now, was alarmed; my usual hearty appetite disappeared, and I was picking at my food.

I went to a number of doctors, who gave me all sorts of tests, but they found no specific cause for my exhaustion. One doctor, however, did prescribe a cure, suggesting that a three-month vacation someplace warm and sunny, with plenty of sleep and food, would cure me of my undiagnosed ailments.

I continued to work ten-hour days, waking in the cold, dark morning and returning home exhausted, barely able to stay awake through my half-eaten dinner.

Finally, spring arrived. It began wet and cold, but I had hopes for recovery. I looked forward to the warm sun, for it reminded me of my childhood in Jerusalem, of skies that were clean and clear and nights that were bright with stars. But on March 26, for the first time in many years, I missed a day of work. Using the Kaslows' phone, I called Joel and told him I would not be in the shop, and he, concerned, asked if I needed any help. I told him no, it was only a question of rest. Mrs.

Kaslow, listening, told me to wait a minute and brought me a small package from the butcher shop.

"Here—a little extra for you, Chaim. Eat it, and be strong."

I barely made it up the four flights to our apartment. Yona unwrapped the package; inside were two chicken breasts, and she immediately boiled them, and for the first time in a week, I was able to eat with appetite.

In the afternoon, feeling better, I went out with Yona. She carried our son downstairs and put him in the stroller. With Mrs. Kaslow watching from the window of her butcher shop, I followed, and the three of us set out on a shopping expedition.

We had walked one short block on Saratoga Avenue, when the world began spinning. I stopped, swayed, and reached for Yona.

"Chaim, what's wrong?"

Cars, people, and buildings were whirling around me.

"Chaim!"

I don't know how long I was unconscious, but Yona and some passersby helped me to my feet, and with sheer willpower and holding on to Yona, I somehow got home. Mrs. Kaslow saw us coming, and her husband ran out in his bloodstained apron and, with his powerful butcher's arm around my waist, got me upstairs.

"Can I use your phone?" Yona asked Mrs. Kaslow.

"Of course, of course."

An hour later, our family doctor arrived. With my wife and child looking on with frightened stares, Dr. Lerner took my pulse. Her eyes opened wide.

"Get dressed," she ordered. She turned to Yona. "Call the butcher."

Mr. Kaslow carried me down to the street and put me in Dr. Lerner's car.

I woke in a hospital bed. I looked about, completely disoriented. Food was placed before me, but I did not even try to eat. A nurse and doctor examined me and left.

Around me was much noise and activity, but quickly, the noises retreated to a soothing whisper. Outside, the light was fading. It was time to sleep. I closed my eyes, and soon I was weightless, floating higher and higher into endless white clouds with the faint whispering noises below. There was no pain, only a soft white peace. For the first time in so long, I was free of worry, and I floated higher and higher into the soft white clouds.

Someone was speaking to me.

"Mr. Linder, can you open your eyes?"

When I did, it was dark outside.

"I'm Dr. Greenberg. Mr. Linder, I have good news for you. Very early this morning, your wife gave birth to a boy. They're both doing very well."

The doctor was watching me closely, and I should have smiled, thanked him, and asked about my wife and new son, but I was completely indifferent to what he had just told me. I wanted to float on the soft white clouds, sleep for a long time, and be without worry. The doctor was talking again, but I did not hear him. I was able, however, to see that he was a tall, healthy-looking young man, and I thought that if I were as healthy as he, I would have gotten out of bed and left the hospital. I closed my eyes, and soon he stopped talking and left, and I let my body rise again into the cool white clouds.

There was warmth on my eyelids, warm and yellow, and on my face and hands. I was still cool, but now there was this new warmth. I stirred and opened my eyes but was blinded by morning light and immediately closed them. The warmth remained on my face and eyes even as I grew colder inside, until I was filled with it, and the warmth no longer mattered. I let myself rise into the soft whiteness, the cold spreading through me.

Now, a nurse was speaking my name, saying that she would be taking a blood count and that I would feel a little prick on my finger, which I felt but did not mind at all. I barely heard her clinking a test tube and then shouting for Dr. Goldberg, and after that, I heard nothing at all.

I was floating higher and higher, leaving everything behind, even my wife, child, and new son, and I did not care.

Chapter 70

I would have been named Chaim if my father had died, as it seemed he most likely would after collapsing on the street that day; thanks, however, to the heroic efforts of our family doctor, Mr. Kaslow the butcher, and the hospital staff who leaped into full emergency alert when the nurse took his blood count and discovered, as my father tells it, that his blood was "as thin as water," by Sunday afternoon, he had regained consciousness.

I was born in the early morning hours of March 27, 1944. I was named Mark.

My mother was still in the maternity ward, and my father's only visitor that Sunday was my grandmother Rivka, whom we called Buba. She brought a bag of home-baked soft bagels, which she promptly began feeding my father as he lay in bed, hooked up to two IVs.

"Baruch HaShem!" she exclaimed. "He eats."

From the foot of the bed, Dr. Greenberg watched my father chew and swallow. "This is almost a miracle."

"Mr. Linder," Dr. Greenberg asked, "did you know that you have pernicious anemia?"

"I was never diagnosed. But I know what anemia is."

"Pernicious anemia is a chronic severe shortage of red blood cells. If the condition isn't corrected, it can lead to death. You had a very acute episode, probably brought on by poor nutrition. You're fortunate to be alive."

Imma cried out. *"Mein Gott!"*

"It can be treated with iron supplements," Dr. Greenberg said. "You're going to be fine."

Buba wept. "Baruch HaShem," she said, holding out another piece of bagel.

At that time, pernicious anemia was thought to be the result of a lack of iron in the diet interfering with the formation of red blood cells. My father was told to eat more red meat, particularly liver, which my mother served once a week for many years, a meal my brothers and I detested. Other organ meats, lung and heart, were also rich in iron, and on occasion those perverse delicacies found their way onto our plates. Adhering as closely as possible to the Jewish dietary laws that forbid the eating of blood, my mother broiled the steer liver over an open flame on the range, reducing its moisture content to the absolute minimum and producing a flat, stiff gray-brown slab with a taste and texture akin to pressed, metallic sawdust. Fried onions would have helped, but for some reason, they did not appear.

In addition to the liver regimen, my father gave himself weekly injections of liver extract using a hypodermic syringe, which he kept in a little case in a drawer of his bedroom chest. In a few years, capsules of dried liver extract replaced the liquid injections. Later research showed that pernicious anemia not a deficiency of iron but a lack of what is called the intrinsic factor, which in turns prevents the absorption of vitamin B12, the catalyst without which the body cannot utilize the iron to produce red blood cells. Monthly injections of B12 fixed that problem.

My father possessed certain mechanical skills. Standard household tools were not his forte, and he was unhandy around the house. He never learned to drive a car—he did not even try, because, he explained, the quick decisions necessary for successful maneuver of a moving mechanism, such as a car, among other moving and stationary objects was beyond him.

However, he had specific areas of expertise where his small-motor skills were put to excellent use. He could disassemble and repair a complicated Linotype machine the size of a small bathroom. As a child, I went to his printing shop a number of times and watched him on his small swivel seat as his fingers flew over the keys, and the Linotype whirred and clacked as parts turned, slid, and dropped. Then he'd lock the slugs into a quoin and, with his thin arms, carry the heavy form to a press for a quick proof.

Once, I asked him what the "-8-" at the end of a column meant.

"It's a typographer's mark that means the article is finished."

"But not all columns have them."

"That's right, because an article goes on for many columns."

"So why don't you write 'The End'?"

"Because another word might be confusing to the typesetter. That's why we use the number eight with two dashes. There's no mistake. It means the end of the story."

After I was born, my father stayed in the hospital for two weeks, and when he finally returned home, it was, he said, wonderful to see his wife, child and new born son, and be back in his sunny, bright home.

*

I was born at a relatively auspicious time during World War II. We were three months from D-day, and the Allies were making good and steady progress. The front page of the *New York Times* for March 27, 1944, reported that the Red army was attacking the German Feldgrau with a relentless fury. Churchill proclaimed, "The hour of our greatest effort and action is approaching." Led by a ferocious bombardment by the RAF, five hundred American Flying Fortresses of the United States Eighth Army Air Force completed the destruction of Frankfurt's industrial center. They obliterated IG Farbenindustrie's chemical warfare plants. As the Nazis rushed their armored columns to the Danube, Turkey sent its divisions through Hungary and Romania to prevent a German breakout. Meanwhile, in Rome, the Nazis, furious that twenty-four Gestapo officers and fourteen Fascistas had been killed by Italian partisans, executed about a thousand citizens of Rome, immediately killed those without identity cards, and then dragged an additional three hundred unlucky souls into the Coliseum and mowed them down with machine guns.

In the Pacific, American bombers widened their attack on the Japanese Kuril Islands. My uncle Moe was stationed in New Guinea. He moved around the Pacific with his camera and special high-resolution lenses, part of the offensive.

CHAPTER 71

As I regained my strength, I decided to end my business partnership with Joel Shapiro. Our personal and professional relationship was good, and there was an abundance of composition work, but the Modern Linotype Company was not going to achieve the level of success I desired.

Our location was not the best. The profitable publishing work was in Manhattan, and we were losing time, money, and business in Brooklyn. Manhattan was the center of its own universe, and though a trip over the bridge might seem a minor inconvenience, it was a major impediment for us. Last but not least, we had opened with too little capital, and the money for upgrading and maintenance was not available. We were working long hours for little money, with no prospects of improvement.

We ended the partnership in the same pleasant, professional manner we'd begun it; Joel remained with the typesetting plant, and I once again went looking for work.

My efforts bore immediate fruit. The Hebrew-American Typographical Union, Local 83, was actively looking for new members. The president of the union made a personal visit to Saratoga Avenue to tell me that the union would look favorably upon my membership application. With my union card in hand, I never lacked for work.

CHAPTER 72

After the war, nations and individuals began to reconstruct their shattered lands and lives. All peoples, victorious and defeated, enemies and allies, joined together to rebuild that which had been destroyed—all peoples except one, that is. The Jewish people, who were the most brutalized of the war, could not rebuild.

They had neither land nor home.

There were more than six million who would never need a home again. They had died of starvation and disease and had been put to death in concentration camps, buried alive, tortured in diabolical Nazi medical experiments, and killed in gas chambers.

Years earlier, after the deaths of my cousins in Hebron at the hands of an Arab mob, my mother had asked me to read to her from the Midrash, and now, after the terrible atrocities visited upon my people, I heard myself speaking those words yet again: "The Assembly of Israel asked of God: Your Torah forbids us to slaughter a cow and her young baby-calf in the same day because of the tender feelings of the mother for her baby-calf. Why were You silent when the enemy slaughtered our mothers with their children in the same day? We are obliged to sacrifice our lives for Your Name, but Heaven remains silent when we are annihilated."

I weep still and close my eyes against the images.

Angels do not always come on time.

CHAPTER 73

My brother came home from New Guinea via the Philippines; married a woman he had known in New York, Adele; bought a photo studio on East Tremont Avenue in the Bronx and a house nearby; and began a family.

Yona's brother, Hy, Number Five, returned from the battleground of Europe, found part-time work during the day, and went to school at night. He got his high school degree and then married Mildred, a college graduate, and, using the benefits of the GI Bill, went on to college and began a family.

Dave Engel, the husband of Pnina, Number Four, came back from Japan; moved to Williamsburg, and began a family.

Jack Yarmosky was discharged from the merchant marine, and he and Shoshana, Number Three, moved to Baltimore, where within a short time, they bought their own pharmacy and began a family.

In June 1945, our third son, Michael, was born.

In December 1947, Yona and I had our fourth child, a boy. We named him Raphael Gabriel.

Yona and I agreed that he would be our last child.

I was thirty-seven years old, and Yona was twenty-seven.

Moe, New Guinea

CHAPTER 74

I was a little more than a year old when my brother Michael showed up in June of 1945, and I remember very little about his arrival. I was old enough to have memories of the birth of my youngest brother, Raphe, in December of 1947 and of the great snowstorm that paralyzed New York City—both events my father writes of, giving more attention to the snowstorm and how he and hundreds of other New Yorkers had to abandon their subway cars and trudge home through the mountainous drifts.

His emphasis on the weather is understandable, for my brother's birth was merely a family event, and not an uncommon one, while the snowstorm was a historical, universal phenomenon that dramatically altered the lives of the citizenry for a week.

While my mother was in the hospital and my father was working, my grandparents and aunts looked after my brothers and me. We were living in the same house, so the logistics were easy.

The house, which my grandparents Buba and Zeda owned, was in Sheepshead Bay, a residential neighborhood in the south of Brooklyn. The address was 1909 Avenue X. Many people found it hard to fathom that we lived on a street called X, so my brothers and I took our cue from our mother and always gave our address with the coda, "X as in x-ray," which produced a thoughtful silence.

It was a semi attached two-family house, its wood frame covered with rippled gray stucco. It had been built just after World War I, in 1919. The house cost $6,600.

When my grandparents returned to Jerusalem in 1961, they sold the house to us for $14,000, and we moved upstairs so we could have the extra bedroom.

*

My brother Michael almost didn't make it. He was allergic to milk; formula didn't work either. Our family doctor, Dr. Lerner, was alarmed; Michael was losing weight and becoming weak. After much trial and error, Dr. Lerner discovered that a mixture of ordinary milk and banana powder mitigated Michael's allergic reaction. There was a second: the war. Banana powder was one of the indispensable ingredients of food rations in the Pacific theater, and domestic supplies were restricted.

With Michael's survival at stake, my father was not going to wait for any angels. He took all his vacation time, and scoured the city for the precious powder. From morning to night, in Brooklyn, Manhattan and the Bronx, he went from one pharmacy to another and knocked on doors of medical supply and specialty food stores. He returned home late in the evening, exhausted and depressed. Every night, he gave himself an extra injection of liver extract to fortify himself for the next day, and then fell into a fitful sleep.

On the afternoon of the fifth day, he walked into a dark and dingy pharmacy on Rivington and Norfolk Streets on the Lower East Side. Instinct told him that his quest was over. He returned home with enough powder for almost six months.

It worked.

Michael thrived.

The moral of this tale, as my father explained it, was that you can usually find a miracle if you look hard enough.

There were times when you had to be your own angel.

*

My father was a writer who had not answered the call—or, rather, had answered the call of economic necessity. Still, he worked with words all his life. He had put his mother's thoughts and feelings on paper, as well as those of other forlorn women, and then, as a linotypist and compositor, he had composed, edited, and printed the words of others.

Our mother, however, had answered her own call for story telling in the form of family photography. It was her obsession. She carried a camera at all times; all family events, great and small, were recorded.

We have shelves of albums, hundreds of hours of film. It was her way, I think, of holding back Time's tide.

On Liberty Island in New York Harbor, our family portrait can be found in the collection of immigrant families. The six of us stand in full frontal display. My brothers and I, barely teenagers, wear my father's ties, though our youngest brother, Raphael, sports a bow tie and, not old enough to manage a belt, suspenders. The photograph is an American classic: immigrant parents and their native sons. The winter of war had given way to the sun of the Eisenhower era.

Thus, I was aware of these two narrative modes. My mother's movie making and photography gave our family a strong visual orientation, and our father provided the oral, literary one.

He wrote,

While our youngest boy, Raphael, slept in a crib, his older brothers, Chuck, Mark, and Michael, shared one large bedroom—at least it was large compared to the rooms of my childhood—and almost every night, I sat on one of their beds and read children's stories.

> We had in the house a small library of children's books and an encyclopedia set, but it wasn't enough, and we went often, usually on Friday night, to the Sheepshead Bay Public Library, and took out books from there.
>
> It still wasn't enough, and in addition to these books, we made up our own stories.

My father, very much taken with the short stories he had read in Mr. Power's home library, and at the American Library in Jerusalem, tried his hand at short fiction when he attended Seward Park High School in Manhattan during the Depression. His teacher complimented him on his skills and then asked, "Will you depend on your writing to earn a living?"

"I have no other source of income than what I earn," he said.

"It's very difficult to make money on just writing." The teacher had had his own disappointments. "Learn a trade, and try to write at night."

But his nights were for resting.

Our mother was tireless in her pursuit of supplemental income. For a year, she sold greeting cards. She'd buy boxes of them from a mail-order company at wholesale prices and then peddle them to friends, neighbors, and relatives at retail. She soon saturated her neighborhood market. So she started a home business in women's alterations. Her first customers were neighbors and friends, but her natural talents at sewing and design soon got her a much broader customer base. She set up shop in the front room of our apartment—we called it the sun parlor because it had five windows. We had only five rooms, so my older brother had his bed there. Customer visits ended at four o'clock. My mother did the machine sewing during the day, shifting to the living room for her handwork. That way Chuck had the room to himself in the evening.

We were a family of six, five of us men, and our mother was on the perpetual lookout for labor-saving devices; with the additional income her dressmaking brought in, she embarked upon a household modernization program.

"Not on children or books does one live," my father wrote, "but Yona and I had to buy things. You see, we had money. I had steady work and often worked overtime. And Yona did dress alterations for neighborhood women, who were willing to pay to be fitted exactly as they wanted."

My father said they "had money," though that was only in comparison to the impoverishment of his life in Batei Warsaw. Our income was always limited, but with careful management, we were able to ride the cutting edge of postwar consumer technology. Initially, that is. It was the follow-through that we couldn't afford. We bought early and quick and kept things forever.

We were one of the first households on our stretch of Avenue X to get a television. It was a necessary expense—my younger brothers were spending too much time watching television at other people's homes. Our television was a dark wood console about the size of a small chest of drawers. Its screen was eleven inches on the diagonal and used vacuum-tube technology; it took a full a minute to warm up. As the television aged, we had to max the brightness to keep the image visible. We got four channels. The big attraction was *The Milton Berle Show* every Tuesday night at 8:00, and within a month of getting our Crosby, our living room was jammed with neighbors watching Uncle Miltie do his shtick.

We were also one of the first to get a vacuum cleaner, a true American miracle that freed our mother at last from a life of sweeping and mopping that had begun when she was a child in Jerusalem. It was a genuine Hoover, and she bought it from a salesman who came to our house. He wore a spiffy gray suit and brought a selection of dirts and refuse. I was there during the event, and it was impressive to see all his dirt swept into the insatiable mouth at the end of the machine's long throat. The vacuum was a long, wide cylinder that slid on metal runners and howled like a plane on takeoff. The first time my grandparents borrowed it, they couldn't quite figure out the in-suck and out-blow, and my uncle Hy came down to tell me, alarmed, that the vaccum was broken.

"There's hot air coming out the back. If we broke it, we'll of course pay for a new one."

"Oh no," I assured him. "It always does that."

"It does?"

"That's the way it works." I was a precocious child of seven and remembered how the salesman had explained it. "The motor pulls in air through the hose and leaves the dirt in the machine and then goes out the back, like a balloon."

My uncle was relieved.

We kept that vacuum for almost twenty years.

We also kept our television beyond the point of functionality. Because the screen was so small, we hooked up a huge water-filled magnifying glass in front of it. There was a contraption made especially for this purpose—a slide mechanism was screwed to the top of the television cabinet, at the end of which was a clamping device that held the magnifying glass. The magnifier was a big hollow, plastic concave device filled with water. Fortunately, the television was so big and heavy that there was no danger of it toppling forward. We moved the glass back and forth in front of the screen to get the best combination of enlargement and focus. However, if we sat too much off to the side, the images were distorted through the magnifier's curves, so my brothers and I arranged ourselves single file on the living room floor in size places: Chuck sat in the back; Raphael in the front; and Michael and I, because we were almost the same height, squeezed together in the middle and watched TV with heads tilted out and eyes trained in.

My mother also bought a washing machine and, shortly thereafter, a gas dryer. But unless it rained, we hung the clothes in the backyard, Jerusalem style.

As a child, I didn't have a true sense of our family's financial status. My parents never spoke about money, and my brothers and I got an allowance that covered our daily needs. An ice cream cone was ten cents, a candy bar a nickel, so a dollar a week kept us in sweets. For Hanukkah, we got two crisp dollar bills from Zeda and a dollar here or there from aunts and uncles—a true fortune. Our family's food supply was plentiful. I didn't care about clothing. I never thought about money and didn't know there were vast differences in incomes.

My older brother Chuck was considerably worldlier. One day at supper, the six of us were eating in our kitchen at 1909 Avenue X, and I asked my father about his income. I had just come from Hebrew school, which I went to four days a week after public school, and my teacher had been teaching us about Rosh Hashanah and Yom Kippur.

"On Yom Kippur," he told us, "God determines your fate for the coming year. That means he decides everything that will happen to you."

"You mean," one student asked, "if you're going to live or die?"

"Everything, big or little. Between Rosh Hashanah and Yom Kippur, you have a chance to influence things by thinking about your behavior and what you want to change. On Yom Kippur, your time is up. Let's say that it's written down that your father will make twenty-five thousand dollars that year—that's what he'll make."

I was ten, and had no idea what twenty five thousand dollars meant. I had a question for my father that night.

"Dad, do you make twenty-five thousand dollars a year?"

"What!" That was Chuck, scoffing.

My father looked up from his plate. "No, I don't make twenty-five thousand dollars."

"Do you think if Dad made twenty-five thousand dollars we'd be living in a dump like this?" Chuck said.

"It doesn't seem like a dump to me."

My two younger brothers were listening.

"It's not a dump," my father said. "We have five rooms and a bathroom."

By old Jerusalem standards, a veritable mansion.

"We're working class," my brother said. He was only twelve but light-years ahead of me in socioeconomic reality.

Knowing what I know now, I can state with certainty that our house was not a dump at all: as a piece of real estate, 1909 Avenue X was, and remains, right smack in the middle of the socio-economic spectrum, and though the demographics of ownership have changed, its value has held up well through the decades. After my parents sold the house, the new owners covered the stucco with aluminum siding, and the whip of a tree that my grandfather and uncle planted on the sidewalk in front of the house when I was a child had opened into a fully crowned maple. The house suited us well, and the dumpiness was in the eyes of my brother.

My father's sense of our economic status was the assessment of a man coming from a deep, pervasive poverty. We were never, by any stretch of the imagination, wealthy. When I entered City College, I was getting a New York State scholarship. I had to give my parents' income as proof of need. My father's gross income for 1962 was $9,760, including overtime—good journeyman printer's wages. On this, my family of six lived without obvious want or deprivation.

His overtime work was the key to our financial solvency. He was one of the few multilingual Linotype compositors working on the East Coast, and was in great demand. He took as much overtime as he could get. He rose at 5:45 every morning, and from my bedroom in the front of the house, I could hear the radio playing "The Star-Spangled Banner," the sign-in music of WQXR, the *New York Times* radio station, which began broadcasting at 6:00 a.m. By the time my brothers and I were getting ready for school, my father was on the train heading into Manhattan. He'd return at six, and by 6:15 we'd be having supper in our eat-in kitchen. On Saturday, he would rise early too and go into Manhattan and work half a day.

I realized only later how extraordinary that was and how much the overtime meant for our finances. For our father, brought up in a strictly Orthodox environment in which the Sabbath was the holiest of all days, to work on Saturday revealed a high level of need.

On Sunday, he slept much of the day, and on Monday morning, he was up at 5:30 to begin the week.

*

In the 1950's, the mailman made his rounds a twice a day, first at about eleven o'clock, and again in mid afternoon. There was practically no junk mail; personal correspondence formed the bulk of the deliveries, and our two little mailboxes in the jamb between our entry doors got more than their fair share. My grandparents and parents corresponded regularly with their families and friends in Jerusalem. Transatlantic mail went by boat, and a letter might take six weeks to reach its destination. Airmail was expensive; the planes were props and weight was a factor, and you had to go to the post office so the letter could be weighed. There were special prepaid envelopes you could use. They were made of lightweight, blue-tinted paper and were both envelope and writing surface in one. You wrote on the main body and then on the outer flaps, numbering each flap so that the reader could go from one panel to the next, then folded everything in proper sequence and licked three edges. My mother's letters were masterpieces of micro script. She wrote in Hebrew, so the page had an ancient glyphic look. As soon as the ink was dry, I dropped the letter in the mailbox across the street.

The appearance of our mailman was always an event. He bore a striking resemblance to Captain Video, the hero of a primitive TV show called *Captain Video and His Video Rangers*, and I dashed out of the house as he approached our stoop. I liked to take hand delivery of our mail; even before I learned to read, I was able to distinguish the names Linder and Levy. Most of the mail was from Jerusalem, par avion, with the addresses written in English, and I distributed it between our two households. The return address was often in Hebrew and sometimes in English, and I quickly was able to read it in either language: Jerusalem, Palestine.

I was a social little boy, and liked to talk to my grandparents.

"Zeda, what's the news from Palestine?" I asked my grandfather, and he would open the letter while I stood there and, after reading the first few lines, reply.

"The news is good. Everyone is healthy."

I would reply, "That's good," and then go downstairs to play.

I learned later that things had not been that good in Palestine.

CHAPTER 75

Zalman Leib, my father-in-law, had a number of careers in America. He first was a collector for various charities in Jerusalem, traveling to Jewish communities in the United States. When he brought his family to America in 1937, he lived in Baltimore, Maryland. In 1943, he and his wife and seven children moved to Brooklyn, New York.

Then a friend from Jerusalem got him a job in a luggage factory; it was a time of much travel, and valises of all sizes and shapes were in great demand. That lasted about a year, and then, for unspecified reasons, Zalman Leib opened a meat market.

Never in a million years did I think my father-in-law would be a butcher, but his brother-in-law sold meat in Bensonhurst, Brooklyn, and enticed him with prospects of economic independence. Zalman Leib was reluctant. What did he know about being a butcher?

The brother-in-law was encouraging.

"Zalman Leib, what's there to know? Believe me, you won't travel far on your valises. Come work for me for a month, and you'll learn all there is to know. What do you have to lose?"

My father-in-law's store was just four blocks from our house on Avenue X. He bought carcasses wholesale, and carved and chopped them into smaller cuts. My mother-in-law sat on a small stool plucking chickens and pulling out their innards, saving the liver and gizzard for sale, and discarding the entrails into a big metal bucket at her feet. Every part was sold, including their little hearts and gizzards and their feet, which, when thrown in a pot of boiling water, did amazing things for the flavor of chicken soup.

Zalman Leib was a good butcher, and honest, and he did well during the war years; meat was rationed and commanded a high price. Soon, however, his lack of experience made it difficult to judge demand, and often he ran out of the favorite cuts. He lost more by not trimming the carcasses properly. Then the war ended; the supply of meat increased;

two supermarkets opened in our neighborhood and, and after a year of struggle, my father-in-law closed his meat market.

He looked again for a sexton position and found a large synagogue not far from Brooklyn College in the Flatbush section; due to the shortage of apartments after the war, he spent a good part of his day traveling from home to work. On the Sabbath and other Holy Days, he spent the night at congregants' houses. This went on for two long years. On rainy days and during the cold winter months, Yona made the round trip with him in our new Ford. Then the congregation found an apartment near the synagogue, and my in-laws moved out.

I missed them. There was a lot of life in the house when we lived together; people came and went; there was a great deal of cooking and eating. Conversation was constant. Almost every evening, after supper, Zalman Leib came down to our apartment. Yona was not interested in politics or current events, but my father-in-law was, and we both were avid readers of newspapers. Our conversations covered a lot of ground.

But one doesn't live on words alone, and Yona always offered dessert.

"Would you like some fruit? Maybe an orange?"

"No, no."

She then offered him cake. "Abba, I just finished baking. Have some."

"No, no." He would pull his silver watch from his vest pocket. He adhered to a strict schedule and did not take any food for an hour before going to bed. "I have to go to sleep soon. But I will take a glass of tea."

My wife made him tea, serving it always in a glass

"I do not drink from a porcelain cup," he insisted. "I am not an aristocrat."

CHAPTER 76

But as his grandson, I knew that in a way, he was. But it was only later, when I was more familiar with the sociological, economic and political history of the world, that I understood the broader context of his comment. My grandfather thought of himself as an ordinary man, a wage earner, and preferred a simple, plain glass placed on a flat plate with a lump of sugar at its side.

Zeda and my father were both skillful talkers who liked the big themes, so they usually talked about the state of the world, past and present. My grandfather's interest was the Jewish people. His family had fled the pogroms of Russia, and then he, born in Jerusalem, was forced to immigrate to America because of economic need. He longed to return to Jerusalem.

He believed that exile created many problems.

"Look, Chaim," he often said to my father, "even the individual, the single man or woman, suffers when he or she has no home."

My grandfather was a follower of Jabotinsky, whose call for the immediate creation of a Jewish homeland touched a deep chord in my father as well. In Jerusalem, my father heard Jabotinsky speak, and he recalled with great vividness how Jabotinsky poured forth his anger and hope.

"The Torah begins, 'In the beginning God created heaven and earth.'" Jabotinsky's voice was raised and his hand pointed to the heavens. "Our sages have explained that this means the entire earth belongs to God and thence to all of mankind. The earth does not belong only to one country or people. Why should the Arab peoples have so many nations and possess so much land, while the Jewish people have neither nation nor land?"

My father and grandfather agreed that Jabotinsky had read the future correctly, foreseeing not only the creation of a Jewish state but also the holocaust that would precede it; in the years preceding World War II, he sounded the alarm to European Jewry, urging them to flee before the horrors began. Unfortunately, when the reality descended the exit doors were already closing. Even had they managed to flee, there was no country that would have them.

"Words alone," Jabotinsky said, "do not make things happen. We must act."

CHAPTER 77

One morning in early June of 1948 I did my junior postman's rounds. I took the letters for my grandparents upstairs and gave them to Buba, who gave me a piece of cinnamon strudel. There were two crinkly letters from Jerusalem, par avion, their edges etched in the blue-and-red stripes. Downstairs, I went about my business in the backyard, digging a small mud hole and climbing into the fork of our peach tree. There was a garage-like building on our rear property line, and my grandfather had planted roses at the base of the wall. The air was full of scent and buzzing bumblebees. My grandfather and our next-door neighbor, Tony Buonovero, had also planted peach trees, one in each yard, and I sat in the low fork of our tree and tried to count the hundreds of small, hard, unripe green peaches on the branches. My youngest brother, Raphael, was watching me from under the hood of his carriage, and I threw some leaves at him to see his reaction. Below me, in the yard, my other younger brother, Michael, was watching an anthill. Chuck, in the first grade, was at school.

Later, I went up to my grandparents' apartment. Zeda was reading a letter at the kitchen table.

"Zeda, is everything good in Palestine?"

He looked up. "It's no longer Palestine," he said. His eyes were full. "Today it's Israel."

CHAPTER 78

Early one evening I received a phone call: my cousin Yitzhak was in New York.

"I'm here for a very brief visit," he told me. "Can I see you?"

"Of course! When? Tomorrow?"

"Tonight," he said.

Yitzhak, my cousin and oldest, best friend from Jerusalem, was visiting!

An hour later, his car pulled up. I had been waiting on the front steps, and I rushed down and embraced him as he stepped out of the car.

Alas, it was a sad reunion.

I did not know it, but from an early age, my cousin had had heart troubles, and now, with his condition deteriorating, he had come to America to seek treatment.

Outwardly, he was the same happy and smiling young man I had said goodbye to in 1929 many years ago. He had always been bigger and stronger than I, full of life and jokes and amusing ironies, and even now he stood tall and strong. We sat and sipped tea, and reminisced over all the mischief we had managed to do during our childhoods in Jerusalem.

"I have to go now, Chaim. Could you call a taxi?"

"So soon?" There were still so many memories to share, questions to ask about my sisters and mother and our aunts and uncles, so many smiles to exchange. "Stay for tonight. You can go in the morning."

He looked at his watch. He had to go. He had an appointment at Johns Hopkins Medical center tomorrow. "I really have to rest."

We embraced.

"Shalom," I said.

"Shalom, Chaim."

And he was gone.

He died a month later, in Jerusalem.

He was forty-seven years old.

My dear cousin Yitzhak.

CHAPTER 79

My father loved America, loved its freedom and its possibility. Like his brother Moe, he was fond of telling us, "this is America." He had no desire to return to Jerusalem, but my grandparents did, and in 1961 they returned to the land of their birth, once called Palestine and now Israel.

Then, on a day in March 1967, my mother got a phone call. Coming home, I found my mother weeping. Zeda had died of a heart attack that morning in Jerusalem.

Three months later, the Israelis defeated Egypt, Syria, and Jordan in the Six-Day War, and Jerusalem was reunited under Jewish sovereignty for the first time in two thousand years.

My mother was both joyful and sad.

"If only Abba, your grandfather, had lived to see this day," she told me.

He would have wept with joy.

CHAPTER 80

February 6, 1980, at one o'clock in the morning, the telephone rang. Moe's son was calling from Chicago.

"Uncle Chaim, my father died a few minutes earlier."

Later that morning I flew to my brother's funeral in Chicago.

I had visited him in Chicago every summer for the last twenty years; for the last ten Moshe had been in poor health, confined to a wheelchair.

Moshe was seventy-eight years old.

I must sing my dear brother's praises.

He had been an active man all his life, and though in his old age he had lost much strength, his heart and mind were always young and vibrant.

An eternal optimist, Moshe loved life, and America.

He had never attended any school other than our Talmud Torah in Batei Warsaw, but had educated himself to the level of a college graduate. He had a special talent for language, and read and wrote Hebrew, Yiddish, and English, and was fluent in Arabic and Italian. He had taught himself to play the piano and was a natural photographer.

For all the days of my youth in Jerusalem, and for five long decades in America, Moshe was a source of strength and happiness.

He has passed on to another world.

Moshe, my brother, Moshe, how I miss you.

CHAPTER 81

My father's tales will soon end with his return to Jerusalem in the summer of 1965.

Like many of his generation, he was a voyager, crossing oceans and cultures in search of a different life. Despite hunger, deprivation, danger, and poor health, he strove, always, to earn a living, raise a family, and be part of something greater than himself. With his marriage and the birth of his children, he had laid down cornerstones in America, and had achieved a full measure of those goals.

He had left Batei Warsaw a young man, and he returned in 1965 as a middle-aged gentleman. He told me how the stones of his childhood streets had voices, the very air, a taste.

He had not looked upon his mother's face for almost forty years.

She lived in a home for the aged; she went to Hinda's house for his visit.

She had a question.

"Chaim, are you happy?"

He had not expected that out of the mouth of his ninety-two-year-old mother; when he was a child, there was little talk of happiness.

"Yes, I'm happy."

"Ah, Chaim," she replied, "you always kept your thoughts to yourself. How do I know you are really happy?"

He assured her he was.

He told me, when he returned to New York two weeks later, he had never thought about happiness, not even now.

"You don't live on a steady diet of happiness. You have to do things."

All his years he had been so busy living—running through the streets of Jerusalem, studying Talmud, trying his hand at different trades, selling neckties in New York bars, learning English in night school, learning the craft of printing, trying to keep warm in his furnished rooms, working overtime at his Linotype—that he never stopped to think about being happy. Happiness was doing, such as marrying his dancing girl and having children to love.

His mother died shortly after his visit and then, one by one, his aunts, uncles, brothers, sisters, and childhood friends, all, passed on.

Many years after that visit, I visited him in Florida. My father was weak, yet alert. I had flown down for a quick visit. The hospital room was sunny and pleasant. I held his hand, a hand that had spent a lifetime on a Linotype keyboard and then on a typewriter—a warm, finely shaped hand, still strong. His hearing was failing, but we talked. I told him that he looked better than I'd thought he would, which made him smile, in part because he knew I was lying, in part because he was pleased that it might be true. I gave him the news of New York, of my wife, Katherine, and our children, his grandchildren, Samuel and Anne.

"Ah, yes," he said, of Anne, " the girl with the million-dollar smile."

He asked me if I would look into his memoir, as he put it, and do something with it, meaning edit it into a publishable book.

"It has many fine things in it," he said.

He was a true author to the end, puffing his work.

He said he wanted his words to see the light of day.

I said I would.

Outside, it was a beautiful, sunny day, and I found some shade beneath a palm tree by the side of a small man-made lake and stretched out on the grass. I knew my father would never be outside again. He was dying and would spend whatever little time he had inside a room, never to feel the sun and air on his face. I stood. I wanted to take him outside and would walk with him in the sunlight, one last time.

My request was greeted with incredulity by the nursing staff. He was attached to too many tubes and machines, they told me, and the legal liabilities and hospital protocols made it impossible.

I returned to New York.

My two younger brothers flew down and visited him.

A week later, following a surgical procedure, our father was taken to a hospice.

A rabbi administered the appropriate Jewish ritual in contemplation of death, and left. My mother, his dancing girl, sat on the bed. She put in his hearing aid, took his hand, and spoke into his ear.

"My dear Chaim, I thank you for a wonderful life. For our four wonderful sons and all that you have done for us. I would do it all again—all of it, my dear husband. I will see you again—much later, I hope, but I will see you."

Two days later, our father died.

His body was brought to New York for burial.

Our oldest brother flew in from Israel.

In keeping with custom, there was no formal viewing of the body. The funeral director asked our mother if she wanted to see him one last time, and she said no, then changed her mind. In the rear of the hearse, the director opened the coffin. In keeping with custom, it was a plain, unadorned pine box, for there is no need to preserve the body after death; dust unto dust. My mother looked in. I did too. He was wrapped in a white, wool prayer shawl. About him was aura of serenity. At last, after a lifetime of striving, he was at peace. My older brother, whose son lies in a cemetery in Israel, reached out and touched our father's prayer shawl and then brought his fingers to his lips, a final kiss.

A family friend, a rabbi, conducted the service at the gravesite. The weather was mild for February. Our mother, my brothers and I stood over the open earth. Around us were our wives and children, aunts, uncles, and cousins. We lowered the coffin, and threw handfuls of earth into the grave. After the Kaddish, we left and returned to my parents' apartment in Sheepshead Bay for the shivah.

CHAPTER 82

In August 1965, I returned to Jerusalem.

I was fifty eight years old.

Thirty-six years earlier, I had taken my first ocean voyage, traveling from Jaffa, Palestine, to Providence, Rhode Island. The trip lasted thirty-one days. Now I flew from New York to Israel in sixteen hours, arriving at Lod Airport on Sunday afternoon. My mother wasn't at the airport, but had told my family to give me a warm welcome, and after passing through customs, I was greeted by a crowd of waving, shouting relatives.

I recognized my three sisters, Chaya Sara, Yehoved, and Hinda, whom I hadn't seen in almost four decades, but I didn't know that the man with the dark beard and big smile was my youngest brother, Fishel, who had been ten when I left Jerusalem in 1929.

Fishel led me through the crowd to a waiting taxi, and we sped off to Jerusalem through the dark night. I hadn't slept in twenty-four hours but wasn't tired. We climbed higher and higher, the traffic thick around us, and then, without warning, we were in the midst of the city, its streets lit by electric lamps, with not a kerosene lantern to be seen.

The taxi pulled up at a narrow alley with wide, flat steps—the entrance to Batei Warsaw.

I couldn't wait. I rushed up the steps and turned to the left, but Fishel, laughing, stopped me. Other tenants now occupied our old house.

"To the right," he said. "To Hinda's house."

Through the open windows, I saw a crowd of people, and from the street, I heard loud talking—the steady buzz of Yiddish, so familiar.

A boy's voice shouted from the yard, "He's here!"

Everyone stopped talking.

Fishel led me through the silent crowd, guided me to the far side of the room. All eyes were upon me; not a word was spoken, not even a whisper. At the window, my mother was sitting on a wooden chair. She stood.

I was tense and excited and didn't know what to do or say.

My mother had changed, and she had not. She looked at me for a long moment and then lifted her right hand. In it was her old siddur, the prayer book given to her by my grandfather Fishel so many years ago. I stepped closer, and she put her left hand on my breast. My mother was a careful talker, measuring her words and silences and measuring her actions too. I remembered how, when we had parted thirty-six years before, the two of us had stood at the Jaffa port, and she had put her hand on my chest, fastened the buttons of my coat in the cold morning, and told me to take care of myself.

I had never left Jerusalem.

I couldn't see my mother clearly.

She held the siddur open between us and, in a quivering voice, sang the blessing of Shecheyanu: "Blessed are thou, Eternal God, King of the universe, who has preserved our life and health and brought us to this season once again."

The entire room answered with a loud "Amen!" and then they burst into song.

On the tables were trays of cakes, fruits, candy, nuts, wine, and soda.

My sister Hinda's house had electric lights.

"See? Just like America," she said.

Everyone was talking at once—the way it should be.

"So that's Uncle Chaim."

"Yeah, from America."

"He looks like any one of us."

"But he's much different."

"Only because he's dressed different."

"He's dressed like a German."

"No, that's not German; that's how they dress in America."

"Where are his earlocks and beard?"

"Where do you think they are?"

"He comes from America—that's why."

"Everything is upside down there."

"Where are his children?"

"Where do you think they are?"

Suddenly, one of the little boys standing watch ran in.

"Uncle Yisrael Yitzhak is coming!" He stood in the doorway in his yarmulke and fringed garment, pointing out the door, very excited. "I saw him with my own eyes! He's coming!"

Everyone stopped talking. The men and women separated. The men who were wearing only yarmulkes quickly put on their formal fur-trimmed streimels, and used their fingers to comb out their beards and tighten their earlocks. Everyone stood in a deep silence, ready to welcome their beloved and distinguished relative, my favorite uncle, the highly regarded and well-known rabbinical judge, Dayon Yisrael Yitzhak Ha'levi Reisman.

My mother walked to the entrance door.

"He's coming right now!"

"Shush!"

Suddenly, my uncle stood in the doorway. He looked like a king in his beautiful frock and streimel trimmed with fur, his long gray beard combed out. No one uttered a word.

Now, a minor dispute arose between my mother and her brother: Who should walk first into the room, age or Torah?

My mother was ninety-two years old; her brother the dayon was a mere eighty-nine. My uncle insisted she go before him. My mother refused; her brother, the renowned judge and Talmudic scholar, wore the crown of Torah, and she demanded that he precede her.

Finally, displaying the respect and social skills of a scholar and judge, he did as she insisted and walked slowly and with great dignity until he stood in front of me. He looked at me in silence. I looked back. This was the same uncle who, many years ago, had caught me reading the biographies of poets and had questioned me about Pushkin's duel. In his eyes was the memory of that conversation. He continued to stare at me, no doubt regarding my mode of dress as strange as Pushkin's. Waiting for the response of the distinguished dayon to the secular, junior uncle from America, the entire room held its breath.

Long moments passed. There had been so much love between us long ago, a lifetime of years. I had sat on his lap when he and my father studied together in the soft light of a kerosene lantern; I had prayed with him and sang and danced arm in arm with him. So much love! Had it vanished? Where does love go during the years? And where do friendship, laughter, and sorrow go? Do they just disappear into the air, or does the world have a place for everything—in the heart perhaps? We stood face-to-face and looked into each other's eyes. Yes, the love was there. There was more—there was, in his eyes, respect. We had missed each other.

Uncle Yisrael Yitzhak put his hand in his pocket, put something in my hand.

"Have a sweet, Chaim."

At once, the room exhaled, and everyone was calling out, "Shalom aleichem! Shalom Aleichem!"

Conversation resumed in a loud, animated buzz.

My uncle sat with my mother and then, holding informal court, nodded and smiled as guests lined up one by one to greet him.

In a few minutes, he signaled with a raised hand that he was ready to leave. Again, everyone fell silent. Those who were seated rose. My mother stood and escorted him to the door.

"Chaim," uncle Yisrael Yitzhak said, "you must visit me tomorrow."

With that final stamp of acceptance, he left. Two of my nephews, sons of my sister Yehoved, accompanied my uncle to his home, ensuring his safe return.

Almost immediately, the little boy on lookout rushed back into the house.

"Uncle Yoshke is coming! And he's walking very fast!"

This was none other than Yosef, my sister Chaya Sara's husband.

Uncle Yoshke's arrival didn't generate the same furor of respect and silence as Uncle Yitzhak's, but as he stepped over the threshold the room fell silent. Everyone parted, opening a path.

He entered quickly and stood before me. He looked me up and down.

I waited.

Uncle Yoshke continued measuring me with a sharp eye.

"You aren't the same Chaim!"

"That's true, but I'm close enough."

After a long moment, he smiled, extending his hand. "Shalom Aleichem."

"Aleichem shalom."

Uncle Yoshke didn't stay long, and soon the others left. My mother had been sitting all night long, and now she stood.

"My child," she said, "you must be tired. Better go to sleep now."

My child! I hadn't heard those words in more than half a lifetime.

It had been a long day and a long night, and I hadn't slept since leaving New York. My sister Hinda gave me the best bed in her house, and I slept once again in the place where I'd first drawn breath: in Batei Warsaw, my home in the center of the universe.

*

I woke early at dawn.

Overwhelmed with emotions, I lay in bed and looked around.

Why, this was the house my grandparents, Netanel and Nechama, had lived in. I got out of bed. There were the bent nails on the closet frame that held the door shut—the same nails.

On the little bedside table was the lemon candy Uncle Yisrael Yitzhak had given me the night before. I looked at it for a long time and then picked it up and put it in my valise. I took a deep breath. Away with nostalgia! I was in Jerusalem to experience the present and to return to New York with hope and inspiration.

My sister and her family were still sleeping, and I went out to the front yard and greeted Batei Warsaw with a loud "Shalom aleichem!"

Batei Warsaw did not respond. Evidently, my return after thirty-six years of self-imposed exile did not warrant attention.

I stepped through the gate. The narrow unpaved paths, washed with dew and sparkling with early light, ran off in all directions.

A few chickens pecked at the earth.

A young Hasid, holding his tallit and tefillin under his arm, kicked an empty tin can down the dirt path to the Hasidic Ohel Shmuel Shul.

Peaceful, sleepy Batei Warsaw was still the village of my youth.

After breakfast, three of my nephews entered, chattering about where I was to go and what I was to do. They had been assigned to be my guides. I politely declined their offer, explaining that I preferred to explore Jerusalem myself.

Avram, my sister's son, insisted, "Uncle Chaim, Jerusalem isn't the same as thirty-six years ago. You may get lost."

"Me? Get lost in Jerusalem?" I smiled at them. "Never."

"But, Uncle Chaim, it's different now."

"I'm sure the streets are the same. I'll find my way."

The three young Hasids looked at each other, retreated to a corner, whispered together.

Avran spoke. "At least let us follow you."

But I sent them away; Jerusalem was my home

My first stop was the Mea Shearim.

I walked through quiet streets, wondering, *It isn't Shabbos, so why is it so empty?*

The Mea Shearim was a ghost town. Gone was the big, open market full of shops and stalls with their tumble of goods and the vendors selling food and drink. Gone were the crowds of talking men and bargaining women. Gone were the Arab peasant women who came down from the villages outside Jerusalem with their baskets of fruits and vegetables.

I left the Mea Shearim and walked through the twisting, narrow streets to Batei Hungary. There too the bustle of life was nowhere to be found; even the stones were subdued. I continued east and then south, taking one of my favorite routes to the Old City that passed the Italian hospital. Walking briskly through the morning light, I continued east, then south, and then, without warning, there was a wall.

Stretching north and south was a high, ugly barrier of cement and stone.

I looked up. I looked down. I looked to the left and then the right.

I stood in amazement.

Jerusalem had been cut in half.

I stood and stared. I understood now what my nephews had been trying to tell me. The streets were the same, but they led only to this dead wall.

It's called the Green Line. It's drawn on the maps with a line of green and is a barrier made of old houses, broken walls, stones, and fences. I walked south along the wall toward the Old City, but nowhere could I enter. Here and there were little breaks and cracks to which I could put my eye. I saw that to the east, on the other side of the wall, was a brief stretch of no-man's-land, a narrow band of ruin and rubble, and beyond that, Jordan. I detoured south along Shivtei Yisra'el, hoping to pick up Jaffa Road and to follow that to the old Jaffa Gate, and at least get close to the ancient stones, but the green wall suddenly appeared again.

Jerusalem, The Green Line

I stood in silence. I could not enter the Old City. I wanted to go to the Kotel and tell the ancient stones that I had kept my promise to return. I wanted to tell them too that I had never forgotten or forsaken Jerusalem, and never would.

I turned, and not looking back, returned to my sister Hinda's house.

"Just as good, Chaim," my brother Fishel told me. "The houses and synagogues in the Old City are destroyed. The Kotel has huts built against it. We're not allowed in."

We were forbidden entry, even though a treaty signed with the Jordanians in 1949 guaranteed Jewish access to the Mount of Olives and our other holy places in the Old City.

"Ah, but its even worse," said Fishel.

I learned later that the Jordanians had taken some of the stones of our old synagogues and even some tombstones and used them to construct public urinals for the Arabs of Jerusalem.

I had wished to stand over the resting places of my father, grandfather, uncles, and aunts, all of them buried on the Mount of Olives, but that part of Jerusalem was in Jordanian hands, and no Jew was permitted to walk upon that holy earth for the briefest of moments. As a solace, one afternoon, Elazar, Zipporah's husband, drove me to a high hill near the Zion Gate. Telescopes had been installed on the hill's crest. I scanned the rows of gravestones, but was unable to find those of my ancestors. From where I stood upon the hill, I could see Jordanian soldiers in a watchtower in the Old City, pointing rifles at us.

"Don't worry," said Elazar. "They won't shoot. They only want to frighten us."

We drove back in silence. I was sad and bitter. Jerusalem's Old City was now Judenfrei, just as the Nazis would have wished. Yet New Jerusalem, in Israel, was home to many Arabs. They had mosques and cemeteries, and they walked freely among us.

As we drove slowly back to Batei Warsaw, I made a promise to myself that I would return when all of Jerusalem was united and free.

"May it be," I murmured to myself, "in my lifetime."

Elazar heard. "Amen," he responded.

May it be so.

The next night I had dinner at my brother's home. The talk around the table and the Shabbos foods—the savory meats and kugel, the sweets, all the tastes of so many things—were a wonderful visit to my childhood.

All my days, never to be forgotten.

*

One afternoon, Fishel and I, and one of his younger daughters, went to visit our mother at the home for the aged. We stopped at the Mahaneh Yehuda open market and bought some fruit to take to the home. As we continued, the little girl asked if she could have an orange, and when Fishel said she couldn't, she persisted.

"But, Abba," she said, "I only want one. There's a lot more."

"The fruit was bought for your grandmother," Fishel replied, "and it already belongs to her."

"Maybe she'll give me an orange if I ask her."

"I'm sure you won't have to ask. And you'll get more than an orange. But there's another reason you can't have one now."

"I know," she said. "All food must be washed or cleaned before we eat it."

"That's right. And also, you know, only animals eat in the street. People are different. We eat only within our gates."

We walked on, carrying the fruit to the home for the aged.

We eat the foods we are permitted to eat within the gates of our houses, for Leviticus prohibits eating food on the run, for that is what animals and uncivilized people do. Food is sustenance and must be treated with respect, for then we are elevated; thus, hands and food are washed, a blessing is said, and then one eats. Appetite is something of value, and the needs of the body are happily met, but with grace and thanks.

*

Three days before I left, Fishel took me to his father-in-law, Amram Blau. Religious to the highest degree, and the founding member of the Neturei Karta—Guardians of the City--Amram was well educated and worked as an administrator in a civil court in Jerusalem. We visited him in his home, where, even though I was obviously not nearly as frum—observant---as he thought I should be, I was received with the respect befitting the older brother of Fishel Linder.

Amram was eager to hear about the United States, which he called the Other World. He questioned me avidly. After asking about my children and their education, he was surprised, and disappointed, that my two older sons were not yet married. He reminded me that according to custom, boys should be married by the time they were eighteen.

Acknowledging that I was well aware of that particular guideline, I offered, shall we say, a variant interpretation.

"At the time our sages were discussing this issue," I said, "the life span of the average person was very short, and illness and accident further lessened everyone's years, so people had to marry young. Now, however, there's time before we start families."

He was upset. "Atheism will always find reasons. Our Holy Torah is never outdated. It is eternal truth forever and ever."

For the sake of a harmonious visit, and because the host is allowed the last word in his own house, I did not argue; the Talmud itself, however, is not of divine origin but is the product of men and women and, as Amram well knew, subject to change and refinement.

For a change from the old to the new, I took a two-day trip to the Upper and Lower Galilee. The itinerary followed the trip I had made in the happy spring of 1929 with my cousin Yitzhak and the other yeshiva students from Hebron. As in my youth, I walked the hills and valleys of Galilee and along the shores of Lake Kinneret—or, as it called, the Sea of Galilee.

Hovering about me, however, were the dark memories of those terrible events in Hebron, when my cousins Yaakov and Moshe Aaron were killed by angry mobs. Had we lost the war in 1948, all my family, all of Israel, I feared, would have suffered the same terrible fate.

Yet as I rode through the beautiful countryside, my cousins were, in some measure, still alive in my memories. I saw them dancing in the star lit night, the flicker of the fire upon their faces, their voices lifted with mine in happy song. I stood upon the shores of the Kinneret, closed my eyes, and offered a prayer of thanks.

Never to be forgotten, never to happen again.

The memory of the departed will be for a blessing.

*

During every visit to my mother in the home for the aged, she urged me, "Chaim, *l'man HaShem*"—in God's name—"visit our shul."

And so I went. Wanting the place to myself, I stopped in after morning services.

Nothing had changed during the thirty-six years of my absence. There were the same wall closets, long tables, and backless benches. The old brick oven near the entrance door, however, had been replaced with a kerosene heater.

Suddenly, I was bereft; the old brick oven had belonged to me. My boyhood friends and I had searched the fields for wood scraps to keep the synagogue warm in the winter; we'd baked potatoes on the hot bricks and then devoured them steaming at our benches, burning our tongues.

There, near the east corner, was my father's favorite seat. On the flat, stone windowsill was the same crack where my father had tucked his little packet of snuff.

In one of the wall closets, I found a volume of Talmud with my footnotes and remarks in Hebrew on its worn pages. That was one of my youthful transgressions: writing critical commentary on matters I knew so little of.

Before I left Jerusalem, I returned to the synagogue for the last service of the Sabbath. Uncle Yisrael Yitzhak, the president of the shul, invited me to sit near him on the eastern wall, the wall facing the site of the temple in Old Jerusalem, a seat of high distinction.

The cantor began with the first line of Psalm 95.

"Come, let us sing to the Lord," he sang. The congregation murmured the second line, and then, as the cantor raised his voice, the men, feeling the melody, began singing.

"Come, my friend, to meet the bride; let us welcome the Sabbath."

Each verse generated more and more excitement, and their voices rose louder and louder.

"Shake off your sorrows! Arise! Put on your glorious garments, my people, and pray."

The old walls of the synagogue were shaking, the voices touching the heavens.

After the service, the few congregants who still remembered me shook my hand and wished me peace. His grandson led one of them, now old and almost blind. Happy to hear my voice, he could not stop saying my name. "Oh, Chaim, Chaim! You have returned! Of course I remember you! Chaim, Chaim, you have returned!"

The next morning, Sunday, I sped to Ben Gurion Airport, and early that evening I was back home in Brooklyn. The next day, Monday, I took the subway to Prompt Press on Ninth Avenue in Manhattan, and soon was sitting at my Linotype machine, working.

*

One cannot erase the past.

Nor can one relive it.

On my visit to Israel, I had wandered about the streets and narrow alleys of Jerusalem searching for the place I had left thirty-six years ago. During all my years in America, when I thought about the past, I was always a child in Jerusalem, and when I went back to Batei Warsaw I expected to meet that little boy running barefoot through the streets with his earlocks bouncing behind. But the Old City and the fields were now in Jordanian hands, and I could not find my lonely pear tree in whose friendly, leafy arms I had spent so many pleasant hours.

I was a middle-aged man looking for ghosts.

But there were moments—intense, strange moments—when, walking in an alley of Batei Warsaw, I did see myself. The child Chaim was in front of me, walking in the bright sunlight. Yes, it was I, the quiet, intense child, leaving my footprints in the dusty stones of Jerusalem. It was so very real I wanted to tap him on the shoulder and say shalom.

Or was it a dream?

This morning, sitting on my little seat and working the keys of my Linotype machine, my fingers flew without thinking; my mind was elsewhere. I had gone to Jerusalem to find a part of the past, my youth, memories of which I had carried with me during the years of my exile.

But I did not find it.

Who was to blame?

My mother had kissed me in farewell and blessed me; my sisters and brother had cried at my leaving.

Could I blame Jerusalem for not saving itself for me and keeping me safe from time?

My wife, my dancing girl, met me at the airport when I returned, waiting for me to pass through customs. My four sons, strong and healthy, greeted me with interest and then went about their own business. They had no time for their middle-aged father and his memories.

Later, I thought, *when they have children of their own, and perhaps grandchildren, they will want to know, for they will be old enough to know that my life is, in a sense, theirs, and what I lived they have lived too.*

I shall give them these memories, these cornerstones to build upon, for lives, like buildings, require foundations; as others have done for me, I shall do for them.

May they do the same for their children and for the generations to come.

CHAPTER 83

Years earlier, while my father was writing these tales, and before his Parkinson's had established its debilitating grip on his nimble fingers, I dropped by for a visit. He was in the spare bedroom, his writing room. He greeted me with his big smile and pushed his chair away from the typewriter. He was working on the third draft of his memoir.

"This should be your last draft," I said to him. "I think you know that."

He shook his head, smiled. "I enjoy it too much to stop."

There was always another interesting story or funny episode to put down.

"Dad, too much of a good thing is too much. It's a surfeit of honey."

Not hearing me, he said, "I sit and think about my life, and my thoughts are like rainbows. I see them like colors in the air, and I look at them and wonder."

I knew what he meant; the written word has a special power, for it holds a gleam just beyond our reach.

"Your mother is shopping," he said. "Do you want something to eat?"

"Just something to drink."

He shuffled off to the kitchen, and I glanced at the page. He was working on the section about meeting my mother: "Destiny was the butter on my daily bread."

He had written, "the sudden and unexpected meeting with the dancing girl, who I knew now as Yona Levi, couldn't have been an accident. Thoughts of her consumed my mind and heart. Was this the bigness that had been part of my life since I was a child?"

He was in the kitchen, taking something out of the refrigerator—soda perhaps.

His writing desk was small, and the typewriter took up most of it. The pages were in a neat stack; a lifetime of Linotype work had taught him to work cleanly. This was his life: fourteen hundred pages filled with words. An aura hovered over the desk. Presences abounded. He had lived his destiny—more, he had seized it, welcoming it with all his strength. His ancestors had had their destinies, he his. He had sailed to the *goldene medina*, the golden land of America.

His days were dwindling, and he had become smaller and bent, but there remained a bigness in his life, and that bigness was part of mine. He saw his life as a path reaching back to generations beyond Jerusalem and beyond Poland, a life intertwined with the lives of others, past and future. The world, he often told me, has a place for everyone. Indeed, there had been a place for his grandfather and a place for his father, and here in America my father had found his. *Think big*, he often said. Our lives are full of chance, but there is a bigness into which we can step.

There I stood in his little writing room in New York and read his words.

I was transported to Jerusalem all those many years ago.

"My thoughts are like rainbows," my father had said. "I see them like colors in the air. I can touch them."

Like rainbows, I thought.

I sat with him at the small table off the kitchen, and watched him drink his tea.

Now, at last, with his words going forth, my father is alive in his wonderful rainbow, part of the eternal light.

-8-

ABOUT THE AUTHOR

Chaim Linder was born in Jerusalem in 1907, one of seven children in an ultra-orthodox Jewish family that lived just outside Jerusalem's walls in Batei Warsaw, a community that housed Polish immigrants. As a child, he lived through the deprivations and chaos of World War I when the British, in their quest for empire, fought the Turks and their German allies. At the end of the war, Palestine, and Jerusalem, became a mandate of Britain, and Chaim and his family experienced once more the hard, brutal hand of another imperial power. After the Arab riots of 1929, in which two of Chaim's cousins were slaughtered in Hebron, he left Jerusalem for America. There, expecting to find gold at his feet, he encountered the harsh realities of the Great Depression. He taught himself English, became a tri-lingual linotypist. In New York, he met an émigré from Jerusalem. They married and moved to Brooklyn, where they raised a family of four sons. Chaim retired in 1972 and began working on his memoir. Now, twenty years after his death, one of his sons, a professional writer, has edited the manuscript, and the story of Chaim Linder, and his ancestors, comes to life in ANGELS ALWAYS COME ON TIME.

CPSIA information can be obtained
at www.ICGtesting.com
Printed in the USA
BVHW030749030319
541639BV00001B/2/P